Modern Police Leadership

Mark Roycroft • Lindsey Brine
Editors

Modern Police Leadership

Operational Effectiveness at Every Level

palgrave
macmillan

Editors
Mark Roycroft
Rabdan Academy
Al Bhustan, Abu Dhabi, United Arab
Emirates

Lindsey Brine
Rabdan Academy
Al Bhustan, Abu Dhabi, United Arab
Emirates

ISBN 978-3-030-63929-7   ISBN 978-3-030-63930-3   (eBook)
https://doi.org/10.1007/978-3-030-63930-3

Contents

Part I   Introduction   **1**

Introduction... 3
Mark Roycroft

Human Rights... 13
Lindsey Brine

Accountability and Governance 19
Mark Roycroft

Local Partnerships and International Agencies...................... 29
Mark Roycroft

Part II   Use of Force   **45**

Use of Force and Public Order 47
James Law and Mark Roycroft

Armed Policing... 59
Mark Roycroft

Management of Deadly Force 73
Gordon Harper

The Grainger Firearms Case Study 79
Mark Roycroft

Part III   International Policing   **83**

UN Peacekeeping Operations. 85
Lindsey Brine

**Crisis and Disaster Management and Disaster Victim
Identification (DVI).** 97
Lindsey Brine and Mark Roycroft

**Cybercrime in the Age of Digital Transformation,
Rising Nationalism and the Demise of Global Governance** 109
Larry Poe

Part IV   Investigation   127

Investigation. 129
Mark Roycroft

Cybercrime 143
Nikola Protrka

Child Protection 157
Andrew Bailey and Mark Roycroft

Sexual Assault Investigations in the UK and Canada 171
Lindsey Brine and Mark Roycroft

Investigative Interviewing 183
Mark Roycroft and Lindsey Brine

**Police Practice in Dealing with Severe Addictions and/or
Mental Illness: Treatment or Arrest?** 199
Katherine Brine, Lindsey Brine, and Mark Roycroft

Part V   Forensic Investigations   221

Forensics: The Golden Hour 223
Andrew Rose

The Crime Scene Expert 235
Scott Fairgrieve

Forensic Intelligence 245
Andrew Williamson

Part VI   Counter-Terrorism   261

Counterterrorism 263
Lindsey Brine and Mark Roycroft

Homegrown and Lone-Actor Terrorism 281
Ian Brine and Lindsey Brine

The Nexus Between Terrorist Organizations and Organized Crime 293
Michał Matyasik

Extraterritorial Investigations of Terrorist-Related Kidnappings 303
Lindsey Brine

Part VII   Intelligence   325

Knowledge Management (KM) and Intelligence-Led Policing (ILP) 327
Larry Poe, Nikola Protrka, Mark Roycroft, and Tiina Koivuniemi

Part VIII   Mental Wellbeing   345

Global Policing Leadership and Security Sector Reform 347
Kurt Eyre

Personal Resilience in High-Risk Domains 367
Amadeus Kubicek

Mental Health Awareness for Police Officers 381
Mark Roycroft and Lindsey Brine

Decision-Making in Law Enforcement 389
Mark Roycroft

Part IX   Community Policing   403

Community Policing 405
Johannes Oosthuizen

Building Communities from the Inside Out 423
Nigel Lloyd

Part X   Conclusion   435

Conclusion 437
Mark Roycroft

Glossary 453

Appendices 457

Glossary Chapter 13 Cyber Crime 477

References. 481

Index 509

Notes on Contributors

Andrew Bailey served in the police in Northern Ireland for 28 years. He was the lead detective for Child Abuse, Sexual Offences and Vulnerable Adults. His main areas of interest were the protection of children and vulnerable adults, criminal investigation, extradition, international mutual legal assistance, pre-employment vetting, project management, intelligence disclosure/management and sex offender risk management. After retirement, Bailey was appointed Child Protection Advisor to Northern Ireland Cooperation Overseas (NICO) and was deployed on various missions funded by the European Union, primarily training police and judges in child abuse. Andrew holds a PhD in......... (Ulster University, YEAR??).

Ian Brine holds a Bachelor of Arts in Criminology and Criminal Justice (Carleton University, 2016) and a Master of Terrorism and Security Studies (Charles Sturt University, 2019).

Brine has diverse experience in working with the public, including as Jail Guard for the RCMP in the Arctic, and providing security and protective services for clients that included the Royal Embassy of Saudi Arabia. Brine has worked extensively with vulnerable populations in homeless shelters in Ottawa and Vancouver. Most recently, Brine provided harm reduction services at a Supervised Injection Site.

Katherine Brine holds a Bachelor of Arts (Highest Honours) in Psychology (Carleton University, 2013) and a Master of Arts in Criminology (Simon Fraser University, 2015). Her research focused on protective factors in post-release Canadian federal offenders with mental health issues, and health service accessibility and police response to mental-health-related emergencies in Northern British

Columbia. Brine's interest in these areas stems from working as a mental health counsellor, extensive experience residing in a number of Canadian rural and remote settings including the Arctic, and her father's work as an Royal Canadian Mounted Police (RCMP) officer. Katherine has been employed as a Youth Reintegration Support Worker at a full-time attendance program (alternative to custody) for female youth with severe substance addictions. She worked as a Government Youth Probation Officer, and is working as a Child Protection Social Worker in Greater Vancouver.

Lindsey Brine joined the Royal Canadian Mounted Police (RCMP) in 1987 after completing his First Class Honours BA in Philosophy (McGill University, 1986). He performed uniform policing duties in Canada's Arctic and the Atlantic coast. Brine also worked as a Constable, a Corporal, and a Sergeant conducting and managing complex investigations including on armed robberies, arson, homicides, narcotics, and serious sexual assaults. He was commissioned in 2003 and worked in Human Resources as an Inspector and a Superintendent. In 2008, Lindsey became the RCMP Liaison Officer for the Senate of Canada Committee on National Security and Defence. In 2009, he worked as Team Commander for two high profile terrorist related kidnappings.

Lindsey led a Canada Labour Code investigation into the deaths of two RCMP members who perished in the 2010 Haiti Earthquake. He was also assigned to senior positions at the Vancouver 2010 Olympics and the Toronto G20 Summit. Lindsey was seconded to the UN Peacekeeping Mission in post-earthquake Haiti for a year, as the Senior Advisor to the Deputy Commander, Operations, and as Chief of Staff for over 4400 UN police officers.

In 2012, Lindsey was promoted to Chief Superintendent as Commanding Officer of Nunavut Territory. During this time, Lindsey completed a Master of Police Leadership and Management (Charles Sturt University, 2014).

Since retiring from policing, Lindsey has lectured at universities in Australia and the United Arab Emirates. He continues to place an emphasis on the mental toll exacted on those in frontline public service.

Lindsey has been awarded the following honours and recognition:

- Queen's Diamond and Golden Jubilee Medals 2012 and 2002
- Canadian Peacekeeping Services Medal 2012
- United Nations Peacekeeping Medal 2011
- Queen's Operational Service Medal - Expedition (Mali and Somalia) 2009
- RCMP 20 Year Long Service Medal and 25 Year Bronze Clasp
- Commanding Officer's Commendation 2000 (investigation of Organized Crime Group)

Lindsey is the proud father of two adult children, both of whom have chosen careers in front line public service assisting vulnerable populations and ensuring the safety and security of Canadians.

Lindsey is an avid hiker, cyclist, reader, and traveller.

Kurt Eyre has over 30 years of experience working across a variety of executive, command and advisory military, policing and security sector roles, specialising in international leadership, learning, training and organisational development. Eyre has worked with the Geneva Centre for Security Sector Governance and Geneva Centre for Security Sector Governance (DCAF) (International Security Sector Advisory Team (ISSAT)) and was head of the UK College of Policing's International Academy (Bramshill). He was a UK Policing Advisor for Latin America and the Caribbean and an Officer in Her Majesty's Royal Marines. Eyre holds an MSc in Security Sector Reform (Cranfield University, 2010).

Scott Fairgrieve is Professor of Science in Policing and Security at Rabdan Academy (United Arab Emirates) and Professor of Forensic Science at Laurentian University (Canada). Fairgrieve researches human skeletal biology and forensic anthropology and has widely authored in the areas of forensic anthropology, microscopy of bone, and the analysis of intentionally burned human remains. He is Director of the Forensic Osteology Laboratory and Forensic Anthropology consultant to the Office of the Chief Coroner of Ontario (Canada) and the Ontario Forensic Pathology Service. He has testified as an expert witness in Canada and the United States. Fairgrieve holds a Bachelor of Science (University of Toronto, 1986), a Master of Philosophy (Cambridge University, 1987), and a Doctor of Philosophy (University of Toronto, 2003)—all in Physical and Biological Anthropology.

Gordon Harper retired from the Police Service for Northern Ireland in 2014 after 32 years of service. His policing career focused primarily on National Security, Counter Terrorism and High-Risk Crime in Action. He was a nationally qualified Gold and Silver Commander and a Trainer and Tactical Advisor, in both Specialist Firearms Operations and Public Order. He has had strategic responsibility for the delivery of a number of UK Government sponsored security sector reform projects. Since retirement, Harper has worked in the Middle East in education and project management. He holds a Master of Arts in Leadership and Management for Learning (Canterbury Christ Church University, 2011).

Tiina Koivuniemi is a member of European Union Agency for Law Enforcement Training (CEPOL) and lectures in Finland on leadership issues. She is presently at

Rabdan Academy in Abu Dhabi and will take up a new post in Albania in January 2020 lecturing on leadership issues to the Albanian Police. She has written extensively on leadership issues.

Amadeus Kubicek is an Assistant Professor of Resilience at Rabdan Academy (UAE) with a professional background in law enforcement, aviation, and academia. With a strong industry-based experience reinforced by an academic background in risk management and risk management behaviour, Kubicek has focused research on professional practice applications that minimise risk in cross-cultural environments. Kubicek holds a Bachelor of Aviation (Western Sydney University, 2003), a Master of Business in Human Resource Management (CSU, 2008), and a Doctorate in Business Administration in Behavioral Risk Management (Charles Sturt University, 2015).

James Law was a police officer in operations and training in the United Kingdom for thirty years. He was a lecturer at the University of Ulster and Rabdan Academy (United Arab Emirates). After retirement, Law worked in the field of community policing in the refugee camps of Jordan. He holds a Bachelor of Arts in Professional Development in Leadership and Management, a Master's Degree in Human Rights and a Master's Degree in Child Care Law and Practice.

Nigel Lloyd joined the UK police in 1977 and retired at the rank of Superintendent after 30 years of policing. Having been Director of the Core Leadership Programme at the Police Staff College, after retirement, Lloyd continued to deliver Leadership courses and Neighbourhood Policing courses to forces across England and Wales. He later continued to specialise in Leadership development at the Leadership Centre for Saudi Aramco and Rabdan Academy (United Arab Emirates). Lloyd holds a First Class Honours Degree in Education (1998), a Masters (Distinction) Degree in Leadership and Management (2007), and he has been a Fellow of the Chartered Management Institute since 2007.

Michał Matyasik holds a PhD in Political Science (Jagiellonian University, 2006). He has lectured at Jagiellonian University, the American University in the Emirates, and Rabdan Academy (UAE) on many topics related to International Relations and Security. Matyasik was deployed to Afghanistan (NATO ISAF) as Civil-Military functional specialist responsible for provision of humanitarian assistance, negotiation, and civil environment evaluation.

Johannes Oosthuizen has 24 years of experience with the South African Defence Force and the Dorset Police (UK) where he retired at the rank of Inspector.

Oosthuizen has lectured at the University of West London, the University of Greenwich (London), the University of Winchester, and the John Jay College of Criminal Justice (New York). He is currently an Assistant Professor at Rabdan Academy (UAE). Oosthuizen holds a Bachelor of Science in Policing (2007), a Master of Science in Criminology and Criminal Justice (2009) and a PhD in Neighbourhood Policing (2020), all from the University of Portsmouth.

Larry Poe served in the United States Navy on active duty and as a reserve officer. His military tours of duty include US Pacific Command, the Middle East and the Pentagon. He also specialized in coordinating international law enforcement operations and training for various US government departments and INTERPOL. Poe holds an Executive Master's Degree in International Emergency and Disaster Management (Georgetown University, 2018) and has attended executive training at Harvard University and the Massachusetts Institute of Technology (MIT).

Nikola Protrka joined the Croatian Police in 1998. As a national expert on Cybercrime, he worked in most investigative areas related to Cybercrime from computer fraud, ransomware, and DDOS attacks. He became a senior lecturer at the Police Academy Zagreb in 2009 and represented the Croatian Ministry of the Interior internationally, designing and delivering training. Protrka remains a serving police officer and lectures at the Police Academy in Zagreb. He has considerable operational experience in criminal investigations and he is a member of European Union Agency for Law Enforcement Training. He lectures on Cybercrime, Digital Evidence, and Computer Forensics. He has written extensively on Cyber Crime. Protrka holds a PhD in International Co-operation and Security (University of Zadar, 2018).

Andrew Rose joined the Metropolitan Police (London, U.K.) in 1980 and served for 32 years, retiring as a Detective Inspector. As a career detective, he worked in most investigative areas from volume crime to homicide and terrorism. He became an instructor at the Metropolitan Police Detective Training School in 1999 and represented Scotland Yard internationally, designing and delivering training. Immediately after retiring, Rose was security manager at a venue for the 2012 London Olympics. He is currently a senior lecturer at the University of West London where he is the School Lead for Policing and the PEQF Link Tutor. He lectures on Policing, Criminology, Forensic Science and Forensic Psychology. Rose has a Master of Science in Investigative Forensic Psychology (London South Bank, 2010) and is a Fellow of the Higher Education Academy.

Mark Roycroft served in the Metropolitan Police (UK) for 30 years with postings as a Senior Detective in homicide, counterterrorism, and criminal intelligence. Roycroft secured a Fulbright Scholarship (2001) to research major investigations in the USA. He has authored two books, *Police Chiefs in the UK* (2017) and *Decision Making in Police Enquires and Critical Incidents* (2019), and has written extensively on extremism, investigative issues, private policing, and the history of sexual assault investigations. Roycroft is currently an Assistant Professor at Rabdan Academy (UAE) and has also lectured at the University of East London and the Open University (UK). He holds a PhD from Surrey University (2008).

Andrew Williamson served with the Royal Air Force, UK National Police and the Abu Dhabi Police for over 39 years in a variety of operational and training roles. He has fulfilled all of the roles of operational crime scene investigation. Williamson has also worked with the UK and foreign governments conducting reviews and developing national policing projects. He has worked as a team leader and lecturer at Rabdan Academy (UAE). Williamson holds a Diploma in Higher Education (Edinburgh Napier, 2014) and a Master of Letters in Terrorism Studies (St. Andrew's, 2019).

List of Figures

Use of Force and Public Order

Fig. 1   Conflict management model...................................54

Armed Policing

Fig. 1   THE RCMP Incident Management Intervention Model'
          (IMIM) model of force......................................65
Fig. 2   Number of armed officers 2010 to 2019.......................68

Investigative Interviewing

Fig. 1   Achieving best evidence and PEACE model 190
Fig. 2   PEACE model...191
Fig. 3   ABE in criminal proceedings...............................192

Counterterrorism

Fig. 1   Terror attacks and deaths in Western Europe, 1970–2015 270

Knowledge Management (KM) and Intelligence-Led Policing (ILP)

Fig. 1   Intelligence tradecraft terminology 328
Fig. 2   The SARA model..338

Global Policing Leadership and Security Sector Reform

Fig. 1   Innovation in leadership 353
Fig. 2   Innovation in leadership training: balance 355
Fig. 3   Innovation in leadership training: blended 357
Fig. 4   Leadership and advisory professional development and training
          delivery model 358
Fig. 5   Leadership and Advisory Professional Development
          (LAPD) framework......................................363

Personal Resilience in High-Risk Domains

Fig. 1   Hofstede's dimensions of culture 374

Building Communities from the Inside Out

Fig. 1   Traditional services model 425
Fig. 2   ABCD approach 425

List of Tables

Accountability and Governance

Table 1   Potential benefits of private/public policing..24

Table 2   Who performs what policing task? 26

Armed Policing

Table 1   Notable UK police shooting incidents 60

Table 2   The advantages/disadvantages of routinely arming the police.............64

Sexual Assault Investigations in the UK and Canada

Table 1   CPS rape case outcomes 2017–2019 174

Table 2   The development of rape policy in the UK timetable 176

Knowledge Management (KM) and Intelligence-Led Policing (ILP)

Table 1   The differences between IM and KM 331

Table 2   Five regimes of intelligence 335

Global Policing Leadership and Security Sector Reform

Table 1   Pillar 1 SSR..363

Building Communities from the Inside Out

Table 1   Public services model versus ABCD model.......................................427

Conclusion

Table 1   Skills described in the chapters..439

Part I

Introduction

Introduction

Mark Roycroft

The global policing landscape has changed dramatically due to significant advances in Information and Communications Technology (ICT) and new crime types. In addition, consequential movements of population and a rising demand for police services set the agenda for the modern police officer at all levels. The police must deal with counter-terrorism and public order issues as well as combating organized criminal activity. Police forces are now more accountable and are subject to increased governance and accountability, not just from formal oversight bodies, but also from the public who can record and transmit police behavior within seconds. Furthermore, crime has moved indoors and on line. This book was designed and written with the intent of providing a comprehensive overview of the most significant operational and strategic challenges facing modern policing and the post Covid19 world. These challenges are impacted by leadership at all levels, regardless of rank. This new world has provided significant new challenges for the police such as the spontaneous global public order Black Lives Matter protests following the death of George Floyd in Minneapolis on May 25, 2020.

Research by Deloitte (2018) stated that the police are now in the 4th stage or 4th evolution of policing following the ICT revolution. Furthermore, crime has increasingly moved indoors and on line. The previous stages started with the

M. Roycroft (✉)
Rabdan Academy, Al Bhustan, Abu Dhabi, United Arab Emirates
e-mail: mroycroft@ra.ac.ae

© The Author(s), under exclusive license to Springer Nature Switzerland AG 2021
M. Roycroft, L. Brine (eds.), *Modern Police Leadership*,
https://doi.org/10.1007/978-3-030-63930-3_1

3

inception of the modern police in London in 1829. While Sir Robert Peel's Nine Principles still apply (see Appendix 1) the "public police (Roycroft 2016) "have taken on more and more responsibilities". It is critical to reflect on Peelian Principles, and in particular, his belief that "*the police are the public and that the public are the police*", the police being only members of the public who are paid to give full time attention to duties which are incumbent on every citizen in the interests of community welfare and existence".

https://www.gov.uk/government/publications/policing-by-consent/definition-of-policing-by-consent

Roycroft (2016) explored the issue of rising demand for police services in his book "Police Chiefs in the UK". One Chief Officer stated "that modern technology is changing both the demand on policing and the structure of Policing" (Roycroft 2016). Another Chief mentioned that the "totality of the policing mission is based on vulnerability of risk whether it is flooding, crime or firearms crime. We are there to protect life". These demands require different skills and leadership and this book sets out to illustrate the plethora of demands facing the Police. Jackson states that (2012) the Police must be futurist. Another Police Chief (2016: 65) stated that the modern Police need education, engineering, and enforcement to disrupt and create barriers. "*These three Es show the complexity and wide reaching response required by the Police in the modern era*".

In addition, the police are expected to, and must, act with the highest degree of ethics in their day to day contact with the public and during investigations. Even when off-duty, there is an expectation that a police officer will maintain this behavior. This is reflected in the Code of Ethics that the UK police follow (see Appendix 2) and the guiding core values of the Royal Canadian Mounted Police (RCMP) (see Appendix 3). In fact, the RCMP Act (1985) legislates that RCMP members carry out their responsibilities in a specific and ethical manner. (See Appendix 5 "ROYAL CANADIAN MOUNTED POLICE REGULATIONS, 2014") https://laws-lois.justice.gc.ca/eng/acts/R-10/page-7.html#h-421417).

There are many similarities in these expectations across police organizations in the Commonwealth, Western countries, and the Middle East. The attributes of honesty, integrity, professionalism, compassion, accountability, and respect are key for police for officers. These are aimed as a guide to assist the ethical decision making of members. These principles highlight the standards by which the public expect their police officers and other employees to behave.

Ever-changing demographics in most parts of the world mean that police are faced with an increasingly aging and multi-cultural society, as well as significant advances in how individual sexuality is viewed. The police themselves must not only reflect that community, but also have the skill set to deal with both traditional and modern crimes. Increasingly, police are confronted with mental health issues in many of their duties, including depression, psychosis, and substance addiction. In addition, police leadership is recognizing the toll that policing takes on first responders and investigators (see chapter "Mental Health Awareness for Police Officers"). This requires leadership at all levels of the police force.

The UK College of Policing (2013) stated that "it must create a police service more confident in the professional judgment and discretion of individual officers "The International Association of Chief Officers (IACP) mentions the concept of *dispersed "leadership and that every Police Officer is a leader"*. Fletcher (2007) comments that it will become increasingly unlikely that, in a world of growing complexity, a single leader will possess the capability and competence to understand, solve and improve leadership problems in order to achieve effective team outcomes. It must be the entire team that possesses leadership skills. The onus is therefore placed on every police officer, under the maxim of dispersed leadership, to display leadership skills and ethical decision making in their respective area of policing, whether that is specialized or not. The police are often seen as a Command and Control organization but the rank of constable enjoys a great deal of discretion. By default, it will invariably be the most junior officers who first attend a critical incident and therefore their "golden hour" can have a significant effect on the reputation of a police force. The book talks of dispersed leadership and sets out to explore whether leadership is dispersed or part of an integrated structure that accommodates leadership at all levels.

The leader at the top of the organization needs to balance local, regional, national, and international issues, but it is the officers at the operational level that take the greatest physical risks and can influence the reputation of the police by their actions. These issues affect each level of the police service with The Price Waterhouse Cooper (PWC) report "Policing in a connected world" (2018) stating that *"an emerging set of challenges threatens to undermine both the capability of police organizations to stay ahead of crime and crucially the public perception that they are doing so"*. Well and Schafer (2006) discuss the future trends affecting Policing including demographic, economic, political, and technological trends. All of these simultaneously offer challenges and opportunities for the global police service.

The police operate in a challenging environment and are often seen as the primary social agency. Manning (2008) comments that the police should be built around the core goals of accountability, legitimacy and innovation. Stone and Travis (2011) state that the 'New professionalism' of policing should be built around the same goal.

The contributors to this book set out some of the issues the modern police, at all ranks, in the early twenty-first century face, while offering informed comment from the viewpoints of both an academic and practitioner. These 'pracademics' contribute to the ongoing debate on how these trends and themes can be managed. The book concentrates on the skill set needed for the modern police leader at every level of a police organization. The Chapters are researched and written by a unique body of experts who have both practitioner experience and academic knowledge.

There are links between the Chapters with many core themes such as, community relations, decision making, fast time intelligence, Human Rights, and mental health. This is deliberate and emphasizes the fact that policing can no longer be compartmentalized. Maintaining security and preserving life and freedom demand that the police leader has to balance many competing priorities such as community policing, counter-terrorism, crime fighting, and the maintenance of public order. This needs to be further balanced against a backdrop of preserving Human Rights and accountability. In the modern world, these areas are inextricably intertwined.

The 2017 radical Islam terror attacks in Manchester and London (UK) saw 36 victims killed and hundreds injured; yet prior to this tragedy, the UK Police and security services thwarted 20 similarly planned attacks. The subsequent report by Anderson (2017 gov.uk) illustrates the complexities of policing in the early twenty-first century. These attacks showed the professionalism of the police and security services along with the resilience of the British public. Leadership was displayed at all levels. The three main issues were how the police use data, the need for intelligence sharing with local agencies and dealing with extreme ideology. It is the role of the police leader to promote and drive tolerance while deterring and disrupting those who do not share these values.

The rise of suicide bombing, as a form of asymmetric warfare of the 'weak' against the 'strong, has grown exponentially. Of the 10 worst bombings between 2011 and 2108, seven were suicide bombings (Overton 2019 The Price of Paradise). Over 55 countries have been affected by suicide bombers using this inexpensive and effective method. Overton (2019) comments that this is not Islamist extremism but these are extremists who use Islam as a facade. So how does one counter the radicalization of young people? The modern police leader must build a counter-terror strategy based on humanitarianism, engagement and understanding. The numerous global ideological based attacks have been far reaching and impact many countries. In addition, active or spree shooting attacks have complicated the situation. The response to firearms incidents, in countries where the general duty police officer is not armed, requires a balanced approach by the Firearms Commander with a need to preserve life and arrest suspects. In countries where the generally duty police officer is armed, there is extensive 'active shooter' scenario training for the first responders. The use of technology, the need for local intelligence, and the ease of travel are all critical aspects of counter-terrorism policing in the twenty-first century.

The 2019 Christchurch (New Zealand) attack was the first to be live-streamed on a social media platform by the perpetrator. Despite being removed quickly from

Facebook, the company admitted that its Artificial Intelligence (AI) moderation failed. The evidential and public responsibility issues and legal consequences exposed by this attack provide dilemmas for any police leader. Yet, as much as these attacks necessitate new understanding and knowledge, they also still require the best of the more traditional techniques of local policing, including evidence gathering with robust decision making.

A multilayered approach, including police leadership, is needed to disrupt and monitor not only terror groups, but also organized crime syndicates that they often work in concert with.

Fact Sheet

Poly Groups Europol

Poly-criminality

Some 45% of the Organized Crime Groups (OCGs) reported for the SOCTA 2017 are involved in more than one criminal activity. The share of these poly-criminal groups has increased sharply compared to 2013.

OCGs also often engage in more than one criminal activity to mitigate risks, reduce operational costs, and increase profit margins. The OCGs involved in the trafficking of illicit goods are the most poly-criminal groups in the EU. These groups typically traffic more than one illicit commodity such as counterfeit goods or different types of illicit drugs.

Many OCGs are highly flexible and able to shift from one criminal activity to another or to add new criminal activities to their crime portfolio. In many cases, OCGs operate on an on-demand basis and only become active once new profit opportunities emerge.

Both traditional acquisitive and new crime types require police investigators at all levels to upskill and lead enquiries. This includes not only hands on standard tactical investigations methods, but also cybercrime, forensics, forensic intelligence, and interviewing, and risk management.

The management of risk is a recurring theme throughout the book. The UK College of policing (see www.app.college.police.uk/app-content/risk-) lays out 10 different principles of risk. (See Appendix 9) Principle 3 states that: Decision makers must be able to exercise sound judgment in coming to an appropriate decision. They should consider how to make the benefits more likely and valuable and the harms less likely and less serious. Fleming (2015) in her book *Rising to the Top* states that police officers hold a unique role in liberal democracies and their ability to lead is generally regarded as key to performance. This ability to exercise sound judgment, decision making, and transformational leadership in moments of high stress is a significant theme throughout this book.

Although technology has assisted evidence retrieval, it has also brought about the challenge of being able to retrieve it all for evidentiary purposes. This need to collate passive data mixed with the need to deal with the media, reassure vulnerable communities, and conduct international enquiries illustrates the complex milieu in which modern police leaders operate. A Chief Constable in "Police Chiefs in the UK" (Roycroft 2016) comments that the police were facing a tidal wave of cyber facilitated crime. Police officers need new skills and modernized legislation. The head of Britain's National Cyber Crime Unit (NCCU) states (Times 9/4/19) that laws dealing with cybercrime in the UK were outdated and failed to punish suspects adequately. Cybercrime has now become the volume crime overtaking traditional acquisitive crime as the major crime type. In November 2018 (3rd Special report 19/4/19 HL paper 222) the Joint Parliamentary Committee on National Security Strategy (JCNSS) states that the government was failing to grapple with "potentially devastating" cyber threats to energy, health services, transport and water. There is a role for internet and social media providers, and new laws are needed to deal with new crimes. The police leader needs to work with private companies to deal with cyber issues. Assistant Commissioner Neil Basu the head of Scotland Yard's Counter-Terrorism warned in March 2019 that, following the attack in New Zealand, mainstream media websites were contributing to the radicalization of extremists. Cybercrime involves cyber enabled and cyber dependent crime and requires international partnerships and industry liaison to help combat it. The Darknet provides anonymization for criminals and the police, government, and the private sector must deter and disrupt these activities.

Public order policing remains a major issue in the twenty-first century as is illustrated by the Gilets jaunes (yellow vests) Protests in Paris (2018/2019), the Ferguson Missouri Riots (2014) and the Black Lives Matter Protests (2020). In France, the French National Police riot squad, the Compagnies républicaines de sécurité (CRS), have been strongly criticized for using sting-ball grenades that contain 25 g of TNT high-explosive. France is the only European country where crowd-control police use such powerful grenades. Mega events and international conferences demonstrate the need for 'hard' and 'soft' options in dealing with both preplanned and spontaneous protests. This issue is explored in chapter "Use of Force and Public Order". In some respects, public order policing has been made easier by the advent of CCTV and drones, but more difficult by the increased mobility and coordination offered to protestors by the technology of social media.

Crisis and disaster management also poses significant new challenges for policing in the twenty-first century. Police officers and other public service organizations deploy as the first responders in a wide variety of unforeseen situations. These officers are required to develop new knowledge, skills, and abilities in order to cope and adapt to a changing, more globalized environment. These challenges range from natural disasters to man-made accidents and intentional human malevolence. Not only has the probability of such events increased, their consequences and impact have wider implications. Public security agencies that fail to respond rapidly and efficiently to such emergency events run the risk of reputational damage and the loss of public trust.

The need to protect vulnerable victims from abuse and exploitation requires specialist investigational skills coupled with reliable third party reporting. The global movement of people as commodities, including human trafficking, means that victim reports can come from various sources. For example, the Darknet was the subject of an investigation by Europol in 2017 that saw 39 arrests for Live Distant Child Abuse (LDCA). Historical child abuse enquires consume £1 billion of resources annually in the UK (Times 22 March 16). A similar situation exists in relation to the historic residential schools of Canada which were run by Catholic and Anglican missionaries in the mid-1900s.

Organized crime and transnational organized crime (TOC) deal with a multitude of commodities, including counterfeit goods, drugs, firearms, humans (including kidnapping for ransom), and wildlife. The modern police leader must ensure a thorough response at regional, national, and international levels. This requires coordination and collaboration with other agencies. The judicious use of informants, intelligence gathering from all sources and global evidence retrieval demand an in-depth skill set from police leaders. TOC is ever changing and adapts to markets. Over the past two decades, as the world economy has globalized, so have its illicit counterparts. The global impact of transnational crime has risen to unprecedented levels. Criminal groups have appropriated new technologies, adapted horizontal network structures that are difficult to trace and stop, and diversified their activities.

Fleming (2015) notes that the effective working of partnership was vital for identifying local problems, delivering preventive solutions, and ensuring an accurate understanding of the needs of young people and their families. He states that where coordination is well-organized through effective partnerships, there are significant benefits to community safety, crime prevention, and deradicalization. Partnerships can now be found in diverse areas of policing, such as domestic violence, child abuse, mental health, public protection, and road traffic (HM Government 2011). Many of these 'policing' issues can also be tackled using a 'whole-of-government' approach while working closely with international allies. Chapter "Global Policing Leadership and Security Sector Reform" discusses the link between security and development and highlights the importance of security in the establishment of sustainable peace and development.

Community Policing forms the backbone of policing and builds on the Peelian principle of "the police are the public and the public are the police". Tilley (2003: 315) explains that Community Policing is done with the community and for the community rather than being viewed as policing of the community. Community policing allows

the community to come up with solutions that will work within their own neighbor-
hood and to change or eliminate those that do not work. Local policing in the UK involves Police and Community Support officers as well as warranted officers and has
recently been extended to community responders who act as firefighters, medics and
police officers in rural areas (Times 10/4/19). This multi layered approach adds to the
complexity of leadership and requires additional skills from police leaders.

There are several themes that are evident throughout this book, including accountability, decision making, governance, human rights,, leadership, mental health issues
in the community and amongst law enforcement officers, intelligence and information, partnerships, the need to work with public and private sector agencies, risk
management at all levels, and vulnerable populations. This book synthesizes many of
the complex facets of modern policing. Decision making forms a significant part of
this skill set and is a critical component of the modern leader. The need to prioritize
and review those decisions in the era of close accountability and governance require
the modern leader to be well versed in multiple areas. This book lays out a strong
foundation for operational and strategic policing in the twenty-first century.

References

Anderson, D. (2017). *Attacks in London and Manchester*. March-June 2017. London: David
    Anderson.
Brown, J. (Ed.). (2013). *The Future of Policing*. Routledge, UK.
Caless, B. (2015). *Leading Policing in Europe an empirical study of strategic police manage-
    ment*. Policy Press.
Deloitte Policing 4.0. (2018). *Deciding the future of policing in the UK*.
Fleming, J. (2015). *Police Leadership: Rising to the Top*. Oxford, UK.
Fletcher, J. (2007). Leadership, power and positive relationships. In J. Dutton & B. R. Ragins
    (Eds.), *Exploring positive relationships at work: Building a theoretical and research
    foundation* (pp. 347–371). Mahwah: Lawrence Erlbaum Publishers.
Friedman, L. (2015). *Strategy: A history*. New York: Oxford University Press.
HM Government. (2011). https://www.theguardian.com/world/2015/nov/20/mali-attack-
    highlights-global-spread-extremist-violence
Kind, S. (1987). *The Scientific Investigation of Crime*. Manchester: John Sherratt and Son.
Kirby, S. (2013). *Effective Policing?: Implementation in Theory and Practice*. Palgrave
    Macmillan.
Manning. (2008). *The technology of Policing*. UK: Policing Journal.
Overton, I. (2019). *The price of paradise*. Oxford University Press.

Price Waterhouse (PWC). (2018). *Policing in a connected world.* https://www.pwc.com›gx›en›industries›government-public-services›public

Roycroft, M. (2016). *Police chiefs in the UK.* UK: Palgrave.

Roycroft, M. (2019). *Decision making in major enquires.* UK: Palgrave.

Stone, C., & Travis, J. (2011, March). *"Toward a New Professionalism in Policing." New Perspectives in Policing.* Executive Session on Policing and Public Safety.

Tilley, N. (2003). Community policing, problem-orientated policing and intelligence-led transnational organized crime. *Director of National Intelligence.* Available at: https://www.dni.gov/. Accessed 15 Sept 2019.

Wells, W., & Schafer, J. A. (2006). Officer perceptions of police responses to persons with a mental illness. *Policing: An International Journal of Police Strategies & Management, 29*(4), 578–601.

Fact Sheet Human Rights

Article 8
Article 2

Human Rights

Lindsey Brine

The United Nations defines Human Rights as:

> *rights inherent to all human beings, regardless of race, sex, nationality, ethnicity, language, religion, or any other status. Human rights include the right to life and liberty, freedom from slavery and torture, freedom of opinion and expression, the right to work and education, and many more. Everyone is entitled to these rights, without discrimination.* (https://www.un.org/en/sections/issues-depth/human-rights/)

In order to understand how Human Rights impact policing, it is critical to have an understanding of the history of Human Rights. Religions have had a significant impact on civilization and Human Rights for thousands of years. Abrahamic religions are based on the concept of only one God, that being the God of Abraham. This stream of religion includes the main religions Christianity, Islam, and Judaism. Approximately 55 percent of the population of the earth belongs to this stream. Dharmic religions originated in the Indian sub-continent and include Buddhism, Hinduism, and Sikhism. These account for approximately 25 percent of the world population. There are other religions in various parts of the world, including many indigenous religions. However, Christianity, Islam, and Judaism have had the greatest impact on Human Rights issues in the West and in the Middle East. All of these religions, including the Dharmic, in their own way, essentially since their

L. Brine (✉)
Rabdan Academy, Al Bhustan, Abu Dhabi, United Arab Emirates

© The Author(s), under exclusive license to Springer Nature Switzerland AG 2021
M. Roycroft, L. Brine (eds.), *Modern Police Leadership*,
https://doi.org/10.1007/978-3-030-63930-3_2

inception, have laid out some of the rights and responsibilities of their followers in addition to ensuring that individual and collective rights are protected to some degree.

The first known non-religious documentation of the rights of individuals and groups was in 1215 AD with the creation of the Magna Carta Libertatum (commonly referred to as the Magna Carta). This Latin document was written by the Archbishop of Canterbury at the behest of King John of England with the intent of settling an escalating feud between the King and a group of barons who were dismayed with the actions of the King. This was the very first time that the principle that all citizens, including the King, are subject to the law. The initial version of the Magna Carta included clauses that protected the rights of the church, and also protected barons from being jailed illegally and giving them access to swift justice. A subsequent war between King John and the barons resulted in the Magna Carta being nullified. In 1225 AD, a new version of the Magna Carta was created by King Henry III, the son of King John.

The most critical clause of the Magna Carta states:

> *No free man shall be seized or imprisoned, or stripped of his rights or possessions, or outlawed or exiled, or deprived of his standing in any other way, nor will we proceed with force against him, or send others to do so, except by the lawful judgement of his equals or by the law of the land. To no one will we sell, to no one deny or delay right or justice.*

Although the Magna Carta only applied to 'free men', not the entire population, this clause has set the foundation for many other Human Rights decisions or documents over the ensuing centuries, including: the guarantee of a jury trial by Parliament (fourteenth century), a seventeenth century interpretation in England of individual liberties, Sir Edward Coke interpreted it as a declaration of individual liberty in his conflict with the early Stuart kings in the 17th century; and it echoes in the American Bill of Rights (1791) and the United Nations Universal Declaration of Human Rights (1948). This Declaration was proclaimed primarily in response to the significant abuse of Human Rights in World War Two. Eight hundred years later, the Magna Carta remains the foundation of both the British and Canadian Constitutions. (https://www.bl.uk/magna-carta/articles/magna-carta-an-introduction)

Until World War Two, the protection of Human Rights had been considered a matter primarily between states and persons under their jurisdiction; the concept of national sovereignty had prevented states or the international community from interfering with the way Human Rights were safeguarded in other states. Where such interference had taken place, it was in the form of diplomatic protection of a country's own citizens under the jurisdiction of another state. The European

Convention on Human Rights was ratified and entered into force in 1953. Many former Soviet bloc countries joined the Convention in the 1990s after the collapse of the Union of Soviet Socialist Republics. Two key Articles in relation to domestic and international policing deal with the right to life of human beings (Article 2) and the right to privacy (Article 8). Of note, Articles 3 and 4 deal with torture and forced labor (slavery). These Articles play an important role in how law enforcement agencies investigate and try to combat forced prostitution, human trafficking, and migrant (human) smuggling. Further articles related specifically to the justice system include: Article 5 (the right to liberty, and by extension prohibits unlawful arrest and detention), and Article 6 (the right to a fair trial). (see Appendix 7) (https://www.echr.coe.int/Documents/Convention_ENG.pdf)

The original constitution of Canada (1867) was an act of the British Parliament. As a result, only Britain had the authority to change it. After extensive community and parliamentary collaborative consultation, Prime Minister Pierre Trudeau led the effort in receiving approval from Britain for one last time by creating the Canada Act (1982) which allowed Canada independence from Britain in amending the Canadian constitution. At the same time, Queen Elizabeth II also signed the Canadian Charter of Rights and Freedoms, which is a binding list of the most important rights of Canadians.

As with many Human Rights charters, the Canadian Charter ensures the primacy of both Human Rights and basic freedoms. There are other Human Rights charters and documents within Canada. These include legislation and policy from federal, provincial and territorial governments, as well as common law and international laws and treaties An additional right or freedom can be added at any level of government, so long as it contradicts neither rights enshrined in the Canadian Charter of Rights and Freedoms, nor any relevant case law at the level of the Supreme Court of Canada. The Canadian Bill of Rights (1960) and the Canadian Human Rights Act (1977) both still in force today, are often still used in court decisions in relation to specific rights not mentioned in the Canadian Charter of Rights and Freedoms.

As a result of the European Convention on Human Rights (1950), many countries felt compelled to create domestic legislation based on the rights found in that document. As a result, the United Kingdom created the Human Rights Act (1998). In essence, this legislation created law which makes it unlawful to contravene those rights found in the European Convention on Human Rights (1950). (https://www.bl.uk/collection-items/human-rights-act-1998)

"It enabled British courts to enforce the Convention without referring to the European Court in Strasbourg. The Act repeats verbatim the Articles of the European Convention, and in so doing re-establishes in British law the ideals of

civil liberty inspired by Magna Carta" (https://bl.uk/collection-items/human-rights-act-1998). The Human Rights Act (1998) very closely mirrors many of the pieces of legislation noted above.

Similarly, the Charter of Fundamental Rights of the European Union was proclaimed in 2000. It did not come into full force until 2009 as the result of numerous political and legal issues. This Charter is comprised of 54 articles embedded in seven titles. The key titles that relate to policing and justice include: Dignity, Freedoms, Equality, and Justice. Again, this legislation very closely reflects the various declarations and pieces of legislation noted above.

The JAPAN Mnemonic Explaining Human Rights Ethos

The following mnemonic describes some of the key elements to which all police officers should adhere. The key principles are in accordance with Human Rights directives and legislation and are fundamental in decision making and critical incidents.

- J ustification (legality)—reasonable grounds to suspect criminal activity
- A uthorisation—that proper procedures have been followed and recorded
- P roportionality—nature of interference is proportional to matter under investigation
- A ccountability—all options considered and recorded
- N ecessity—the methods used are necessary for the enquiry. Activities are in accordance with law and are necessary in a democratic society in pursuit of one or more aims specified in Article (2) ECHR. The Regulation of Investigatory Powers Act (2000), 1997 Act and 1994 Act all stipulate that the police officer granting an authorization or judge issuing a warrant for directed or intrusive surveillance, or interference with property, must believe that the activities to be authorized are necessary on one or more grounds. This involves balancing the seriousness of the intrusion into the privacy of the subject and proportionate to what is sought to be achieved. Police decisions must be recorded.

Sammy Yatim Case Study

Minutes before midnight on July 26, 2013 the Toronto (Canada) Police Service responded to a 911 call of an irate male on a public streetcar (tram) brandishing a switchblade knife and threatening the passengers. Eighteen-year-old Yatim initially told the passengers to remain on the streetcar and then ordered them off. Yatim appeared to be mentally unstable and at one point held his exposed genitals in one hand and the switchblade in the other. One of the first responding officers, with his firearm drawn, ordered Yatim not to move and to drop the knife. This same officer requested a nearby officer deploy a Conducted Energy Weapon (CEW- TASER). Yatim moved forward, although still on the street car, and the police officer fired three shots at Yatim, hitting him and causing him to fall to the floor of the streetcar. Moments later, Yatim made an attempt to get up and the same officer fired an additional six rounds at him. Approximately, thirty seconds later, a nearby officer deployed his CEW striking Yatim. At autopsy, it was determined that Yatim was killed by the first three shots fired. The entire incident was captured on a private cell phone camera and the footage was watched widely around the world.

The Ontario Special Investigations Unit immediately took over the investigation as the independent authority mandated to investigate police related deaths. Approximately three weeks later, the police officer who fired the shots was charged with Second Degree Murder (Section 230 Criminal Code of Canada, 1985). He was also charged with Attempted Murder (Section 239 Criminal Code of Canada, 1985).

Eventually the case went to a jury trial in 2015/2016 and the accused police officer was found Not Guilty of Second Degree Murder, as the jury believed that the first three shots were necessary, proportionate, and justifiable. However, the police officer was found Guilty of Attempted Murder as the jury believed that the final six shots were not justified. The police officer was sentenced to six years in jail. He appealed the decision and sentence to the Ontario Court of Appeal and the appeal was denied. The police officer then applied to the Supreme Court of Canada for leave to appeal the conviction and sentence. His application was denied.

In August 2013, the Chief of the Toronto Police Service mandated a review of the police response to the incidents involving those suffering from mental health issues. The report,

Police Encounters with People in Crisis—Toronto Police Service (TPS) (https://www.torontopolice.on.ca/publications/files/reports/police_encounters_with_people_in_crisis_2014.pdf), was completed by The Honourable Frank Iacobucci, a retired Supreme Court of Canada Justice. This study was ordered as a result of the Yatim shooting, but the mandate did not include a review of the actual incident itself. Rather, it was meant to be an independent review of "the policies, practices, and procedures of, and the services provided by, the TPS with respect to the use of lethal force or potentially lethal force, in particular in encounters with persons who are or may be emotionally disturbed, mentally disturbed or cognitively impaired." The report is over 400 pages long and made 84 recommendations. Although the report was written for a municipal police force, it had wide ranging implications for all law enforcement organizations across Canada, including the federal Royal Canadian Mounted Police. The recommendations of the report focused on crisis intervention, equipment, the mental health system, mental health of police officers, police culture, police training, recruiting, supervision, and the use of force, (https:// www.thestar.com/news/gta/sammyyatim.html)

Questions

Seminar Questions

Using the JAPAN mnemonic, analyze each component in relation to the above incident.

Do the same rules of proportionality apply to situations involving mental health?

Should any of the other officers present at the shooting have been held responsible for what occurred?

Without considering the court's verdict, argue why or why not lethal force was justified in this case.

All police actions in the UK must be proportionate and necessary. Define these two terms in relation to the *McCann and Others v United Kingdom* (1995) case involving the Irish Republican Army (IRA) mentioned in the chapter "Accountability and Governance".

Exam Questions

Canada has The Canadian Bill of Rights (1960) and the Canadian Human Rights Act (1977) while Britain has its own Human Rights Act (1998). Discuss how these are important to ensure transparency and fault in the Criminal Justice systems of both countries?

Accountability and Governance

Mark Roycroft

Police in democratic societies are held accountable through independent governance bodies that oversee their behaviour and performance. It is only correct that police officers are held to the highest levels of behaviour and performance to preserve public confidence. Goldstein (1977) points out that, "The police, by the very nature of their function, are an anomaly in a free society. They are invested with a great deal of authority under a system of government in which authority is reluctantly granted and, when granted, sharply curtailed" (p. xi). The Royal Commission of Police (UK, 1962) recommends (Recommendation #6) that in relation to specific operational decision-making, the Chief Constable would enjoy complete "political independence" with respect to "quasi-judicial" law enforcement decisions (i.e. decisions re: investigation, arrest and prosecution in individual cases) (Stenning 2007, p. 18).

The police in the UK are accountable to a number of different organisations as noted below. These organisations have increased their scope and commentary on policing and, as a result, the police enjoy increased transparency. The governance model in the UK is sometimes referred to as a triangle between the Chief Constable, the Home Office and the Police and Crime Commissioner (PCC). The PCCs are elected (see below) every four years and the Home Secretary is an elected Member

M. Roycroft (✉)
Rabdan Academy, Al Bhustan, Abu Dhabi, United Arab Emirates
e-mail: mroycroft@ra.ac.ae

© The Author(s), under exclusive license to Springer Nature Switzerland AG 2021
M. Roycroft, L. Brine (eds.), *Modern Police Leadership*,
https://doi.org/10.1007/978-3-030-63930-3_3

of Parliament. The Police are expected to maintain independence from political control while performing their duties but conforming to legislative standards. The election of the PCCs saw a return to the "calculative and contractual" model of accountability (Reiner 1993) albeit on a horizontal axis rather than a formal triangle. As Reiner states the model is based on financial management. The axis is now between the PCC and the Chief Constable. The PCC can (and has) removed Chief constables under their section 38 powers of the 2011. In Canada, there are different arrangements for the Royal Canadian Mounted Police (RCMP) and provincial and municipal forces (see below).

The police in both countries are also accountable to the Courts and to the public. In England and Wales, prosecutions are undertaken by the Crown Prosecution Service in England and Wales, The Crown Office and Procurator Fiscal Service (COPFS) in Scotland, and Public Prosecution Service for Northern Ireland (PPS). This level of scrutiny appears proper for an organisation which enjoys the level of powers given to the police. There is a need for checks and balances in the system. The Public Prosecution Service of Canada (PPSC) prosecutes federal offences and provides advice to law enforcement agencies; it also has jurisdiction in the three Northern territories. In the provinces, the prosecution service is governed by each provincial government. In British Columbia, the police require pre-charge approval from the Crown Prosecutor for most offences. In the vast majority of provinces and territories, the police are able to lay a charge without this.

The police in both countries have both a discipline and an ethics code (see Introduction Chapter and Appendices 2 and 3) set out by the appropriate authorities of legislation.

The UK Independent Office for Police Conduct (IOPC)

Police complaints agencies are faced with the age old dictum of "Who polices the police?". The irony is that the police have the best skill set to investigate themselves. Roycroft (2016) finds that many PCCs and CCs commented on the good work that their Professional Standards Units (PSDs) do. Many felt that their PSDs were tougher on recalcitrant police officers than the general public.

In the UK, the Independent Office for Police Conduct succeeded the IPCC, The Independent Police Complaints Commission in 2018. The IPCC replaced the previous Police Complaints Authority in 2004. It is led by a Director General who leads the executive team and chairs the Board of the IOPC, which includes six non-executive directors. The Director is supported by two Deputy Director Generals none of whom can ever have worked for the police. There are six regional offices. The director general is appointed by the Queen and is accountable for individual casework decisions, including in respect of the investigation of the most serious and sensitive allegations involving the police. Corporate governance is provided by a board comprising a majority of non-executive directors appointed by the Home Secretary to challenge and have oversight of the overall running of the organisation (PP 11 February 2016).

It reflects a process of greater civilian oversight of the police. Bucke (2008, p. 142) comments on the debate between complainants, police forces and police staff associations about 'how proportionate the complaints system is and what an efficient and fair system should look like'. The internal Professional Standards Departments (PSDs) of each force deals with the majority of complaints.

Policing Ombudsman for Northern Ireland (PONI)

The Policing Ombudsman was created in November 2000 to give civilian oversight of police complaints in the province. Within the four nations of the UK, PONI has different terms of reference than the other three nations. The law does not permit the police in Northern Ireland to investigate complaints made by members of the public about police officers. These must be referred to the Police Ombudsman's Office for independent investigation. The Ombudsman has two offices: current investigations and historical investigation. The Ombudsman has a staff of 150, about 120 of whom work within the investigations teams. The PONI looks at evidence to decide whether police officers have acted properly, including cases of excessive force, rude or aggressive behaviour or officers acting inappropriately. PONI investigates complaints about some, but not all, civilian employees of the police. This includes those performing custody and escort duties. Chief Constable Hamilton in *Police chiefs in the UK* (2016) described PONI as offering, "Undiluted accountability a great model of accountability it has teeth and has the full powers of constables, very expensive, but we agree a joint strategy after appointing a full investigative team".

Police Investigations and Review Commissioner (PIRC) Scotland

In 2013, the Police and Fire Reform (Scotland) Act 2012 brought together Scotland's eight police services, the Scottish Crime and Drug Enforcement Agency and the Scottish Police Services Authority into the single Police Scotland. The

PIRC was created out of the old Police complaints system and is an independent organisation. The role of the PIRC is to undertake independent investigations into the most serious incidents involving the police.

Her Majesty's Inspectorate of Constabulary and Fire and Rescue Service (HMICFRS)

Her Majesty's Inspectorate like the IPCC is independent of government and the Police Service. By inspecting the forces throughout the UK, it assists in understanding the efficiency and effectiveness of the forces. Its present role and the appointment of its first civilian, Chief Inspector Sir Tom Winsor, marked another move by the Government to reform policing bodies in the UK. HMICFRS is there to challenge forces.

The HMICFRS function is to inspect police forces and fire and rescue organisations in England, Wales and Northern Ireland, carrying out inspections or reviews ranging from individual functional areas through to force-level performance and leadership. The HMICFRS looks at critical national issues and themes across the Police Service. The PEEL process looks at police effectiveness, efficiency and legitimacy (PEEL). There is a similar organisation in Scotland (HM Inspectorate of Constabulary in Scotland) that inspects Police Scotland and has powers under the Police and Fire Reform Act (Scotland) in 2012.

Police and Crime Commissioners

The introduction of elected Police and Crime Commissioners (PCCs) in England and Wales in The Police Reform and Social Responsibility Act (2011) was the biggest change to policing in a generation. The policy behind the introduction of PCCs seems analogous to the increasingly devolved model of government as exemplified by the debate over localism and the introduction of mayors.

Public elections for the first PCCs took place on 15 November 2012 in 41 police force areas across England and Wales, not including London. New elections took place in May 2016. The Deputy Mayor for Policing (MOPAC) is responsible for the PCC office in the Metropolis. When PCCs took office in 2012, they became responsible for a combined police force budget of £8 billion.

The 2011 Act establishes PCCs within each force area in England and Wales with the exception of the City of London and gives these PCCs responsibility for the totality of policing within their area. It further requires them to hold the CC in each Force to account for the operational delivery of policing in relation to the Strategic Policing Requirement (see Appendix 6) published by the Home Secretary. The ethos behind the introduction of PCCs has the principle of increased local democracy with some academics portraying the relationship as one of 'Principal/ agent' association (Davies and Johnson 2015). They examined the new power dynamics that have emerged with this shift, paying particular attention to the role of conflict in relationships between PCCs and CCs, compounded by the one-on-one dynamic.

The UK created an office to oversee Terrorist legislation named the Independent Reviewer of Terrorist legislation (IRTL). Independence is particularly vital where the oversight of intelligence and anti-terrorism is concerned, since each area is characterised by laws whose scope is controversial and publicly available information is scarce. Their role is to inform the public and political debate on anti-terrorism law including police use of the laws.

Accountability in Canada

Canada has independent civilian agencies to ensure that the police are accountable for their actions. Only six provinces—British Columbia, Alberta, Manitoba, Ontario, Quebec, and Nova Scotia—have a civilian oversight agency that independently investigate cases of serious injury and death involving police and the public. However, this excludes the RCMP in Ontario and Quebec because these independent agencies only have authority to investigate serious injury and death involving municipal, regional and provincial police. The RCMP only enforces federal laws in Ontario and Quebec, so these oversight agencies have no jurisdiction to investigate the RCMP. The RCMP conducts federal enforcement AND municipal and provincial/territorial enforcement in all of the other provinces and territories.

The seven other Canadian jurisdictions—Saskatchewan, New Brunswick, Prince Edward Island, Newfoundland and Labrador, Yukon, Northwest Territories and Nunavut—do not have a civilian oversight agency that investigates police misconduct. In some of these provinces, the oversight agency from another province or an independent police force will often be asked to investigate.

Justice Tulloch's report (https://www.attorneygeneral.jus.gov.on.ca/english/ about/pubs/police_oversight_review/ 2017) on police governance in Ontario found several issues with the Special Investigations Unit which was formed in Ontario in 1990 The report made 129 recommendations to the province's three police oversight agencies—chief among them was for better transparency of the independent Special Investigations Unit in Ontario (SIU).

The Civilian Review and Complaints Commission is an independent agency that reviews public complaints concerning the conduct of RCMP members but has no authority to investigate incidents of death or injury involving the RCMP. It also can only make a non-binding recommendation to the Commissioner of the RCMP. Otherwise, another police service or an RCMP investigative team from another jurisdiction will investigate the RCMP. For example, the Government of Nunavut Territory contracts the Ottawa Police Service to investigate cases of serious injury and death involving the RCMP in the Territory.

Private and Public Policing

As Rawlings states (2002:130), the majority of policing has traditionally been done by organisations and people other than the police (Table 1). In the 1990s, the Posen review distinguished between core and ancillary tasks with a reduction in police undertaking the latter and private security taking on the escorting wide loads, custody services and prisoner escorts. Bayley, Shearing (1996:585) argue that this, could be seen as "when one system of policing finished and another took its place".

Lamenting the end of public policing is somewhat premature. What has progressively occurred over the last several decades is an extension of policing

Table 1 Potential benefits of private/public policing

Potential benefits	Concerns
Cost saving in times of austerity	Failures of private sector leave public sector as
Freeing up expertise allowing trained	agency of last resort,
staff to undertake public police roles	Dispersed governance networks
Flexibility and innovation	Use of force by non-licensed or regulated staff
New skill sets acquired from mentoring	Leaving the public police to deal with difficult
in business practices and process	confrontations
engineering	Pluralisation of services, may lead to unequal
Better quality of service in routine	service distribution and exacerbate social
matters	division
Better running of middle and back room	Complaints procedure and transparency
functions.	Perceived failure of state policing
Raises the profile of the public police	Lack of training in private sector
officer.	Private security is accountable to paying
	clients/shareholders rather than tax payer
	Possibility of strike action
	Increased surveillance culture with much
	surveillance in private hands.

activities by non-state agencies and the emergence of plural provision of police services (Bayley and Shearing 1996). This can be seen as a transformation or modernisation.

A Home Office Circular (114/83) placed limits on Chief Constables on the acquisition of additional resources and requires them to consider greater cost efficiencies.

There are arguments about private sector involvement and how 'outsourcing' may be seen either as a crucial element in the modernisation agenda. This may free up trained officers to 'front line' duties or it may be seen as a creeping 'privatisation' with the state losing control of policing. Some commentators see private–public partnerships as working together in order to transform policing in the twenty-first century. Johnston (1992) for example states "fragmented, diverse, networked policing is to all intents and purposes here to stay indeed, current developments serve in many respects merely to accentuate and extend what has in fact long been a world of multiple provisions".

This gradual fracturing of the monopoly of the public police over the last 30 years is due to several factors:

1. An increase in PCSOs and the introduction of tiered policing.
2. Private security provision has risen as a consequence of liberalising powers granted in the Police Act (1994).
3. The changing nature of public places has led to an increase in private security.
4. Private sector has been a response to cost cutting in the public police forces.
5. The liberalisation of the consumption of alcohol through changes to licensing laws has stimulated expansion in the private policing of pubs, clubs etc. (Table 2).

What Should Remain in the Private Sector?

The detection of crime, both low volume and high volume, should remain part of the core function of the public police. There is a public expectation that these are part of public sector responsibilities and that a warranted officer, with the underpinning governance must deal with serious crimes such as murder and rape in a professional and sensitive way. It is unlikely that the multi-faceted aspects of such investigations involving covert surveillance, undercover operations, family liaison and forensic retrieval could ever be appropriately carried out by private companies.

Table 2 Who performs what policing task?

Task	Public police	Private provision	Combined
Minor crime investigation	Need for warranted powers for arrest	Routine statement taking Custody duties Scenes of crime	Interviewing Victim support Crime pattern analysis
Major crime investigations	Need for warranted powers for arrest/ detention/use of force Family liaison	Routine statement taking custody duties Scenes of crime Asset recovery Transporting prisoners Forensic science analysis	Specialist investigations such as E crime and fraud Victim support Behavioural investigative advice
Public order	Political protest, national prestige events	Football matches and smaller scale policing of events.	Special events
Administration	Some file production	Back office administration	Middle office administration
Intelligence gathering	Covert surveillance, undercover work Electronic intercepts	Back office, routine intelligence gathering	Cyber crime
Emergency response	'Fire-brigade' policing	Managing police call centres	Disaster management
Counter-terrorism	Covert surveillance, undercover work Electronic intercepts Local intelligence gathering Major operations	Routine statement taking Custody duties Scenes of crime Forensic science analysis	Combined arrest teams
Road traffic accidents	Fatal accidents, major traffic disruption	Routine patrolling traffic officers	Traffic investigation
Community engagement	Reassurance policing	Rostering duties	Community liaison Monitoring community tension indicators MAPPA

Public Order

Public order situations, such as the London Riots of 2011, require large reserves of uniformed officers who are garnered through mutual aid arrangements. It is difficult to envisage there being an economic benefit for the private sector given the unpredictability of such occurrences or their scale. Specialist activities such as missing person searches, firearms teams and counter-terrorism should also remain within the public sector with their complex mix of demands and potential sensitivity of issues.

Redefining the Role of the Police

The primary aim of the public police is to protect the citizen, by handling emergencies, resolving conflicts and where necessary utilising force. In addition, there may be a requirement to arrest thereby depriving the individual of their liberty. This involves the direct public–police contact with differing levels of risk and their attendant consequences. Consensus must be based on cultural, political and organisational issues (Lea 2009).

A good example of private/public policing in the UK is the use of the Highways Agency to carry out routine patrolling and minor road safety issues. The number of roads policing officers has been greatly reduced; over the last five years, it has fallen by 27%, or 1437 officers (Police Professional 26 May 2016). Roads Policing is now partly carried out by cameras and technology along with the Highways Agency.

The number of detected motoring offences fell from 4.3 million in 2001 to 1.62 million in 2013. In *Police Chiefs in the UK* (Roycroft 2016) one Chief Constable comments that, "We do not have enough resources to make the roads totally safe and secure, we have a huge reduction in permanent road policing officers, we need to be capable guardians of the roads, a lack of presence could lead to a lack of habitual compliance, cameras are a visible deterrence". But like other Chiefs and PCCs he felt that "we do not have enough officers who can make the roads safer by offering discretion and enforcing the law against dangerous drivers". He was concerned with the Big 4 issues:

- Drink and drive
- Wearing seatbelts
- Motorist using distractions such as mobile phones
- Speeding

Many forces now have shared motorway units such as the West Midlands and Staffordshire Central motorway group. However, another Chief Constable felt that roads policing was ineffective and should go completely to the Highways Agency. The National Police Chiefs Council (NPCC) "Policing the Roads in Partnership 2015–2020 for England, Wales and Northern Ireland" has the following priorities:

- Reducing road casualties
- Disrupting criminality
- Countering terrorism
- Patrolling the roads

Technology now plays, and must continue to play, a major part in Roads Policing.

Conclusion

It is clear that there is growing transparency that the modern police officer must face. The Courts, elected officials and independent bodies all hold the police to account. This is made more complex by the public police having to work with a blended model of policing. The public police are still a necessary and vital part of the state. The public and private police can work in this "blended model" especially in the areas of cybercrime. The policing role is evolving to meet new demands and this involves a new 'continuum mode' where public and private contributors exchange expertise, key personnel and importantly, accommodate shifting parameters of operations and priorities. There are new demands for police managers and leaders. Partnerships have matured and reflect the changing nature of the multifaceted private policing and security world.

Local Partnerships and International Agencies

Mark Roycroft

Partnerships, at a local, regional, national and international level, have now become an accepted and essential part of modern policing. They provide many advantages by adding to the early identification of risk at every level of policing and by assisting in information gathering and inducing a coordinated response to critical incidents.

Partnership working recognises that there is no single-agency solution to crime or social problems. Crawford (2015: 75) states that there is "need for social responses which reflect crimes' multiple etiology". It allows for the "policing of expertise, information and resources". In *Police Chiefs in the UK* (Roycroft 2016) Alun Michael, the PCC for South Wales, states that there should be a tenth Peel principle around partnership working. He states, "we need to expand our horizons beyond the 20th Century policing landscape to develop an effective partnership approach with other agencies particularly local authorities and health."

Partnership working has been a common feature in UK police forces for about 30 years. In the 1980s, police officers were not allowed in schools without permission. There was little or no multi-agency working until Section 106 of the Police and Criminal Evidence Act 1984 was proclaimed, which stipulates *"Arrangements for obtaining the views of the community on policing shall be made in each police*

M. Roycroft (✉)
Rabdan Academy, Al Bhustan, Abu Dhabi, United Arab Emirates
e-mail: mroycroft@ra.ac.ae

M. Roycroft, L. Brine (eds.), *Modern Police Leadership*,
https://doi.org/10.1007/978-3-030-63930-3_4

29

area for obtaining the views of people in that area about matters concerning the policing of the area and for obtaining their cooperation with the police in preventing crime in the area". This was the first time that the police had a statutory obligation to work with other agencies.

This section was created because of Home Affairs Committee reports (1982 and 1986) into racial attacks and harassment. Partnership working under MARAC provisions (see below) provides a statutory framework for protecting vulnerable members of society.

Until the mid-1980s, crime reduction efforts were mainly of the reaction and prevention variety. In 1988, the Home Office launched a five year 'Safer Cities' programme in 20 urban areas. A co-ordinator in each locality had the remit to bring local agencies together, consider methods of crime prevention and bid to carry out projects. The aims of the programme were to reduce crime, reduce fear of crime and create conditions for community life to flourish, using a problem-solving approach facilitated by a wide range of resources, powers and expertise. The initiative generated a hybrid form of crime reduction which became known as 'community safety', and was later mandated by the Crime and Disorder Act 1998. The Act requires the police and local authorities to establish formal partnerships, and "'formulate and implement a strategy for the reduction of crime and disorder in the area". Within this broad requirement, no particular organisational structures or working protocols were required, allowing a plethora of interpretations. There was no specific expectation in terms of results or cost-benefit. Partnership activity reached its peak in approximately 2010, in tandem with the size of neighbourhood policing teams. In fact, records of activity levels and their impacts are scarce. Since that time, financial cutbacks and burgeoning reactive demand have put this form of policing under increasing pressure.

The Benefits of Partnership Working

A US theoretical perspective on multi-agency models of crime reduction identifies seven potential benefits of *effective partnership working* (Rosenbaum 2002) including the maxim that partnerships are better able to develop creative and targeted interventions. Partnerships bring more resources and new ideas to the problem-solving arena. Furthermore, multiple interventions are likely to maximise the impact on any particular issue. The UK is witnessing a phenomenon of "County Lines Policing Crime". This phenomenon involves Organized Crime Groups (OCGs) employing young people and using modern technology to deal drugs in small provincial towns away from major cities where the police have less resources. This illustrates the modern complexity of OCGs who use modern communications and vulnerable people to deal drugs on a country wide basis. These problems require comprehensive solutions.

Why Partnerships?

Partnerships aid in the implementation of the Crime Prevention Model which is comprised of:

- Primary Prevention (situation and social prevention) and is directed at stopping a problem before it happens. This involves reducing the opportunities for crime, addressing social and / or environmental factors that increase risk of offending, and strengthening community and social structures.
- Secondary Prevention seeks to change people, typically those at high risk of embarking upon a criminal career. The focus can be on rapid/effective early interventions (e.g., youth programmes) and/or high risk neighbourhoods.
- Tertiary Prevention focuses is on dealing with offending after it has happened. The focus is on intervention in the lives of known offenders in an attempt to prevent them from re-offending.

Cunningham in *Rising to the Top* (Fleming 2015) outlines seven characteristics of effective partnerships:

- There is a need to Focus on the problem
- There is a concentration on Problem Orientated Policing (PoP)
- There has to be Trust between the partners
- Co-location of services
- A Sharing of success
- A Retaining of Professional identity
- A display of Leadership

There are many specific examples of partnership bodies such as Multi Agency Safeguarding Hub (MASH) and MARAC (see below), which provide triage and multi- agency assessment of safeguarding concerns for vulnerable adults and children. They share information from every agency and they agree on the best intervention.They provide early effective risk identification joint decision making. This provides for coordinated action to assess, manage and reduce risk.

Fact Sheet

The College of Policing under their Partnership working and multi-agency responses/mechanisms App discusses the merits of Multi-agency risk assessment conferences for domestic abuse (MARAC). A MARAC is a meeting where information on the highest-risk domestic abuse cases is shared between representatives of local police, probation services, health, child protection, housing practitioners, IDVAs and other specialists from the statutory and voluntary sectors. Once the representatives have shared all relevant information they have about a victim, potential risks are outlined and options are discussed to improve the safety of the victim. These are turned into a coordinated action plan. The primary focus of the MARAC is to safeguard the adult victim and children, and ultimately address the perpetrator's behaviour. The MARAC also makes links with other forums, including child protection case conferences, to safeguard children and manage perpetrator behaviour. The underlying principle of MARAC is that no single agency or individual can see the complete picture, but all may have insights that are crucial to the victim's safety. The victim, children or perpetrator do not attend the meeting, but the victim is represented by an Independent Domestic Violence Advisor (IDVA) who speaks on their behalf. There are currently over 270 MARACs operating across England, Wales, and Scotland and Northern Ireland managing more than 64,000 cases a year.

The partnership agenda was driven by the Crime and Disorder Act, and the Police Reform and Social Responsibility Act 2011 (section 34) which introduced the Police and Crime Commissioners for England and Wales. The PCCs must engage with local people and each Chief Constable "must make arrangements for obtaining the views of people within each neighbourhood about crime and disorder and make arrangements for providing such people with information about policing in that neighbourhood". The Police Reform and Social Responsibility Act 2011 is particularly important because it places a legal responsibility on the Chief Officer to ensure that the police are successfully engaging local communities.

The Development of the Partnership Approach

Police and Crime Commissioners (PCCs) were introduced in England and Wales in 2012 and while they are not a responsible authority for the purpose of membership of the Community Safety Partnership (CSP), they must work together with their local CSP to develop local approaches to reduce and prevent crime. They must have regard to each other's priorities when developing their respective plans.

'Metro Mayors' were introduced in May 2017 and are the PCCs for that area as is the Mayor for London who delegates their responsibilities to the Deputy Mayors Office for Policing (MOPAC).The PCCs and Mayors provide another level of accountability and governance.

The Morgan Report (1991) identifies the local authority as being central to the delivery of crime prevention strategy. The HO circular 8/1994 stated that Crime prevention cannot be left to the police alone. Crime and crime prevention strategies are two of the most socio-political important issues facing Britain in the contemporary era. The crime prevention strategies that were in place for the vast majority of the twentieth century were established to deal with nineteenth century social and political problems pertaining to urban expansion—itself a direct cause of industrialisation and the expansion of technology in the Victorian era (Elmsley 2003: 66–84). The Morgan Report (1991 para 3.15) states that "at present crime prevention is a peripheral concern of all the agencies involved and a truly core activity for none of them". It has 19 major recommendations and saw a move from voluntary to statutory responsibility on local authorities.

An example of good local working is the Merseyside Crime Prevention Fund (PCC)in Liverpool, UK (see *https://www.merseysidepcc.info/CrimePreventionFund.aspx*).

The local PCC has a Commissioner's Crime Prevention Fund which is used to help charities, community groups and social enterprises stop crime and corollary issues before they occur. This is done by reducing the opportunities for crime and by deterring people away from becoming involved in anti-social and illegal behaviour thus Bb ringing partnership agencies together in a cohesive form as noted by many PCCs (Roycroft 2016). One (PCC38) states he had set up a victims' health centre with two specialists in mental health and hate crime. Stopping the revolving door of justice and keeping young offenders out of prison was mentioned by the PCCs. The Home Affairs Select Committee Report (HASC, 2016 www.parliament.uk) describes the different ways in which the PCCs are working with local agencies and services including universities, mental health providers and victim services.

The aim of the Neighbourhood Policing Team (NPT) is to engage and network with communities so they are more reliant on each other and become independent of outside assistance, transforming their members from consumers to active citizens. In addition, NPTs should provide information on local policing activity and be accountable for that activity to provide reassurance to the public through visibility and to allow the public to discuss their individual issues and give them an opportunity to influence their local community priorities.

► Case Study: Bourne Valley Action Group (BVAG): Poole   BVAG is a volunteer group that was set up by local residents in 2010 to tackle concerns such as ASB in partnership with the local Rossmore & Alderney NPT, local authority and housing associations. Recognising that there was a strong need in the community to develop self-belief and change the negative mindset of the people living in what was labelled "a deprived area", the group wanted to encourage the development of a positive community spirit whilst addressing the underlying needs of the people living there.

Some of their initiatives include the building of a £100,000 part-National Lottery funded local outdoor play park where over 350 local people were consulted about the play area's location. They have also funded the provision of youth football coaching, environmental improvement projects, the provision of multimedia equipment in the local youth centre, organised and run several large scale outdoor events to improve community engagement and are currently carrying out a consultation exercise to determine the further needs of the residents.

BVAG were also awarded a £1million Big Lottery Award in 2012 and shortly thereafter were given a Big Society Award (2012) by the Prime Minister Mr. David Cameron, an award that 'recognises the outstanding people and organizations who are dedicated to strengthening their communities and improving lives'.

BVAG is a superb local example of local residents transforming themselves from consumers of a public service, to active citizens who are independently addressing and meeting the needs of their local community.

Police Consultancy Groups (PCGs)

Dorset Police (UK) has established 3 police consultation groups: Race Equality Council, Access Dorset and The Intercom Trust. Their role is to:

1. Be consulted on policy review and equality impact assessments (as required)
2. Provide advice on the systems and processes developed to support our People, Confidence and Equality Strategy
3. Be consulted on strategic matters (as required)
4. Provide constructive advice to the organisation on ways to improve the quality of service delivery to different religions or beliefs, Black and Minority Ethnic (BME), disabled and lesbian, gay, bisexual and transgendered (LGB&T) communities
5. Support key Force initiatives

The concept of Independent Advisory Groups (IAGs) was introduced as a result of the Macpherson Report (1999). Their role has evolved significantly and they now play an important part in ensuring that the police service effectively involves and considers the views of all communities. Independent advisors can be called upon to give guidance in the event of:

1. Any internal or external critical incident or emerging problem.
2. In the development of policy and business plans within a police force area.
3. Their terms of reference are to act as 'critical friends' who volunteer their time to help inform and improve the police service.

Fact sheet Independent Advisory Group (IAG)
An Independent Advisory Group (IAG) is comprised of members of the public and they consider local issues such as stop and search figures, hate crime statistics, critical incidents or issues. IAGs aim to maximise the trust and confidence of the diverse communities through communication, exchanges of views and discussing police issues and provide a provide a forum for the community to help shape service delivery.

* *To enable the police to develop policies and procedures that are both accessible and transparent*
* *To increase engagement with communities and help expand the potential for community resilience through the Neighbourhood Policing plan*
* *To act as a 'critical friend' to scrutinise policing and policy decisions and debrief incidents and operations*

Their role is not one of formal scrutiny, but ensures that the policies, procedures and practices of the police meet the strategic aims of the ECHR strategy and provide a safeguard against the service disadvantaging any section of the community through lack of understanding, ignorance or mistaken beliefs. The Macpherson Report recommends that more should be done to generate trust and confidence in the community while providing senior police officers with the opportunity to have open dialogue with members of the diverse community. They should receive individual independent advice from members.

Community Safety Partnerships (CSPs)

CSPs were formed in accordance with the Crime and Disorder Act 1998, and are not only committed to tackling crime and the fear of crime, but also the causes of crime. CSPs are made up of representatives from the *'responsible authorities'*, which are the:

- Police
- Local authorities
- Fire and rescue authorities
- Probation service
- Health

These groups have a statutory duty to work with other local agencies to develop and implement strategies to tackle crime and disorder. This includes issues such as crime, anti-social behaviour, drug misuse and reduction in re-offending. Section 115 of the Crime and Disorder Act 1998 gives any person the power to lawfully disclose information, for the prevention of crime and disorder, to the police, local authorities, probation service or health authorities and it is this element of partnership working that many neighbourhood policing officers find particularly useful.

Developments in Partnership Working

The Police and Justice Act (2006) gives CSPs the responsibility to complete a 3 year rolling delivery plan and an annual strategic assessment. PCSPs (Policing and Community Safety Partnerships) are local bodies made up of councillors and independent citizens from each council area who strive to make their community safer though practical and realistic plans.

PCSPs have a range of duties which are set in legislation:

- **consult and engage** with the local community on the issues of concern in relation to policing and community safety. Each PCSP has a Policing Committee with a distinct responsibility to provide views to the relevant district commander and the Policing Board on policing matters;
- **identify and prioritise** the particular issues of concern and prepare plans for how these can be tackled;
- **monitor** the performance of the police and work to gain the co-operation of the public with the police in preventing crime; and
- **deliver** a reduction in crime and enhance community safety in each district, directly through interventions, through the work of delivery groups or through support for the work of others.

Partnership Working

In many jurisdictions, the police work in partnership with social workers to investigate child abuse. There are a number of key reasons why the police and other relevant agencies cooperate in the investigations. There are also wide variations across the world in terms of what these arrangements look like. Typically, the police, social workers, health, education and charities or NGOs are involved in these investigations.

First, there is the need for a legal basis. For cooperation and joint working, agencies and Governments can take the view that no special legal basis is required. From this standpoint, agencies cooperate because they think it is best for them or their client group and/or because current laws, constitutions or codes of practice allow or encourage it. For example, data protection laws already allow data sharing for particular relevant reasons or a children's charity might be established by Royal Charter and be charged with promoting the health and well-being of children.

The State may take the view that specific enabling legislation is required. Legal provisions might be passed to enable or compel certain agencies to work together. This can be important in making sure that the best protection is provided for children.

From an EU perspective, there are a number of tests that policy makers consider when introducing new policies, including legal basis and proportionality. Agencies could, in theory, refuse to cooperate and share data for example if they feel that they require a specific legal basis to do so. In reality, agencies may agree to cooperate while legislation is enacted. The ideal starting point for joint working could include:

- the existence of a sound legal basis,
- having a champion for the policy at a senior level,
- proper funding and training,
- support from the Public Prosecutor/Courts
- a wide acceptance of detailed well thought out policies and protocols

Models of Joint Working

There are three basic models of cooperation in children's crimes investigation (Casey Family Programs (2018).)

Model 1: Minimal law enforcement involvement or coordination: This is the traditional model for child protection services. There may be a formal or informal agreement between police and social workers to share information and to notify each other about reports of child abuse and neglect, but the agencies do not participate in joint activities for reports or investigations. Both agencies may investigate the same case, but each retains its own responsibilities. (see https://www.casey.org/are-there-good-examples-of-how-child-welfare-agencies-are-collaborating-with-law-enforcement/).

Model 2: Joint collaborative child abuse and neglect investigations: In this model, the police play a more routine, more collaborative role by participating in joint investigations with social workers or child protection services. The coordination may involve a statute that prescribes cooperation in investigations, a Memorandum of Understanding, or a multidisciplinary team or a Children's Advocacy Center.

Model 3: Sole law enforcement investigation responsibility: The police are solely responsible for investigation of a substantial portion of cases, usually determined by the seriousness of the case. In this model, the responsibility of social services is triggered, usually after the investigation, if services and/or placement are warranted. Police also make decisions about whether the child should be removed from the home. Within this model, there are differing degrees of police control.

Merits of Joint Working

- Being collocated in the same office, training together and sharing information systems, makes for a more seamless policy.
- Child interviews may be reduced as the police and social services can get the information they need from the same single interview.

- Each of the agencies may well need vital information that the partner agency holds
- Staff can gain a better understanding of each other's roles
- Co-location and joint working will be more efficient
- Disagreements can be resolved quickly
- Different agency views about time scales and emergencies can be resolved
- Child protection centres can be a one stop shop
- Specialist child protection centres that have key professionals may facilitate initiatives such as joint forensic medical exams by a police surgeon and community paediatric/consultant doctor.

Demerits

- Significant organising and maintenance
- Some people may be against the idea and detailed policies and training may be required
- Data sharing laws need to be considered
- There may be vetting issues for staff working alongside the police
- Staff may start to identify more with the partner agency rather than their own
- Staff may see the arrangements as trying to make police officers out of social workers and vice versa.

Outcomes of Joint Working

Using data from the National Survey of Child and Adolescent Well-Being, Cross, Finkelhor, and Ormond (2005) conducted an analysis comparing child abuse investigations that involved the police with those that did not.

The outcomes examined were that (1) the abuse would be found credible; (2) the child would be placed out of the home; (3) services would be provided.

The analysis reveals that the presence of a police investigation increases the likelihood that the referral would be deemed 'credible' and that services would be provided. Service provision also increased when police were involved in case planning and when a multidisciplinary team was used. The authors concluded that "Overall, police do not appear to hinder CPS effectiveness and may, in fact, promote it".

International Partnerships

There are significant number of international agencies and bodies that are not police forces but act on behalf of the national force to disrupt and detect crime. Globalisation and increased mobility have considerably changed the face of crime and the demands on police. Disrupting criminal networks requires a response that is based on international cooperation and coordination. Criminals are now engaging in 'Poly criminality (Chapter 1)' and dealing in numerous commodities at the one time. They develop tactical alliances with local criminal groups while exploiting the internationalisation of financial systems to conduct money laundering operations.

The Organisations

Interpol has 194 members and it was established in 1923 to facilitate communications and provide intelligence analysis and databases. It uses a number of coloured notices:

Red—global circulation of a wanted person
Blue—requests for information on named persons
Green—circulations with information on suspects

The United Nations often focuses on capacity building of the police in host countries. The Security Council has the power to deploy Formed Police Units (i.e., public order units, sometimes armed) from member states to peacekeeping missions. This programme is known as CIVPOL (i.e., Civilian Police). The United Nations Office of Drugs and Crime (UNODC) provides data and analysis on drugs, organised crime, corruption and terrorism.

Europol was established in 1992 and is bound to certain areas of investigation. It is based in The Hague. It supports Police operations throughout the 27 member states and has a cybercrime.

ASEANPOL is the Association of South East Asian Nations Police and was founded in 1967. In the USA, the Department for Homeland Security was formed in 2002 and brought together 22 Federal agencies. These regional and global hubs and are focused on law enforcement issues.

The Five Eyes (FVEY) is an intelligence alliance comprising Australia, Canada, New Zealand, the United Kingdom and the United States. These countries are parties to the multilateral UKUSA Agreement.

The Financial Action Task Force (FATF-UK) is an inter-governmental body established in 1989 by the Ministers of its Member jurisdictions. The objectives of the FATF are to set standards and promote effective implementation of legal, regulatory and operational measures for combating money laundering, terrorist financing and other related threats to the integrity of the international financial system. The FATF is therefore a 'policy-making body' which works to generate the necessary political will to bring about national legislative and regulatory reforms in these areas.

Frontex is the European Border and Coast Guard agency that focuses on preventing terrorism, smuggling and human trafficking.

GCC POL, the Gulf Cooperation Council in the Middle East is comprised of six states in the Gulf area of the Middle East (i.e., Bahrain, Kuwait, Oman, Qatar, Saudi Arabia and the United Arab Emirates).

It is part of the "Dialogue on multilateral Policing" overseen by Interpol which gathers leading regional organisations together to share information and minimise duplication between key stakeholders. It was set up to overcome obstacles to information sharing between organisations and ensure accessibility of information to frontline police and borders staff to be able to intercept the movement of terrorists and organised criminals.

Case Study: Encrochat

The National Crime Agency (NCA), after a four year investigation work by international police units stated that in 2020 the French and Dutch Police managed to access Encrochat, an encrypted platform used by 60,000 people worldwide. The encrypted handsets allowed users to securely communicate on a platform that until now was encrypted. Encrochat charged £1500 for a device on a six-month contract. After the platform was accessed, investigators were able to monitor thousands of Encrochat handsets and analyse millions of messages to get information on drug dealing, the sale of illegal guns and money laundering.

In 2020 law enforcement agencies across Europe shared data obtained from Encrochat with police forces across the UK. Th in the UK described this investigation as unprecedented in scale, officers in the UK have arrested 746 suspects and seized more than £54 million in cash, as well as 55 sports cars and 73 luxury watches. They have taken control of more than two tonnes of Class A and B drugs, as well as 28 million street Valium pills. A total of 77 guns, including submachine guns, as well as 1800 rounds of ammunition and four grenades, have also been seized. A joint operation focused on an OCG spanning the UK, Europe and UAE involved in the importation and distribution of cocaine and firearms.

The head of the Police in London Commissioner Cressida Dick stated that the Operation (2/7/20) is the most significant activity that the "Met" has carried out against serious and organised criminality across London. She stated that OCGs have used encrypted communications to enable their offending. They have openly discussed plots to murder, launder money, deal drugs and sell firearms capable of causing atrocious scenes in our communities. "Organised crime does not respect geographical boundaries. This operation has enabled us to target those at the top of the hierarchy and individuals we have known about for years but have not been able to tackle head on. "Through this work with our international partners, we have significantly developed our understanding of organized criminality in London and the ways in which some of our most prolific and dangerous offenders operate". This shows that the modern detective has to utilise a set of skills on a local and international level.

Seminar Questions

- What are the benefits of international partnerships such as Interpol?
- Why do we increasingly need international cooperation?
- What are the potential benefits of working with the private sector around security issues?
- What do FATF do?
- Name the Crime issues in two different regions of the world.
- What is the role of Interpol in defeating TOC?

Exam Questions

Using two international policing organisations discuss and compare their effectiveness in dealing with transnational crime. What are the benefits of cooperation over "silo" working?

References

Crawford, A. and Cunningham, M. (2015) 'Working in Partnership: The challenges of working across organisational boundaries, cultures and practices', in J. Fleming (ed.) Police Leadership - Rising to the Top, Oxford: Oxford University Press, pp. 71–94.

Cross, T. P., Finkelhor, D., & Ormrod, R. (2005). Police involvement in child protective services investigations: Literature review and secondary data analysis. Child Maltreatment, 10(3), 1–21. Retrieved from http://www.unh.edu/ccrc/pdf/CV83.pdf.

Elmsley, C. (2003). The birth and development of the police. In T. Newburn (Ed.), A handbook of policing. Uffculme: Willan Publishing.

Fleming, J. (2015). Police leadership, rising to the top. Oxford: Oxford University Press.

(Rosenbaum, 2002) seven potential benefits of effective partnership working

Roycroft (2016). Police Chiefs in the UK " Palgarve MacMillan

Metro Mayors see info@centreforcities.org

Part II

Use of Force

Use of Force and Public Order

James Law and Mark Roycroft

Police officers are often required to make crucial life and death decisions in relation to themselves, colleagues, or members of the public. On many occasions this decision making process is undertaken during extremely stressful conditions.[1] It is imperative that when force is used it is accountable, necessary, lawful, and proportionate.

No one can predict what an individual police officer will do in a particular situation[2] as each situation is unique based on a multitude of factors (e.g. age, knowledge, emotional intelligence, personal experiences, time of day, training etc.) The decision making process is influenced by prevailing and ongoing circumstances. It must be emphasised that the decision to use force in any particular situation is a personal choice that the individual should be able to defend ethically, morally, and at an inquiry or in a court of law. When force is used, there are always conse-

---

[1] D. Grossman et al., '*On Combat: The Psychology and Physiology of Deadly Conflict in War and in Peace*', (Belleville PPCT Research Publications 2007), K. Murray, *Training at the Speed of Life Volume One*, (2004 Armiger Publications, Inc. Florida).

[2] D. Grossman et al., '*On Combat: The Psychology and Physiology of Deadly Conflict in War and in Peace*', (Belleville PPCT Research Publications 2007).

J. Law (✉) • M. Roycroft
Rabdan Academy, Al Bhustan, Abu Dhabi, United Arab Emirates
e-mail: mroycroft@ra.ac.ae

M. Roycroft, L. Brine (eds.), *Modern Police Leadership*,
https://doi.org/10.1007/978-3-030-63930-3_5

quences, including investigations and a psychological toll on those involved. This was the case in the UK following the death of Ian Tomlinson after the G20 in London in 2009 and the death of George Floyd in Minneapolis in 2020 and also following the shooting of Michael Brown in 2014 in Ferguson, Missouri. MacIntyre (Times 22 August 2014) comments that "Ferguson is a textbook example of how the lessons from Kerner (1960s report into USA Riots) went unlearnt" and the media controlled events. There has been a huge increase in the reach of the media since the publication of the Kerner report in the 1960s and the police must learn to control events properly and ethically. Public order situations require large reserves of uniformed officers who are garnered through mutual aid arrangements in most countries. Officers are justifiably concerned with their unpredictability and their scale.

There are various pieces of literature and legislation that govern the use of force either in general terms (i.e. religious texts, human rights legislation etc.) that are discussed in other areas of this book.

Article 2 of the European Convention of Human Rights: The Right to Life (see Appendix 7)

Police in countries that are included in the above legislation are legally empowered to use force. However, *"peaceful means should be attempted before use of force, and only minimum levels of force are to be applied in any event"*.[3] Even though force can be used, Kleinig argues, *"it is intrinsically wrong, because it conflicts with the ethics of duty, and specifically with the dignity and personal autonomy of its subject"*.[4]

The right to life, which is an absolute right, is one of the fundamental rights of all people and is encapsulated in Article 2 of the European Convention of Human Rights. Crawshaw (1999) states that an *"individual's right to life is a fundamental human right, if not the fundamental right"*.[5]

---

[3] R. Crawshaw. Police *And Human Rights A Manual for Teachers, Resource Persons and Participants in Human Rights Programmes* (2nd Ed. Martinus Nijhoff Publishers. Lisbon 2009) p. 76.

[4] Neyroud P. et al. Policing, *Ethics and Human Rights*, (Willan Publishing 2001) p. 137.

[5] R. Crawshaw, International standards on the right to life and the use of force by police', The International Journal of Human Rights, 3: 4 Routledge, London 1999. p. 67.

Alpert et al. (1994) state, *"we live in a world that increasingly displays distaste for the use of physical force to direct or control the behaviour of others"*.[6] However, the use of force is a necessary tool for police officers and can conflict, albeit justifiably, with their moral obligation to protect life and preserve order. The attitude and behaviour of the officer in responding in an appropriate manner can impact how a society perceives whether their human rights are being protected or abused. This ultimately reflects upon public confidence in policing. Police, unlike criminals, are governed by rules and regulations, but are often challenged over the legitimacy of the use of force. In fact, the police can use force, even lethal, within the confines of the rule of law.

Article 2(1) European Convention of Human Rights states:

> Everyone's right to life shall be protected by law. No one shall be deprived of his life intentionally save in the execution of a sentence of a court following his conviction of a crime for which this penalty is provided by law.

The same Convention has a caveat in the Article 2(2) which allows for the taking of life. It states, *"when it results from the use of force which is no more than absolutely necessary"*,[7] in the following circumstances:

(a) in defence of any person from unlawful violence[8];
(b) in order to effect a lawful arrest or to prevent escape of a person lawfully detained[9];
(c) in action lawfully taken for the purpose of quelling a riot or insurrection.[10]

Lethal force may be justifiable under Article 2(2) if it is both proportionate and *"the use of force which is no more than absolutely necessary"*.

The mindset of a rational police officer is to preserve and protect life, not take it, sometimes even sacrificing themselves in order to protect others.[11] Murray also states that, *"the preservation of human life is one of the strongest urges of the human spirit, so strong that the noble will sacrifice their own lives in the defence*

---

[6] G. Alpert et al., How Reasonable is the Reasonable Man? Police and Excessive Force. The Journal of Criminal Law and Criminology 1994. p. 481.

[7] Ibid., p. 92.

[8] Wolfgram v Germany 1986 49 DR 213; Diaz Ruano v Spain A/285-B 1994.

[9] Farrell v UK 1982 30 DR 96; Kelly v UK1999 EHRLR 214; Aytekin v Turkey 1997 25 EHRR 251.

[10] Stewart v UK 10 July 1984. DR39/162; X v Belgium 1969 12 Yearbook 174.

[11] K. Murray, *Training at the Speed of Life Volume One*, (2004 Armiger Publications, Inc. Florida).

of the helpless",[12] Any force used must be in accordance with Article 2(2) of the Convention and must be 'strictly proportionate'.

The expectations of society, often through accountability mechanisms, demand that even in the course of a life and death altercation an officer must render immediate decisions.[13] The officer who hesitates in such a conflict while endeavouring to *"navigate through the maelstrom of uncertainty that often accompanies a lethal force encounter"* is probably destined to failure since their opponent has prepared in advance to take life in a lethal encounter.[14]

European Code of Police Ethics and United Nations Basic Principles on the Use of Force and Firearms by Law Enforcement

Police Officers have the right to defend themselves and other members of society against unlawful physical violence. Article 31 of the Code of Conduct for Law Enforcement Officials states that police have the same rights as other citizens.[15]

Training in use of force is essential for police officers to enhance their attitude, behaviour, knowledge, skills, and understanding. Article 19, United Nations Basic Principles on the Use of Force and Firearms by Law Enforcement states:

• *Governments and law enforcement agencies shall ensure that all law enforcement officials are provided with training and are tested in accordance with appropriate proficiency standards in the use of force. Those law enforcement officials who are required to carry firearms should be authorized to do so only upon completion of special training in their use.*[16]

It also states that there is a need to improve the working conditions of police officers and emphasise that a threat to the life and safety of police officers must be seen as a threat to the stability of society.[17]

---

[12] Ibid., p. 18

[13] Ibid.

[14] Ibid.

[15] R. Crawshaw et al. *Human Rights and Policing* (2nd edn. Martinus Nijhoff Publishers Leiden/Boston 2007).

[16] Basic Principles on the Use of Force and Firearms by Law Enforcement Officials Adopted by the Eighth United Nations Congress on the Prevention of Crime and the Treatment of Offenders, Havana, Cuba, 27 August to 7 September 1990.

[17] R. Crawshaw, 'International standards on the right to life and the use of force by police', The International Journal of Human Rights, 3: 4 Routledge, London 1999.

Lawful Execution of Duties and Reasonableness

The vast majority of police services around the world have some form of a code relating to conduct, ethics and discipline. The Police Service of Northern Ireland Code of Ethics 2008 was put in place following extensive consultation with the public and a range of statutory organisations. It provides an ethical framework for the decisions and actions taken by police officers. It also ensures that police officers are aware of their rights and obligations under the Human Rights Act 1998 and the European Convention of Human Rights(year). As with many documents of this nature worldwide, it has its foundations in human rights legislation, United Nations guidelines, and various other documents. The vast majority of police organisations in the Commonwealth and Europe have similar documents based upon the same foundations. These documents are readily available to the public so that there is openness and transparency in the rules that govern police conduct. The force used must fall under the four key principles of Legality, Necessity, Proportionality and Accountability (mnemonic: Laws, Need, Protection, Always) or Proportionate, Lawful, Accountable, Necessary (mnemonic: PLAN). These powers are scrutinised by police accountability agencies, and often by public opinion (e.g. Minneapolis death of George Floyd 2020) Crawshaw (1999) states that *"Compliance will reduce the likelihood of violations of the right to life enhance the lawful and expert use of force"*.[18]

Reasonable Force

In many countries, reasonable force has been enshrined in case law, and in some cases legislation for many years. In Beckford v The Queen, Lord Griffiths states:

> The test to be applied for self-defence is that a person may use such force as is reasonable in the circumstances, as he honestly believes them to be in the defence of himself or another.

Forrester v Leckey the judges in this appeal case state:

> In our view such force as is reasonable does require an objective test, based on the subjective belief. The degree of force used by an accused may not be regarded as reasonable if he uses excessive force or has overreacted.

---

[18] R. Crawshaw, 'International standards on the right to life and the use of force by police', The International Journal of Human Rights, 3: 4 Routledge, London 1999. p. 67.

The objective test, in relation to 'reasonable force' is extremely important. It assesses whether a person acted reasonably. This will be judged by considering how a reasonable person who finds themselves in the same situation and circumstances as that of the accused person would act.

The Owino judgement (date) further elaborates on the test for 'reasonableness' and held that:

> The test of the appropriate degree of force a person was entitled to use in self defence was not any degree of force which he believed was reasonable, however well founded this belief. A jury must decide whether a defendant honestly believed that the circumstances were such as required him to use force to defend himself from an attack or a threatened attack. A defendant must be judged in accordance with his honest belief, even though that belief may be mistaken. But the jury has then to decide whether the force used was reasonable in the circumstances as he believed them to be…

The fact that an act was considered necessary does not mean that the resulting action was reasonable. This is supported by the judgement in the Clegg case (1995):

> That where a person used a greater degree of force in self-defense than was necessary in the circumstances he was guilty of murder: that there was no distinction to be made between the use of excessive force in the prevention of crime or in arresting an offender; and that it made no difference that the person using it was a soldier or police officer acting in the course of his duty.

Article 4 of the European Charter of Human Rights states that "Police officers, in carrying out their duties, shall as far as possible apply non-violent methods before resorting to any use of force". There is no simple definition of what force is reasonable. It is based on the individual set of circumstances and governed by common and statute law.

Necessary

The lawfulness and reasonableness of the use of force is intertwined within the key principles of necessity and proportionality.[19] The use of force must be absolutely necessary, meaning that in a democratic society it is for a legitimate purpose or pressing social need.[20,21]

---

[19] M. Dawes, *Understanding Reasonable Force*, (The Derwent Press, Derbyshire, England 2006).

[20] Ibid.

[21] P. Neyroud et al. *Policing, Ethics and Human Rights*, (Willan Publishing. Devon 2001).

Proportional

Proportionality has a significant influence on what is deemed to be reasonable force and requires 'the active side of discretion'[22] finding a just balance between the protection of individual rights and the interests of the community. The proportionality aspect of use of force must bear in mind the right to life. Accordingly, only as much force as is necessary to resolve the issue must be used. A review of proportionality must be ongoing during the course of an intervention/operation.

The Ten Key Principles Governing the Use of Force by the Police Service are shown in Appendix 10. The main principles are:

1. *Police officers may, consistent with this duty, use force in the exercise of particular statutory powers, for the prevention of crime or in effecting a lawful arrest.*
2. *Police officers shall, as far as possible, apply non-violent methods before resorting to any use of force. They should use force only when other methods have proved ineffective, or when it is honestly and reasonably judged that there is no realistic prospect of achieving the lawful objective identified without force.*
3. *When force is used it shall be exercised with restraint.*
4. *Lethal or potentially lethal force should only be used when absolutely necessary in self- defence, or in the defence of others against the threat of death or serious injury; HMIC Rules of engagement (2011)*

Use of Force Models Used in Police Officer Decision Making

Policing is a complex vocation and on-duty conflict can range from verbal engagement to lethal force. Police officers are individuals and it is necessary to implement methods of training and thinking where there is relative consistency for different police officers faced with similar situations. Ultimately, a police officer needs to control and neutralise any potential threat in order to preserve the peace and uphold the rule of law.

The Conflict Management Model is a cyclic problem-solving model with five elements and has been devised to guide police officers when they are dealing with conflict situations and when the use of force is considered as an option to resolve a situation. Using this model, police officers should gather intelligence about an in-

---

[22] Ibid., p. 65.

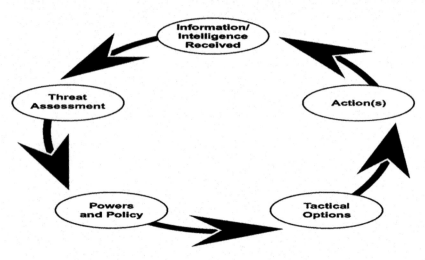

Fig. 1 Conflict management model

cident, create a threat assessment, and then consider what powers to use. Officers should consider Human Rights and hopefully arrive at a peaceful situation. Spontaneous incidents of protest do not always allow time for this sort of model to function fully (Fig. 1).

Public Order

The policing of, and preparation for protests and major events has changed significantly over the last few decades. The police are continually faced with balancing the competing rights of those who wish to protest, with the rights of the whole community, and their duty to protect life and property from the threat of harm or injury. The police are accountable and public order policing must be able to adapt to the ever-changing times and yet remain consistent in the implementation of command and tactics (NPIA Manual of Guidance on Keeping the Peace 2010).

Policing major public order events is hugely demanding of police resources. It also puts large numbers of police on display wearing aggressive looking full public order equipment, carrying batons, shields, carrying controversial weapons, using tear-gas and deploying such vehicles as water-cannons. Police actions are highly scrutinised now that the press and individuals can video with a smart phone and upload onto social media within seconds. Often, these videos show only short snippets of a police-suspect interaction, leading to a misinterpretation of what actually happened. What is fair in terms of policing for one section of society will remain unfair for another (Brogden 2005).

Following the Patten Report (1999) the Police Service of Northern Ireland aimed at keeping in close contact with community leaders and treating the public as customers rather than 'objects' of policing. In some instances, it took the view that, in public order situations, keeping people safe was much more of a priority than to confront and end law breaking. This is within the original British policing model, with its approachable, impartial, accountable style of policing based on the use of minimal force. The vast majority of public order events pass off with minimal police intervention. However, a small number of these events result in some form of protest and the police are quite often placed in a position between opposing sides.

The College of Policing Authorised Professional Practice (APP) for Public Order guidelines have been adapted by police in England, Wales, and Northern Ireland and contain the following six basic principles:

- Policing Style and Tone
- Communication
- Use of National Decision Model (NDM)
- Command
- Proportionate Response
- Capacity and Capability

The joint planning of police public order operations should include local community representatives/leaders from the specific location of the event, local marshals, and protest organisers. The main aim of the joint planning of events should help to minimise the opportunities for confrontation to take place.

Mediation minimises the risk of confrontation before an event or protest, and mechanisms should also be put in place to de-escalate and contain problems that may arise. It may be suitable at times to allow the policing of an event to be conducted by the organisers and their own marshals, while the police can provide assistance with physical barriers and traffic control. These types of events are normally of a minor nature and the police should always be in a position to take control and maintain the peace. Any intervention by police at an event should be done with a graduated response and a range of tactical options should be at their disposal.

Police should always avoid deploying resources and using tactics that are disproportionate to the threat they face (ACPO Guide to Public Order Policing 2006).

Public Order events especially those that are pre planned can see the use of a Public Order Tactical Advisor (POTAC) who can provide advice, guidance, and information in line with legislation, policy, and standards, as well as tactical options. They are able to review emerging information and intelligence, including updated threat, risk, and community impact assessments to ascertain the implications for the public order operation.

Case Study (Comes in 2 Parts)

A. Maria a 32 year old slightly built 5′4″ tall single parent has called police in relation to a domestic incident with her boyfriend.

Maria has a bruise to her left cheek threatening that if police did not do anything about her boyfriend she would take things into her own hands.

Considering the Decision Making Model and the Conflict Management Model highlight what you would consider and what is the rationale for your decisions.

B. The following day you are again tasked to a similar call. On arrival, you are met by Maria who is holding a blood stained knife and is covered with blood and in a hysterical state. You observe a male lying on the floor with blood over his chest.

Considering the Decision Making Model and the Conflict Management Model, highlight what you would consider and What would be the rationale for your decisions on this occasion.

References

Alpert, G., et al. (1994). How reasonable is the reasonable man?: Police and excessive force. *The Journal of Criminal Law and Criminology, 85*(2), 481–501.

Brogden, M. (2005). "Horses for Courses" and "Thin Blue Lines": Community Policing in Transitional Society. *Police Quarterly, 8*(1), 64–98. https://doi.org/10.1177/1098611104267328.

Crawford, A., Lister, S., Blackburn, S., & Burnett, J. (2005). Plural Policing: The Mixed economy of visible patrols in England and Wales. Policy Press.

Crawford, A., & Cunningham, M. (2015). 'Working in Partnership: The challenges of working across organisational boundaries, cultures and practices', in J. Fleming (ed.) Police Leadership - Rising to the Top, Oxford: Oxford University Press, pp. 71–94.

Crawshaw, R. (1999). International standards on the right to life and the use of force by police. *The International Journal of Human Rights, 3*(4), 67.

Association of Chief Police Officers. (2006). *Manual of guidance on police use of firearms.* ACPO London Revised.

Basic Principles on the Use of Force and Firearms by Law Enforcement Officials, Adopted by the Eighth United Nations Congress on the Prevention of Crime and the Treatment of Offenders, Havana, Cuba, 27 August to 7 September 1990

Code of Conduct for Law Enforcement Officials Adopted by General Assembly resolution 34/169 of 17 December 1979 Office of the United Nations High Commissioner for Human Rights

Websites

BBC News—Ian Tomlinson unlawfully killed by Pc at G20 protests. http://www.bbc.co.uk/news/uk-13268633

Cases

McCann v UK (1996) 23 EHRR 97
R v Clegg [1995] 1 AC 482
Stewart v UK (10044/82)39 DR 162

Armed Policing

Mark Roycroft

The traditional social 'contract' on the UK mainland between the public and the police involves the ideal of an unarmed police service. This wider social contract applies in all developed countries advocated by philosophers such as John Locke and Thomas Hobbes, citizens surrender their freedom to use force and entrust a public agency to use force to protect society for the protection of that society. This is a protective measure. In recent years, the public has accepted the more visible role of specialist armed officers on security duties in airports and strategic positions, however, the majority of officers in the UK remain unarmed. This is the result of increased prevalence of firearms and also terrorist attacks.

Following the 7/7 bombings in London and the Derrick Bird (2 June 2010) case in Cumbria (see Table 1), there have been media calls for more police officers to be armed on a routine basis. This would fundamentally change the social contract and the relationship with the British public. All the Chief Constables and PCCs (Police and Crime Commissioner) interviewed for *Police Chiefs in the UK* (2016) commented that the principle of unarmed policing and the idea of the citizen in uniform are the fundamental tenets of British policing. Historically, the only forces in the UK in which officers are routinely armed are the Police Service of Northern Ireland, the Ministry of Defence Police, and the Civil Nuclear Constabulary.

M. Roycroft (✉)
Rabdan Academy, Al Bhustan, Abu Dhabi, United Arab Emirates
e-mail: mroycroft@ra.ac.ae

© The Author(s), under exclusive license to Springer Nature Switzerland AG 2021
M. Roycroft, L. Brine (eds.), *Modern Police Leadership*,
https://doi.org/10.1007/978-3-030-63930-3_6

Table 1 Notable UK police shooting incidents

Name of person shot or location	Date	Circumstances	Consequences
Hungerford	19 August 1987	A series of random shootings in Hungerford, England when Michael Robert Ryan, an unemployed antiques dealer and handyman, shot dead 16 people, including a police officer and his own mother, before shooting himself.	Under the Firearms Act 1988, semi-automatic and pump-action rifles and shotguns were banned. The Act prohibited more dangerous forms of ammunition such as that which explodes or contains noxious substances. Shotguns with barrels of 24 inches or longer required a firearms certificate
Azelle Rodeny	30 April 1995	Rodney was driven by associates Wesley Lovell and Frank Graham across North London after they were observed by police to pick up three weapons, believed to be MAC 10 sub-machine guns. MPS specialist firearms officers performed a 'hard stop' manoeuvre in which one officer fired eight shots, 6 of which hit Rodney in the head, neck, and chest. A hard stop is a tactic in a planned operation that involves armed officers deliberately intercepting a vehicle to confront suspects	In July 2013, the public inquiry by Lord Bach concluded that the armed police officer who fired the fatal shots had "no lawful justification" for killing Rodney. The report of the inquiry noted that eight shots were fired from close range in 2.1 seconds,. It resulted in the case for prosecution of the officer who fired the fatal shots for the charges of murder. However, the jury found the officer not guilty
Dunblane	13 March 1996	The Dunblane school massacre took place at Dunblane Primary School near Stirling, Scotland, on 13 March 1996, when Thomas Hamilton shot 16 children and one teacher dead, injured 15 others, before killing himself. It remains the deadliest mass shooting in British history.	Firearms Amendment Act 1997 banned all handguns

(*continued*)

Table 1 (continued)

Name of person shot or location	Date	Circumstances	Consequences
De Menezes	22 July 2005	De Menezes was a Brazilian man killed by officers of the London Metropolitan Police Service at Stockwell Station on the London Underground after he was wrongly deemed to be one of the fugitives involved in the previous day's failed bombing attempts. These events took place two weeks after the London bombings of 7 July 2005, in which 52 people were killed. The Independent Police Complaints Commission (IPCC) launched two investigations. In July 2006, the Crown Prosecution Service said that there was insufficient evidence to prosecute any named individual police officers in a personal capacity, although a criminal prosecution of the Police was brought under the Health and Safety at Work. Act 1974, on the failure of the duty of care due to Menezes. The Commissioner was found guilty and his office was fined	IPCC report Stockwell 2 www.jesip.org see command below
Derrick bird	2 June 2010	This was a shooting spree which occurred on 2 June 2010 when a lone gunman, taxi driver Derrick Bird, killed twelve people and injured 11 others before killing himself in Cumbria, England, United Kingdom.	Chesterman report
Mark Duggan	4 August 2011 London	Police officers were attempting to arrest Duggan on suspicion of planning an attack, and being in possession of a handgun. Duggan died from a gunshot wound to the chest. The circumstances of Duggan's killing resulted in public protests in Tottenham, which led to conflict with police and escalated into riots across London and other English cities.	In January 2014 a jury returned the verdict of lawful killing

(*continued*)

Table 1 (continued)

Name of person shot or location	Date	Circumstances	Consequences
Khuram Shazad butt Rachid Redouane Youssef Zaghba	3 June 2017	Southwark, London Terrorists shot during the June 2017 London Bridge attack by Police in an Armed response vehicle after killing 7 people and injuring 48 people.	
Usman Khan	29 November 2019	Usman khan stabbed 5 people including two who later died in the vicinity of London Bridge. It is reported the attacker was wearing a "hoax" suicide vest. The attacker was shot twice by police and died at the scene	
Sudesh Amman	2 February 2020	Streatham, London, UK	Having stabbed and injured three people using a machete, Sudesh Amman was shot and killed by metropolitan police. Amman was reported to be wearing a fake suicide vest,

In contrast, all major police forces in Europe, as well as the US, Canada and Australia, routinely carry firearms. The two main exceptions are the Republic of Ireland and New Zealand. In Norway, officers carry firearms in their cars but not on their person.

History of Firearms Policing in the UK

New armed policing guidelines (see Rules of Engagement below) were introduced in the wake of the 1983 shooting of film editor Stephen Waldorf in London, UK. Waldorf was shot five times in error after being misidentified as a wanted suspect. The present firearms arrangements are included in the College of Policing "app" on armed policing (*www.app.college.police.uk/app-content/armed-policing/*) and include guidance on the legal context and rules of engagement.

The UK police must comply with Article 2 of the ECHR on the right to life (see Appendix 7) and the UN Basic Principles on the Use of Force and Firearms (see

Appendix 10) which states that governments and law enforcement agencies shall adopt and implement rules and regulations on the use of force and firearms against persons by law enforcement officials. In addition, a legal case following the shooting deaths of three Provisional IRA members by British Armed Forces in Gibraltar on 6 March 1988 has impacted on how armed police must act. British authorities had received information that a bomb was about to be planted in Gibraltar The case went before the European Court and it rejected the notion that the UK had specifically planned an execution mission and not an arrest mission. The police in the UK are allowed discretion to shoot, but must adhere to the UN 26 rule that "Obedience to superior orders shall be no defence if the law enforcement officials knew that an order to use force and firearms resulting in the death or serious injury of a person was manifestly unlawful".

Rules of Engagement

1) Officers must identify themselves (introduced after Waldorf shooting)
2) Aim for the biggest target—centre mass
3) It is a last resort
4) Officers should reassess the situation after each shot. The Royal Canadian Mounted Police (RCMP) follow the principle of two initial shots to centre mass. If this fails and the suspect is still approaching them as a continued threat and in close proximity, they are trained to aim for the head for a subsequent shot. This is routine training. The RCMP have a continuum of Force model called the Incident Management Intervention Model' (IMIM) see Table 2
5) Has reasonable force been used, under S3(1) Criminal Law Act 2008; reasonable force is to be assessed by the Court based on the question, was it necessary and proportionate?

UN Basic principles on the use of Force and firearms by Law enforcement Officers (1990) set out the rules and regulations on the Use of Force and firearms and allow for differentiated use of firearms. These principles state the development and deployment of non-lethal incapacitating force and stipulate that officers must apply non-violent means before resorting to the use of force and firearms. As in the shootings at Borough Market in 2017 (see Table 1), this may not always be a possibility.

The RCMP (IMIM) Incident Management Intervention Model' model discusses situational factors and takes the officer through "soft" tactics including verbal commands, then intermediate weapons and then at the top "Lethal Force". However

Table 2 The advantages/disadvantages of routinely arming the police

For	Against
Deterrent effect? An armed police force will deter criminal behaviour. This is not a rationale for the arming of police in Canada	Arming the police will cause an escalation in criminal violence i.e. the ratchet effect Would it stop or deter suicide bombers/shooters?
Ensures greater safety for officers and the public.	Would lead to a 'ratchet' effect with criminals. Changes the contract with the public. Will it lead to a reduction in the continuum of force i.e. would it mean less use of less harmful alternatives such as tasers, 'stun guns', CS spray, and negotiation. A police officer must justify their use of force. The 'ambush' or marauding terrorist attack (i.e. Mumbai and London attacks) by armed criminals on police or public can never be controlled whether or not officers are armed. These are rare events.
The routine arming of officers will lead to better protection	The risk of greater use of weapons against the public and/or offenders when the police are armed, mistakes will lead to innocent people getting shot i.e. De Menezes
The police should be equipped to react to contemporary problems such as terrorism and organised crime	Will it lead to a reduction in the continuum of force i.e. would it mean less use of less harmful alternatives such as tasers, 'stun guns', CS spray, and negotiation. The gun is only one option open to officers
Routine arming did not affect recruitment to the RUC during the troubles	Recruitment will be adversely affected if the police are armed. The contrary may prevail in North America where disarming the police may have a negative effect on recruitment.
It would deter firearm offences.	Gun control following Dunblane with relatively few guns in public hands, there is less need for police officers to be armed than in countries where gun ownership is less strictly controlled.
A quicker response to armed incidents	Would this stop a Dunblane or Hungerford? In Canada, all front line officers are trained in 'active shooter' techniques. The first police officer at the scene tries to eliminate the suspect.
Fewer police casualties? i.e. PC Keith palmer outside the London houses of parliament was unarmed	The cost of supplying firearms and training,

this is a guide and (like the UK Police) the authority to use force is derived from and bounded by the Criminal Code of Canada and related common law and case law principles, not by any use of force model or similar framework. A police officer must be able to totally and legally justify which use of force option they choose and it must conform to the IMIM. A police officer cannot immediately go for the side-arm option if a less lethal option would be suitable.

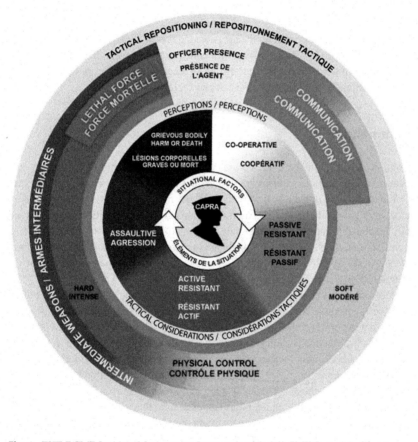

Fig. 1 THE RCMP Incident Management Intervention Model' (IMIM) model of force

The United Nations Basic Principles on the Use of Force and Firearms by Law Enforcement Official states that Law enforcement officials should:

- exercise restraint in such use and act in proportion to the seriousness of the offence and the legitimate objective to be achieved
- minimise damage and injury, and respect and preserve human life
- ensure that assistance and medical aid are rendered to any injured or affected persons at the earliest possible moment

Many factors will impact on the decision and it is not practical to pre-determine the most appropriate options as part of a **continuum of force**, that is, to continue each option in strict hierarchy, in terms of an escalation of force, or to use each in turn on that basis until the objective has been achieved.

Command

Commanders and authorised firearms officers (AFOs) are trained to analyse and determine appropriate courses of action in the course of armed deployments. Commanders and those involved with the assessment of intelligence, provision of tactical advice and relaying of communications. They are legally and professionally responsible for decisions that they make, and tasks or authorisations that they give. All directions must be 'reasonable in the circumstances' and where appropriate the tests of 'absolute necessity' (Article 2 of the European Convention on Human Rights) and 'proportionality' will be applied.

Operation Kratos refers to tactics developed by London's Metropolitan Police Service for dealing with suspected suicide bombers, most notably firing shots to the head without warning. The tactics were developed shortly after the 11 September 2001 attacks, based in part on consultation with Israeli and Sri Lankan law enforcement agencies on how to deal with suicide bombers. After the shooting of Jean Charles de Menezes on 22 July 2005, in the wake of the 7 July 2005 London bombings (see Table 1 above). The term 'Operation Kratos' is no longer used by the Metropolitan Police, although similar tactics remain in force.

When asked, UK police officers overwhelmingly indicate that they wish to remain unarmed. A 2006 survey of 47,328 Police Federation of England and Wales' members found 82 per cent did not want officers to be routinely armed on duty. It is a position shared by the Police Superintendents' Association of England and

Wales and the Association of Chief Police Officers (ACPO now NPCC). An ICM poll in April 2004 found 47 per cent of the public supported arming all police, compared to 48 per cent against. Sir Hugh Orde (ex-President NPCC) stated, "It is strikingly obvious that bringing firearms into the policing equation does not solve the problem of violent crime, or protect officers from being injured or killed" (The Guardian, 20 September 2012). He further states, "The police service collectively does not want to routinely carry guns – we agree our relationship with the public we serve is too precious to jeopardise".

There appears to be competing agendas for the police to contend with. These have been illustrated by a recent controversy in Scotland about a standing authority that allowed a small number of officers to carry guns when attending non-firearms incidents. Politicians and community leaders attacked the nationwide rollout of officers with a standing authority to carry guns on routine patrols since the formation of Scotland's single police force. The force's armed police monitoring group recommended keeping the standing authority in place after it was given intelligence on serious organised crime groups in 2014. Her Majesty's Inspectorate of Constabulary in Scotland (HMICS) in its 2014 review of the authority said the operational need for the authority is justified by the national intelligence and threat levels. However, as well as not considering the impact on public perception, HMICS said a full and informed debate around the deployment of firearms officers to incidents and duties that do not require a firearms response was not conducted. Responding to those who have asked why armed officers are required in quiet country areas such as the Highlands, Chief Constable Sir Stephen House cited the gun massacres at Dunblane and Hungerford and also the shootings by Derrick Bird in Cumbria, saying that they had taken place in areas where violent crime was uncommon. This report shows that the police felt they had sound operational reasons to routinely deploy armed officers but they 'crossed the line' in what was publicly acceptable.

The situation and history in Canada are somewhat different. All police officers in Canada are routinely armed with a sidearm, and many jurisdictions also carry tactical high powered rifles in each patrol car. When the RCMP was formed in 1873, it was armed in order to deal with sometimes violent illegal American whiskey traders crossing the border into Canada and selling their goods to Aboriginals. (https://www.rcmp-grc.gc.ca/en/history-rcmp) Because of its rural nature, there is a high level of gun ownership in rural areas and the vast distances mean that backup from other police officers can take several hours.

Why Should Police Officers Be Armed?

Balance of Armed to Unarmed UK Police Officers?

The number of firearms officers in the UK is low and all are specially trained and selected for their role. Of the 32,500 officers in the Metropolitan Police Service (MPS), just 2740 were 'authorised firearms officers' (MPS 2013). There were a total of 4432 deployments by armed officers in London in 2011, compared to 4656 the previous year. The number of times armed officers responded to emergency calls has also fallen in recent years, partly as a result of fewer people reporting the use of guns on the streets (see Home Office figures below right). Armed response vehicles (ARVs) are called to around 3000 incidents a year in London and 13,346 in the rest of the UK. Outside the capital, the entire territory of England and Wales is policed with the help of just 4128 armed officers. There were **6653 armed officers** as at March 2019, a **3 per cent increase** (+194) and continuing the recent rise in the number of armed officers.

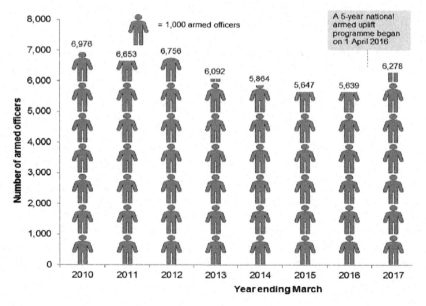

Fig. 2 Number of armed officers 2010 to 2019

There are 431 authorised firearms officers in Scotland of which 275 are performing dedicated ARV duties. Presently, only a small proportion of officers are authorised to use firearms, about 5 per cent of the total number in the UK. The Home Office states that in 2010–2011, firearms officers were involved in 17,209 operations, a fall of 1347 (7 per cent) on the previous year.

The opinion of Chief Constables was divided on the use of Conducted Energy Weapon (i.e. CEW, also known as TASER). Some Chiefs and Police and Crime Commisioners (PCCs) felt they were a suitable midway option between firearms and a truncheon while others (including the Staff associations) were opposed to every officer having to use them. One Chief Constable (CC19) stated they had been an authorised firearm officers for 10 years of their Service and they were "concerned about cross border protocols especially around the issue of marauding terrorists, 16% of my force are trained for using Tasers or CEW Conducted Energy Weapons". The geography of the Force area concentrated the Chief officers minds and many shared firearms operability across regional units. One Chief Constable (Police Chiefs in the UK, 2016) remarked that they had a mixture of urban and rural areas to police and they felt they had the right number of armed officers. They stated that CEWs are good and they were introducing it to single patrol officers. The CC reactions depended on the geography of their Force area and the problems their officers had to cope with. CC18 stated, "We need guns, poaching is an issue, we have 2 ARVs on patrol at any one time". Similarly, CC38 was of the opinion that "we have large rural areas with single crews , we need more Tasers/CEWs to combat 'edge weapons'". CC11 commented, "the Police service has become a target and we have to protect officers". A retired Chief Constable (RCC3) was concerned that "the Police do not overarm, we have less armed officers than 1997 but better organised, but they could disconnect the Police form the Community". Chief Constable 13 stated that less than 2 per cent of officers are armed and the public had forgotten the cases of Dunblane and Hungerford. He further stated, "why shouldn't ARVs (Armed Response vehicles) take ordinary calls if they are close to an incident. Look at the way the police dealt with Lee Rigby's killers, they shot them and then gave them first aid".

One Chief Constable (CC17) felt there were too many armed officers while retired Chief Constable 2 wanted smaller numbers of armed officers but better trained. A number of Chiefs had concerns over attracting a sufficient number of volunteers for armed duties after the recent charging of a Firearms officer in London following a pre-planned operation by the Mets SO19. One Chief felt that the UK Police had the right balance at present (CC21) especially with 'Counter Terrorism' concerns; "Charlie Hebdo (Paris shootings, 2015) showed that we need to be prepared for a variation of officers in the UK who are taser trained 15% or

5%, why do people focus on the negatives of taser but it has positives I looked/reviewed a police killing in ...where the suspect was shot dead by police as he was wielding a sword and he was full of drugs, a Taser may have stopped him and prevented him being killed". The use of tasers *at* Leytonstone Tube on 5 December 2015 showed how these weapons could be used effectively.

One Chief was concerned about the lack of diversity on their ARVS and were actively trying to recruit more ethnic minorities and women onto the ARVs (CC30). CC Creedon stated on 12/15 (Police Oracle) that he did not believe officers should be routinely armed in the UK and it flew in the face of the British Policing model, the Police needed to balance the public perception along with safety requirements of the officers and the cost of equipment and training.

Many critics state that the routine arming of the police would lead to further tragic mistakes as have been discussed above. However, these are rare and are investigated fully by the Independent of Police Conduct IOPC previously the Independent Police Complaints Commission (IPCC). The deployment of specialised firearms officers to prevent marauding attacks has concerned UK law enforcement since the Mumbai Attacks(2008) when 166 people were killed by 10 marauding terrorists. Like Brussels (2016) and Paris (2015), these attacks concentrate on transport hubs and key locations. The Chief Constables were concerned with having sufficiently trained officers to cope with this type of attack especially across a number of key locations. One PCC (PCC7) felt that Chief officers were too protective over their concerns about armed policing and they should learn to share their views with the PCCs.

Conclusion

The UK along with Norway, New Zealand, and Ireland are unique in their model of largely unarmed policing. The RCMP model of a continuum of Force (the IMIM) illustrates how officers can move through a range of options before firing a shot. In many circumstances, these options are not always available and the officer has to make an instant decision based on the prevailing circumstances. Officers are there primarily to save the lives of the public and their colleagues. There are differences in the deployment of officers on pre-planned operations where firearms are deployed and instantaneous situations such as the Borough market shootings of 2017 in London. This chapter has examined how the police use and carry firearms in the UK and whether all police officers should be routinely armed. Today's firearms officers are well trained and are mindful of their legal and moral obligations. It is clear that the routine arming of police is a tradition that has carried on since the inception of policing in Canada. The use of a firearm by a police officer is an option, but only one of last resort.

Seminar Questions

1. The Royal Canadian Mounted Police (see Fig. 1) discuss the continuum of Force, what stages should an officer contemplate before using lethal force?
2. What were the learning issues for the Police from the De Menezes case in London 2005.
3. Discuss the implications of Human Rights legislation in firearms Policing.
4. Should all Police officers in the UK be routinely armed?

Exam Question

Take 2 examples from Table 1 of the advantages and disadvantages of armed policing above and discuss the implications for British Policing?

Management of Deadly Force

Gordon Harper

The Joint Services Specialist Firearms Commander Programme (JSP) (JSSFCDP 2014) defines the environment of Specialist Firearms Operations (SFO) as being:

> *An Operation conducted in relation to National Security, Counter Terrorism or where the nature of the circumstances surrounding the incident are deemed so serious by an accredited Strategic Commander that he/she directs that the incident should be commanded by an accredited Specialist Tactical Firearms Commander.* (JSSFCDP Manual 2010, PSNI)

While Specialist Firearms Commanders may be designated as a 'Strategic Commander' or 'Tactical Commander' within an Operation, they are carrying out a strategic leadership role, having the responsibility to translate organisational strategy into effective operational performance within a complex intelligence led multi-agency operation.

Police commanders within SFO often face a number of challenges, including short collapsing time frames that impact on the ability of the police to complete certain desirable actions. This factor, combined with an often incomplete intelligence picture, requires the police commander to be able to hypothesise quickly in order to fill these information gaps to counter any immediate threats and reach the

G. Harper (✉)
Rabdan Academy, Al Bhustan, Abu Dhabi, United Arab Emirates
e-mail: mroycroft@ra.ac.ae

© The Author(s), under exclusive license to Springer Nature Switzerland AG 2021
M. Roycroft, L. Brine (eds.), *Modern Police Leadership*,
https://doi.org/10.1007/978-3-030-63930-3_7

objectives of the police operation. The task of the police commander may be further burdened by the high stakes involved, such as the threat not being countered. *A Commander's role is to make decisions, give clear directions and ensure that those directions are carried out* (APP, Operations 2018).

There is potential that SFO commanders faced with this complexity, uncertainty, and extreme risk within a SFO may become risk averse or avoid making a difficult decision. Uncertainty is a major obstacle to effective decision making and is manifest as a sense of doubt that blocks or delays action (Lipshitz and Strauss 1997). By accepting this complexity and uncertainty from the onset, through training and preparation, it is hoped that risk can be reduced and dynamic decision making improved.

> *It is essential that everyone involved in the police response clearly understands what they are required to do, how they are required to do it and when. This is particularly important where a multi-agency response is required, as confusion and uncertainty can lead to command paralysis where commanders are unable to make and/or communicate decisions effectively.* (APP, Operations, Command 2013)

Simon argues that decision makers do not operate within the confines of perfect rationality. Instead, they make decisions by simplifying models that extract the essential elements of the problem, without their full complexity. That is to say, individuals operate within a bounded rationality. An implication of bounded rationality is that decision makers are '*satisficers*'. '*Satisfice' is a word which combines 'satisfy' and 'suffice'.* Satisficing means that decision criteria and alternatives are pragmatically developed based on meeting requirements in a timely manner. These alternatives are reviewed based on previous experiences and current knowledge. Satisficers do not perform a full review of alternatives, but they continue until a 'good enough' alternative is identified. A possible downside to this approach, however, is that the best option may never get to the evaluation stage.

Both naturalistic decision making (satisficers) and classical decision making (optimisers, maximisers) are relevant to decision making within SFO. The naturalistic decision making approach focuses on experienced decision making in dynamic, uncertain environments. Complex and uncertain SFO operations in many ways are similar to military operations:

> *An essential component of expertise in military command and control is the ability to make and implement decisions in a timely, efficient and effective manner, most often with very limited information, in an increasingly fluid and multidimensional battle space.* (Serfaty et al. 1997)

In contrast, Lehto and Nah (2006) describe classical decision making as "The choice between two or more alternatives, one of which may, of course, be to do nothing."

The ability of the commander to apply naturalistic decision making is essential and often involves the following:

1. Ill structured problems—problems rarely present themselves in a neat, complete form which means that commanders need to be situationally aware, generate hypotheses and then determine whether or not the situation is one where a decision is required.
2. Uncertain dynamic environments—incomplete, poor, rapidly changing and/or ambiguous information.
3. Shifting, ill-defined, or competing goals—some of which may directly oppose other goals, resulting in goals being traded. These conflicts and trade-offs may be made more complex by virtue of the dynamic environment in which they exist as new goals emerge.
4. Action/feedback loops—a commander may encounter a series of decision actions in a problem if it is dealt with or explored more.
5. Time stress—significant time pressure often results in the commander experiencing high levels of personal stress, which may lead to exhaustion or loss of vigilance.
6. High stakes—potential loss of one's own life or the lives of others.
7. Multiple players—decision may involve more than one decision maker, who may not be co-located, and may or may not act cooperatively and/or competitively. There must be shared situational awareness and an understanding of the goals.
8. Organisational goals and norms—goals must reflect the organisational strategy and decision making approaches should adhere to standard operation procedures.

Commanders should be aware of the possible presence of heuristics and cognitive bias in making decisions in uncertain conditions. Heuristics is any approach to a problem that uses a practical method that is likely not perfect, but is sufficient for reaching an immediate and/or short-term goal.

The heuristics may include:

• Representativeness—the tendency to judge someone or something according to similar patterns, happenings, events or things.

- Availability—the tendency to consider an instance or event as being more probable if it can be easily imagined, as opposed to being difficult to bring to mind
- Adjustment and anchoring– the tendency to give more weight to evidence that is consistent with their initial hypothesis (or 'anchor') than to contrary information.

Cognitive biases include:

- Overconfidence—being more confident than is justified may lead to prematurely closing off the search for information.
- Confirmatory—seeking information and cues that confirm the tentative hypothesis yet fails to seek (or discount) information that supports a contrary view.

The UK police service trains commanders in the use of a number of decision making models, including, the primary model—the National Decision Model (NDM). The UK College of Policing Approved Professional Practice (APP) describes the NDM as an aid to assist operational officers, planners, advisers and commanders to manage their response to a situation in a reasonable and proportionate way. The NDM reinforces the need for a commander to be able to apply both conventional decision making and naturalistic decision making supported by the learning, skills, experience and competencies gained throughout their lives.

Training alone cannot equip commanders to make critical decisions within specialist firearms operations. Support is available to the commander through the provision of tactical advice with the premise being *"to advise and not to make command decisions. The responsibility for the validity and reliability of the advice lies with the advisor, but the responsibility for the use of that advice rests with the commander."* (APP, Command 2014). The commander must possess enhanced tactical and technical competence and a knowledge of abilities and capacities of others involved in the operations. This enables the tactical advisor to concentrate on which specific tactic would be the most appropriate, especially in time sensitive situations. Accordingly, there will be less of a need for the commander to be briefed on the fine details of the tactics being considered. The overall knowledge of the operation by the commander coupled with the specialist operational knowledge of the tactical advisor allows for an effective and high performing partnership. In addition, partnerships of this nature must clearly delineate the decision making authority of the commander as opposed to the advisory nature of the tactical expert.

Kolditz describes leadership within environments similar to that of SFO as "in extremis leadership" (2007). He suggests that 'in extremis leadership' involves giving purpose, motivation, and direction to people when there is imminent physical danger and where followers believe that the behaviour of the leader will influence their physical wellbeing or survival. 'In extremis' leaders are self-selected, as they willingly place themselves in the position of leadership as opposed to 'crisis leaders' who are "thrust unexpectedly into extreme challenge, disaster or circumstances". It should be noted that Specialist Firearms Commanders volunteer to lead in operations where uncertainty and high risk are prevalent. They also know that their behaviour will be scrutinised by their team, and that they have a significant duty of care to the team and the public.

"When allocating roles consideration should be given to the appropriateness of the task to the individual's training, experience and competence." (ACPO Guidance on Command and Control 2009, p. 11) Rank and training alone cannot prepare a police commander to exercise 'command' in SFOs. In fact, the APP, Armed Policing (2014) states that the command structure within armed operations "is functional rather than based on rank".

Leadership and the ability to command within SFO require a commander to practise and promote the following:

- Trust and criticality
- High standards
- Emotional intelligence
- Acceptance of uncertainty and complexity
- Fallibility
- Acceptance of risk
- Acceptance of accountability
- Shared leadership
- Knowledge of skills and abilities of team members
- Tactical and technical competence
- Physical and moral courage
- Modelling (displaying consistency and authenticity in what they say and do)

Past experience has shown that a lack of clarity of command and a holistic response has had a negative impact on the ability of the police to respond appropriately and effectively to extreme threats. In the investigation into the 2005 shooting death of Jean Charles de Menezes by the Metropolitan Police(UK) as the result of mistaken identity (Stockwell One, Independent Police Complaints Commission 2007), five key areas that were highlighted for improvement in the Stockwell report were: Governance, Command and Control, Interoperability, Fusion of Tactics and Training.

Seminar Questions

The ability of the commander to apply naturalistic decision making within SFO is essential and often involves what elements?

What do you understand by the term naturalistic decision making and how does it apply to Firearms policing?

What five key elements were highlighted by the report into the killing of Jean Charles de Menezes in London (and explain each one)?

Exam Questions

Leadership and the ability to command within SFO require a commander to practise and promote which issues?

References

APP = Association of Chief Police Officers (ACPO), Manual of Guidance on Police use of Firearms, (ACPO) Firearms www.app.college.police.uk/appcontent/armed-policing/

Association of Chief Police Officers (ACPO) Guidance on Command and Control, 2009, p.11) London, ACPO College of Policing app website. www.app.college.police.ac.uk www.app.college.police.uk.

JSSFCDP = The Anthony Grainger Inquiry - Gov.uk https://assets.publishing.service.gov. uk › uploads › file.

Kolditz (2007). *In Extremis Leadership: Leading As If Your Life Depended On It.* HB Printing.

Lehto, M.R. and Nah, F. (2006). Decision-Making Models and Decision Support. In Handbook of Human Factors and Ergonomics, G. Salvendy (Ed.). https://doi. org/10.1002/0470048204.ch8.

Lipshitz, R., & Strauss, O. (1997). Coping with uncertainty: A naturalistic decision-making analysis. Organizational Behavior and Human Decision Processes, 69(2), 149–163. https:// doi.org/10.1006/obhd.1997.2679.

Serfaty, D., MacMillan, J., Entin, E. E., & Entin, E. B. (1997). The decision-making expertise of battle commanders. In C. E. Zsambok & G. Klein (Eds.), Expertise: Research and applications. Naturalistic decision making (p. 233–246). Lawrence Erlbaum Associates, Inc.

Sweeney, M. Matthews, & P. Lester (Eds.), Leading in dangerous contexts. Annapolis, MD: Naval Institute Press, pp. 218–229.

The Grainger Firearms Case Study

Mark Roycroft

The Anthony Grainger Inquiry (July 2019) was an independent public inquiry that examined the circumstances surrounding the death of Anthony Grainger, a suspect who was shot and killed as he sat in a car, by the Greater Manchester Police (GMP) during a Mobile Armed Support to Surveillance (MASTS) operation (Operation Shire) on 3 March 2012. Police believed that he and two others were planning to commit an armed robbery on a supermarket and that he had access to firearms, although none were found. The inquiry found that the police armed response unit lacked the necessary level of operational competence, did not follow proper procedures, and had adopted a culture of "secrecy" and "arrogant disdain for the views of others". Ultimately, the Chief Constable of GMP was charged under the Health and Safety at Work Act as he had ultimate responsibility for those who reported to him.

The Inquiry report states that *"Overall, Mr Grainger died because GMP failed to authorise, plan or conduct the MASTS operation on 3 March in such a way as to minimise, to the greatest extent possible, recourse to the use of lethal force"*. (Chap. 1, Para. 75).

The Executive Summary highlights the lack of professional competence of some of those involved including the Tactical Commander (Chap. 1, P. 20, Para

M. Roycroft (✉)
Rabdan Academy, Al Bhustan, Abu Dhabi, United Arab Emirates
e-mail: mroycroft@ra.ac.ae

1.73). The report is critical of the senior officers for being complacent with regard to their duties in dealing with failings highlighted during training,

> *Some of the officers who commanded or participated in the mobile armed support to surveillance (MASTS).operation of 3 March 2012, including the tactical firearms commander ("TFC") and the operational firearms commander ("OFC"), lacked the requisite level of professional competence:*

- *The TFC, (a Superintendent), had recently failed a specialist Police Service of Northern Ireland Joint Services training course. Before allowing (the Superintendent) to resume a tactical command role, GMP should have considered whether to remove him from firearms command responsibilities pending further assessment of his operational competence but did not do so.*
- *The OFC had not attended his mandatory annual refresher training and had recently failed a counter-terrorist specialist firearms officer ("CTSFO") course for the second time. He was not occupationally competent at the date of the MASTS operation and, by reason of his second CTSFO failure, was no longer eligible to participate in a MASTS operation in any capacity.*
- *One of the AFOs had also recently failed a CTSFO course. GMP should have suspended him from AFO duties pending remedial training but did not do so until after the death of Mr Grainger.*
- *A tactical adviser ("TA"), had never been trained as a MASTS AFO and was not occupationally competent to act as TA in a MASTS operation.*

The commanders lack of knowledge in the tactics authorised during the operation were also highlighted by the report (Chap. 1, Para. 59).

> *While GMP had received no intelligence suggesting that the subjects of the operation were armed or had immediate access to firearms, the three men collectively posed sufficient danger to justify the deployment of a firearms team in support of surveillance officers according to the orthodox view of the MASTS methodology. However, the firearms commanders who authorised and planned the armed deployment of 3 March 2012 held an unorthodox and fundamentally flawed view of MASTS, treating it less as a means of deploying firearms officers in support of a surveillance operation and more as a means of deploying surveillance officers in support of a firearms operation, the predetermined purpose of which was to carry out arrests.*

In its conclusion, the report states, *"GMP failed to ensure that all those who commanded and participated in the MASTS operation were occupationally and operationally competent to fulfil their designated roles"* (Chap. 12, Para 11, Page 320).

The actions or inactions of the senior leadership of GMP must considered within the context of the wider organisational culture that existed at that time.

Seminar Questions

How can chains of command be addressed when there are multiple specialised units working on an investigation?

Why was the Chief Constable held accountable and charged?

Should anyone else have been charged under the Health and Safety at Work Act?

Part III

International Policing

UN Peacekeeping Operations

Lindsey Brine

Multilateral cooperation, particularly on the world stage, grows increasingly important as the relationships between countries, international bodies, and policing organizations have a broader impact on international security. As a result of globalization, events such as conflicts, government instability, and terrorist incidents are having a significantly greater impact on the world stage now than they were in previous decades (Stibli, 2010). Due to the advent of social and network media, it is evident that an event in an isolated part of the world now has a more pronounced global effect. This was clear during the Arab Spring when political unrest and attempts at democratization quickly spread beyond the Middle East and drew attention from around the world (Yigit & Tarman, 2013). This is also the case in Haiti, when the world became refocused on this small country as a result of the 2010 Earthquake. Political instability in Haiti has been problematic since it was colonized in 1492. There have been over 30 coups, a successful slave revolution, foreign invasions, and assassinations. Since the early 1990s, the international community has focused on assisting Haiti in reforming its government and strengthening its economy in order to improve living conditions (Foreign Affairs, Trade and Development Canada, 2013). As part of this, multilateral cooperation in the area of police reform has become a critical component of stabilizing Haiti.

L. Brine (✉)
Rabdan Academy, Al Bhustan, Abu Dhabi, United Arab Emirates

M. Roycroft, L. Brine (eds.), *Modern Police Leadership*,
https://doi.org/10.1007/978-3-030-63930-3_9

Peacekeeping efforts in Haiti have focused on three main areas: operational support to the Haitian National police with the goal of increasing security and stability, reforming and restructuring the Haitian National Police, (Resolution 1892 as adopted on October 13, 2009 reaffirms the previous resolutions in Haiti.) and strengthening a weak 'rule of law'—all components of Security Sector Reform. One of the unexpected consequences of peacekeeping in Haiti, which in many ways has been somewhat lawless for years, was an upsurge in criminal activity. Research shows (https://www.researchgate.net/publication/334777526_ Peacekeepers_against_Criminal_Violence-Unintended_Effects_of_ Peacekeeping_Operations) that a reduction in internal political conflict has the unintended effect of increasing violence. A smaller degree of conflict leads to a greater degree of economic opportunities. An unfortunate impact is that while the community, in general, is safer, "violent competition among criminal groups" has increased. Also, because peacekeeping tends to demobilize those involved in the violent political conflict, those same individuals have limited employment opportunities because of a lack of schooling and experience. This often sees them turning to crime as a result.

In November 2013, as reported by the Miami Herald, armed bandits who referred to themselves as 'rebels' escalated their violent attacks on unsuspecting locals in the small community of Petit-Goave, which is about 60 kilometres west of Port-au-Prince. These 'rebels' attempted to take control of the highway leading through the city, as this is the gateway to three major regions in the south of the country. An important trade route, this is the only highway to or from the capital of Port-au-Prince. The gangs of violent offenders were successful in slowing down or stopping merchant vehicles, and stole money and other items of value. In some cases, they disarmed Haitian National Police officers and private security guards. Extreme acts of violence have included hostage takings and the shooting of United Nations civilian police officers (Charles, 2013). This is not surprising in a country that is ranked 161 out of 180 countries for corruption (Transparency International, 2013).

These violent Haitian gangs are symptomatic of far more than roving bandits seeking treasure. Haiti has been in a state of civil unrest for decades, and arguably even centuries. Because of this, the internal infrastructure has never been developed sufficiently to deal with a porous land border with the Dominican Republic and other neighbouring Caribbean countries easily accessible by water. The proximity to Dominican Republic and the other islands has allowed parts of Haiti to become a haven for drug traffickers, gun runners, and human traffickers (United States Department of State, 2013).

In the context of the armed gangs of the Haitian bandits noted, it is important to have an understanding of the concept of 'transnational crime'. In 1995, the definition of transnational crime became "offences whose inception, prevention and/or direct or indirect effects involved more than one country" (United Nations Secretariat, 1995). With ever increasing globalization, the prominence of transnational crime has exploded and the United Nations and its contributing countries continue to attempt to find ways to combat it, albeit with little success. So, although the Haitian 'bandits' may seem like a small and isolated local problem, they are symptomatic of the grassroots of transnational crime. Based on their location and the fact that they are heavily armed, it can be postulated that they are involved in illegal drugs and arms activity.

Since the initial United Nations incursion in 1993, there has been little democratic progress or economic reform. The country is still rife with corruption and this even manifests itself through fraudulent and corrupt election practices (Schmall, 2010). Just prior to the 2010 election, while working as the Chief of Staff of the UN Peacekeeping Mission in Haiti, the author located bundles of thousands of new, unused ballots for the upcoming election in a ditch on the side of the road. The situation has been further compounded by repeated natural disasters. The most infamous of these is the January 2010 Earthquake in which over 230,000 people were killed and 1,300,000 displaced (Foreign Affairs, Trade and Development Canada, 2013). In addition, 96 UN peacekeepers were killed. The author was appointed as Lead Investigator for a Canada Labour Code investigation into the deaths of two Royal Canadian Mounted Police members who perished during the Earthquake. He provided significant and lasting recommendations to improve the level of safety for Canadian police officers posted to all peacekeeping missions worldwide. Unbeknownst to most in the industrialized world, the country is also plagued by annual devastating hurricanes, flooding, deforestation, and significant diseases. These situations further destabilize all aspects of the country and the government, and allow for increased transnational criminal activity. If the sparse resources of the government are continually focusing on dealing with natural disasters, then there is little ability to focus on other issues such as 'rule of law'.

It is impossible to achieve 'rule of law' in a failed state. As defined by the Reference Dictionary, a 'failed state' is "a weak state where social and political structures have collapsed to the point where the government has little or no control". Gros aptly points out that Haiti is a failed state (p. 63). In 1998, a private plane from South America flew over a remote portion of Haiti and distributed packets of cocaine. Some locals hid the packets away while others went to tell the Haitian National Police of their find. The police arrived a short time later and brutally attacked the residents and seized the packets of cocaine. Afterwards, it was determined that it was actually a case of drug importation with the consent and wilful participation of the local police. This is demonstrative of not only a failed state, but also transnational crime in its most rudimentary form.

This example is closely paralleled by the current situation involving armed gangs in Petit-Goave. The blockades and the attacks by the armed bandits may seem like a rather insignificant problem, but it is directly tied to the complex issues of the increase in transnational organized crime due to Haiti being a 'failed state'. This situation and response by both the Haitian National Police and the United Nations Police demonstrates the ever increasing need for multilateral cooperation in policing issues in 'failed states', as ultimately there is an international impact related to crime from these countries. Further complicating this particular matter, and indeed contributing to the whole 'failed state' premise, the blockades established by the 'rebels' have restricted the local economy and jeopardized the health of locals as it has precluded travel by doctors, health workers, and non-government organizations (NGOs) (Charles, 2013).

International aid is not uncommon and is provided by many industrialized nations to third world and developing nations.

The United Nations has had to act swiftly and strongly in relation to the rule of law in Haiti. The Haitian National Police, which is approximately 15,000 strong, was created in 1995. https://www.miamiherald.com/news/nation-world/world/americas/haiti/article228678394.html. As the result of several incarnations of United Nations missions in Haiti, in 2004 it was decided that one of the main components of the mission would be focused on developing and supporting the fledgling police force (MINUSTAH, 2013). Aid in the form of both economic donations and 'boots on the ground' tends to increase dramatically after a significant natural disaster. Many countries see participation in these post-disaster missions as glamorous because it potentially increases the international profile of the participating country. For example, prior to the 2010 Earthquake, United Nations Resolution 1892 authorized up to 2211 foreign police officers representing approximately 20 countries. The post-earthquake United Nations Resolution authorized up to 4391 police officers. This marked an increase of 2180 foreign police personnel flooding into Haiti. At this time, there were 54 contributing countries. Security Resolution 2119 in 2013 only permitted up to 2601 police. This is a decrease of 40% from immediately after the Earthquake (United Nations, 2013). In 2017, the MINUSTAH ended and the United Nations Mission for Justice Support in Haiti (MINUJUSTH) commenced. The mandate of MINUJUSTH:

MINUJUSTH will assist the Government of Haiti to further develop the Haitian National Police (HNP); to strengthen Haiti's rule of law institutions, including the justice and prisons; and to promote and protect human rights – all with a view to improving the everyday lives of the Haitian people.

The UN peacekeeping mission was reduced to only just over a thousand employees including police, corrections officers and civilians—from a significantly lower number of contributing countries. However, Haiti was no longer at the forefront of international news, especially with the ongoing impact from the Arab Spring, the Western withdrawal from Iraq and Afghanistan, and the political turmoil and civil war in much of central Africa. MINUJUSTH ended in 2019.

Although there are many countries contributing to the United Nations civilian police component in Haiti, Canada remained the largest contributing country with anywhere between 100 and 150 Canadian police officers deployed to Haiti at any one time. The vast majority of these are members of the Royal Canadian Mounted Police (Royal Canadian Mounted Police, 2013). The Government of Canada became actively involved in the United Nations peacekeeping mission to Haiti in 1994. These missions include:

- UNMIH United Nations Mission in Haiti—1993–1996
- UNSMIH United Nations Support Mission in Haiti—1996–1997
- UNTMIH United Nations Transition Mission in Haiti—1997
- MIPONUH United Nations Civilian Police Mission in Haiti—1997–2000
- MINUSTAH United Nations Stabilization Mission in Haiti—2004–2017 (pp. 17–20, White, 2007)

Although one may think that is altruistic on the part of the Government of Canada, this is not the case. Canada is the home to significant populations of Haitians in Montreal and Ottawa. In total, there are over 160,000 Haitians living in Canada (Statistics Canada, 2007). Clearly, the impact of transnational crime is a significant threat not only due to this high population but also due to the geographic proximity to Haiti, as it is only a three hour flight from Canada. In concert with the Government of Canada, the Royal Canadian Mounted Police has recognized the need for a strong civilian police peacekeeping and mentoring presence in Haiti. The fragility of the Haitian government, the porous border with the Dominican Republic and neighbouring islands and the high rate of corruption has been compounded by border skirmishes, the lack of effective policing, and no maritime patrol, human and drug trafficking, gun running, and other types of transnational organized crime. Canada does not want internal issues in Haiti to be transposed to the Haitian population in Canada. The Royal Canadian Mounted Police have regularly been given senior leadership positions within the mission. The author served as Senior Advisor to the Deputy Police Commissioner of Operations and then as Chief of Staff in MINUSTAH from 2010 to 2011.

A sound policing model, which in many countries has taken centuries to create, is unlikely to happen quickly in a country that is rife with centuries of economic, political, and social chaos. There is a need to establish trust and to encourage people from formerly disenfranchised groups to enter the mainstream. The establishment of a fair criminal justice system is important for all states emerging from years of strife. (https://minustah.unmissions.org/sites/default/files/rsgsept09.pdf). Gros (2003) argues that there is a direct link between 'failed states' and the ever increasing global criminalization or transnational crime. He properly recognizes that a 'failed state' lacks a span of control, and by default becomes both a victim and a perpetrator of international crime. (p. 64). Along with this, not only does the state fail, but so too do the institutions within that state.

The instability in Haiti, especially post-earthquake, has continued and in fact increased. Although the United Nations civilian police complement diminished, the challenges for the Haitian National Police in combating both domestic and transnational crime continue.

FACT SHEET
Homicides continue to be a major concern. In 2018, there were 757 reported homicides, with 73% occurring in the West Department, which includes Port-au-Prince. There were nine known U.S. citizen victims of murder. While reported homicides are down from 2017 levels, the statistics show a sharp increase in the second half of the year, to levels higher than 2017. Gang-on-gang violence continues to increase.

The HNP reported 53 kidnappings in 2018 compared to 63 in 2017. While the overall number is lower than 2017, it could be more due to underreporting than a true decrease in crime.

The Haitian National Police (HNP) has about 15,000 officers, approximately two-thirds of whom serve in the greater Port-au-Prince metropolitan area (home to approximately three million residents). As a result, some communities do not have reliable means to report crimes. The HNP has a limited response capability, which hinders the deterrent effect on criminals, who operate without fear of the uniformed or traffic police. Investigations are frequently limited by a lack of resources. In 2018, 18 HNP officers were murdered and 54 injured in the line of duty. https://www.osac. gov/Country/Haiti/Content/Detail/Report/b038d0a0-cc5a-4427-a753-15f4aebea7a9

These issues create significant challenges for the fledgling police force, especially in light of the fact that the Haitian National Police is working in an environment where conflict and corruption have been prevalent since the inception of the country (MINUSTAH, 2013). Many of the current senior leadership in the Haitian

National Police are former military personnel from a time when the military still existed. Haiti no longer has a military structure, so many of the former soldiers turned to policing and continued in their heavy handed and corrupt ways. Capacity building will assist the Haitian National Police to eventually build and maintain a professional police service that conforms to the norms of a stable democracy. Accordingly, the key goals of the United Nations civilian police mission within Haiti have been to provide stability and security, and to assist in the development and reformation of the Haitian National Police. These legacy issues have been seen in other countries such as Northern Ireland, and Kosovo. It is difficult to move from a para-military policing model to one of policing where the needs and concerns of the community are addressed as a priority.

Within the United Nations mission in Haiti, there are two main pillars that have facilitated the cooperation between the United Nations civilian police and the Haitian National Police—Operations (tactical) and Development (capacity building). Operations consists of the following functions: hands on mentoring, coaching, and demonstrating to the Haitian National Police how to conduct proper investigations and how to implement effective community-based policing models. Operations is also involved in duties that support the security and stability of Haiti. For much of the MINUSTAH tenure, there was no senior level Haitian National Police officer embedded in Operations at the strategic level so as to demonstrate United Nations commitment to ensuring the success of the Haitian National Police. This would clearly be beneficial and although the author has made this recommendation to senior level United Nations officials a number of times, it was clearly not a priority. During the unrest and banditry in Petit-Goave, the United Nations police monitored events and gave operational guidance, but did not directly intervene (Charles, 2013).

'Capacity development' refers to the approaches, strategies, and methodologies used to improve the performance of a developing organization. Its objective is to enhance, or more effectively utilize, skills, abilities, and resources. It should also strengthen understandings and relationships while addressing issues of values, attitudes, motivations, and conditions in order to support sustainable development. This must be founded, in any peacekeeping mission, on broad-based participation and a locally driven agenda, building on local capacities, ongoing learning and adaptation, long term investments, and the integration of activities at various levels to address complex problems. (Foreign Affairs, Trade and Development Canada, 2013) The United Nations police have assisted the Haitian National Police in this area by developing robust training, recruiting, hiring, and vetting processes in order to professionalize the administrative capacity (MINUSTAH, 2013).

The bandits of Petit-Goave have demonstrated that the policing environment in Haiti is highly complex. The United Nations police must have a good understanding of the local legal and policing systems, as well as culture and customs that are specific to the country where the mission is taking place. In Haiti, not only did the United Nations police use a radio system completely independent of the Haitian National Police, but also many of the peacekeepers did not speak French or Creole, thereby making bilateral communication almost impossible. It was a misconception that the UN peacekeepers should be recruited from francophone countries. The vast majority of Haitians do not speak or understand French, but instead speak Haitian Creole.

Under the constant scrutiny of the international media and the Haitian population, the United Nations police were often faulted for many situations over which they had no control, or rarely given credit for their operational successes. Mutual cooperation is almost impossible at times as the rules of engagement for the United Nations police are very limited in relation to day-to-day criminal activities (MINUSTAH, 2013). The Haitian National Police were often reluctant to accept theUnited Nations mandate, and were willing to turn a blind eye to corruption issues in both the police and the government.

The United Nations Resolutions with respect to Haiti confirm that neighbouring states, whilst respecting its territorial integrity and sovereignty, will support Haiti's efforts in the prevention of cross-border illegal activities (especially the trafficking of persons, weapons, drugs, and taxable goods) that undermine Haiti's economic, socio-political, and internal security.

The United Nations Department of Peacekeeping Operations, Concept of Operations for the Police Component for MINUSTAH incorporates the following principles:

1. Ensuring that the United Nations police operate in a manner conducive to establishing local ownership of the reform process.
2. Ensuring that the United Nations police provide operational support to the Haitian National Police in the conduct of their day-to-day policing activities, including in the Internally Displaced Persons camps.
3. Assisting the Haitian authorities in the establishment of effective governance, oversight, and accountability in the policing system.
4. Assisting the Haitian authorities in improving the delivery of policing services.
5. Assisting the Haitian authorities in developing a sustainable police service based on democratic norms, and sound principles of governance and the rule of law.

6. Adjusting to a more dynamic approach to operational support and mentoring of the Haitian National Police through an enhanced program of co-location, joint patrols, and the development of robust hiring and administrative processes.
7. Ensuring effective donor coordination in support of priorities related to operational and investigative aspects, infrastructure development, logistics and communication.
8. Contributing to strengthening capacity in the areas of combating cross-border trafficking of persons (especially women and children) drugs, arms and other illegal activities.
9. Providing technical expertise in support of efforts to implement an integrated border management approach, with emphasis on state capacity-building.
10. Ensuring that the United Nations Police are prepared to, on an exceptional basis, give limited logistical support to the Haitian National Police in order to enable the continuance of operations and basic services.

All of these critical points should eventually enable a well-equipped, well-trained, and self-sustaining Haitian National Police that provides a professional and community-based police service to the people of Haiti. 'Failed states' lead to failed institutions, as is demonstrated in the developments in Petit-Goave, the bandits are at arm's length from any type of sustainable enforcement capacity, thereby making it relatively easy for them to operate with impunity. Of note is the fact that one of those detained by the Haitian National Police during a tactical sweep of Petit-Goave was the campaign manager for a high profile politician closely linked to President Michel Martelly. There was strong speculation that the release of this individual was facilitated by the mayor of Petit-Goave who, not so coincidentally, was appointed to her chair by President Martelly (Charles, 2013). This supports the theory of Gros and demonstrates the almost insurmountable challenge for the United Nations of creating and maintaining a professional police service for the people of Haiti.

Globally, there is great support for international law enforcement cooperation directed at fighting transnational organized crime, but this clearly begins at the local level and through multilateral cooperation. This has been brought forward by many world leaders and discussed widely at international forums including the G8 and the United Nations (Kadono, 1999). While the example cited in the *Miami Herald* may seem innocuous, it is evident that it has far-reaching implications and that it is tied in directly to both bilateral cooperation and transnational organized crime.

As Mobekk (2005) notes,

> International policing is an essential part of post-conflict reconstruction and peace
> building and plays a crucial role in establishing stability in post-conflict societies. Ir-
> respective of the breadth of the mandate, a successful police operation is necessary to
> ensure long term peace in the mission country since the policing forces oversee the
> development of the public security forces – which often determines whether there will
> be peace or the resumption of conflict. International policing has for a long time been
> undervalued and its role not sufficiently understood or investigated. This has changed
> considerably, but a number of challenges remain which must be overcome in order to
> have not only successful policing operations, but also successful peace building.
> (p. 1).

The accumulation of private wealth and material goods is one of the prime objectives of the armed bandits of Petit-Goave. Within a 'failed state', the collapsed
economy leaves the opportunity for the political elite and for the common criminals to garner wealth. This is compounded by the disinterest and apathy of the police or other government entities to move the country forward. Fuelled by years of
corruption, poor morale, and low (if any) wages, many police begin to engage in
illegal activities themselves, or merely turn a blind eye in exchange for payoffs.
With the situation in Petit-Goave, and actually Haiti in general, the role of international cooperation and peacekeeping operations becomes clear. The United Nations
has clearly stated in its resolutions that any United Nations police force in Haiti
must not only assist with security and stability in the country, but also focus on
capacity building. In Petit-Goave, the United Nations police became frustrated at
their inability to directly intervene, but were reminded of their mandate of standing
by and coaching and mentoring (Charles, 2013).

There is little doubt that any continued United Nations intervention in Haiti will
attempt to address the issues of 'rule of law' and transnational crime. Unfortunately,
in a country that has suffered from internal conflict and criminality for centuries, it
is unlikely multilateral cooperation will create lasting change. The history of the
UN in Haiti is a remarkable learning opportunity for future UN missions.

Seminar Questions

Peacekeeping efforts in Haiti have focused on three main areas, what were they?
What problems faced the UN peacekeeping Force when they arrived in Haiti?
How many Homicides were recorded in Haiti in 2018 and what was the general
    level of crime at the time?
What were the key goals of the United Nations civilian police mission deployed to
    Haiti?

Exam Question

The United Nations Department of Peacekeeping Operations, Concept of Operations for the Police Component for MINUSTAH incorporates a number of principles, name and discuss five of these?

References

Charles, J. (2013, October 15). Armed bandits testing Haiti's understaffed police forces. *Miami Herald*. Retrieved from http://www.miamiherald.com/2013/10/15/3691691/armed-bandits-testing-haitis.html

Foreign Affairs, Trade and Development Canada. (2013). *Haiti – Facts at a glance*. Retrieved from http://www.acdi-cida.gc.ca/acdi-cida/acdi-cida.nsf/En/NIC-223124146-NRN

Gros, J. (2003). Trouble in paradise: Crime and collapsed states in the age of globalization. *British Journal of Criminology, 43*, 63–80. Retrieved from http://bjc.oxford journals.org/content/43/1/63.full.pdf.

Kadono, N. (1999). How can we fight 21st century crime? International cooperation against transnational organized crime. In *Transnational crime and regional security in the Asia Pacific* (pp. 119–125). Manila: CSCAP/ISDS.

MINUSTAH (Mission des Nations Unies pour la stabilisation en Haiti). (2013). *Developpement de la police nationale d'haiti: cap sur 2016*. Retrieved from website: http://www.minustah.org/developpement-de-la-police-nationale-dhaiti-cap-sur-2016/

Mobekk, E. Geneva Centre for the Democratic Control of Armed Forces (DCAF). (2005). *Identifying lessons in United Nations international policing missions* (Policy paper no. 9). Retrieved from website: http://www.dcaf.ch/Publications/Identifying-Lessons-in-United-Nations-International-Policing-Missions

Royal Canadian Mounted Police. (2013). *International peace operations branch – Current operations*. Retrieved from http://www.rcmp-grc.gc.ca/po-mp/missions-curr-cour-eng.htm#n4

Schmall, E. (2010, November 28). Allegations of fraud and corruption mar Haiti elections. *The Huffington Post*. Retrieved from http://www.huffingtonpost.com/emily-schmall/allegations-of-fraud-corr_b_788906.html

Statistics Canada. (2007). *The Haitian community in Canada*. Retrieved from: http://www.statcan.gc.ca/pub/89-621-x/89-621-x2007011-eng.htm

Stibli, F. (2010). Terrorism in the context of globalization. *Academic and Applied Research in Military Science, 9*(1), 1–7. Retrieved from http://www.zmne.hu/aarms/docs/Volume9/Issue1/pdf/01.pdf.

Transparency International. (2013). Corruption perceptions index 2013. Retrieved from http://www.transparency.org/cpi2013/results

United Nations. (2013). *MINUSTAH – Facts and figures*. Retrieved from http://www.un.org/en/peacekeeping/missions/minustah/facts.shtml

United Nations Office on Drugs and Crime (1995), Ninth United Nations Congress on the Prevention of Crime and the Treatment of Offenders, Cairo, Egypt. Retrieved from: https://

www.unodc.org/documents/congress/Previous_Congresses/9th_Congress_1995/017_
ACONF.169.15.ADD.1_Interim_Report_Strengthening_the_Rule_of_Law.pdf
United States Department of State, Bureau of Diplomatic Security. (2013). *Haiti 2013 crime
and safety report*. Retrieved from https://www.osac.gov/pages/ContentReportDetails.
aspx?cid=14000
White, K. (2007). *The Canadian contribution to United Nations peacekeeping*. Retrieved
from United Nations Association in Canada website: http://peacekeeping.unac.org:8080/
en/pdf/CdnUNPkpgBooklet_e.pdf
Yigit, M. F., & Tarman, B. (2013). The impact of social media on globalization, democratization, and participative leadership. *Journal of Social Science Education, 12*(1), 75–80.
Retrieved from http://www.jsse.org/index.php/jsse/article/view/84/1169.

Crisis and Disaster Management and Disaster Victim Identification (DVI)

Lindsey Brine and Mark Roycroft

The police play a complex and critical role during times of crises and disasters. This includes ensuring public order, safety and security. As funding and dynamics change, police leadership are often required to fulfill the same role with lower budgets and fewer resources. There are many aspects of crisis and disaster management, including communications, interoperability, leadership, and police responsibility. These have been further complicated as a result of the increasing presence of the internet, digital communications and social media, all of which create both opportunities and challenges.

Risk management is a process that assists with the identification and management of potential risks and liability that an organization may encounter. Risk management and identification is an essential part of dealing with crises and disasters. To adequately understand and address various crises and disasters, it is critical to understand what risk entails. It was only following a significant rise in natural, social, and technological disasters and their devastating impacts during the 1980s that risk assessment, health and safety culture and crisis and disaster management made their entry into the public service and not-for-profit sectors.

Challenges have become more numerous, widespread and increasingly complex. Public service organizations and policing agencies are currently facing new

L. Brine (✉) • M. Roycroft
Rabdan Academy, Al Bhustan, Abu Dhabi, United Arab Emirates
e-mail: mroycroft@ra.ac.ae

challenges and taking on new responsibilities. This has led to a more diversified approach to risk management, often referred to as *risk governance*. Crises and disasters can include natural disasters, transnational-armed conflict, transnational organized criminal, cybercrime, and terrorism. Risk can adopt two forms, that which is known and can be measured, and that which we label as 'uncertainty.' Identifying risks and planning and preparing for those risks is a key element of readying for crises and disasters. There is a significant threat to organizational reputation and public trust for any police or security organization that depends entirely on how that organization responds to a crisis or disaster. Public agencies, including the police, are accountable to the public and to oversight organizations.

The International Organization for Standardization in its guidelines on risk management (i.e., ISO 3100 https://www.iso.org/iso-31000-risk-management), states that an organization can assess risk through identification, analysis, and evaluation. This requires a systematic and collaborative approach that draws on the knowledge and perspective of stakeholders. Fink defines a crisis, as "…a fluid and dynamic state of affairs containing equal parts danger and opportunity." Lerbinger sees risk as closely related to the media coverage an emergency event generates and remarks that there exist extremes in perception of what constitutes a crisis. Boin (2005, p. 163) draws a connection between crises and disasters by noting that a "crisis… pertains to the process of perceived disruption; whereas disaster applies to the collectively arrived-at appraisal of such a process in negative terms. In this perspective, a disaster is a crisis with a bad ending."

A critical incident defines the tipping point between what constitutes an emergency and a crisis. The 2019 Christchurch mosque shootings was a critical incident. A critical incident, if poorly managed, can rapidly develop into a crisis. The terrorist attacks of September 11, 2001 were a crisis. A crisis is an event that exceeds the capacity, ability, or resources to respond effectively. A disaster generally presumes large-scale damage of infrastructure and loss of life and is often associated with natural events such as earthquakes, hurricanes, flooding and fires. Hurricane Katrina (2005) was a disaster and the overall response by multiple stakeholders provides valuable lessons.

The management of crises and disasters is a cyclical process. It includes risk assessment, planning, preparation, mitigation and contingency, response, recovery and finally, an evaluation. The final phases, those of recovery and evaluation, are critical. The initial phase of risk assessment is undertaken during planning and preparation. Prior to developing plans and preparing to deal with various threats, specific hazards need to be identified, analyzed and evaluated. Following this are planning and preparation. The planning and preparation phases must be sufficiently emphasized and supported. Otherwise, it will be almost impossible to develop a culture of crisis management within the organization and subsequent stages of the cycle will suffer from the lack of planning and preparation.

The police and other emergency services organizations face significant challenges and responsibilities during crises and disasters. In addition to their routine duties, they must cope with, and respond to, issues such as communications (internal and external), effective resource management, emergency medical treatment, interoperability, looting, logistics, mass evacuation, rioting, and victim identification.

As a result of the response to major disasters such as Hurricane Katrina in New Orleans, Louisiana, USA in 2005, there has been increased awareness about the roles and responsibilities of the police and other emergency services organizations during these types of events. Sound recommendations on what planning and structures should be in place to support operational command during future major disasters must be developed from any major incident. The identification of key command and control structures and the overall response, along with the pre-event emergency preparedness of the police and other organizations in New Orleans can also provide insight regarding lessons learned from strategic and tactical errors, and best practices to improve future responses. By reviewing the prerequisite preparation of major agencies involved in pre-disaster planning, it is possible to demonstrate how the collaborative and participative style of command sits with the principle of overall command. Campbell and Kodz (2011) point out that leadership in policing is somewhat different from other areas as it blends 'command and control' with collaboration.

Hurricane Katrina has been classified by many experts as the "most devastating hurricane in the history of the United States (National Hurricane Center, 2012)." In late August 2005, Hurricane Katrina formed in the Atlantic Ocean and traversed Florida in a westerly direction as a low level Category 1 hurricane (Drye, 2005). The path of the hurricane, as predicted by the National Hurricane Center (2012), led the Governor of Louisiana to declare a state of emergency on Friday, August 26. This triggered the activation of emergency support, including federal troops, to plan with the Federal Emergency Management Agency (FEMA). As noted on their website, "FEMA's mission is to support our citizens and first responders to ensure that as a nation we work together to build, sustain and improve our capability to prepare for, protect against, respond to, recover from and mitigate all hazards." (U.S. Department of Homeland Security, 2013) The primary intent of the activation of FEMA was to enable the immediate implementation of cross jurisdictional communication and cooperation in order to have all three levels of government (i.e., local, state, federal) and non-governmental organizations (NGO) work strategically and collaboratively to deal with the impact of the looming Hurricane Katrina.

Over the following two days, several areas of the Gulf Coast were evacuated and President George Bush declared a federal disaster allowing for federal assistance and funding to be released to the disaster response. Once the hurricane passed westwards over Florida, it intensified to a Category 5 hurricane; the highest level of hurricane classification on the Saffir-Simpson hurricane wind scale (SSHWS). It then pushed north, and although weakened, pounded the north coast of the Gulf of Mexico. Katrina wreaked tremendous damage all the way from Florida to Texas. Although there was significant damage due to wind and rain, the majority of damage in New Orleans was the result of a powerful storm surge that caused the levee system to fail completely (Drye, 2005). The levee system is a highly complex system of dams and locks that have been built and improved upon over the last three hundred years to deal with flooding in the low lying coastal area of New Orleans (Sills et al., 2008). Within hours, the vast majority of New Orleans and the surrounding areas were completely inundated with water. Chaos erupted amidst the search and rescue efforts, with widespread looting as a major issue. In total, almost 2000 people were killed by the effects of the storm (Drye, 2005).

As Hurricane Katrina approached New Orleans, and the devastation started, it was very quickly evident that the concept of unity of command and mutual cooperation were fragmented. Much of this chaos was a result of the unforeseen scale of damage incurred in the early hours of the hurricane. As noted by the U.S. House of Representatives (2006), "Local governments' command and control was often paralyzed by the complete destruction of their entire emergency management infrastructure." (p. 184) Despite extensive planning and training for events such as this, there was a catastrophic breakdown in the emergency response in New Orleans.

Over the ensuing days and weeks, multiple agencies of the local, state, federal, and international levels worked to restore order, locate survivors, and recover victims. Since then, the response has received much criticism (e.g., lengthy delays in rescue, confusion amongst agencies, lack of basic supplies, etc.,) from the public and the media for its lack of cohesion (Manjoo et al., 2005). To a certain extent, this criticism is valid, as there was almost a complete breakdown of a coordinated strategic response. This lack of coordinated response led to ineffective rescue, recovery, relief operations, and communications (media) strategies. Local, state, and federal organizations failed to coordinate and control in any effective way. Evacuations, search and rescue operations, the provision of food and water to stranded citizens, and other key elements of a major rescue and recovery response were largely inadequate (U.S. House of Representatives, 2006). Planning and organizing are key elements of preparedness, yet all of this quickly went by the wayside during the response due to the magnitude of the disaster and complications arising largely from poor communications and confusion over jurisdiction. The most serious problems in New Orleans did not really begin until the levees were breached and there was mass flooding in virtually the entire city. The police were completely unprepared for this, and many of their own police stations and command centers were rendered useless as a result. As the water rose, not only did the citizens fear for their lives because of drowning, but they also began to panic about their homes. This was significantly compounded when the realization was made that food, water, and other supplies were virtually nonexistent. As a result, looting and rioting erupted in some areas (U.S. House of Representatives, 2006). A complete lack of communication about evacuation plans for the residents worsened the situation. It should be noted that even if an effective communications plan had been in place, it likely would not have been deliverable as most communications means were destroyed in the early hours of Hurricane Katrina (U.S. House of Representatives, 2006).

The infamous evacuation to the Superdome and to the Convention Center, although with the best of intentions, turned into a disaster in its own right. There was no clear plan for this being an evacuation center, there was a shortage of food and water, and worst of all, the New Orleans Police and the National Guard were unable to determine who was in charge. The New Orleans Police had been tasked with command and control and the National Guard were there in support of the police. At varying times, both agencies stated that the other was in charge, and when FEMA contacted officials at the Superdome, it was clear that "nobody was in charge." (U.S. House of Representatives, 2006) This led to even more confusion and the inability to make effective decisions. As noted, "in New Orleans, for at least some period of time, emergency managers, the police, and the military lost command and control over their own personnel and lost unity of command with the other local, state, and federal agencies that needed to be involved in the relief efforts." (U.S. House of Representatives, 2006) This clearly illustrates the absence of leadership and unified command.

Superintendent Compass, the police chief of New Orleans during Hurricane Katrina became personally involved in rescue operations and day to day low level operational issues. Furthermore, his involvement with the media was not strategic and rather than relying on professional communications strategists, Compass gave numerous 'off the cuff' interviews throughout the day (PBS, 2010). This fed directly into the media hype and misreporting that further complicated the emergency response by all levels of government. Trim notes that "ineffective forms of communication can create problems that militate against effective disaster planning." (2004) This holds true both within and amongst the responding agencies and in dealings with the public and the media.

The role played by Superintendent Compass during Hurricane Katrina clearly illustrates the complete lack of both unity of command and unified command principles. Arguably, these actions by Compass demonstrate that the New Orleans Police Department "did not adopt a clear plan, and no well-defined roles were established for the officers dealing with various elements of the disaster." (Deflem and Sutphin, 2009, p. 49) "Leading effectively ... requires sensitivity and interpersonal skills, directive task-oriented skills, and the resilience, hardness and flexibility to know when to use which. ... Prior planning and familiarity of procedures, grounded in a knowledge of likely challenges." (Alison and Crego, 2012) Compass was the antithesis of this approach.

The planning phase must be carried out with relevant stakeholders at all levels of government and also include NGOs. An exercise in which possible crises and disasters are examined must occur. These must then be broken down further into appropriate responses, jurisdiction, communications protocols and strategies, contingency plans, and risk mitigation strategies. The ability to build, manage, and maintain effective relationships with external partners and the community before a major incident is essential. This allows the potential negative impact or influences of these groups to be mitigated during the incident. Effective command requires that there is a solid foundation in community policing. By building themselves into the community, the police are seen as part of the community rather than strictly law-enforcement personnel. The community, in this instance, is defined not only as the citizens of an area, but all other agencies, different levels of government, humanitarian groups, and the media.

As relationships are built with other agencies and with the government before the disaster, the police leader should ensure that open and honest frank communication and dialogue is maintained. This dialogue should lead into mutual training, desktop exercises, and the ability to ensure that there is interoperability between agencies if there is a disaster. Cooperation and a familiarity with each the role of each agency and NGO will allow for proper and appropriate tasking during a crisis which will make the response more effective and lessen the burden on the police commander. Police are seen as leaders in major disasters. We need to instill confidence in the community and in our partners and the government.

→ **Features of a Crisis or Disaster**

Agencies may blame each other for shortfalls in response.
A threat manifests itself unexpectedly
Communication (internal and external) becomes difficult
to manage (e.g., technical failures, overload, media, etc.)
Increased risk of reputational damage
Lack of organization
Numerous requests for information from and to multiple
sources
Standard Operating Procedures (SOPs) may no longer apply
Stress factors continue to increase
Urgent need for immediate decision-making

→ **Elements of Effective Crisis Response**

Maintaining reputational integrity
Sound planning and preparedness
Solid leadership
Effective and timely communications
Strategic, well-organized interagency collaboration and
resource allocation
Successful operational tactics
Post-crisis evaluation and recommendations

→ **Fact Sheet on Kerslake Enquiry 2019 into the Manchester
Bombing**

*The investment in multi-agency planning and exercising as part of the Greater
Manchester Resilience Forum resulted in the partner agencies being generally
able to act with a high level of confidence there was not a shared communication across the agencies of the declaration of Operation PLATO, which is the*

(continued)

(continued)

agreed operational response to a suspected Marauding Terrorist Firearms Attack, nor was there a shared understanding of its implications. In the event, pragmatic judgements were made on the night that ensured that the response remained effective. However, we think that during any future events, it is essential that this communication across the agencies happens and happens early. We recommend that the Operation PLATO principles should be reviewed nationally and referred to as the Joint Operating Principles for Responding to a Terrorist Attack, regardless of whether firearms are thought to be involved. (kerslakearenareview.co.uk)

Powerful events call for powerful leadership. During a crisis or disaster, two fundamental requirements are that an organization responds effectively and that there is a leader to direct the efforts. It is clear that there are several prerequisite skills and attributes required of an effective operational commander. Essentially, the prerequisite skills of this commander can be categorized into the basic values of honesty, integrity, professionalism, compassion, accountability, and respect (i.e., these are the RCMP Core Values). In addition, the competencies of thinking skills and people skills are critical. Thinking skills incorporate planning and organizing, problem solving, strategic thinking, and decisiveness. People skills include communication, persuasiveness, courage of convictions, teamwork, team leadership (the ability to appropriately delegate), self-control, and composure. Tying these very important attributes in with job knowledge and practical hands-on experience is critical (RCMP Competency Dictionary, 2011).

A combination of Active Leadership and Situational Leadership can be of great benefit in these major incident command situations. Active leaders who lead from the front by setting a good example and by implementing 'role modeling strategies' will have a greater impact on influencing those on their team, even if they are not from the same organization. Situational leaders who are able to subtly change their behavior in order to address the current situation can take account of each team member's years of experience, formal position of power, and each individual's specific training or expertise. (Campbell & Kodz, 2011) This is critical in major incidents.

Although there is no exact formula for identifying an effective operational or incident commander, it is clear that most modern police agencies have reached the same conclusions as to the necessary attributes.

In order to maximize the effectiveness of operational command, there is a clear need for the police organization to recognize its importance. In most situations, there are generally lives at stake, both of the victims and potentially the rescuers and emergency personnel. There is a moral and ethical obligation to the community, and also a legal responsibility within its mandate to fulfill the operational command role. This legal responsibility ties into a significant liability risk for the police organization, should the response to situations not be handled in a defendable and conscientious manner.

Disaster Victim Identification (DVI)

DVI is a police discipline that has developed out of lessons learnt from dealing with incidents of mass casualties around the world. Natural disasters (2004 Tsunami), terrorist attacks (9/11) and transport disasters (1999 Paddington rail crash) are just some of the critical incidents where DVI officers have been employed. During the 2004 Tsunami response, the international response, which involved 31 countries, led to numerous agencies from the host countries and abroad assisting with the approximately 230,000 fatalities. In Indonesia, the military coordinated 42 different agencies. A Tsunami Identification Centre was set up in Thailand in partnership with Interpol in an effort to identify the many bodies. The British response (i.e., Operation Bracknell) involved more than 700 staff from 40 police organizations. Their duties included: body recovery, Family Liaison Officers, identification of more than 3000 victims, investigation of missing persons, and the repatriation of human remains.

The Canadian Armed Forces deployed its Disaster Assistance Response Team immediately after the 2004 Tsunami to assist with emergency relief operations. Shortly after, the Royal Canadian Mounted Police deployed ten forensic specialists to assist with identifying victims. Using an advanced fingerprinting technique, the Royal Canadian Mounted Police had a 70–80 percent identification success rate with lifting fingerprints off of the victims—the average of some teams from other countries was half of that. https://www.theglobeandmail.com/news/world/canadians-lead-effort-to-identify-tsunami-victims/article18219513/

A 'Closed Disaster' is a situation where the victims are from a fixed, identifiable group, such as a plane crash where there is a passenger manifest. In contrast, the 2004 Tsunami was an 'Open Disaster.' In this case, there are "unknown individuals for whom no prior records or descriptive data are available. It is difficult to obtain information about the actual number of victims following such events." (Disaster Victim Identification Guide, Interpol 2009 https://www.cmu.edu/chrs/conferences/eppi/docs/Interpol%20DVI%20Guide.pdf)

In the UK, DVI is within the remit of the National Police Chiefs Council (NPCC) National Police Coordination Centre (NPoCC).The role of UK DVI is to coordinate the national capability of the police service to respond to mass fatality incidents in the UK. Fire Service may assist when there are structural issues and collapse. The DVI guidance is contained within the College of Policing APP on Major Incidents. (https://www.app.college.police.uk/app-content/civil-emergencies/).

UK DVI Recovery Teams consist of 6 members and they use the Joint Decision Making Model under Jesip (Joint Doctrine, the interoperability framework) to deal with four distinct phases of a critical incident:

Phase 1: Scene Coordination.
Phase 2: Post-Mortem Coordination.
Phase 3: Ante-Mortem Coordination.
Phase 4: Reconciliation Coordination
Category 1 No difficult access
Category 2 Restricted access
Category 3 Difficult access area

Some of the Post incident considerations involve the setting up of MFCG Mass Fatality Coordination Group (MFCG) and locating a temporary mortuary. The teams are tasked with collecting and categorizing fragmented remains. The standards for DVI officers are set by Interpol internationally. The police work with third sector organizations such as the Red Cross or Red Crescent Societies.

Objective 4 of the UK DVI strategy is to implement a national standard in respect of a Casualty Bureau that operates as a Single Point of Contact (SPOC) for receiving and processing information about missing people in an incident. During the 2004 Tsunami, the UK Casualty Bureau worked with the third sector and overseas agencies to facilitate the identification of victims and coordinate missing person reports with casualty and evacuee records. The Bureau also provides information and intelligence for the investigation process. The Casualty Bureau manager implements information sharing protocols. The Bureau is comprised of trained staff from various police Forces in the UK.

In the Case of the Royal Canadian Mounted Police, DVI Is Comprised of the Following

* Family Liaison Assistance Group who assist victims' families

- Assessment Team evaluates the total scope of the DVI operation including logistical requirements, team size, subject matter expertise required and morgue location
- Body Recovery Teams collect the bodies and personal effects from the disaster site and document all available relevant information about the individual
- Ante-mortem Teams prepare missing persons files which include information required for the victim's identification such as medical records, original dental records, fingerprints and DNA
- Post-mortem Teams collect all post-mortem data including relevant dental, medical and forensic data from the victims during autopsy
- The Reconciliation Teams are responsible for searching the ante-mortem and post-mortem records and ultimately presenting a report and recommendation to the Identification Board

  The Identification Board confirms whether the victim's identity has been established (https://www.grc-rcmp.gc.ca/fsis-ssji/fis-sij/dvi-ivc-eng.htm; https://www.rcmp-grc.gc.ca/fsis-ssji/fis-sij/dvi-ivc-eng.htm; https://www.theglobeandmail.com/news/world/canadians-lead-effort-to-identify-tsunami-victims/article18219513/)

Exam Questions

1. Why is maintaining the reputational integrity of the police of such importance during a major crisis/disaster?
2. Why is planning an important component of Crisis and Disaster Management?
3. What is the fundamental principle relating to crisis communications?
4. What are the competencies that a successful police leader requires during a critical incident, crisis, or disaster?
5. Despite the growing importance of online and digital communications, why is it important to maintain ties with traditional media?
6. What are the main components of the recovery process

References

Alison, L., & Crego, J. (2012). *Policing critical incidents: Leadership and critical incident management*. Oxford: Willan Publishing. Retrieved from http://csuau.eblib.com.ezproxy.csu.edu.au/patron/FullRecord.aspxp=449567&echo=1&userid=UPUx6QtlF2YKCeynpalTg==&tstamp=1366056843&id=85181280FD72A772F22B8F600999D60F180EE96E

Boin, A et al. (2005). *The Politics of Crisis Management: Public Leadership Under Pressure.* Arjen Boin, Paul 't Hart, Eric Stern, and Bengt Sundelius. New York: Cambridge University Press. ISBN 0521845378.

Campbell, I., & Kodz, J. (2011). *What Makes Great Police Leadership? What Research Can Tell Us About the Effectiveness of Different Leadership Styles, Competencies and Behaviours: A Rapid Evidence Review.* London: National Police Improvement Agency.

Deflem, M., & Sutphin, S. (2009). Policing Katrina: Managing law enforcement in New Orleans. *Policing: A Journal of Policy and Practise, 3*(1), 41–49. Retrieved from http://policing.oxfordjournals.org.ezproxy.csu.edu.au/content/3/1/41.full

Drye, W. (2005, September 14). Hurricane Katrina: The essential time line. *National Geographic News.* Retrieved from http://news.nationalgeographic.com/news/2005/09/0914_050914_katrina_timeline.html

Manjoo, F., Rockwell, P. & Kinney, A., Timeline to disaster. (2005, September 15). *Salon.* Retrieved from http://www.salon.com/2005/09/15/katrina_timeline/

National Hurricane Center. (2012). *Hurricane Katrina.* Retrieved from http://www.nhc.noaa.gov/outreach/history/

PBS. (2010). *Hurricane Katrina crime and disorder and the storm.* http://www.pbs.org, USA.

RCMP Competency Dicytionary. (2011). http://www.policeofficerleadership.com/RCMP Organizational Core Competencies...

Royal Canadian Mounted Police. (2013). *About the RCMP.* Retrieved from http://www.rcmp-grc.gc.ca/about-ausujet/index-eng.htm

Sills, G. L., Vroman, N. D., Wahl, P. E., & Schwanz, P. E. (2008). Overview of New Orleans levee failures: Lessons learned and their impact on national levee design and assessment. *Journal of Geotechnical and Geoenvironmental Engineering, 134*(5), 556–565. Retrieved from http://champs.cecs.ucf.edu/Library/Journal_Articles/pdfs/Sills_Overview_of_New_Orleans.pdf

Trim, P. R. J. (2004). An integrative approach to disaster management and planning. *Disaster Prevention and Management, 13*(3), 218–225. Retrieved from http://www.emeraldinsight.com/journals.htm?articleid=871051.

U.S. Department of Homeland Security. (2013). *Federal emergency management agency.* Retrieved from http://www.fema.gov/

U.S. House of Representatives. (2006). *A failure of initiative: Final report of the select bipartisan committee to investigate the preparation for and response to Hurricane Katrina.* Retrieved from http://repositories.lib.utexas.edu/handle/2152/13152?show=full

Cybercrime in the Age of Digital Transformation, Rising Nationalism and the Demise of Global Governance

Larry Poe

According to the World Economic Forum (WEF), the Fourth Industrial Revolution (4IR, also known as digital transformation) "has the potential to raise global income levels and improve the quality of life for populations around the world".[1] However, WEF President Klaus Schwab puts this forecast in context by stating, "there has never been a time of greater promise (combating climate change, global economic growth) or potential peril (increased cybercrime)".[2] Key amongst these perils is the rapid increase of cybercrime, which now affects every sector of society. Furthermore, one must understand how the willful negligence and pursuit of nationalistic cyber policies and objectives of China, Russia and the United States (US) (i.e., the Big Three) have given rise to a lawless and under governed cyber space where so-called state actors (i.e., national security agencies) and non-state actors (i.e., criminal and political activists) further political-military objectives, spread disinformation (so-called infodemics, e.g., false COVID-19 medical information), interfere with democratic elections, collect ransoms and compromise

[1] Schwab, Klaus. "The Fourth Industrial Revolution: What It Means and How to Respond." *World Economic Forum*, 16 Jan. 2016, www.weforum.org/agenda/2016/01/the-fourth-industrial-revolution-what-it-means-and-how-to-respond/

[2] Schwab, Klaus. *The Fourth Industrial Revolution*. Portfolio Penguin, 2017.

L. Poe (✉)
Rabdan Academy, Al Bhustan, Abu Dhabi, United Arab Emirates

© The Author(s), under exclusive license to Springer Nature Switzerland AG 2021
M. Roycroft, L. Brine (eds.), *Modern Police Leadership*,
https://doi.org/10.1007/978-3-030-63930-3_11

critical infrastructure (e.g., electrical grids/public facilities/medical centers). This permissive environment has even facilitated crime in ways that no one could have previously imagined (e.g., the use of social media as a "megaphone" to spread hate speech, incite murder, and then broadcast these acts via the internet).

This chapter will also address how these vexing circumstances undermine the global governance efforts of the United Nations (UN) to regularize and promote a more stringent multilateral and global standard for cybercrime. The efforts of the UN are not compatible with the national interests of the so-called Big Three, as attaining their nationalistic objectives (i.e., offensive cyber operations) requires the legal boundaries of cyber space to remain murky and ill-defined. This current situation has, at times, strengthened long standing security agreements such as the Five Eyes Intelligence sharing alliance (FVEY) between the Australia, Canada, New Zealand, United Kingdom, and US, while deepening mistrust in public (i.e., law enforcement) and private sector (i.e., technology companies) partnerships (PPP).

Simply put, the lack of stringent cyber security laws and the unyielding pursuit of the national interests of three nations, now leave global law enforcement (LE) with the daunting task of checking these new cyber "perils" without adequate laws for the task. Under these conditions, harmful acts will undermine the growth and stability of society as state actors (i.e., national intelligence services) and non-state actors (i.e., criminals and political hackers) seek to capitalize on purposefully weakened law enforcement agreements for criminal gains.

More "Connected" Means More "Efficiency"...and More Crime

The spectacular nature of the digital transformation of society (i.e., 4th Industrial Revolution (4IR)) is met in contrast with a woeful lack of global governance and international laws to regularize and enforce the lawful use of these transformative technologies. The digital transformation of society has created a quantum leap in human existence (i.e., social media, digital economy, reducing climate change, advances in medical science) brought about by "the confluence of four information technologies (Artificial Intelligence, Big Data, Cloud Computing and the Internet of Things)"[3] which are drastically revolutionizing every sector of the economy (i.e., communications, energy, medicine, transportation). The WEF describes this dynamic, as follows, "It (4IR) is characterized by a range of new technologies that

---

[3] Siebel, Thomas M. *Digital Transformation: Survive and Thrive in an Era of Mass Extinction*. Rosetta Books, 2019.

are fusing the physical, digital and biological worlds, impacting all disciplines, economies and industries, and even challenging ideas about what it means to be human".[4] This is to say that internet technologies (IT) are now the backbone of manufacturing, energy, agriculture, and transportation and accounts for nearly two-thirds of the world's gross domestic product (GDP).[5] While IT has hastened productivity, the very global connectivity which spells success, also presents new threats and challenges as malicious actors (both state and non-state) enter this milieu to advance their goals and objectives.

(A) Criminals (Non-State Actors)

The fully automated programs and tools to conduct malicious cyberattacks are now widely available on the Dark Web (a portion of the internet only accessible with a special web browser called Tor, which guarantees complete anonymity). These fully automated programs work relentlessly around the clock hacking computers and testing cyber defenses. This alarming threat is dynamic and adaptable and requires global law enforcement stakeholders to develop an integrated and joint response. However, an adequate defense remains elusive, as demonstrated by the recent surge of criminal cyberattacks targeting medical facilities worldwide during the COVID-19 pandemic. While medical personnel valiantly labor to treat the ill, criminals quietly exploit under protected medical facilities by seizing the personal data of patients, hindering medical operations by disabling computers, spreading disinformation (e.g., false medical scares) and swindling money through scams which capitalize on fears of the pandemic.

However, the targeting of critical infrastructure essential to public welfare and security is not new, as cyber criminals have preyed upon civil authorities, especially targeting law enforcement and emergency medical personnel.[6] In fact, at present, defenseless local and state governments account for 70 percent of all ransomware attacks in the US. Estimates for 2020, by London-based insurance com-

---

[4] Schwab, Klaus. "The Fourth Industrial Revolution: What It Means and How to Respond." *World Economic Forum*, 16 Jan. 2016, www.weforum.org/agenda/2016/01/the-fourth-indus-trial-revolution-what-it-means-and-how-to-respond/

[5] Schwab, Klaus. "The Fourth Industrial Revolution: What It Means and How to Respond." *World Economic Forum*, 16 Jan. 2016, www.weforum.org/agenda/2016/01/the-fourth-indus-trial-revolution-what-it-means-and-how-to-respond/

[6] Muggah, Robert. "Our Cities Are under Cyberattack. Here's Why – And What They Should Do about It." *World Economic Forum*, 30 Sept. 2019, www.weforum.org/agenda/2019/09/our-cities-are-increasingly-vulnerable-to-cyberattacks-heres-how-they-can-fight-back/

pany Lloyd's, estimates that the public and private sectors in New York City, alone, could lose over US $2.3 billion in cybercrime related incidents. In 2018 and 2019, ransomware attacks crippled the US city of Baltimore by disabling servers and the 911 emergency center. Equally alarming are the hundreds of thousands of dollars of ransom paid in digital currencies, such as Bitcoin, by 22 small towns across the US state of Texas. Attacks against medical facilities and critical infrastructure are truly a global phenomenon: clear examples are Dublin (i.e., municipal tram system), Hyderabad and Johannesburg (i.e., power plants) and Stockholm (i.e., air traffic control and railway ticketing).[7]

(B) State Actors

The tacit approval of state-sponsored cybercrime is a subject of great debate. However, China, Russia, and the US continue to allow international laws to languish, in favor of offensive cyber operations that permit nations to strike deep within sovereign territories with "plausible deniability".

• Cyber Influencing: Elections Tampering (Russia)

In 2016, Russia used social media to influence voter opinions in support of the Republican Party candidate, Donald Trump. The existence of this invasive operation is widely acknowledged and subsequently led the two dominant US political parties (Democratic and Republican) to consider election fraud countermeasures to protect the upcoming 2020 presidential election.

In 2017, while meeting with Russian officials, Trump expressed his disbelief about the effectiveness of such cyber operations. He even suggested that conducting offensive cyber operations is legitimate, as the US has frequently interfered in the elections of other nations. In 2019, in stark contrast, Democratic presidential candidate Andrew Yang not only confirmed illegal US interference in foreign elections, but also called for a halt to these operations, "We've tampered (US) with other elections. You've tampered (Russia) with our elections. And now it has to stop".[8]

---

[7] Muggah, Robert. "Our Cities Are under Cyberattack. Here's Why – And What They Should Do about It." *World Economic Forum*, 30 Sept. 2019, www.weforum.org/agenda/2019/09/our-cities-are-increasingly-vulnerable-to-cyberattacks-heres-how-they-can-fight-back/

[8] Knake, Robert K. "Banning Covert Foreign Election Interference." *Council on Foreign Relations*, Council on Foreign Relations, 29 May 2020, www.cfr.org/report/banning-covert-foreign-election-interference

- **Cyberattack on Critical Infrastructure: Stuxnet and the Iranian Nuclear Power Program (Believed to be the Israel and the US)**

In 2010, the US and Israel allegedly conducted an offensive cyberattack on Iran's Natanz and Bashear Nuclear Power Facilities, as punishment for Tehran's attempts to enrich uranium.[9] This attack involved using malware to take control of the computers operating the centrifuges (i.e., a device which uses centrifugal force to enrich uranium) supporting Iran's nuclear energy program. This malware successfully damaged the centrifuges and resulted in the first cyberattack to "leave cyberspace" and cause actual physical damage.

In 2018, Iranian hackers executed the largest cyberattack recorded against a US city (Atlanta), resulting in closing the city hall for five days, halting police services and canceling court cases. Additionally, the city's airport, Hartsfield International (the busiest in the country), was affected. It is believed that this cyberattack, along with many others, are retaliation for the Stuxnet attack and part of the ongoing cyberwar between nations.

- **Cyber Hacking: Impeding Criminal Investigations (Russia)**

In 2018, Dutch officials intercepted and foiled operatives of the GRU (Russian Military Intelligence Service) while conducting offensive cyberattacks against the Organization for the Prevention of Chemical Weapons (OPCW). This operation was in retaliation for the organization's criminal investigation of Russian chemical weapons deployments to Syria.[10]

In 2016, Russian hackers, known as Tsar Team (APT28) or Fancy Bear, executed a cyberattack against the World Anti-Doping Agency (WADA) which was conducting an investigation on the abuse of performance enhancing drugs by Russian athletes. Russian hackers successfully gained access to the private data of international athletes and posted this stolen information on the internet. The WADA was also threatened with further breaches, if the investigation of Russian athletes did not cease.[11]

---

[9] Segal, Adam, and Hannah Pitts. *Cyber Conflict after Stuxnet: Essays from the Other Bank of the Rubicon.* Cyber Conflict Studies, 2016.

[10] Ministerie van Algemene Zaken. "Netherlands Defence Intelligence and Security Service Disrupts Russian Cyber Operation Targeting OPCW." *News Item | Government.nl*, Ministerie, 4 Oct. 2018, www.government.nl/latest/news/2018/10/04/netherlands-defence-intelligence-and-security-service-disrupts-russian-cyber-operation-targeting-opcw

[11] WADA Confirms Attack by Russian Cyber Espionage Group | World. Retrieved July 5, 2020, from https://www.wada-ama.org/en/media/news/2016-09/wada-confirms-attack-by-russian-cyber-espionage-group

In 2014, Russian intelligence operatives attempted to hinder the criminal investigation of the negligent downing of Malaysian Airlines flight MH 17. This flight was en route to Kuala Lumpur from Amsterdam when it was shot down over eastern Ukraine, by Russian forces engaged in combat operations there.[12]

• **Cyber Hacking of Critical Infrastructure: Medical Facilities (Believed to be China)**

In March 2020, Europe's largest private hospital operator, and key supplier of kidney dialysis supplies, was targeted by ransomware. This attack is most vexing, as COVID-19 patients often experience kidney failure. Similar cyberattacks occurred around the world and involved both seizing private data (i.e., patient medical records, public health analysis, sensitive medical research) and demands for ransom money paid in a digital currency, such as Bitcoin.[13] Noncompliance resulted in the loss of valuable data and computer systems and the posting of sensitive information on the internet. The aggressive nature of these cyberattacks, combined with the COVID-19 pandemic, presented a unique risk to global medical infrastructure and led the US Department of Homeland Security (DHS) and the UK's National Cyber Security Centre (NCSC) to issue a joint alert. This warning indicated that state-sponsored hackers (also known as "APT" or advanced persistent threats) were targeting "frontline healthcare providers" engaged in combating COVID-19. The alert further states that, "APT actors frequently target organizations in order to collect bulk personal information, intellectual property, and intelligence that aligns with national priorities".[14] While this document does not explicitly indicate Chinese involvement, the characteristics of the attack (i.e., theft of intellectual property and intelligence collection) do mirror Beijing's tactics.

---

[12] Ministerie van Algemene Zaken. "MH17 Incident." *Government.nl*, Ministerie Van Algemene Zaken, 25 May 2018, www.government.nl/topics/mh17-incident

[13] Krebs, Brian. "Europe's Largest Private Hospital Operator Fresenius Hit by Ransomware." *Brian Krebs*, May 2020, krebsonsecurity.com/2020/05/europes-largest-private-hospital-operator-fresenius-hit-by-ransomware/.

[14] US Department of Homeland Security and UK National Cyber Security Center. "Alert (AA20-126A)." *Cybersecurity and Infrastructure Security Agency CISA*, 2020, www.us-cert.gov/ncas/alerts/AA20126A

(C) Political "Hacktivists"

The killing of unarmed citizen George Floyd by police in Minneapolis, Minnesota, sparked global protests and debate over police brutality and injustice. At the same time, internet activity surrounding this event also peaked, and with it, a dramatic increase in Distributed Denial of Service (i.e., DDOS, a large number of requests to access a website sent with the intention of overwhelming the website and knock it offline) cyberattacks against anti-racism groups. According to Cloudflare, a cybersecurity company, it blocked 19 billion DDOS attacks in the days following the killing of George Floyd and the subsequent rioting after his death. Cloudflare further reports that a certain anti-racism advocacy group targeted by DDOS attacks received 20,000 requests per second.[15]

This Is Everybody's Problem: Why Isn't More Being Done?

Recent cyberattacks on the World Health Organization (WHO) and critical health care facilities, around the world, led US Secretary of State, Mike Pompeo to urge both Washington and international partners to promote "responsible behavior in cyberspace". Instead of calling for stringent international laws, Pompeo suggested that the world community adopt "nonbinding norms" at the height of the global COVID-19 pandemic. This alarming activity eventually led UN Undersecretary General Fabrizio Hochschild to call for a "global digital ceasefire". The future of regulating cyberspace appears bleak, as not even a matter of life and death, such as the Covid-19 pandemic, will unite the world and force the "Big Three" to adhere.[16]

Across all nations many public and private sector organizations have fallen prey to hacking and cybercrime. The victims are a veritable "who's who" of Fortune 500 companies and influential government agencies.[17] These incidents highlight the paradox of the digital economy and cyber security. IT has greatly augmented the convenience, efficiency and the creation of wealth creation in society. As such, corporations are eager to expand connectivity. However, this eagerness is only

---

[15] BBC News. "George Floyd Death: Anti-Racism Sites Hit by Wave of Cyber-Attacks." *BBC News*, BBC, 3 June 2020, www.bbc.com/news/technology-52912881

[16] Gold, Josh. "Amid COVID-Related Cyber Threats, the Netherlands Leads UN Efforts." *Council on Foreign Relations*, Council on Foreign Relations, 4 May 2020, www.cfr.org/blog/amid-covid-related-cyber-threats-netherlands-leads-un-efforts

[17] Shull, Aaron. *Governing Cyberspace during a Crisis in Trust.* 11 Aug. 2019, www.cigionline.org/articles/governing-cyberspace-during-crisis-trust

equaled by a lack of consideration for the increased threats that an increasingly digitized society will face. This precarious situation is further aggravated by the fact that a deeply fragmented and underdeveloped system of global governance is the only mechanism in place to confront global cybercrime.

In 2019, the UN Secretary-General convened a panel to strengthen the architecture for global digital cooperation. This group of experts was tasked with identifying gaps and challenges in current security regimes and to propose three options for global governance of cyberspace. First amongst these recommendations is that the international community should better leverage the established mechanisms for digital cooperation that currently exist. This includes fora and networks of governments, industry, technical bodies and civil society, as well as existing regulations and 'soft law' such as norms, guidelines, and codes of conduct. Second, the UN must promote global commitment to digital trust and security by promulgating a shared vision of digital responsibility and strengthen use of norms for legal uses of technology. Third, is to promote global digital cooperation. To achieve this, the UN Secretary-General can facilitate this process developing updated mechanisms for global digital cooperation.[18]

In 2018, WEF analysis indicated that global governance protocols already exist that can aid in regulating the internet. These tools include laws, conventions, private sector industry initiatives, and information-sharing platforms.[19] However, these tools are not enough, as cybercrime cannot be successfully contained through unilateral actions. Instead, public and private sectors must work in unison to find effective ways of dealing with this issue. The cornerstone of any solution to cybercrime is trust and this is brought about through transparency, on both sides.

The following are recommendations for drafting agreements on the fundamental steps required to make real global progress: (1) enhanced public-private sector information sharing on threats, vulnerability assessments and consequences, (2) create new platforms, strengthen existing platforms and coordination to improve investigations and prosecutions, (3) promote wider adoption of the Budapest Convention (i.e., the first international treaty on cybercrime) and the principles it contains, (4) work to build trust and provide a forum for contentious topics related to cybercrime (i.e., encryption, cloud services, data access and privacy) and (5) engage in other initiatives which reduce cybercrime.

---

[18] United Nations. "Secretary-General's High-Level Panel on Digital Cooperation." *United Nations*, United Nations, 2019, www.un.org/en/digital-cooperation-panel/

[19] Schwab, Klaus. *The Fourth Industrial Revolution*. Portfolio Penguin, 2017.

Five Eyes (FVEY) and the PPP: Together We Stand, Divided We Fall

The FVEY alliance was created during World War II, remained strong throughout the Cold War, and is now facing the new challenges of the 4IR. However, the challenges and opportunities presented by digital transformation have tested the vitality of this alliance. The dynamic nature of this new era of digital transformation highlighted a unique "blind spot"—the inability of FVEY nations to detect and contain social media usage of transnational white nationalist. This is best exemplified by the right wing extremism mosque attacks that occurred in Christchurch, New Zealand in 2019. These events also suggest that the FVEY Nations must reassess how they jointly determine strategic threats and more specifically the unique challenges caused by white nationalist. These individuals now present a transnational threat, as similar attacks have occurred in Canada, the United Kingdom, and the United States. Furthermore, such attacks can be expected in the future, as white nationalists view themselves as combatants in a war that is only just beginning. This is evidenced by the manifestos posted online by various white nationalists, before executing their attacks.[20]

For the FVEY nations the duality of benefit and "peril" of the digital transformation of society is best exemplified by the under regulated rise of social media and the role it has played in the mass shootings in the US (e.g., Charleston, El Paso, Pittsburgh) and New Zealand (i.e., Christchurch). While social media has radically changed how we socialize and exchange ideas. The same forum that unites family and friends, also brings together hate groups and serves as "a megaphone for mass shooters, and a recruiting platform for violent white nationalists".[21] These technology-based (social media) crimes clearly demonstrate the "Achilles' heel" of international cooperation and remind us that the PPP has failed miserably at preventing, protecting, and mitigating the effects of serious cybercrimes.

By 2018, law enforcement officials of the FVEY nations were well-aware of emerging technology-based threats. To curtail this threat, they issued a joint statement (i.e., Statement of Principles on Access to Evidence and Encryption) strongly urging technology companies to cooperate with law enforcement and provide ac-

---

[20] Laub, Zachary. "Hate Speech on Social Media: Global Comparisons." *Council on Foreign Relations*, Council on Foreign Relations, Jan. 2019, www.cfr.org/backgrounder/hate-speech-social-media-global-comparisons

[21] Laub, Zachary. "Hate Speech on Social Media: Global Comparisons." *Council on Foreign Relations*, Council on Foreign Relations, Jan. 2019, www.cfr.org/backgrounder/hate-speech-social-media-global-comparisons

cess to encrypted data related to ongoing criminal investigations. In response to the "absolutist" stance (lawful access is incompatible with privacy concerns) taken by many technology companies, FVEY officials reaffirmed their commitment to protecting personal rights and privacy. This statement further warned that noncompliance may have consequences, "we may pursue technological, enforcement, legislative or other measures to achieve lawful access solutions".[22] In December 2019, FVEY leadership met again to discuss international cooperation and to devise a solution acceptable to both the public and private sectors. Concerning their proactive and conciliatory approach, United States Attorney General William Barr noted that, "making our virtual world more secure should not come at the expense of making us more vulnerable in the real world".[23]

The FVEY nations have also sought to attack the problem of PPP independently. Since 2015, these same concerns led the New York County District Attorney to vehemently object to opposition from Apple and Google and to seek legislative support for legal access to private data on IT devices. The District Attorney further suggests that the tech industry perspective of "either we have user privacy or lawful access, but we can't have both"[24] simply is not true. This position clearly threatens public safety and order, as lawful hacking of IT devices may require more time than statutes of limitation or speedy trial requirements may allow. Additionally, the costs for these services are often prohibitive. For example, in 2015 the FBI paid US $900,000 dollars to access evidence on the phone of a mass murder in San Bernardino, California. Apple refused to offer assistance.[25]

---

[22] Vance, Cyrus. "Written Testimony for the United States Senate Committee on the Judiciary on Smartphone Encryption and Public Safety." *Manhattan District Attorney's Office*, 10 Dec 2019, www.manhattanda.org/written-testimony-for-the-united-states-senate-committee-on-the-judiciary-on-smartphone-encryption-and-public-safety/

[23] Vance, Cyrus. "Written Testimony for the United States Senate Committee on the Judiciary on Smartphone Encryption and Public Safety." *Manhattan District Attorney's Office*, 10 Dec. 2019, www.manhattanda.org/written-testimony-for-the-united-states-senate-committee-on-the-judiciary-on-smartphone-encryption-and-public-safety/

[24] Vance, Cyrus. "Written Testimony for the United States Senate Committee on the Judiciary on Smartphone Encryption and Public Safety." *Manhattan District Attorney's Office*, 10 Dec. 2019, www.manhattanda.org/written-testimony-for-the-united-states-senate-committee-on-the-judiciary-on-smartphone-encryption-and-public-safety/

[25] Vance, Cyrus. "Written Testimony for the United States Senate Committee on the Judiciary on Smartphone Encryption and Public Safety." *Manhattan District Attorney's Office*, 10 Dec. 2019, www.manhattanda.org/written-testimony-for-the-united-states-senate-committee-on-the-judiciary-on-smartphone-encryption-and-public-safety/

In November 2018, the UK faced similar challenges. This led the Government Communications Headquarters (GCHQ), National Cyber Security Centre (NCSC) to formally request the assistance of technology companies in gaining so-called exceptional access—the ability to gain case-by-case access (approved by authorities) to encrypted end-to-end communications of individuals under criminal investigation or engaged in terrorism. GCHQ further suggested that, "the service provider usually controls the identity system and so really decides who's who and which devices are involved in introducing the parties to a chat or call. You end up with everything still being end-to-end encrypted, but there's an extra end".[26] While this process sounds simple, tech companies view this activity as a violation of privacy agreements and it may have significant legal implications.

In 2019, similar concerns led the Australian Parliament to pass a law (i.e., Telecommunications and Other Legislation Amendment) which endeavors to provide exceptional access, without inducing the, "systemic weakness or systemic vulnerability" of IT devices.[27]

(A) The Failed PPP (Social Media and Hate Crime)

The technologies which support the 4IR are overwhelmingly owned and operated by privately held entities. However, regulation and law enforcement in cyberspace are uniquely the responsibility of the public sector. The economies and national welfare of most nations are now fully dependent upon digital transformation and 4IR technologies. In response, the PPP should ideally serve as a mechanism to jointly leverage law enforcement and security resources to counter cybercrime. As such, the PPP should be the "cornerstone" or "hub" of any LE cybercrime strategy.

However, conflicting roles and responsibilities of the two sectors limits the effectiveness of the PPP. The focus of the private sector on profit will always take precedence over national security (undeniably a public sector responsibility). To gain trust and confidence, the public sector must always respect this fact. One must also acknowledge that government oversight alone cannot successfully monitor

---

[26] Levy, Ian, and Crispin Robinson. "Principles for a More Informed Exceptional Access Debate." *Lawfare*, 31 Oct. 2019, www.lawfareblog.com/principles-more-informed-exceptional-access-debate

[27] Vance, Cyrus. "Written Testimony for the United States Senate Committee on the Judiciary on Smartphone Encryption and Public Safety." *Manhattan District Attorney's Office*, 10 Dec. 2019, www.manhattanda.org/written-testimony-for-the-united-states-senate-committee-on-the-judiciary-on-smartphone-encryption-and-public-safety/

and counter the advanced crimes of the 4IR. What is required is a PPP capable of harnessing private sector innovation, while limiting the public sector role to coordinating and advising. Ultimately, the mechanisms and know-how for keeping cyberspace safe reside in the private sector. As such, the lead for these endeavors should remain in the private sector. The public sector must make every effort to lessen private sector mistrust by encouraging open dialogue (i.e., mutual threat information sharing) and regulatory transparency (e.g., are you here to help us or issue fines?) to build mutual trust.

(B) The Fine Line Between Regulation and Cooperation

Law enforcement must remain transparent concerning cybersecurity regulatory frameworks and render assistance, in order to promote private sector cooperation while investigating cybercrime. The failure to do so will ultimately undermine the trust required, between the two sides, to facilitate the joint development of strategies for criminal investigations and information sharing.

The issue of regulating social media is truly global in proportion. The difficulties encountered in regulation are as nuanced and varied as the citizens that access social media. The enormity of this complex issue is brought into context by the fact that almost one third of the world's population currently uses Facebook. In fact, in some long-isolated regions of the world, such as authoritarian Myanmar, Facebook "is the internet"[28] for most residents.

While the lives of most citizens are influenced positively by social media, a small segment of society is leveraging technology to express racist, misogynistic, and homophobic sentiments. The same tool which positively bolsters social inclusion also reinforces these negative views and goads a small few to harm others. This concept was recently taken a step further in New Zealand when a white extremist gunman posted a live broadcast on Facebook of his attack against the Muslim community in the city of Christchurch.[29] Experts clearly indicate that hate speech, expressed via social media, can promote violence. Evidence to support this fact comes from both the developing and industrialized nations.

---

[28] Chernenko, Elena. "Increasing International Cooperation in Cybersecurity and Adapting Cyber Norms." *Council on Foreign Relations,* Council on Foreign Relations, February 2018, www.cfr.org/report/increasing-international-cooperation-cybersecurity-and-adapting-cyber-norms

[29] Laub, Zachary. "Hate Speech on Social Media: Global Comparisons." *Council on Foreign Relations*, Council on Foreign Relations, Jan. 2019, www.cfr.org/backgrounder/hate-speech-social-media-global-comparisons

Continued criticism of Facebook's ability to monitor violence inducing hate speech online led CEO Mark Zuckerberg to seek assistance from governments in many of the markets served by his company. While Zuckerberg viewed this move as a safe way to navigate disparate legal systems and avoid intrusive investigations, critics characterized this initiative as a method to appease oppressive regimes and retain access to markets that restrict free speech. Project Dragonfly, a proposal for adherence to Chinese internet restrictions, is a prime example.[30] However, this criticism is inconsistent with the cancelation by Facebook of the accounts of senior ranking officials in Myanmar and the addition of several native speakers to monitor inflammatory speech in the region. Both actions directly prevented further persecution of the Muslim Rohingya minority.[31]

Freedom of expression, equality, and rule of law are strictly public sector functions which each nation must reevaluate, given the current advances in communication technology. The technical challenges of how to monitor hate speech, and avert the criminal acts this may cause, is a public matter that each nation must resolve independently.

In the US, social media previously enjoyed tremendous leeway to establish standards for content and regimes for enforcement through the Communications Decency Act (CDA). Social media's ability to exercise discretion over its content was best exemplified by protections against liability for "actionable speech" by their customers. Print and television media outlets were never favored in this way and were always liable if they knowingly released defamatory information.[32]

Social media lost this privilege with the stroke of a pen and a heated exchange with US President Donald Trump. This incident all began with a violent Twitter entry by Trump in reference to looters that took to the streets after the death of George Floyd--"when the looting starts, the shooting starts".[33] In an attempt to

---

[30] Vance, Cyrus. "Written Testimony for the United States Senate Committee on the Judiciary on Smartphone Encryption and Public Safety." *Manhattan District Attorney's Office*, 10 Dec. 2019, www.manhattanda.org/written-testimony-for-the-united-states-senate-committee-on-the-judiciary-on-smartphone-encryption-and-public-safety/

[31] Chernenko, Elena. "Increasing International Cooperation in Cybersecurity and Adapting Cyber Norms." *Council on Foreign Relations,* Council on Foreign Relations, February 2018, www.cfr.org/report/increasing-international-cooperation-cybersecurity-and-adapting-cyber-norms

[32] Laub, Zachary. "Hate Speech on Social Media: Global Comparisons." *Council on Foreign Relations*, Council on Foreign Relations, Jan. 2019, www.cfr.org/backgrounder/hate-speech-social-media-global-comparisons

[33] Alba, Davey, et al. "Twitter Adds Warnings to Trump and White House Tweets, Fueling Tensions." *The New York Times*, The New York Times, 29 May 2020, www.nytimes.com/2020/05/29/technology/trump-twitter-minneapolis-george-floyd.html

moderate hate speech, Twitter prevented readers from accessing the post without reading a warning statement indicating that the entry "glorified violence". In response, Trump issued an executive order placing limits on the legal protections from liability under the Communications Decency Act (Section 230). In other words, technology companies are now being penalized for their attempts for moderating hate speech and averting possible acts of crime. In response, Twitter said it will "continue to place warning labels on content which incite violence and/or spread false information concerning elections and Coronavirus".[34] Additionally, political factions have long debated that the moderation of hate speech attempts to limit conservative political expression. Donald Trump is an active supporter of this point of view.

This highly contentious point was the subject of much congressional testimony and debate in the US Congress shortly after the attacks in New Zealand. In one hearing Democratic Congressman Jerry Nadler expressed concerns that the internet aided white nationalism's international proliferation. Republican Senator Ted Cruz suggested that social media suppressed conservative speech with threats of federal regulations.[35] According to US Congressman Nadler, "The President's rhetoric fans the flames with language that—whether intentional or not—may motivate and embolden white supremacist movements".[36] Politicians around the world continue to make use of hate speech to gain influence and power. The August 2019 attack in El Paso quickly gave fuel to the debate on the correlation between hate speech, social media, and violence.

In the European Union (EU), the 28 member nations confront hate speech in different ways. However, some similarity in laws exists. This disparity in the treatment of hate speech is increasingly exacerbated by the rise of anti-immigrant sentiments and the return of anti-Semitism. To avoid more stringent regulation, companies agreed to proactively investigate content complaints made by users and delete them within 24 hours. As of February 2019, the EU indicated that tech companies

---

[34] Alba, Davey, et al. "Twitter Adds Warnings to Trump and White House Tweets, Fueling Tensions." *The New York Times*, The New York Times, 29 May 2020, www.nytimes.com/2020/05/29/technology/trump-twitter-minneapolis-george-floyd.html

[35] Chernenko, Elena. "Increasing International Cooperation in Cybersecurity and Adapting Cyber Norms." *Council on Foreign Relations,* Council on Foreign Relations, February 2018, www.cfr.org/report/increasing-international-cooperation-cybersecurity-and-adapting-cyber-norms

[36] Chernenko, Elena. "Increasing International Cooperation in Cybersecurity and Adapting Cyber Norms." *Council on Foreign Relations,* Council on Foreign Relations, February 2018, www.cfr.org/report/increasing-international-cooperation-cybersecurity-and-adapting-cyber-norms

complied with agreement three quarters of the time.[37] While the EU's measures are a step in the right direction, truly comprehensive oversight remains bedeviled by unclear definitions of prohibited material and the limitations associated with private sector enforcement.

The European Union (EU) also recently issued new guidelines requiring social media companies (Facebook, Google, Twitter) to provide monthly reports on their efforts to counter COVID-19 disinformation. According to the EU mandate, these companies must report, "on their actions to promote authoritative content, improve user awareness and limit Coronavirus disinformation and advertising related to it". The EU further maintains that Russia and China are actively promoting a Coronavirus "infodemic", "seeking to undermine democratic debate and exacerbate social polarization and improve their own image in the COVID-19 context".[38]

Conclusion

Global connectivity is the cornerstone of the 4IR and brings a uniquely international aspect to cybercrime. However, enhanced multi-national cooperation is required to effectively prevent, protect against, and mitigate the harmful effects of under governed cyber space. This can only occur through better cooperation and coordination between the public and private sector. This will truly reinforce the vitality of the PPP, which faces unique challenges when exercised across borders. Equally vexing are the dysfunctional and inadequate global governance laws and mechanisms used to check malicious actors in cyberspace. In fact, at present, there is a lack of a globally accepted definition of prohibited cyber activity, upon which to base national laws. This has created an expanding crisis in law enforcement, resulting in a continued increase in cybercrime across nations. Even the venerable and time tested FVEY Alliance, which stood firm against the Axis powers, Soviet expansion and global jihadists, is now straining under the rapid advance of technology. One must expect these problems to persist, as the US, China and Russia will likely continue to choose short-term national priorities over sustainable global governance agreements which will lead the 4IR toward continued safe and productive growth. From a crime prevention perspective, law enforcement is at a disadvan-

---

[37] Laub, Zachary. "Hate Speech on Social Media: Global Comparisons." *Council on Foreign Relations*, Council on Foreign Relations, Jan. 2019, ww.cfr.org/backgrounder/hate-speech-social-media-global-comparisonswww.cfr.org/backg

[38] CFR, EU Requests Monthly Reports on COVID-19 Disinformation From Social Media Giants, https://www.cfr.org/blog/cyber-week-review-june-12-2020

tage, as acts of cybercrime do not require the offender to be located in the same country as the victim. This explains why many cybercrime offenses have a transnational dimension. Successful prevention and combating of cybercrime, therefore, requires effective international cooperation through adequate legal protocols and well-trained law enforcement personnel.

Digital Economy/Magnitude of Damage

There is an urgent need for cooperation among states to mitigate threats such as cybercrime, cyberattacks on critical infrastructure, electronic espionage, bulk data interception, and offensive operations intended to project power by the application of force in and through cyberspace. Emerging cyber threats could precipitate massive economic and societal damage, and international efforts need to be recalibrated to account for this new reality. However, going forward, expect China, Russia, and the US to continue undermining the strengthening of international norms and protocols, by choosing to act unilaterally, through sanctions, indictments, and offensive cyberattacks (so-called defending forward). This approach gives the appearance of being tough on cybercrime, while leveraging under governed cyberspace and "plausible deniability" to gain strategic advantage.

Seminar Questions

What do we mean by the" Five Eyes" Intelligence community and why is it important in the modern world?
There is a fine line between cooperation and legislation. How should the police and governments respond to cybercrime in the twenty-first Century?

Exam Questions

Cyber-attacks on critical infrastructure in different countries are now a matter of routine. What measures can be taken to deal with these attacks?

References

Alba, Davey, et al. (2020, May 29). Twitter adds warnings to trump and white house tweets, fueling tensions. *The New York Times*. www.nytimes.com/2020/05/29/technology/trump-twitter-minneapolis-george-floyd.html

BBC News. (2020, June 3). George Floyd death: Anti-racism sites hit by wave of cyber-attacks. *BBC News*. www.bbc.com/news/technology-52912881

Chernenko, Elena. (2018, February). Increasing international cooperation in cybersecurity and adapting cyber norms. *Council on foreign relations*. www.cfr.org/report/increasing-international-cooperation-cybersecurity-and-adapting-cyber-norms

Gold, Josh. (2020, May 4). Amid COVID-related cyber threats, the Netherlands leads UN efforts. *Council on foreign relations*. www.cfr.org/blog/amid-covid-related-cyber-threats-netherlands-leads-un-efforts

Knake, Robert K. (2020, May 29). Banning covert foreign election interference. *Council on foreign relations*. www.cfr.org/report/banning-covert-foreign-election-interference

Krebs, Brian. (2020, May). *Europe's largest private hospital operator Fresenius hit by ransomware*. krebsonsecurity.com/2020/05/europes-largest-private-hospital-operator-fresenius-hit-by-ransomware/

Laub, Zachary. (2019, January). Hate speech on social media: Global comparisons. *Council on foreign relations*. www.cfr.org/backgrounder/hate-speech-social-media-global-comparisons

Levy, Ian, & Crispin Robinson. (2019, October 3). Principles for a more informed exceptional access debate. *Lawfare*. www.lawfareblog.com/principles-more-informed-exceptional-access-debate

Ministerie van Algemene Zaken. (2018a, May 25). MH17 Incident. *Government.nl*. www.government.nl/topics/mh17-incident

Ministerie van Algemene Zaken. (2018b, October 4). Netherlands defence intelligence and security service disrupts Russian cyber operation targeting OPCW. *News Item | Government.nl*. www.government.nl/latest/news/2018/10/04/netherlands-defence-intelligence-and-security-service-disrupts-russian-cyber-operation-targeting-opcw

Muggah, Robert. (2019, September 30). Our cities are under cyberattack. Here's why – And what they should do about it. *World Economic* Forum. www.weforum.org/agenda/2019/09/our-cities-are-increasingly-vulnerable-to-cyberattacks-heres-how-they-can-fight-back/

National Crime Agency. (2020, July 2). NCA and police smash thousands of criminal conspiracies after infiltration of encrypted communication platform in UK's biggest ever law enforcement operation. *National crime agency*. www.nationalcrimeagency.gov.uk/news/operation-venetic

Schwab, Klaus. (2016, January 16). The fourth industrial revolution: What it means and how to respond. *World Economic Forum*. www.weforum.org/agenda/2016/01/the-fourth-industrial-revolution-what-it-means-and-how-to-respond/

Schwab, K. (2017). *The fourth industrial revolution*. London: Portfolio Penguin.

Segal, Adam, and Hannah Pitts. (2016). *Cyber conflict after Stuxnet: Essays from the other bank of the Rubicon*. Cyber Conflict Studies.

Shull, Aaron. (2019, August 11). *Governing cyberspace during a crisis in trust*. www.cigionline.org/articles/governing-cyberspace-during-crisis-trust

Siebel, T. M. (2019). *Digital transformation: Survive and thrive in an era of mass extinction.* New York: Rosetta Books.

United Nations. (2019). Secretary-general's high-level panel on digital cooperation. *United Nations.* www.un.org/en/digital-cooperation-panel/

US Department of Homeland Security and UK National Cyber Security Center. (2020). Alert (AA20-126A). Cybersecurity and infrastructure security agency CISA. www.us-cert. gov/ncas/alerts/AA20126A

Vance, Cyrus. (2019, December 10). *Written testimony for the United States senate committee on the judiciary on smartphone encryption and public safety.* Manhattan district attorney's office. www.manhattanda.org/written-testimony-for-the-united-states-senate-committee-on-the-judiciary-on-smartphone-encryption-and-public-safety/

WADA Confirms Attack by Russian Cyber Espionage Group | World. Retrieved July 5, 2020, from https://www.wada-ama.org/en/media/news/2016-09/wada-confirms-attack-by-russian-cyber-espionage-group

Part IV

Investigation

Investigation

Mark Roycroft

This chapter will explore some of the issues behind decision making and the attributes of a good decision maker in major investigations, along with an examination of lessons from the last 40 years of public enquiries and reviews. The chapter further discusses some of the research carried out into 166 murder cases in London, England and the lessons learnt. Bryant (2018) states, "Judgment involves reasoning in practical, non-abstract circumstances and gives rise to action and hence in police critical decision-making is of particular importance". West/Donnelly *(2019)* talked of the acquisition of knowledge that is needed for good decision makers in investigations and good policing versus human factors. They talk of the timeliness involved (the Golden Hour principle) along with the phases and pressures of homicide investigation today.

In researching public enquires and reviews into murder cases over the last 40 years seven clear themes emerged:

- The Clarity and leadership needed among Senior Officers
- The Skills of SIOs required
- Systematic failures
- The Phasing of enquires required

M. Roycroft (✉)
Rabdan Academy, Al Bhustan, Abu Dhabi, United Arab Emirates
e-mail: mroycroft@ra.ac.ae

© The Author(s), under exclusive license to Springer Nature Switzerland AG 2021
M. Roycroft, L. Brine (eds.), *Modern Police Leadership*,
https://doi.org/10.1007/978-3-030-63930-3_12

- The role of the Major Incident Room
- Information management and
- Individual investigative strategy failures.

These are explained as follows:

Clarity and Leadership Among Senior Officers

Smith and Flanagan (2000) explore leadership as one of their 22 skill clusters for reflective Senior Investigating Officers (SIOs). SIOs in the UK are usually a Detective Chief Inspector or Superintendent who have qualified for the Professionalising Investigative Practice (PIP) curriculum to Level 3 standard. They state that as a good leader the SIO has to be seen to be responsible for the investigation by maintaining control, inspiring and drawing information from the investigative team whilst ensuring they have the most appropriate direction based on his/her decisions (ibid.).

During the late 1970s and early 1980s the Yorkshire Ripper, a case involving a serial killer, demonstrated how the direction given by the SIO can influence the rest of the enquiry. For example, Peter Sutcliffe, who was later convicted of 13 murders as the Yorkshire Ripper, was interviewed nine times by the Police between 1975 and his arrest in January 1981. Interviewing officers were influenced by the credence given to the letters and the tape sent by a hoaxer.

The common theme running through inquiries into cases such as the Yorkshire Ripper, the Harold Shipman serial murders, the murder of Stephen Lawrence in London and the murders of Holly Wells and Jessica Chapman in Soham, relate to the competencies of the SIO. Effective leadership is a key skill for SIOs and is crucial to the success of the investigation and it appeared problematic in inquiries such as those above. The question of leadership was not confined to multiple investigations but was subject to comment in single homicide cases such as the Damilola Taylor case. In both the Taylor case and the Yorkshire Ripper cases, the lack of a clear leader at the very top compromised the effective deploying of resources. One person cannot solve the case by themselves and it is the responsibility of all those who assume even partial leadership to be effective as a leader, to share information and to coordinate the investigation.

The Stevens (2002) review of the investigation in to the murder of Damilola Taylor commented how the primary investigation was well resourced but clarity was missing as to where the overall responsibility for the investigation lay.

During the Inquiry into the serial killer, Harold Shipman, Smith (2003) commented how one of the primary reasons why the investigation failed was that the Chief Superintendent kept to himself the responsibility for supervision.

Decision Making Styles of Investigators

During research conducted by the author, it was highlighted how the type of management style adopted by the SIO was of importance when solving the crime. The type of management style and the ability of the SIO to constantly review his/her strategy were critical. There is also a need to assess future SIOs for their potential decision-making processes prior to their initial deployment investigating serious crimes with, for example, the ability to choose the correct approach for the murder investigation at the right time being one of the key elements of success. Democratic management of the murder investigation team (MIT) emerged as a critical trait along with the ability to manage the different phases of the enquiry over long periods of time. The SIO has to have the ability to constantly review all the information and potential evidence before him or her, be open to feedback from the team and have the ability to use "the collective brain of the team", this democratic approach is key to managing successful investigations. The key to bringing the right offender to justice is a flexible and creative approach which includes being proactive and evaluating alternative interpretations as evidence grows.

Fact Sheet

Major Incident Room (MIR) the MIR is the formal organisation of a major police enquiry with, specifically, the use of information technology to assist the enquiry. In most cases this will refer to the 'HOLMES' arrangements. (Holmes is the Home Office Large Major Enquiry System brought in after the Yorkshire Ripper case and the subsequent Byford Report). The standardised operating procedures are outlined in the 280 page Major Incident Room Standardised Administrative Procedures (MIRSAP) manual, providing a template for the linking and interchange between enquiries nationwide.

Central to effective decision making is the idea of diagnostic inclination in which the SIO brings skills and disposition to approach the investigation in a systematic and analytic fashion. The SIO diagnoses an unfamiliar situation and designs a course of action to deal with it. The heuristics that SIOs develop will enable them to utilise a framework to understand complex investigations. This enables

SIOs to order their decision making, by systemising the decision-making process. The SIO can then start to prioritise lines of enquiry and order the phasing of the case before them. Diagnostic inclination embodies a need to assess incoming information, quickly reviewing all information and prioritising certain actions. This systematic approach to investigation reduces the time taken for the investigation, with the more proactive SIOs being able to reduce this time by up to 5 months. As a result, a good SIO needs an ability to balance all the needs of the enquiry simultaneously while responding quickly to ongoing issues within the investigation.

Decision-Making Techniques by the SIO

The SIO needs to be able to identify and apply the appropriate solving factor as well as handling the simultaneous maintenance of multiple solving factors critical to the success of an enquiry. The need to construct a case with up to 12 potential solving factors at one time is a key element of success.

The SIO needs to:

- Work through the evaluative stage in the decision frame employing a creative management style and prioritising the initial actions
- Ensure all lines of enquiry are adequately resourced,
- Ensure the policy is fully implemented.
- Ensure that all the Incident Room actions relate to the SIOs strategy are executed

Crucial decision-making skills include:

- Constant review of the enquiry
- Selection of the correct solving factors for particular types of enquiry
- Holding regular briefings/meetings to listen to the views of members of the team while retaining overall responsibility for decision making

It is imperative that throughout the process the SIO records their decisions in the decision/policy logs, as this enables an accurate record to be established of the progress of the enquiry. This also helps to explain to a court or review team why certain decisions were made at particular times. The policy log should act as a chronological description of the progress of the enquiry and should reflect the SIOs thought process.

SIOs discussed the following seven broad solving themes comprising 36 individual solving factors:

1. Police Strategies
2. Suspects Behaviour
3. Technical Strategies
4. Intelligence Strategies
5. Media strategies
6. Use of outside experts
7. Legal strategy

The author's research further showed the importance of choosing the correct solving factors for the type of enquiry being investigated at that time. The seven broad themes and the 36 individual solving factors uncovered by the research show the breadth and complexity of solving major crimes in the UK. The identification of factors serves as a guide for SIOs in how these most challenging of enquiries can be solved. The use of Forensic techniques was the most used strategy followed by the management of witnesses, the use of police intelligence, the use of CCTV footage and passive data analysis. The passive data techniques highlight the scale of material that detectives have to analyse. The SIOs considered many of the factors shown but did not actually deploy them. One of the key solving factors to emerge was the SIOs ability to identify the theme of the murder quickly (e.g. whether this was likely to be a gang related killing or resulting from some domestic dispute) and to keep reviewing the progress of the investigation. Forensic management was the single most important factor SIOs identified but interestingly it was the management of witnesses that was a decisive factor revealed through the secondary analysis. A statistically significant variable from the research predicting whether the case was solved or not was the number of police investigative strategies used. The weight for this was 2.15 meaning that for every additional strategy used there was a doubling of the likelihood of solving the cases.

Management of the Major Incident Room (MIR)

In the Yorkshire Ripper case, the report by Lord Byford (Home Office, 2006) criticised the amount of information which was held within the MIR. Bilton (2003) comments that the Byford inquiry into the Yorkshire Ripper case found the management of the investigation to be totally disorganised. The so called 'Byford team' also highlighted a lack of opportunity for the investigative team to stand back, reflect upon and review existing evidence. The MIR became overwhelmed and had the direct effect of frustrating the work of SIOs and junior detectives alike. The management of the flow of information into the MIR was the subject of concern in many of the inquiries. The Yorkshire Ripper case was the most glaring example of the failure to provide an adequate database or system to link cases or identify killers across force boundaries. MacPherson (1999) also highlighted failings within the incident room during the investigation in to the murder of Stephen Lawrence. This was also the case with other investigations into murders such as those of Maxwell, Hogg and Harper.

The use of Information management is an effective tool to support both the MIR and other force enquiries through informing the decision makers. For example the inquiry by Laming (2003) into the death of Victoria Climbie, made a recommendation that the police must be provided with effective information technology to ensure that Child Protection Teams have an effective Child Protection database and IT management system. This is just one example of how the effective management of information is paramount to the success of an investigation.

Individual Investigative Strategy Failures

Laming (2003, https://assets.publishing.service.gov.) states that the investigation into the death of Victoria Climbie should have begun as soon as the police were notified of the original problems and that the investigators did not adopt numerous detailed investigative leads. They were also criticised for not taking the basic steps required in a major investigation and therefore vital evidence was lost.

In the Soham murder case the Flanagan (2004) report stated that there could have been a greater sense of urgency during the early stages of the investigation.

Flanagan (2004) continued that high priority leads were not acted on for more than one week, with an inability to appreciate the Golden Hour's value in relation to the information generated by the enquiry, with senior officers failing to act on valuable evidential leads gathered by officers on the ground. The report also stated that the first SIO made the decision not to deploy additional officers on the night the victims went missing.

In many of the cases explained here, witnesses were reluctant to come forward and these necessitated the SIO seeking a proactive use of recruiting informants and seeking intelligence from other means. Whilst in the Soham inquiry, they were overwhelmed with information to the extent that they could not cope so in essence underestimated the potential information that had to be managed and used to inform decisions.

Following the initial evaluation of the available knowledge, one approach adopted by the SIO may lead them to draw upon procedural knowledge and past experience in a reactive manner and apply rigid processes. An alternative approach is one where the SIO is empowered to be more flexible, creative and able to differentiate the potential value of the available solving factors.

Main Issues: Phasing of Enquires

The timeliness of decision making is challenging for the management of enquiries, not only initially in regard to timeliness of, for example the response, but also as to sequencing of events. Jones, Grieve and Milne (2008) argue that the historical context is important when examining, for example, murder investigations.

The sequence of events is, self-evidently, a critical tool in understanding the relationship of cause and effect contained within the evidence gathered. This is more than just the intellectual construct of a 'story' which helps the understanding of investigators, prosecutors and those presenting the evidence to a jury. Time and place are central elements of the SIOs initial parameters and are often the basis of eliminations from enquiries where there is no direct physical evidence as elimination criteria. This phasing aspect became evident in the author's research of 166 murder cases. The SIOs interviewed stated that "Phasing" played a major part in their enquiries and described how they divided particular cases into distinct phases. In broad terms, a first phase was concerned with meeting the requirements of legislative time limits and obtaining sufficient evidence to bring the suspect to court.

A second phase was concerned with obtaining further evidence and constructing a case for trial at Court. The second phase was a long term one with the need for effective coordination of forensic evidence gathering, witness statements and advice from other experts. One SIO commented that in a long running case he had to "build in blocks of time" to deal with the particular case but also the seven other cases his team were dealing with at the time. At the other end of the investigative phase, one SIO described the benefit of a "long war" in keeping a case open. One SIO dealt with a murder enquiry which took place over 4 years with distinct phases throughout. The initial stage of the enquiry generated a large number of actions for the police to follow up and report upon. The second stage of the enquiry took place around the arrest stage and post arrest stage.

The third distinct phase took place over the period of the trial becoming a phase in its own right.

The synthesis of the evidence may be used several times in the course of any enquiry, with initial interest in the events relating to the victim, and then subsequent concentration relating to the events associated with the offender. It must be acknowledged that the arrest of the offender is in no way the end of the enquiry and all of the phases must come together to be successful.

The importance of Evidence Based Policing research is borne out by the research carried out by the author (Roycroft, 2019) on what solves murder cases and similarly research carries out by Fashing and Ask (2016) in Norway. They compared UK and Norwegian senior detectives discovering significant and impactful points during investigations. These were predominantly focused upon deciding to make an arrest and deciding on investigative strategies.

The planning and phasing of major enquiries were referred to during the Victoria Climbie inquiry in 2003, where Laming (2003) stated how an investigation should have started straight after the incident. Apart from leaving a message with the police photographic department and doing a police database check to see if the family were known, the first police officer at the scene did absolutely nothing to begin investigating the crime before going off duty. Lord Laming continues to identify issues such as investigative leads that should have been followed including identifying the scene, arranging statements, medical examinations, identifying suspects and speaking directly to the victim.

The identification of the crime scene is a general theme which emerges in various enquiries.

MacPherson (1999) reported into the death of Stephen Lawrence and stated that decisions made early on in the investigation were sometimes the wrong ones leading to delays in arrests.

Fact Sheet
MacPherson Report
Lord MacPherson was tasked in 1997 at looking at the circumstances around the murder of Stephen Lawrence in South London. The report found the Metropolitan Police "institutionally racist". The investigation into the killing had been "marred by a combination of professional incompetence, institutional racism and a failure of leadership". Specific officers in the Metropolitan police were named and the entire force was criticised. It made 70 recommendations and for major investigations, it led to the setting up of Family Liaison Officers (FLOs) and decision logs for Senior Investigators to record all their decisions in a major investigation.

MacPherson (ibid.) also comments that the Detective Chief Superintendent allowed himself to go along with the weak and unenterprising decisions made by his SIOs in which he had been himself directly involved. The report criticises the failure to arrest one of the main suspects and to remove him from the scene, suggesting that there can be no excuses for such a series of errors, failures and lack of direction and control. Each failure was compounded by the failure to acknowledge and to detect errors.

The next phase occurs after the arrest and interview of a suspect. There begins the selection, ordering and presentation of investigative material. Savage and Milne (2007) suggest caution as even at the stage of the interview an investigator must maintain a critical mind-set and not close down investigative options, refer to this as the time when a shift occurs from establishing a sequence of events to confirming what has really happened.

Roycroft's research (2019) of 166 murder cases in London showed that the successful SIOs tended to avoid replicated decision making and tailored their decision making to the type of crime being investigated rather than a generic template. The final deliberative stage of differentiated alternatives led to the selection of solving factors by reviewing the decision process. As Simon (1945) stated "decision-makers reduce information processing demands by constructing limited representations of options. Successful SIOs were those who choose strategies in the early phase of the enquiry and had the ability to quickly make decisions and a period of initial activity was followed by a period of review. The "innovative" SIOs were creative and flexible in their decision-making processes and looked at all possible methods to help solve the crimes. They were consultative in their management of specialist teams and sought to use "the creative brain" of their respective teams. They, in short, brought a complete "tool kit" of management and investigative skills to their enquiries.

Central to effective decision making is the idea of diagnostic inclination in which the SIO brings skills and disposition to approach the investigation in a systematic and analytic fashion. The SIO diagnoses an unfamiliar situation and designs a course of action to deal with it. The heuristics that SIOs develop enable them to utilise a framework to understand complex investigations. This enables SIOs to order their decision making. By systemising the decision-making process, the SIO can start to prioritise lines of enquiry and order the phasing of the case before them. Diagnostic inclination embodies a need to assess incoming information, quickly reviewing all information and prioritising certain actions. This systematic approach to investigation reduced the time taken and the more proactive SIOs reduced the time taken by up to five months. The good SIO needs an ability to balance all the needs of the enquiry simultaneously while responding quickly to ongoing issues within the case.

The SIOs management style was an important factor in the decision-making process and the inclusive approach (involving all the team in office meetings) was used by successful SIOs. One SIO stated that he liked to use "the collective brain of the team" to help solve cases. The less successful SIOs had a more reactive style responding to events rather than anticipating them. The inclusive style and the prioritisation of lines of enquiry were significant. The inclusive style encouraged the team to participate. The lack of a post charge strategy in one Category A case shows that individual strategy failures can occur. Senior Investigators need to undergo a Constant review of the inquiry and undertake a prioritisation of lines of enquiry. The senior Investigator needs to select the correct solving factors for particular types of enquiry.

The SIO needs to be able to identify and apply the appropriate solving factors in the enquiry. The simultaneous maintenance of multiple solving factors is critical to the success of an enquiry. The need to construct a case with up to 12 individual potential solving factors at one time is a key element of success. The recording of the SIOs thought process in the SIO decision log enables an accurate record to be established of the progress of the enquiry. It helps to explain to a court or review team why certain decisions were made at particular times. The policy log should act as a chronological description of the progress of the enquiry and should reflect the SIOs thought process. Maintenance of the enquiry may entail numerous decision logs and they may be themed (e.g., Search Strategy, Forensic Strategy etc.).

The SIO needs to work through the evaluative stage in the early stages of an investigation employing a creative management style and prioritising the initial actions. Following this in the investigative stage the key investigative strategies are identified and engage a proactive response. The enquiry then moves into an evidence processing phase there needs to be a conscious decision to employ analytic strategies rather than simply following the manual and engaging in non-productive replicative behaviour.

The SIOs decision-making skills are crucial to the investigation. There needs to be a Constant review of the enquiry as it progresses.

Dealing with Different Crime Types

Drugs and Firearms Crime

The Policing of Drugs/narcotics is complex with a host of interactions between health, crime, different groups of users, mental illness and addiction. Drugs Policy is concerned with protecting people and helping the most vulnerable. Society is harmed by the cost both physically and medically from drug addiction. The Portuguese model of drug policing which we refer to as the Health model within Europe model started in 2001 and allowed for users not to be criminalised within the Criminal justice system but to be treated on a health basis via dissuasion boards.

The "War on Drugs" phrase was first coined by President Richard Nixon in the 1970s in the USA and there is common agreement among police professionals that this has been lost. The Global Commission on Crime (UN, 2011) stated, "The global war on drugs has failed, with devastating consequences for individuals and societies around the world. Vast expenditures on criminalization and repressive measures directed at producers, traffickers and consumers of illegal drugs have clearly failed to curtail supply or consumption".

The demand for all types of drugs has remained high and the price of drugs has remained comparatively low. We are facing a crisis over opioid drugs and in the UK, we have the phenomenon of "County Lines" drug supply whereby drug dealers in the major cities use vulnerable youths to distribute drugs via social media. The UK Police have to use anti-slavery legislation to deal with this issue and it has caused havoc in some of the provincial forces. The growth of opioid drugs such as fentanyl has caused problems particularly in the USA. Some see the phrase "War on Drugs" as redundant and law enforcement is moving towards a combination of the following models:

- A Health model as per the Portuguese model and the use of needle exchanges and treatment rooms for addicts.
- A Legal model with new legal measures such as de criminalisation of certain drugs that is, cannabis as seen in 11 states in the USA.
- A Financial model that involves disrupting and seizing Drug barons assets with new measures such as Unexplained Wealth Orders (UWOs) and increasing the investigation and analysis of passive data.
- A "Poly Criminality" model whereby criminals deal in a range of commodities (polymath) see Europol SOCTA report and the UK NCA report of May 2019 which stated there were 4629 OCGs within the UK. These groups deal not only in drugs but also in other commodities.
- A deterrence model where the curbing of the Importation of Drugs and the restriction of the supply of drugs via Border Forces and Frontex in Europe restricts the supply of drugs.

Dealing with Drugs took up a major part of my Policing career and I saw lives ruined by this menace, we have to work smarter to curb drug demand. It fuels gang wars particularly in London and other urban areas. It finances terrorism and organised crime. This is a problem that cuts across all social divides. A 2007 Home Office report in the UK found that the illegal drug markets underpinned the criminal economy and assisted illegal use of firearms. Firearms possession was reported in relation to robberies of drug dealers, territorial disputes, personal protection and sanctioning of drug market participants.

Organisations like Europol have led a crackdown on the illegal trade in firearms. Organised criminal groups often rely on the availability of weapons to carry out their activities. However, the market for firearms in the EU remains modest in size. Trafficking occurs on a small scale, and the weapons trafficked are intended for either personal use or to meet specific orders.

Weapons trafficking is almost exclusively a supplementary rather than a primary source of income for the small number of organised criminal groups involved. Most groups enter the weapons-trafficking business through other criminal activity, which may offer contacts, knowledge of existing routes and infrastructure related to the smuggling of weapons. Europol's European Counter Terrorism Centre (ECTC) supports Member States in information-sharing and operational cooperation with regard to monitoring traffic in illegal firearms. In addition, Europol's European Migrant Smuggling Centre (EMSC) is seeking to identify and analyse links between the facilitation of illegal immigration and other crime areas, including firearms trafficking.

Interpol try to "join the dots" in illegal firearms activity by using the I – arms database which provides links across all member states. See Chap. 2 on International Partnership and Operation Trigger which is now in its fifth phase and concentrates on firearm dealing hotspots. Legally, the United Nations Convention against Transnational Organized Crime, and the Protocol against the Illicit Manufacturing of and Trafficking in Firearms, adopted by United Nations General Assembly resolutions 55/25 (2000) and 55/255 (2001) respectively, provide statute for dealing with firearms crime internationally. This is the first legally binding instrument on small arms to be adopted at the global level.

Investigating Money

Following the money trail has always been part of the Detectives lexicon. A financial investigation is defined as any investigation into a person or person's financial matters or those of a business or private limited company. A financial investigation can determine where money comes from, how it is moved and how it is used. Financial investigation techniques can be used in all types of investigations, and investigators are able to use powerful legislative tools that target the proceeds of crime. A financial investigation may involve some element of asset recovery but may be for other reasons such as to inform a criminal money laundering investigation, trace missing persons or witnesses, or simply to enhance the quality of any criminal investigation.

Unexplained-wealth orders in the (UK) will make the seizing of such assets easier. Where there is a significant disparity between what an individual earns and what they own including their houses and vehicles. Law-enforcement officials will be able to apply to a judge for an order to demand evidence that such items were purchased legitimately.

Financial institutions are expected to report Suspicious activities in accounts or the use of large amounts of cash; these are known as SARS, Suspicious activity reports. These are dealt with by Financial Intelligence Units both within the Police and in private financial institutions.

Three conditions must be met: the subject must be a "politically exposed person" from outside the European Economic Area or someone reasonably suspected of involvement in serious crime; their known income must be insufficient to have purchased the property in question; and the asset must be worth more than £50,000. Most significantly, the orders will shift the burden of proof towards the accused, who will have to demonstrate that their assets were acquired legally. If they cannot, the assets may be frozen. The benefits of financial crime include:

- Disruption of organised crime groups.
- Take assets of criminals
- Reduces acquisitive crime
- Reassures the public.

In America, Police and Federal agencies use the Racketeer Influenced and Corrupt Organizations (RICO) Act. This can be used to prosecute all individuals involved in a corrupt organisation.

Seminar Questions

What were the 7 main Solving themes from Roycroft's research into 166 murder cases in London?

What was the significance of the MacPherson report to major investigations in the UK? Name two of the recommendations that are still in force today.

Why are financial investigations important in police enquiries and what methods can be used to arrest and disrupt criminals?

Exam Question

What were the 7 clear themes that emerged from Roycroft's research into 40 years of public inquires and reviews into murder cases in the UK?

References

Bryant, R., Bryant, S., Graça, S., Lawton-Barrett, K., Gilbert, P., Hooper, G., Jones, N., Blackburn, B., McCormack, T., & Mitchell, S. (2017). *Blackstone's Handbook for Policing Students 2018.*

Blackburn, B., McCormack, T., & Mitchell, S. (2017). *Blackstone's Handbook for Policing Students 2018.*

Dr Ivar Fahsing (2013, June). Decision making and decisional tipping points in homicide investigations: An interview study of British and Norwegian detectives. *Journal of Investigative Psychology and Offender Profiling, 10*(2), 155–165.

Jones, Grieve and Milne. (2008). The case to review murder investigations. *Policing, 2*(4), 470–480.

Lord Laming Report. (2003). *The Victoria Climbie inquiry: Report of an inquiry by Lord Laming.* https://www.gov.uk/government/publications/the-victoria-climbie-inquiry-report-of-an-inquiry-by-lord-laming

MacPherson, W. (1999). *The Stephen Lawrence inquiry* (Cm 4262-I). London: Home Office.

Roycroft, M., & Roach, J. (Ed.). (2019). *Decision making in Police Enquires and Critical Incidents: What really works.* London: Palgrave.

Savage, S., & Milne, B. (2007). Miscarriages of justice. In T. Newburn, T. Williamson, & A. Wright (Eds.), *Handbook of criminal investigation* (pp. 610–627). Cullompton: Willan Publishing.

Simon , H. (1945). *Administrative Behaviour.* New York: MacMillan.

Sir William MacPherson Report on the death of Stephen Lawrence CM 4261. (1999, February 1). *Stationary Office.*

Smith, N., & Flanagan, C. (2000). *The effective detective: Identifying the skills of an effective SIO* (Police research series paper 122).

Smith, J. (2003). *The Shipman inquiry 2nd report: The police investigation of March 1998* (CM 5853). London: HMSO.

Stevens, J. (2002). *Damilola Taylor: The review of the investigation and prosecution arising from the murder of Damilola Taylor.* London: New Scotland Yard. http://image.guardian.co.uk/sys-files/Guardian/documents/2002/12/09/damilola.pdf

Cybercrime

Nikola Protrka

Unlike traditional crime, cybercrime has no borders. There are now only e borders that require new skills and a new approach from police investigators. The police are faced with the prospect of dealing with victims in one country and the suspects in another. As a result of the Covid-19 crisis, our dependence on IT has increased dramatically. The term 'cybercrime' is defined by Thomas and Loader (2000: 3) as "computer-mediated activities which are either illegal or considered illicit by certain parties and which can be conducted through global electronic networks". Wall (2007) subdivides cybercrime into four categories:

1. Cyber-trespass (Crossing boundaries into other people's property) e.g., hacking, defacement, viruses
2. Cyber deception and thefts
3. Cyberpornogarphy
4. Cyber Violence or Cyber stalking

The largely positive development of ICT, also has a downside. Cybercrime is a global phenomenon. While some countries have adopted the recommendations of the Convention on Cybercrime of the Council of Europe (which has been signed by

N. Protrka (✉)
Rabdan Academy, Al Bhustan, Abu Dhabi, United Arab Emirates

143
M. Roycroft, L. Brine (eds.), *Modern Police Leadership*,
https://doi.org/10.1007/978-3-030-63930-3_13

some non-European countries) and changed legislation, others have not.[1] The police must deal with huge leaps in technical developments and ensure they have
sufficiently trained personnel. Underreporting of cybercrime makes it difficult to
gauge the true extent of the crime.

Cyber-dependent crimes are offences committed using a computer, computer
networks, or other forms of information communications technology (ICT). These
acts include the spread of viruses, malware, ransomware, and hacking, and distributed denial of service (DDoS) attacks (McGuire and Dowlingm, 2013). These activities are primarily directed at computers or network resources, although there
may be secondary outcomes. For example, data gathered by hacking into an email
account may subsequently be used to commit a fraud. Cyber-enabled crimes are
traditional crimes that have increased through the use of computers. Unlike cyber-
dependent crimes, they can still be committed without the use of ICT. Examples
can include fraud (e.g., phishing, online scams), theft, and sexual offences against
children (Furnel, 2019). The police use relatively new skills to detect and surveil
cybercrime.

Modern society largely depends on the smooth functioning of information and
communication systems that are critical to all the key systems of the police, hospitals, and traffic services. National and international infrastructure depend on reliable and functioning IT. Since all these systems are increasingly interconnected,
the danger of these systems being attacked is also increasing. The wide availability
of technology enables increased automation of attacks and the use of sophisticated
tools for attacking.

Researchers from the University of Sydney and Commonwealth Scientific and
Industrial Research Organisation's (CSIRO) Data 61, found that Google Play store
contains thousands of possible malware-laden counterfeit apps and games
(Rajasegaran and others, 2019). These apps and games mimic popular alternatives,
making users susceptible to downloading the wrong one. Focusing on a set of about
50,000 apps that were masquerading as other popular apps, researchers found that
2040 were malware, 1565 potentially compromised security, and 1407 had suspi-
ciously large amounts of advertising. This is more than 10%. The apps were then
checked for malware using the private API of VirusTotal, and investigated further
if they asked for a suspicious amount of permission. The authors state that once the
app is downloaded, it is easy to determine if it is malicious, but difficult to know
this before the app is downloaded.

---

[1] Chart of signatures and ratifications of Treaty 185, Convention on Cybercrime Status as of
31/07/2019 available at: https://www.coe.int/en/web/conventions/full-list/-/conventions/
treaty/185/signatures

The Convention on Cybercrime has introduced the term 'cybercrime' in to legal profession, which has assisted in the co-operation of signatory states in combating cybercrime. Nations need to define the following:

1. Data protection
2. Technical co-ordination in the processing of computer security incidents
3. International co-operation
4. Education, research, development and raised awareness of security in cyberspace

There are two key cyber threats: the use of cyber tools to cause financial loss to businesses and governments, and the desire to disrupt and penetrate computer networks. Annual reports by relevant regulatory and governmental institutions in the (e.g., European Network and Information Security Agency (ENISA) and EUROPOL) depict the continuing rise in the number and complexity of detected attacks on information systems and data (Katulić and Protrka, 2019). Businesses are more likely to be targeted by more severe, complex hacking and DDoS attacks. Cybercrimes that require more skill (due to higher security) have fewer victims, but a higher profit.

The Levels of Police Response

As cybercrime increases, police must keep pace with new technologies. The challenge for police leaders is the need to deal with these demands with the right skills and resources over a 24/7 period. There are National Contact Points in every EU country related to cybercrime matters.[2]

Countries are encouraged to co-operate and to exchange information as the perpetrator may be anywhere and the offence may have been committed (Protrka, 2018). International co-operation has thus become essential many co-operative

---

[2] For example, in the UK this response is met regionally by the 10 Regional Organised Crime Units (ROCUs), nationally by the NCCU of the National Crime Agency (NCA www.nationalcrimeagency.gov.uk/) and European wide by the UK contribution to Europol's EC3.The ROCUs deal with cybercrime investigation and the NCCU leadership role enables it to harness skills across government, law enforcement, industry and internationally. It works in partnership with all these stakeholders to assess and prioritise cyber threats. The National Cyber Security Centre acts as a conduit between industry and government, providing a unified source of advice, guidance, and support on cyber security, including the management of cyber security incidents.

organizations have been formed (e.g., Interpol—Cyber Fusion Centre,[3] Europol—European Centre for cybercrime—EC3[4] etc.). The Interpol Cyber Fusion Centre brings together cyber experts from law enforcement and industry to gather and analyse all available information on criminal activities in cyberspace and provide countries with coherent, actionable intelligence. Supported by the Singapore Ministry of Home Affairs, the desk was opened in 2018 and assists law enforcement officials to combat cybercrime through a combination of intelligence development, investigative support and operational coordination. The Internet Organised Crime threat assessment (IOCTA)[5] published by EC3 outlines the need for the police to deal with Child Sexual Exploitation on line (CSE), Distributed Denial-Of-Service (DDOS attack) and card fraud.

The internet can be divided into three categories—the Surface web, the Deep web, and the Dark web or Darknet. The Surface web is the normal web which is visible for all is indexed by search engines. The Deep web and Dark web are the hidden portions of the web that are not visible to the normal user. The Deep web consists of a website or any page on the website which is not indexed by search engines. The user can only access it with specific permissions (i.e., web address, username, and password etc.,). The Deep web is used to store most personal information such as Cloud storage, any organizational personal data, and military data and so on. The majority of criminal activities are carried out on the Darknet. The user can only access it if the user has a Tor Browser which means The Onion Router. It was developed in the mid-1990s by United States Naval Research Laboratory for the purpose of protecting U.S. intelligence communications online. It can make layers of many IPs and the user can surf the internet anonymously.[6]

The anonymous Darknet or TOR allows users to communicate more freely. Darknet sites such as the Silk Road or AlphaBay were used for supplying drugs and other illicit goods. The Silk Road darknet site was taken down by EC3 on 12 November 2014 Operation 'Onymousco' coordinated by EC3, the FBI, US Immigration and Customs.[7] The action was aimed at stopping the sale, distribution,

---

[3] Interpol—Cyber Fusion Centre, available at: https://www.interpol.int/en/Crimes/Cybercrime/Investigative-support-for-cybercrime

[4] Europol—European Centre for cybercrime, available at: https://www.europol.europa.eu/about-europol/european-cybercrime-centre-ec3

[5] Europol—Internet Organised Crime Threat Assessment, available at: https://www.europol.europa.eu/internet-organised-crime-threat-assessment-2018

[6] Medium. What is Surface Web, Deep Web and Dark Web? Available at: https://medium.com/@hackersleague/what-is-surface-web-deep-web-and-dark-web-cdbaf71b30d5

[7] Europol, Operation Onymous, available at: https://www.europol.europa.eu/activities-services/europol-in-action/operations/operation-onymous

and promotion of illegal and harmful items including weapons and drugs. As a result, 410 hidden services were shut down, 17 vendors and administrators were arrested, and USD 1 million worth of Bitcoins, EUR 180,000 in cash, drugs, gold, and silver were seized. The Darknet is a network, built on top of the internet, that is purposefully hidden. It has been designed specifically for anonymity. Unlike the deep web, the darknet is accessible only with special tools and software (i.e., browsers and other protocol beyond direct links or credentials).

The Darknet will continue to facilitate online criminal markets, where criminals sell illicit products in order to engage in other criminal activity or avoid surface net traceability. Among the technologies used to achieve this are anonymization services, encrypted communication services and cryptocurrencies—each of which mitigates the risk of detection. Anonymization services allow buyers and sellers to interact without revealing their identities. However, for complete anonymity to be achieved, the financial side of the transaction must also be carried out anonymously. Darknet marketplaces achieve this through the use of cryptocurrencies. Probably the most well-known example is Bitcoin, introduced in 2008 by an anonymous individual (or group) using the name Satoshi Nakamoto. The aim was to remove the need to trust governments or other political and financial institutions (as is inherent in all fiat currencies) and instead base it on a trust in cryptography. Bitcoins are designed to be free from control and interference from outside institutions and to be self-managed by an online community (Nakamoto, 2009).

The use of modern technologies poses certain security risks. Without the use of protective technologies (such as firewalls or antivirus software), IT systems will be vulnerable. The aims of criminal investigation into cybercrime applications are:

- Obtaining evidence indicating the commission of a criminal offence,
- Identify the perpetrator's identity,
- Identify the identity of the injured person/victim,
- Identify the identity of other victims and perpetrators,
- Prosecute the perpetrator.

▶ **Case Study 1: First Documented Darknet Murder Case** Police in Russia are investigating what could be the world's first documented case of a contract killing ordered via the so-called Darknet. High-ranking police investigator Yevgeniya Shishkinawas shot dead outside her home near Moscow in October 2018. Five months later, local police announced they had arrested two people in connection with the killing. Preliminary details of the case, which has shocked Russian investigators, have been shared unofficially with BBC by sources close to the investigation. The documents allege that the pair was paid one million roubles (£12,000) to carry out the murder. According to the police reports, the order was placed by the owner of a drug-dealing site on an illegal online trading platform on part of what is known as the Darknet. (BC, UK, 2019, https://www.bbc.com/news/technology-47747357)

Cyber-dependent crime: Viruses, Worms, Trojans, Spyware (generally labelled as Malware (Malicious Software)), Hacking, Denial of Service or Distributed Denial of Service attacks, Spam and Botnets.

Cyber-enabled crimes: Traditional crimes committed using modern ICT such as, frauds, fraudulent sales, Phishing scams, sexual exploitation and even 'Online romance'[8] frauds.

Phishing (or masking) means when one person uses the identity of another person to access computer infrastructure. Security methods used by computer infrastructure protection systems must be sufficiently active to detect and prevent phishing. There are two main types of phishing—physical and electronic. Physical representation occurs when a perpetrator uses an authorized user identity or access card to access confidential areas of computer infrastructure and data. False representation occurs when the perpetrator uses an authorized user ID or password to register in a computer system, thus obtaining data and information.

Hacking investigations detect unauthorized access to data or computer systems is dependent on the type of data and computer system and the ways in which it is protected against unauthorized access. The investigation finds traces that point to deviations from data protection mechanisms and computer systems. Depending on the size of the geographical and network coverage of the data, the investigation can include either a single system or a wider network. It is crucial to determine who has proper access to the system or data, the timing of the access, and then compile this information with information obtained from those systems that show by whom and when it was determined and by whom and when it was really accessed.

Ransomware is a type of malicious software (malware) designed to deny access to a computer system or data until a ransom is paid. Ransomware typically spreads through phishing emails or by unknowingly visiting an infected website. Ransomware can be devastating to an individual or an organization. Anyone with important data stored on a computer or network is at risk, including government or law enforcement agencies, healthcare systems, and other infrastructure entities.

---

[8] Individuals may be contacted via social networking or dating sites and persuaded to part with personal information or money following a lengthy online 'relationship'.

Recovery can be a difficult process that may require the services of a reputable data recovery specialist, and some victims (including large organizations) even pay to recover their files. However, there is no guarantee that individuals will recover their files if they pay the ransom.[9]

Interception

Investigation that detects unauthorized interception of computer data is extremely complex. In most cases, it is about detecting copies of data obtained by interception, and actions based on this data must prove that there was interception of data. Generally, the 'attack tools' can be found within the data. The existence of the tool can be ambiguous because they are often used as aids for the administration of computer systems, especially wireless computer networks. It is necessary to compare the copied data found with that from the computer system for evidentiary purposes, and to determine what the degree of similarity is. As each electronic system produces a specific electromagnetic communication that can be recorded and reproduced by the appropriate device, it is relatively simple to wire the CRT or LCD monitor, which can then be tracked to within several dozen metres.[10]

Botnets and DOS/DDOS

'Botnets' refer to clusters of computers infected by malicious software (malware). They are used to send out spam, phishing emails, or other malicious email traffic automatically and repeatedly to specified targets (Alhomoud et al., 2013). They are often termed 'zombies' as the networks are controlled centrally by a 'botmaster' (or 'herder'). Denial Of Service and Distributed Denial Of Service (DDOS) attack relate to the flooding of internet servers with so many requests (e.g., links that have been clicked) that they are unable to respond quickly enough. This can overload servers causing them to freeze or crash.

---

[9] The Cybersecurity and Infrastructure Security Agency (CISA), available at: https://www.us-cert.gov/Ransomware

[10] Van Eck phreaking is a form of eavesdropping in which special equipment is used to pick up telecommunication signals or data within a computer device by monitoring and picking up the electromagnetic fields (EM fields) that are produced by the signals or movement of the data.

Identity Theft

Identity theft rarely involves the unauthorized taking personal possessions of a victim, rather it involves the perpetrator of the crime taking personal information of the victim and using it in an unauthorized way for their own personal gain. Criminals can even use seemingly harmless pieces of information, such as your date of birth, to commit identity theft. The date of birth may enable the criminal to access other personal information.[11]

Computer Fraud

Computer fraud involves various types of data manipulation, usually related to finances. Such manipulations may occur during data entry, processing, storage, distribution of data, and data exchange within a computer network or through telephone and other communication channels. The development of ATMs and their widespread introduction into regular bank operations has opened up new possibilities of manipulation with computer-stored data on cards or within the system. Security researchers discovered a never-before-seen Trojan used in attacks on compromised bank networks. To make the fraudulent withdrawals, hackers first breach targeted bank networks and compromise the switch application servers handling ATM transactions (Symantec, 2018). Once these servers are compromised, previously unknown malware—Trojan. Fastcash—is deployed. This malware intercepts fraudulent cash withdrawal requests and sends fake approval responses, allowing the attackers to steal cash from ATMs.

Child Sexual Exploitation (CSE)

CSE is the sexual exploitation of children and young people **under 18** years of age involving exploitative situations. The act of CSE is generally a hidden activity and is much more likely to occur in private dwellings than in public venues.

---

[11] Identity Theft, available at: https://www.identitytheft.org.uk/

Challenges for the Police

▶ **Case Study 2: Spyware** A 28-year-old man who allegedly hacked into thousands of computers to watch and listen to users has been indicted in Ohio, US. Federal prosecutors say Phillip Durachinsky created malware that enabled him to remotely access and turn on the cameras and microphones of computers. Prosecutors say he has been hacking into computers for over 13 years from the basement of his parents' house. Security researchers say people may have unwittingly opened an infected computer or file from a website, and once the malware gets on the computer it has the ability to listen to people's conversations, turn on the webcam, take screen captures, record keystrokes. It's almost a complete surveillance device. The malware was named Fruitfly because it was initially found on computers in medical labs where researchers were studying fruit flies. It was first detected on computers at Case Western Reserve University, which reported it to the FBI 2017. Many victims were in Ohio, but they were also as far away as California. (Department of Justice, District Ohio, US, 2018, https://www.justice. gov/opa/press-release/file/1024116/download)

▶ **Case Study 3: Mirai and Clickfraud Botnet** Three cybercriminals, who were all between 18 and 20 years old when they built and launched Mirai, pleaded guilty to creating the malware Mirai, which hijacked hundreds of thousands of internet-of-things devices and united them as a digital army. Begun as a way to attack rival Minecraft videogame hosts, it evolved into an online tsunami of nefarious traffic that knocked entire web-hosting companies offline. A broad 'denial of service' attack waged using the Mirai botnet knocked services such as Twitter and Netflix offline in October 2016. (Department of Justice, US, 2017, https://www. justice.gov/opa/pr/justice-department-announces-charges-and-guilty-pleas-three-computer-crime-cases-involving)

▶ **Case Study 4: Phishing Scam** Scammers are using fake vacation rental ads. Rental scammers try to get your rental booking and take your money. But, when you show up for the vacation, you have no place to stay and your money is gone. Scammers start with real rental listings. Then they take off the owner's contact information, put in their own, and place the new listing on a different site—though they might continue to use the name of the actual owner. In other cases, scammers hijack the email accounts of property owners on reputable vacation rental websites. Some scammers don't bother with real rentals—they make up listings for places that aren't really for rent or don't exist. To get people to act fast, they often ask for lower than average rent or promise great amenities. Their goal is to get your money before you find out the truth. (Federal Trade Commission, US, 2018, https://www.consumer.ftc. gov/blog/2018/07/getting-vacation-rental-watch-out-scams)

Forensic Investigation of Cybercrime and Electronic Evidence

Digital Investigation

As the number of devices owned by the general public rises, the need for digital evidence and its use has quickly become a major component of forensic investigation. There is a high demand for digital data analytics. Digital forensics is a rapidly expanding field and it faces specific challenges.

Digital forensics is the process by which information is extracted from data storage media (e.g., devices, remote storage and systems associated with computing, imaging, image comparison, video processing and enhancement [including CCTV], audio analysis, satellite navigation, communications), rendered into a useable form, processed and interpreted for the purpose of obtaining intelligence for use in investigations, or evidence for use in criminal proceedings. (UK College of Policing APP)

This definition is wide and includes automatic number plate recognition, manual classification of indecent images of children, crime scene photography, eFit, recovery from a working CCTV system, CCTV replay for viewing with no further analysis, and so on.

A 2019 report by the UK House of Lords stated, "Digital evidence will become even more prevalent in trials in the coming years. There needs to be a better understanding among legal practitioners of the timescales involved in interrogating and analysing digital evidence where modern technology is not used"(Forensic Science and the Criminal Justice system 2019).

The College of Policing now has set up training of Digital Media Investigator (DMIs). The role involves being tactical advisors to Senior Investigating Officers and Police Leaders on the most effective and efficient strategies to harness communications data and other digital media, having advised and agreed on the strategy, work with the investigative team to lawfully acquire the data, reduce it into an admissible format, and attend court to present the findings.

The Cellebrite Report Digital Intelligence Industry Benchmark Report (2020) states that "lab examiners are drowning in data and device overload and data sources are continuing to grow". There is a high demand for digital data analytics for investigations. They state that AI is needed to sort through the mountains of incoming data. Seizure of mobile phones, smartphones, laptops, and desktops is a critical part of modern police procedure. Specially designed bags (i.e., Faraday) such as Faraday Bags can isolate devices from external signals and thus preserve evidence. The police need to establish, if the devices(s) of the suspect contain(s) evidence of the crime being investigated, the source of that evidence, and if it can be attributed to the suspect. Accessing Cloud storage presents other challenges such as, What are the legal constraints and who has legal access?, Who has ownership of the device?, How do police preserve evidential integrity?, Can the relevant information be accessed without damaging the relevant information sought? Is the date stored in another jurisdiction?.

Police in the UK must abide by the following principles of digital investigation from the ACPO Good Practice Advice on digital evidence 2012:

Principle 1: No action taken by law enforcement agencies, should change data which may subsequently be relied upon in court.

Principle 2: On accessing original data, that person must be competent to do so and be able to give evidence explaining the relevance and the implications of their actions.

Principle 3: An audit trail or other record of all processes applied to digital evidence should be created and preserved. An independent third party should be able to examine those processes and achieve the same result.

Principle 4: The person in charge of the investigation has overall responsibility for ensuring that the law and these principles are adhered to.

Data collection and data evidence is the most sensitive step of Computer Forensic Analysis (CFA). Any mistakes at this stage may mean irretrievable loss of evidence, either as a result of damage or credibility due to inappropriate collection methods. Therefore, it is necessary to carefully plan the process of collecting evidence, with particular emphasis on vulnerable evidence, and use the appropriate software tools. To determine electronic evidence content, forensics is used to compile content tools. The two most commonly used algorithms in all of these tools are MD5 and SHA1. All collected electronic evidence must be authentic, or identical, as well as at the time of collection.

State Sponsored Cybercrime

Some nation states are involved in Cybercrime. As cybercrime evolves, governments and businesses are faced with an expanding threat landscape from malicious nation-states that are seeking to further their own national agenda and prosperity. For example, the following nationalized hacking groups: Chinese APT10, Russian Fancy Bear or Syrian Electronic Army and so on. Campaigns by nation states are characterized by focusing on espionage and intellectual property theft and usually take place over a long period of time using significant technical capability. The Russian attack on Estonia 2007 involved disabling the websites of its parliament, ministries, banks and media organizations.

Challenges to the Police

Cyber criminals are generally younger than the average age range of suspects. Many suspects in the UK are under the age of 20. "Cyber Crime: A review of the Evidence" (UK Home Office 2013) indicates that under 2% of business online incidents are reported to the police and many private individuals do not report to the police as the banks reimburse them to save reputational damage (McGuire and Dowling, 2013). As technologies advance, there are clearly new opportunities to be had via routes such as the Internet of Things (IoT), smart homes, and autonomous vehicles. The IoT is a system of interrelated computing devices, mechanical and digital machines, objects, animals, or people that are provided with unique identifiers (UIDs) and the ability to transfer data over a network without requiring human-to-human or human-to-computer interaction. As the number of connected devices continues to rise, our living and working environments will become filled with smart products—assuming we are willing to accept the security and privacy trade-offs.

Seminar Questions

1. What illegal activity can be found on Darknet and how they are available?
2. Research and compare cost of cybercrime with some other traditional crimes?
3. Explain the main forms of cyber-enabled crimes.
4. What is known about cyber-enabled fraud and theft?
5. Try to connect traditional crimes with main forms of cyber-enabled crimes.
6. What skills must have forensic investigator for dealing with cyber-crime?

Exam Questions

1. After seizing a suspect's IT devices, what methods can the Police use to 'attribute' guilt to that suspect?
2. What is meant mean by the term 'Cyber Criminal' and how can the Police deal with them?
3. What is the role of a Digital Media Investigator (DMI) in a major enquiry? How can they assist the SIO?

References

Alhomoud, A., Awan, I., Disso, J. P., & Younas, M. (2013). Cyber security next generation toolkit against botnets. *Computer, 46*(4), 62–66. Available at: https://www.researchgate. net/publication/260584111_A_Next-Generation_Approach_to_Combating_Botnets.

European Network and Information Security Agency. (2019). *ENISA threat landscape report 2018*. Available at: https://www.enisa.europa.eu/publications/enisa-threatlandscape-report-2018

Europol. (2017). *Drugs and the darknet, perspectives for enforcement, research and policy.* Available at: https://www.europol.europa.eu/sites/default/files/documents/drugs_and_ the_darknet_-_td0417834enn.pdf

Furnel, S. M. (2019). Cyber crime: A portrait of the landscape. *Journal of Criminological Research, Policy and Practice.* University of Plymouth. Available at: https://pearl. plymouth.ac.uk/bitstream/handle/10026.1/13345/Cyber%20crime%20-%20A%20portrait%20of%20the%20landscape.PDF?sequence=1&isAllowed=y

Katulić, T., & Protrka, N. (2019). *Information security in principles and provisions of the EU data protection law* (pp. 1420–1426). 42nd international convention on information and communication technology, electronics and microelectronics (MIPRO), Opatija, Croatia. Available at: https://ieeexplore.ieee.org/document/8757153

McGuire, M., & Dowling, S. (2013). *Home office UK. "Cyber crime: A review of the evidence".* Research report 75, Chapter 1: Cyber-dependent crimes, Home Office, London. Available at: https://www.gov.uk/government/publications/cyber-crime-a-review-of-the-evidence

Nakamoto, S. (2009). *Bitcoin: A peer-to-peer electronic cash system.* Bitcoin. Available at: https://bitcoin.org/bitcoin.pdf

Protrka, N. (2018). *International cooperation and security in combating crime in cyberspace.* Available at: https://urn.nsk.hr/urn:nbn:hr:162:834428

Rajasegaran, J. and others. (2019). *A multi-modal neural embeddings approach for detecting mobile counterfeit apps* (pp. 3165–3171). WWW '19 the world wide web conference, San Francisco. Available at: https://dl.acm.org/citation.cfm?id=3313427

Symantec. (2018). *FASTCash: How the Lazarus group is emptying millions from ATMs.* Available at: https://www.symantec.com/blogs/threat-intelligence/fastcash-lazarus-atm-malware

Thomas, D., & Loader, B. (2000). *Cybercrime: Security and surveillance in the information age Routledge.*

Wall, D. (2007). *Cybercrime.* Polity.

Child Protection

Andrew Bailey and Mark Roycroft

It is critical for the police and other public sector agencies to be aware at all levels of the complexities of child abuse investigations. States are often judged on how they treat the most vulnerable in society and child abuse victims must receive appropriate access to justice. There are wide ranging definitions and ages of child abuse across countries and regions. Generally, the age at which children or young people can give informed consent to sexual activity is between 15 and 18 years. Child pornography (i.e., indecent images) is generally demarcated by the age of 18 years. Abuse and neglect are forms of maltreatment of a child, usually committed by inflicting harm (either physical or psychological), or by failing to act to prevent harm to a child. Children may be abused in a wide variety of settings including: community, family, friends, institutions, and strangers.

A. Bailey (✉) • M. Roycroft
Rabdan Academy, Al Bhustan, Abu Dhabi, United Arab Emirates
e-mail: mroycroft@ra.ac.ae

M. Roycroft, L. Brine (eds.), *Modern Police Leadership*,
https://doi.org/10.1007/978-3-030-63930-3_14

157

Sexual Abuse

Sexual abuse is often perpetrated by people who are known and trusted by the child (e.g., relatives, family friends, neighbours, babysitters, people working with the child in school, faith settings, clubs, or activities). It is often planned and systematic—people do not sexually abuse children by accident.

- Grooming the child—people who abuse children take care to choose a vulnerable child and often spend time making them dependent.
- Grooming the child's environment—abusers try to ensure that potential adult protectors (e.g., parents and other caregivers) are not suspicious of their motives.

Child Protection Policies

Child protection policies are developed in a specific national or local policy context. Public policy development in this area is complicated by the need for particular agencies to have their own guidance and the need in most jurisdictions, to formulate joint protocols and working relationships with other relevant agencies. Obviously, cultural, legal, political, and financial contexts will form the backdrop to a particular policy.

The main question that underpins public policy development is, 'Does the child protection policy specify the who, when, how and why of what can be complex and sometimes ambiguous reports and suspicions relating to child crimes?'. Policies develop and improve over time, and this can be driven by various factors such as improved understanding of child abuse, public pressure, and legislative changes. One point to consider when reviewing or revisiting previous or historic cases, is that at one level, they can only be judged by the policies and available investigative techniques of that era.

Often as a result of a public inquiry or media coverage of a child death or a child sex abuse ring, the revision of child protection policies occurs. (See Appendix A for examples of this from the UK.) Public inquiries can be cumbersome and expensive. Between 1990 and 2017, 10% of full public inquiries* in the UK concerned child abuse (Norris and Shepheard 2017). These likely consist of the most serious or newsworthy cases. A full public inquiry in the UK tends to mean that the inquiry was convened by a Minister or the Prime Minister and was funded with public money but has been conducted independent of government. However, there are thousands of other reviews in the UK where Local Authorities, Councils, and Police Forces have conducted internal or multi-agency reviews of cases to learn lessons for the future. The situation is similar in most Western countries and the Commonwealth.

https://www.instituteforgovernment.org.uk/sites/default/files/publications/Public%20Inquiries%20%28final%29.pdf

Serious Case Reviews

In keeping with other protocols for reviewing criminal cases and investigations, including major unsolved criminal investigations, child protection in the UK has specific arrangements for reviewing certain categories of cases.

When a child dies or is seriously harmed as a result of neglect or abuse, an examination of the case is conducted to identify ways that professionals and agencies can improve joint working to safeguard children and prevent similar incidents from occurring. The reviews are conducted by multi-agency panels comprised of relevant senior professionals. The review team tasks a senior officer from each agency involved to develop a complete chronology of contact between the agency and the impacted child. The focus is not to allocate blame but to learn lessons for the future. Terminology and guidance for carrying out and sharing 'lessons learned' from the reviews may differ depending on the jurisdiction.

The reviews are known as:

- child safeguarding practice reviews in England
- case management reviews in Northern Ireland
- significant case reviews in Scotland
- child practice reviews in Wales.

https://learning.nspcc.org.uk/case-reviews/process-in-each-uk-nation/

Case Study 1

Samantha was a 2 year old female. Her parents were intravenous drug users and the father was an alcoholic and had been arrested on a number of occasions for assault and theft. Her mother has three other children to different fathers and previously one had been removed from the mother and placed in the care of the Local Authority for 6 months due to neglect. The mother has had ongoing interventions by social work staff from the local authority and attended three programmes run by NGOs concerning parenting skills. The family was well known to the police and

*local medical community. Two siblings of Samantha sustained 'accidental injuries'
associated with a spilled saucepan and an unguarded coal fire. When Samantha's
mother became pregnant with Samantha, her attendance at ante-natal services was
regular. Home visits were conducted by the Community Midwife. Regular advice on
preventing Sudden Infant Death or Cot-Death was provided throughout the preg-
nancy and in the postnatal stage by Midwives and the Health Visitor. This included
advice on smoking cessation, placing babies on their back to sleep, and not co-
sleeping.*

*Prior to the birth of Samantha, a multi-disciplinary case conference decided
that once released from hospital, the child could be cared for by her mother at
home. Three days after arriving home, the child had been sleeping in her father's
bed with the father and when the father woke in the morning, Samantha was dead.
The cause was found to be 'Cot-death' or 'Sudden and Unexplained Infant Death'.*

Findings for this type of case review will typically include:

1. *A need for greater education to parents on 'cot-death'.*
2. *Identifying shortcomings in the data sharing at the multi-disciplinary case conference concerning the criminal history of both parents from both police and the
   Probation Service.*
3. *There was a need for greater collaboration from family doctors.*
4. *Some consideration was given to requiring the father to provide samples for
   toxicology analysis for future cases.*

Major Issues Arising from Public Inquiries

Significant analytical research on child abuse cases from the UK and Europe has
determined that there are 23 main themes in relation to child abuse. This research
indicates that these themes apply equally to children, young adults, and individuals
with a learning disability (Bailey 2001).

1. A perception that police and/or social workers did not believe the victim or the
   parents of the victim and that children/vulnerable adults may not make good
   court witnesses.
2. A lack of cooperation between other agencies such as medical, teaching, or
   residential care staff in terms of reporting suspicions or protecting children.
3. Over-zealousness on the part of professionals in diagnosing child abuse.

4. Failures in legislation or social work procedures relating to foster care or emergency protection orders. In particular, where children could or should have been removed from abusive situations and were not, and subsequently were murdered, abused, or harmed.

5. Failure to properly interview child victims in an evidentially sound and non-leading manner.

6. A lack of support for parents.

7. An over-use and indeed an under-use of emergency protection orders to re-move the child from abusive situations.

8. Failure to treat the child as a person and not an object of concern.

9. Repeated interviews with children and multiple medical examinations.

10. Failure to act in the best interests of the child (the welfare of the child should be the paramount principle).

11. In serious cases, a lack of designated senior staff from both police and social services to coordinate the investigation and child protection work.

12. Child protection should be seen as a specialist area and staff from different areas should train together.

13. Failure to protect children in the care of the state from a 'wide-ranging con-spiracy' involving prominent persons and others with the objective of sexual activity with children in care (e.g., Jimmy Saville Inquiry), where prominent British disc jockeys and other media personalities were 'allowed' to commit a wide range of sexual assaults on children over many years despite concerns being raised. See https://www.bbc.com/news/uk-35657868, NSPCC (2013) Giving Victims a Voice.

14. Church, social workers and other caregivers accused or suspected of child abuse being removed from the area where the allegations relate to, but being allowed to continue in roles giving them access to children or vulnerable adults.

15. Political correctness being allowed to limit the criminal investigation. For ex-ample, in the UK a child prostitution ring involving almost all the suspects being from one particular ethnic minority discouraged officers from properly investigating the cases because they feared they might be accused of being racist as all the suspects were from the same overseas location (Jay 2014).

16. On occasion, a complete breakdown in the multi-agency child protection sys-tem established by law and procedure involving health, police, housing chari-ties and social services failing to work together effectively to protect child victims. Most significant has been the problem of senior managers failing to take responsibility for the failings of their organisations.

17. Poor record keeping.

18. Allegations of deliberate harm to a child being marked as case closed without the following recommended steps having been taken:

- A. The child has been spoken to alone.
- B. The caretakers of the child should be seen and spoken to.
- C. The accommodation in which the child is to live has been visited.
- D. The views of all professionals involved have been sought/considered.
- E. A plan for the promotion and safeguarding of the welfare of the child has been agreed.

19. Whenever a joint investigation by police and social services is required into possible injury or harm to a child, a failure to involve a manager from each agency at the referral stage, and in any further strategy discussion.
20. A lack of training for child protection officers to equip them with the confidence to question the views of professionals in other agencies, including doctors.
21. A failure to follow key principles of good information management (i.e., capture, review, retention, deletion, and sharing) while having regard to the police role, the law, and the rights of the individual.
22. Delays in post mortem results being supplied to the police, in particular in cases of neglect, non-accidental injury, sudden/unexplained infant death, and infants delivered in secret by teenage girls.
23. Police reluctance to arrest parents suspected in serious abuse cases because the parents involved are going through a sensitive time/grief.

Many of the 23 points share a common theme related to poor leadership and supervision.

Case Study 2

Basma is a 14 year old girl living in the care of the Local Authority. She has a key social worker from the nearby social work department who has a caseload of 12 similar cases. Basma was sexually assaulted three years ago by her uncle who was living in the family home. Her parents did not believe her allegations and refused to protect her. The suspect was arrested and charged with indecent assault but the case was dropped by the Public Prosecution Service due to a lack of corroboration. During the investigation, the suspect indicated that Basma agreed to various sexual encounters with him despite the fact that she was not legally able to consent.

Basma is relatively happy living in a public funded home for children and is doing well at school. She was however recently accused at school of a minor physical assault on an 18-year-old male student. He declined to prosecute and declined to cooperate with the school or the police.

The residents at the home for children where Basma stays are asked to be back in the facility by 21:30 hours each evening and staff at the facility consist of five qualified social workers in the role of team leader and a number of unqualified staff and student social workers on different shifts.

Basma has failed to return to the facility by 21:30 hours on six occasions and claims that her watch and phone were not working. Staff suspect she had been drinking alcohol and smoking cannabis. On one occasion, she was reported missing and turned up the following morning claiming she fell asleep at a house party after drinking too much alcohol. On one occasion, she returned to the facility with a brand new smartphone leather jacket.

Questions

What avenues of her life need to be explored and by who?

   What interagency liaison should take place if any?

   Can the social worker with a caseload of 12 similar teenagers invest significant time in this case?

   Can the police help?

   Is the drinking and drug taking unusual, risky, normal, or suspicious?

   What inquiries should be undertaken concerning the gifts, house party, and the uncle from the previous allegations?

   Is it relevant to know whether she is still in contact with the uncle?

   What might be behind the physical assault she committed on the 18 year old man?

   Was the victim of the assault trying to recruit Basma for sexual exploitation?

   What self-protection work could be delivered to Basma?

   Is she able to access contraception and sexual health services?

   Are there any cultural or language issues that should be considered?

Wadeema's Law (2016)

Wadeema's Law (Federal Law No. 3/2016), as it is known in the United Arab Emirates, is unusual because it is considered a good example of a relatively new law and procedure underpinning child protection that did not originate from a long line of similar previous policies or laws. The law is designed to ensure that children are provided with appropriate living standards, services, equal opportunities and be protected from abuse and neglect. The provisions allow childcare specialists to remove children from the care of their parents without their permission and allow mandatory inspection visits by social services staff and specialists.

This law was created as the result of a child abuse case involving an eight year old girl from Dubai named Wadeema. After her body was found buried in the desert, it was discovered that she had been tortured to death by her father and his girlfriend. Investigation revealed that Wadeema and her younger sister had been regularly burnt with cigarettes and stun guns and beaten. On the day of her death, her father had beaten her with an iron bar and then locked her in the bathroom where she died.

Wadeema's Law includes:

• compulsory reporting by educational establishments, other professionals, and caregivers
• a register of those convicted of crimes against children
• terms of reference for the Child Protection Unit
• preventative and protection measures
• foster family responsibilities
• age restrictions on child labour
• vetting procedures for child protection specialists
• a level of anonymity to those reporting abuse

In addition, those convicted of sexual offences and possessing indecent images of children are barred from employment that provides them access to children, and they cannot reside within five kilometres of the victim. Article 12 of the legislation states that the views of the child must be taken into account concerning the 'measures' taken in his/her regard. Article 33 gives the child a legal right to protection from abuse in a wide variety of contexts. This puts the UAE much further ahead than many jurisdictions. The child will have a right to protection from such situations as:

• Exposure to abuse, neglect, rejection etc.,
• Exposure to exploitation by illegal organisations or organised crime groups (including 'planting ideas of intolerance and hatred')
• Exposure to begging or other forms of exploitation

A critical component of the law prohibits the possession and distribution of indecent images of children. It also specifies the powers and duties of child protection specialists. At the end of any period of imprisonment, the offender can be given mandatory treatment at a special therapeutic treatment centre.

(U.A.E. Federal Law No. 3/2016, Issued 8/3/16, Corresponding to 28 Jumada Al-Awwal 1437 H. on Child Rights (Wadeema's Law))

The UAE now gives child related issues a priority, as a result of a clear commitment to offering the optimal environment for the child growth and protection of their rights. The UAE is a signatory to the International Convention on Children's Rights (1997), and after Wadeema's Law was implemented, other agencies were quick to issue detailed policy guidance and child protection policies. (e.g., The Central School Dubai, Child protection and Safeguarding policy 2019 revised edition available at https://www.centraldxb.com/wp-content/uploads/Child-protection-and-safeguarding-policy-2019-20.pdf).

Forensic Interviews Relating to Child Abuse

In the mid-1970s, the initial professional response to child sexual abuse was to gather information "by any means necessary", including interviewing the child multiple times, asking leading questions, and using other suggestive techniques. (Faller 2015) In the mid-1980s, however, concerns about false allegations began to drive interview practices in many Western countries. Events that led to this "backlash" included a series of multi-victim cases. The cases received a great deal of media attention, initially focused on the enormity of harm to children and later highlighting questionable interview practices and doubting the children's disclosures (Faller 2015). A subsequent major inquiry helped the UK to formulate detailed policies and dedicated child abuse investigation teams.

Professional views about the veracity of the sexual and other abuse described in these multi-victim cases remains mixed. Nevertheless, these high-profile cases have played a major role in shaping forensic interview practice. They have driven interview strategies that avoid false positives (i.e., children determined to have been sexually abused, but who were not) as opposed to false negatives (i.e., children who were sexually abused but were not identified in the investigative process). In addition to the development of joint interagency practice, the Children's Advocacy Centre model was introduced by many jurisdictions. The interview was able to be observed, either through a one-way mirror or on a TV monitor, by all relevant professionals.

There are divergent views across concerning who is qualified to conduct specialised forensic interviews with child abuse victims. In the UK and most of the Commonwealth, experienced detectives can qualify after 9–15 days training and a quality assurance of their interviews. In Ireland, only specialised and experienced psychiatrists or clinical psychologists acting as special advisers to an investigative judge or in some cases a state prosecutor are qualified (Odeljan et al. 2015).

Central Aims of the Criminal Investigation

It must be understood that the protection, welfare, and wellbeing of the child are more important than criminal proceedings. Also, it may be difficult to secure evidence for a wide variety of reasons, including the reluctance of the child. A criminal investigation is conducted with a view as to whether a person should be charged with an offence. This will include:

- whether a child needs to be safeguarded or removed from a situation.
- identifying the most appropriate line(s) of enquiry to pursue and the objectives taking into account resources, priorities, necessity and proportionality
- directing and conducting investigations to gather the maximum amount of evidence
- understanding and managing community impact and wider child protection considerations including pre-employment vetting and repeat victimisation

It is critical that the investigator of child abuse be open to the following possibilities:

- the child has been abused than more than one offender
- there may be other victims
- the victim may have been told to lie
- the offender may be interested in both genders and multiple ages
- a person engaging in prostitution who is under the age of consent is a victim of crime

There are three key phases for investigators:

1. Instigation and initial response—strategy discussion and record checks amongst partner agencies, deploying of investigators to the incident, preserving life, securing the scene, arresting offenders, locating evidence.
2. Investigation—developing strategies for suitable victim and witness interviews, generating and testing hypotheses, gathering the evidence needed to establish what occurred, identifying and arresting suspects, and gathering material for prosecution.
3. Case management—post-charge enquiries, preparing the evidence for prosecution, managing witnesses and exhibits, updating and arranging special measures for the victim.

In most jurisdictions, the prosecutor will determine whether there is sufficient evidence to secure a conviction, and decide whether the prosecution is in the public interest.

Investigation is a core duty of policing. Interviewing victims, witnesses, and suspects is central to the success of an investigation and the highest standards need to be upheld. A police organisation must develop and maintain skilled investigators and interviewers. Those that are conducted professionally can:

- an investigation and gather material, which in turn can lead to a successful prosecution or the early release of an innocent person
- the prosecution case, thereby saving time, money, and resources
- public confidence in the police service, particularly with witnesses and victims of crimes.

Without the accounts of those who played a central role in the crime, (i.e., victims, witnesses, suspects, etc.,), other evidence (e.g., CCTV, DNA, fingerprints, etc.,) may have little value. Investigators must act ethically, fairly, and impartially, and comply with all legislation and policy, when interviewing victims, witnesses, and suspects.

Victims and witnesses with clear or perceived vulnerabilities (including age) should be treated with particular care. It is also incorrect to assume that people with a developmental disability will make poor witnesses. Often providing them proper support will assist them in being good witnesses for the court (Bailey et al. 2001; McAllister et al. 2002).

The European Court of Human Rights has identified five key components to investigations: (https://www.echr.coe.int/Documents/Guide_Art_6_criminal_ ENG.pdf, 2020).

- Effective: Police must show that they followed a process of investigation which was capable of leading to a result. In order to do this, they must have taken all reasonable steps available to them to secure the evidence concerning the incident (i.e., autopsy, eyewitness testimony, forensic evidence, etc.,).
- Independent: Where there is an allegation of unlawful killing by state agents, the persons responsible for, and carrying out, the investigation should be independent from those implicated in the events.
- Prompt: While there may be obstacles that prevent progress in an investigation, a prompt response by the authorities in investigating the use of lethal force may generally be regarded as essential in maintaining public confidence in their adherence to the rule of law and in preventing any appearance of collusion in or

intolerance of unlawful acts. Clear records should be kept throughout an investigation which detail why action was taken, or in appropriate cases, why action was not taken.

- Subject to public scrutiny: Police have a duty to keep full records of all their actions in order that at some later stage they are capable of scrutiny. Decisions whether or not to disclose information during the investigation should be carefully justified.
- Involve the next of kin to the extent necessary to safeguard their interest.

It is clear that jurisdictions may have differing policies and legislation concerning how a child abuse investigation should properly unfold. These may be impacted by cultural considerations and the roles and responsibilities of each involved organisation. That said, whatever the current arrangements are, one must stress the criticality of accountability, collaboration, cooperation, and complexity of child abuse investigations. Training for staff, and awareness for the public are essential. The underlying principle of policy makers and advisors should be the prevention and detection of child abuse combined with enabling child abuse victims' proper access to justice and/or civil remedies. Clearly, effective child abuse investigation requires strong leadership and supervision from all agencies involved.

References

Frozen watchfulness (http://www.body-languages.net/2014/02/frozen-watchfulness/)
Norris, E., & Shepheard, M. (2017). *How public inquiries lead to change*. London: Institute for Government.

WADEEMA'S LAW

https://www.khda.gov.ae/CMS/WebParts/TextEditor/Documents/Children_Law_English.pdf. Accessed Sept 2019.
Bailey, A. (2001). Ph.D. Thesis 'Factors influencing police investigation of sexual crimes committed against people who have a learning disability and implications for public policy'.
Protocol On the Procedure in case of Abuse and Neglect of Children (Croatia). https://www.mup.hr/UserDocsImages/Savjeti/2015/PROTOCOL%20ON%20THE%20PROCEDURE%20IN%20CASE%20OF%20ABUSE%20AND%20NEGLECT%20OF%20CHILDREN%20(2).pdf. Accessed Sept 2019.
(Guidance on Article 6 of the European Convention on Human Rights updated 2018. https://www.echr.coe.int/Documents/Guide_Art_6_criminal_ENG.pdf). Accessed Sept 2019.

Protocol for Joint Investigation by Social workers and Police Officers of Alleged or Suspected Cases of Child Abuse-Northern Ireland, PSNI/HSC. http://www.hscboard. hscni.net/download/PUBLICATIONS/policies-protocols-and-guidelines/Protocol-for-joint-investigation-by-social-workers-and-police-officers-of-alledged-and-suspected-cases-of-child-abuse-NI.pdf. Accessed Sept 2019.

Recantation and False Allegations of Child Abuse. The National Children's Advocacy Center US, 2011.

https://www.icmec.org/wp-content/uploads/2015/10/Recantations-and-False-Allegations-Bibliography.pdf. Accessed Aug 2019.

https://en.wikipedia.org/wiki/False_allegation_of_child_sexual_abuse. Accessed Aug 2019.

The Criminal Justice (Northern Ireland) Order 2008 (UK). https://www.legislation.gov.uk/nisi/2008/1216/contents. Accessed Aug 2019.

The Casey Family Programs. Are there good examples of how child welfare agencies are collaborating with law enforcement? https://www.casey.org/are-there-good-examples-of-how-child-welfare-agencies-are-collaborating-with-law-enforcement/. Accessed Dec 2018.

Achieving Best Evidence in Criminal Proceedings. Guidance on interviewing victims and witnesses, and guidance on using special measures. Ministry of Justice (2011). https://www.cps.gov.uk/sites/default/files/documents/legal_guidance/best_evidence_in_criminal_proceedings.pdf. Accessed Aug 2019.

Guidance on Interviewing Suspects (the P.E.A.C.E. Model). https://assets.publishing.service.gov.uk/government/uploads/system/uploads/attachment_data/file/757585/BAGT-Interviewing-suspects-v4.0ext_archive.pdf. Accessed Aug 2019

Child Welfare Information Gateway (2016). https://www.childwelfare.gov/topics/can/. Accessed Sept 2019.

Guidance on the UN Convention on the Rights of the Child. https://www.ohchr.org/en/professionalinterest/pages/crc.aspx. Accessed Aug 2019.

UN Convention of the Rights of the Child. https://www.ohchr.org/en/professionalinterest/pages/crc.aspx. Accessed Aug 2019.

Cleveland Inquiry. https://www.thetcj.org/child-care-history-policy/the-cleveland-reportby-judge-elizabeth-butler-sloss. Accessed Aug 2019

Orkney Inquiry. https://www.gov.uk/government/publications/inquiry-into-the-removal-of-children-from-orkney-in-february-1991. Accessed Aug 2019.

Publications

Bailey, A., Barr, O., & Bunting, B. (2001). Police attitudes toward people who have intellectual disabilities an evaluation of awareness training. *Intellectual Disability Research, 45,* 1–7.

Faller, K. C. (2015). Forty years of forensic interviewing of children suspected of sexual abuse. *Social Science, 4,* 34–65.

Jay. (2014). *Independent inquiry into child sexual exploitation in Rotherham (England) 1997–2013.* Rotherham: Rotherham Metropolitan Borough Council.

McAllister, A., Bailey, A., & Barr, O. (2002). Training in joint investigation of alleged crimes against people with learning disabilities in Northern Ireland. *Journal of Adult Protection, 4*(2), 21–27.

Odeljan, R., Butorac, K., & Bailey, A. (2015). Investigative interviews with children. *European Law Enforcement Research Bulletin*, (12), 18–24.

Sexual Assault Investigations in the UK and Canada

Lindsey Brine and Mark Roycroft

A report by Dame Elish Angiolini report (2 June 15) into rape investigations in The Metropolitan Police in London, UK, highlights the issues in modern day rape investigations and makes a list of recommendations (See Table 2). The report states that *"Rape is one of the most serious but misunderstood crimes and presents investigators and prosecutors with unique challenges. In its variety and complexity rape often presents difficulties fa*r in *excess of those encountered in investigating other crimes, including homicide"*. This reflects the author's experience managing detective units and investigating rape in London. The Home Office Research Study in 2005 saw rape as, 'a unique crime, representing both a physical and psychological violation'. In 2010, Baroness Stern went further, observing, 'It is unique in the way it strikes at the bodily integrity and self-respect of the complainant, in the demands it makes on those public authorities required to respond to it and in the controversy it generates'. This chapter will examine these recommendations and place them in the context of 40 years of changing policy towards rape investigation, legal changes, and the change in the social milieu, in both the UK and Canada.

L. Brine (✉) • M. Roycroft
Rabdan Academy, Al Bhustan, Abu Dhabi, United Arab Emirates
e-mail: mroycroft@ra.ac.ae

© The Author(s), under exclusive license to Springer Nature Switzerland AG 2021
M. Roycroft, L. Brine (eds.), *Modern Police Leadership*,
https://doi.org/10.1007/978-3-030-63930-3_15

Definition of Rape Under the Sexual Offences Act 2003

The Sexual Offences Act sets out the offences requiring the prosecution to prove absence of consent. They are, rape; assault by penetration; sexual assault; and causing a person to engage in sexual activity.

In relation to these offences, a person (A) is guilty of an offence if she/he: Acts intentionally, (B) does not consent to the act, and (A) does not reasonably believe that (B) consents.

Sexual assault in Canada as defined in the Criminal Code of Canada (1985) is fundamentally different from equivalent offences as defined in many other developed nations. In addition, the factors that determine what level of sexual assault charge (or the equivalent in other nations) is laid also differ. The Canadian definition of sexual assault is an assault, within any one of the definitions of that concept in s. 265(1) Canadian Criminal Code, is committed in circumstances of a sexual nature such that the sexual integrity of the victim is violated. What would be defined as rape in other countries (and used to be defined as rape in Canada) could fall under the Criminal Code's sexual assault level 1, sexual assault level 2, or sexual assault level 3, depending on the severity of the assault. Canada has a broad definition of sexual assault. It includes all unwanted sexual activity, such as unwanted sexual grabbing, kissing, and fondling, as well as rape. However, Canada stopped using the term 'rape' in the 1980s. The Handbook *for Legislation on Violence against Women* from the UN Department of Economic and Social Affairs Division for the Advancement of Women postulates that the term "Rape" should be replaced by the term sexual assault graded on harm. This in turn should be defined as a violation of bodily integrity and sexual autonomy. Sexual activity is only legal when both parties consent.

Police in the UK, Canada, and many other countries have implemented many beneficial and significant changes in sexual assault investigations over the last 40 years, including the following:

- Creation of Specialist teams and specially trained officers Sexual Offences SOITs
- The increased use of Forensic material including digital evidence
- Multi agency working particularly with medical professionals
- Third party reporting
- Improved training for Police officers
- Continual support for victims along with victim Impact statements read to the Court
- The use of Havens or Sexual Offences Referral Centre

- Fact Sheet the Havens are Sexual Assault Referral Centres that have been set up as a joint initiative by the MPS and the NHS to ensure that victims of rape and sexual assault get the help they need. This partnership combines the best possible initial case management by skilled officers with the best available victim care from the health service.

The Havens provide ongoing treatment, advice and counselling, and specialist and forensically trained doctors and nurses. It aims to provide a one-stop-shop service to victims of rape, regardless of whether they are male, female, trans*, young or old.

Scale of the Issue

The number of rapes recorded by the police in England and Wales has risen to 54,035 for the 2017/2018 in the past year (2018–2019) according to the Office for National Statistics (ONS). This increase in reporting may be the result of improved public confidence in steps taken by authorities in how these offences are investigated (Table 1).

This type of crime is prevalent worldwide. Using Canada and the UK as an example some cities and many police forces face issues around reporting of such cases and then the high "attrition" rate(the length of time from first complaint to court trial) of such crimes. The Globe and Mail (3/2/17) newspaper in Canada found that police in 115 communities dismiss at least one-third of sex-assault complaints as unfounded while large cities such as Toronto, Winnipeg, Windsor, have single-digit unfounded rates.

The 1980s and 1990s were watershed decades for sexual-assault legislation in Canada. The crimes of rape and indecent assault were replaced with three tiers of sexual-assault offences (see above), encompassing a fuller spectrum of sexual violence. Restrictions were put on the circumstances in which a victim's sexual history could be introduced in court. The corroboration requirement was removed, meaning that a complainant's word, even without third-party testimony or physical evidence, became enough to secure a conviction. Restrictions were put on a suspect's ability to claim that he had "mistakenly believed" a complainant had consented to sexual activity.

In February 2017, The Globe and Mail newspaper in Canada published a report after spending 20 months investigating how 870 Canadian police services manage sexual-assault investigations. As part of the reporting, The Globe and Mail looked at the rate at which police dismiss sex-assault complaints as unfounded, meaning, the rate at which investigating officer and his/her supervisor do not believe a crime

Table 1 CPS rape case outcomes 2017–2019

England and Wales, CPS rape outcomes[4]	Number of post-charge finalisations (caseload)	Number of convictions	Conviction rate	Number of cases which were contested	Number of convictions after contest	Number of acquittals/ dismissed after trial	Number of prosecutions dropped	Convictions after contest rate	Number of guilty pleas	Guilty plea rate
Year ending March 2019	3034	1925	63.4%	1468	833	635	426	56.7%	1092	36.0%
Year ending March 2018	4517	2635	58.3%	2255	1112	1143	659	49.3%	1522	33.7%
Year ending March 2017	5190	2991	57.6%	2731	1264	1467	642	46.3%	1727	33.3%

Source: Crown Prosecution Service

occurred. The data showed that, on average, one out of every five sex-assault cases is classified as unfounded. But regionally, unfounded rates were notably higher in the North. The North refers to the Arctic region of Canada and includes Northwest Territories, Nunavut Territory, and Yukon Territory. These areas are largely populated with First Nations Aboriginals, and Inuit. Language barriers with these populations, high turnover among police officers, substance-abuse issues and fewer resources compound an already fraught dynamic, where the realities of small-town living mean the personal lives of police officers, complainants, suspects and support workers are likely to intersect outside the legal process. As a consequence of the Globe and Mail report, the Royal Canadian Mounted Police (RCMP) examined all sexual assault files classified as unfounded from 2016 to ensure that investigations followed RCMP operational policy. The RCMP and many other police organizations have changed their policies in relation to Police training and awareness, investigation accountability, victim support and public education.

In Canada in 2017, there were 24,672 incidents of sexual assault (levels 1, 2 and 3) reported by police and 98% of them were categorized as level 1. This represents an increase from 22,246 incidents in 2006. From 2006 to 2016, the quantity of incidents reported by police fluctuated slightly. However, from 2016 to 2017, the number of police-reported level 1 sexual assaults increased 14% (from 21,072 to 24,094), the number of level 2 sexual assaults increased 6% (from 395 to 417), and the number of level 3 sexual assaults increased 44% (from 112 to 161). The proportion of the total number of all sexual assaults reported to police that were cleared by charge was mostly constant from 1998 to 2015, varying from 41% to 46%. In the past two years, the cleared-by-charge rate dropped considerably to 37% in 2016 and 34% in 2017.

Policy Changes in the UK

Walklate (2004, 153) concludes, "it is clearly the case that there has been a remarkable change of direction in terms of policing policy in this issue". The major turning point in rape investigation in the UK in recent times was the BBC documentary by Roger Graef in 1982 entitled "Police". In episode three, 'A Complaint of Rape', a woman with a history of psychiatric treatment claims she has been raped by three strangers and is, in turn, cajoled by three male officers who dismiss her story out of hand. Transmitted soon after an infamous court decision (in which a judge had accused a hitchhiker of "contributory negligence" in her own rape), 'A Complaint of Rape' caused a public outcry and led to a change in the way police forces handled rape cases. An HMIC report in 2012 report (see Table 2) stated that great progress had been made and commented that there were now specially trained officers and access to Havens and Sexual Assault referral centres (SARCs).

Table 2 The development of rape policy in the UK timetable

Event	Issues	Consequences and improvements
BBC documentary Police 1982	Treatment of victims	HO circular to chief constables (25/1983) advice on how investigations should be conducted, on the timing and conduct of medical examinations, the number of officers involved in an investigation & the importance of having female officers.
Working party *Violence Against Women* (Women's National Commission, 1985)	To ensure that victims receive the legal, medical, social and psychological help which they. Offered practical advice to the police and to court personnel on their procedures and to bring home to them that these procedures could be contributing to a lack of effectiveness	Home Office circular 69/1986 which dealt with victims, police forces should consider setting up special victim examination suites, More advice and information for rape victims, follow-up visits, and enhanced training for officers
Abolition of rape within marriage clause 1991 by the house of lords, in the case of *R v R*	Abolition of the marital rape exclusion clause.	The first attempted prosecution of a husband for the rape of his wife was *R v Clarke*
Introduction of havens or sexual assault referral centers 2000	Rape victims often had to wait for many hours, unable to drink, eat, or wash, before a forensic medical examination or other services could be provided. Lack of female doctors with the training to carry out forensic medical examinations	Victims can be prescribed emergency contraception and receive treatment, availability of counselling and support
Sexual Offences Act 2003	Clarified consent issues Definition of consent given "a person consents if he agrees by choice and has the freedom and capacity to make that choice."	Broadened the definition of rape, widened definitions of family in relation to familial sex offences, created new offences shifting the focus from purely physical to include other abusive behaviours such as sexual grooming

(continued)

Table 2 (continued)

Event	Issues	Consequences and improvements
Baroness stern report 2010	Deplored conflicting police and crown prosecution service performance targets Commented on the need for intelligence gathering	23 recommendations made including: Transfer of commissioning of sexual assault referral Centres from the police to the NHS; and sexual assault referral Centres in every police force area
IPCC report in Warboys	Individual and systemic failings in investigating complaints of assaults by Worboys and a failure to challenge or investigate inconsistencies in Worboys' account Serious errors of judgement and the investigations lacked rigour Failure to secure evidence such as CCTV footage, forensic swabs and blood and urine tests promptly, Failure to interview key witnesses to corroborate victims' accounts Victims were not kept informed	Recommendations: Making information available for victims online and regular case updates with victims Sharing of information and intelligence with local agencies where there is a high risk to the community Working with the voluntary sector to formalise structures to encourage women to report to third parties
HMIC report Forging the links: Rape investigation and prosecution February 2012	HMIC report in 2012 report stated that great progress had been made and commented that: Call handling systems are more responsive Specially trained officers or their equivalents have been widely introduced Training for police and prosecutors is improved Access to sexual assault referral centres (SARCs) is in place Use of early evidence kits is widespread	Stressed the importance of the importance of intelligence material in preventing, investigating and prosecuting rape

(continued)

Table 2 (continued)

Event	Issues	Consequences and improvements
Dame Elish Angilioni report 2015	A key finding was the consistent approval of the policies applied to the investigation and prosecution of rape, and the identification of an inability to implement those same policies comprehensively and successfully	47 recommendations including the havens are key to increasing reporting of rape and reducing attrition Increase in numbers of independent sexual violence advisors (ISVAs) Need for joint case building between the CPS and the MPS. Need for extra resources and a 24 hour response to victims.
Creation of rape performance group led by her Majesty's inspectorate of constabulary (HMIC) and the crown prosecution service (CPS)	This unit will monitor police and CPS performance in handling allegations and undertake the assessments as part of the new measures to improve the investigation and prosecution in rape cases. An extra £1.8 million in funding will be provided to sexual assault referral centres (SARCs) and independent sexual violence advisors (ISVA) to increase the support network available to rape victims.	Each police force in England and Wales will be expected to ensure all rape victims are seen by a specially trained officer within an hour of reporting and specialist sexual violence voluntary sector services should be involved in delivering training programmes on rape to police forces, so that all officers know what action to take when a rape is first reported.
London rape review 2016	Examined the attrition rate of rape cases, reasons for victim/survivor withdrawal were complex and often interrelated. 95% of victims/survivors had at least one need present that is, mental health.	The review tried to predict attrition By procedural characteristics Where the victim was less than 18 years old Victim/survivor mental health
Liam Allen rape case 2017	"Texts" from his accuser proved his innocence but had not been given to his defence lawyer.	Noted as a "firework case" that highlighted the issue of disclosure and social media messages in the modern age. It acted as a catalyst for a review by the CPS and MPS below.

The report stated that there should be greater emphasis on intelligence gathering and analysis through local forces and the Serious Crime Analysis Section (SCAS) now based within the NCA. This was reflected in the Independent Police Complaints Commission (now IPOC) IPCC recommendations following the conviction of John Warboys, a London taxi driver who between 2003 and 2008 drugged, raped and sexually assaulted 85 victims. At least 10 victims reported attacks to the police before he was eventually arrested and charged in 2008 The IPCC identified "individual and systemic" issues within the Metropolitan police (see Table 2 for full list), some of the key findings showed that there were Individual and systemic failings in investigating complaints of assaults by Warboys and a failure to challenge or investigate inconsistencies in Wordbooks' account with crucial investigative issues missed. The report made several recommendations (see Table 2) including making information available for victims online and regular case updates with victims. J.Bindell (28 February 2014) writing in the Guardian stated that "Not just the Police but the criminal justice system was partly to blame,... evidentially rape cases are difficult to prosecute but new forensic methods and passive data collection can assist greatly". The Timetable shown in Table 2 highlights the main issues in UK Policy on Rape since 1982 including Home office circulars (25/1983 and 69/1986) advocating best practice. Dame Elish Angiolini's report builds on the number of reports and increasing resources, the number of Havens and specially trained officers.

Adequacy Standards Regulations in Canada requires a police services board to have a policy on investigations into sexual assaults. It also requires the Chief of Police to develop and maintain procedures on and processes for undertaking and managing investigations of sexual assaults.

Consent

Dame Elish's report states that the capacity to consent is a major issue in rape investigations. Proving that the complainant did not consent and the defendant did not reasonably believe that the complainant consented, is the key issue in many rape cases. The Sexual Offences Act 2003 states, "a person consents if he agrees by choice and has the freedom and capacity to make that choice". Today, many cases investigated by the Metropolitan Police Service involve a complainant who is incapacitated by alcohol or drugs. The legislation, unlike the corresponding legislation in Scotland, does not address the issue of self-induced intoxication and it has been left to the Court of Appeal in the case of R v Bree (2007) to clarify the situation. The issue of consent has been highlighted by the trial of Liam Allen in 2017 in the

UK whereby "texts" from his accuser proved his innocence but had not been given to his defence lawyer. This case highlighted the issue of disclosure and social media messages in the modern age. It acted as a catalyst for a review by The CPS and MPS. This stated that the disclosure problems in this case were caused by a combination of error, lack of challenge, and lack of knowledge.

This trial collapsed over non-disclosure of a mobile phone download which cast doubt on the claim the sex was non-consensual. A review stated that the disclosure problem was caused "by a combination of error, lack of challenge and lack of knowledge". There were a total of 57,000 messages in the alleged victim's phone and revealed that the alleged victim had pestered him for casual sex. This illustrates the difficulties the Police are having in processing digital evidence.

Consent is defined in Canada's *Criminal Code* in s. 273.1(1), as the voluntary agreement to engage in the sexual activity in question. The law focuses on what the person was actually thinking and feeling at the time of the sexual activity. Sexual touching is only lawful if the person affirmatively communicated their consent, whether through words or conduct. Silence or passivity does not equal consent.

The Role of the Law

Carrabine, Cox et al. (2014: 208) state that the law can be both instrumental and symbolic so the practical instrumental role wishes to stop rape while symbolically the state also displays changing social concerns around rape in marriage which was criminalised in 1991 and the 2003 Sexual Offences Act the most radical overhaul of sex offences for over 50 years. The 2003 Act broadened the definition of rape, widened definitions of family in relation to familial sex offences, created new offences shifting the focus from purely physical to include other abusive behaviours such as sexual grooming. A key change was the re definition of consent, defendants had to show that they have reasonable grounds to support their belief and show what steps they took to elicit consent. Sex crimes are and can create "moral panics" described by Jock Young in 1971 and Cohen in 1992;they appear to be triggered by alarming media stories and reinforced by reactive laws and public policy, of exaggerated or misdirected public concern, anxiety, fear, or anger over a perceived threat to social order. It was only in 1991 after over 20 years of feminist campaigns on the issue that rape within marriage (of a wife by a husband) was made formally illegal with the abolition of the marital rape exclusion clause.

The Victims Commissioners office in the UK is highlighting the plight of rape victims and the Victims Commissioners website *victim's commissioner .org.uk* has guidance on the various stages of a victim's journey through the criminal justice process.

Social Changes

Society has seen many changes over the last 40 years and some of the issues shown in Table 2 could be seen as what criminologists suggest are the "moral panics" mentioned above. The report by Dame Elish Angiolini continues a significant increase in the awareness of issues surrounding the role and status of women. The traditional advice (Walklate 2004) to women was of the "don't variety" that is, don't go out late at night by yourself, don't use public transport late at night and so on. Hopefully society has moved from this concept of victim precipitated rape (see Temkin and Krahe 2008: 32) to one where all victims are treated as victims within the criminal justice system. The myths around rape and the typology attributed to different types of rape that is, date rape, stranger rape and rape in conflict situations are now seen as redundant. It was only in 1991 after over 20 years of feminist campaigns on the issue that rape within marriage (of a wife by a husband) was made formally illegal with the abolition of the marital rape exclusion clause.

Conclusion

Great progress has been made by the UK Police and Canadian police in the area of rape and sexual assault investigation but they cannot be complacent. While rape remains one the most difficult crimes to investigate, intelligence gathering, multi-agency working and passive data collection are areas of importance mentioned in various reports. Dame Elish adds to recent reports by well-judged comments that broadly support current practices while suggesting how they can be improved with case building between the CPS and the Police one of the major issues.

Seminar Questions

Describe how sexual assault legislation has changed in Canada over the last three decades.

The IPCC report into the Warboys case dealt with many issues surrounding the investigation and made several recommendations. Discuss these recommendations.

Consent is a major issue in all sexual assault cases, using the Liam Allen case (2019) shown in Table 2 please discuss the needs of the victim against CPS charging policy in rape/sexual assault cases. See https://www.**cps**.gov.uk/publication/**cps-policy**-prosecuting-cases-**rape**

Exam Questions

Describe the development of Rape/ sexual assault policy in the UK using some of the examples in Table 2.

References

Walklate (2004). Gender, Crime, and Criminal Justice, Willan.
Temkin and Krahe (2008:32). Elisabeth McDonald, Temkin & Krahe, Sexual Assault and the Justice Gap: A Question of Attitude, 29 Pace L. Rev. 349 (2009). Tensions." The New York Times, The New York Times, 29 May 2020.
Carrabine, Cox et al (2014:208). Criminology A Sociological Introduction. Routledge. UK.

Investigative Interviewing

Mark Roycroft and Lindsey Brine

Investigation is a core duty of policing and the extent will depend (inter-alia) on the type of legal system that prevails. The role of public prosecutors and the police will differ depending on the legal tradition adopted in a particular country. Two types of legal traditions dominate the nature of investigation and adjudication around the world. These are the adversarial and inquisitorial legal systems. Common law countries use an adversarial system to determine facts in the adjudication and investigation process. The prosecution and defence compete against each other, and the judge serves as a referee. The adversarial system assumes that the best way to get to the truth of a matter is through a competitive process to determine the facts and application of the law accurately. In this system, the police are often tasked with the main bulk of responsibilities around gathering evidence and conducting witness and suspect interviews.

They can also seek pre-charge advice from the State or Public Prosecutor. (https://www.unodc.org/e4j/en/organized-crime/module-9/key-issues/adversarial-vs-inquisitorial-legal-systems.html).

The inquisitorial system is associated with civil law legal systems and is characterised by extensive pre-trial investigation and interrogations with the objective to avoid bringing an innocent person to trial. The inquisitorial process can be

M. Roycroft (✉) • L. Brine
Rabdan Academy, Al Bhustan, Abu Dhabi, United Arab Emirates
e-mail: mroycroft@ra.ac.ae

M. Roycroft, L. Brine (eds.), *Modern Police Leadership*,
https://doi.org/10.1007/978-3-030-63930-3_16

183

described as an official inquiry to ascertain the truth, whereas the adversarial system uses a competitive process between the two sides to determine the facts. The inquisitorial process grants more power to the judge who oversees the process and state prosecutors of special advisers to the judge may have a more active role in investigative interviews.

In the Course of any major investigation, Police will interview victims, witnesses and suspects. The Police are there to determine what happened and "discover who did what" (Milne and Bull 2006). An interview has been described as "a conversation with a purpose" (Hodgson 1987). It is important to understand how those "conversations" are managed by the Police to ensure that information pertinent to the enquiry is adduced within an ethical framework.

Williamson (1993) surmised that in relation to interviewing skills of investigating officers, a study by Moston et al. (1992) had found

> the degree of questioning skill often to be quite low. The interviewers frequently gave up at the slightest obstacle (e.g. the suspect exercising the right to silence and/or saying "no comment"). Many interviews appeared chaotic and unstructured. In many interviews the questioning appeared to lack basic preparation and planning. Many of the officers seemed more nervous than the suspect. (Williamson 1993, pp. 89–99)

Interviewing victims, witnesses and suspects is central to the success of an investigation in either legal system and the highest standards need to be upheld. The Maxwell Confait case in the UK in 1972 led to a Royal Commission and subsequently the introduction of the Police and Criminal evidence Act that placed formal regulations on custody and interviewing. Interviews were to be tape recorded. Confait was murdered and 3 suspects "confessed" to the murder including one defendant who had learning difficulties and was illiterate. All suspects were later exonerated and released from prison. The previous emphasis on "confession evidence" alone to convict defendants was now a thing of the past. This fundamentally changed police enquiries, and the emphasis was now on 'fact finding'. The Police now had to fully prepare for interviews and follow the PACE guidelines. As Roycroft found in his research of 166 murder cases, there was an average of 4 "solving factors" that is, those factors that helped solve the murder case. In only 4 cases out of the 166 murder cases were confessions obtained. This represents 2.4% of the total solving factors for the case. Confession evidence was controversial in the Birmingham 6 case and the Guildford 4 where the defendants were charged with terrorist offences and later their convictions were overturned. The Police and Criminal Evidence Act of 1984 (PACE) introduced tape recorded interviews and as Milne and Bull (2003) since the introduction of PACE regarding audio-taping interviews with suspects, police interviews have become better planned, more structured, and the use of trickery and deceit has all but vanished" (p. 121).

Having skilled interviewers is a key part of any police organisation. Good professional interviews can support the prosecution case. The suspect interview can fill in gaps in the enquiry. Even if a suspect lies during an interview, the police can then further investigate and disprove those lies, thereby impacting the credibility of the suspect.

Police organisations need to develop and maintain the valuable resource of a cohort of skilled interviewers. Interviews that are conducted professionally and that are quality assured realise several benefits. In particular, they can assist an investigation and help corroborate evidence obtained from other sources. An interview can support the prosecution case. Interviews with witnesses and victims are important to maintain public confidence in the Police. The College of Policing app states.

> *Without the accounts of those who played a central role in the crime, or those who have witnessed an important aspect of the commission of a crime, other sources of material such as CCTV images, fingerprints and forensic material, although extremely important, may have little value.*

Body Worn Cameras

The majority of officers have now been issued Body worn Cameras (BWC) and these present an opportunity for "live" interviews at the scene of a crime or after an incident. This information can be shared with the Crown Prosecution Service, which can lead to swifter justice. Lord Justice Leveson said in his 2015 *Review of Efficiency in Criminal Proceedings* that presentation of evidence was a key aspiration and BWC cameras on police officers will have a huge impact on the trial process. The report said digital evidence gathering is to be encouraged and the technology is proving reliable. Presently the footage can be downloaded into computers at the Police Station and an audit trail can be implemented. The suspect is given a caution and warned that they are on camera while the camera records the proceedings.

Changes in the law may be needed for BWC at the scene of a crime to deliver swifter, fairer and more cost effective service for victims.

Professionalism and Integrity

Interviewing is complex. An interview should not be used solely for obtaining information about an investigation. It may also be used to provide witnesses and victims with important information, for example, about court proceedings, protection of identity and disclosure. In interviews with victims, the interview should be victim friendly, non-leading and in cases of child or vulnerable adult abuse, some victims might find it therapeutic.

Establish a Professional Relationship

Witnesses and victims will require empathetic treatment from the police handling the case. Witnesses can come in various guises. The CPS guidelines (w.cps.gov.uk ABE in Criminal Proceedings) refer to Hostile Witnesses, Intimidated witnesses, significant witnesses and vulnerable witnesses. The interviewee should be treated fairly and in accordance with legislative guidelines. Interviewers must not allow their personal opinions or beliefs to affect the way in which they deal with witnesses, victims or suspects. This is important in cases such as child abuse, sexual offences and vulnerable adult abuse where stereotypical attitudes can (if not checked) interfere with the appraisal of the merits of the case (Bailey 2001; Bailey et al. 2001).

The Importance of Being Methodical

Using the PEACE model below should allow for good Preparation and Planning for the interview. This model started in the 1990s with a collaboration between psychologists and Police officers in the UK. Commander Tom Williamson of the Metropolitan Police worked with psychologists to develop a model of interviewing that drastically reduces the possibility of "false confessions". The model is widely used in Canada, UK, Australia and New Zealand.

Personal Style

Rapport building can have a significant impact on interview outcomes and successful communication with the interviewee is vital. Establishing a good rapport means adopting an open style as well as showing empathy for the interviewee.

The rapport phase contains three elements: preliminaries, neutral topics and ground rules. The preliminaries are an introduction to the interview. Setting ground rules reduces the anxiety that witnesses may feel in a new situation. Dr. K Smith states (Counsel 2014). A protracted rapport phase obviously lengthens the witness's evidence, increasing the duration of the trial and thus costs.

WISCI

Witness interview strategies for critical incidents (WISCI) should always complement and be complemented by a witness care strategy that is intended to provide support to all witnesses identified by the investigation, irrespective of the extent of their cooperation. Witness care strategies describe the practical arrangements for taking action when a witness's safety is at risk and the mechanisms that have been put in place for their therapeutic support (see Smith and Milne 2017 for further information). (The Journal of Forensic Practice 2018 Witness Interview Strategy)

Roycroft found that witness management was a crucial solving factor in murder enquires (2019) Better management of witnesses may lead to more convictions at court and perhaps more likelihood of suspects being picked out on identity parades.

A witness management strategy should include taking early statements from witnesses and managing them over the period of the enquiry. The management of witnesses over the lifespan of an enquiry is important. This highlights the need for the police to protect and monitor witnesses after interviewing them... This can place an enormous strain on police resources which SIOs need to be aware of and take into account.

Interview Location

The physical setting can have an effect on the establishment of the relationship between those involved especially with children and vulnerable victims. In sexual offences cases, a full Police interview suite which consists of a comfortable interview room with discreet cameras and microphones and full recording facilities will be available. Specially trained officers will be employed in these rooms.

Dealing with Suggestibility

This is when an interviewee is influenced by what they believe the interviewer wants or expects them to say. People vary in the degree to which they are suggestible. Vulnerable people, people with learning difficulties and children, for example, may be more suggestible and require special protection.

The aim of all professional interviewers is to obtain a full and accurate account. To do this they must ask the appropriate questions. The history of police interviews from the Maxwell Confait through to the Birmingham 6 and Guildford 4 course demonstrate how confession evidence can be limited.

The chances of obtaining a high-quality account are increased by the application of good investigative interviewing techniques, underpinned by seven key principles.

These are designed to guide investigators on how to use the cognitive framework for investigative interviewing, for interviewing of crime suspects in operational situations.

These 7 principles are underpinned by Human rights legislation particularly the following (see Appendix 15):

- Article 3: no one shall be subject to torture or inhuman, degrading treatment or punishment… and
- Article 5: everyone has the right to liberty and security and when arrested and deprived of such liberty everyone must be informed promptly.
- *see also Code C of the PACE Codes of Practice in the UK https://www.gov.uk/guidance/police-and-criminal-evidence-act-1984-pace*

Expert Advice

The National Crime Agency (NCA) Specialist operations team can assist major enquires with their The Witness Intermediary Team. This provides support to police officers and prosecutors in the use of *Registered Intermediaries* and offers advice on interview strategies for vulnerable and intimidated witnesses. The dedicated team matches Registered Intermediaries to the needs of vulnerable victims and witnesses in order to achieve best evidence. Registered Intermediaries (RIs) during investigations and during trials has become an established practice. RIs are professional people who have the skills to communicate with vulnerable witnesses.

Most are Speech and Language Therapists, some are also psychologists, occupational therapists, advocates, social workers, nurses and teachers.

Downstream Monitoring or Remote Monitoring of Interviews

The remote monitoring of interviews can improve the quality of an investigative interview by ensuring all the questions are properly covered, The author has used this technique in murder enquires and it further allows appropriate interview techniques to be employed and that all investigative options are explored. .Suspects and their legal representatives must be made fully aware if remote monitoring of the interview is to take place. Home Office Circular 50/1995 Remote Monitoring of Interviews with Suspects (as agreed between ACPO and the Law Society) refers and sets out the minimum standards for doing so. In other jurisdictions, such as Canada, the interviewee is advised in a standard formatted preamble that the interview is being recorded and monitored.

Cognitive Interview Model (P.E.A.C.E. for Suspects and A.B.E. for Victims)

This cognitive interview model is considered to be best practice in many parts of the UK, Australia, Canada, New Zealand and some jurisdictions in the USA. It is highly recommended in terms of both the results that can be obtained and the ethical nature of the model. It has been widely researched and is the preferred model in the UK, Eire and Croatia and many jurisdictions in North America. The ABE model has been used widely for child abuse victims and is also suitable for interviewing adults who have a developmental disability (Bailey et al. 2001; Odeljan et al. 2015). Shepherd (1991, p. 43) used the term 'ethical interviewing' to describe interview techniques where the officer demonstrates a willingness to accept that the interviewee has "the right to be treated with dignity and the right to make free choices – to decide whether or not to engage in the exchange, and to evaluate and to respond to the content and the conduct of the exchange" (Fig. 1).

Achieving Best Evidence in Criminal Proceedings. – Guidance on interviewing victims and witnesses, and guidance on using special measures. https://www.cps. gov.uk/sites/default/files/documents/legal_guidance/best_evidence_in_criminal_ proceedings.pdf.

Achieving best evidence	PEACE
Planning and preparation	Planning and preparation
Establishing rapport	Engage and explain
Initiating and supporting a free narrative account questioning	Account, clarify and challenge
Closing the interview	Closure
Evaluation	Evaluation

Fig. 1 Achieving best evidence and PEACE model

Guidance on Interviewing Suspects under the terms of the P.E.A.C.E. Model, https://assets.publishing.service.gov.uk/government/uploads/system/uploads/attachment_data/file/757585/BAGT-Interviewing-suspects-v4.0ext_archive.pdf.

The basic goal of an interview with a witness is to obtain an accurate and reliable account in a fair way and which is acceptable to the court. The cognitive interview starts with a free narrative phase and then gradually becomes more and more specific in the nature of the questioning in order to elicit further detail.

The Broad Outline of the PEACE Framework for Suspect Interviews

PEACE finds its origins in England in the 1990s and was designed as A non-accusatory, information-gathering approach to investigative interviewing, the PEACE model is considered to be best practice and is suitable for any type of interview; victim, witness or suspect. It was developed in a joint effort between law enforcement and psychologists in England and Wales, and was intended to be used in a way to stem the number of false confessions that were resulting from an accusatory style of interviewing (Fig. 2).

Achieving Best Evidence Model

Lord Levenson in his 2015 report stated that around Achieving Best Evidence (or 'ABE') interview there is "a pressing need to distinguish between the two quite different purposes of the interview: the first is as an investigative tool; and the second is as a means by which evidence of an offence is adduced in court."

The ABE Model consists of four parts:

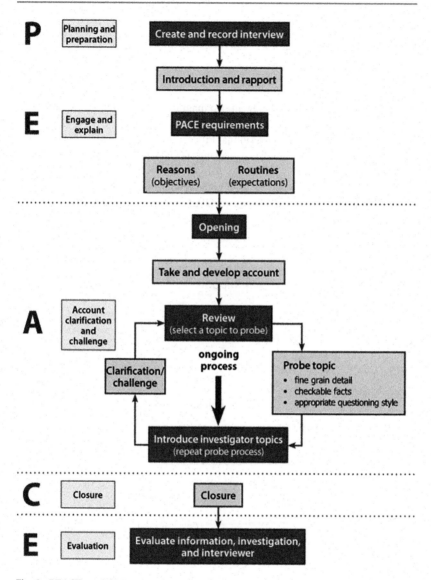

Fig. 2 PEACE model

- Establishing rapport;
- Initiating and supporting a **free narrative** account;
- Questioning; and
- Closure.

The model is represented below in two diagrams. From CPS ABE in Criminal Proceedings, reproduce table (Fig. 3).

Achieving Best Evidence in Criminal Proceedings—Guidance on interviewing victims and witnesses, and guidance on using special measures, Ministry of Justice (2011).

Various question types may be used in the models, but in witness interviews, it is considered good practice to use free recall to encourage the individual to give an account of the situation.

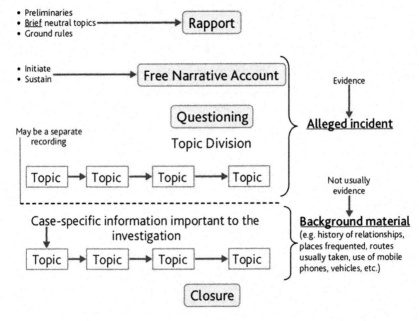

Fig. 3 ABE in criminal proceedings

Free Recall and the Way That Memory Is Stored

Free recall is a system which can be used in interviews to encourage interviewees to put themselves back into the situation they were in when they witnessed the incident.

A free recall interview includes:

- asking the witness to provide an account of the relevant event(s) in their own words (e.g., 'Earlier today you told me that you saw something last week, please tell me about that in your own words')
- adopting a posture of active listening, allowing the witness to pause, and using minimal prompts that do not go beyond the witness's account
- reflecting back what the witness has said, as appropriate
- avoiding interrupting
- identifying manageable topics or episodes in the witness's account to be expanded on and clarified

On video, any specific and detailed questions about the incident asked before the free narrative stage can erroneously become part of the narrative.

Extensive research has found evidence of large and significant increase in correct details and a small increase in errors when using the cognitive model and no differences between the cognitive model and other models when it comes to rates of confabulation (Memon et al. 2010). A direct comparison of the amount of information retrieved by detectives using the cognitive model by Fisher et al. (1989) found that detectives trained in the model elicited 47% more information after than before training, and 63% more information than did the untrained detectives.

Based on what is known about the encoding specificity principle, the interviewer can encourage the witness to revisit their state of mind at the time of the incident, or other details. This an attempt to put the witness back to the context of the incident, called context reinstatement. The interviewer makes every effort to assist the witness to remain in a state of focused concentration and encourages the witnesses' participation, by using open-ended questions.

In terms of retrieval, the interviewer may ask the witness to mentally revisit the incident. The interviewer may ask them to form a mental picture or map of the environment and this could include the placement of objects such as windows or weapons, the lighting or even the temperature. The purpose of this process is to increase the feature overlap between initial witnessing and subsequent retrieval contexts.. At times, it may be beneficial to suggest to the interviewee that they close their eyes and bring their mind back to the location or event.

The interviewer might encourage the witness to report of every detail of the incident that they can recall because a. the witness may not realise what information is significant or not and the recalling of some of these details might allow the witness to remember other details that they initially did not retrieve.

The participant is asked to report the event from several different perspectives; like that of another witness or even a participant. If the participant witnessed a robbery, the interviewer may ask 'What do you think the cashier saw?' and then ask for the participant's perspective. Or, "Pretend you are a fly on the wall during the robbery, tell me what you see".

A related technique is to ask the witness to think about the incident from a different perspective. The witness may be asked to report the event from, for example. The context of not what the witness saw but what he/she heard or smelt. This technique is particularly powerful in sexual assault investigations as victims often remember a distinct smell (e.g., body odour, cologne, sweat etc.,) or tactile feeling (e.g., hair on the suspect's back, clean shaven, unshaven etc.,).

The Four Phases in ABE

Phase 1
Looking at each of four the ABE phases, the rapport stage is first.

- It introduces all those present to the witness using the name by which the witness prefers to be known
- States date, time, and location of interview
- Explanation of the possible use of recording in court and check for witness consent re interview, interviewer selection and possible use in court
- Explanation of the format and structure of the interview process
- Uses neutral topics to relax the child to identify appropriate questioning styles and prepare child for same and to assess the interviewees emotional/social and cognitive development
- Explains that the witness is free to say that they don't know or can't remember when asked a question

Phase 2: Free Narrative
The purpose of this phase is to encourage the child to give an account in his/her own words

- It is important to try in this stage to encourage the child to provide uncontaminated information- the opening question is important
- Try to expand on this without influencing this (use open-ended prompts e.g. "What happened next?")
- At no stage should the child be questioned in this phase about the information they are providing

The Do's and Dont's for this phase are

Do's	Don'ts
- Encourage to speak freely.	- Use known information which has not been mentioned by the child
- Act as facilitator	- Overuse prompts
- Use open-ended prompts e.g. " Did anything else happen"	- Use any indication of approval or disapproval of answers given
- Use active listening - Be tolerant- pauses and silences	

Phase 3 Questioning
The questioning phase is where the witness is asked questions about what they have disclosed in phase 2. Their account will be typically broken down into a number of relatively discrete areas and each will be examined in turn. There are four main types of question and they are less evidentially sound as we progress down from the A to D.

A.
- Questions which provide an unrestricted answers
- Tell me....
- Explain what....
- Describe the....
- This must be appropriate to age/development of the child

B.
- Who....
- What....
- Where....
- When....
- Why...
- How

These are commonly known as the five WH questions.
I keep six honest serving-men
(They taught me all I knew);
Their names are What and Why and When
And How and Where and Who.
Rudyard Kipling, 1902

C. Closed questions
- Provides a limited number of alternative responses
- Children under 6 will normally choose last option
- Always try to give an alternative

For example, "Was the earring in his left ear or his right ear, or you can't remember" (Best option: Describe the person's neck starting at the neck and go from part to part.)

D. Leading questions
- Questions that imply the answer
- Questions that assume facts that are likely to be in dispute
- "Was he wearing a hat?"—where this has not been mentioned before
- Use these with caution particularly regarding central matters in the case

Phase 4 Closure

- This allows the interviewer to check his/her understanding of child's account
- Recap using child's language
- Ensure that the child is not distressed
- Return to neutral topics
- Thank the child/check if there's anything more
- Explain what may happen next

Seminar Questions

Explain the PEACE model for interviewing, how does it contribute to better interviewing of suspects and witnesses?

What are the Four phases of Achieving best Event interviews. Explain how ABE interviews lead to a greater understanding of victims and their needs.

Exam Questions

The Police and Criminal evidence Act that placed formal regulations on custody and interviewing suspects. How did PACE safeguard suspects rights?

References

Bailey, A. (2001) *Factors influencing police investigation of sexual crimes committed against people who have a learning disability and implications for public policy*. Ph.D. thesis.

Bailey, A., Barr, O., & Bunting, B. (2001). Police attitudes toward people who have intellectual disabilities: An evaluation of awareness training. *Intellectual Disability Research, 45*, 1–7.

Fisher, R. P., Geiselman, R. E., & Amador, M. (1989). Field test of the cognitive interview: Enhancing the recollection of actual victims and witnesses of crime. *Journal of Applied Psychology, 74*(5), 722–727.

Frozen watchfulness (http://www.body-languages.net/2014/02/frozen-watchfulness/).

https://www.icmec.org/wp-content/uploads/2015/10/Recantations-and-False-Allegations-Bibliography.pdf. Accessed Aug 2019.

Hodgson, P. (1987). *A practical guide to successful interviewing*. Maidenhead: McGraw Hill.

Memon, A., Meissner, C. A., & Fraser, J. (2010). The cognitive interview: A meta-analytic review and study space analysis of the past 25 years. *Psychology, Public Policy, and Law, 16*(4), 340–372.

Milne, B., & Bull, R. (2003). Interviewing by the police. In D. Carson, & R. Bull (Eds.), *Handbook of Pychology in Legal Contexts* (pp. 111–125).

Milne, B., & Bull, R. (2006). Interviewing victims, including children and people with intellectual disabilities. In G. Davies & M. Kebbell (Eds.), *Practical psychology for forensic investigations* (pp. 8–23). Chichester: Wiley.

Moston. et al. (1992, published 1993). The effects of case characteristics on suspect behaviour during police questioning. *British Journal of Criminology, 32*(1), 23–40. https://doi.org/10.1093/oxfordjournals.bjc.a048178

Odeljan, R., Butorac, K., & Bailey, A. (2015). Investigative Interviews with Children. *European Law Enforcement Research Bulletin, 12*, 18–24.

Recantation and False Allegations of Child Abuse. The National Children's Advocacy Centre US, 2011.

Roycroft, M., & Roach, J. Ed. (2019). *Decision making in Police Enquires and Critical Incidents: What really works*. London: Palgrave.

Shepherd, E. (1991). Ethical interviewing. *Policing, 7*, 42–60.

Williamson, T. (1993). From interrogation to investigative interviewing; strategic trends in police questioning. *Journal of Community and Applied Social Psychology*.

Websites

Investigative interviewing – College of Policing APP https://www.app.college.police.uk/app-content/investigations

Police Practice in Dealing with Severe Addictions and/or Mental Illness: Treatment or Arrest?

Katherine Brine, Lindsey Brine, and Mark Roycroft

Introduction

The interaction between individuals with severe addictions and/or mental illness and police has been the continuing focus of media and public inquiries in many countries. In some cases, the interaction results in the death of the individual due to police utilizing deadly force. Many jurisdictions continue to study this phenomenon with the intent of implementing approach and policy changes so that the use of deadly force can be minimized. This requires a strategy that involves not only the police, but also other community partners including, but not limited to, community programs, homeless shelters, mental health practitioners, social services, and supervised injections sites.

According to the World Health Organization (2020), mental illness is defined as "a combination of abnormal thoughts, emotions, behaviour, and relationships with others. Examples are schizophrenia, depression, intellectual disabilities, and disorders due to drug abuse." Severe addiction, also known as substance use disorder or drug abuse falls under the category of mental illness and occurs when the "recurrent use of alcohol and/or drugs causes clinically significant impairment, including health problems, disability, and failure to meet major responsibilities at work,

K. Brine (✉) • L. Brine • M. Roycroft
Rabdan Academy, Al Bhustan, Abu Dhabi, United Arab Emirates
e-mail: mroycroft@ra.ac.ae

© The Author(s), under exclusive license to Springer Nature Switzerland AG 2021
M. Roycroft, L. Brine (eds.), *Modern Police Leadership*,
https://doi.org/10.1007/978-3-030-63930-3_17

school, or home (SAMHSA 2020)". The most common substances used in this context are alcohol, cocaine, methamphetamines, opioids, and some prescribed medications.

While it is possible for a person with mental health issues to live a seemingly outward life of normalcy and be an effective and contributing member of the community, severe addiction and mental illness often significantly impact daily functioning and require intervention from a medical professional. Unfortunately, these conditions often go undiagnosed or untreated, as the individual afflicted with them seeks no treatment or lacks insight to their mental health related symptoms.

In the context of police encounters, a person with severe addiction and/or mental illness is

> a member of the public whose behaviour brings them into contact with police either because of an apparent need for urgent care within the mental health system, or because they are otherwise experiencing a mental or emotional crisis involving behaviour that is sufficiently erratic, threatening or dangerous that the police are called in order to protect the person or those around them. (Iacobucci 2014, p. 4)

Certainly, front line police officers encounter individuals with severe addictions and/or mental health issues on a daily basis. It has been argued that deinstitutionalization (the shift of persons with mental illness from large scale institutions to the community) was not met with adequate community support and has considerably increased the prevalence of persons with mental illness diverted into the criminal justice system and coming into contact with police (Gur 2010). Police involvement tends to increase in rural and remote communities due a lack of alternative resources. Notably, individuals with severe mental illness/addiction are also significantly more likely to be victimized. For example, the organization Pettitt et al. (2013) outlines that people in the UK with a severe mental illness are:

- Three times more likely to be a victim of crime
- Five times more likely to experience an assault
- Women are 10 times more likely to experience assault
- Both men and women are seven times more likely to experience three or more crimes in a year

Unfortunately, a subset of police encounters escalates into violent confrontations, which are usually the result of an individual wanting to harm themselves or others. These circumstances are of increasing concern and have led to the development of a collaborative community approach centred on evidence-based policing. This approach is based on diverting people away from the formal criminal justice system.

A Policing Approach

Persons with severe addiction and/or mental illness are part of the wider perspective of policing vulnerability. The police have started to employ an Evidence Base Approach (EBP) in their decision making. In Roycroft's Chapter (29), we have seen how the police use the National decision making model and Naturalistic Decision Making. An Evidence Base Policing (EBP) approach informs that decision making on both a tactical and strategic level. The police should create an evidence base to inform that decision making process, helping to identify vulnerable factors at the early stages of interaction with people who have mental health issues. EBP can assist in helping those with mental health issues by achieving the appropriate response upon police arrival. The second goal is to ensure that the vulnerable person avoids unnecessary involvement in the criminal justice system (Williams 2018). This might avoid repeat victimization of vulnerable people.

Dr. Shepherd of the Cardiff Model stated that evidence-informed police services are important to the health of citizens, and formal police–public health partnerships provide a mechanism to uphold public policy. More specifically,

> The Cardiff Violence Prevention Model provides a way for communities to gain a clearer picture about where violence is occurring by combining and mapping both hospital and police data on violence. But more than just an approach to map and understand violence, the Cardiff Model provides a straightforward framework for hospitals, law enforcement agencies, public health agencies, community groups, and others interested in violence prevention to work together and develop collaborative violence prevention strategies. (Mercer Kollar et al. 2017, p. 1)

Mental health policing has seen significant change in recent years with the emphasis on collaboration with mental health professionals. The Police and Crime Commissioners (PCCs) in the UK are victim focused and in places like Staffordshire Police, National Health Service (NHS) staff and police work together to ensure individuals get the right support. This has reduced the number of people detained in police custody under the Mental Health Act by 80% from 168 in 2012 to 33 in 2015/16 (PCC annual report). The police work with local crisis teams and provide the initial response for patrol officers engaged with people with mental health issues.

Fact Sheet
Evidence Based Policing (EBP)
   The term was first used by professor Larry Sherman in 1998 and refers to building an evidence base to inform police decision making. It is informed practice that

examines what works in a practical context, base. According to Sherman EBP is comprised of the "3 T's": (1) targeting, (2) testing, and (3) tracking. **Targeting** *deals with systematic ranking and a comparison of levels of harm/risk in certain locations and times (see Hotspots Intelligence Chapter).* **Testing** *by empirical research methods allows the police to implement strategies and* **track** *their effectiveness.*

Evidence Based Policing seeks to assist the understanding of why and how the police act or behave in certain situations. This can establish a base of evidence that can then inform police staff on how future situations should be dealt with. This knowledge exchange is important to enhance the legitimacy of the police and improve public safety (Sherman 1998). This establishment of best practice and a complex body of knowledge are important for the standing of the Police Service. Nowhere is EBP more important than the study of police interaction with those suffering from mental health issues. The HMICFRS report of 2018 (see below) concluded that "police forces have an inadequate picture of the extent and nature of the demand they face from people with mental health problems."

A UK Perspective

In the book *Police Chiefs in the UK,* most of those engaged at the top of British policing advocated that there was a greater need for Integration and cross-agency working to protect the vulnerable in society (Roycroft 2016). One Police and Crime Commissioner (PCC20) talked of the need for integrated authorities and information sharing 'with a need to overcome data sharing barriers especially with regards to multi-agency tackling of the most problematic people and families'. PCC38 stated that he had set up a victims help centre with two specialists in mental health and hate crime. Stopping the revolving door of justice and keeping young offenders out of prison by working with courts and local prisons was mentioned by a number of PCCs. One PCC stated that he paid for training in doctor's surgeries to help understand mental health issues. He commented that 30% of calls to the Police were for mental health. When dealing with mental health issues many of those interviewed felt responses by the most appropriate agency and information sharing were the key to success.

Several Chief Constables mentioned the Cardiff Model (see above) which allows for deeper integration with Children's Services, mental health professionals and the National Health Service (NHS). Dr. Shepherd who formed the unit (see above) in 1997 felt that this was essential to deal with the threat, harm, and risk (under the UK strategic policing requirement see Appendix) and to assist victims and future victims. This has been further enhanced by the Care Concordat signed by 27 different agencies in 2014 including the police who see their function as:-

- Access to support before crisis point
- Urgent and emergency access to crisis care
- The right quality of treatment and care when in crisis
- Recovery and preventing future crises

Legislation

The Police in the UK are given powers under the Mental Health Act of 2007 to deal with members of the public who need immediate attention.

Fact Sheet; Police Powers in the UK to deal with mental illness.

A police officer has a power under section 136(1)(a) MHA 2007 to remove a person who appears to be suffering from a mental disorder and to be in need of immediate care or control to a place of safety (or keep them at a place of safety). Previously, a person could only be removed to a place of safety if he or she was found in a place "to which the public have access". This power can be exercised where the person is in any place other than, broadly, a "private dwelling" or its associated buildings or grounds. A Police station cannot be used for those under 18 years of age as a place of safety.

The Care Act 2014 provides a method by which the police are able to refer and direct an individual towards services provided by the relevant local authority. If an individual comes to the attention of the police because they are in need of care, police may submit a referral request for assessment of needs to their local authority.

The Bradley Report (2009) was an independent review set up the report made 82 recommendations for improving the treatment of people with mental health problems and people with learning difficulties in the criminal justice system in England and Wales. The development of liaison and diversion services and a single Operating Model by NHS England is a significant change that should bring about major improvements to the criminal justice system. It provided this definition of Diversion:

'Diversion' is a process whereby people are assessed and their needs identified as early as possible in the offender pathway (including prevention and early intervention), thus informing subsequent decisions about where an individual is best placed to receive treatment, taking into account public safety, safety of the individual and punishment of an offence.

In a follow report in 2013 the Bradley report reported progress in the use of street triage' and "having mental health practitioners in police control centres seems to be ….useful. Where street triage, in whatever form, works well it provides two key components

1) Immediate mental health expertise,
2) Immediate access to information on people known to services. Some areas have taken this latter point further by having miniature care plans for known individuals prominent on the police information system".

The HMICFRS (2018) report "Picking up the Pieces" stated that too many people were being directed to the Police where they should have been receiving treatment from healthcare professionals. The treatment and response needs to concentrate on long term care rather than immediate point of contact between the Police and the vulnerable. Many Forces have introduced street triage systems to deal with these issues.

Street Triage System: The Police and Partner Agencies

The street triage system has been adopted in the UK and versions of it have been used in North America. In the West Midlands Police Force, at a 'Mental Health Triage Pilot' run by the Department of Health, police officers work with mental health nurses and paramedics in an unmarked car. This has seen a reduction of people brought into police custody under S136 MHA, which was used 176 times during 1058 call-outs. Only two were subsequently taken to police stations (PCC report).

In Manchester, the local Force Greater Manchester Police (GMP) have trained constables in comprehensive mental health awareness training to become crisis intervention officers (CIOs). CIOs are trained to attend incidents involving people who are seen to be experiencing mental health issues, understand the issues and provide support accordingly. Like Staffs and GMP, Leicestershire Police have a street triage car which has reduced the section 136 MHA detention rate by 33% from the level prior to the introduction of the car.

The Canadian Experience

Although similar to the UK in many ways, including history and legislation, Canada is significantly different in the way it deals with severe addictions and mental health largely because of its vast geography and alternative approaches.

Rural and Remote Communities

Owing to the immense number of police encounters involving those with severe addictions and mental illness, and the numerous unfortunate consequences that can occur, it is apparent that further research needs to address the nature of these interactions so that appropriate resources to handle these situations effectively may be established. Notably, the primary focus of much research on policing has been in the context of urban and suburban police organizations (Payne et al. 2005; Weisheit et al. 1994; Wood and Trostle 1997). While this research has provided a wealth of information pertaining to policing issues, it is important to consider the differences that exist in rural and northern police departments, particularly in a Canadian context. Prior to discussing the implications these differences have in the context of police response to mental-health-related emergencies, it is important to highlight the literature that differentiates police roles in urban versus rural environments.

Generally, from urban to rural environments, police roles contrast between that of the "urban" law enforcer who primarily utilizes methods of crime control, and the "rural" officer who emphasizes crime prevention and performs various service activities within the community (Landau 1996; Payne et al. 2005). Consequently, research consistently stipulates that police duties in small communities extend beyond those of urban police officers and that officers working in rural or northern settings carry out a wider range of tasks than in urban departments; many of which are unrelated to crime incidents (Weisheit et al. 1994). Furthermore, rural police "fulfill several roles simultaneously," many of which fall outside the traditional law-enforcement-oriented policing mandate (Payne et al. 2005, p. 38; Wood and Trostle 1997).

Evidently, there are numerous considerations with regard to policing these communities that may not be apparent in urban settings. To highlight police roles in rural settings, Weisheit, Wells, and Falcone (1994) identify three themes that are related to the relationship between police and their community based on observations in small town regions of the United States. They state that in rural environments: (1) police are accountable for their community, (2) police are more connected with, and integrated into their communities owing to personal level interactions, and (3) rural police are oriented towards solving general problems rather than crime incidents exclusively.

As illustrated by Weisheit et al. (1994), in small towns, police are recognized as an integral part of the community. Moreover, as members of the community themselves, they often know offenders and victims personally. Owing to this high level of personal interaction, the level of formality for resolving incidents also varies from rural to urban environments (Payne et al. 2005). Close personal relationships with community members often provide police with the opportunity to informally resolve issues as an alternative to arrest or formal processing. However, the small population and close connections may also result in higher expectations of the police by the public and leave officer actions highly visible, thus reducing their level of discretion and increasing their level of accountability (Weisheit et al. 1994).

To further emphasize the contrast between policing in urban versus rural settings, Wood and Trostle (1997) explore police roles in remote Arctic communities; specifically in Canada's Baffin Region, using RCMP file data collected for a multi-year Baffin Region Crime and Justice study. Findings from their analysis suggest that, in light of geographic isolation and a considerable lack of economy, police in Arctic and sub-Arctic communities perform an extensive number of tasks that go beyond the duties of officers working in urban regions. Moreover, police officers originally from the south of Canada and who primarily work in these communities are often unfamiliar with the various environmental and cultural differences, possibly impacting the effectiveness of their policing strategies.

In their review of Yukon's Royal Canadian Mounted Police (RCMP) "M" Division, Arnold, Clark, and Cooley (2010) encapsulate the responsibilities of police in northern communities:

> Policing in northern communities is a high-demand, high-expectation occupation: there is a high demand on members' resourcefulness and creativity and high expectations by citizens, who expect members to not only engage in law enforcement but also be visible and participate in community life. The process by which members become accepted by the community and establish relationships with community members is one of the most crucial aspects of policing in northern communities. (p. 7–8).

Evidently, as previously asserted (Landau 1996; Payne et al. 2005), a "law enforcement" approach may be ideal in urban settings, albeit, in remote and rural regions, establishing a strong relationship with the community is essential (Wood and Trostle 1997).

Access to Services

Accessibility and a lack of appropriate services in rural and northern communities is a recurring theme throughout the literature. Specifically, the availability of psychiatric and social services in these communities is either non-existent or not easily accessible (Landau 1996; Payne et al. 2005; Weisheit et al. 1994). As a result, police are the primary 24-hour resource available for responding to mental health emergencies.

The general lack of resources in these settings may be attributed to a scarcity of qualified permanent employees, (Landau 1996) and minimal staffing in health centres (Herrington 2012). Particularly, the significant shortage of health care professionals can be credited to the remoteness and isolation that restricts medical professionals from interacting with other medical peers and furthering their education (Kirby and Keon 2006).

Additionally, in rural communities, resources are often spread thin; police have longer distances to travel to the nearest health centre (Herrington 2012; Ontario Mental Health and Addictions Knowledge Exchange Network [OMHAKEN] 2009), and fewer transportation options are available (OMHAKEN 2009). While 80% of Canada's population lives in urban settings, many live in remote regions where the nearest mental health service may be a far commute, or not accessible by road (Cotton and Coleman 2010). Moreover, most mental-health-related calls generally occur in the late evening and on weekends when the fewest resources are available (Lee et al. 2008). It is noteworthy that lack of access, owing to both geographical barriers and limited available services, greatly contributes to the criminalization of individuals with mental illness who live in rural regions. A study conducted in Mississippi exploring the criminalization of people with serious mental illness living in rural areas found that 60% of SAMI individuals are held in jail without criminal charges (Sullivan and Spritzer 1997). When hospital beds, access to mental health services, or transportation to hospitals is not immediately available, SAMI individuals are detained in jails without criminal charges and without appropriate treatment (Sullivan and Spritzer 1997).

The evident "difficulty of geographic access" (Wood and Trostle 1997, p. 378) and need for services generate various obstacles for police; and thus, communities highly reliant on medical and mental health services are left without basic resources necessary to address these prevalent issues.

Prevalence and Nature of Police Interactions

Since the mid-1950s, it has been argued that deinstitutionalization (the shift of persons with mental illness from institutions to the community) has considerably increased the prevalence of persons with mental illness diverted into the criminal justice system and coming into contact with police (Gur 2010). Notably, however, the true impact of deinstitutionalization on mental-health-related police contacts is under debate within the literature.

In a comprehensive review of several Canadian studies, Brink et al. (2011) established that approximately 5% of police dispatches or encounters involve mental illness; although the prevalence of these interactions has been found to range from 1% to as high as 31% (Brink et al. 2011). For example, research conducted in a mid-sized Canadian city, examining rates and patterns of police encounters among individuals with and without mental illness, found that 3% of police interactions involve mental illness (Crocker et al. 2009). In contrast, a 2007 Vancouver Police Department (VPD) survey found that of 1154 dispatch calls, 31% involved a person with mental illness (Wilson-Bates 2008). It is also noteworthy that prevalence rates may include multiple contacts with the same individual, as repetitive encounters are a common finding throughout the literature (e.g. Crocker et al. 2009; Reuland et al. 2009).

The high volume of police contact with mental illness is conducive to extreme variation in the nature of these encounters. Cotton and Coleman (2010) outline the general nature of police interactions with mental illness in a Canadian context. The extent of these formal and informal interactions include: apprehensions under the Mental Health Act (MHA), arrests and disturbances in which the person turns out to be mentally ill, disturbances in which an individual appears to be mentally ill, situations in which a mental illness is the victim of a crime, and social support and informal contacts by police (p. 303).

The extremely diverse nature of police encounters with mental illness is further demonstrated in findings from a British Columbia (BC) study relating to how people with mental illness perceive and interact with the police (Brink et al. 2011). While the most common type of interaction was being transported by police to hospital or jail (90%), reasons for police contact also included: mental health crises, intoxication, being served with a warrant, request for assistance (to report a crime, as a witness to a crime, or as a victim of a crime), commission of a violent or non-violent criminal offence, and public disturbance (Brink et al. 2011).

Evidently, police interactions with mental illness can be both formal and informal in nature. Moreover, through these encounters, police have the discretion to choose between both formal and informal means of resolving the situation (Wells and Schafer 2006). Informal resolutions include leaving the individual at the scene, in the care of another person (e.g. family member), or recommending treatment options/available services (Ritter et al. 2011; Teplin 1986, as cited in Lurigio et al. 2008; Wells and Schafer 2006). Conversely, formal police interventions may include diversion into the mental health or criminal justice system through means of apprehension under the Mental Health Act, or arrest (Wells and Schafer 2006).

Mental health legislation is at the provincial or territorial level in Canada, not federal. It is similar legislation amongst the jurisdictions. Section 28 of the British Columbia Mental Health Act involves the apprehension by police of individuals (based on personal observations or information received), who are acting in a manner likely to endanger themselves or others and who exhibit apparent signs of mental disorder. According to section one, a 'person with a mental disorder' is someone "who has a disorder of the mind that requires treatment and seriously impairs the person's ability: (a) to react appropriately to the person's environment, or (b) to associate with others" (Mental Health Act [MHA] 1996). Generally, following apprehension, the police bring the individual to a physician for examination; usually in the Emergency Department of the local hospital. Notably, however, not all hospitals are 'designated facilities' for the purpose of civil commitment, and in less populated regions, the nearest designated facility may be far away.

Specifically, s. 28 states:

(1) A police officer or constable may apprehend and immediately take a person to a physician for examination if satisfied from personal observations, or information received, that the person

  (a) is acting in a manner likely to endanger that person's own safety or the safety of others, and

  (b) is apparently a person with a mental disorder.

(2) A person apprehended under subsection (1) must be released if a physician does not complete a medical certificate in accordance with section 22 (3) and (4).

Mental Health Act apprehensions vary greatly in terms of individual characteristics and outcomes. Through their investigation of patients brought to the ER by police under MHA provisions in Victoria, Australia, Al-Khafaji, Loy, and Kelly (2014), established that the most common reason for apprehension is a threat of harm to one's self (65%). Of the 197 presentations analysed in the study, the most common diagnosis following assessment was self-harm ideation or intent; the second being drug or alcohol effect. With regard to apprehension outcome, 67% were discharged to home, 13% resulted in voluntary psychiatric admission, and 13% in involuntary psychiatric admission (Al-Khafaji et al. 2014).

In the context of mental health emergencies, recent research in British Columbia states that 17% of mental illness are apprehended or detained under the MHA and 15% are taken to hospital for psychiatric treatment (Brink et al. 2011). In 2007, an Ontario Police Services survey documented 40,000 mental illness/police contacts; over 16,000 of which were MHA apprehensions (40%) (Durbin et al. 2010). Arrest or apprehension of mental illness momentarily protects the public and the mental illness, best serving the needs of both the individual and society. However, the long-term consequences of quick release and a lack of adequate treatment contribute to the revolving door phenomenon whereby individuals cycle in and out of the criminal justice system (Durbin et al. 2010; Gur 2010).

Best Practices for Diversion

▶ **The Vancouver Police Mental Health Unit: A Role Model** In October of 2011, the VPD and Vancouver Coastal Health Authority (VCH) committed to work together to improve the quality of life for their mutual clients who suffer from mental illness and problematic substance use and addiction. The collaboration was aimed at reducing harm to clients and to the community, as well as reducing the clients' involvement with the criminal justice system, law enforcement, and emergency health services. The VPD's Mental Health Unit and involvement with the VCH Assertive Community Treatment (ACT) teams and the Assertive Outreach Team (AOT) were the result of this agreement.

Assertive Community Treatment (ACT) Teams

Assertive Community Treatment teams are full-service mental health programs providing "wrap-around" care. The first ACT team was created in January of 2012. The five Vancouver ACT teams are managed by Vancouver Coastal Health. There are 10 to 12 people on an ACT team, including psychiatrists, social workers, nurses, vocational counsellors, occupational and recreational therapists, and peer counsellors, among others. Two full-time VPD officers work with the teams, providing daily police support. Teams focus on the well-being of clients who are experiencing challenges related to community living, and who have an extensive history of police involvement and high use of health services. They have high-risk behaviour and long-standing complex mental health issues. Their goal is to provide longer-term psychosocial support to prepare clients for a successful transition to community-based care. ACT teams may assist with finding long-term 24/7 health care, support with life skills, job training, assistance with housing, and help maintaining physical and mental wellness.

Assertive Outreach Team (AOT)

The Assertive Outreach Team is a VPD / Vancouver Coastal Health mental health program, which began in March 2014. The team provides short-term transitional support for clients with moderate to severe substance use and/or mental health issues as they go from hospital or jail to a community service provider. The clients are often experiencing challenges living in the community, and have a history of police involvement and complex mental health issues. Team members are psychiatrists, nurses, clinical supervisors, and police officers. During a one- to two-month period, the team connects individuals with their primary care provider and uses a creative and collaborative problem-solving approach. The goal is to reduce incidents of violence and self-harm, prevent further deterioration in their quality of life, and reduce their involvement with the criminal justice system. Police officers play a larger role in the AOT than the ACT, including locating clients who may be at-risk and preventing issues before they happen.

Car 87- Mental Health Car

Car 87 teams a Vancouver Police constable with a registered nurse or a registered psychiatric nurse to provide on-site assessments and intervention for people living with mental illness. The nurse and the police officer work as a team in assessing, managing, and deciding about the most appropriate action, which may include referrals for community-based mental health follow-up or emergency intervention. The Car 87 program is a partnership between the Vancouver Police Department and Vancouver Coastal Health's Access & Assessment Centre's Crisis Response Team. The Car 87 program started on a trial basis in 1978 and was formalized in 1987. In addition to Car 87, the Access & Assessment Centre operates a telephone crisis line where nurses assist callers in crisis, provide information pertaining to resources and triage situations to the appropriate resources: Car 87, ambulance ors police as required.

Harm Reduction- Best Practice

Closely tied into the concept of caring for those with mental health issues, is the ever-growing response to severe addictions by using "harm reduction" or "harm minimization" approach. Traditionally, the war on drugs has been a two pillared approach focusing on supply reduction and demand reduction. Reducing the supply of drugs from source countries often has little known corollary impacts such as increasing local poverty levels, decreasing school attendance, and impacting the health of locals through chemically driven crop eradication., Similarly, attempts to reduce the demand for drugs by way of the death penalty, harsh jail terms, and mandatory drug treatment have had minimal success. Despite this, illicit drugs continue to be a major source of revenue for both organized crime and terrorist groups. In the World Drug Report (2015), the United Nations Office on Drugs and Crime indicated that "… the harm caused by illicit drugs has a significant impact on peace, security, and development".

Furthermore, the report supports the use of evidence-based intervention in all three of the areas noted above.

The third pillar, "harm reduction", has had a significant impact on drug use by allowing a human rights based approach to illicit drug use.

> The ideal of a 'drug free world' (to quote from the declaration adopted by the UN General Assembly in 1998), and its required prohibitionist, punitive approach, may be based on an overarching concern for the 'health and welfare of mankind.' But in practice, the health and welfare of those in need of special care and assistance—people who use drugs, those most at risk from drug related harm, and the most marginalized communities—have not been a priority. They have instead been overshadowed, and often badly damaged, by the pursuit of that drug-free ideal. (Barrett et al. 2008, p. 3)

In essence, the drive to helping those vulnerable people who have severe addictions through safer drug use, treatment and rehabilitation should be one of the primary goals of the police and government response. Some estimates indicate that drug rehabilitation for one person costs only a quarter of a prison term (NIDA 2020).

Canada has taken a highly progressive and proactive approach to "harm reduction" since the late 1990s. An international study on the relationship between the police and supervised injection sites that included Australia, Canada, Denmark, France, Germany, Netherlands, and Spain indicated that: "Five key contributors to cooperative SIS-police relationships emerged from the data: early engagement and dialogues; supportive police chiefs; dedicated police liaisons; negotiated boundary agreements; and regular face-to-face contact. Most participants perceived the less formalized, on-the-ground approach to relationship-building between police and SIS adopted in their city to be working well in general. SIS managers and police participants reported a lack of formal police training on harm reduction, and some thought that training was unnecessary given the relatively positive local SIS-police relationships they reported." (https://www.sciencedirect.com/journal/international-journal-of-drug-policy/vol/61/suppl/C).

With the ever-increasing global opioid crisis, these are valuable points for those cities or countries establishing these sites. A 2020 study in Scotland noted that 75% of people who use illegal intravenous drugs support the creation of supervised injections sites to address their concerns about drug related harm, including the transmission of infectious diseases (Trayner et al. 2020).

▶ **A Canadian Approach to Harm Reduction and Mental Health: Providing Supervised Injection Sites**

encourage abstinence from drugs, reduction in drug use, drug substitute therapies, or needle syringe programs.

provide counselling, education, and support to addicts

reach problematic IV drug users and provide pathways and opportunities for treatment and support

reduce drug-related loitering, drug dealing, and petty crime

reduce healthcare costs including ambulance call-outs and hospital admission.

reduce overdoses (fatal and non-fatal)

reduce public littering of injecting equipment

reduce the harm caused by blood borne diseases such as Hepatitis C and HIV/AIDS and other medical maladies.

ensure trained staff are able to provide immediate medical interventions in the case of overdoses uphold and promote the dignity of all people who use the service and promote awareness and understanding in the community

▶ Human Rights and Mental Health in Canada: Supreme Court of Canada 2011

Supervised injection sites

In 2003, health authorities in British Columbia opened a supervised drug injection site to combat the epidemic of HIV/AIDS and hepatitis C in the Downtown Eastside of Vancouver. In order for the operation of these sites to be considered legal, the federal Minister of Health must grant an exemption from the prohibitions of possession and trafficking of controlled substances. In 2008, the BC health authorities made an application for a new exemption before the previous one expired. The Minister denied the application. The organization that ran the site and a number of its clients argued that the Minister's decision violated the right to life, liberty and security of the person.

The Supreme Court found that the Minister's decision would prevent injection drug users from accessing life-saving health services. As a result, the health of the clients would be threatened and their lives would be endangered. Evidence showed that in over the 8 years of its operation, the safe injection site had proven to save lives with no known negative impact on public safety or health. The Minister's decision went against the public safety objectives it was supposed to be pursuing. It was also arbitrary, meaning it had no rational connection to the government's stated purpose of protecting lives and health. The Court ordered the Minister to grant the exemption.

Canada (Attorney General) v. PHS Community Services Society, 2011 SCC 44

Case Study

Thomas Orchard case

Thomas Orchard, 32, died in hospital seven days after being arrested and brought to Heavitree Road police station in Exeter, Devon, in October 2012. Mr. Orchard, who had paranoid schizophrenia, was held down in Police Custody suites, handcuffed and a large webbing belt placed across his face. Police officers entered the call 12 minutes later and found him dead. Mr. Orchard was experiencing a mental health crisis having not taken his medication. The Police officers involved in the restrain of Mr. Orchard were charged and subject to a trail at Court. A pathologist found he died from severe hypoxic-ischemic brain damage, caused by a prolonged cardio-respiratory arrest "following a violent struggle and period of physical restraint". An Emergency Response Belt (ERB) was placed on Mr. Orchard and Devon and Cornwall Police were subsequently fined under the Health and Safety Act.

A review into policing and mental health in the county found that 15–25% of police time was connected to mental health issues. A mental health programme manager was recruited by the police and crime commissioner (PCC) who led several programmes to address mental health issues.

Mental Health and Counter-Terrorism

Mental Health affects all sections of society and we have seen Government Policy in the UK formalize safeguarding as a central part of the country's counter-terrorism prevent strand of the Contest strategy. When referencing the management of terrorist offenders, the strategy also cited 'mental health issues' as a distinct terrorism-related 'vulnerability' (HM Government 2018, p. 41). It created hubs collaborating between National Counter-Terrorism Policing, the NHS (National Health Service) through the Department of Health, as well as the Home Office (National Police Chiefs' Council). The hubs received joint funding from each of these bodies. The aim of the hubs was to assess the value of mental health professionals working alongside counter-terrorism police officers. This is in relation to the management of individuals referred to the police with known or suspected mental disorders who may be vulnerable to radicalization and extremism. The hubs could challenge the traditional roles of a mental health care provider, is that they open for diverting vulnerable people away from prosecution and into 'urgent care pathway' treatment (only) if they are considered at risk of radicalisation or of committing a terrorism-related offence. The 2018 UK counter-terrorism strategy implicitly proposed a partial discursive recasting of counter-terrorism: from being about protecting (the public and the state) from security risks, to providing support (to individuals) in managing and overcoming The formalization of mental health vulnerability and safeguarding in UK counter-terrorism seems not to have changed counter-terrorism's overall risk calculus, but simply incorporated vulnerability as 'early' type of (potential) risk. While 'vulnerability' from the perspective of the state has conventionally been connected with lack of capacity and with care needs (e.g. UK Care Act 2014), UK counter-terrorism now appears to be increasingly direct in linking mental health vulnerability to a potential capacity for involvement in terrorism. From a primary conceptual location within a domain of care, 'vulnerability' now seems relatively more closely associated with an early stage of a foreseen pre-attack timeline, prompting responses emphasizing crime risk management such as surveillance and investigation rather than a treatment pathway.

Their remit is to identify referrals to Prevent (see Counter Terrorism Chapter), that may have mental health difficulties at the earliest possible opportunity and, where appropriate, to assist them in accessing mainstream services for help.

The pilot, which was launched in April 2016, is split across three areas—West Midlands, North West and London—and will conclude in March 2017. These areas were chosen because of their existing close links with NHS partners. Collectively the three hubs aim to provide a national resource although the majority of their cases will be local referrals.

The development of the service was based on a programme of work undertaken by Birmingham and Solihull Mental Health NHS Foundation Trust between 2012–2016. The aim of this work was to explore the mental health needs of individuals referred to Prevent and develop effective ways of providing help and diverting them to mental health services. Activities included an evaluation of current pathways, joint working and training courses, research and case management. The research included a review of 657 individuals referred to Prevent nationally to explore the prevalence of a broad range of mental health and psychological difficulties. This was identified in up to half of the cases.

The cases related to a range of ideologies—mainly Islamist but also extreme right wing, animal rights or where no clear ideology was identified.

The Mental Health Hubs also incorporate best practice from other established mental health services, such as Street Triage and Liaison and Diversion services and FTAC (the Fixated Threat assessment Centre) where NHS and Police work in close partnership to identify and support vulnerable individuals with mental health difficulties.

Funding for the pilot and the evaluation is provided by national counter-terrorism policing, the NHS and the Home Office.

Conclusion

There have been deep-seated changes in the mental health policing milieu over recent years. Deinstitutionalization has led to greater emphasis on community care. The Police found themselves in the invidious role of being the primary 24/7 service that could answer and deal with mental health episodes. The move to triage vehicles and joint collaboration enables vulnerable people to receive the treatment they need and to divert them from the criminal justice system. Clearly, only a few short years ago, many of these initiative such as supervised injection sites and a mental health triage system, would have been unheard of. The mental health crisis continues and with the ongoing Covid-19 pandemic, there has been a significant increase.

Mental illness is an omnipresent social problem in our society. Its impact is compounded in rural northern communities by the very nature of their small size and limited infrastructures. The pervasive effect of mental health issues in these contexts is detrimental to patients, families, communities, health services, and to the police. Addressing the issue of mental health and its associated impact requires a collaborative multi-agency approach. The cooperation of multiple stakeholders is required to define and implement an effective and lasting solution.

Seminar Questions

- Is a police station the right place for a mentally ill person in an urban environment?
- Is a police station the right place for a mentally ill person in a remote or rural environment?
- How should Police deal with a person who presents mental health problems?
- Is a multi-disciplinary approach to mental health and severe addictions possible regardless of the community size? How would you overcome the challenges of lack of resources and great distances if so?
- How can triage assist the police in dealing with mental health?
- Discuss how different agencies can work together to deal with mental health issues in the community?
- What do we mean by diversion in dealing with mentally ill members of the public?
- Are supporting harm reductions strategies such as supervised injection sites really the role of police?

Exam Question

In dealing with mentally ill vulnerable people, how can the Police divert such vulnerable people from the criminal justice system? Explain your answer by elaborating current Police practice and the potential benefits for society and the individuals concerned.

References

Al-Khafaji, K., Loy, J., & Kelly, A. M. (2014). Characteristics and outcome of patients brought to an emergency department by police under the provisions (Section 10) of the Mental Health Act in Victoria, Australia. *International Journal of Law and Psychiatry, 37*(4), 415–419.

Arnold, S., Clark, P., & Cooley, D. (2010). *Sharing common ground: Review of Yukon's Police Force: Executive summary*. Retrieved from the Yukon Government website: http://www.policereview2010.gov.yk.ca/

Barrett, D., Lines, R., Schleifer, R., Elliott, R., & Bewley-Taylor, D. (2008). *Recalibrating the regime: The need for a human rights-based approach to drug policy*. London: Beckley Foundation and International Harm Reduction Association.

Bradley, K. (2009). *The Bradley Report: Lord Bradley's review of people with mental health problems or learning disabilities in the criminal justice system*. Retrieved from https://webarchive.nationalarchives.gov.uk/20130105193845/ http://www.dh.gov.uk/prod_consum_dh/groups/dh_digitalassets/documents/digitalasset/MentalHealthCrisisCareConcordat https://www.crisiscareconcordat.org.uk

Brink, J., Livingston, J., Desmarais, S., Greaves, C., Maxwell, V., Michalak, E., Parent, R., Verdun-Jones, S., & Weaver, C. (2011). *A study of how people with mental illness perceive and interact with the police*. Calgary: Mental Health Commission of Canada.

Care Act, UK Public General Acts (2014, c.23). Retrieved from http://www.legislation.gov.uk/ukpga/2014/23/contents/enacted

Cotton, D., & Coleman, T. G. (2010). Canadian police agencies and their interactions with persons with a mental illness: A systems approach. *Police Practice and Research, 11*(4), 301–314.

Crocker, A. G., Hartford, K., & Heslop, L. (2009). Gender differences in police encounters among persons with and without serious mental illness. *Psychiatric Services (Washington, D.C.), 60*(1), 86–93.

Durbin, J., Lin, E., & Zaslavaska, N. (2010). Police-citizen encounters that involve mental health concerns: Results of an Ontario police services survey. *Canadian Journal of Community Mental Health, 29*, 53–72.

Gur, O. M. (2010). Persons with mental illness in the criminal justice system: Police interventions to prevent violence and criminalization. *Journal of Police Crisis Negotiations, 10*(1–2), 220–240.

Her Majesty's Inspectorate of the Constabulary and Fire & Rescue Services [HMICFRS]. (2018). *Policing and mental health: Picking up the pieces*. Retrieved from: https://www.

justiceinspectorates.gov.uk/hmicfrs/wp-content/uploads/policing-and-mental-health-picking-up-the-pieces.pdf

Herrington, V. (2012). Inter-agency cooperation and joined-up working in police responses to persons with a mental illness: Lessons from new South Wales. *Policing, 6*(4), 388–397.

Iacobucci, F. (2014) *Police encounters with people in crisis: An independent review of the use of lethal force by the Toronto Police Service.* Retrieved from http://www.tpsreview. ca/docs/Police-Encounters-With-People-In-Crisis.pdf

Kirby, M. J., & Keon, W. J. (2006). *Out of the shadows at last: Transforming mental health, mental illness and addiction services in Canada.* Retrieved from http://www.mental-healthcommission.ca/English/system/files/private/t/out_of_the_shadows_at_last_-_full_0.pdf

Landau, T. (1996). Policing and security in four remote aboriginal communities: A challenge to coercive models of police work. *Canadian Journal of Criminology, 38*(1), 1–32.

Lee, S., Brunero, S., Fairbrother, G., & Cowan, D. (2008). Profiling police presentations of mental health consumers to an emergency department. *International Journal of Mental Health Nursing, 17*, 311–316.

Lurigio, A. J., Smith, A., & Harris, A. (2008). The challenge of responding to people with mental illness: Police officer training and special programmes. *The Police Journal, 81*, 295–323. https://doi.org/10.1358/pojo.2008.81.4.431.

Mental Health Act, Revised Statutes of British Columbia (1996, c. 288). Retrieved from http://www.bclaws.ca/civix/document/id/complete/statreg/96288_01

Mental Health Crisis Care Concord at https://www.crisiscareconcordat.org.uk

Mercer Kollar, L. M., Jacoby, S. F., Ridgeway, G., & Sumner, S. A. (2017). *Cardiff model toolkit: Community Guidance for violence prevention.* Division of Violence Prevention, National Center for Injury Prevention and Control, Centers for Disease Control and Prevention: Atlanta.

National Institute on Drug Abuse [NIDA]. (2020). *Is providing drug abuse treatment to offenders worth the financial investment?.* Retrieved from https://www.drugabuse.gov/publications/principles-drug-abuse-treatment-criminal-justice-populations-research-based-guide/providing-drug-abuse-treatment-to-offenders-worth-financial-investment on 2020, July 6

Ontario Mental Health and Addictions Knowledge Exchange Network. (2009). *Building bridges between community mental health and justice sectors: A work in progress.* Retrieved from http://eenet.ca/wpcontent/uploads/2013/10/10_09_Building-Bridges-Supp-Report-FINAL.pdf

Payne, B. K., Berg, B. L., & Sun, I. Y. (2005). Policing in small town America: Dogs, drunks, disorder, and dysfunction. *Journal of Criminal Justice, 33*(1), 31–41.

Pettitt, B., Greenhead, S., Khalifeh, H., Drennan, V., Hart, T., Hogg, J., Borschmann, R., Mamo, E., & Moran, P. (2013). *At risk, yet dismissed: The criminal victimisation of people with mental health problems* (Project Report). London: Victim Support, Mind.

Reuland, M. M., Schwarzfeld, M., & Draper, L. (2009). *Law enforcement responses to people with mental illnesses: A guide to research-informed policy and practice.* Retrieved from https://www.bja.gov/Publications/CSG_le-research.pdf

Ritter, C., Teller, J. L. S., Marcussen, K., Munetz, M. R., & Teasdale, B. (2011). Crisis intervention team officer dispatch, assessment, and disposition: Interactions with individuals with severe mental illness. *International Journal of Law and Psychiatry, 34*(1), 30–38. https://doi.org/10.1016/j.ijlp.2010.11.005.

Roycroft, M. (2016). *Police chiefs in the UK: Politicians, HR managers or cops?* Palgrave Macmillan.

Shepherd JP, Sumner SA. (2017). Policing and Public Health—Strategies for Collaboration. *JAMA, 317*(15):1525–1526. https://doi.org/10.1001/jama.2017.1854

Sherman, L. W. (1998). *Evidence based policing.* Washington, DC: Police Foundation.

Sullivan, G., & Spritzer, K. (1997). The criminalization of persons with serious mental illness living in rural areas. *The Journal of Rural Health, 13*(1), 6–13.

Trayner, K., et al. (2020). High willingness to use drug consumption rooms among people who inject drugs in Scotland: Findings from a national bio-behavioural survey among people who inject drugs. *International Journal of Drug Policy.* https://doi.org/10.1016/j.drugpo.2020.102731.

United Nations Office on Drugs and Crime. (2015). *World Drug Report 2015* (United Nations publication, Sales No. E.15.XI.6).

Wells, W., & Schafer, J. A. (2006). Officer perceptions of police responses to persons with a mental illness. *Policing: An International Journal of Police Strategies & Management, 29*(4), 578–601. https://doi.org/10.1108/13639510610711556.

Weisheit, R., Wells, L. E., & Falcone, D. N. (1994). Community policing in small town and rural America. *Crime & Delinquency, 40*(4), 549–567.

World Health Organization. (2020). *Mental health: Mental disorders.* Retrieved from https://www.who.int/mental_health/management/en/

Williams, D. R. (2018) Stress and the mental health of populations of color. Advancing our understanding of race-related stressors. *Journal of Health and Social Behavior, 59*(4), 466–485. https://doi.org/10.1177/0022146518814251.

Wilson-Bates, F. (2008). *Lost in transition: How a lack of capacity in the mental health system is failing Vancouver's mentally ill and draining police resources.* Retrieved from http://vancouver.ca/police/assets/pdf/reports-policies/vpd-lost-in-transition.pdf ok

Wood, D. S., & Trostle, L. C. (1997). The nonenforcement role of police in western Alaska and the eastern Canadian arctic: An analysis of police tasks in remote arctic communities. *Journal of Criminal Justice, 25*(5), 367–379.

PCC Annual Report

William's, Norman, & Nixon (2018)

The Bradley Report (2009)

IPOC report into the death of Thomas Orchard www.gov.uk/government/news/independent-office-for-police

Independent Commission on Mental Health and Policing Report (2013)

Mental Health Crisis Care Concordat (2014)

The Welfare of Vulnerable People in Custody (2015)

The MHA 1983 definition of mental disorder and the Police and Criminal Evidence Act 1984 (PACE) Code C definition of mentally vulnerable

Part V

Forensic Investigations

Forensics: The Golden Hour

Andrew Rose

It is said that one never gets a second chance to make a first impression. By the same token, in forensic scene examination, one never gets a second chance to recover evidence that has been destroyed or damaged by poor decision making in its identification, retrieval and subsequent handling.

As science develops, and more and more opportunities exist to retrieve and examine trace evidence, the importance of the decisions made at the scene become ever more vital to the recovery of that evidence and its continuity. Retrieval, packaging, transportation and storage all take place before moving to laboratory examination and then, if necessary, production at court.

The days of scene preservation being a matter of just keeping 'your hands in your pockets' and hoping to collect a few fingerprints and, maybe, some blood that could be typed and narrowed down to half the population are long gone. Today every cough, sneeze and inadvertent movement can distribute skin cells, hair, fibres, saliva and other sources of DNA from the first responders, the investigative team and anyone else who happens to find their way into a crime scene.

One of the mantras that must be instilled in forensic science students is *"Just because you can't see it, doesn't mean it isn't there"*. We are all now familiar with the paper suited, double gloved, hood wearing, mask-breathing scene examiner painstakingly searching for and recovering evidence in its various forms. But,

A. Rose (✉)
Rabdan Academy, Al Bhustan, Abu Dhabi, United Arab Emirates

M. Roycroft, L. Brine (eds.), *Modern Police Leadership*,
https://doi.org/10.1007/978-3-030-63930-3_18

223

unless the correct decisions have been made prior to the arrival of these experts, and every step meticulously recorded and accounted for, then whatever they find, or do not find, may be completely useless to any subsequent investigation.

The advances in science, and the ability to find ever smaller and smaller pieces of trace evidence means that often the defence team no longer looks to deny that the trace evidence belongs to the defendant, but will question how that piece of evidence got to be where it was found and what relevance it has to the matter at hand. The fact that I can shake hands with someone and, sometime later, they can put my DNA on a light switch, door handle or piece of clothing that I have been nowhere near must raise concerns for the forensic investigator. The multiple occasions where people, literally, rub shoulders with each other on public transport, at concerts, festivals, in lifts and other enclosed spaces provide a myriad of opportunities for the transference of trace evidence and correct retrieval and interpretation of its meaning is vital in the modern world of investigation.

When Edmund Locard in the 19th century, posited the theory that *"Every contact leaves a trace"* (Byard et al. 2016), he may not have known that, over 100 years later it would still be the principle by which every forensic scientist and investigator ran their decision making processes. And, Locard certainly would have had no concept of the type of trace evidence that would be capable of identification.

Everyone involved in the forensic scene management and investigation process has to make decisions that may never be able to be reversed or saved if wrong. This chapter will look to provide some guidance and processes to make it as straightforward as possible to reach good, sound, decisions at every stage of the investigative process.

First, it is useful to explore what is meant by 'crime scene'. It may not just be the place where a homicide or serious sexual assault took place, or the vehicle involved in a fatal collision but will include, potentially, any land, water, form of transportation, witnesses, victims, suspects and so on (Sutton et al. 2017). A crime scene is, quite literally, anywhere or anything that can provide evidence of the commission of an offence, or provide corroboration of a victim's allegation or suspect's defence.

One must examine what this crime scene can provide by way of evidence and then use this evidence to:

- Prove an offence has been committed and which one
- Link a suspect to a scene
- Link a scene to a suspect
- Link a suspect or scenes to other suspects or scenes
- Support, or disprove, statements made by any victim, witness or suspect
- Provide potential lines of enquiry

The evidence available to assist these areas may be short-lived, so the action taken in those first important moments is crucial to the success of the investigation.

A useful memory aid for initial crime scene preservation is the mnemonic MEAL. It suggests a simple, yet effective, way of understanding what needs to be done at all stages of the investigation and should be borne in mind when making decisions in areas that may affect retrieval of evidence.

To Prevent:

- **M**ovement of evidence
- **E**vidence being obliterated
- **A**ddition of material
- **L**oss of material

Depending on the type of incident, a number of different first responders might attend and obtain access to the scene. The overriding principle for any incident where injury or death is a possible outcome, is the preservation of life (Suboch, 2016). This could mean that, in order to preserve life, first responders might *MOVE EVIDENCE* in order to gain access to an injured person, they will almost certainly *OBLITERATE EVIDENCE* within the scene, on the approach to the scene and on the victim. Their clothing, especially their footwear will *ADD MATERIAL* from outside and from other scenes they have attended, as they also will by shedding hairs, fibres, skin cells and so on. When they remove the injured parties or leave the scene, there will be a *LOSS of MATERIAL* either by the deliberate removal of clothing, cleaning of wounds, or by the inadvertent removal of evidence on the responder's clothing, footwear and so on.

Whilst nothing in this guidance is intended to delay the immediate response to preserve life, there are some decisions that could be taken by all potential first responders in order to increase the opportunities for recovery of physical and trace evidence from a scene. Carrying disposable gloves, overshoes and a facemask as part of your standard kit allows a quick and simple means of protection for both the responder and the scene, without delaying any action needing to be taken. A mental preparation on arrival at the scene allows for some thought to be given to noting the position of certain items or any responses from victims, witnesses and allow for the responder to be able to give an account detailing how the scene may have changed between their arrival and the position it is now in, as handed over to the first investigator.

It is critical to understand the concept of the Forensic Value of an item. This is an expression designed to get you to ask yourself a series of questions about any item of potential evidence in order to aid your decision making in following the five principles of exhibit management to ensure that throughout its life it remains viable as evidence in any investigation. Those principles are:

Integrity—Will this item be in the same condition when it is examined as it was at the scene and time of retrieval?

Continuity—Can I account for every second of the whereabouts of this item from the moment it was seized to the time it is produced in court?

Identification—How will I demonstrate that this item, or any evidence obtained from it, is the same as the one seized at the scene?

Preservation—How will I ensure that from the moment I seize the item, I can ensure that whatever evidence I hope to get from it will remain on it until it is examined?

Protection—How can I protect the item from being damaged or harming or injuring anyone that may need to handle it?

The Forensic Value invites you to ask the following questions with regard to each item of potential evidence:

What is it?

What do I hope to get from it, evidentially?

How does that assist the investigation?

How should I retrieve it?

How should I package it?

Within your decision making process, the answer to those questions will inform your actions and give you a series of points for your decision log as a memory aid to act as a reference point for what you knew, when you knew it and what you did as a result.

Nothing in this guidance is intended to take any priority over saving life. It is, of course, quite clear that the preservation of life comes first and all other considerations are second to that. The need to reiterate these basic thoughts and decision making models is clearly demonstrated in a decision by a U.K. judge:

> *R v Hoey 2007 Judgement by Weir, J*
>
> *It is not my function to criticise the seemingly thoughtless and slapdash approach of police and SOCO (Scene of Crime Officer) officers to the collection, storage and transmission of what must have been potential exhibits in a possible future criminal trial, but it is difficult to avoid some expression of surprise that, in an era in which the potential for fibre, if not DNA, contamination was well known to the police such items were so widely and routinely handled with cavalier disregard for their integrity*
>
> *(R v Hoey [2007] NICC 49 (20 December, 2007))*
>
> (In Bryant, Graça, Lawton-Barrett, Gilbert, Hooper, Jones, Blackburn, McCormack and Mitchell, 2017)

Your role at a scene should now concentrate on understanding and applying Locard's principle that every contact leaves a trace and one must avoid cross contamination. As discussed above, your job is simply to retrieve anything, however small, that may be of evidential value and ensure that its efficacy is maintained through whatever testing process is needed to obtain best evidence. At the current level of science there is now often less dispute about the finding of blood, DNA or other trace evidence and its belonging to any particular subject. The focus now tends to be on trying to show that the evidence was found there because of poor cross contamination control, or a lack of secure handling or control of the item throughout the examination process. In a judicial system that relies on a court being satisfied "beyond all reasonable doubt" that the evidence shows what is being suggested it shows, the opportunity for a defence team to show any doubt in the veracity of the evidence could well lead to the acquittal of a guilty person (Hamer 2007). To that end, cross contamination can be defined as the accidental or incidental contamination of the suspected person or object by material from a source other than the specific exchange as a consequence of the offence.

So, in simple terms, one must reduce the accidental or incidental exchange of material in order to ensure that the material that is found is from the specific exchange one seeks to prove. Following a crowded bus or train journey, packed lift or the mosh pit at a concert, we leave covered in hairs, fibres and DNA from other people, and those people leave with bits of us all over them. In the normal course of events, this is just part of life and we give it no thought. But, in practical terms, imagine that you, as a forensic scene examiner have just been to the site of a murder. You then leave the scene and drive back to your office. Your colleague then takes the car and drives to a burglary scene. Inside that scene, your colleague unknowingly deposits material from your murder scene at the burglary scene, which is then recovered and ends up providing a link between the scenes, However, the link is based only on the movements of you and your colleague. It is not an actual investigative link. At some stage in the future, someone is arrested for the burglary and also becomes a suspect in the murder. And, this is a direct result of you and your forensic colleague failing to consider the issues of cross contamination between the two unrelated crime scenes.

When a crime is committed there is evidence left behind. This may be physical, such as a murder weapon; trace, such as DNA, finger marks, or blood; or digital, such as an IP address or attempts to delete data from a hard drive or memory stick. Whatever the medium involved, the principles discussed above remain true. Take whatever action is necessary to deliver the item for examination in the same condition as it was found at the scene.

At many scenes, there may already have been others in attendance (e.g. family members, fire services, first responding police offers, media, paramedics, etc.). Once it has been satisfied that all efforts have been taken to preserve life and remove injured parties, then the forensic officer needs to take control of the scene in order for the best opportunity to recover the specific transfer and other relevant evidence whilst minimising or eradicating any accidental or incidental cross contamination. In this "Golden Hour" there are a number of actions that can be taken to aid in achieving the best possible evidence and the best possible outcome from the initial actions of the forensic officer.

Understanding that anyone who entered or left the scene is likely to have deposited material (i.e., Locard's principle) therein will allow a determination of the best way of gaining entrance to the scene, for the forensic officer and others (only if absolutely necessary), whilst avoiding any areas where that material is most likely to be. One must determine this route of least contamination. This is known as the common approach path and it should be delineated in some way so that all people who need to access the scene can do so with the chances of cross contamination being minimised.

In order to protect and manage the scene and limit access, it is essential that cordons be placed at an appropriate distance from the scene. The basic principle in establishing a crime scene cordon is that it is much easier to start with a large crime cordon and reduce it, than to start with a small crime scene and increase it. The crime scene cordon should be placed thoughtfully and in accordance with the overall forensic strategy. In addition, the crime scene cordon will require police staff to monitor it to prevent breaches, to speak to interested parties, and to direct enquiries.

The best way to protect this area is to designate a single and specific point of entry through the cordon and ensure that a police officer manages and records entry to the scene by utilising a cordon control log. This log should be designed to show a chronological list of everyone who enters the scene, why they are entering the scene, who authorised their entry and their time of exit. The personnel on this cordon control need to be experienced so that unauthorised people (including senior officers) do not try to enter the scene without due authority or valid reason.

In the early stages of response, cordon placement may not be the priority but it is something that should be considered as soon as practicable. Do not fall into the trap of using easy landmarks to delineate the cordon lines but take the time to consider exactly where they should be placed based on the evidence and information at the scene. For example, just because a fence or wall seems to be a natural and convenient barrier, consider that a suspect could have jumped over that barrier in their escape and may have left some type of evidence thereby creating a secondary crime scene that will need examination.

For more complex incidents, it is important to consider how the arrival of support staff and services is managed whilst keeping clear of the scene. A complex scene may involve the use of a number of specialised support services and experts, including but not limited to:

- Anthropologist
- Biologist
- Collision Reconstructionist
- Computer expert
- Coroners Officer
- Entomologist
- Fingerprint Identification Officers
- Fire Investigator
- Firearms
- Graphic/Plan Drawer
- Marine Search
- Medical Examiner
- Odontologist
- Palynologist
- Pathologist
- Photographer
- POLSA (Police Search Advisor)
- Specialist Evidence Recovery Unit
- Surveyors/Builders
- Traffic Officers
- Vehicle Examiner

It is now important that you clearly define your role as the Crime Scene Manager (CSM) and, in consultation with the Senior Investigating Officer (SIO), set a forensic strategy. This strategy should include a clear chain of command and your role will be to advise and support the SIO by recommending the best people for the best roles within the scene. It should also take into account an order of examination such that the different expert roles complement rather than conflict within the scene.

At this point, it is also critical that the CSM advises the SIO what elements of the forensic recovery should and should not be mentioned outside of the police investigators. There may be details about the crime scene that should not be made public, as only the perpetrator would know them. In these cases, it is critical that these details are not mentioned to other non-police entities or the media. Having said that, it is important to have a media strategy, and a place where press photographers and others can be directed to allow them to carry out their roles without interfering with the crime scene. Experience suggests that an openness and willingness to understand their needs and accommodate them will lessen the chances of anyone trying to breach the cordon in order to get that 'exclusive' picture.

There are certain things that can be done at a crime scene once only. There may be only a limited window of opportunity to examine certain things before the evidence they can provide us is lost forever. Specifically, when first entering a scene and making the initial assessment, the forensic officer's decision-making process and log must reflect the possible competing demands and options.

Imagine walking into a house and discovering an apparently lifeless body. The initial priority is to provide aid if the person is alive. For a forensic officer, this step will have already been taken care of. The main decision making must include touch nothing, move nothing, note everything and preserve the scene. However, there may be items in the scene that can afford potential evidence, but only if immediate action is taken. Specifically in a domestic setting, there may very well be an appliance (e.g. kettle, oven etc.) that shows evidence of recent use, but only if you examine them now. For example, a kettle may still be hot from recent use, warm from use a short while ago, or cold. An immediate examination provides evidence that would not be available a few minutes or hours later.

As noted from above, there is no set of fixed rules to follow that will answer every situation or questions a forensic officer may encounter. Advice from more experienced forensic officers, critical thinking, knowledge and personal experience will give the forensic officer the ability to weigh the pros and cons and make a well thought out and defendable decision. Hindsight is a wonderful and exacting science, often employed by defence attorneys, but the forensic officer should never be afraid to take unpopular or difficult decisions if they are the correct and defendable.

In some cases, other pressures may influence your decision making (e.g. demands from colleagues, senior officers, media, the public etc.). For example, if a fatal collision occurs on a major road feeding into a major airport, there will likely be large numbers of potential witnesses and evidence (i.e. debris, tyre marks, etc.) It is likely that this scene will have been heavily contaminated by fire officers, paramedics, police officers and witnesses. There will be significant pressure to open the road as quickly as possible to get traffic and trade flowing again, and to allow people to catch their flights. This scene should be looked at no differently than a death in a private dwelling where there is very little pressure to work quickly. The forensic officer must remember that their duty, first and foremost, is to locate and preserve evidence in order to assist in determining what happened and to support any charges that may arise from the overall investigation.

It is important to note that a fire scene is another challenging scene for forensic investigation. Nothing is designed more favourably to destroy evidence than a fire. By its very nature, it will burn evidence from items, potentially destroy human remains beyond recognition and make the scene a dangerous place with structural damage and chemical hazards. During the actual burning phase of a fire, the fire brigade has full responsibility. Only once a scene has been declared safe by them can anyone else enter for the purposes of investigation. In the UK and Canada, it is the responsibility of the police to detect and investigate any crime and report the facts to the relevant coroner.

A fire is any burning, combustion or flaming which results in injury to any person or animal or damage to property. The role of the investigator is to establish where the fire originated. This is known as the seat of the fire and is usually the area where there is likely to be the most extensive damage and the greatest intensity of burning. Often, if it can be established where the fire started, it can be obvious how the fire started. Not all fires are deliberately started, but until you establish that the cause is innocent, it must be investigated as suspicious in order to maximise the retrieval of evidence. Some innocent causes may be:

• Careless disposal of cigarettes/matches
• Chemical Reaction
• Clothing placed to near a fire or heat source
• Electrical Fault
• Focus of sun's rays onto combustible material
• Lightning Strikes
• Overheating of machinery, particularly rotating parts
• Sparks from fire, welding equipment, grinding machines

A deliberate fire might include:

• Allowing a candle to burn down
• Incendiary/explosive device
• Naked flames applied to combustible material
• Petrol Bomb
• Using an accelerant with the above

One of the investigative methods that may be used in a laboratory setting is a test burning by taking material from the scene and igniting similar material to see the rate of burn, whether or not it needs an accelerant, how it combusts and so on.

It must not be overlooked that a fire may have been deliberately started in order to disguise the presence or commission of other criminal activity. So, it isn't just about the what, where, how of the forensic scene, but a deeper look into the surrounding circumstances and factors. Because it is such a difficult crime to investigate, the forensic officer must undertake a slow and methodical investigation with extensive contemporaneous notes to provide a detailed record of their scene examination. Of course, the chemical identification of potential accelerants is a vital part of this preliminary examination given that they contaminate other items that evaporate over time. Given the peculiar nature of fire investigation, it is even more important to ensure you remain aware of, and protect where appropriate, against cross contamination, bear in mind the issues of random and specific exchanges and maintain the highest level of continuity and integrity. Basically, treat a death by fire as murder until it can be proven otherwise.

From the moment someone first arrives at a crime scene, there is potential for the correct recovery of an item to provide good quality evidence to assist in the investigation and to support prosecutions. There is also, however, potential for a poor decision or lack of knowledge to destroy that piece of evidence and thereby hinder or even completely ruin any prospect of a reasonable outcome. Care must be taken from the outset. Even officers not trained in the specific expert techniques of recovery should be trained to a level where they recognise the importance of the processes described above and can follow the suggested protocols to increase the likelihood of best evidence retrieval. Robbers (2008) shows that, more and more often, juries are conflating fact and fiction with regards to forensic evidence as a result of a plethora of TV programmes and almost expect such evidence to be produced in every case. It is, therefore, vital that any lack of forensic evidence is because there was not any to be found rather than a poorly trained or inexperienced first responder not carrying out their role effectively.

Seminar Questions

The author states that an officer needs to "understand the concept of an item's Forensic Value". Explain this concept.

Name and describe the role of four experts mentioned in the text that can assist an investigator. How can these individuals assist an investigation?

What do we mean by the term "Golden Hour" in Forensic terms?

Exam Question

What does the mnemonic MEAL stand for and why are its key headings important at a crime scene?

References

Bryant, R., Bryant, S., Graça, S., Lawton-Barrett, K., Gilbert, P., Hooper, G., Jones, N., Blackburn, B., McCormack, T., & Mitchell, S. (2017). *Blackstone's handbook for policing students 2018*. Oxford: Oxford University Press.

Byard, R. W., James, H., Berketa, J., & Heath, K. (2016). Locard's principle of exchange, dental examination and fragments of skin. *Journal of forensic sciences, 03, 61*(2).

Hamer, D. (2007). The Presumption of innocence and reverse burdens: A balancing Act. *The Cambridge Law Journal, 66*(1).

Robbers, M. L. P. (2008). Blinded by science: The social construction of reality in forensic television shows and its effect on criminal jury trials. *Criminal Justice Policy Review, 19*(1).

Suboch, G. (2016). *Real-world crime scene investigation: A step-by-step procedure manual*. Boca Raton: CRC Press.

Sutton, R., Trueman, K., & Moran, C. (2017). *Crime scene management: Scene specific methods*. Chichester: Wiley.

The Crime Scene Expert

Scott Fairgrieve

In order to fully understand the role of crime scene experts, this chapter focuses on the expertise of the author who is a consulting Forensic Anthropologist (FA) with over 30 years of experience in the Province of Ontario, Canada. Ontario is the most populous province in Canada with over 15 million people.

All death investigations in Ontario fall under the Coroner's Act of Ontario (R.S.O. 1990, C. C.37, s. 31(1)). This act grants coroners in Ontario extraordinary powers to investigate deaths. The context of these death investigations center around a mandated list of five key questions:

(a) who the deceased was;
(b) how the deceased came to his or her death;
(c) when the deceased came of his or her death;
(d) where the deceased came to his or her death; and
(e) by what means the deceased came to his or her death.

Within the Coroner's Act, a pathologist is assigned to be responsible for the postmortem examination of the remains. A forensic pathologist is vetted by the Ontario Forensic Pathology Service in order to conduct medico-legal autopsies.

S. Fairgrieve (✉)
Rabdan Academy, Al Bhustan, Abu Dhabi, United Arab Emirates
e-mail: mroycroft@ra.ac.ae

M. Roycroft, L. Brine (eds.), *Modern Police Leadership*,
https://doi.org/10.1007/978-3-030-63930-3_19

More typically, these pathologists have gone through a fellowship program in forensic pathology. (https://www.mcscs.jus.gov.on.ca/english/DeathInvestigations/Pathology/pathology_main.html, accessed on 23/09/2019). These registered forensic pathologists have the discretionary power to "...conduct or direct any person other than a coroner to conduct other such examinations and analyses as he or she considers appropriate in the circumstances" (2009, c. 15. S. 18). This facilitates the forensic pathologist ability to ask for specialized assistance in the examination of human remains. Yet, it is under the authority of the Coroner that he or she may "... direct any person, other than the pathologist to whom the warrant is issued, to conduct such examinations and analyses" (2009, C.15, S. 18). In this instance, the Coroner may bring into the crime scene investigation, an FA to assist with the recognition, documentation, and ultimately, the recovery of human remains.

The Coroner's Act provides both the Coroner and the Forensic Pathologist the authority to bring in personnel with specialized expertise to the scene and at the postmortem examination, and after a revision of the Coroner's Act it permits experts to be brought into an investigation.

Prior to bringing an expert to the crime scene or autopsy room, the problem of defining forensic fields in which expertise may be required, as well as who was recognized as an expert became an issue. Therefore, it is important to explore how one becomes an expert in his or her field, while also becoming recognized as an expert upon whom the Coroner and Forensic Pathologist may call upon.

Who Are the Experts?

Experts who are not attached to a particular forensic service tend to be academics who are predominantly faculty at universities who teach and undertake research in their area of expertise. In order to be considered as experts they must have some form of recognition in their own field of expertise. This recognition comes in the form of having elements in their curriculum vitae that would potentially be acceptable for being recognized in a court of law as being an expert. It is important to examine the type of qualifications that need to be in the background of an academic in order for them to be considered an expert in the eyes of either investigators or the courts. University faculty members who wish to be recognized as forensic experts in their field have usually had some sort of forensic training, either through an accredited University, or through a professional organization such as the American Academy of Forensic Sciences. However, their training must be relevant to their field of expertise. Recently, many universities in the United States and Canada have established undergraduate degrees in forensic science, usually with a concentration in a particular scientific area of study, such as biology, chemistry, and biological anthropology. However, such programs are generally not enough to permit the holder of such a degree at this level to be an expert witness. It is more typical that experts in various fields who hold post graduate degrees will have undergone more rigorous training in their field of expertise. However, it is at the level of the PhD thesis where the research skills may be honed to the level of a world expert.

Areas where forensic scientists may be experts, who are not regularly employed by a forensic laboratory, may include forensic anthropology, forensic entomology, and forensic botany. Other specialists who are regularly employed by forensic laboratories or police in their forensic units may include those with expertise in fingerprint analysis, footwear analysis, bloodstain pattern, and general criminalists.

Even this does not guarantee that the individual will be a recognized forensic expert. There may be further training through professional associations, additional certifications offered through various professional boards, and research publications in forensic journals add to the legitimacy of the scientist having a forensic orientation. Ultimately, the forensic scientist must get some casework experience. Initially, this can be done by working with a colleague or mentor in the area and being part of the team that comes to the crime scene or is provided samples that have been collected for analysis. Gradually, their role in forensic cases transitions from being an analyst to being the lead on casework. Although this seems vague, such a pathway will familiarize the scientist with forensic standards and their standard operating procedures for both crime scene work and how to collect, analyze and interpret data in an unbiased fashion. Without using an unbiased process and being capable of presenting one's findings without bias in a court of law, one cannot be an expert witness. Forensic science is entirely dependent upon the integrity of both the individuals involved at the scene and those involved in the analysis and interpretation of such evidence.

An Illustration of Involving an Expert from the Scene to the Courtroom

It is important to provide context to this area of expertise so as to understand how and why such an expert is dispatched to a crime scene. An FA is an expert in the discovery, documentation, recovery, and analysis of human remains that have typically undergone significant decomposition to the point where at least some portion of the human skeleton is exposed. This decomposition can be due to the natural processes of tissue degradation, be it through insect activity or faunal (animal) scavenging, or degradation where a human agent has undertaken a process to make the body unrecognizable, such as burning a body (Fairgrieve, 2008). An FA has expertise in the skeletal structure of the human body, to the point where they are able to experience and identify the type and anatomical location of bones in a fragmentary state. Such training and experience is necessary for the recognition of human skeletal elements (bones) in a variety of contexts. It is not atypical for an FA to have to work with crime scene personnel and search an area for bone fragments. Hence, the specialized nature of these remains makes it essential to have an FA at the scene. In addition to the scene, the FA is involved in the examination of the human remains with a forensic pathologist. In so doing, the FA is asked to analyze the skeletal remains for indications of their age at death, their biological sex (i.e., not gender), ancestry (i.e., not race), evidence of how long ago they died, and to chronicle any and all damage to skeletal elements, be they due to animal or human actions (such as trauma). Hence, the FA has value both at the crime scene and at the autopsy.

Dispatching an Expert

Police are typically the first responders to death scenes. If intact human remains are found, and there is minimal disturbance to the body, an FA may not be needed at the scene. However, if remains are found to be in a fragmentary or unrecognizable state or in a stage of decomposition where the remains are starting to disarticulate, then an FA is likely needed. The determination of whether an FA is needed is generally made by a specialized investigator in conjunction with the local coroner, who is a qualified medical doctor, and forensic police officers. In many jurisdictions, these forensic police officers have been trained in the recovery of human remains and will be aware of whether a FA, botanist, or entomologist is needed at the scene. This investigator will follow the protocol of the police organization for requesting a FA.

There are instances where the postmortem interval (i.e., the interval of time that has elapsed between the death of the individual and the discovery of the remains) has been an issue that can be resolved using entomological and/or botanical evidence. The FA is provided relevant information including: location, scene context (e.g., wooded area, backyard, garage, wooded area, etc.,), weather, and so on. Once at the scene, the FA will consult with the police and coroner on how to proceed with the investigation of the remains.

How the Expert Works with the Case Coroner and the Police

Upon arrival at the scene, the FA will check in with the officer in charge of the crime scene entry log and follow all other routine crime scene protocol. The case will be discussed in its entirety with the coroner, the investigator in charge, and the lead forensic officer. It is usually at this time that the responsibilities of all involved are clearly outlined. Although not formally recognized as such, this is the point where the role of the FA is clearly indicated to the police. In Ontario, the death investigation is under the control of the Coroner. The Coroner's Act (1990) clearly defines their role in the investigation. The FA is there through the Coroner and as such reports directly to that office. Hence, the FA works with the police to coordinate any search for the remains, in a supporting role. Police searchers flag any items that appear to be bone and the FA determines if it is bone, and if so, if it is human. In the case where remains are clearly human, arrangements are made with the forensic team to have a standard series of photographs of each item and have an evidence number assigned to each skeletal element. The location of this bone and the evidence number are marked with a flag or an evidence marker. This will facilitate later mapping of the scene so that the distribution of the bones may be considered in the subsequent analysis. This process is consistent with the processing of evidence in a 'routine' crime investigation. Prior to the FA touching the bone, or conducting any sort of an excavation, a forensic botanist must examine the scene to ascertain the relevance of any botanical association with the remains.

The FA is only involved with the human remains. Other associated evidence is the responsibility of the forensic officers at the scene. If evidence is directly associated with the body and it is decided not to remove that evidence from the body, it will go with the body to the autopsy. Then at the autopsy, the evidence will be collected by or with the forensic pathologist for the case, and the forensic officer will be present to photograph and process the evidence.

Once all of the remains have been recovered from the scene, the police arrange for the transportation of the remains to a morgue where the forensic pathologist will conduct the autopsy. The scene duties of the FA are complete at this point, however, the FA will receive a copy of the scene investigation report along with a map showing the location of the human remains from the police. The FA then generates a comprehensive report about their involvement at the scene and an inventory, with a map, of all the remains found at the scene. This report will go to the Office of the Chief Coroner and the Ontario Forensic Pathology Service for peer review by the Service prior to being released to the investigating officers and the case coroner. This is done as a quality control measure.

The Postmortem Examination

The involvement of an FA in a postmortem examination also operates on a set policy under the Coroner's Act of Ontario. Specifically, the assigned forensic pathologist for the case has the obligation to call in the assistance of an external approved expert should one be necessary. In this system, the forensic pathologist is always the lead on any postmortem examination of human remains. The FA assists in the examination of the remains. Although the FA does not have the same status as the forensic pathologist, the FA does make significant contributions as part of this investigative team. The forensic pathologist will request the FA assess the remains and make recommendations on how to proceed.

The nature of these cases will range from an inventory of the bones present, to a full analysis for an age at death estimation, sex, ancestry, postmortem interval, stature, evidence of skeletal anomalies that will assist in identification of the victim, and evidence of antemortem, postmortem, and perimortem (i.e., around the time of death) trauma. When presented with a dry bone (i.e., a bone that no longer has any associated soft tissue) exhibits a cut mark, for example, it is not possible to say if that cut mark happened prior to the death of the individual, at the time of death, or after. All the FA can do is chronicle the type and position of the injury. If there is soft tissue present and the death was recent we would still have to say that the injury to the bone is perimortem unless there is evidence of bleeding at the wound site which, as the forensic pathologist would interpret, as being at or around the time of death. However, it is the responsibility of the forensic pathologist to make that determination.

The general rule for the involvement of an FA in a postmortem examination is to deal with any aspects that concern the human skeleton. FAs may also be able to contribute information concerning bone trauma in cases where significant soft tissue is present, such as in a recent death. For example, in a case where a victim suffered multiple blows to the head resulting in a series of fractures, the FA may be able to reassemble the bone fragments, thereby providing a sequence to the blows to the head, and an estimate of the minimum number of blows.

The FA also contributes to establishing a positive identification of the victim. If there are antemortem medical records indicating past surgeries involving bone, or even radiographs (X-rays) from prior medical assessments, these can be used in the identification process. For example, it has been found through many studies that the pattern of the sinuses in the frontal bone show significant enough variation that they have been accepted as a means of achieving a positive identification (Cox et al., 2009). Of course, there are other radiographic comparisons that may be utilized from other areas of the body, including aspects of vertebral form, marrow cavity shape in long bones of the arm or leg. Similarly, a forensic odontologist deals with any issues that are dental. This specialist is able to make a formal identification based on dental records of the victim. It is interesting to note that with advances in dental care, there seem to be fewer cases where dental restorations are present. Generally speaking, tissue samples are taken for DNA analysis. Once the analysis of the remains is complete, a forensic anthropology analysis report will be created concerning the remains.

The Expert Witness

Assuming that criminal charges have been brought against someone for the death, and a trial will ensue, the FA must provide a curriculum vitae (CV). The CV is necessary as it will go into evidence as proof of the qualifications during the process to be certified as an expert witness. This process only goes forward if the FA is being called upon to provide testimony concerning their reports. As noted above, after being called to the stand, the attorney (i.e., Crown or defense) who has called the FA to provide testimony, will then question the FA concerning the relevance of their education, training, and experience and how it relates to the matter at hand. Once finished, the court is asked to certify the FA as an expert in a specified area that pertains to that particular case. The judge will then ask the opposing counsel if there is an objection or if they have any questions of the FA at this stage. Once certified by the court, the FA is now in a position to provide expert testimony to assist the court in providing relevant evidence about the case. Rather than having the experts provide their evidence as a long diatribe concerning the contents of their report, skilled attorneys will ask very specific questions concerning the reports so that responses will be short and to the point. However, it is always advisable for the FA to meet with the attorney prior to court proceedings in order to provide context to the report. The context in this case is to provide information concerning the limits of the analysis. The expert will provide information as to what the data actually indicate and, more importantly, the limits of their analysis so that the conclusions are not overstated. This is the key to providing an unbiased testimony. In Canada, there was a significant

Public Inquiry in the case of a pediatric pathologist who was providing expert evidence in cases involving child decedents (http://www.attorneygeneral.jus. gov.on.ca/inquiries/goudge/index.html). One of the findings was that the pathologist in question did not have any forensic training, and hence was not qualified to provide an expert opinion. However, at the time, because he was a pathologist, he was recognized as having the qualifications to do forensic casework involving children. This report eventually led to the founding of the Ontario Forensic Pathology Service to oversee the vetting of qualifications of forensic pathologists and other experts, including FAs, to provide a system of quality assurance. This also includes the system for peer review of all reports generated by these experts.

Conclusions

An established process for having a non- police expert in a particular area of forensic science become involved in an investigation is critical. The key aspect of this process is to have a system in place to evaluate the credentials of forensic experts prior needing them to respond to an incident. It is beneficial to have a roster of experts for various areas of expertise so that they can be utilized to gather valuable forensic evidence in death investigations conducted by the police.

Seminar Questions

What is forensic Pathology?
How can an FA contribute to a homicide investigation?

Exam Questions

How does the FA expert work with the Police and Coroner to deal with serious inquires?

References

Coroner's Act of Ontario R.S.O. (1990). C. C.37, s. 31(1).

Cox, M., Malcolm, M., & Fairgrieve, S. (2009). A new digital method for the objective comparison of frontal sinuses for identification. *Journal of Forensic Sciences, 54*(4), 761–772. https://doi.org/10.1111/j.1556-4029.2009.01075.x.

Death Investigations in Ontario. https://www.mcscs.jus.gov.on.ca/english/DeathInvestigations/Pathology/pathology_main.html. Accessed 23 Sept 2019.

Fairgrieve, S. (2008). *Forensic cremation analysis and interpretation.* Boca Raton: CRC Press.

Goudge, S. T. (2008). *The inquiry into pediatric forensic pathology in Ontario.* http://www.attorneygeneral.jus.gov.on.ca/inquiries/goudge/index.html. Accessed 11 Mar 2020.

Forensic Intelligence

Andrew Williamson

There is confusion around the labelling and function of FORINT, with a multitude of different labels, descriptions and practices. This misunderstanding of FORINT may stem from the fact that both the police and security services have a limited awareness of forensic processes, its' realities and more importantly how it can be used proactively to combat crime and terrorism.

When researching the Intelligence Led Policing (ILP) model, several challenges within ILP presented difficulties which render FORINT ineffective. UK Police foster a culture of relying on 'traditional' methods of investigation; traditional methods tend to view forensic science as a purely reactive resource within a legal framework. Much of this culture is centred on a 'need-to-know' principle, which James (2011) suggests is often applied to a 'ridiculous extreme[s]', resulting in intelligence being kept within intelligence spheres which prefer to exclude those without a 'need to know'.

When researching cases of terrorism where forensics was used, nearly all the FORINT was reactive to an event. It became apparent that many of the terrorists were involved in criminal activities before progressing to terrorism; this presented a different perspective to the research. Being involved in Illegal activity suggests that these individuals would have been the focus of police attention and therefore,

A. Williamson (✉)
Rabdan Academy, Al Bhustan, Abu Dhabi, United Arab Emirates
e-mail: mroycroft@ra.ac.ae

M. Roycroft, L. Brine (eds.), *Modern Police Leadership*,
https://doi.org/10.1007/978-3-030-63930-3_20

they present an opportunity at this criminal stage for FORINT to be proactive and preventative to identify suspects before they become terrorists.

The extensive use of intelligence within the policing and military sectors clearly demonstrates FORINT can play a role in identifying terrorists' pre-event. However, due to the confidentiality and sensitivity surrounding the intelligence-gathering methods and outcomes, it would, in most situations, be challenging to uncover any evidence other than anecdotal. Criminalistics forensic has long played in supporting law enforcement by providing intelligence and evidence to combat criminality. Crime scene examinations and trace evidence are typically utilised to explain what has happened in a scene, and assists juries, and court officials.

Proactive Intelligence

Given the investigative possibilities and potential value of FORINT in the fight against terrorism, it is clear that proactive FORINT should be used more as a proactive means of gathering actionable intelligence for the *'deterrence and reduction of crime'* (Almog, 2014), in the prevention of attacks, and in early intervention of terrorist planning. However, Ribaux and Caneppele (2018) suggest the forensic personnel who work in this environment are only permitted to offer opinions to an investigation if the opinion which they express is based on existing evidence, and the evidence is *'confined to technical and scientific considerations (e.g., the cause of a technical failure, cause of a fire, etc.)'* FORINT actually offers a tangible and unique means of collating information from forensics for the identification and prevention of terrorism and criminal activity. Vogel and Legrand (2014) discuss how, in 1989, Birkett, deliberated on the indexing of forensic data from numerous crime scenes to assist in the linking of crime scenes and the identification of suspects, though the concept of *'FORINT' was* first presented by Margot and Ribeaux (1999). Ribeaux and Margot 'aimed to show that the study of inferences drawn by investigators during problem-solving is a useful approach to analyse how forensic science data should be integrated into criminal intelligence.'

As forensic science and related technologies develop at pace, new collection techniques, analytical methods and processes enable data to be collected and analysed accurately, promptly and at reducing costs. *'Such approach [es] can not only resolve crimes that might be unresolvable otherwise but also save time, manpower and resources. Furthermore, they may prevent certain crimes from being committed in the first place'* (Almog, 2014).

Unfortunately, forensic practitioners appear to be unwittingly undermining the progress and development of FORINT; awareness and education of practitioners are therefore likely to be beneficial. Ross (2015) reports, *'forensic scientists do not routinely supply relevant intelligence for several reasons:*

- *It does not comply with traditional quality assurance;*
- *There is a reticence among forensic scientists to disseminate 'soft' information (not empirical information) for fear it will be engaged in a Court process; and*
- *There is a lack of awareness about the needs of partners in policing.'*

'it is not easy to convince policymakers of the importance of proactive forensics' (Almog, 2014). Policymakers are nervous about utilising methods and sources which they cannot verify and trust. Milne (2012) comments that *'forensics is often viewed by crime intelligence analysts as the domain of the Crime Scene Investigator. This compartmentalisation of thinking can and has led to disastrous failures in major investigations.'* Buckley (2014) argued that police officers have an alarming lack of understanding of sciences involved in forensics, *'and in many cases overwhelmed by the technical aspects of it, and most forensic scientists have little, if any, experience in relation to intelligence management.'* He further suggests that police staff and law enforcement policymakers are risk-averse and therefore tend not to be influenced by the 'unproven' features of FORINT; they take the path they understand best – traditional policing.

Intelligence-Led Policing

ILP is the overarching management philosophy and organisational strategy of which FORINT is a subsection. Intelligence-led policing (ILP) is a policing model built around the assessment and management of risk. UK Police forces have broadly adopted ILP as a *'collaborative enforcement approach combining problemsolving, information sharing and police accountability, with enhanced intelligence operations with a focus on gathering, compiling, and analysing data to inform decision making'* (Ribaux & Caneppele, 2018), to ultimately prevent and reduce crime. One crucial element of any successful ILP strategy is the timely processing and effective analysis of the diverse sources of intelligence which will inform longer-term policing challenges. Ribaux et al. (2018) further argue that forensic examinations and FORINT are iterative and can empower ILP. By proactively linking activities and persons through FORINT, the traditional role of reactive policing can be fulfilled; what is required is a more in-depth analysis which will provide an *'understanding of crime systems and mechanisms. This knowledge, in turn, allows the design of proactive actions aimed at disrupting those activities. From investigating the past, forensic intelligence turns to anticipate the future.'*

The challenge is, to see FORINT as being proactive, not just as reactive. The profile of terrorists shows a large percentage of actors who have criminal careers before they graduate to terrorism; this offers unique opportunities to track and identify offenders, supporters, resources and targets. Intelligence gathering may include what may appear to be irrelevant and isolated evidential materials and intelligence, much of which would not meet the stringent requirements of the counterterrorist agencies and judiciary, but when viewed in the context of the terrorist jigsaw puzzle, adds knowledge to build the overall intelligence picture.

FORINT

FORINT combines Forensic and Intelligence disciplines to form a sub-category of ILP. FORINT is not new to UK policing and has been in use by operational policing resources since 1960s. However, it was not till the late 1990s that policing, and academia formalised a process (Raymond & Julian, 2015).' FORINT is viewed by mainstream policing as *'additional 'type' of intelligence. As an emerging form of intelligence, its meaning and value are yet to be widely understood.'* They define FORINT as *'the accurate, timely and useful product of logically processing (analysis of) forensic case data (information) for investigation and/or intelligence purposes.'* FORINT is viewed as a piece of mainly reactive evidence and intelligence that can provide investigations with valuable information to ultimately influence the investigation. The fundamental principle of this type of evidence should not be to examine cases on an individual basis, but should include a holistic approach and absorb all possible FORINT creating a multi-case focus. By collecting and collating evidence and turning this evidence into intelligence using structured processes, the data from the crime scene reports and scientific examinations can be subject to qualitative and quantitative analysis. This analysis seeks to find patterns and links in criminal behaviour from physical and documentary evidence recovered from scenes. This intelligence will generate many different patterns including identifications to individuals, scene to scene, scene to individuals, linking modus operandi, chemical trace and physical fit.

'Intelligence involves a process of bringing a vast body of information, often meaningless in isolation, together in the hope of discerning links and underlying patterns that, over time, create a meaningful picture' (McCulloch & Pickering, 2009). In past decades, the police have been endowed with new proactive powers and a pre-crime legislative framework. These powers and the framework are vital if the police and security agencies are to gather useful proactive intelligence, which, taken in isolation may have no relation to crime or terrorism context.

The fear of terrorism and extremism is a paramount concern for public safety officials. Recent 'melee' attacks in the UK have caused concern, as they are simple to plan and execute; all that is required is a desire to kill and a weapon. To counter such threats, Policing and Public Safety strategies are turning to technological innovations and physical solutions to minimise the risk. For example, the use of the military to guard locations, concrete barriers, strict gun laws and banning knives at public events.

The gathering of crime intelligence has grown to such an extent that it is seen as a potential threat to human rights. The UK *'permits the indefinite retention of DNA profiles of most convicted individuals and temporal retention for some first-time convicted minors and innocent individuals on the National DNA Database (NDNAD)'* (Amankwaa & McCartney, 2018). It could be viewed that a legal framework which distinguishes between intelligence and criminal legal standards, one that tries to *'see into the future inevitably blurs the line between evidence and intelligence'* (McCulloch & Pickering, 2009) By its nature intelligence alone is unsuitable for charging or convicting a suspect directly, intelligence is often used to construct a picture of threats and risks. Intelligence is frequently gathered for crime prevention and *typically, terrorism prosecutions under pre-crime regimes, are commenced based on vast amounts of 'circumstantial evidence'*. Intelligence agencies are compelled to accumulate vast amounts of information and analyse the information in such a way to connect people, occurrences and criminal actions. This can enable the police to understand the relevance of threats, risks and vulnerabilities; it may well detect and prevent crime and terrorist activities.

Criminal Background

In 2006, McGarrell, Freilich, and Chermak (2007) discussed a study which analysed over 60 terrorist 'pre-incident indicators. The study scrutinised the incident histories, including the planning phases looking to establish if there had been intelligence gathering opportunities. They concluded; *'The study provides support for the conclusion that law enforcement agencies can prevent a terrorist attack if able to access the right types of data and intelligence in [a] timely manner'*. There is a relevance to ILP and FORINT here as the study asserted:

- Terrorist Incidents have a planning and equipping phase; this phase does not occur impulsively or in isolation. The analysis established that *'on average, approximately 2 to 3 months elapse between planning and commission.'*
- Terrorists and terrorist groups are prone to have been involved in crime and are likely to be 'chronic offenders' known to police.
- Nearly 50% of the terrorists carried out the planning and preparation of the attack within 30 miles of where they lived.

During the investigations following the attacks in Paris and Brussels, it was revealed that forensic opportunities were exploited from *'traces left at the scene of the crimes, including cellular phones and DNA'* (Cusson, 2018a, b). This intelligence was used proactively in this case as police identified other persons, with criminal records, on the periphery of the attacks.

A more proactive stance is therefore needed employing FORINT. Both these studies support the theory that a significant proportion of terrorists operating in Europe have a criminal background and they are known to police. After the many recent terror attacks in Europe, a former Belgium Defence Minister Heisbourg, noted; *'every time there is an attack, we discover that the perpetrators were known to the authorities'* Cusson (2018a, b). also argues that terrorists often have criminal behaviours and criminal records; criminologists would recognise the behaviours as those of 'common criminals'. Terrorists often commit a crime in several different categories during their 'criminal careers' where they may have seen themselves as above the law.

The Intelligence Is Out There

Many of the attackers involved in the recent attacks in Europe had criminal records and they were known to police or the security services. The offences involved covered a wide range, including drug dealing, drug-taking, robberies, burglaries and assaults. *'Two of the suicide bombers in the Brussels attacks, Ibrahim el-Bakraoui and his younger brother Khalid, both residents on Max Roos Street since the beginning of the year, had managed to go undetected for so long? And all this despite a record of violent crime in Belgium and, in the case of the older brother, a clear warning from Turkey in June that he was on his way back to Europe after being arrested as a suspected terrorist while on his way to Syria?'* (Higgins and de Freytas-Tamura 2016). The open report on the Westminster, London Bridge and Finsbury Park, London and the Manchester arena attacks of March–June 2017 (Anderson, 2017), also corroborates this theory (See Appendix 1).

Missed Opportunities for Harvesting Intelligence

This evidence of criminal activity and missed opportunities reinforces the hypothesis that there are FORINT opportunities pre-attack that could help identify future terrorists. McGarrell et al. (2007) contemplated that intelligence should target criminal groups and complex organisations as *a clear pattern of precursor activity across diverse terrorist organizations are discovered. They discovered that 'all terrorist organizations require money, material, transportation, identity papers, communication systems, and safe havens to accomplish their aims. Crimes to finance these operations should be the top priority for investigators.'* If criminal activity is suspected or detected, there should be ample opportunity to harvest numerous evidence types to produce FORINT from the various scenes.

Knowledge of how these individuals or groups operate in the build-up to terrorism can help target criminal intelligence collection methods and counter risks and threat FORINT can assist in pre-crime interventions where intelligence links *substantial and continuing coercive action to suspicion without the need for evidence, charge and conviction. Other measures, such as the criminalization of association and 'preparatory' offences, are pre-crimes that expand the remit of the criminal law by fulfilling the demand for security that 'dictates earlier and earlier intervention to reduce opportunity.'* (McCulloch & Pickering, 2009) In pre-crime intervention, the intention is to use intelligence proactively and encourage the subjects to disengage from a violent future.

Criminals Identified in Terror

A further example of a connection between crime, terrorism and missed forensic opportunities is in the aftermath of the terrorist attack in Maalbeek, Brussels, in 2016. After the incident, which killed 20 people, the criminal investigation led the police to discover a cache of firearms in accommodation near Paris. Unfortunately, it was not until 2018 that the rifles were forensically examined, and positive DNA profiles uploaded to the French national database. The Dutch DNA database was able to identify four suspects who were resident in The Netherlands. The suspects had come to the attention of the Dutch police sometime before the attacks. Dutch legislation allowed the police to secure DNA from; *'suspects and individuals convicted of offences or crimes for which preventative custody is allowed, or by a judicial order,'* (Williams & Johnson, 2005) therefore, providing evidence that the group was involved in criminal activity.

On 18 June 2018, the four were located and arrested with one individual already in prison. When FORINT information suggested, *'the four Dutch suspects may have provided the arms to the French jihadi cell. The arrests are further evidence of the role the Netherlands plays in international gun-running'* (DutchNews.NL, 2018). FORINT provided the investigators with the evidence to apprehend the group, which may even have prevented further attacks. This is an example of the social and criminal environment becoming 'uncomfortable and unattractive' as in the aftermath of the attack the international policing community used all its resources to track down the perpetrators and supporters. The suspects will have known that forensic traces could be found and identified, as such did this result in the individuals remaining in the crime stage and not progressing to terror, keeping their 'heads down'? It is difficult to judge whether the group were in the phase of criminality pre-terrorism, but there is no doubt they had access to weapons and explosives.

Targeted Forensics'

ILP, as a concept, has a focus on building intelligence within a problem-solving framework which attempts to encompass POP, COP, and engagement of partnerships agencies and local government. The United Kingdom framework contains some conflicts, for example, *'community policing calls for decentralized, geographic-based structure* (see Chapter "Community Policing"), *but ILP is likely to include a centralized intelligence function. The danger, given the challenges of organizational change, is that integration of ILP, COP, POP, and partnerships results in a watered-down model whereby little meaningful change occurs'* (McGarrell et al., 2007). As can be seen in the following case study, multiple agency partnerships and intelligence sharing proved somewhat successful.

An intelligence collection strategy is required to combat crime and terrorism, one which is capable of harvesting FORINT through directed targeting, local knowledge and available intelligence. The following example of FORINT demonstrates how the successful integrated ILP and FORINT can be effective. This operation, 'Anvil' applied historic FORINT, and other intelligence, to gather information which proactively targeted crimes of theft from motor vehicles (See Box 1).

▶   **Box 1 Operation Anvil** It was identified that our 'forensic hits' for theft from motor vehicle offences was poor. This was mainly because capacity issues meant that it was never a high priority for scenes of crime officers to attend such crimes. This had to change to help make the impact we were aiming for; therefore, a forensic strategy for this crime within Middlesbrough was developed. This strategy was aimed at supporting investigating officers and District Criminal Investigation departments to detect and reduce crime by the effective use of scientific techniques and forensic intelligence. This strategy guided officers in best practice and pledged a more comprehensive response by scenes of crime officers to specified crime. Furthermore, a dedicated scene of crime officer was tasked to cover any calls to vehicles parked within Middlesbrough football club's vicinity during match days (as this was constantly on the location target list). A more thorough crime scene assessment was agreed on, which would greatly increase the chances of gaining the amount of relevant evidence to detect and prosecute. Any intelligence gained during crime scene assessments was fed back through the intelligence office for further dissemination. Since its inception in early September 06, forensic 'hits' alone have led to 24 auto crime arrests. (Sellars, 2007)

The FORINT model focuses on traces, does not differentiate between the types of traces and treats them generically to ensure, 'the continuous follow-up of problems' (Ribaux & Caneppele, 2018). The result is that it only relates to specific criminal investigations and not the full spectrum of crime. For example, if a serial offender is suspected of committing offences and other scenes are identified where the modus operandi (MO) is similar, these scenes should be examined further to establish if further links can be identified. Any intelligence generated can then be used to establish a pattern of behaviour, which may allow future events to be anticipated.

FORINT Challenges

As an intelligence product, FORINT has been used with some success in both a national and international context to supplement criminal intelligence, though it has still to be valued and absorbed entirely into ILP as a proactive product in the UK. '*When this potential is fully realised, the value of trace evidence will also be upgraded because it can be seen as a crucial source of information in an investigative or intelligence framework*' (Roux et al., 2007). Recently, the Home Office Transforming Forensics Project (2017), whose task it is to '*investigating the possible transformation of the delivery of forensic services using an evidence-based approach, by developing options and making recommendations that lead to a more effective, efficient and economical model, thereby delivering enhanced public safety and public confidence'*. This project is a driver for delivering a 'fit-for-purpose' forensic service for the UK policing but unfortunately decided to, 'exclude digital investigations and intelligence, and communications intelligence', yet another impediment and missed opportunity.

In today's policing, there are many objectives, demands and drivers which mould and direct the focus of policing. The government attaches performance requirements which police forces must attain. For example, *'Avon and Somerset Police adopted a 100% attendance policy (for Forensics??) to provide a high-level service to the public. While this was put in place to try to improve public satisfaction and overall performance, the latter was not achieved. It is clear that a balance between serving our public and utilising the time of our valuable CSI resources is essential, and a balance between the plans needs to be found'* (Williams, 2014). Forensic resources, who were already overstretched and under-resourced, were not only being tasked to attend 100% of house burglaries. The official government records show that nationally attendance rates for house burglaries were actually between 100% and 67% (NPIA Forensics21 Project, 2009). The actual recovery rates of forensic evidence varied significantly across the country with identification of offender rates declining as the project continued. As the adverse outcomes of the project started to show in the published statistics, the NPIA Forensics21 Project (2009) recommended:

- *Reduce [forensic] data collected by 80.4%*
- *Get rid of the irritating bits* [the negative aspects of the data]
- *Report back on* [forensic] *Data provided*
- *Demonstrate the contribution of forensics to major crime and contribute to national communications plan* [public reassurance]

This effort to give public reassurance was driven by several recent critical policing failures, where issues arise there are questions raised in relation to intelligence. "...the British Crime Survey published in March found less than half of those questioned had confidence in the force's ability to deal with crime and antisocial behavior. While researchers know that while people's opinion of the NHS goes up if they have recently used it personally, the reverse is true for the police" (McVeigh et al., 2009).

CSI departments and resources were motivated by the Home Office data that was generated monthly, and under pressure, to ensure departments were reaching the government's key performance indicators for crime reduction. The recommendations given by The NPIA Forensics21 Project were eventually implemented, and this had a negative effect on the CSI community to collect evidence at crime scenes. With the focus shifted to public reassurance, the priority shifted to attending crimes to placate an irritated public who saw the police as failing in its role.

The 'public reassurance' strategy resulted in the under-resourced CSIs being sent to all crimes as a public relations exercise. There were a significant number of tasks that had no potential for the CSI's to harvest meaningful FORINT. The situation was aggravated further as the tasking was often initiated by 'TV show' untrained police staff. This misconceived policy and a belief that the more tasks forensic resources attend, the more intelligence will be collected was wrong. If there are no realistic prospects of harvesting forensic evidence, there is no forensic requirement to attend. The tasking criteria had a negative impact on the forensic community and attracted criticism from the public, and within policing as outwardly, it appeared FORINT was failing The collection of trace evidence diminished, and the identification rates declined significantly. What was required was carefully considered tasking criteria to target evidential retrieval and areas of intelligence interest. This strategy could encompass an all 'viable' crimes approach.

The value of FORINT is significant when it operates in a proactive and preventative stance. For this to be successful, it needs some significant harmonisation in several areas including terminology, definition, legislation, forensic submission policy, results in standardisation and policies and processes at a national and international level. There is a demonstrated need for a driver for Forensics intelligence to be integrated and accepted into the intelligence cycle. For this to happen, there are many historic challenges to overcome, involving not just those in policing, but the wider community or those that can provide intelligence products.

Weston (2015) suggests, the sources of intelligence ultimately decide the direction of the response to the intelligence machine. Though ILP may be a desirable strategy, there is a general absence of empirical knowledge of how effective this strategy is, particularly concerning terrorism. As discussed, this challenge could, in part, be due to the unwillingness, or inability due to legal restraints, of those who take part in intelligence gathering to be open and discuss sensitive matters.

There is no doubt that criminalistics forensics and FORINT are powerful tools for fighting crime, with proven success in reacting to crime and terrorist incidents. The continued reactive deployment of this form of intelligence is driven by the forensic disciplines themselves, traditional policing culture and a widespread lack of awareness in the capabilities of government to offer a proactive choice. A change in police culture is needed to accept FORINT and embrace multi-disciplinary crime analysis that embraces a holistic view of the challenge of identifying criminals who are pre-terrorism. In the UK, the *National Ballistics Intelligence Service (NABIS)*, compiles FORINT relating to firearms and ballistics. The intelligence is currently limited to reactive Investigation of crime though there is potential and *'permits strategic analysis of the 'extent of illegal possession, supply and use of firearms and directing proactive work upstream'* (www.nabis.police.uk/Database, *accessed 14 June 2016). This latter is clearly preventive in orientation'* (Tilly & French, 2018). Again, to take advantage of this FORINT requires training and education to promote at a minimum, partnership working and sharing of information.

The notion that FORINT is ambiguous to many is easy to understand as FORINT appears to be 'fuzzy' and have no clear remit. *'While the concepts of 'forensics' and 'intelligence' separately describe two far-reaching fields of policing, their combination does not bring much into focus'* (Legrand & Vogel, 2014a, b). In its current state FORINT is unlikely to be developed in mainstream policing and taught as a subject to policing resources.

There is enough research to establish that there are opportunities to identify criminal behaviours which many terrorists have been proven to exhibit before committing terror offences. More research to generate strategy and policy should be conducted in FORINT by combining skills of criminology, social sciences and law enforcement. By collaborating and understanding each other's priorities, they work together to detect patterns of criminal behaviour to identify suspects and possibly deter future terrorists. Any advantage that might be gained through actively identifying criminals likely to become terrorists or those involved in crime networks could be lost; the advantage must be recognised by forensic resources which should strive to promote FORINT and proactively seek to break into the 'need to know' world of the intelligence cycle.

In partnership with other specialist professionals, FORINT can identify links that other disciplines cannot; without cooperation and collaboration, opportunities to prevent crime may be lost. Being proactive is difficult with the continued lack of intelligence sharing and continuation of a 'need to know' culture, as well as resource constraints. Trusted partnerships should be encouraged and developed amongst the forensic providers, government and non-government agencies as Intelligence systems should be a hub to analyse and share information with partners and experts, including forensic resources and specialists. Sharing intelligence, with the appropriate risk measures, must be embraced by the intelligence community and subject matter experts to aid intelligence-led decisions. Education and ongoing training could produce a starting point to solve some of these challenges, providing police and security staff with the awareness required to at least start the conversation around FORINT. Accordingly, *'Consideration should be given to including FORINT elements in any induction course.'* (Raymond & Julian, 2015).

To provide FORINT with the credibility required by the intelligence community, and to give strategic, tactical and operational focus, a process must be supported by a robust FORINT framework which unites forensic resources, the police, the intelligence and forensic science services, encouraging an environment where FORINT is shared to prevent crime. For these changes to be realistic, there should be *'a more holistic integration of information conveyed by traces and behavioural analysis into the intelligence process'* (Ribaux et al., 2014). To realise this potential, a comprehensive and inclusive intelligence framework should be developed, which integrates the operators involved in harvesting intelligence and utilises the specialist skills of experts.

The framework and its operatives should recognise FORINT as a unique intelligence product specifically focused on the analysis of forensic traces from multiple scenes. The trace intelligence can assist analysts to identify patterns of offence, offending, criminal behaviour and MO. Patterns of consistency and inferences can also be formed to assess the individual's behaviours, therefore, assisting with anticipating their future activities. *'Intelligence partly provided by traces, thus indicates how preventive/repressive measures can be envisaged and planned to mitigate an activity causing harm. This switch from reactive to proactive policing changes the reference for forensic science and also connects to the global field of security and policing, in particular to problem-solving or, broadly, to the so-called intelligence-led style of policing'* (Ribaux & Caneppele, 2018).

To ensure that such a framework is properly implemented and that it produces effective outcomes, education and training of all those involved in the forensic processes is best practice and delivered to facilitate an understanding of the significance of the FORINT to preventative intelligence. Education should prompt operational staff and 'analysts' to peer out of their discipline onto the broader intelligence landscape, sharing intelligence and hopefully acquiring a holistic view of the big picture. Co-operation and collaboration are key to making links between intelligence sources and intelligence to provide a proactive tool which positively impacts and contributes to the fight against terrorism.

It is difficult to define and measure success of FORINT; we can quantify the successful use of FORINT where there are quantifiable and known positive outcomes. What cannot be measured are the proactive and preventative outcomes that result in offenders being dissuaded from progressing from criminal behaviour to terrorist activity.

Unfortunately, even after the terrorist events of 7/7 and 21/7, the UK intelligence community are still, for the most part, extremely fragmented with intelligence staff often operating in a knowledge vacuum. Until the sharing of intelligence informatics becomes standard practice and subject matter experts are involved in analysis of intelligence and use of an intelligence cycle to put the information into context, FORINT will continue to be ineffective and misunderstood when used to prevent crime and terrorist activity.

Seminar Questions

1. "Law enforcement agencies can prevent a terrorist attack if able to access the right types of data and intelligence in [a] timely manner." How can FORINT assist in this process?
2. What are the Challenges facing FORINT?
3. According to the author "Targeted Forensics" can assist the Police prevent crime and terrorism, explain how this can be done?

Exam Questions

What is Forensic Intelligence (FORINT) and how can it be used to deal with criminal and Terrorist offences?

Why is FORINT important in detecting and detecting serious crime?

References

Almog, J. (2014). Forensics as a proactive science. *Science and Justice*, 325–326. Retrieved from https://doi.org/10.1016/j.scijus.2014.05.008

Anderson, D. (2017). *Attacks in London and Manchester: March–June 2017*. London: David Anderson.

Buckley, J. (2014). *Managing intelligence: A guide for professional law enforcement professionals*. Florida: CRC Press.

Cusson, M. (2018a). A method that combines criminology and forensic science. Considering the case of antiterrorism. In Q. Rossy (Ed.), *The Routledge international handbook of forensic intelligence and criminology* (Routledge international handbooks) (pp. 39–46). London/New York: Taylor & Francis. Kindle Edition.

Cusson, M. (2018b). *The Routledge international handbook of forensic intelligence and criminology*. (Q. Rossy, D. Decary-Hetu, O. Delemont, & M. Mulone, Eds.). New York: Routledge.

DutchNews.NL. (2018, June 19). *Three arrested in the Netherlands after DNA links them to Paris IS safe house*. Retrieved from DutchNews.NL. https://www.dutchnews.nl/news/2018/06/three-arrested-in-the-netherlands-after-dna-links-them-to-paris-is-safe-house/

Higgins, G. (2009). Quantitative versus Qualitative Methods: Understanding why Quantitative Methods are Predominant in Criminology and Criminal Justice. *Journal of Theoretical and Philosophical Criminology, 1*, 23–27.

Home Office. (2017). *Transforming forensics*. NPCC Forensics Portfolio Board. London: Home Office.

James, A. (2011, September). *The London school of economics and political science the influence of intelligence-led policing models on investigative policy and practice in mainstream policing 1993–2007: Division, resistance and investigative orthodoxy.* Retrieved June 2019, from Academia.edu. https://www.academia.edu/34382308/Thesis_-_examining_intelligence-led_policing

Legrand, T., & Vogel, L. (2014a, December). *Forensic intelligence.* Retrieved from ResearchGate. https://www.researchgate.net/publication/271820268

Legrand, T., & Vogel, L. (2014b, June 23). *The landscape of forensic intelligence research.* Retrieved from Taylor & Francis Online: https://doi.org/10.1080/00450618.2014.928830

Margot, P., & Ribaux, O. (1999). Inference structures for crime analysis and intelligence: The example of burglary using forensic science data. *Forensic Science International,* 193–210.

McCulloch, J., & Pickering, S. (2009, August). Pre-crime and counter-terrorism imagining; future crime in the 'war on terror'. *British Journal of Criminology, 49,* 629–645.

McGarrell, E., Freilich, J., & Chermak, S. (2007). Intelligence Led Policing as a framework for responding to terrorism. *Journal of Contemporary Criminal Justice, 23*(142), 142–158.

McVeigh, T., Syal, R., & Hinsliff, G. (2009, April 19). G20 protests: How the image of UK police took a beating. *The Guardian.*

Milne, R. (2012). *Forensic intelligence.* Florida: CRC Press.

NPIA Forensics21 Project. (2009, February 13). Forensic data returns 2009–10 and beyond. *PowerPoint.* London: NPIA

Ribaux, O., & Caneppele, S. (2018). *The Routledge International Handbook of Forensic Intelligence and Criminology.* (Q. Rossy, D. Decary-Hetu, O. Delemont, & M. Mulone, Eds.). New York: Routledge.

Ribaux, O., Crispino, F., & Roux, C. (2014). Forensic intelligence: Deregulation or return to the roots of forensic science? *Australian Journal of Forensic Sciences,* 1–15.

Rooss, Roux etc = Eva Bruenisholz, Sameer Prakash, Alastair Ross, Marie Morelato, Troy O'Malley, Michael Anthony Raymond, Olivier Ribaux, Claude Patrick.

Sellars, S. (2007). *Middlesbrough theft from motor vehicle initiative* (pp. 171–181). Middlesbrough: Cleveland Police.

Tilly, N., & French, J. (2018). *The Routledge international handbook of forensic intelligence and criminology.* (Q. Rossy, D. Decary-Hetu, O. Delemont, & M. Mulone, Eds.). New York: Routledge

Vogel, L., & Legrand, T. (2014). The landscape of forensic intelligence research. *Australian Journal of Forensic Sciences, 47*(1), 16–26. https://doi.org/10.1080/00450618.2014.928830

Weston, C. (2015). Hunting for 'Paper Gangsters'; an institutional analysis of intelligence led policing in Canadian context. Wilfrid Laurier University, Department of Criminology. Thesis and Dissertations (Comprehensive)

Part VI

Counter-Terrorism

Counterterrorism

Lindsey Brine and Mark Roycroft

The vast majority of countries have experienced some form of terrorism. To counterterrorism, one must understand the reasons behind terrorism. There are common characteristics among all terrorist campaigns regardless of their cause. There have been seminal moments throughout the history of terrorism, particularly 9/11 in the USA, which have changed our daily routine, lives and transportation. They have also influenced the law enforcement and central government response.

Rapoport (2002) states that terrorism has evolved in waves and "identifies four such waves: the anarchists who originated in 1880s Russia; the anti-colonial terrorists that followed the First World War; the new left which emerged in the 1960s; and the religious wave which dominates the current threat landscape. Lone actors have been active during each wave."[1] This means that governments and the police have had to adapt their techniques and response. As the Provisional Irish Republican Army (PIRA) said after the massive assassination attempt attack on the

---

[1] Pantucci, Raffaello, Clare Ellis, and Lorien Chaplais. "Lone-Actor Terrorism" (2016).

L. Brine (✉) • M. Roycroft
Rabdan Academy, Al Bhustan, Abu Dhabi, United Arab Emirates
e-mail: mroycroft@ra.ac.ae

© The Author(s), under exclusive license to Springer Nature Switzerland AG 2021
M. Roycroft, L. Brine (eds.), *Modern Police Leadership*,
https://doi.org/10.1007/978-3-030-63930-3_21

British Prime Minister in 1984, "Today we were unlucky, but remember, we only have to be lucky once; you (The Government) will have to be lucky always."

Terrorist conflicts also have a direct impact on the rise of transnational crime through cybercrime, kidnapping for ransom, and drugs, arms and human trafficking, all of which are used to fund radical Islam-based terrorist organizations or rebels such as the Taliban in Afghanistan (Transnational Organized Crime, 2019). Due to the rise of these types of terror-related crimes, especially post 9/11, legislation was introduced amending the Criminal Code of Canada with the Anti-terrorism Act, 2002, and subsequently the Combating Terrorism Act, 2012. These allow for the prosecution of individuals. These cases show that financial intelligence and good legislation are needed to combat terrorism. The government cannot legislate its way out of the current problems. Any legislation must be appropriate and not counterproductive. Internment in Northern Ireland was introduced in 1971 and lasted for four years. In retrospect, it aided Irish Republican Army (IRA) recruitment. While it had been successful in the IRA's 1956–1961 campaign, this was largely due to the fact that it relied on good, current intelligence and the Irish Government introduced the measure simultaneously in the South of Ireland. This highlights two of the major prongs of anti-extremism policy: good intelligence and a transnational approach to dealing with potential extremists.

Modern counterterrorism demands that each state retains a high state of vigilance along with a proportionate legal response and a robust intelligence-gathering capacity. However, it is critical to note that effectively combating terrorism demands more than just decisive enforcement and legislation—it also demands a strong counter-radicalization, education and prevention strategy. Former Counterterrorist Commander John Grieve (in the *Future of Policing* [2014]) believes that states need to "find a balance between protecting a community and keeping its confidence".

Definition of Terrorism

There are a number of definitions for terrorism. However, the simplest and most widely accepted one is that terrorism is the use of violence or the threat of violence against non-combatants or civilians, usually motivated by political, religious or ideological beliefs in order to compel a government to do something or to refrain from doing something. In many countries, the legal definition also includes terrorist acts against its citizens overseas.

There are many examples throughout history where someone is seen as a 'terrorist' by the government, but as a 'freedom fighter' by large segments of the population. In some cases, these individuals have eventually entered politics. Some of these campaigns have revolved around self-determination in the post-colonial era, while others have been economic, political, religious or social. Examples of these include the following: Nelson Mandela who eventually became President of South Africa in 1994; Jomo Kenyatta who, after the Mau Mau rebellion, became President of Kenya in 1964, and Archbishop Makarios who became President of Cyprus in 1960 after the Ethnikí Orgánosis Kipriakoú Agónos (EOKA) rebellion against British rule.

As noted, there is a multitude of definitions of terrorism. Likewise, there are varying views of what the main types of terrorism are. Generally speaking, the most widely held view is that there are five main types of terrorism:

- **State-sponsored terrorism:** terrorist acts on a state or government by a state or government.
- **Dissent terrorism:** groups which have rebelled against their government.
- **Terrorists and the Left and Right:** groups rooted in political ideology.
- **Religious terrorism:** extremists who are motivated by religion.
- **Criminal terrorism:** terrorists acts used to aid in crime and criminal profit.

Terrorist groups have an ideological or political motive for their actions. Their main weapon is, as their name suggests, terror or fear, but with modern technology, many groups also commit cyberattacks or fraud. The ability to strike anywhere, at any time, is one of their greatest assets. This was evident with the PIRA campaign in Ireland and the Spanish Fuerzas Armadas Revolucionarias de Colombia (FARC; Revolutionary Armed Forces of Colombia) campaign in Colombia, both of which continued for decades. Many of these groups believe they are engaged in a battle of the weak (terrorist group) against the strong (the state). Silke (2014, p. 330) discusses the role of asymmetrical warfare of the weak against the stronger forces. Silke states that there are four main phases involved in terrorist campaigns: provocation, blame, escalation and endurance. Initially, the terrorists 'provoke' the state into a strong reaction and then escalates the violence so that each side blames the other for atrocities. The final phase, the endurance phase, is aimed at breaking the will of state to sustain the conflict.

The origins of terrorist behaviour according to Margolin (1977, pp. 273–4) are a "response to the frustration of various political, economic, and personal needs or objectives". Wilkinson (1977) states that the causes of political violence in general also cause terrorism. These include ethnic conflicts, religious and ideological conflicts, poverty, modernization stresses, political inequities, lack of peaceful communications channels, traditions of violence, the existence of a revolutionary group, governmental weakness and ineptness, erosions of confidence in a regime, and deep divisions within governing elites and leadership groups. Shaw (1986, p. 365) provides a strong case for "The Personal Pathway Model", by which terrorists join terrorist groups. The components of this pathway include early socialization processes, narcissistic injuries, escalatory events (particularly confrontation with police) and personal connections to terrorist group members.

By understanding the reasons for terrorism and why young people join terrorist groups, one may begin to form some ideas about counterterrorism and how to encourage disengagement from terrorist group, including diverting people from radicalization. Counterterrorism policy should flow from the recognition that social factors tend to surpass political ones in the making and deterrence of terrorists.

The Canadian Experience

Throughout the twentieth century and into the twenty-first century, Canada experienced multiple domestic terrorism events. These have included assassinations, bombings, hijackings and kidnappings. The Canadian experience with terrorism, especially since the 1960s, has provided many valuable lessons about dealing with complex terrorism investigations. One of the most significant terrorist events in the history of Canada occurred in the late 1960s with the now infamous 'October Crisis', which the Government of Canada, under the leadership of Prime Minister Pierre Trudeau, managed with strength and resilience. Radical elements in the Province of Quebec, one of the thirteen provinces and territories in Canada pushed forward a violent agenda of terrorism with the hopes of securing total political independence for the province. The Front de la Liberation du Quebec (FLQ), or the Front for the Liberation of Quebec, was created by extremist separatists in this predominantly French-speaking province. Tension between the French and English remained flared up in the late 1960s and reached a peak in October 1970. The creation of the FLQ, which can be seen as nothing less than a terrorist organization, resulted in a small group of extremists employing violence as a means to their ultimate goal of creating their own country. Over the course of eight years, the FLQ committed over 200 violent crimes, including bombings and shootings (Canadian Broadcasting Corporation, 2019).

Canada was originally settled by explorers and migrants from England and France. As the result of a war between the two countries in the 1700s, the colony of Canada was formed, with England having won the war. All French lands were declared as spoils for England and annexed to the colony (Citizenship and Immigration Canada, 2019); hence, the FLQ bombings of the 1960s targeted federal government agencies such as the Royal Canadian Mounted Police and financial venues such as the Montreal Stock Exchange that represented a united Canada. On October 5, 1970, the FLQ abducted an Irish-born British diplomat and five days later kidnapped the Quebec Minister of Labour, Pierre Laporte. On October 13, Prime Minister Pierre Trudeau ordered the military into Ottawa to support the police. Trudeau was asked by reporters how far he would go to eliminate the terrorist threat in order to maintain peace and security within Canada, including Quebec. The following exchange took place:

Reporter:	"Sir what is it with all these men with guns around here?"
Trudeau:	"There's a lot of bleeding hearts around who don't like to see people with helmets and guns. All I can say is 'go ahead and bleed' but it's more important to keep law and order in this society than to be worried about weak-kneed people who don't like the looks of…".
Reporter:	"At what cost? How far would you go? To what extent?"
Trudeau:	"Well, just watch me." (Canadian Broadcasting Corporation, 2014).

On October 16, as a result of increasingly violent acts by the FLQ, Prime Minister Trudeau declared martial law under the authority of the War Measures Act (1914). The following day, the body of Laporte was discovered in the trunk of a car. On the same day as that, the FLQ secretly informed the government that the execution of Cross was indefinitely suspended and that his status was as a 'political prisoner'. Cross was ultimately released several weeks later. After a protracted investigation targeting the FLQ, the insurrection ended after almost a decade, with many of the suspects either dead or in prison. Some were granted political asylum in Cuba after a deal was negotiated with Fidel Castro (Canadian Broadcasting Corporation, 2019).

This firm-handed approach and the refusal by Trudeau to acquiesce to the separatist demands of the FLQ established the precedent for Canada's future dealings with terrorist threats, both domestic and extra-territorial. In the decades following the 'October Crisis', Canada postured itself on the international stage as a country that had successfully dealt with domestic terrorism. Current scholarly readings on terrorism fail to mention that Canada has undergone a period of significant domestic terrorism since the 1960s. Authors such as Innes and Theil (2012) focus primarily on the experiences of the USA and UK despite the fact that the Canadian experience has valuable lessons for many Western democracies. One such example is the domestic deployment of the military during peacetime, similar to the deployment of the UK military during the Troubles in Northern Ireland. There is a tendency for both domestic and foreign police and governments to look towards the Northern Ireland experience for proposed solutions to current problems, however rarely is the Canadian October Crisis examined. The bilateral cooperation between the military and Royal

Canadian Mounted Police demonstrated that the country was a capable and willing force in taking a strong stance against approaching terrorist threats.

Fact Sheet

Military Aid to the civil power is an important democratic decision. Any tactic like this requires careful planning and the Army need to understand the social and legal context they operate in. The Army in Northern Ireland had a Yellow Card system which they had to consult. The deployment of troops raises issues of the capacity and capability of the civil powers.

In the late 1970s, largely as a result of the October Crisis, the Canadian Security Intelligence Service was established by transferring the purely security intelligence function from the Royal Canadian Mounted Police. It was determined that during the October Crisis, officers from the Royal Canadian Mounted Police used many illegal investigative techniques such as unauthorized electronic surveillance and break-ins. A Royal Commission was established with one of the key recommendations being the creation of a new security service devolved from the Royal Canadian Mounted Police (Canadian Encyclopedia, 2019). However, the Royal Canadian Mounted Police retained responsibility, and still does, for criminal investigations associated with terrorist threats and attacks (Royal Canadian Mounted Police, 2019).

Despite its reputation as a peaceful country, Canada also has a lengthy history of terrorist events with an international dimension. In more recent times, significant plots or successful attacks have been primarily related to extra-territorial extremists with the most infamous probably being the dual Air India attacks that targeted flights originating in Vancouver, Canada. Babbar Khalsa is a militant Sikh extremist group seeking political independence from India. Canadian Pacific Air Lines Flight 60 left Vancouver in June 1985 destined for Toronto. A bomb was hidden in checked luggage and subsequently transferred to Air India Flight 182 which was bound for Delhi, India, with stops in Montreal, Canada, and London, UK, en route. A mid-flight intentional explosion on Air India Flight 182 occurred in June 1985 at an altitude of 9400 metres approximately 190 kilometres southwest of County Cork in the Republic of Ireland. This resulted in 329 deaths and placed the recovery operation in the hands of the Republic of Ireland. Simultaneously, a bomb exploded at Narita International Airport in Japan and killed two baggage handlers. Canadian Pacific Air Lines Flight 003 had originated in Vancouver and luggage had been checked there that was due to be transferred in Japan to Air India Flight 301 which was ultimately bound for Bangkok, Thailand. Both attacks were attributed to Sikh extremists residing in Canada. Inderjit Singh Reyat, a Canadian resident, was the only person convicted for these bombings. Numerous other Babbar Khalsa Sikh extremists were implicated, and some charged. Others either fled Canada and have never been located or were killed by Punjabi police during incidents there (Bolan, 2017). A subsequent Commission of Inquiry (2010) determined that there needed to be improved cooperation and communication between the Royal Canadian Mounted Police and the Canadian Security Intelligence Service with the goal of successfully investigating and combatting terrorism.

The prevalence of terrorist violence in Canada continues to this day. Throughout previous decades, Canada has dealt with a number of terrorism issues such as oil pipeline bombings and the assassination of a Turkish diplomat in Ottawa (The Canadian Encyclopedia, 2019). According to Innes and Thiel (2012), "terrorist violence tends to be highly dramatic, attacking signal targets (people, places, events) to attract media attention to amplify its effect. Terrorists are in the business of fear, and their operating practices reflect this" (p. 556).

In order to effectively address terrorism, Canada has adapted its model of policing and implemented some of the best practices and lessons learnt by the UK. The current focus in the Royal Canadian Mounted Police, the agency legislated as the lead investigator and oversight body for all criminal terrorist activities in Canada, is primarily centred on 'high policing'. 'High policing' focuses on collecting intelligence and infiltrating and disrupting criminal groups (Bayley, 2006). On the other hand, 'low policing' deals with everyday crime in order to protect the public and is completed by preventing and solving smaller crimes. Generally, it is a reactive form of policing. Canada has done a good job of focusing on 'high policing' in order to deal with terrorism. As noted by Innes and Thiel (2012), 'beyond policing' is typically defined by military action, both domestic and international, such as the declaration of martial law by Prime Minister Trudeau during the October Crisis or Canadian military deployment to Afghanistan, Iraq and Mali. 'High policing' also includes actions and activities by the Canadian Security Intelligence Service, the Royal Canadian Mounted Police (RCMP) and the Communications Security Establishment. However, Canada has gone one step further by offering the services of RCMP members in combat zones in order to deal with intelligence gathering and, equally importantly, to coach and mentor foreign police officers in these 'failed states'. Canada has deployed police officers on both training missions and investigations to such terrorist hotspots as Afghanistan, Iraq, Libya, Mali, Palestine, Sudan and Syria.

The UK Experience

The UK first dealt with organized terrorism in 1858 when an Irish 'Fenain' terrorist planted a bomb in London. The 1970s saw a resurgence of bombs on the mainland of the UK as a consequence of the 'Troubles' in Northern Ireland from 1969 to the Good Friday agreement of 1998. In a long-running campaign, both the Royal Ulster Constabulary and the Metropolitan Police Anti-terrorist branch developed significant expertise in counterterrorism. (Fig. 1).

The use of technology, the need for local intelligence, and the ease of travel are all aspects of counterterrorism policing in the twenty-first century. The Police Chiefs were concerned with establishing adequate structures to deal with counterterrorism. As English states, the UK Rule of Law model (2010, p. 303) is a highly effective system facilitating a uniquely collaborative interaction between police and the intelligence services. Successful counterterrorism will rely most heavily on

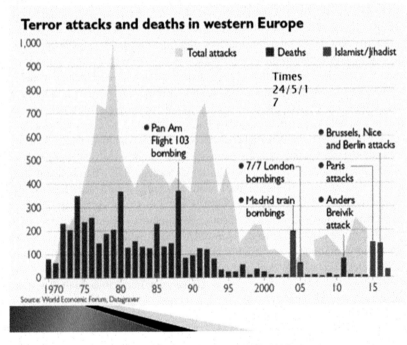

Fig. 1 Terror attacks and deaths in Western Europe, 1970–2015

police work and on respect for the existing legal framework of civilian authority and power.

Chief Constables and Police and Crime Commissioners (PCCs) in "Police Chiefs in the UK" reflected on the issue of radicalization. One Chief Constable stated that radicalization is corrosive and with segregated classrooms we need better joined up thinking. The Trojan Horse report into alleged extremism in Birmingham schools led by Peter Clarke, ex-head of the Counterterrorism Branch, concluded that "there was an agenda to introduce an intolerant and aggressive Islamist ethos" into some Birmingham schools. He further found a "sustained and co-ordinated agenda to impose upon children in a number of Birmingham schools the segregationist attitudes and practices of a hardline and politicised strain of Sunni Islam". He made a total of 14 recommendations around school governance; inspection processes add local authority and Department of Education responsibilities. This report illustrates the reach and scale of the extremism problem. The approach to dealing with the issue reaches across public bodies including education, local authorities and policing. Local government and PCCs along with the urban mayors in the UK are well placed to tackle these issues, locally supported by an effective and fair national programme.

The UK police have to balance maintaining public confidence with arresting terrorists. Many Chief Constables (Roycroft, 2016) felt that police neighbourhood teams were as important to counterterrorism policing as specialist officers in the regional Counterterrorism Units (CTUs). One Chief Constable added that "with the growth of ISIS and ISIL the first responsibility of Government is to protect the public by supporting local policing". Another Chief Officer believed that "Counterterrorism is linked to Community Policing, we now have individuals involved in terrorism with no individual objective they are operating within a disorganised franchise. We cannot afford communities to feel disconnected from their communities if they have no cops to talk to, they may not tell us what is happening." One Chief Constable stated that "we are building good relationships with the Asian Muslim community, as the demographics change".

One Police and Crime Commissioner (PCC) reflected this viewpoint and stated that while local police officers were protecting the Muslim community's right to worship with patrols outside mosques, it would allow radicalization issues to be dealt with in a non-threatening way. This local model of terrorism policing was seen as "not negotiable, we need a laminate model for policing involving PCSOs in Asian Communities, it is the nexus between counter Terrorism and other crimes". Other Chiefs felt that counterterrorism should be changed and not just led by the security demand but linked to community policing.

One Chief Constable faced problems reaching out to local Muslim communities who felt they were being berated and isolated because of terrorist activity and child sexual exploitation claims. The Chief commented that the group became very hard to engage with and it took time to restore trust. The Independent Reviewer of Terrorism (IRTL), David Anderson QC stated in his 2014 report that he was concerned with the number of arrests of 18–20-year-old males. This key demographic group demands attention and appropriate measures to divert it from extremist activity.

The Police Role in Counterterrorism

While nothing is easier than to denounce the evildoer, nothing is more difficult than to understand him.

Fyodor Mikhailovich Dostoevsky
One of the keys to understanding how to deal with terrorism is to understand those who commit such crimes. The police and related agencies need to 'understand' the demands, motivations and organization of terrorist groups. Counterterrorism demands a proactive investigative response blended with local community policing. In "Police Chiefs in the UK, Politicians, HR Managers or Cops?" (Roycroft, 2017), Chief Constables and Police and Crime Commissioners were primarily concerned with the risk of dealing with spontaneous terrorist activity such as marauding attacks. This requires keeping a standing army of specialist firearms officers with a certain radius of likely targets and equipping the regional counterterrorist units (CTUs) within the UK to enable them to respond appropriately. The disruption of terrorist activity involves intelligence gathering and using the theme of convergence. This enables the police to recognize ordinary crimes that terrorists have committed in preparation for their operational attack: committing traffic violations, obtaining fake identification papers, smuggling, human trafficking, counterfeiting, committing piracy, drug trafficking and so on. Local police serve as the eyes and ears of communities; they are best positioned to observe behaviours that have a nexus to terrorism (Downing, 2009a).

Islamic State of Iraq and the Levant (ISIL) is a new type of terrorist organization with unique funding streams. There is a need to freeze terrorist funds and stop terrorist financing to deprive terrorists of funds. This can involve sanctions in using the financial system and disruption of cross border cash movements and blocking shell companies. In Canada the Financial Transactions and Reports Analysis of Canada (FINTRAC) (see fintrac-canadafe.gc.ca) uses financial intelligence to assist money laundering and terrorist financing investigations. Terrorists, however, also use informal value transfer systems, fraud, counterfeit goods, tax evasion and drug trafficking. The UK is a member of Financial Action Task Force (FATF), and it introduced the Criminal Finances Act in 2017 to investigate terrorist financing by permitting law enforcement to request more Suspicious Activity report (SARs) and share terrorist financing information.

Counterterrorism Strategies

Intelligence

Wardlaw (1988) states that "the first line of defence against political terrorism is good intelligence" (*1998 2nd Edition Political Terrorism*). He articulates that 95% of the important action in any campaign consists of intelligence and police work whereby suspects are identified, movements are infiltrated, and police seek international collaboration to disrupt terrorists. The secret of winning the battle against terrorism in an open democratic society is winning the intelligence war and thwarting terrorist conspiracies before they happen. Neil Basu, head of the London Metropolitan, stated in 2019 (BBC News 19/9/19) that 22 terrorist plots had been disrupted in the UK from March 2017 to 2019 with 7 of those being orchestrated by members of Right wing organizations.

Investment in the process of acquiring such intelligence is, arguably, the crucial foundation upon which other interlinked aspects of response can then be built. Without such high-quality intelligence, it is likely that all aspects of state response will stumble ineffectively. English (2009) states, "Intelligence is the most vital element in successful counter terrorism."

In the USA prior to the 9/11 attacks, a report entitled "Countering the Changing Threat of International Terrorism", the National Commission on terrorism identified that lack of information sharing was addressed by the inception of the Department of Homeland Security post 9/11. The US National Intelligence Community now has 17 members (see US Intelligence Community www.intelligence.gov) from the Central Intelligence Agency (CIA) to the armed forces to the Drug Enforcement Agency (DEA) and Fedearl Bureau of Investigation (FBI).

Intelligence-Led Policing—Why It Is Needed?

Michael Clarke Royal United Services Institute (RUSI) sees intelligence-led policing (ILP) helping to prevent and disrupt terrorism. It is intended to help build a base that offers two-way communication between the community and the police. It helps to offer reassurance that they are not isolated, misunderstood or mistrusted. When they try to deal with radicalization within their own community (Clarke 2019: 259 Jihadist Terror), this assists in isolating the violent extremists from their support networks.

The 'balkanization' of apps and the web has rapidly accelerated, creating an enormous social media network that is difficult to monitor, let alone enforce. Intelligence-led policing is struggling to keep up with social media intelligence (SOCINT). Some countries are attempting to ban certain social media platforms that originate in other countries. The scope for criminal and terrorist groups to be able to communicate through social networks and apps is vast and without technical limits. Under the Prevent scheme, the Metropolitan Police Counter-Terrorism Internet Referral Unit removed 32,057 pieces of content from websites in 2017. And since its inception in 2010, it has removed 310,039 pieces of content (see Freedom of Information (FOI) request January 1, 2018).

Deradicalization programmes, such as those run by Saudi Arabia and Sweden, have had mixed results. The UK has had some success with attempts by the Channel programme, part of the UK government's counterterrorism strategy (see Prevent), to divert young people from extremism. Such efforts, with police, social services and local authorities working together, draw on methods used to help young people leave gangs (*Economist* August 30, 2014). The International Centre for the Study of Radicalisation and Political Violence (ICSR, 2013) report on Countering Online Radicalization found that reducing the appeal of extremist views and working with multi agencies would have an impact on extremists' behaviour along with strategic prosecutions of offenders. The report found that cultural awareness is an important part of deradicalization and that people should appreciate what is acceptable in their societies.

Community Engagement

Effective community engagement will be a key enabler of gathering community intelligence to support the wider intelligence picture. This strategy is required to prevent and detect terrorist activity within the UK. Most terrorist operations are 'disrupted' and stopped before they take place.

The UK's Strategy for Countering Terrorism is by collecting community intelligence across a wider and much broader demographic area. This is referred to by Brine and the Canadian counterterrorism strategy as 'low policing'. It has also become apparent that Police and Community Support Officer (PCSOs) have developed a greater intelligence-gathering role than their colleagues from non-police agencies (e.g., local authorities, housing associations, etc.) (Robinson, 2006, p. 15), an approach that has been highlighted by Loveday as being one of the advantages that have accrued to PCSOs besides community relationships (Loveday, 2015, p. 3).

It may be argued that this 'intelligence-gathering role' which PCSOs have developed could now be in direct conflict with their original core purposes, namely community engagement and problem solving. Gaining the trust of the local community for community engagement in particular will become increasingly more difficult when that community feels they are being 'spied' on, a point made quite public when a PCSO working with Cambridge's Muslim community in 2014 was found to be gathering intelligence on behalf of Special Branch (Cambridge News, 2014). In this case, the Muslim leaders of that community stated that the revelation 'left a bitter taste in their mouths', and it would have taken a significant amount of work by Cambridgeshire Constabulary to restore any trust between the local Muslim community and their Neighbourhood Policing team.

This approach is not an original one and was most prominently highlighted by the 9/11 Commission Report (2004, p. 417) which stated that there are "no punishments for not sharing information [and] … agencies uphold a 'need to know' culture of information protection rather than promoting a 'need to share' culture of integration". This reasoning led to the 9/11 Commission recommending that "information procedures should provide incentives for sharing, to restore a better balance between security and shared knowledge" and that a decentralized model should be sharing that intelligence horizontally, allowing different databases to be searchable across agency lines (National Commission on Terrorist Attacks Upon the United States, 2004, p. 418). This concept is closely followed by the CONTEST strategy (see below) in the UK, particularly within the PREVENT strand, and has been responsible for encouraging and operationally deploying PCSOs within local neighbourhoods in order to collect as much relevant information and intelligence as possible.

Fact Sheet: The UK Government's Anti-terrorism Strategy Under CONTEST

Prevent is the first strand of CONTEST, the government's anti-terrorism strategy.

Prevent aims to stop people becoming terrorists by halting the spread of extremist ideology and mentoring young people at risk.
Pursue is the name given to the work of the security services in identifying and investigating plots and prosecuting terrorists.

Prepare refers to the work of responding to an attack, including the deployment of armed police and medical crews.

Protect is the name given to the work of defending Britain's borders, reducing the vulnerability of the transport network and protecting crowded places such as shopping centres.

As part of the overall Contest strategy to stop the growth of terrorism, the 4P strategy, shown above, is in place to protect the public. Nazir Afzal, an ex-Crown Prosecution Service (UK) (CPS) Chief Prosecutor, comments (*The Times* June 3, 2017, The Prosecutor 2020) that with Prevent "there's an industry which is trying to undermine Prevent". The key question Nazir raises is: who represents a particular community and who should the public authorities liaise with to curb extremism?

The UK Government Prevent strategy defines extremism as vocal or active opposition to fundamental British values, including democracy, the rule of law, individual liberty, and mutual respect and tolerance of different faiths and beliefs. Extremism also includes calls for the death of members of the armed forces (Revised Prevent Duty Guidance for England and Wales, originally issued on March 12, 2015, and revised on July 16, 2015, paragraph 7).

The UK Prevent strategy has proved controversial and has even been commented on by the head of the Counter-Terrorism Branch Assistant Commissioner Neil Basu, who stated "that up to 80% of those who wanted to attack the UK were British-born or raised, which strongly indicated domestic social issues were among the root causes". Neil Basu told the *Guardian*, "Counter-terrorism operations increased by 50% from 2015 to 2017 and have since remained at a high level … the deeper causes need examining and we need to stop the flow of recruits into terrorism." Don't forget that 70%–80% of the people we arrest, disrupt or commit an attack here, are born and raised here. Grievances held by people who were "malleable" to terrorist recruitment were highly dangerous, he said, calling for sociologists and criminologists to take a leading role in helping police tackle the problem. Giving a personal view on the best ways to reduce terrorism", Basu said: "Policies that go towards more social inclusion, more social mobility and more education are much more likely to drive down violence … than all the policing and state security apparatus put together. It is much more likely to have a positive effect on society."

"The prescription for me is around social inclusion – its social mobility, its education, its opportunity." Basu said Prevent, which he sees as the most important plank of Britain's counterterrorism strategy, had been "badly handled", but its work was vital and had to become more transparent and community led.

Goldsmith (2016) sees the response by central government as multi-faceted and that "there is no single response but rather there are many". This nuanced-layered response demands a multinational effort from bodies like the UN and a transnational response particularly intelligence sharing.

Elements of Counterterrorism Policy in Canada, Australia and New Zealand

Most countries in the developed world have a coordinated counterterrorism strategy that brings together public agencies, the police and intelligence services. The UK 4P strategy is similar to Canada's *Prevent, Detect, Deny* and *Respond* (see https://www.publicsafety.gc.ca›cntr-trrrsm›index-en   *Accessed   7.9.19*).   The Canadian 'Building Resilience Against Terrorism', Canada's first counterterrorism strategy, was released in 2012. This comprehensive strategy guides more than 20 federal departments and agencies to better align them to 'prevent, detect, deny and respond' to terrorist threats by using a whole-of-government approach. The Federal Terrorism Response Plan (FTRP) strengthens coordination among security and intelligence departments and agencies, and others, and facilitates a collective response to a terrorist threat or incident occurring in Canada.

Australia talks of Preparedness, Prevention, Response and Recovery, all remarkably similar to the 4P counterterrorism strategy discussed previously in the UK. The different responses to Counter terrorist (CT) illustrate the different political constitutions of countries such as Canada with a more federal composition. Nevertheless, the national CT policies remain remarkably consistent https://www.nationalsecurity.gov.au/Pages/default.aspx (accessed September 7, 2019).

The New Zealand approach to managing the risk of terrorism is known as the 4Rs:

Reduction—identifying and analysing long-term risks and taking steps to eliminate these risks.

Readiness—developing operational systems and capabilities before an emergency happens.

Response—taking action immediately before, during or directly after a significant event.

Recovery—using coordinated efforts and processes to bring about immediate, medium-term and long-term regeneration.

This was sorely tested after the shootings at the Christchurch mosque by Bretton Tarrant in March 2019 (https://dpmc.govt.nz›NationalSecurity, *Accessed September 7, 2019*).

In conclusion, counterterrorism demands a multi-faceted response from all police and security services, and ultimately the government as a whole. It requires intelligence gathering, community engagement and deradicalization programmes. It must embrace legislation, policing (local and national), education, local government, international cooperation and the third-sector voluntary organizations. This can be done under the banner of programmes such as Prevent, but it must be targeted carefully and consistently. This is a long-term issue with long-term solutions.

Case Study Mumbai Attacks

On November 26–29, 2008, Mumbai was attacked by ten determined members of a radical Islam terror group entered the city from the largely unprotected Arabian Sea aboard dinghies having started their voyage in coastal Pakistan. The attackers spread out to assault high-profile targets throughout the urban centre of Mumbai firing at victims randomly and throwing explosives. Hostages were taken and buildings set on fire. A hospital, hotels, a Jewish centre, restaurants and tourist sites were specifically selected for their symbolic value and to inflict maximum casualties. Police, commandos and regular military troops were deployed. Dozens of hostages were freed over the course of the four-day attack. Over 300 people were injured, 166 killed (including 20 police and soldiers), and 9 of the 10 terrorists were killed. It is clear that Indian security forces were caught off guard by the scope and violence of the assault. The lone survivor among the terrorists signed a seven-page confession approximately two weeks after the attack, in which he confirmed that the men were members of Lashkar-e-Taiba (Army of the Pure), a Pakistan-based radical Islam terror organization. He described his weapons training at several Lashkar camps in Pakistan and his indoctrination on alleged Indian atrocities against Muslims. Training in Karachi, Pakistan, included how to operate fast boats. When he and nine others embarked on a ship in late November, each man was issued an AK-47 assault rifle, hand grenades and ammunition. They were ordered to maximize casualties on their mission (https://fas.org/irp/eprint/mumbai.pdf).

Seminar Questions

Does faith-based natural law justify acts of violence?
Name three of the elements of counterterrorism?

Why is international cooperation necessary to combat terrorism and what groups can assist individual countries?

Discuss and compare two separate countries' counterterrorism policies. What are the differences and similarities?

Is there any way to prevent an attack such as the one that took place in Mumbai in 2008?

In a large-scale attack with multiple targets and perpetrators, who should have overall responsibility for coordinating the response and why?

Is sound and robust intelligence able to stop all terrorist attacks? If not, why not?

Exam Question

Prevent has been seen as a controversial approach to stooping terrorism and radicalization. Assess its effectiveness.

References

Berger, J. M., & Strathearn, B. (2013, March). *Who matters online: Measuring influence, evaluating content and countering violent extremism in online social networks.* International Centre for the Study of Radicalisation (ICSR).]

Downing, P. (2009a, February). *Methods: Information, systems and contexts.* Oxford: Chandos Publishing.

Downing, M. P. (2009b, February). Policing terrorism in the United States: The Los Angeles police department's convergence strategy. *Police Chief, 76*(2), 28,30–36,39,40,43.

English, R. (2009). *Terrorism how to respond.* Oxford.

Margolin, J. (1977). Psychological perspectives in terrorism. In Y. Alexander & S. M. Finger (Eds.), *Terrorism: Interdisciplinary perspectives* (pp. 273–274). New York: John Jay.

Prevent Duty Guidance for England and Wales (originally issued on 12th March 2015 and revised on 16th July 2015, paragraph 7).

Rapoport. (2002, September 11). The four waves of rebel terror and D.C. *Journal of Generative Anthropology* (Spring/summer).

Silke, A. (2014). *Terrorism all that matters.* Hodder & Stoughton.

The future of policing. (2014). (Prof J. Brown, Ed.). Routledge.

Homegrown and Lone-Actor Terrorism

Ian Brine and Lindsey Brine

Lone-actor and homegrown terrorism poses a credible threat to the safety and security of the globe, specifically the West. Lone-actor terrorism, also known as lone-wolf terrorism, is essentially "a person who acts on his or her own without orders from—or even connections to—an organization".[1] There have been numerous examples of lone-actor and homegrown terrorism in recent years, such as the Norway attack carried out by Anders Breivik in 2011 which resulted in 77 deaths. Breivik, a Norwegian national, became radicalized in far-right ideology and committed the violent attack to send a message to opposing belief systems.[2] Lone-actor and homegrown terrorism will continue to increase and evolve through the systematic targeting of susceptible individuals in the West by terrorist organizations.

It is clear that certain individuals, such as Breivik, are more vulnerable to radicalization due to factors such as mental health, sociological belonging, and upbringing. These individuals are targeted through the media operations branches of well-established terrorist organizations such as the Islamic State, al-Qaeda, and

---

[1] Spaaij, Ramón. Understanding Lone Wolf Terrorism: Global Patterns, Motivations and Prevention, Springer, 2011.

[2] Pantucci, Raffaello. "What have we learned about lone wolves from Anders Behring Breivik?." *Perspectives on Terrorism* 5, no. 5–6 (2011).

I. Brine (✉) • L. Brine
Rabdan Academy, Al Bhustan, Abu Dhabi, United Arab Emirates

© The Author(s), under exclusive license to Springer Nature Switzerland
AG 2021
M. Roycroft, L. Brine (eds.), *Modern Police Leadership*,
https://doi.org/10.1007/978-3-030-63930-3_22

extreme right-wing organizations. The need to combat homegrown terrorism was voiced by former American President Barack Obama (2011), who stated that "the risk that we're especially concerned over right now is the lone wolf terrorist, somebody with a single weapon being able to carry out wide-scale massacres of the sort that we saw in Norway recently. You know, when you've got one person who is deranged or driven by a hateful ideology, they can do a lot of damage, and it's a lot harder to trace those lone wolf operators."[3]

As previously stated, the threat of lone-actor and homegrown terrorism is credible and will continue to be so until the means of radicalization are combatted. According to an analysis of lone-actor terrorism in 30 European countries, "98 lone-actor terrorist plots were identified between 1 January 2000 and 31 December 2014, including 79 led by individuals, 12 by dyads and 7 by triads".[4] In order to thwart the radicalization efforts of terrorist organizations, it is critical that counterterrorism operations target social media campaigns aimed at individuals susceptible to radicalization. Also, imperative to successfully hindering the rise in homegrown terrorism is intra-agency cooperation on operations, such as sharing data linked to the profiles of lone-wolf terrorists. Lastly, it is important for law enforcement agencies to communicate with their communities. Oftentimes, signs of self-radicalization are apparent before an attack is carried out. Communication with the community may signal law enforcement to individuals at a high risk of self-radicalization.

In order to combat the threat of lone-actor and homegrown terrorism, it is crucial to understand the history of the phenomenon of self-radicalization and lone-actor attacks. Rapoport (2012) states that terrorism has evolved in waves and "identifies four such waves" (see chapter "The Crime Scene Expert"). This notion of a long-standing existence of lone-actor terrorism is solidified by Bates who states that it was evident in the "writings of ... The People's Will, a Russian revolutionary group which championed the concept of 'propaganda by deed' in the middle of the 19th century. The 'propaganda by deed,' committed by a lone wolf terrorist, appears to have been resurrected in the latter half of the 20th century primarily by radical right-wing extremists, Islamic jihadists."[5]

---

[3] McCauley, Clark, Sophia Moskalenko, and Benjamin Van Son. "Characteristics of lone-wolf violent offenders: A comparison of assassins and school attackers." Perspectives on Terrorism 7, no. 1 (2013): 4–24.

[4] Ellis, Clare, Raffaello Pantucci, van Zuijdewijn J. de Roy, Edwin Bakker, Benoît Gomis, Simon Palombi, and Melanie Smith. "Lone-Actor Terrorism: Analysis Paper." Countering Lone-Actor Terrorism Series (2016): 24.

[5] Bates, Rodger A. "Dancing with wolves: Today's lone wolf terrorists." The Journal of Public and Professional Sociology 4, no. 1 (2012): 1.

The profile of a lone-actor terrorist is complex and one must consider numerous psychological and sociological factors including mental health, social involvement, upbringing, and victimization. Each individual is influenced by different factors. However, there are a number of commonalities among these individuals. "First and foremost, 96.6 percent of lone-actor terrorists are male according to research conducted in 2014.[6]" In addition, only 13 percent communicate their motivations through detailed manifestos.[7] Breivik's 2011 manifesto "2083: A European Declaration of Independence" is mentioned by Brenton Tarrant in his manifesto. Tarrant, a lone-wolf terrorist, massacred 51 people in March 2019 at a New Zealand mosque while livestreaming the entire shooting on Facebook. The New Zealand attack of 2019 was the first to be broadcast and recorded live by the suspect and seen on Facebook. Despite being removed quickly, Facebook admitted that its Artificial Intelligence (AI) moderation failed. The evidential, public responsibility issues and legal consequences exposed by this attack provide dilemmas for any police leader. Yet as much as these attacks necessitate new understanding and knowledge, they also still require the best of more traditional techniques of local policing and evidence gathering with robust decision making.

Broadcasting extremist attacks live through social media is a disturbing, but increasingly common trend. In his far-right manifesto 'The Great Replacement', Tarrant argues a white-supremacist, anti-immigrant stance. Tarrant also pays homage to Alexandre Bissonnette, the perpetrator of a white-supremacist attack on a mosque in Quebec City, Canada, in January 2017 that killed six people. Tarrant painted Bissonnette's name on one of the weapons used in the Christchurch massacre. In August 2019, Patrick Crusius shot and killed 23 people at a Walmart store in Texas. His attack was also based on white supremacy and anti-immigration was titled 'The Inconvenient Truth' and was posted on 8chan shortly before the attack. In this document, he praises the perpetrator of the Christchurch shooting.

The majority of lone wolves are active online, often posting their motivations and propaganda on internet forums, and are often socially isolated. Social isolation, though, does not equate to increased mental health issues. "Terrorists are no more likely to suffer from psychopathology than non-terrorists from the same backgrounds. Nor are terrorists more economically deprived or disadvantaged.

---

[6] Gill, Paul, John Horgan, and Paige Deckert. "Bombing alone: Tracing the motivations and antecedent behaviors of lone-actor terrorists." Journal of forensic sciences 59, no. 2 (2014): 425–435.

[7] Ellis, Clare, Raffaello Pantucci, van Zuijdewijn J. de Roy, Edwin Bakker, Benoît Gomis, Simon Palombi, and Melanie Smith. "Lone-Actor Terrorism: Analysis Paper." Countering Lone-Actor Terrorism Series (2016): 24.

Thus research has turned most analysts away from the idea that there is some profile of individual characteristics that can be used to identify potential terrorists."[8]

It is also important to distinguish between true lone-actor attacks and attacks committed because of severe mental health issues. In October 2014, the War Memorial and the Federal Parliament Buildings in Ottawa, Canada, were attacked by a lone gunman. A Canadian soldier on sentry duty at the War Memorial was killed. The perpetrator was subsequently killed inside the Parliament Buildings by responding police officers. He was homeless, had an extensive criminal record, was addicted to intravenous drugs, and suffered from serious mental health issues. Although the perpetrator had claimed allegiance to the Islamic State, no evidence was uncovered that he had become radicalized. Similarly, the December 2014 Lindt Café siege, in which the perpetrator and two others were killed, appeared to be a lone-wolf attack based on support to the Islamic State, but there are many persuasive arguments that the perpetrator had long-standing severe mental health issues and extensive criminality.

It is interesting to note that an analysis of lone-actor terrorism clearly demonstrates that there is a significant difference in age groupings between religiously inspired and right-wing ideologies. "[T]he majority of religiously inspired perpetrators were younger than 25 years old, with the number of perpetrators declining as age increased; this is in direct contrast to right-wing lone-actor terrorists where the majority were at least 40 years old."[9] This reaffirms the notion that although profiles can be useful during investigations, they cannot guarantee certainty in determining who is a lone wolf. Another varying factor in lone-actor terrorists is previous military training. Lone-actor terrorists who have prior military training are far more lethal than their untrained counterparts, "accounting for 19 percent of perpetrators but 29 percent of fatalities".[10] It is clear that this increases the threat as "attacks planned by those with military training or experience were prevented in only 18 percent of cases, a substantially lower proportion than the 36 percent of perpetrators who had no comparable training or experience".[11] Law enforcement agencies must consider this when assessing individual threat levels.

---

[8] McCauley, Clark, Sophia Moskalenko, and Benjamin Van Son. "Characteristics of lone-wolf violent offenders: A comparison of assassins and school attackers." *Perspectives on Terrorism* 7, no. 1 (2013): 4–24.

[9] Ellis, Clare, Raffaello Pantucci, van Zuijdewijn J. de Roy, Edwin Bakker, Benoît Gomis, Simon Palombi, and Melanie Smith. "Lone-Actor Terrorism: Analysis Paper." Countering Lone-Actor Terrorism Series (2016): 24.

[10] Ibid.

[11] Ibid.

The process toward radicalization is long and complex and involves numerous psychological and social factors. Radicalization is essentially "the process of adopting an extremist belief system, including the willingness to use, support, or facilitate violence, as a method to effect societal change".[12] The New York City Police Department has developed a four-stage model in relation to Jihadization. Phased models, such as this, "aspire to denote the most important causes of radicalization and to give a chronological definition of the different stages people allegedly go through in a radicalization process".[13] The New York City Police Department defines four stages: pre-radicalization, self-identification, indoctrination, and Jihadization.

> Pre-radicalization characterizes the period before an individual is exposed to jihadi-Salafi ideology. Self-Identification marks the process of exploring Salafi Islam, adopting its ideological tenets, and affiliating with its proponents. Indoctrination is the intensification stage, both for the individual's beliefs and for his commitment to the ideas, to action, and to his like-minded collective. Finally, … 'jihadization'. The hallmark is the individual's acceptance of, and commitment to, his individual duty to act on behalf of the cause.[14]

One must recognize that it is not simply the religion or belief that causes an individual to become radicalized, but a series of events that turns a belief into a radical ideology. "After four decades of research on radicalization, no common socio-economic or religious pathway toward violence has been found, and the term itself is characterized by considerable contestability."[15] Radicalization must be understood as a process rather than a singular event.

Lone-actor and homegrown terrorism poses a substantial risk to the safety and security of the West. It is imperative that law enforcement agencies understand both the current risk level of identified self-radicalized individuals and the risk of attack from unknown, lone actors. The rise of social media and online propaganda sites has enabled terrorist organizations to anonymously radicalize and recruit followers. For example, al-Qaeda in the Arabian Peninsula has published 16 issues of

---

[12] Vidino, Lorenzo, and James Brandon. "Countering radicalization in Europe." London: The International Centre for the Study of Radicalisation and Political Violence 9 (2012).

[13] Veldhuis, Tinka, and Jørgen Staun. *Islamist radicalisation: A root cause model*. The Hague: Netherlands Institute of International Relations Clingendael, 2009.

[14] Borum, R. (2011). 'Radicalization into Violent Extremism I: A Review of Social Science Theories', Journal of Strategic Security, 4(4), 7–36. Available here: http://scholarcommons. usf.edu/cgi/viewcontent.cgi?article=1139&context=jss

[15] Aly, Anne, Stuart Macdonald, Lee Jarvis, and Thomas M. Chen. "Introduction to the special issue: Terrorist online propaganda and radicalization." (2017): 1–9.

a magazine titled *Inspire*. It aims to provide a "variety of instructional advice it provides supporters, from methods requiring relatively high levels of sophistication, such as improvised explosive devices, to vehicular and arson attacks. The technical advice gained from Open Source Jihad has been cited by law enforcement in many successful and foiled terrorist attacks, most notably the 2013 Boston Bombing in which the pressure cooker bomb used was based on Open Source Jihad instructions."[16]

As access to the internet increases, so will self-radicalization. In fact, "50 percent of perpetrators conducted at least part of their engagement in a virtual setting. Some of these cases involve the downloading of videos, images and literature as well as interaction on official forums and pages."[17] Online propaganda is specially crafted toward a target population, that being young males susceptible to radical ideology. This is evident in al-Qaeda's media campaign which targets individuals who have already begun to self-radicalize. Often the content seems to be "aimed at a less informed and intellectually engaged audience … Most notably, rather than concentrating on shaping the ideas of its readers, Inspire focuses more on driving them to action. One especially interesting development in Inspire that sets it apart from other examples of al Qaeda propaganda is that it targets an English-speaking readership and emphasizes a do-it-yourself ethos, publishing in each issue a section called 'Open Source Jihad'."[18] Between 2010 and 2016, al-Qaeda published 16 editions of *Inspire*. These carried 'how-to' articles on subjects including assassinations, bomb-making, hiding bombs, lone-wolf attacks, marauding vehicle attacks, radicalizing African Americans, and suicide attacks. The current risk level of homegrown terrorism and lone actors will continue to rise as the ability to access information on the internet becomes more widespread.

When analyzing the threat level of a specific individual, an instrument called the Terrorist Radicalization Assessment Protocol (TRAP-18) can be utilized to assess the risk of attack. The TRAP-18 comprises "eight proximal warning behaviors (such as pathway, fixation, identification, and last resort) and ten longer term distal characteristics (such as personal grievance, ideological framing, failure of sexual

---

[16] Reed, A. 2017. 'Exploring the role of instructional material in AQAP's Inspire and ISIS' Rumiyah', Europol.

[17] Ellis, Clare, Raffaello Pantucci, van Zuijdewijn J. de Roy, Edwin Bakker, Benoît Gomis, Simon Palombi, and Melanie Smith. "Lone-Actor Terrorism: Analysis Paper." Countering Lone-Actor Terrorism Series (2016): 24.

[18] Lemieux, A. F., Brachman, J. M., Levitt, J., & Wood, J. (2014). Inspire magazine: A critical analysis of its significance and potential impact through the lens of the information, motivation, and behavioural skills model. Terrorism and Political Violence, 26(2), 354–371.

pair bonding, and mental disorder)."[19] Ultimately, the instrument is a useful and effective tool for law enforcement agencies in prioritizing potentially radicalized individuals for further investigation. TRAP-18 has been used and tested extensively on American and European jihadism-inspired lone actors.[20] The most recent research indicates that it is a more reliable predictor of lone-actor behavior in American cases than European. It is believed that TRAP-18 is being utilized by law enforcement agencies in North America and Europe, but understandably, this information is not being released.

TRAP-18: Analysis of Anders Breivik

As previously mentioned, the use of TRAP-18 is effective in gauging the risk level of a self-radicalized individual in engaging in violent behavior. The application of TRAP-18 to the case of the Norway attack by Breivik demonstrates the effectiveness of the instrument.

Warning Behavior Typology

The first section of TRAP-18 analyzes the eight warning behavior typologies. First, the 'Pathway' warning behavior deals with the preliminary planning and research of the potential attack. Breivik "was meticulous in his long-term planning for every aspect of his operation. Having defined what he is going to do, he then goes about preparing for it building cover stories at every stage. If he is to be believed this was his focus for nine years, though it is likely that actual planning was conducted over a much shorter time period."[21] The second warning behavior is 'Fixation' which "indicates an increasingly pathological preoccupation with a person or a cause, accompanied by a deterioration in social and occupational life".[22] Breivik, a far-

---

[19] Meloy, J. Reid, and Paul Gill. "The lone-actor terrorist and the TRAP-18." *Journal of Threat Assessment and Management* 3, no. 1 (2016): 37.

[20] Christine Shahan Brugh, Sarah L. Desmarais & Joseph Simons-Rudolph (2020) Application of the TRAP-18 Framework to U.S. and Western European Lone Actor Terrorists, Studies in Conflict & Terrorism, DOI: https://doi.org/10.1080/1057610X.2020.1758372

[21] Pantucci, Raffaello. "What have we learned about lone wolves from Anders Behring Breivik?." *Perspectives on Terrorism* 5, no. 5–6 (2011).

[22] Meloy, J. Reid, and Paul Gill. "The lone-actor terrorist and the TRAP-18." *Journal of Threat Assessment and Management* 3, no. 1 (2016): 37.

right Norwegian outcast, "even warns other potential terrorists they will increase their chance of being apprehended by 100% for every other person they involve in their plans: 'Don't trust anyone unless you absolutely need to (which should never be the case). Do absolutely everything by yourself', he writes in his manifesto."[23] The complete social isolation demonstrates the deterioration in the social life of Breivik. The third warning is 'Identification', which "indicates a psychological desire to be a pseudo-commando, have a warrior mentality, closely associate with weapons or other military or law enforcement paraphernalia, identify with previous attackers or assassins, or identify oneself as an agent to advance a particular cause or belief system".[24] Breivik often posed in military clothing and held weapons prior to the 2011 attacks. In fact, Breivik admired the Israeli Defense Force and wore one of their vests during the attack. "He deeply identified with the Knights Templar of the 12th century, the 'special forces' of the Christian Crusades against Islam, and claimed that he attended a meeting of the Knights in London in 2002 ... He referred to himself as 'Commander Breivik who just performed an operation on behalf of the Knights Templar' while talking to the police by telephone during his attack."[25]

The fourth warning behavior 'Novel Aggression' deals with a prior act of violence to demonstrate the capabilities of an individual. Breivik lived a quiet life prior to the attacks in Norway, as such this warning behavior is not overtly evident.

The 'Energy Burst', a fifth warning behavior, is "an increase in the frequency or variety of any noted activities related to the target, even if the activities themselves are relatively innocuous, usually in the days, weeks, or hours before the attack".[26] This behavior is clearly present as Breivik underwent immense preparation in the days prior to the attack. In his manifesto, the Norwegian lone wolf states, "In any case; I feel I've been really slacking the last week and I really need to step up the pace now. At least now, everything is set so I do not have to research any more techniques and methods." Breivik goes on to speak of his change in dietary regime

---

[23] Bakker, Edwin, and B. A. de Graaf. "Preventing lone wolf terrorism: Some CT approaches addressed." *Perspectives* 5 (2011): 8.

[24] Meloy, J. Reid, and Paul Gill. "The lone-actor terrorist and the TRAP-18." *Journal of Threat Assessment and Management* 3, no. 1 (2016): 37.

[25] Meloy, J. Reid, Elmar Habermeyer, and Angela Guldimann. "The warning behaviors of Anders Breivik." *Journal of Threat Assessment and Management* 2, no. 3–4 (2015): 164.

[26] Meloy, J. Reid, and Paul Gill. "The lone-actor terrorist and the TRAP-18." *Journal of Threat Assessment and Management* 3, no. 1 (2016): 37.

in the days prior, speaking of increasing his workout supplements and feasting at a local restaurant.[27]

The leakage warning behavior (sixth) is arguably one of the most present warning behaviors in Breivik. This is communication with another party prior to the attack. Breivik "read and sometimes posted material on anti-Islamic internet sites such as Gates of Vienna, New English Review, Brussels Journal, Stormfront and the Norwegian document no".[28] Most notably, Breivik emailed a 1500-page manifesto to over 1000 email addresses outlining his ideology and life 90 minutes before the attack.[29] This leakage of ideology is a crucial time for law enforcement to intercept a lone actor, as it provides physical evidence of a premeditated attack that can be used to disrupt, apprehend, and charge the individual.

The seventh warning behavior 'Last Resort' is the time in which the lone actor decides that violence is necessary to enforce their ideology. As per his testimony, Breivik felt the need to kill to share his views. Breivik stated before the court: "I did this out of goodness, not evil. I acted in self-defense on behalf of my people, my city, my country. I would have done it again."[30] The eighth warning behavior is a 'Directly Communicated Threat' to the target and/or law enforcement. Breivik chose to keep a very low profile in the time prior to attack and did not fulfill this behavior.

Ten Distal Behaviors

The next stage of the TRAP-18 model used for gauging the risk of self-radicalized individuals is to analyze ten distal behaviors. Although there are ten, only the highly relevant ones of Breivik will be assessed. A 'Failure to Affiliate with an Extremist Group' behavior clearly meets the behavior of Breivik. Although he was involved with the far-right and anti-Islam online community prior to the attacks, Breivik "seems (also) to have concluded that they are not to be trusted with information and do not necessarily share his goals".[31] This move to not join an extremist

---

[27] Meloy, J. Reid, Elmar Habermeyer, and Angela Guldimann. "The warning behaviors of Anders Breivik." *Journal of Threat Assessment and Management* 2, no. 3–4 (2015): 164

[28] Sandberg, Sveinung. "Are self-narratives strategic or determined, unified or fragmented? Reading Breivik's Manifesto in light of narrative criminology." *Acta Sociologica* 56, no. 1 (2013): 69–83.

[29] Ibid.

[30] Breivik Testimony. 2012. New York Times, p. A9.

[31] Pantucci, Raffaello. "What have we learned about lone wolves from Anders Behring Breivik?" *Perspectives on Terrorism* 5, no. 5–6 (2011).

group is what pushed Breivik to become a lone actor. However, the online presence of Breivik does demonstrate a distal behavior entitled 'Dependence on the Virtual Community'. As noted, he distributed his manifesto online prior to the attack. This was done so that the online communities could reaffirm his actions. Furthermore, the manifesto was distributed in an attempt to inspire similar attacks. Another distal behavior that was evident in Breivik was a 'Mental Disorder'. According to a psychology evaluation prior to the attacks, "Breivik during a long period of time has developed the mental disorder of paranoid schizophrenia, which has changed him and made him into the person he is today ... [they uncovered] grandiose delusions whereby he believes he is to determine who is to live and who is to die."[32] The analysis of various distal behaviors is clearly an effective tool in determining the risk level of a homegrown terrorist.

In 2011, the US "created its first Federal Countering Violent Extremism (CVE) strategy, which revolves around countering the radicalization of all types of potential terrorists".[33] A portion of the CVE strategy revolves around the need to engage with the community and inform the public of warning behaviors of self-radicalization. The strategy states that "studies indicate that family members, friends, or close acquaintances are the most likely to observe activities or behaviours suggesting an individual is being radicalized or has violent intent".[34] According to the Global Terrorism Index, since 2006, 98 percent of all deaths from terrorism in the US have resulted from attacks carried out by lone actors, resulting in 156 deaths.[35] It is clear that due to the immense political turmoil in many places on the globe, the risk of a lone-wolf attack remains very high.

The risk of homegrown and lone-actor attacks poses a credible threat to the safety and security of nations across the globe. In order to combat the threat of lone-actor attacks, it is imperative that law enforcement gains an in-depth understanding of the factors contributing to self-radicalization. The process of radicalization is long and complex, and it is crucial to intercept an individual in the infancy of their radicalization process. Law enforcement must endeavor to analyze and understand the profiles of lone actors, in order to successfully intervene in

---

[32] Ibid.

[33] Liang, Christina Schori. "Cyber Jihad: Understanding and Countering Islamic State Propaganda." GSCP Policy Paper 2 (2015): 4.

[34] House, White. "Strategic implementation plan for empowering local partners to prevent violent extremism in the United States." (2011).

[35] McCauley, Clark and Sophia Moskalenko. 2017. "Lone Wolf Terrorists: What Motivates Them?" *Defence Procurement International* (March).

potential pre-meditated attacks. In the end, as the ability to access online propaganda and communicate with various communities increases, so will the threat of homegrown terrorism.

Seminar Questions

- Using two examples from the text, describe the lone actors' behavior during the incidents they instigated and what appeared to be their motivation?
- How can the police and Western societies try to prevent and disrupt lone actors' behavior?
- TRAP-18 analysis uses eight warning behavior typologies; describe how these illustrate the effectiveness of the system.

Exam Question

Using Andres Breivik in Norway as an example comment on how the stages of TRAP-18 analysis can be used to describe his behavior during the 22nd July attacks in 2011.

References

Aly, A., Macdonald, S., Jarvis, L., & Chen, T. M. (2017). Introduction to the special issue: Terrorist online propaganda and radicalization. *Studies in Conflict & Terrorism, 40*(1), 1–9.

Australian National Security. (2019). *National terrorism threat advisory system.*

Bakker, E., & de Graaf, B. A. (2011). Preventing lone wolf terrorism: Some CT approaches addressed. *Perspectives, 5*, 8.

Bartlett, J., Birdwell, J., & King, M. (2010). *The edge of violence: A radical approach to extremism* (pp. 5–75). London: Demos.

Bates, R. A. (2012). Dancing with wolves: Today's lone wolf terrorists. *The Journal of Public and Professional Sociology, 4*(1), 1.

Borum, R. (2011). Radicalization into violent extremism I: A review of social science theories. *Journal of Strategic Security, 4*(4), 7–36. Available here: http://scholarcommons.usf.edu/cgi/viewcontent.cgi?article=1139&context=jss

Breivik Testimony. (2012, April 18). *New York Times*, p. A9.

Ellis, C., Pantucci, R., de Roy, Z. J., Bakker, E., Gomis, B., Palombi, S., & Smith, M.. (2016). *Lone-actor terrorism: Analysis paper* (Countering Lone-Actor Terrorism Series, 24).

Gill, P., Horgan, J., & Deckert, P. (2014). Bombing alone: Tracing the motivations and ante-
    cedent behaviors of lone-actor terrorists. *Journal of Forensic Sciences, 59*(2), 425–435.
Lemieux, A. F., Brachman, J. M., Levitt, J., & Wood, J. (2014). Inspire magazine: A critical
    analysis of its significance and potential impact through the lens of the information, mo-
    tivation, and behavioral skills model. *Terrorism and Political Violence, 26*(2), 354–371.
McCauley, C. R. (2019). Explaining Homegrown Western Jihadists: The importance of
    Western Foreign Policy. *International Journal of Conflict and Violence (IJCV), 12*, 643.
McCauley, C., & Moskalenko, S. (2017, March). Lone wolf terrorists: What motivates them?
    Defence Procurement International.
McCauley, C., Moskalenko, S., & Van Son, B. (2013). Characteristics of lone-wolf violent
    offenders: A comparison of assassins and school attackers. *Perspectives on Terrorism,
    7*(1), 4–24.
Meloy, J. R., & Gill, P. (2016). The lone-actor terrorist and the TRAP-18. *Journal of Threat
    Assessment and Management, 3*(1), 37.
Meloy, J. R., Habermeyer, E., & Guldimann, A. (2015). The warning behaviors of Anders
    Breivik. *Journal of Threat Assessment and Management, 2*(3–4), 164.
Mullins, S. (2011a). Islamist terrorism and Australia: An empirical examination of the
    'home-grown' threat. *Terrorism and Political Violence, 23*(2), 254–285.
Mullins, S. J. (2011b). *Australian Jihad: Radicalisation and counter-terrorism* (p. 1).
Olteanu, A., Castillo, C., Boy, J., & Varshney, K. R. (2018). The effect of extremist violence
    on hateful speech online. In *Twelfth International AAAIConference on Web and Social
    Media.*
Pantucci, R. (2011). What have we learned about lone wolves from Anders Behring Breivik?
    Perspectives on Terrorism, 5(5–6).
Pantucci, R., Ellis, C., & Chaplais, L. (2016). *Lone-actor terrorism.*
Phillips, B. J. (2017). Deadlier in the US? On lone wolves, terrorist groups, and attack lethal-
    ity. *Terrorism and Political Violence, 29*(3), 533–549.
Reed, A. (2017). Exploring the role of instructional material in AQAP's Inspire and ISIS'
    Rumiyah. *Europol.*
Sandberg, S. (2013). Are self-narratives strategic or determined, unified or fragmented?
    Reading Breivik's Manifesto in light of narrative criminology. *Acta Sociologica, 56*(1),
    69–83.
Spaaij, R. (2011). *Understanding lone wolf terrorism: Global patterns, motivations and pre-
    vention.* Springer. ProQuest Ebook Central, http://ebookcentral.proquest.com/lib/csuau/
    detail.action?docID=886210
The White House. (2011). *Strategic implementation plan for empowering local partners to
    prevent violent extremism in the United States.* Washington, DC: The White House.
Veldhuis, T., & Staun, J. (2009). *Islamist radicalisation: A root cause model.* The Hague:
    Netherlands Institute of International Relations Clingendael.

The Nexus Between Terrorist Organizations and Organized Crime

Michał Matyasik

EUROPOL's Serious and Organized Crime Threat Assessment (SOCTA) states that terrorist organizations (TOs) may engage in the exploitation of organized crime groups(OCGs) infrastructure in two ways: to procure tools such as firearms, fraudulent documents, and moving goods and people necessary to conduct terrorist activities; and to generate funds to finance terrorist operations (SOCTA 2017: 55). With the increasing threat of cooperation between TOs and OCGs, it is necessary to have a solid understanding of terrorism and organized crime. There is no commonly accepted definition of terrorism, nor that of an organized crime. In addition, different countries take a different approach to defining and addressing these issues.

Academics and practitioners have created over 260 various definitions of terrorism (Schmid 2016: 10). International organizations such as the United Nations (UN) and the European Union (EU) have been unable to find common ground and adopt a single, legally binding, definition that would be acceptable to all the states and other involved actors such as non-governmental organizations (NGOs). The main reasons behind the failure to reach consensus are historical and political. The use of violence and terror by an individual or a group of people pursuing a political agenda may be described at the same time as both an unacceptable act of terror and an act of heroism justified by the struggle for independence.

M. Matyasik (✉)
Rabdan Academy, Al Bhustan, Abu Dhabi, United Arab Emirates

© The Author(s), under exclusive license to Springer Nature Switzerland AG 2021
M. Roycroft, L. Brine (eds.), *Modern Police Leadership*,
https://doi.org/10.1007/978-3-030-63930-3_23

One of the first attempts, in 1793, to define "a terrorist" and "political terrorism" was undertaken by Francois-Noël Babeuf, who was a member of "The Conspiracy of the Equals" in France. He wrote,

> Terror is, first of all, a state of mind characterized by intense fear of a threatening danger on an individual level and, by a climate of fear, on the collective level. If the production of terror and exploitation thereof is a deliberate policy of a conflict party, we are dealing with political terror. [...] Terrorists play on our fear of sudden violent death and try to maximize uncertainty and hence anxiety to manipulate actual and prospective victims and those who have reasons to identify with them. (Schmid 2016: 6)

The League of Nations drafted the Convention for the Prevention and Punishment of Terrorism (CPPT) defined terrorism in 1937 as follows: "[...] all criminal acts directed against a State and intended or calculated to create a state of terror in the minds of particular persons, or a group of persons or the general public" (CPPT art. 1.1).

The United Nations attempted to define terrorism in 1972 and after seven years failed to reach a consensus. This topic was reconvened in 1996 and presented a draft of Comprehensive Convention against International Terrorism (CCIT) in which, according to art. 2, terrorism was defined as follows:

(a) Death or serious injury to any person; or
(b) Serious damage to public or private property [...]; or
(c) Damage to property, places, facilities or systems [...], resulting or likely to result in major economic loss, when the purpose of the conduct, by its nature or context, is to intimidate a population, or to compel a Government or an international organization to do or abstain from doing any act. (CCIT art. 2)

This has not yet entered into force.

At the European Union, as a result of 9/11 attacks, member states adopted the EU Council Framework Decision on Combating Terrorism (EU CFDCT 2002). The Framework sets out a list of offences and requires the member states to align their legislation and introduce penalties regarding terrorist offences. Offences can be qualified as acts of terrorism, if

1.1   *[...] given their nature or context, may seriously damage a country or an international organization where committed with the aim of:*
   – seriously intimidating a population, or
   – unduly compelling a Government or international organizations to perform or abstain from performing any act, or

- seriously destabilizing or destroying the fundamental political, constitutional, economic or social structure of a country or an international organization [...]. (EU CFDCT art. 1.1)

It further provides a definition of a "terrorist group":

A structured group of more than two persons, established over a period of time and acting in concert to commit terrorist offences. Structured group shall mean a group that is not randomly formed for the immediate commission of an offence and that does not need to have formally defined roles for its members, continuity of its membership or a developed structure. (EU CFDCT art. 2.1)

There are several recurring elements in the definitions of terrorism, namely the use of violence, spreading fear among population, coercing governments to take action or refrain from taking one and, finally, being part of a plan to achieve various ideological objectives.

An international standard addressing the challenge of organized crime was agreed upon in 2000 by the United Nations General Assembly Resolution no. 55/25 with the introduction of the Convention against Transnational Organized Crime (UNTOC or the Palermo Convention). The Palermo Convention represents a major step forward in the fight against organized crime and has fostered cooperation between member states. By 2019, the Convention had been signed by 147 countries, which committed themselves to adopt specific measures against transnational organized crime. These measures include an obligation to penalize, in domestic law, offences such as participation in an OCG, money laundering, corruption and obstruction of justice, and requests from countries to enhance inter-state cooperation in cases of extradition, mutual legal assistance and law enforcement cooperation. The Convention does not provide any definition of "organized crime," which was a conscious decision made by the negotiators of the draft (Puttonen and Romiti, 2020: 1). Due to the rapid development of the world and with the expansion of the actions in which criminal organizations are involved, any attempt to create a comprehensive inventory of illicit activities would result in the list becoming outdated very quickly. Instead of that, the Convention defines an OCG as

a structured group of three or more persons, existing for a period of time and acting in concert with the aim of committing one or more serious crimes or offences established in accordance with this Convention, in order to obtain, directly or indirectly, a financial or other material benefit. (UNTOC art. 2a)

According to some authors, both organized crime and terrorism can endanger the security of a country and the international community (Blazevska Andonovska and Glavinov 2016: 108). Both groups employ similar tactics, organizational structure, secrecy and a tendency to use violence. However, at the same time, they are distinct from each other in respect to their motivations and objectives.

S. Mullins, J.K. Wither and R. Monaco compare the characteristics of TOs and OCGs and classify them into four categories: profiles, methods, organization and motives (Mullins et al. 2016: 67–71). The single and the biggest risk factor of becoming a criminal or a terrorist is being a young male, whereas a high socioeconomic status and stable family affairs are mitigating factors. A.P. Schmid collected the major differences and similarities between terrorists and criminals (ICCT 2018: 13–14). What distinguishes terrorists from criminals is the fact that the first ones are usually highly motivated by ideology, strive for followers, use less discriminating violence and victimization, seek publicity and compete with governments in pursuit of legitimacy and their overall objective is to cause political changes. Both groups use similar tactics (e.g. kidnappings, assassinations, illegal taxation, extortion, etc.), operating in secrecy and possessing "underground" structures.

United Nations Security Council Resolution no. 2195 expressed concern that terrorists benefit from transnational organized crime through the trafficking of arms, people, drugs, art artefacts and from the illicit trade in natural resources, as well as from kidnapping for ransom, extortion and bank robbery (S/RES/2195: 1). Additionally, a combination of terrorism, violent extremism and transnational organized crime may aggravate conflicts and, in specific cases, complicate conflict prevention and resolution efforts (S/RES/2195: 2). The resolution neither provided a definition of a nexus nor elaborated on its characteristics. Instead, it focused on threat mitigation and prevention, calling on member states to enhance their activities in regard to capacity building activities, adoption of international legal instruments and the enhancement of info-sharing activities (S/RES/2195: 3–7).

The phenomenon of cooperation between terrorists and organized crime has taken on a whole new meaning after the Cold War. Earlier, major terrorist organizations enjoyed a considerable financial stabilization relying mostly on the money flow from states sponsoring terrorist activities. With the end of the Cold War, and the beginning of a new world order in the 1990s, that support began to decline and terrorist organizations were forced to look for alternative sources of income, pioneering new models of nexus and "business logic to terrorism" (Ligeti and Lassalle 2018: 3). Additionally, the international community, as well as several states, has employed new improved tactics and procedures to address the threat of terrorism. Consequently, this change in the security environment compelled terrorist organizations to look for a new partnership, namely with OCGs, which could provide logistics and assistance to sustain their daily operations.

The United Nations Interregional Crime and Justice Research Institute (2016) categorizes three different phases of the nexus evolution: conflict and instability, transition and convergence (UNICRI 2019: 2–7). The first phase—conflict and instability—is the period when organized crime and terrorist groups form their structures and commence their activity separately. If a nexus occurs, it might be of a spontaneous and temporary character. At this phase, mitigating or combatting the nexus and illegal activities is most challenging for the security forces due to the overall instability in a given region (e.g. in the case of countries affected by armed conflicts and failed states). In specific cases, terrorists and criminals may even compete for access to the territory and a monopoly on illegal activity.

The second phase—transition—takes place when the peace process is introduced and the state enters a reconstruction stage, rebuilding its security forces and consolidating the rules of good governance. In that phase, terrorists and criminals tend to coexist and enhance their cooperation as a counterbalance to more effective state security forces.

The third phase—convergence—is when the state becomes stronger, with effective security apparatus helping to reduce violence and criminal activity. The nexus between TOs and OCGs may change into being unified or hybrid. The hybrid criminal-terrorist organizations are less eager to challenge the state with violence, refocusing their activities towards corruption of officials and underground operations outside of the general public and media attention. In some instances, one organization may even change its character and evolve from a terrorist organization into an OCG. In others, OCGs may begin to employ tactics of terrorism, or TOs may engage in criminal activities typical of crime syndicates.

Makarenko developed a model which was based predominantly on post 9/11 countries affected by high levels of destabilization and violence, for example, torn by civil wars or inter-state conflicts (Europe's Crime-Terror Nexus 2012: 16). The model divides the progression of the nexus into four steps (Makarenko 2004: 131). First is a form of alliance or loose cooperation between OCG and TO with the aim of mutual benefit. Second is the adoption of the tactics of the other group. Third is the evolution of motivations, when an organized criminal group develops a political agenda having a priority over a financial interest, or a terrorist organization refocuses its operations mainly on profit maximization. And the final stage takes place when both OCG and TO are operating in the same zone of fragile or failed state, and the organizations merge into one, combining both political violence with activities characteristic of criminal enterprises.

In 2017 the Italian Guardia di Finanza—a fiscal law enforcement agency—warned the authorities that oil is allegedly being shipped from the territories under the control of the so-called Islamic State of Iraq and Syria (ISIS), with the help of

Italian Mafia. The specific role of the OCG and the logistics were not determined, but the fact that such alliance exists remains unquestionable (Foschini and Tonacci 2017). Another interesting example is the role of Al-Qaida in the Islamic Maghreb (AQIM) and its cooperation with OCGs in the Sahel region. The Algerian security forces reported in 2010 that they clashed repeatedly with AQIM fighters, providing security escorts for convoys of drug smugglers. The terrorists were utilizing their knowledge of the region and terrain as well as the access to small and heavy arms, in return for money from drug smugglers. The authorities assume that such cooperation makes both groups even a more potent threat (Chikhi 2010).

The importance of combating the terrorism and organized crime nexus was raised again in the United Nations Security Council Resolution 2482(2019). The Security Council expressed its concern that specific individuals and criminal groups facilitate procurement networks for ISIL (Islamic State of Iraq and the Levant) and Al-Qaida to obtain military grade equipment such as unmanned aircraft systems and improvised explosive devices (S/RES/2482: 2). The Security Council called upon all member states to strengthen border protection, adopt appropriate laws and mechanisms, implement their obligations fully to collect and analyse advance passenger information systems, develop the expertise of their financial intelligence units, consider the ratification and implementation of relevant international instruments and enhance the exchange of information between the public sector and relevant private sector entities (S/RES/2482: 15a-f).

Best Practices in Combating Terrorism-Organized Crime Nexus

As noted, the attempt to combat the relationship between terrorism and organized crime has been addressed by the UN Security Council, international legal instruments and law enforcement. The difficulty in being effective is the result of the complexities of time, geography, political systems, leadership styles, financial support and the operational capabilities of each group. Nevertheless, two well-thought-out projects analysed and collected best practices and advised those who are engaged in combating crime-terror nexus on the best possible course of action.

Clearly, one of the biggest problems in dealing with the nexus is the fact that the attention of the international community is predominantly allocated to combat terrorism, which takes priority over the threats posed by OCGs (Clarke 2018: 3). The nexuses are often of local and transnational character, and only focus on tactical objectives in combating them, undermining long-term strategic plans (Clarke 2018: 7–9). Subject matter experts have identified five best practices:

- prevention is a key to success;
- any response plans need to be tailor-made;
- the importance of intelligence and info-sharing;
- the need for transnational exchange of info and learning process;
- cooperation is a key to success: "it takes nexus to combat a nexus" (Clarke 2018: 10–11).

The nexus between terrorism and OCGs, especially after the terrorist attacks on 9/11, is a critical challenge. The activities of TOs and OCGs ignore borders which makes law enforcement extremely challenging. Moreover, the nexus has many different characteristics, from rudimentary ad hoc cooperation to sophisticated forms of hybrids. Additionally, every form of cooperation between TOs and OCGs has a unique character. The key is to understand, mitigate and combat the phenomenon of a nexus through careful observation, cooperation, collection and analysis of intelligence, and a robust engagement by the appropriate authorities including both effective legislation and law enforcement activities.

Seminar Questions

1. Define "terrorism" and identify the five main types.
2. Evaluate different definitions of "terrorism" and explain their shortcomings.
3. How does the UN Convention against Transnational Organized Crime (UNTOC) define an "organized criminal group"?
4. Present three current examples of an "organized criminal group" in accordance with the UNTOC definition.
5. What are the major similarities and differences between terrorist organizations (TOs) and OCGs?
6. Explain, why the nexuses between TOs and OCGs have increased in number after the end of the Cold War?
7. Working in groups, prepare one case study for each different level of the nexus evolution (operational, conceptual and evolutional).

Exam Question

8. Based on your own research, what kind of best practices/strategies in combating the nexus would you recommend?

References

Blazevska Andonovska, V., & Glavinov, A. (2016). Connection between organized crime and terrorism as a new security threat. *Contemporary Macedonian Defence, 16*(30), 97–110.

Chikhi, L. (2010, February 22). Algeria says al Qaeda guards Sahara drug smugglers. *Reuters*. Available at: https://www.reuters.com/article/us-security-qaeda-algeria/algeria-says-al-qaeda-guards-sahara-drug-smugglers-idUSTRE61L3KL20100222. Accessed 15 Nov 2019.

Clarke, C. P. (2018, July). Investigating and prosecuting cases of the Nexus between organized crime and terrorism: Best practices and lessons learned for practitioners. *International Center for Counter-Terrorism – The Hague Report*. Available at: https://icct.nl/publication/investigating-and-prosecuting-cases-of-the-nexus-between-organised-crime-and-terrorism-best-practices-and-lessons-learned-for-practitioners/. Accessed 12 Dec 2019.

Convention for the Prevention and Punishment of Terrorism [CPPT]. The League of Nations, Geneva (1937, November 16). Available at: https://www.wdl.org/en/item/11579/. Accessed 10 Dec 2019.

Europe's Crime-Terror Nexus: Links between terrorist and organized crime groups in the European Union [Europe's Crime-Terror Nexus]. (2012). Available at: https://www.europarl.europa.eu/RegData/etudes/etudes/join/2012/462503/IPOL-LIBE_ET(2012)462503_EN.pdf. Accessed 10 Dec 2019.

European Union Council Framework Decision 2002/475/JHA, on combating terrorism [EU CFDCT]. (2002, June 13). Available at: https://eur-lex.europa.eu/legal-content/EN/TXT/?uri=CELEX:02002F0475-20081209. Accessed 10 Nov 2019.

Foschini, G., & Tonacci, F. (2017, July 31). Il petrolio dell'Isis finisce in Italia: la Guardia di Finanza indaga sulle 'navi fantasma. *la Repubblica*. Available at: https://www.repubblica.it/cronaca/2017/07/31/news/il_petrolio_dell_isis_finisce_in_italia_la_guardia_di_finanza_indaga_sulle_navi_fantasma_-172011799/. Accessed 15 Nov 2019.

Ligeti, K., & Lassalle, M. (2018). The organised crime-terror nexus: How to address the issue of ISIS benefitting from lucrative criminal activities? *Law Working Paper Series, 9*, 2–26.

Makarenko, T. (2004). The crime-terror continuum: Tracing the interplay between transnational organized crime and terrorism. *Global Crime, 6*(1), 129–145.

Mullins, S., Wither, J. K., & Monaco, S. R. (2016). Terrorism and crime. In J. K. Wither & S. Mullins (Eds.), *Combating transnational terrorism* (pp. 67–84). Sofia: Procon Ltd..

Policy Toolkit on the Hague Good Practices on the Nexus Between Transnational Organized Crime and Terrorism [UNICRI]. (2019). United Nations Interregional Crime and Justice Research Institute. Available at: http://www.unicri.it/news/article/Toolkit_nexus_crime_terrorism. Accessed 2 Feb 2020.

Puttonen, R., & Romiti F. (2020). The linkages between organized crime and terrorism. *Studies in Conflict & Terrorism*. Available at: https://doi.org/10.1080/10576 10X.2019.1678871. Accessed 20 Feb 2020.

Schmid, A. P. (2016). Defining terrorism. In J. K. Wither & S. Mullins (Eds.), *Combating transnational terrorism* (pp. 1–16). Sofia: Procon Ltd.

Schmid, A. P. (2018). *Revisiting the relationship between international terrorism and transnational organized crime 22 years later [ICCT]*. International Centre for Counter-Terrorism – The Hague Research paper. Available at: https://icct.nl/publication/revisiting-the-relationship-between-international-terrorism-and-transnational-organised-crime-22-years-later/. Accessed 10 Jan 2020.

Serious and Organized Crime Threat Assessment [SOCTA]. (2017). Available at: https://www.europol.europa.eu/socta-report. Accessed 5 Feb 2020.

United Nations Security Council resolution [S/RES/2482]. (2019, July 19). *Threats to international peace and security*. Available at: http://unscr.com/en/resolutions/2482. Accessed 5 Jan 2020.

Extraterritorial Investigations of Terrorist-Related Kidnappings

Lindsey Brine

Canada has not been spared from radical Islam-based terrorism. Terrorism is a form of 'transnational crime' as defined by the United Nations (UN) in the 1970s. Transnational crime classifies a group of criminal activities that go beyond the borders of a single country. It can be soundly argued that even radical Islam-based 'domestic terrorism' fits into this definition as it is inspired beyond the borders of Canada (Peace Palace Library 2013). Criminal terrorism consists of terrorist acts used to aid crime and criminal profit. In 1995, the definition of transnational crime became "offences whose inception, prevention and/or direct or indirect effects involved more than one country" (UN Secretariat 1995). With ever-increasing globalization, the prominence of transnational crime has increased, and the UN and contributing countries continue to look for ways to combat it. Despite the clear nexus, in some cases, between terrorist groups and organized crime, some terrorist organizations actually engage in criminal activity to raise funds for their terrorist acts. This could consist of a multitude of crimes, including bank robberies, cyber-crime, drug production, drug smuggling, drug trafficking, human trafficking, illegal arms, kidnapping for ransom, and so on.

In Canada, the presence of radical Islam-based terrorism was relatively insignificant until the large, highly coordinated Al Qaeda terrorist attack on September 11, 2001 (9/11), in the United States. During this attack, four American-operated

L. Brine (✉)
Rabdan Academy, Al Bhustan, Abu Dhabi, United Arab Emirates

© The Author(s), under exclusive license to Springer Nature Switzerland AG 2021
M. Roycroft, L. Brine (eds.), *Modern Police Leadership*,
https://doi.org/10.1007/978-3-030-63930-3_24

airlines on the Eastern seaboard of the United States were hijacked and forced to crash into famous American landmarks—resulting in thousands of deaths. Initial reports from the American government and media indicated that the 9/11 terrorists had prepared for their mission in Canada and then entered the United States. This was eventually clearly disproven. However, Canada was later discovered to have been the residence for the Millennium Bomber, Ahmed Ressam, who was a radical Algerian Islamist terrorist who planned to detonate a bomb at the Los Angeles International Airport on January 1, 2000. He was apprehended after disembarking from a ferry, arriving in the United States from Canada, and was found to be in possession of a significant quantity of bomb-making materials. The Royal Canadian Mounted Police (RCMP) determined that his plan had been developed and operationalized while he was residing in Montreal. Despite extensive multilateral cooperation between the RCMP and federal authorities in the United States, Canada was 'accused' of harbouring terrorists who were intent on attacking America. Ressam was convicted in the United States of terrorism-related offences and sentenced to thirty-seven years in jail (The Canadian Encyclopedia, 2019).

Terrorism and terrorist-based plots and, by extension, transnational crime within the borders of Canada have included both foreign-born citizens and first- and second-generation Canadians with roots in failed states. Often, they have travelled to these failed states to enrol in terrorist camps or to fight in civil wars. Although these terrorist-based wars may seem distant and isolated from day-to-day life in Canada, they are symptomatic of the terrorist threat to Canada and its allies. These conflicts also have a direct impact on the rise of transnational crimes which are all used to fund radical Islam-based terrorist organizations or rebels such as the Taliban in Afghanistan (Transnational Organized Crime 2019).

Effective legislation is crucial to combatting terrorism. Due to the rise of these types of terror-related crimes, especially post-9/11, legislation amending the Criminal Code of Canada with the Anti-Terrorism Act, 2002, and subsequently the Combating Terrorism Act, 2012, was created. These allow for the prosecution of individuals responsible for terrorist-related offences targeting Canadian citizens and permanent residents, and interests outside of Canada (Legislative Services Branch 2019). As a result, the mandate of the RCMP is not confined within the borders of Canada; it extends internationally as a result of these extraterritorial provisions of the Criminal Code of Canada. Prior to this, the RCMP had virtually no power to charge suspects in investigations where the terror crimes were committed abroad.

The 9/11 attacks and the subsequent naming of Canada as a target country by Al Qaeda during the war in Afghanistan heightened Canada's response to the terrorist threat. Post 9/11, the majority of Canadian terrorists have been homegrown and influenced by radical Islam. This has included the 'Digibomber' who was convicted of, and jailed for, assisting British radical Islamists with a plot to set off bombs in the United Kingdom in 2004. The 'Toronto 18' had plans to seize the Canadian Parliament and behead the Prime Minister in 2006. This plot was successfully disrupted by Canadian Security Intelligence Service (CSIS) and the RCMP, which resulted in eleven of these individuals being convicted of terrorist-related offences. In late 2013, the RCMP arrested and charged two foreign nationals, both Canadian residents, but one originally from Tunisia and the other from Palestine. They had planned to bomb a commuter train travelling between Toronto and New York City (Ha et al. 2013).

In order to work on terrorist-related investigations that have an international component, there is a requirement for all investigators to have a security clearance of Top Secret Indoctrinated. The indoctrination component allows for the investigator to be given access to Compartmented Information which is "information derived from sensitive sources and methods" (Government of Canada Treasury Board Secretariat 2019). Compartmented Information in this context refers to intercepted signal intelligence (SIGINT) or private communications between individuals or governments. This can include cell phone communications, computer apps and games, radios, transmitters, etc. Although the author of this chapter was privy to significant amounts of SIGINT in these two kidnapping investigations, all of the information in this chapter is open source and can be readily found on the internet or in published memoirs by the victims.

In 2008, I was transferred to the counterterrorism programme, where I served for two years. I was named as Team Commander for two high-profile terrorist-related kidnappings of Canadian citizens by Al Qaeda and Al Shabaab in Africa. By outlining my experiences in these situations, I aim to explain the most important lessons of such operations while highlighting their complexity. Around this time, there was a rash of kidnappings of Canadian citizens overseas by radical Islamist terror groups. There was an increase in these types of crimes as many terrorist groups realized that some countries would facilitate ransom payments. However, Canada was not one of those countries. One of the first kidnappings was in Niger and had been perpetrated by Al Qaeda in the Islamic Maghreb (AQIM), and the other was in Somalia, which was carried out by Al Shabaab. Managing and investigating these crimes is a highly complex task with multiple domestic and foreign partners, coupled with extremely high expectations and pressures placed on the primary investigating agency. These real-world examples will be used to illustrate the whole-of-government approach used by Canada and will focus on the police component of that approach.

The first investigation involved the kidnapping of two UN diplomats in Niger on December 14, 2008. The two victims were Canadian citizens, with one (Robert Fowler) having just been appointed as the UN Special Envoy to Niger. His assistant, also a career diplomat, Louis Guay, was with him. Fowler had been appointed by UN Secretary-General Ban Ki-Moon to attempt to find a diplomatic solution to the ongoing Tuareg rebel conflict in the Agadez region of northern Niger. This high-level diplomatically sensitive appointment was purportedly done on a 'need to know' basis, and without the blessing of the Government of Niger. Fowler and Guay were presumably chosen as targets as they were high-profile international diplomats working for the UN on a contentious issue. Generally, those kidnapped in Niger were quickly transported to the vast northern regions of Mali.

Initially, the Tuareg-backed rebel group Front des Forces de Redressement claimed responsibility, but early on, suspicions indicated that the kidnapping had either been committed by or at the behest of Al Qaeda in the Islamic Maghreb (AQIM). The kidnapping had apparently been orchestrated by Mokhtar Belmokhtar, also known as 'One Eye', as he lost his left eye during his terrorist escapades; he was one of the original founders of AQIM. AQIM was founded in the 1990s as a result of the Algerian civil war (BBC 2013). The mandate of AQIM is made exceedingly clear in the words of Mokhtar Belmokhtar released in a propaganda video in 2012 (Wojtanik 2015):

> We vow to all those who planned and participated in the aggression against the right of our Muslim people to be ruled by Islamic Shari'a on our land, we will respond with all available force and you will hear from us on the battlefield. It is our promise to you that we will fight you in your own homes, you will experience the heat of wounds in your own countries and we will threaten your interests.

Within days, the Government of Canada, and by default the RCMP, was asked by the UN to lead the investigation into the kidnapping of the two diplomats, and RCMP officers were deployed to both Mali and Niger. The initial deployment by the RCMP included forensics specialists, hostage negotiators, investigators, intelligence analysts, a Team Commander, and an Executive Leadership position. Due to the extremely difficult work and living conditions, the working-level team members were rotated every three weeks, with the Team Commander remaining for six weeks before rotation. The Executive Leadership position was eliminated fairly quickly into the investigation, with those responsibilities being taken over by the Team Commander. All major RCMP major investigations are given a unique title. In this case, the name was Project Seigle.

Since the 1990s, Canada has been a world leader in utilizing a 'whole-of-government' approach to solving complex issues. It allows for a collaborative interdepartmental approach to achieving a common goal. Law enforcement and security organizations in Canada have been at the forefront of developing 'whole-of-government' solutions. For example, with the current rise of radicalized citizens returning from war zones in Syria, Iraq, and Afghanistan, a broad system of collaboration and cooperation has been developed to manage the threat.

> Canada's law enforcement, security and intelligence, and defence departments and agencies continue to monitor and respond to the threat of Canadian extremist travellers (CET) through a coordinated, whole-of-government approach. When the Government learns that a CET may be seeking to return, federal departments and agencies come together to tailor an approach to address the threat he/she may pose. Key departments and agencies, including Public Safety Canada, Global Affairs Canada (GAC), the RCMP, CSIS, the Integrated Terrorism Assessment Centre (ITAC), the Department of National Defence and the Canadian Armed Forces (DND/CAF), Canada Border Services Agency (CBSA), Immigration, Refugee and Citizenship Canada (IRCC), Transport Canada (TC) and the Privy Council Office (PCO) work together to assess risks, develop options and manage the return of CETs. The whole-of-government approach enables the collective identification of measures needed to deal with the threat. (Public Safety Canada 2018)

The synergy and power that is created in delivering this approach not only is formidable but also creates unique challenges. Within a multi-agency approach, the team, including the RCMP, was co-located at the Embassy of Canada in Bamako, Mali, with representatives from the CSIS, the Communication Security Establishment (CSE), the Department of National Defence (DND), the Department of Foreign Affairs and International Trade (DFAIT), and a Task Force Leader who was selected by the Government of Canada. This individual was a close colleague of the captives. Their relationship created an additional layer of complexity as there was a risk that when decisions were made, or about to be made, they were based, or appeared to be based, on the relationship as opposed to what was best for the investigation and resolution. It also created a tremendous amount of individual pressure on this person as his stake in resolving the kidnapping was at a personal level. To further complicate matters, both Fowler and Guay personally knew the Prime Minister of Canada and the Secretary-General of the UN.

Each agency had a specific mandate but with the specific goal that the work of all of the organizations would complement one another in order to provide a high-quality diplomatic and investigative ability that would successfully garner the release of the two Canadian hostages. The role of CSE, a key security and intelligence organization, was to focus on foreign signal intelligence. DND was to provide high-level military expertise and guidance should a tactical response be mounted, as other Western countries had done in previous kidnappings. DFAIT was to use every diplomatic channel possible to garner support from the Mali government and its African neighbours.

I flew to Bamako with three other RCMP members from Paris. Upon arrival, the luggage for every passenger came out on the carrousel except for the four of us. We waited over an hour for our luggage to come out, and by this time, the Arrivals Hall was virtually empty. It was clear when we received our luggage that it had been opened and thoroughly searched by the local police who had obviously been given advance notice of our arrival. I took this as a sign that our time in Bamako would not be easy.

The RCMP team that we were replacing met us at the airport. It was late in the evening and I was shocked when they immediately took us to a nightclub in the Hippodrome district of Bamako rather than to our hotel. La Terrasse was an outdoor rooftop bar that was frequented by a wide variety of people of ill repute. I felt uncomfortable at the nightclub from both a moral and a security and safety standpoint, and we departed soon after. The next day, I made it clear to my team that we were in Mali representing the Government of Canada and the RCMP with the sole mission of trying to secure freedom for the hostages. It was clear to me that it was inappropriate to be visiting places such as this during our off time and that should the media get a hold of it, it would be devastating for Canada on the world stage. The following day, I met with the Task Force Leader and advised him of this. Much to my dismay, he informed me that this had been a frequent pattern. Again, it reflected poorly on Canada, particularly in light of strong government policy against human trafficking in third world countries. I immediately reported to RCMP HQ in Ottawa what had happened. Rather than dealing with the situation as it should have been, I was advised by HQ that those employees would simply not be sent back in the future.

Of note, on March 7, 2015, the La Terrasse rooftop bar was stormed by masked AQIM gunmen who killed five people, including expatriates, and wounded nine (BBC 2015). This only reinforced in my mind the appropriateness of the decision I had made a few years earlier during the kidnapping investigation.

Upon arrival in Mali, it was clear that the investigation was suffering in part due to tension between some of the Government of Canada partners. This was likely caused by a number of factors: unclear objectives, the newness of the first 'whole of government' deployment to a terrorist kidnapping, personalities, and the normal transition of group development (i.e., forming–storming–norming–performing). There appeared to be a lack of trust, a feeling that information was not being shared, and each agency had its own view on the best way to resolve the kidnapping. This is not atypical in team dynamics, especially when the team comprises many different partners each with their own mandate. Through negotiation, consensus building, and the understanding of the respective role of each agency, I was able to create a positive atmosphere that resulted in significantly improved relations amongst the various groups. I worked collaboratively with the Task Force Leader, the Canadian Ambassador to Mali, the Canadian Ambassador to Burkina Faso, the Resident Representative of the United Nations Development Programme in Mali, the UN Under-Secretary-General for Safety and Security in New York City, and the top commander of the police and military for the Government of Mali.

This was a highly sensitive investigation that required cooperation, tact, and diplomacy with many organizations and many senior-level stakeholders, with all of them expecting a full debriefing. However, only certain information could be shared with certain partners, and this caused tension at times. It was difficult to manage the expectations of some of the Canadian partners as there was a view that all information about everything should be shared. Much of the intelligence that we were gathering from various sources was on a strict 'need-to-know' basis. Many of the partners had never been exposed to criminal investigations or sensitive intelligence. The fear was that if too much information was shared, it might inadvertently be repeated by one of our Government of Canada colleagues and result in harm to the captives. At this point, I also discovered that various team members, including those from the RCMP, were taking their secure computers and USBs with them when they left the Embassy and when they travelled to and from Canada. This was a serious security breach, and as a result, I implemented a standard operating procedure where these items had to remain at the Embassy or be transported in a diplomatic pouch.

Unfortunately, some team members displayed an attitude of supremacy, within the Task Force. There was an overriding sense that these team members felt that they could implement their own decisions and tactics without considering the whole-of-government approach. Often they hatched schemes without consulting the Team Commander, the Task Force Leader, or anyone else. Many of their ideas centred on such outlandish ideas as planning reconnaissance trips in excess of one thousand kilometres one way to the nether regions of northern Mali. Their thought process was that if they were in closer proximity to where the hostages might be being held, they would be able to recruit human sources that would either reveal the location of the hostages or assist in negotiating their release. When I discovered these plans, it was impressed upon them that they would stand out as Westerners and likely end up as hostages themselves. Ultimately, I was placed in the position of having to report their activities to Canada to bring them back in line with the Task Force concept and goals. These investigations must have to be a strong unified approach in order to achieve success.

In this same time period, there were also hostages from a number of other countries being held. These included citizens of Germany, Switzerland, and the United Kingdom (Rice 2009). Multiple hostages from multiple jurisdictions being held in a third world country certainly added a significant layer of complexity to the investigation. The Five Eyes intelligence alliance opened the door for Canada to receive significant SIGINT from its partners that were operating in the region. The United States (including the military) has a significant presence in the Sahel, and both Canada and the United Kingdom had hostages being held in the region. Regular meetings were held with investigators from the United Kingdom, Switzerland, and Germany, who were also located in Bamako. Although these meetings were somewhat productive, it was impossible to negate the reality of not being able to share certain relevant intelligence with countries that did not belong to the Five Eyes. Although there were no French nationals in captivity in this same time period, the Government of France had significant influence and contacts as much of the region comprised former French colonies. Separate meetings were held with other international partners. Throughout the investigation, my team and I also authored daily briefing material to RCMP Senior Executives, which were then used to brief the Minister of Justice and the Prime Minister of Canada. The Prime Minister personally knew Fowler and Guay, so there was a keen interest in knowing what was going on, and virtually unlimited support from the Government of Canada.

As Team Commander, team security for all partners was of the utmost concern. During my tenure in Bamako, we were under surveillance continuously. We were advised by various partners that those watching us were not only from Mali but also from neighbouring African countries—all active players in the AQIM world. It was not unusual to return to our hotel rooms at the Radisson Blu Bamako to find that items had been shuffled about and searched, including the contents of our hotel room safes. We had no doubt that electronic surveillance had also been installed in our rooms. All of this led to extremely guarded conversations and a constant sense of paranoia. Oddly, RCMP sidearms were available to the RCMP team, but we were instructed to leave them at the safe at the Embassy of Canada. Our directions were that we should only take them out of the Embassy if there was a specific need. This clearly made no sense and provided little comfort to us.

At one point, I used an Embassy vehicle to drive to the local market. I was stopped by the Police Nationale du Mali and angrily accused of driving the wrong way on a one-way street, which I had not done. This appeared to me to be nothing more than an excuse to stop me. This happened directly outside a police station, and I was taken inside and ordered to pay an immediate fine for my transgressions, which I refused to do. I was not allowed to leave, and my diplomatic passport was seized. I was able to convince the head of the police station that I was working at the Embassy of Canada, and he eventually permitted me to call the Task Force Leader. Once he spoke to the police, I was allowed to go with no 'fine' paid.

My concern over various safety-related issues led me to instruct our Embassy driver to take different routes between our hotel and work—not only to avoid detection but more importantly to ensure that habits and non-routine routes would make it more difficult for us to be targeted by kidnappers or those wanting to kill us to send a message to the West. Many on the team thought that I was being overly paranoid. On November 20, 2015, the Radisson Blu Bamako was attacked by two AQIM insurgents who took 170 hostages and killed 20 others. The scenes on television of the bullet-ridden lobby, restaurant, and guest rooms where I had spent a significant amount of time were a frank and frightening reminder that one can never be overly cautious when deployed overseas (Walker and English 2015).

Other challenges the team faced included frequent illnesses related to either food poisoning or infections, contracted because of the extremely unhygienic conditions in Bamako. At various times, either my team members or I were bedridden for one or two days at a time with debilitating gastrointestinal problems and high fevers.

Understandably, there was little chance for the team to decompress. We were working twelve to sixteen hour days, seven days a week. Trying to socialize in one of the guest rooms only led to paranoia that our conversations were being monitored. At times, this created tension within the team. As with any workplace setting, there were times when I had to navigate harassment (sexual and otherwise) issues reported to me by and amongst my team members.

It is clear that those who choose a life in law enforcement or a similar occupation have an overwhelming desire to assist those in need and to protect the public. Constantly hanging over our heads was the prospect that the hostages could be executed at any time and that we had not done enough to save them or negotiate their release. This too took a toll on all of us on the team, regardless of which organization we worked for. There were significant psychological impacts on many of us who worked on these investigations. I worked seven days a week, often in excess of sixteen hours a day, from January to June of 2009. Not only were we exposed to the trauma of the investigation, but those of us who travelled to Bamako were witnesses to abject poverty and disease. On the drive to the Embassy of Canada one morning, I witnessed a man on a motorcycle get hit and killed by a vehicle. I had previously been to dozens of fatal collisions in my policing career, but this was different. The locals merely either drove or walked around his body until some bystanders dragged it off the road. This was a loud and clear message to me that life in this part of Africa had little value and that did not bode well for any of the foreign captives held by a terrorist group.

A 'Proof of Life' video of Fowler and Guay was filmed on day five of their ordeal and released some months later. 'Proof of Life' is evidence that the victim of a kidnapping is still alive. In this video, a haggard-looking Fowler and Guay sit with their driver on the desert sand in a makeshift tent. Behind them stand three armed and masked AQIM members with an Al Qaeda flag draped behind them. This was the first definitive proof the RCMP had that Fowler and Guay were in the hands of Al Qaeda. Finally, there was substantive evidence that they were alive—or at least still alive at the time the video was made. Videos filmed over the ensuing months seemed to indicate an increased threat on Fowler and Guay. They had their hands tied behind their backs and were blindfolded and silent. The narrator spoke in Arabic of Al Qaeda, Holy Wars, and Allah. On at least one occasion, the hostages were permitted to call home using cell phones from remote regions of the desert (CBC News 2009a, b).

There were occasional high-level meetings between the Task Force Leader, me, and a senior-ranking military official from the Government of Mali. These were usually last minute and initiated at the request of the Malian official. Our goal was not only to use these meetings to seek information that would benefit the investigation but, more importantly, to see if we could get the Government of Mali to orchestrate or facilitate the release of Fowler and Guay. The meetings were always held in a high-security military compound on the edge of Bamako. The agreed strategy of our team at these types of meetings was to offer only minor concessions, agree to nothing, thank the Government of Mali profusely for supporting Canada, and inform the military official that it would be beneficial to meet again within a day or two. This allowed us to keep the lines of communication open.

The Colonel invited an unnamed intermediary who we were led to believe was in direct contact with the hostage takers. He was well known by AQIM and by the Government of Mali as he had apparently assisted with hostage negotiations in the past. Often the goal of an intermediary of this nature is to negotiate a ransom for the hostages, likely so that he would be paid some sort of commission by AQIM for helping to facilitate it. However, the position of the Government of Canada was exceedingly clear. Canada would not negotiate with terrorists and would not provide any money or other financial aid to release a hostage. Radical Islam terror groups, since the early 2000s, have increasingly used "kidnapping for ransom" as a method to raise finances for their terror attacks (Callimachi 2014). Studies have shown clearly that AQIM is heavily involved in criminal activity to raise funds. Their primary illegal activity is trafficking in contraband (i.e., cocaine, hashish, and counterfeit cigarettes), which is closely followed by human trafficking. However, the largest money-making enterprise for AQIM is the kidnapping of Westerners for ransom. Between 2003 and 2011, it is believed that AQIM raised between 60 and 175 million USD through a total of sixty-three Western hostage takings (Laremont 2011). There was a constant theme in our meetings that a ransom was being demanded.

At one meeting in particular, the intermediary insisted that the Canadian Task Force Leader make arrangements to give him one of the brand new Toyota Land Cruisers from the Embassy of Canada so that he could drive to the north regions of Mali with a reliable vehicle. The intermediary indicated that this would allow him to meet with both the hostages and the kidnappers. I discreetly advised the Task Force Leader that giving a Government of Canada vehicle to the intermediary was a poor idea. First, we would never get the vehicle back, and more importantly, if we were to give a vehicle to him, the Government of Canada would be complicit in aiding the terrorists and could be charged under Section 83.03 of the Criminal Code of Canada, which makes providing or making available property or services for terrorist purposes a criminal offence.

My team and I did prepare care packages for Fowler and Guay with the hopes that the Government of Mali could somehow facilitate their delivery. We wanted to provide some comforts of life to Fowler and Guay (including letters written by their families), but more importantly, they would be seen as a sign by the hostages that there were actually representatives of Canada working in Mali trying to secure their release. We sincerely hoped that these care packages would eventually reach Fowler and Guay intact. It was only after the eventual release of the hostages that it was confirmed that they had—with most of the items still in them. In his memoir, Fowler relates that the kidnappers were extremely suspicious of the contents of the backpacks (Fowler 2012).

Fowler and Guay were released by AQIM on April 21, 2009, after being held hostage for 130 days. They were transported from northern Mali to Gao by an intermediary. Eventually, Fowler and Guay were turned over to two RCMP officers by government officials and flown back to Bamako (Fowler 2012). At the same time, three other European hostages were released. There were allegations that the Swiss and German governments had paid ransoms. Since then, many countries have paid ransom to AQIM (Fanusie and Entz 2017). Prime Minister Stephen Harper of Canada chose his words carefully when he spoke of the release of Fowler and Guay:

> Canada is always willing to pursue a negotiated resolution to these kinds of issues. But, as you know, the Government of Canada's position is clear on these things: we do not pay ransom and we do not release prisoners. Ultimately, as I say, a great deal of effort went into a large number of activities by Canadian government officials from all departments and agencies over the past four months to help secure the release of these hostages. The release was secured in the end by the authorities of Mali and

Burkina Faso and so I once again thank them for their successful efforts …. Well, I'll be clear with you, and I've said this before, the Government of Canada does not pay ransom or money. The Government of Canada does not release prisoners. What efforts or initiatives may have been undertaken by other governments are questions you'll have to put to those governments. (Wherry 2009)

On June 4, 2009, the British hostage Edwin Dyer who had also been held by AQIM was beheaded (Howden 2011). Within months of the release of Fowler and Guay, rumours abounded that they had been released in exchange for four Al Qaeda prisoners being held by Mali and a sum of 1.1 million USD. According to one of the national newspapers of Canada, this was confirmed by government officials from Mali and an intermediary.

In January 2013, following the expulsion of AQIM rebels from Timbuktu in northern Mali by the French military, a treasure trove of correspondence between AQIM leadership was discovered. In one letter to Belmokhtar, written in November 2012, he was admonished: "The obvious incompetencies to have negotiated the release of the most important hostages in the history of AQIM, the Canadian diplomats, at the low price of only 700,000 Euros." Despite some academic interpretations that this correspondence indicates that Canada paid a ransom, there is nothing anywhere in the correspondence that says this. The documents only state that a ransom was paid (Guidère 2014).

Subsequent to the release of the hostages, I authored a substantial document that laid the foundation for the possibility of future criminal charges. The reality of the situation though was that the perpetrators would never be brought to justice. Numerous Western countries had been targeting the suspects for years with no success. The document outlined the investigation and the evidence against Mokhtar Belmokhtar and his deputy Oumar Hamaha. Fowler was readily able to identify both after his release (Fowler 2012). In June 2013, the RCMP laid charges against both. Section II.1 (Terrorism) of the Criminal Code of Canada specifically defines that "terrorist activity" can be "committed in or outside of Canada". Each of them was charged with Section 279.1 of the Criminal Code of Canada under authority of Section 83.2 of the Criminal Code of Canada:

Everyone who commits an indictable offence under this or any other Act of Parliament for the benefit of, at the direction of or in association with a terrorist group is guilty of an indictable offence and liable to imprisonment for life.

Section 279.1 (1) Criminal Code of Canada: Everyone takes a person hostage who—with intent to induce any person, other than the hostage, or any group of persons or any state or international or intergovernmental organization to commit or cause to be committed any act or omission as a condition, whether express or implied, of the release of the hostage—

(a) confines, imprisons, forcibly seizes or detains that person; and

(b) in any manner utters, conveys or causes any person to receive a threat that the death of, or bodily harm to, the hostage will be caused or that the confinement, imprisonment or detention of the hostage will be continued.

(2) Every person who takes a person hostage is guilty of an indictable offence and liable

(a) if a restricted firearm or prohibited firearm is used in the commission of the offence or if any firearm is used in the commission of the offence and the offence is committed for the benefit of, at the direction of, or in association with, a criminal organization, to imprisonment for life and to a minimum punishment of imprisonment for a term of

(i) in the case of a first offence, five years, and

(ii) in the case of a second or subsequent offence, seven years;

(a.1) in any other case where a firearm is used in the commission of the offence, to imprisonment for life and to a minimum punishment of imprisonment for a term of four years; and

(b) in any other case, to imprisonment for life. (Legislative Services Branch 2019)

Documents filed with the court indicate that "both accused are abroad and their whereabouts are unknown. It is therefore in the interest of justice that a warrant for their arrest be issued in order to take measures so that they can be brought before the court to be dealt with according to the law" (Freeze and Perreaux 2013). In March 2014, Oumar Hamaha was confirmed to have been killed in Mali by the French military (Diallo 2014). Belmokhtar has never been captured and his whereabouts remain unknown. In reality, the laying of these charges against Belmokhtar and Hamaha was nothing more than a symbolic effort by the Government of Canada to take a strong stance against terrorists who commit crimes against Canadian citizens and contrary to Canadian legislation.

As noted, the Government of Canada introduced new anti-terrorism legislation in 2002, several months after 9/11. As Nesbitt (2019) notes, "54 individuals have been charged with terrorism offences in Canada under Part II.1 of the Criminal Code between the time that the ATA was first conceived of in September 2001 and September 2018". A total of 151 charges were laid and this resulted in 46 guilty pleas or verdicts. Only three of the individuals were charged in absentia, two of those were Belmokhtar and Hamaha. The remainder were either Canadian citizens or residents.

During the early weeks of the hostage taking, a senior-ranking police official took it upon himself to meet with the family of Robert Fowler. During this meeting he is alleged to have told the wife of Fowler that "as long as I am in charge of this investigation not one cent will be paid for the release of these high muckety-mucks" (Fowler 2012). I was required to meet Fowler several times after his release in order to discuss police exhibits and other matters. Each time I met with him, I was faced with the same anger, albeit legitimate, about how betrayed his family felt when those words were uttered to his wife. In his book, Fowler places a great deal of criticism on how the investigation was handled by the Government of Canada. But he also indicates,

> All this said, a number of individual RCMP officers worked selflessly and tirelessly and to the very best of their abilities, risking their health and abandoning their families, to secure our freedom, and I owe them a debt of gratitude. (Fowler, Robert. *Season in Hell*. HarperCollins Publishers date. Kindle Edition)

Project Seigle was new territory for the RCMP and for the Government of Canada. It was a complex, protracted investigation that thankfully was successful. Although the RCMP, other agencies, and the Government of Canada have been criticized by various individuals or groups, there were many actions taken and decisions made that can never be made public. This can lead to the frustration of never being able to explain the investigative actions of the team fully. There was no formal review process in place during this investigation, but having said that, many lessons were learnt that impacted future extraterritorial kidnapping investigations. These lessons centred around building relationships with key partners (both domestic and foreign), considering multiple legal options to garner their release, operational security, and the criticality of a whole-of-government approach.

Shortly after the release of Fowler and Guay in Mali, I was assigned as Team Commander for yet another extraterritorial kidnapping of a Canadian in Africa. Amanda Lindhout travelled to Mogadishu, Somalia, as a freelance journalist on August 20, 2008, with her Australian boyfriend Nigel Brennan, a photojournalist. Two days after their arrival, they were kidnapped by the radical Islam terror group Al Shabaab. Although this kidnapping was relatively high profile, there were significant differences to the Fowler and Guay kidnapping. The captors almost immediately demanded a ransom of 2.5 million USD and in less than a month, a proof of life video was released directly to the media (Al Jazeera). In October 2008, Al Shabaab released a statement saying both Lindhout and Brennan would be killed if the aforementioned ransom was not paid within fifteen days. During this time, the RCMP and other federal partners deployed investigative teams to the region to conduct an investigation with the hopes of securing the release of Lindhout. The Australian Federal Police and their government partners did the same (https://www.thestar.com/news/canada/held-hostage.html).

The Canadian team worked out of the Canadian High Commission in Nairobi, Kenya, as it was too unsafe to travel to Somalia. Unfortunately, yet again some of the same specialized team members felt that they were in the best position to make decisions that clearly were dangerous and made little sense. It came to my attention that plans were being made to charter a plane to Mogadishu so that these team members could develop human sources and conduct reconnaissance in closer proximity to the hostages. They believed that this would assist in identifying the exact location of the hostages and that contacts would be able to assist in negotiating their release. Again, this became a significant challenge to manage. Mogadishu was in the midst of a protracted violent conflict, and we had no indication of where Lindhout was being held in the vast reaches of the country. It would have been extremely dangerous and foolish to send Western investigators into the country.

The vast majority of my role as Team Commander in the Lindhout investigation revolved around trying to garner intelligence from allies and liaising with the Australian Federal Police. Again, the ultimate goal was to obtain the release of Lindhout and Brennan within the confines of Government of Canada policy that no ransom was to be paid.

It became clear several months into the investigation that the Brennan family had secured a private contractor and negotiators to try to obtain the release of Brennan and by default Lindhout (https://www.thestar.com/news/canada/held-hostage.html). This would in all likelihood require the payment of a ransom to Al Shabaab. This clearly placed the Government of Canada in a difficult situation. It would be impossible to apply pressure to negotiate their release, while at the same time Al Shabaab was bargaining with the Brennan family representatives to settle on a ransom. It should be noted that even if this private line of seeking the release of the hostages had not taken place, it was a completely different scenario to the Fowler and Guay kidnapping. Somalia was a 'failed state' and had essentially been suffering internal conflict and civil war for decades. There was no feasible way to apply pressure on the government as had been done with the AQIM kidnapping. In addition, Lindhout had wilfully chosen to travel to a 'failed state' that was in the midst of a civil war and was constantly being subjected to terrorist attacks initiated by Al Shabaab. Accordingly, unlike Fowler and Guay, there was limited international pressure to seek the release of Lindhout. She was not a United Nations employee, nor did she work for any sort of high-profile media or charity organization. Certainly, the family of Lindhout likely felt that Amanda was not as worthy a victim as other Canadians who had been kidnapped.

Over the course of fifteen months, the RCMP played various roles, but after the private negotiations started, the main focus was to investigate who was responsible, gather evidence, monitor channels of communication in the event of ransom demands or 'proof of life' calls, and liaise closely with the family of Lindhout to offer support. Lindhout and Brennan were released on November 25, 2009. It became clear that Lindhout had been tortured and sexually assaulted multiple times by her Al Shabaab captors during her ordeal. It was also widely reported in the international media that a ransom of 625,000 USD was paid to release Lindhout and Brennan. These funds were raised largely through private donors (https://www. thestar.com/news/canada/held-hostage.html).

The RCMP continued the investigation into the kidnapping of Lindhout for several years after her release. The hope was to be able to charge and extradite those responsible despite the fact that the culprits were likely still living in Somalia. This added its own level of investigational complexity. Due to the length of the investigation, there were many different officers involved during various times. Ali Omar Ader, one of the key hostage takers and the primary ransom negotiator, was lured into not only giving a full confession but also volunteering to travel to Canada. This was done under the guise of a purported book deal in which he would write about the history of Somalia. Shortly after his arrival in Canada in June 2015, Ader was arrested and charged with the same offences that Belmokhtar and Hamaha had been charged with in the Fowler and Guay kidnapping (https://www.cbc.ca/news/ politics/amanda-lindhout-kidnapping-rcmp-charge-somali-national-ali-omar-ader-1.3110671). After a lengthy trial, Ader was found guilty, and in June 2018, he was sentenced to fifteen years in federal prison, the sentence taking into account the three years already served in pre-trial detention. Unfortunately, having a convicted Al Shabaab terrorist serve time in a Canadian prison raises the potential for him to attempt to radicalize his fellow inmates.

Despite the publicity surrounding the Fowler and Guay kidnapping, and the Lindhout kidnapping, many Canadians choose to travel to high-risk areas. The Global Affairs Canada travel warning website clearly articulates the high risk of kidnapping in numerous countries. There have been numerous abductions of Canadians by radical Islam terror groups since the two investigations noted above. The RCMP has been able to form a coordinated proactive response to these extraterritorial kidnappings. However, as evidenced, these already complex investigations become highly complicated on the world stage. There are multiple stakeholders that include national and local governments, the UN, the Five Eyes, neighbouring countries, and multiple terror groups with different aims and motivations.

Radical Islam terror groups continue to inspire many individuals to seize anti-Western extremist ideals and plot to commit terrorist attacks world-wide. Post 9/11, it quickly became evident in the Western world that multilateral cooperation was growing increasingly important in relation to the global threat of terrorism. Sound relationships between countries, international bodies, intelligence agencies, and police organizations are paramount in the effort to deal with globalization, conflicts, and the threat of terrorism (Stibli 2010). Although Canada is ranked ninth out of 177 countries for corruption, many of its partners in the struggle to combat terrorism are ranked close to the bottom of the corruption list (Transparency International 2019). This includes nations such as Algeria, Burkina Faso, Libya, Mali, Niger, Somalia (all key players in the kidnappings discussed in this chapter), and many other 'failed states'. This creates significant challenges in trying to form international strategies to combat global terrorism that directly impact Canada and, in particular, extraterritorial kidnappings of Canadian citizens.

Globally, there is great support for international law enforcement cooperation directed at fighting transnational organized crime, including terrorism, but this must begin at the local level and through multilateral cooperation. This has been highlighted by many world leaders and discussed widely at international forums including the G8 and the United Nations (Kadono 1999). As Mobekk (2005) notes, "international policing is an essential part of post-conflict reconstruction and peace building and plays a crucial role in establishing stability in post-conflict societies" (p 1). Stability in these countries will lead to a reduction in kidnappings of foreign citizens. Although many Western countries have been relatively successful at fighting terrorism at the local level, this is not so in these 'failed states'. There is little hope that terrorist-related kidnappings will ever end. This is particularly true because some governments and private individuals choose to pay ransoms.

Key Factors to Consider in Complex Extraterritorial Investigations

Be aware of the complexity of team dynamics.
Conduct a Health and Safety Review of accommodations and transportation.
Conduct a Risk Assessment of accommodations and transportation.
Ensure all team members are given a thorough briefing prior to deployment about:

- appropriate behaviour
- chain of command
- health and safety
- intelligence and intelligence handling
- investigation to date
- local environment and culture
- security and communications security

Ensure Team Commander has significant input into who is on team.
Be aware of Interagency Rivalry and how to overcome it.
Do regular psychological assessment for all involved.

Seminar Questions

Why do terrorists kidnap hostages and what can be done to prevent such occurrences?

What are the implications of such kidnappings for police forces?

Describe some of the frustrations mentioned in the two cases described above. What are some of the key learning points for team leaders?

Exam Question

What are the key factors to consider in complex extraterritorial investigations?

References

Bayley, D. (2006). *Changing of the guard: Developing democratic police abroad*. New York: Oxford University Press.

BBC. (2013). Profile: Al-Qaeda in North Africa. *BBC News*. Available at: https://www.bbc.com/news/world-africa-17308138. Accessed 15 Sep 2019.

BBC. (2015). Mali bar attack kills five in Bamako. *BBC News*. Available at: https://www.bbc.com/news/world-africa-31775679. Accessed 15 Sep 2019.

Bolan, K. (2017). Air India Flight 182 Bombing. *Air India Flight 182 Bombing | The Canadian Encyclopedia*. Available at: https://thecanadianencyclopedia.ca/en/article/air-india-flight-182-bombing. Accessed 15 Sep 2019.

Callimachi, R. (2014). Paying ransoms, Europe bankrolls Qaeda terror. *The New York Times*. Available at: https://www.nytimes.com/2014/07/30/world/africa/ransoming-citizens-europe-becomes-al-qaedas-patron.html. Accessed 16 Sep 2019.

CBC. (2019). *The October crisis*. Canadian Broadcasting Corporation. Available at: https://www.cbc.ca/history/EPISCONTENTSE1EP16CH1PA4LE.html. Accessed 11 Sep 2019.

CBC News. (2009a). Transcript 1: Robert Fowler interview Sept. 8, 2009 | CBC News. *CBCnews*. Available at: https://www.cbc.ca/news/canada/transcript-1-robert-fowler-interview-sept-8-2009-1.864625. Accessed 16 Sep 2019.

CBC News. (2009b). Transcript 2: Robert Fowler interview Sept. 9, 2009 | CBC News. *CBCnews*. Available at: https://www.cbc.ca/news/canada/transcript-2-robert-fowler-interview-sept-9-2009-1.863593. Accessed 16 Sep 2019.

Citizenship and Immigration Canada. (2014). *Canada's history*. Retrieved from http://www.cic.gc.ca/english/resources/publications/discover/section-06.asp

Commission of Inquiry into the Investigation into the Bombing of Air India Flight 182. http://publications.gc.ca/collections/collection_2010/bcp-pco/CP32-89-5-2010-1-eng.pdf

Diallo, T. (2014). *French air strikes kill wanted Islamist militant "Red Beard" in Mali*. [online] U.S. Available at: https://www.reuters.com/article/us-mali-islamists/french-air-strikes-kill-wanted-islamist-militant-red-beard-in-mali-idUSBREA2D13Z20140314. Accessed 16 Sep 2019.

Donati, J., & Harooni, M. (2014, January 17). Up to 15, mostly foreigners, killed in Kabul suicide attack. *Reuters*. Retrieved from http://www.reuters.com/article/2014/01/17/us-afghanistan-explosion-idUSBREA0G12P20140117

Fanusie, Y., & Entz, A. (2017). Al-Qaeda in the Islamic Maghreb – s3.us-east-2.amazonaws.com. Available at: https://s3.us-east-2.amazonaws.com/defenddemocracy/uploads/documents/CSIF_TFBB_AQIM.pdf. Accessed 16 Sep 2019.

Fowler, R. (2012). *A season in hell* [Kindle]. Toronto: Harper Perennials.

Freeze, C., & Perreaux, L. (2013). Bandit with ties to al-Qaeda charged by RCMP for abducting diplomats. [online] *The Globe and Mail*. Available at: https://www.theglobeandmail.com/news/national/bandit-with-ties-to-al-qaeda-charged-by-rcmp-for-abducting-diplomats/article12820184/. Accessed 16 Sep 2019.

Government of Canada Treasury Board Secretariat. (2019). *Standard on security screening*. [ONLINE] Available at: https://www.tbs-sct.gc.ca/pol/doc-eng.aspx?id=28115§ion=glossary. Accessed 11 Sep 2019.

Gros, J. (2003). Trouble in paradise: Crime and collapsed states in the age of globalization. *British Journal of Criminology, 43*, 63–80. Retrieved from http://bjc.oxfordjournals.org/content/43/1/63.full.pdf

Guidère, M. (2014). The Timbuktu letters: New insights about AQIM. *Res Militaris*. Available at: https://hal.archives-ouvertes.fr/hal-01081769/document. Accessed 16 Sep 2019.

Ha, T. T., Freeze, C., & Leblanc, D. (2013, April 22). RCMP arrest two for 'al-Qaeda-supported' plot to bomb via train. *The Globe and Mail*. Retrieved from http://www.theglobeandmail.com/news/national/rcmp-arrest-two-for-al-qaeda-supported-plot-to-bomb-via-train/article11465138/

Howden, D. (2011). British holidaymaker is 'beheaded by al-Qa'ida'. *The Independent*. Available at: https://www.independent.co.uk/news/world/africa/british-holidaymaker-is-beheaded-by-al-qaida-1696414.html. Accessed 16 Sep 2019.

https://www.cbc.ca/news/politics/amanda-lindhout-kidnapping-rcmp-charge-somali-national-ali-omar-ader-1.3110671

https://www.thestar.com/news/canada/held-hostage.html

Innes, M., & Thiel, D. (2012). Policing terror. In T. Newburn (Ed.), *Handbook of policing* (pp. 553–579). Hoboken: Taylor and Francis.

Kadono, N. (1999). How can we fight 21st century crime? International cooperation against transnational organized crime. *Transnational Crime and Regional Security in the Asia Pacific*, pp. 119–125.

Laremont, R. (2011). *Al Qaeda in the Islamic Maghreb: Terrorism and counterterrorism in the Sahel*. Taylor & Francis. Available at: https://www.tandfonline.com/doi/full/10.1080/19392206.2011.628630. Accessed 16 Sep 2019.

Legislative Services Branch. (2019). Criminal code of Canada. *Criminal Code*. Available at: https://laws-lois.justice.gc.ca/eng/acts/C-46/. Accessed 15 Sep 2019.

Mobekk, E., & Geneva Centre for the Democratic Control of Armed Forces (DCAF). (2005). *Identifying lessons in United Nations international policing missions* (Policy paper No. 9). Retrieved from website: http://www.dcaf.ch/Publications/Identifying-Lessons-in-United-Nations-International-Policing-Missions

Nesbitt, M. (2019). *An empirical study of terrorism charges and terrorism trials in Canada between September 2001 and September 2018.* [Online] Papers.ssrn.com. Available at: https://papers.ssrn.com/sol3/papers.cfm?abstract_id=3325956. Accessed 16 Sep 2019.

Peace Palace Library. (2013). *Transnational crime.* Retrieved from website: http://www.peacepalacelibrary.nl/research-guides/international-criminal-law/transnational-crime/

Public Safety Canada. (2018). 2018 Public report on the terrorism threat to Canada. *Public Safety Canada / Sécurité publique Canada.* Available at: https://www.publicsafety.gc.ca/cnt/rsrcs/pblctns/pblc-rprt-trrrsm-thrt-cnd-2018/index-en.aspx. Accessed 15 Sep 2019.

RCMP. (2014a). *2011–2012 departmental performance report.* Retrieved from http://www.rcmp-grc.gc.ca/dpr-rmr/2011-2012/2012-eng.pdf

RCMP. (2014b). *National security criminal investigations program.* Retrieved from website http://www.rcmp-grc.gc.ca/nsci-ecsn/index-eng.htm

Rice, X. (2009). Briton among four tourists seized by rebels after festival in Mali. *The Guardian.* Available at: https://www.theguardian.com/world/2009/jan/24/mali-niger-hostages. Accessed 15 Sep 2019.

Sallot, J. (2006). Canadian Security Intelligence Service. *The Canadian Encyclopedia.* Available at: https://www.thecanadianencyclopedia.ca/en/article/canadian-security-intelligence-service. Accessed 15 Sep 2019.

Statistics Canada. (2014). *Religion.* Retrieved from: http://www.statcan.gc.ca/search-recherche/bb/info/3000017-eng.htm

Stibli, F. (2010). Terrorism in the context of globalization. *Academic and Applied Research in Military Science, 9*(1), 1–7. Retrieved from http://www.zmne.hu/aarms/docs/Volume9/Issue1/pdf/01.pdf

The Canadian Encyclopedia. (2014). *Terrorism.* Retrieved from http://thecanadianencyclopedia.com/en/article/terrorism/

The Reference Dictionary. (2013). *Definition of 'failed state'.* Retrieved from http://dictionary.reference.com/browse/failed+state

Transnational Organized Crime. *Director of national intelligence.* Available at: https://www.dni.gov/. Accessed 15 Sep 2019.

Transparency International. (2019). *Corruption perceptions index 2018.* Retrieved from http://www.transparency.org/cpi2018/results

United Nations Office on Drugs and Crime (1995). *Ninth United Nations Congress on the Prevention of Crime and the Treatment of Offenders, Cairo, Egypt.* Retrieved from: https://www.unodc.org/documents/congress/Previous_Congresses/9th_Congress_1995/017_ACONF.169.15.ADD.1_Interim_Report_Strengthening_the_Rule_of_Law.pdf

United States Department of State. (2014). *Country reports on terrorism, western hemisphere, Canada.* Retrieved from http://www.state.gov/j/ct/rls/crt/2012/209984.htm

Walker, P., & English, C. (2015). Mali attack: More than 20 dead after terrorist raid on Bamako hotel. *The Guardian.* Available at: https://www.theguardian.com/world/2015/nov/20/mali-attack-highlights-global-spread-extremist-violence

Wallenfeldt, J. The troubles. *Encyclopædia Britannica.* Available at: https://www.britannica.com/event/The-Troubles-Northern-Ireland-history. Accessed 15 Sep 2019.

Wherry, A. (2009). A negotiated release of the hostages was preferable to just about every other conceivable option. *Macleans.ca.* Available at: https://www.macleans.ca/uncategorized/a-negotiated-release-of-the-hostages-was-preferable-to-just-about-every-other-conceivable-option/. Accessed 16 Sep 2019.

White, K. (2007). *The Canadian contribution to United Nations peacekeeping*. Retrieved from United Nations Association in Canada website: http://peacekeeping.unac.org:8080/en/pdf/CdnUNPkpgBooklet_e.pdf

Wojtanik, A. (2015). Mokhtar Belmokhtar: One-eyed firebrand of North Africa and the Sahel. [Online] *Ctc.usma.edu*. Available at: https://ctc.usma.edu/app/uploads/2018/01/CTC_Mokhtar-Belmokhtar-Jihadi-Bio-February2015-2.pdf. Accessed 15 Sep 2019.

York, G. (2009). The secret Mali deal to release two Canadians. *The Globe and Mail*. Available at: https://beta.theglobeandmail.com/news/politics/the-secret-mali-deal-to-release-two-canadians/article4248750/?ref=http://www.theglobeandmail.com. Accessed 16 Sep 2019.

Part VII

Intelligence

Knowledge Management (KM) and Intelligence-Led Policing (ILP)

Larry Poe, Nikola Protrka, Mark Roycroft, and Tiina Koivuniemi

In this era of information overload, effective intelligence-led policing (ILP) operations rely upon efficient knowledge and information management. This facilitates core intelligence functions like the creation of intelligence requirements, devising collection plans, analysing raw intelligence and producing finished intelligence. Additionally, knowledge management (KM) and intelligence management (IM) promote the operational security (OPSEC) required to disseminate finished intelligence (tactical and operational) to law enforcement (LE).

To accomplish this tasking, KM and IM are used to manage the capture, creation, distribution, filtering, security and storage of data.

The Practical Application of KM and IM

According to Wilson (2002), KM is used as a synonym for either IM or the 'management of work practices' used to improve the sharing of knowledge. The main challenge for many organizations is a lack of clarity concerning KM and its relation to IM (Fig. 1).

Generally speaking, KM is the efficient handling of information and resources within an organization. Knowledge is defined as the amalgamation of experience,

L. Poe (✉) • N. Protrka • M. Roycroft • T. Koivuniemi
Rabdan Academy, Al Bhustan, Abu Dhabi, United Arab Emirates

327

M. Roycroft, L. Brine (eds.), *Modern Police Leadership*,
https://doi.org/10.1007/978-3-030-63930-3_25

Intelligence Tradecraft Terminology

Collection Plan: Defines the best sources and methods for collecting intelligence requirements and developing actionable intelligence

Finished Intelligence: Analytical reports which "connect the dots" by putting information into context and drawing conclusions about its implications.

Information Management: The management of data and information.

Intelligence Requirements: Intelligence requirements information that needs to be collected to better understand the threat.

Knowledge Management: The systemic management of an organization's knowledge, to meet tactical and strategic requirements

Operational Intelligence: Actionable intelligence about long-term threats that is used to develop and implement preventive responses.

Operational Security (OPSEC): Measures taken to protect intelligence collection sources, methods, and content.

Tactical Intelligence: Actionable intelligence concerning near-term threats and used by operational units to develop preventive or mitigating response plans.

Raw Intelligence: "the dots"—individual pieces of data before being analyzed and synthesized.

(Carter, 2009)

Fig. 1 Intelligence tradecraft terminology

values, information, insight and strategic awareness—which goes beyond the notions of data and information. Retained, managed and exploited, it can be a valuable source of competitive difference and advantage. Its importance is described as follows: intellectual capital is the hidden value (and capital) tied up in an organization's people which can set it apart from its competitors and be a valuable source of competitive advantage and future earnings—difficult to quantify and add to the balance sheet (Thompson and Martin 2010).

KM is the key facilitator of ILP, one of the most important law enforcement innovations of the twenty-first century. By skilful top-down decision-making and employing a managerial model crime fighting that is guided by effective intelligence gathering and analysis (Kelling and Bratton 2006, 5).

The Elements of Knowledge Management

There are at least three kinds of knowledge in an organization: (1) tacit knowledge, (2) embedded knowledge and (3) explicit knowledge. Tacit knowledge is created through practice, experiment, simulation, observation, personal communication and interaction. It exists in the minds of people and is difficult to transfer from one person. Embedded knowledge exists in the systems and routines of an organization (e.g., regulations, procedures, processes and documents). Explicit knowledge is words, numbers and symbols, and it can be stored electronically or in writing (Federal Authority for Government Human Resource 2017, 14–16).

Intellectual capital, intangible assets, knowledge creation and knowledge capital are strongly linked to KM. Knowledge, if managed well, creates added value for organizations. Knowledge exists in the following forms:

1. Human capital: Staff skills, talents and knowledge such as leadership, influencing, know-how, creativity, strategy, problem solving and decision-making.
2. Information capital: Databases, information systems and infrastructure, information technology.
3. Organization capital: Corporate culture, leadership, teamwork and commitment.

The KM process includes production, classification, storage, dissemination and utilization of knowledge. The process includes formal procedures to collect information such as lessons learned during a police operation. Once knowledge is captured, the real power occurs when the information is used, shared and put into action (Davenport and Prusak 1998; Kumar and Gupta 2012).

KM needs a system to implement its strategy. A well-functioning KM system is a combination of technology, content management and human elements. KM involves an understanding of

- where and in what forms knowledge exists
- what the organization needs to know
- how to promote a culture conducive to learning, sharing and knowledge creation
- how to make the right knowledge available and to the right people at the right time
- how to best generate or acquire new relevant knowledge
- how to manage all of these factors so as to enhance performance in light of the organization's strategic goals and short-term opportunities and threats

An excellent KM strategy requires alignment to the organization's overall strategy. KM strategy consists of five components:

1. Vision and mission
2. Analysis of strengths, weaknesses, opportunities and threats
3. Strategic objectives
4. Initiatives
5. Action plans

On the organizational level, it is necessary to share both explicit knowledge and tacit knowledge. Explicit knowledge sharing needs articulation to define needs, awareness of available knowledge and access to knowledge. Employees need frequent guidance to use knowledge and to share it. Tacit knowledge sharing is challenging, as codification of tacit knowledge is difficult or even impossible. Sharing tacit knowledge requires socialization and partnerships.

Kumar and Gupta (2012, 12) list some methods and techniques which are useful for capturing tacit knowledge:

- Structure conversation with the experts
- Storytelling
- Learning through conversation
- Learning through observation and making films
- Networks for sharing knowledge
- Special meetings for lessons learned
- Learning in virtual places

- Making experts take part in education process
- Creating situations for working together

The key factor that emerges is that of rich, deep and open communications not only within the organization but also with the outside world. Leaders must attempt to apply those same successful environmental aspects to all the organization's stakeholders, and that is what the purest form of KM process aims to do.

Intelligence Management

IM is the process of collecting, storing, managing and maintaining information in all its forms. IM is a broad term that incorporates policies and procedures for centrally managing and sharing information among different individuals, organizations and/or information systems throughout the information life cycle. When used correctly, knowledge is a vital resource that can create quantifiable value that provides reward to the organization. It will usually include the origination or acquisition of data, its storage in databases, its manipulation or processing to produce new (value-added) data and reports via application programmes, and the transmission (communication) of the data or resulting reports. Many companies include the management of voice communications (e.g., telephone systems, voice messaging and, increasingly, computer-telephony integration or CTI) and even intellectual property. There is a significant difference between the terms 'data' and 'information'. Superficially, information results from the processing of raw data (raw intelligence). However, the real issue is getting the right information to the right person at the right time and in a usable form. In this sense, information may be a perishable commodity (Table 1).

Table 1 The differences between IM and KM

Intelligence management	Knowledge management
Data and info, numbers and facts, structured and unstructured	Knowledge, structured info, understanding and wisdom
Technology-driven	People-, process- and management-driven
Explicit, articulated, well-defined, easy to define and share	Tacit, unarticulated, hard to identify and share
Know what, facts, statistics and so on	Know-how, action, experience and innovation
Easy to copy	Hard to copy

http://www.knowledge-management-tools.net/IM_vs_KM.php

Strategies for KM and IM in Policing

Sharing knowledge in policing remains a significant challenge around the world. Manning (1992) states that 'policing is a service occupation whose central "input" and basis for action is information … and the ways in which the police obtain, process, encode, decode and use information are critical to understanding their mandate and function' (p. 352). Police culture can often be an inhibitor preventing best practice with regard to knowledge sharing. Inter office rivalries, departmental hierarchies, agency elitism and other ingrained 'empires' and 'silos' all work against effective knowledge sharing processes for the police. The real challenge is how to promote information sharing, while maintaining adequate OPSEC to protect the integrity of an investigation.

Berg et al. (2008) argue that leadership by police managers is needed to stimulate and encourage knowledge sharing in police investigations. Their study examined management roles and how they affect knowledge sharing. It determined that encouragement from managers is significant, as is networking. Glomseth et al. (2007) indicate that team culture has a significant influence on the extent of knowledge sharing and that a team culture stimulates detectives to work together to solve crimes. Abrahamson and Goodman-Delahunty (2013) further showed that cultures where Canadian police officers take a proactive approach to obtaining and applying new information to respond to changes and to promote innovation show better information use outcomes.

Intelligence-Led Policing (ILP)

A Short History

> In the vision of ILP, synthesizing, linking and spatially distributing the vast amounts of data compiled and stored by police organizations will allow for the most informed and targeted allocation of police resources (Cope 2004).

UK police intelligence, as a practice, was formally established in 1883 as part of the Metropolitan Police, with the formation of the Special Irish Branch, later Special Branch. This unit was established to combat the threat of the Fenian terrorism on the UK mainland, namely the Irish Republican Army (IRA). The unit aimed to gather intelligence on terrorist actors and arrest the domestic opponents of the UK. It was not until the 1960s that the intelligence function was extended to mainstream policing, though ILP would take some time to finally enter the jurisdiction of the police.

McGarrell et al. (2007) noted that it was the US government department who, in the 1970s, 'recommended that all law enforcement in the United States develop an intelligence capacity and that agencies with more than 75 personnel should have a full-time intelligence capacity'. In the 1990s, the UK Audit Commission and Her Majesty's Inspectorate of Constabulary (HMIC) identified an urgent requirement for the police to develop a proactive crime strategy. This strategy would be required to employ law enforcement resources more effectively as the number of offences were outstripping the capability of the police to control crime. The UK Audit Commission understood that forensics, and especially biometrics, 'could be used as both an identifier and an information source' (Raymond and Julian 2015). The commission recommended that ILP was a proactive way forward, particularly when combined with surveillance, informants and other intelligence leads. ILP, the commission suggested, would allow for the targeting of offenders, not just crimes (operational and tactical intelligence). Tilly and French (2018) noted that even when the crime was not strictly organized crime, many crimes such as drug dealing, armed robbery, theft of vehicles for export and terrorism required networks to operate or move goods. Gathering intelligence on such networks would give the police and security services valuable insight into the criminal world (operational intelligence). 'With such understanding, promising methods of disruption can be developed, for example, by focusing enforcement activity on key members. Forensic science has a potential role here in that it can help find out who is related to whom by transferred contact trace materials and the co-presence of trace materials from different individuals who associate with one another in the course of conducting criminal enterprises' (Tilly et al. 2018).

Two influential British government reports, *Helping with Enquiries: Tackling Crime Effectively* (Audit Commission 1993) and *Policing with Intelligence* (HMIC 1997), laid out the government's interpretation of the problems: existing police roles and accountability lacked integration, police were not making the best use of resources, and targeting criminals would be more effective than focusing on crime.

The 1999 HMIC report suggested that prolific and reoffending criminals should be targeted by developing intelligence products on these individuals with the use of informants and surveillance techniques. Kent Police and later Northumbria Police were amongst the first adopters of what was to become known as ILP. ILP was significantly isolated and did not make a major change to the traditional policing methods until the events of 9/11. For various reasons, ignorance, 'need to know', 'dare to share' or protectionism, to name a few, policing and government departments did not share intelligence amongst themselves and preferred to practise intelligence 'isolationism', a major barrier to the successful application of ILP. Kent and Northumbria, in the meantime, used ILP successfully; the strategy at least contributed to a reduction in crime. Once the system was understood and embraced, ILP empowered police officers, and the gathering and dissemination of crime intelligence allowed the police to identify and target serial offenders before they acted. 'As evident in the U.K. experience, the adoption of ILP did not arise solely from the concern with terrorism but rather builds on major developments in law enforcement that emerged in the past two decades of the 20th century' (McGarrell et al. 2007).

There is still no standard definition of intelligence despite research and debate. The definition of intelligence depends on the context where we use it. In the area of law enforcement, intelligence is usually divided into three main areas: strategic, operational and tactical intelligence.

Strategic intelligence focuses on the long-term aims of law enforcement agencies. In this area, data and information are connected to current and emerging trends, changes in the crime environment, threats to public safety and opportunities for controlling actions. Strategic intelligence can be used in the development and change of programmes and legislation.

Operational intelligence provides an investigative team with hypotheses and inferences concerning specific elements of illegal operations of any sort. Operational intelligence is based on information concerning specific criminal networks, individuals or groups involved in unlawful activities, and intelligence could be used for effective law enforcement action. The development of operational intelligence in itself will provide an important source of intelligence to consider from a strategic perspective.

Tactical intelligence is actionable intelligence concerning near-term threats and used by operational units to develop preventive or mitigating response plans.

The law enforcement sector has five regimes of intelligence. These regimes are public order intelligence, criminal intelligence, public tranquillity intelligence, partnership intelligence and managerial/strategy intelligence (Table 2).

Intelligence-led policing has potential to be the most important law enforcement innovation of the twenty-first century, even though its origins trace back to the early 1970s and the term 'intelligence-led policing' (ILP) has been in use at least since the 1990s. The true value of ILP emerged during the last decade.

Ratcliffe (2016, 66) defines intelligence-led policing as policing that 'emphasizes analysis and intelligence as pivotal to an objective, decision making framework that prioritizes crime hotspots, repeat victims, prolific offenders and criminal groups. It facilitates crime and harm reduction, disruption and prevention through strategic and tactical management, deployment and enforcement.' He also mentions

Table 2 Five regimes of intelligence

Intelligence	Targets	Objectives	The time horizon
Public order intelligence	Information about protest movements, terrorism, riots and other forms of violence	Identifying and monitoring potential threats in public areas, preventing violence, predicting how large a police presence will be necessary to maintain or restore order, disrupting terrorist plots and preventing terrorist attacks	Future
Criminal intelligence	Track those who have committed crimes in past or who are committing crimes on an ongoing basis	Collecting intelligence to gather evidence and build cases against suspects in order to bring offenders to justice and facilitate their criminal prosecution and punishment	Future
Public tranquillity intelligence	Commit ground-level actors inside and outside the police to fight against petty crimes and public nuisance, increase quality of life issues, protection of housing stock and property, and increase feeling of security	Ability to respond quickly and effectively to ongoing emergencies, to remove or mitigate hotspots of criminal activity and to restore public confidence in the police	Present
Partnership intelligence	Developing intelligence emphasizes consensus, collective deliberation, participation by heterogeneous actors and involving partners	Recognize which information is gathered, shared and negotiated with partners, collective decisions, divide the tasks, set priorities, elaborate coordinated approaches, enlarge the repertoire of interventions, create synergies and lend reciprocal support	Variable
Managerial/ strategic intelligence	Allocating resources, monitoring crime trends, evaluating the performance of police units and keeping track of police outputs	Identifying enforcement priorities, assuring the most efficient use of police resources and developing efficient and scientifically tested approach to the problems	Longitudinal Comparative

Delpeuch and Ross 2016

that 'intelligence-led policing is the application of criminal intelligence analysis as an objective decision-making tool in order to facilitate crime reduction and prevention through effective policing strategies and external partnership projects drawn from evidential base'.

Some other commonly used definitions are as follows:

> Intelligence-led policing is a collaborative philosophy that starts with information, gathered at all levels of the organization, that is analyzed to create useful intelligence and an improved understanding of the operational environment. This will assist leadership in making the best possible decisions with respect to crime control strategies, allocation of resources, and tactical operations. (New Jersey State Police)

> The collection and analysis of information related to crime and conditions that contribute to crime, resulting in an actionable intelligence product intended to aid law enforcement in developing tactical responses to threats and/or strategic planning related to emerging or changing threats. (Carter)

The main process of ILP is to create intelligence for decision-makers and policing. In this process, data, information, knowledge and intelligence have a significant role. On the first level, there is data which is raw and uninterpreted observations or measurement (crime reports, crime statistics, databases of offenders, etc.). On the next level, data will have a meaning and it is put in context. On this level, we have information. When information is understood and it has been given an interpretation, it will be knowledge. On the highest level is intelligence when data, information and knowledge are evaluated and analysed. In the end, intelligence is presented in decision-making format and for action-oriented purposes.

Intelligence-Led Policing and Evidence-Based Policing

ILP concentrates on individuals or organized crime groups (OCGs) and is concerned with the collection of information; ILP is a traditional law enforcement, but carried out in a smarter way (Ekblom 2003; Tilley 2003).

Intelligence-led policing is a business model and managerial philosophy where data analysis and crime intelligence are pivotal to an objective, decision-making framework that facilitates crime and problem reduction, disruption and prevention through both strategic management and effective enforcement strategies that target prolific and serious offenders (Ratcliffe 2008a: 89). National Intelligence Model

(NIM) is a business process. It is intended to provide focus to operational policing and dependent on a clear framework of analysis of information and intelligence.

The National Intelligence Model used in the UK allows the production of intelligence products, such as strategic and tactical assessments and problem profiles along with target profiles. The UK National Intelligence Model has four elements that concentrate on

- targeting offenders (especially the targeting of active criminals through overt and covert means);
- the management of crime and disorder hotspots;
- the investigation of linked series of crimes and incidents;
- the application of preventative measures, including working with local partnerships to reduce crime and disorder (NCIS 2000).

There is a need for the police to learn the lessons of the past and retain institutional memory. Evidence-based policing allows this function aided by research and empirical evidence. Intelligence analysis uses the ANCAPA (intelligence principles and analytical techniques to enable critical thinking skills) method and software such as I-2 that allows the police to provide timely and accurate products that inform police decision-makers whether it be Senior Investigating Officer (SIOs) in major investigations or police commanders in live critical incidents. There is a distinction between an analyst making recommendations and a police officer making decisions (Cope 2004).

Many chiefs saw the NIM as a framework for intelligence gathering and dissemination. The NIM relies on timely submitting of intelligence reports to the local police station and to central units. One chief constable in Roycroft's *Police Chiefs in the UK* book stated that 'intelligence is from people out on the streets, Covert Human Intelligence Sources (CHISs informants) and Police and Community Support Officers (PCSOs)'. The accent was on the integration of existing data and intelligence coupled with an ability to analyse and disseminate intelligence to where it is needed. Intelligence units use a problem-solving methodology such as SARA—scan, analyse, respond and assess (Eck & Spelman 1987)—as the framework for prioritization. An evidential base is therefore significant to both problem-oriented policing in the analysis and response stage and to intelligence-led policing in the selection of crime reduction plans. (SARA) Crime analysts can 'join the dots' in investigations and against OCGs. Who is connected to whom, which car do they drive, which firearm have they used, and where does their money come from? (Fig. 2)

Fig. 2 The SARA model

The problem-orientated policing (POP) model, introduced by Goldstein in 2001, is a structured approach where information is analysed to enable a long-term strategic objective. This enables the development of specific responses to individual problems (2020 Pepper). Intelligence-driven crime reduction is a three-stage process, requiring that law enforcement interpret the criminal environment and influence decision-makers and finally that decision-maker's impact on the criminal environment. This 3i model (interpret, influence and impact) is used as the framework for an evaluation of the intelligence process.

Something academics have termed 'sousveillance': the recording of actions of the police by members of the public, either text or picture taken from their phone. Mann from the University of Toronto writes as follows:

> We now live in a society in which we have both "the few watching the many" (surveillance), AND "the many watching the few" (sousveillance). Widespread sousveillance will cause a transition from our one-sided surveillance society back to a situation akin to olden times when the sheriff could see what everyone was doing AND everyone could see what the sheriff was doing.

Within the crime analysis of ILP, the intelligence collected is collated and recorded to identify areas of interest (tactical and operational intelligence): 'crime hotspots'. The 'hotspot' approach to policing has been adopted to allow for the effective distribution of resources and surveillance while identifying areas requiring extra attention by policing resources. 'Calculated and purposeful allocation is believed to make the best use of the limited resources at hand' (Weston 2015). The assumption is that 'hotspot' identification supports directed patrols, interventions and proactive arrests which should directly affect and support crime prevention within these areas. In theory, 'crime hotspot' identification fits well with the ILP paradigms by combining ILP with POP, community-orientated policing (COP) and partner agencies.

Intelligence Process

The core of the intelligence-led policing is an intelligence process. In this process, data, information, knowledge and intelligence have a significant role. On the first level, there is raw intelligence, data which is raw and uninterpreted observations or measurement (crime reports, crime statistics, databases of offenders, etc.). On the next level, data will have a meaning and it is put in context. On this level, we have information. When information is understood and it has been given an interpretation, it will be knowledge. On the highest level is finished intelligence when data, information and knowledge are evaluated and analysed. The finished intelligence is presented in decision-making format and for action-oriented purposes (tactical or operational intelligence).

Collection includes the gathering of data and storage of data. Collecting data and information is a challenging process. There are several sources of information. The first way to categorize information is to divide it into two categories using the source of information. We can use official sources (e.g., law enforcement databases, border control data, investigations and public records) and non-official sources (e.g., civil society, social media, anonymous reports and non-governmental organizations). Another way to categorize information is to use the three main types of sources of information:

1. *Open source (OSINT)* is information that is publicly available.
2. *Closed source* is information collected for a specific purpose with limited access and availability to the general public.
3. *Classified* is information collected by specifically tasked covert means including use of human and technical (image and signals intelligence) resources.

A collection plan is a basic tool to manage collection of data and information. The collection plan comprises collection requirements which answer questions like.

• What information?
• Which sources?

- Where to obtain the information?
- How to obtain the information?
- Who is going to collect information?
- How to handle information?
- When to collect information?
- Why to collect all the information?

Evaluation is an assessment of the reliability of the source and the quality of information. The evaluation considers the validity and reliability of information. The evaluation of the information is a critical phase in intelligence process and for final product (output). It has also important role from a human rights and data protection perspective. Next step after evaluation is collation. It means organization of the data into a format from which it can be analysed. The phase has several measures like sorting, prioritizing and referencing of existing information. After collation, information is transferred into a storage system and structured.

One of the most important phases of the intelligence process is data integration and analysis. Analysts prepare association charts, network charts and timelines to assist the investigator to understand the background of a criminal enterprise or crime problem.

It means the careful examination of information. Analysis is usually classified into two categories: strategic analysis and operational analysis. Strategic analysis serves decision-making, policy-making, planning, prioritization and allocation of police resources.

The first phase of this step is data integration. There are various techniques to display the information.

The most common techniques are as follows:

- *Link charting:* to show relationships among entities featuring in the investigation
- *Event charting:* to show chronological relationships among entities or sequences of events
- *Crime pattern analysis:* to identify the nature and scale of emerging and current crime and disorder trends, linked crimes or incidents, hotspots of activity and common characteristics of offenders and offending behaviour
- *Commodity flow charting:* to explore the movement of money, narcotics, stolen goods or other commodities
- *Activity charting:* to identify activities involved in a criminal operation
- *Financial profiling:* to identify concealed income of individuals or business entities and to identify indicators of economic crime

- *Communication analysis* (UNDOC 2011, 14)

The second phase is data interpretation. This phase consists of developing and testing hypotheses. The testing of hypotheses should include hypothesis' pro and contra arguments and processing these in thinking process. A hypothesis inference should contain answers to the following questions:

- Who—key individual/individuals
- What—criminal activities
- How—methods used
- Where—geographical information and scope
- Why—motive
- When—time frame (OSCE 2017, 38)

Analytical methods are useful tools in analysing. Effective proactive law enforcement techniques are crime pattern analysis, demographic/social trend analysis, network analysis, market profiles, criminal business profile, risk analysis, target profile analysis, operational intelligence assessment and result analysis (UNODC 2011, 35–38).

When analyses are completed, it is time to disseminate results. This finished intelligence depends on needs of the customers (intelligence requirements). It can be a strategic, operational or tactical intelligence product. Examples of documents are early warning notifications or intelligence notifications, risk assessment reports, threat assessments, analyses and situation reports. Final products can also take other kind of forms such as structured presentations, weekly overviews and other supporting documentation. One part of the dissemination process is ad-hoc briefings to intelligence or investigation teams.

The analyst interprets the criminal environment and influences the decision-makers with the analysis findings and the decision-makers' impacts on the criminal environment through strategic management, action plans, investigations and operations (Ratcliffe 2016, 83). The successful deployment of intelligence-led policing requires management commitment and the support of leadership.

1. Abrahamson, D.; Goodman-Delahunty, J. (2013). The Impact of Organizational Information Culture on Information Use Outcomes in Policing: An Exploratory Study, Charles Sturt University-Australian Graduate School of Policing; Justice Institute of British Columbia
2. Aims, C. The Hitchhiker's Guide to Intelligence-Led Policing. Chapter 15 May 24, 2016. https://cco.ndu.edu/Portals/96/Documents/books/Impunity/

CHAP_15%20The%20Hitchhiker%E2%80%99s%20Guide.pdf?ver=2017-01-19-102817-930

3. Antosova, M and Csikosova, A (2011). Intellectual Capital in Context of Knowledge Management, The Economic Geography of Globalization, Prof. Piotr Pachura (Ed.), ISBN: 978-953-307-502-0, InTech, Available from: http://www.intechopen.com/books/the-economic-geography-of-globalization/intellectual-capital-incontext-of-knowledge-management

4. Carter, D., L. (2009). *Law Enforcement Intelligence.* Retrieved August 13, 2020 from the World Wide Web: https://www.it.ojp.gov/documents/d/e050919201-IntelGuide_web.pdf

5. Cody W. Telep, Justin Ready and A. Johannes Bottema (2017). Working Towards Intelligence-Led Policing. Volume 12, Number 3, pp. 332–343

6. Davenport, T. & Prusak, L. (1998). Know What You Know. Retrieved February 17, 1999 from the World Wide Web: http://www.brint.com/ km/davenport/cio/know.htm

7. Emil Berg, E., M., Dean, G., Gottschalk, P. and Terje Karlsen, J. (2008), "Police management roles as determinants of knowledge sharing attitude in criminal investigations", International Journal of Public Sector Management, Vol. 21 No. 3, pp. 271–284.

8. Federal Authority for Government Human Resources 2017: Guide of Knowledge Management if the Federal Government

9. Glomseth, R.; Gottschalk, P.; Solli-Sæther, H. (2007). Occupational culture as determinant of knowledge sharing and performance in police investigations. International Journal of the Sociology of Law. 35. 96–107.

10. Knowledge Management Tools, Helpjuice, available at: http://www.knowledge-management-tools.net/

11. Koenig, M.E.D. (1992). Entering state III. The convergence of the stage hypotheses. Journal of the American Society for Information Science Volume 43, Issue 3.

12. Kumar, S & Gupta, S. Role of Knowledge Management Systems (KMS) in Multinational Organization: An Overview International Journal of Advanced Research in Computer Science and Software Engineering Volume 2, Issue 10, October 2012

13. Maguire, M. John, T. Intelligence Led Policing, Managerialism and Community Engagement: Competing Priorities and the Role of the National Intelligence Model in the UK Policing & Society, Vol. 16, No. 1, March 2006, pp. 67–85

14. Manning, P.K. (1992). Information technologies and the police. Crime and Justice, 15, 349–398.

15. McGraw-Hill. (2005). McGraw-Hill Concise Encyclopedia of Engineering
16. OSCE Guidebook Intelligence-Led Policing. 2017 TNTD/SPMU Publication Series Vol 13. https://www.osce.org/chairmanship/327476?download=true
17. Ratcliffe, J.H. 2017 2003 Intelligence-led Policing. Trends & Issues in crime and criminal justice. No. 248. Australian Institute of Criminology
18. Seba, I. and Rowley, J. (2010). Knowledge management in UK police forces. Journal of Knowledge Management, Vol. 14 No. 4, pp. 611–626.
19. Thompson, J.; Martin, F. (2010). Strategic Management: Awareness & Change. Cengage Learning EMEA - Business & Economics
20. UNODC, Criminal Intelligence – Manual for Analysts. United Nations Publication 2011a. https://www.unodc.org/documents/organized-crime/Law-Enforcement/Criminal_Intelligence_for_Analysts.pdf
21. Wattam-Bell, J. (2010). Reviews: The Origins of Object Knowledge. Volume: 39 issue: 5, page(s): 725–726
22. Wilson, T.D. (2002). The nonsense of 'knowledge management'. Information Research, Vol. 8 No. 1
23. WoeiLuen, T.; Hawamdeh, S. (2001). Knowledge management in the public sector: Principles and practices in police work. Journal of Information Science. 27. 311–318.

References

Australian Customs Service (ACS). (2000). *Intelligence Doctrine*. Canberra: Australian Customs Service.
Bruenisholz, E., Prakash, S., Ross, A., Morelato, M., O'Malley, T., Raymond, M. A., Ribaux, O., Roux, C. P., & Walsh, S. (2016). The intelligent use of forensic data: An introduction to the principles. *Forensic Science Policy & Management: An International Journal, 7*(1–2), 21–29. https://doi.org/10.1080/19409044.2015.1084405.
Cope, N. (2004). 'Intelligence led policing or policing led intelligence?': Integrating volume crime analysis into policing (March 2004). *The British Journal of Criminology, 44*(2), 188–203. Available at SSRN: https://ssrn.com/abstract=1160516.
Goldstein, H. (1990). *Problem orientated policing*. New York: McGraw-Hill.
McGarrell, E., Freilich, J., & Chermak, S. (2007). Intelligence-led policing as a framework for responding to terrorism. *Journal of Contemporary Criminal Justice, 23*(2), 142–158.
The National crime Agency in the UK. www.nationalcrimeagency.gov.uk
Tilley, N. (2002). Uses and abuses of evidence in crime prevention. *Community Safety Journal, 1*(1), 13–21.

Part VIII

Mental Wellbeing

Global Policing Leadership and Security Sector Reform

Kurt Eyre

In 1999, former UK Secretary of State for International Development Clare Short made her first reference to Security Sector Reform (SSR), making the link between security and development. It marked the point at which the development community '[redefined] its role in the field of security, while also highlighting the importance of security in the establishment of sustainable peace and development'.[1]

From a UK policing and overseas assistance perspective, the Organisation for Economic Co-operation and Development - Development Assistance Committee (OECD DAC) Guidelines on Security System Reform[2] are most appropriate in terms of definitions and helping inform subsequent learning and development (L&D) programming. Today, Security System Reform and SSR are phrases often used interchangeably—they refer to the broad range of security and justice institutions. Likewise, terms such as 'justice and security reform', 'justice and security providers' and 'justice and security development' are also common.

---

[1] DCAF/ISSAT 2012—SSR in a Nutshell—Manual for Introductory Training on Security Sector Reform.

[2] OECD DAC, (2008), Handbook on Security System Reform: Supporting Security and Justice.

K. Eyre (✉)
Rabdan Academy, Al Bhustan, Abu Dhabi, United Arab Emirates

© The Author(s), under exclusive license to Springer Nature Switzerland AG 2021
M. Roycroft, L. Brine (eds.), *Modern Police Leadership*,
https://doi.org/10.1007/978-3-030-63930-3_26

Accordingly, the description agreed to by EU ministers in 2004 defined the security sector (system) as comprised of the following:

- **Core security actors:** armed forces, border services, gendarmerie, immigration agencies, intelligence and security services, and police
- **Security management and oversight bodies:** relevant government ministries, internal affairs, financial management bodies and public complaints commissions
- **Justice, policing and/or law enforcement institutions:** the judiciary, prisons, prosecution services and traditional justice systems
- **Non-statutory security forces:** private security firms, guerrilla armies and/or private militia

Whilst SSR is a recognised model in 'state-building policy and practice, [and] widely perceived as a precondition for stability and sustainable development in [a post-conflict context]',[3] it also represents a holistic framework for governance and leadership. It views the importance of professionalism and effectiveness of the security sector, such as policing, for example, not through the lens of 'capacity-building' alone but also in how well they are 'managed, monitored and held accountable' (CIGI). Finally, SSR comprises the following three characteristics (SSR 1-2-3):

1. Local ownership is the *one* fundamental approach.
2. Effectiveness and accountability are the *two* core objectives.
3. Political (sensitivity), holistic (perspective) and technical (complexity) are the *three* dimensions.

Above all, SSR focuses on human (and community) rather than regime or state security development. Conceptually, much progress has been made in institutionalising SSR, but as is described later in this chapter, effective and sustainable implementation remains elusive.

In accordance with the Geneva Centre for Security Sector Governance - International Security Sector Advisory Team's (DCAF-ISSAT) core remit to work as a strategic enabler[4] in supporting improved Security Sector Reform (SSR) and institutional and individual capacity to deliver effective assistance, a proposed fo-

---

[3] Centre for International Governance Innovation (CIGI 2010)—SSR—Future of Security Sector Reform (Sedra).

[4] ISSAT Programme of Work 2016–2018: providing support to DCAF-ISSAT members and the wider practitioner community to collectively strengthen and improve international security and justice engagement.

cus for 2018 engagement was in building a specialist leadership and advisory professional development and training capability.

DCAF-ISSAT along with institutions such as the College of Policing international faculty[5] have been supporting the development and integration of SSR (policing)-related training and capacity for over two decades. With a focus on developing trusted relationships, helping translate relevant policy into effective operational practice and identifying capacity needs in implementing coherent security, defence and justice reform processes, such institutions amongst others continue to lead the way in enhancing coordination and harmonisation of SSR (policing) engagement internationally.

The Relevance: International Policing and SSR Leadership Development?

There are increasing political, financial and operational demands, continuous change and complexity impacting on the undertaking of effective and accountable policing and SSR activities. This occurs at the policy, operational and training levels; it is recognised that it is imperative to develop and adapt innovative approaches in leading and advising within an international policing and SSR context. The pressure to justify and evidence the purpose and benefit of engagement is increasing as the uncomfortable truth is that 'despite the significant resources devoted to improving human and institutional capacity across the globe, [most] of the programs [the international community (IC)] fund do not fully achieve their intended outcome'.[6]

Whilst human capital is important in delivering policing and SSR assistance, leadership is critical. Whatever the sector, organisations need capable leadership to guide the programme (and team) through the unprecedented change and complexity being experienced today. Leadership 'awareness' of the strategic plan is one thing, but 'leading' effective implementation by the team is something completely different—the piece 'missing', as constantly expressed by numerous and experienced practitioners in DCAF-ISSAT advanced SSR classes run over the past three years.[7]

---

[5] https://www.college.police.uk/What-we-do/Learning/International-Academy/Pages/International.aspx

[6] Sustainable Capacity Building: Guidelines for Planning and Project Design Communities (Dr N. Gerspacher, Dr Q. Hanlon and N. Weiland)—US Institute of Peace manuscript January 2017.

[7] Captured by the author in his role as DCAF-ISSAT professional training and development coordinator/trainer.

At the International Association of Peacekeeping Training Centres (IAPTC) conference held in Cairo in 2017, the issue of leadership training and performance sat centre stage. The contrast between examples of successful performance improvement within a national context and the reverse being the case in an international 'mission' setting was not in dispute. Moreover, there was agreement of an urgent need amongst a predominantly senior and executive multidisciplinary security, policing and military development group, of the need to transition leadership development to a more integrated, action-learning-based and team-centred approach to improve the status quo. A Development Dimensions International (DDI) forecast (2015)[8] tellingly highlights that of the top ten strategies needed to address the human capital and performance-related challenges in business, four of the highest 'focused on leadership:[improving] leadership development programs, [enhancing] the effectiveness of senior management teams [and improving] the effectiveness of frontline supervisors and managers'. From a policing and SSR leadership and advisory perspective, effective leaders who can direct, coach, develop, manage and inspire their 'globally dispersed' teams in a multi-jurisdictional context is key.

This became the design focus and purpose of a more integrated professional development and training approach in enhancing policing leadership and advisory capacity in SSR.

The Requirement: Integrated Leadership in International Policing and SSR

Leadership is the competency that helps align an understanding of what needs to be done with the capability and behaviour to achieve it. In the interdisciplinary world of SSR and dynamic operational environment of policing, effective leaders will be the ones that demonstrate sound, principled and confident decision-making, underpinned by respect and adaptability. It is also worth noting, however, that leadership is 'not the sole preserve of those in high ranking roles, but a capability that can be instilled and developed at every level'.[9] Be it in the military, policing, wider public services or the private and civilian sectors, leadership applies to four dimensions: *individual, operational, senior and organisational.*

Leadership attributes at both individual and operational levels in terms of role, incident or team management are all important. However, it is decision-making at

---

[8] DDI Global Leadership Forecast 2014|2015—https://www.ddiworld.com/glf2014
[9] Leadership Review Interim report—College of Policing (March 2015).

a senior and organisational level that is vital to achieving tangible SSR, requiring both strategic 'operational' command and executive governance competencies to set the right systemic direction.

To help develop a new type of resilient and adaptable global policing and SSR leader, it will be necessary to better understand the traits expected of such a person today: someone driven by the core values of international engagement, open to challenge, flexible, emotionally intelligent and with the ability to understand and exploit the benefits of partnership, technology and good business practices. Be it as (1) part of the UN's reform of their institutional security and justice pillar, (2) the guidelines laid out in the United Nations Police Monitoring, Mentoring, and Advising UNPOL MMA manual[10] or (3) the concerns acknowledged by peacekeeper practitioners of the ongoing deficiencies in 'mission' leadership performance (IAPTC Cairo), it is clear that in SSR terms, there is an urgent need for a more innovative approach to leadership learning and development today. One that creates leaders who 'empower, trust and support every individual' to succeed and who '[value] difference and diversity; and who [demonstrate] personal accountability while retaining the trust of [partners] and communities'.

As developing more passionate and strategically agile cross-sector leaders, able to adapt to the volatile, uncertain, complex and ambiguous (VUCA[11]) pressures of SSR policing engagement today without compromising these characteristics lies at the heart of the pedagogical 'innovation' explored and advocated further in this chapter.

A Challenge[12]: Pedagogical Innovation in Leadership and SSR Training Design: Now What?[13]

In learning and development terms, certain core training content remains imperative in enhancing a person's knowledge, understanding and skills to fulfil their role. However, particularly in leadership and SSR development for those working in

---

[10] UN Police Dept.—Police Monitoring, Mentoring and Advising in Peace (Manual) 2017 Operations.

[11] DDI report—a world that is volatile, uncertain, complex and ambiguous. First used by the US military to discuss preparedness

[12] Pedagogical Innovation—expanded version of a DCAF presentation given by the author at a Strategic Advising conference held by the Italian Center of Excellence for Stability Police Units (CoESPU) in Nov. 2019.

[13] DDI Global Leadership Forecast 2014|2015—application of this Question Framework.

complex environments, critical in any curricula design is building in the right context, perhaps even more so than the content today. Whilst there is collective success at identifying the 'What Now' (good practices and structure) and indeed the 'So What' (lessons, purpose and process), institutions appear less successful in adapting, evolving and implementing new and relevant needs-based learning approaches, the 'Now What?', for innovative strategic leadership development to emerge. An approach encompassing the components of a 'Beginning, Balance and Blended' is critical.

Shifting from an international SSR and policing development perspective, in identifying a need to shift away from the all-too-common training and capacity building approach (replicated as Train and Equip [T&E] projects in the 'field'[14]), to a more integrated professional development and learning methodology should help re-adjust future leadership design and delivery objectives.

This shift in thinking is necessary in order to re-set the design focus, starting with clarity in the difference between training and learning—the *Beginning*. In pedagogical terms, this means understanding these terms as follows:

- *Training* is about acquiring new skills, but based around short-term activities that are generally narrow in focus or a product-process-centred approach to build capacity, that is, to increase the number of people trained to perform a specific task or role—an approach that has an inherent weakness pedagogically, in SSR leadership and advising training.
- *Learning* is a multi-dimensional approach to integrated learning and professional development (with direct links to Human Resource Management [HRM]) centred on student-centred processes that actively involve, encourage and inspire persons to acquire the relevant skills and knowledge through involvement.

Here the format, approach and skills of the trainer (or facilitator) become just as important as content, that is, the 'contextual' shift needed to improve an L&D impact. The issue still prevalent today[15] is that these more integrated person-centric and problem-solving approaches are generally still missing from many L&D (and HRM) programme designs. The traditional 'performance' learning objective of training remains almost exclusively on developing the technical skills of personnel in isolation of other relevant skills. Yet, in an age of innovation, artificial intelli-

---

[14] 'Field'—a colloquial term for working in country on development projects or multilateral missions.

[15] As feed-back during DCAF-ISSAT SSR Advanced course training discussions and evaluations (2017–2019).

gence (AI) and Internet of Things (IoT), the real need is in recognising that it is no longer enough to simply 'train' for knowledge or skills transfer alone. From the outset, designs must incorporate soft skills and interactive behavioural learning in tandem with technical skills content.

The **Beginning** is not only about a shift away from training but also a move away from the classic training cycle to an alternative learning cycle (Fig. 1).

With a focus on evaluating the business need for leadership development, this then enables more relevant strategic and operational questions to be explored: What are mandatory training requirements to improve organisational performance? What does an increase in public scrutiny or stakeholder expectations look like? Are there political imperatives and/or operational demands to account for? Is the drive to deliver more cost-effective training or simply to make up for a loss of skills due to more employees leaving? Perhaps to increase numbers in the high potential leadership pool in order to increase institutional value or resilience?

This alternative learning cycle in short builds in the much-needed context that is so often missing in the rush to agree terms of reference or cost-effective proposals for the next SSR procurement tender, bilateral training needs project or multilateral T&E component for a complex SSR programme. The reality today is that innovation is urgently needed to better evaluate the operational business need, particularly when it comes to strengthening leadership and governance in SSR theatres—a fact

Fig. 1 Innovation in leadership

that may well lie behind the ongoing reliance on flawed and less sustainable T&E approaches in the field.

Re-balance

With a new Beginning considered and where more integrated knowledge, skills and behavioural learning objectives are defined, then this makes achieving *Balance* in design terms more attainable. A balance that when achieved would further enhance the performance and professional competencies of policing leaders looking to navigate the policy, politics, problem-solving and personality maze that is strategic SSR engagement. The importance of design objectives encompassing the following traditional training areas remains extant, including the following:

1. **Capability:** building capacity, proficiency, skills, aptitude, intelligence, potential and experience (at Organisational, Operational, Technical and Individual levels)
2. **Knowledge** (transfer): of products, service lessons, good practice, case studies and networks (with Partners, Associations and Institutions)
3. **Tools for leadership (SSR):** governance, analysis, direction, decision-making and accountability
4. **Process (system/programmes):** inception/design/implementation/consolidation

These areas of development remain core to an international policing leader's competency. However, the key is in understanding the importance of achieving a balance of the above training areas with a more comprehensive human development (or softer skills) learning focus (Fig. 2).

An ongoing concern with traditional 'training' (or short-term) approaches is that they remain too theoretically based, with not enough time dedicated to knowledge transfer that is practically orientated and building on existing shared experiences. To overcome this one must include 'softer', values-based design elements linked to self-awareness and behavioural change learning objectives. These may include the following:

1. **Values (principles):** encompassing integrity (telling the truth), selflessness (team first and self last), humility (respect diversity and human rights), self-

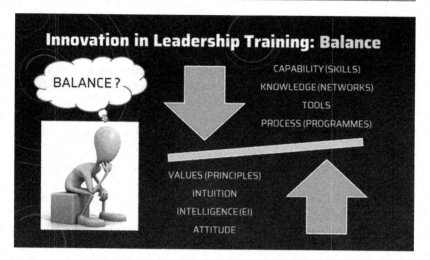

Fig. 2 Innovation in leadership training: balance

discipline (resisting the easy option) and cheerfulness (making humour the heart of morale)[16]

2. **Intuition:** enhancing understanding and instinct (beyond need for conscious reasoning)
3. **Intelligence (emotional):** recognising one's own emotions and those of others and discerning the difference
4. **Attitude:** a settled way of thinking or feeling and reflected in one's own behaviour

Strong Blend

Finally, in applying *Blended* thinking to this more integrated L&D pedagogical approach in terms of both policing leadership and advising in a Security Sector Reform context, it is recognised that people and institutions do not build capacity or change their attitudes, behaviours or practices as a result of knowledge or skills transfer alone. The opportunity to achieve tangible improvement in leadership and

---

[16] Mirroring the ethos and values espoused by Her Majesty's Royal Marines (UK)—a 'State of Mind'.

governance effectiveness requires concerted, collegiate and concurrent change in attitudes and behaviours across multiple levels of an organisation.

Recognising that these are heavily influenced by psycho-social factors such as self-awareness, empathy, stress management, humility and openness and where the development of interrelated competencies such as active listening, respectful communication, executive teamwork, collaboration, cultural awareness and thoughtfulness remains a necessity. Yet, to still see so many leaders at a policy, institutional and/or program levels struggling to achieve this balanced and blended approach is disappointing.

'Now What?' is required then, to do this more effectively in professional development and learning terms. Through the approach outlined above, the real value to be achieved is in developing analytical and critical thinking aligned to improved delegation of authority, decision-making and problem-solving skills that remain operationally relevant; essential leadership responsibilities to be understood, communicated and applied when undertaking effective SSR engagements. Coupled to awareness of the vital impact attitude and behaviour have in combination with topic-specific knowledge, new innovative and Blended leadership curricula will, above all, target two tandem development levels to achieve improvement in Practice, Performance and Professionalism, namely

1. building the right capacity of individuals and teams and
2. changing (evolving) the right attitudes, aptitude and behaviours (Fig. 3).

Integrated Intent: Future Perspectives for Leadership Professional Development and Learning

Principles and Drivers to Leading Sustainable Improvement

Integrated learning, training and development should play a critical part in achieving sustainable capacity and reassuring longer-term government-funded mandate commitments.[17] However, the challenge persists in aligning modern learning and continuous professional development such that it retains a credible theoretical evidence-base whilst being operationally and programmatically applicable. For policing and SSR engagement, where access to timely advice, knowledge, intelligence and tools become ever more important for policymakers and donors, all ac-

---

[17] Politically, operationally and developmentally.

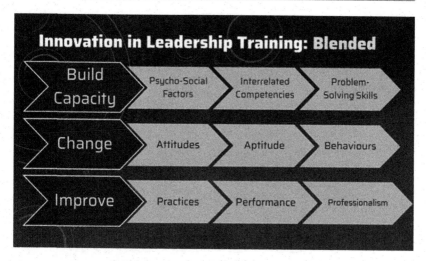

Fig. 3 Innovation in leadership training: blended

knowledge the need to see improved leadership, situational awareness and operational performance management[18] in implementation.

Building sustainable capacity has always been a priority objective. Combining existing, tested and well-established policing and SSR leadership and development services underpinned by globally respected training and project planning curricula, such institutions both in the public and private sectors (see References) do offer a range of strategically orientated and blended leadership, advisory and related training services (including web-based e-learning platforms[19]). However, in most instances, such services are still implemented as stand-alone interventions, lacking coherence and connectivity in programmatic terms to wider-local policing and SSR developments, that is, having minimum impact and contradicting the very context of achieving sustainable benefit. Above all, there has generally been no strategic intent laid out in helping coalesce policy, capacity and approach from the outset.

---

[18] IAPTC (2017) and UN topics that collectively captured these areas of focus included future of peacekeeping in complex environments, leadership, people-centred and inclusive approaches to Peace Support Operations (PSO) engagement, better context (situational) awareness and stronger partnerships.

[19] DCAF-ISSAT—https://issat.dcaf.ch/Learn/E-Learning / EU CEPOL (Policing)—https://www.cepol.europa.eu/education-training/our-approach/types-learning

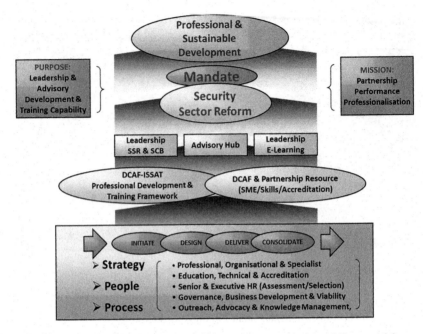

Fig. 4 Leadership and advisory professional development and training delivery model

Conceptually, by integrating SSR and sustainable capacity building (SCB), for example, then this would focus the intent on a more holistic yet operationally relevant strategic approach to a leadership and advisory training 'mission' targeted at improving *Professional*, *Performance* and *Partnership-based* standards, knowledge, competency and behaviours (Fig. 4).[20]

Establishing an integrated but common set of principles for SSR and policing leadership aligned to both SSR and SCB would help deliver consistent training and development support across the vast array of differing donor development models and requirements. Such principles would include but not be limited to the following:

- **Local ownership:** sustainable capacity building of legitimate security and justice reform

---

[20] DCAF-ISSAT Concept paper—Fig. 4 Delivery Model (2017)—Author.

- **Demand (needs) driven:** gender-sensitive approaches to all phases of SSR programming
- **Do no harm:** applying situational awareness, respect, integration and anticipation
- **Build consensus:** creating and achieving commitment, direction and tangible change
- **Intercultural communication:** critical to working in diverse programmes and environments

Policing and SSR Leadership Development: The 'Honest' (Strategic) Need

As previously stated, there is no shortage of endeavour, theories, programmes and intent by the global security and development community in striving to contribute to improved security and justice to help prevent violent conflict, enhance citizen safety and build sustainable peace. However, at a national and donor level, there remains significant variation and 'gaps' in the coherence and consistency in approach to international assistance engagement. What seems apparent is that core to this 'gap' is the lack of quality in international leadership, be that in policing or wider SSR activity:

- **National and organisational misalignment:** at the policy level of Domestic (National Security), Development (Aid and Trade), Diplomacy and Defence (Stabilisation) priorities. Not a design fault, but a failure of leadership to grasp the 'practice of integration' issue.
- **Global security reform:** requires more emotionally intelligent and principled change leaders.
- **Globalisation of 'risk and vulnerability':** operational and reputational risk management in delivering security should not be about personality or self. Requires leaders with courage.
- **Ineffective, uncoordinated and duplicate partnerships:** bilateral and partnership-based overseas activity can be so much more efficient. Needs collective 'gateway' leadership vision.
- **'Missing' national commitment:** international deployments can no longer rely solely on the willing amateur or convenient private-sector 'outsourced' solution. It requires leaders to drive through the professionalisation of international training, development, standards and deployments as a core component of national continuous professional development.

Within the policing, security and SSR context, policy and national security priorities indicate a clear need for a more holistic yet operationally relevant response to leadership development.[21] This will be underpinned by an integrated Leadership, Advisory and Professional Development (LAPD) model that will aim to enhance policing and SSR engagement through the professionalism of leadership and advisory training and support. The strategic objectives of such a model will include the following:

- **Partnership** engagement, to enhance leadership *Performance* and effectiveness
- An **advisory 'hub' (group)**, to identify evidence of what works and share best practice
- Access to an integrated policing and SSR education, knowledge and *Professional* development portfolio of training and support services for uniformed, government and civilian staff

Leading with Purpose in Framing the Future

An honest appraisal of the state of leadership within the context of international policing and SSR development has now been provided. In addition, a more technical investigation into the opportunities available through new innovative pedagogical thinking concerning professional development was explored. If applied with the right intent, this will help enhance the knowledge, skills, aptitude and attitude of future leaders working in an international context. The final 'phase' then is in designing an implementation framework whose sole purpose is to enable the improvement of cross-sector *Professionalisation*, *Performance* and *Partnership* working within the context of improving leadership, advisory and sustainable capacity building.

The LAPD framework[22] will enable policing and related security and justice sector development institutes and/or organisations to provide the following:

1. Better awareness, access and alignment to global policing and SSR governance, professional development, learning, consultancy, and knowledge management capability and capacity.

---

[21] SSR-PSO PKTC draft Concept Paper (K. Eyre) Dec 2017—Global SSR policies; interoperability; PSO organisational and operational practice development; training to improve delivery of effective, efficient and sustainable interventions; tackling corruption; improving professional standards and integrity; inclusivity and human rights; transparency and viability of SSR-PSO practice.

[22] Tailored for SSR development (author), based on the National Police Improvement Agency ten-year improvement strategy published in 2010.

2. Attract multilateral and regional donor support to collaborate and coordinate more effectively on joint policing-SSR leadership and specialist (operational) educational programming to enhance pre-deployment training and advisory access in tandem with increasing the quality, standards and capacity of individual, team and organisational leadership and management.
3. Deliver focused, cross-departmental and interoperable leadership and command programming for senior and operational executives, officers, staff and civilians responsible for improving professional, partnership and operational (practice) performance.

Practical Application

Development of an LAPD framework built around and complementing existing leadership, learning, training and advisory capability as well as aligning to organisational (national) governance, security and development plans will be comprised of five design components:

1. The strategy—improving *Professionalism, Performance* and *Partnerships* in enhancing global security
2. The specific *Areas of Expertise* to be built (or enhanced)—capacity objectives
   - Governance and Accountability (Culture and Organisation)
   - Policing (Justice) and Security Sector Reform
   - Leadership and Command Education
3. The analysis and *Approach*
   - Problem discovery (including identifying 'what works well?')[23]
   - Strategic alignment (governance and structures supporting mandates)
   - Best fit solution (at an individual, team, force/service [local], regional and global level)
   - Finance and programme implementation (priority project/programme management)
   - Manage, monitor and evaluate (reduce bureaucracy and improve decision-making)
4. The Activities—*Capability Pillar* Development
   - *Professional Development and Learning Portfolios (Pillar 1)*

---

[23] Concurrent 'gap' (negative) analysis in tandem with an appreciative enquiry (accounting for the positive).

- Policing and SSR intermediate, senior and customised leadership programmes
- *E-Learning (Pillar 3)*—including blended, web-based learning resource
- *Assessment and Advisory Organisational Support (Pillar 2)*
  - Policing, security and justice support at headquarters and field/project level
  - Undertaking assessments, designing, reviewing and evaluating programmes
  - Coaching (mentoring) strategic and operational officers and staff (link to Pillar 1)
- *Sustainable Organisational and Partnership Development (Pillar 4)*
  - Change and practice-based leadership, planning and decision-making curricula
  - Supporting policing and SSR capacity building in tackling, public order, terrorism (violent extremism), investigation, intelligence, transnational (hybrid) threat, digital, change (technology, organisational development and culture), migration, trafficking, corruption and austerity[24]
- *Advocacy and Knowledge (Pillar 5)*
  - Underpinning all the above capacity with research, production, management and dissemination of practice-based knowledge
5. The organisational and operational *Principles*
  - See Fig. 5 (examples based on mix of policing and SSR-based themes)

The LAPD framework is centred on a partnership-based and coherent process for actors to apply in achieving a more operationally aware and collaborative leadership expertise ready to deliver global security and justice sector improvement. A model not only relevant to building effective individual motivation, confidence and competence at a senior and executive leadership level, but also in directing organisational and cultural change through improved standards, attitude, performance and effectiveness—both nationally (and locally) when deployed abroad.

The structure consists of a multi-annual capability development framework centred on continuous professional development at a national and local level but which is relevant and applicable to international assistance. Under each capability area sits a long-term vision for improvement underpinned by a series of aims and objectives that require allocating to specific teams and with pre-requisite timelines identified. An example of this for Pillar 1 might look as follows (Table 1):

---

[24] Snapshot—curriculum tailored in accordance with the strategic mandate priorities on a case-by-case basis.

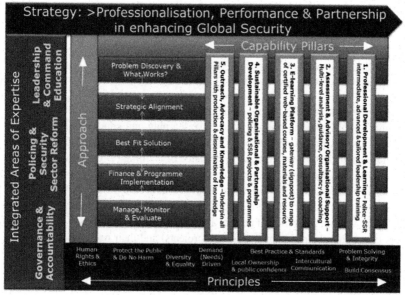

Fig. 5 Leadership and Advisory Professional Development (LAPD) framework

Table 1 Pillar 1 SSR

Pillar 1—Vision (professional development and learning)	
Enhance policing and SSR leadership capability to direct and deliver improved global security	
Aims	
1. Link to effective national/multilateral processes for attracting, identifying, promoting and deploying police and SSR leaders	2. Excellent leadership development at all levels of policing and SSR engagement
Objectives	
1.1 Talent management (nationally) as part of continuous professional development and to enable future leaders to reach their potential	2.1 Leadership capability based on knowledge and evidence of what works, to meet challenges and complexity of policing/SSR
1.2 Improved attraction, selection, development and promotion of cross-national/exchange leaders and L&D experts to increase diversity and shared learning at all levels of leadership	2.2 Development of an International Policing and SSR Leadership and Advisory curricula programme to drive continued improvement in learning and development

Conclusion: Who Is Our Target Audience?

> The emphasis of policing has steadily shifted from [a focus] on crime reduction, performance and targets towards threat, harm and risk and identifying and managing vulnerability. (Police Foundation 2016)

There is a clear case for change in the focus and approach the international community should take in applying innovative learning and educational practices to effect cross-sector strategic and operational reform. At the heart of this effort must be a re-evaluation of the strategic importance of learning (as opposed to training) as a critical policy and practice change instrument. That, and the acceptance amongst executive and senior leaders of an urgent need to re-connect to their 'operational' responsibilities to direct and be accountable for implementation. To stop the 'gap' widening in terms of respect and loyalty between those 'sat' in headquarters (managing their plethora of change projects) and their respective operational teams (where the true strategic impact lies or not) in achieving sustainable improvement.

As highlighted by David Ulrich in 2018, he/she 'who attends [the learning] determines who gets value'. How many senior-level executives and policy leads do we see involved in continuous professional development today—other than when they are looking to change job or for promotional purposes? Furthermore, in terms of learning outcomes that go on to effect improvement, Ulrich et al. in their research entitled 'Victory Through Organization' showed that 'organization-focused learning (i.e. in improving culture, capabilities, or systems) [achieved] four times the impact on business results than individual-focused learning'. Where is the focused executive team development learning helping set the right direction (in operational terms) or facilitated executive meetings honestly accepting the latest feedback from their staff surveys and actually doing something about it? All so vital yet absent in today's complex international environment, which is why the real beneficiaries of working through the LAPD model will in the first instance be executive and senior policy and practice-level participants responsible for effective 'local' (operational) direction and accountability for policing and SSR capacity building.

The framework presents a holistic learning and development opportunity to utilise a blended delivery approach across capability Pillars 1, 2 and 3 whilst enhancing partner and donor access to more coherent and practically focused leadership, command and development programmes for headquarters, programme and field personnel.

Fundamentally, the evidence suggests that there is an ongoing deficit in the quality, consistency, focus and therefore effectiveness of international leadership in policing and SSR today. That in applying a wider-angle lens to the business of pedagogical innovation, there is a clear opportunity to improve the methodology and impact of learning and training such that knowledge and skills transfer take place in tandem with critical behavioural development. And finally, in developing a strategic framework based on a long-term improvement model rather than continual change or reform taking place in isolation, as so often perceived by those implementing and/or those in receipt of support. Combined, these interconnected professional development and leadership perspectives place public-sector learning and education at the centre of a new, future global policing and SSR engagement strategy. Deliberately targeted at international executive and operational leadership professional development and practically applicable across the whole spectrum of security and justice development locally, nationally, regionally and internationally, be that in support of bilateral or multilateral organisations. This is the legitimate goal and commitment for policing and SSR leadership in today's VUCA world.

Seminar Questions

SSR comprises three characteristics, please explain all three.
SSR Leadership, Advisory and Professional Development (LAPD) has five design
   components, what are they and how do they contribute to policing skills?

Exam Question

The author states that SSR offers a re-evaluation of the strategic importance of learning (as opposed to training) as a critical policy and practice change instrument. Please discuss how this approach can influence police leadership.

References

Centre for International Governance Innovation (CIGI). (2010). *SSR – Future of security sector reform.* Sedra.
DCAF/ISSAT. (2012). *SSR in a Nutshell – Manual for introductory training on security sector reform.*
OECD DAC. (2008). *Handbook on security system reform: Supporting security and justice.*

OECD DAC. *Guidelines on security system reform.*

Police Foundation. (2016).

Short, C. from Abrahamse, M. R. *Exporting decentred security governance: The tensions of security sector reform.*

Ulrich, D. A new mandate for human resources from the January–February 1998 issue of Human Resource Management.

Personal Resilience in High-Risk Domains

Amadeus Kubicek

There are many definitions of 'personal resilience'. Some suggest it is the ability, in the face of difficulty, to retain flexible, cognitive, behavioural, and emotional responses (Neenan and Dryden 2002). Other definitions include the ability to lessen the effects of stress—for example, factors such as emotional, cognitive, physiological, behavioural responses to work, work environments, or the organisation (Levi 2000). Most scholars agree it is the ability to deal with perceived adverse situations in a positive and creative way so as to transform a challenge into an opportunity, to absorb any learning offered by setbacks at minimum physical and mental cost.

In the face of adversity or stress, anger, grief, or pain, a sense of hopelessness may develop to the point where professional counselling and/or medical intervention may be required. Contemporary society encourages such interventions. However, in the cycle where prevention and protection is the first course of action, resilient people can keep functioning both physically and psychologically. It allows them to survive and grow and develop as individuals. The notion of being resilient is a safety net to a world of volatility, uncertainty, complexity and ambiguity that harnesses an inner strength to help rebound and develop personally. It may even be said that resilience is a core competency to managing stress.

A. Kubicek (✉)
Rabdan Academy, Al Bhustan, Abu Dhabi, United Arab Emirates

© The Author(s), under exclusive license to Springer Nature Switzerland AG 2021
M. Roycroft, L. Brine (eds.), *Modern Police Leadership*,
https://doi.org/10.1007/978-3-030-63930-3_27

While the narrative of resilience may be simplified, confusion may rest with an outward persona of having everything under control; however, the inner self is in total chaos. This may be exemplified by poor decision-making, non-filtering of conflicting tasks, ambiguity of tasks, and being overloaded by tasks to the point of despondency. Such experiences may be felt on the first day of candidacy at the police academy or at executive decision-making level within the police organisation and between. Regardless of the experience, ensuring a conscious effort to effectively manage those role stressors and harness an inner strength in a cross-cultural environment will help you rebound and reset your mental state.

Cross-Cultural Role Conflict, Ambiguity, and Overload

Cross-cultural role conflict, ambiguity, and overload in this context refer to a process tied to a wider time span. The sequential aspects of role conflict and role overload give reason to expect that these widely experienced perceptions of role difficulties may have different effects on state of mind and task performance, mainly oriented to the limits on choice that are imposed (Hecht 1993). The concept of cultural meanings explained by Hecht (1993) may be in keeping with the idea of adaptability and the proposition of cultural intelligence, whereby cultural adaptability could make a positive contribution to psychological or emotional well-being in a cross-cultural environment.

However, given the conceptual differences that distinguish these processes, it appears that role conflict will have the greater effect on well-being and subsequent decision-making when it comes to risk choices. The most important finding in studies by Hecht (1993) is that role overload and role conflict have different effects on psychological well-being impacting on decision-making. Critical task performance may stimulate role conflict by making significant, and otherwise latent, inconsistencies in priorities and expectations. The stresses in critical tasks may be consequential to role performance structures and organisational frameworks (Peterson et al. 1995), in that role senders may inadvertently create ambiguity, fuelling conflicting expectations with incompatible or difficult-to-prioritise requirements.

Accordingly, there are different concepts and consequences to role conflict and role overload which are often overlooked. Role conflict and role overload refer to different and separate dimensions whereby role conflict occurs when demands associated with one role interfere directly with an ability to satisfy the demands of another role. In contrast, role overload occurs when an individual has too many role demands given the time available to satisfy them (Hecht 1993).

The definition of role conflict implies that competing demands arise during particular or overlapping points in time. When this occurs, there is often a choice of which demand to satisfy, in effect biasing one role over the other. In this sense, role overload refers to a process tied to a wider span of time. The sequential aspects of role conflict and role overload give reason to expect that these widely experienced perceptions of role difficulties may have different effects on mental health and task performance, mainly oriented to the limits on choice that are imposed.

The consequences of role conflict and role overload rest on the assumption that it is the meanings people assign to role experiences, and not the factors that influence exposure to role strains, that influence psychological well-being (Hecht 1993). Thus, people who report greater feelings of role conflict and role overload should report significantly lower levels of psychological well-being compared to those who experience these feelings less frequently. Given the sequential differences which distinguish these processes conceptually, it appears likely that role conflict will have the greater effect on well-being. This is because role conflict, or direct interference between roles (i.e. work and family), is more difficult to manage than role overload, as the demands occur (and need to be satisfied) simultaneously. The most important finding in research published by Hecht (1993) is that role overload and role conflict have different effects on psychological well-being.

This result underscores the importance of making careful distinctions between the two in building and testing theories aimed at understanding the processes by which multiple roles influence psychological well-being. In keeping with this concept, there is a need to understand the predictors for culture and role stresses, and how these may be addressed in approaches to managing environments where task performance and risk may be symbiotic. A conceptual base for predictions about links between culture and role stress is therefore needed.

According to Peterson et al. (1995), these links can be understood by recognising that role stress can originate in stressful work environments or in role structures whose meanings are inadequate or vague. Peterson et al. (1995) assert that task performance may carry ambiguities and complexities not as a result of being unusual or unprecedented, but more so due to not being within people's established interpretive or perceptive mindsets which can generate overload to the performance of a critical task.

Similarly, critical task performance may stimulate role conflicts by making significant otherwise latent inconsistencies in priorities and expectations. The stresses in critical tasks may be consequential to role performance structures and organisational frameworks (Peterson et al. 1995) in the sense that 'role senders' may inadvertently create ambiguous expectations fuelling conflicting expectations with incompatible or difficult-to-prioritise requirements. The research revealed that role overload items have the most consistent structures and the role conflict items the least consistent structures across countries.

The Four-Factor Model of Cultural Intelligence

The works of Earley and Ang (2003) assert that cultural intelligence (CQ) is based on the need to understand why some people are more adept than others at adjusting to new cultural surroundings (i.e. new cultural contexts). However, there are distinctions among concepts of culture, social contexts, and society to suggest a useful definition in that culture consists of patent ways of thinking, feeling, and reacting to various situations and actions acquired and communicated by individuals and groups to include their environments in artefacts (Earley and Ang 2003).

The framework of cultural intelligence holds that it has four factors constituting meta-cognitive (i.e. judgements); cognitive or specific knowledge that people are able to gain and comprehend about a new culture based on various type of cues provided; motivational (i.e. the propensity and commitment to act on the cognitive facet as well as persevere in acquiring knowledge and understanding of a new culture); and behavioural (i.e. the capability of a person to enact their desired and intended actions to a given cultural situation) (Earley and Ang 2003). It requires that an individual observes, comprehends, feels compelled to react/interact, and implements action, in that it is the ability to construct innovating ways of conceptualising, gathering data, and operating in a new culture. This has significance in that diverse cultural groups operating in high-risk industries require a shared comprehension to systems and task performance.

The suggestion therefore is that cultural intelligence offers features of cognition in the form of declarative knowledge, procedural knowledge, and conditional knowledge (Earley and Ang 2003). It also reflects the three questions of identity and self in a social context requiring a certain level of cognitive flexibility since new cultural situations require a constant reshaping and adaptation of self-concept schema, scripts, and so on, to understand and use the setting (Earley and Ang 2003).

A further motivational basis for cultural intelligence is the proposition of a cognitive value approach looking at associated versus abstractive cultures. In associative cultures, people use their own associations among categories when they interact and assume that others share their associations (Earley and Ang 2003). Essentially, this means that in associative cultures, there is an assumption of shared meanings in the framework of the interaction. Unlike other intelligences, cultural intelligence is a learned behaviour and arguably not an innate one. For example, the cognitive component of cultural intelligence highlights a knowledge orientation whereby knowledge is actively sought to gain insight into the cultural dimension.

Similarly, the meta-cognitive components are such that it is how that knowledge is used, that is, judgement in the use of that knowledge. The behavioural component of cultural intelligence is an individual's willingness to utilise knowledge and judgement to display behaviours that are commensurate to the culture, that is to say the individual behaviour aligns to the cultural expectations of the group. The commitment component is the sustainability of the behaviour over the long-term, that is, how committed is the individual to embracing aspects of the culture in their day-to-day activities.

When examining cultural intelligence within multicultural or multi-ethnic environments, the traits of cognition, metacognition, behaviour, and commitment applied to the social interactions an individual may have with the various ethnic communities. While most major cities and towns around the world have a mixed cultural and ethnic dynamic, building relationships with these communities by nurturing and exercising cultural intelligence skills may lead to greater opportunities of trust and cooperation between the community and the police. More importantly, being able to adapt to the mindset of various cultural communities could provide opportunities with understanding community behaviour and issues associated with policing.

Intercultural Communication: Conflict, Ambiguity, and Overload

Intercultural communication is the interpersonal interaction between people of different cultures or shared bodies of knowledge demonstrated in the form of low- and high-context cultures. A low-context culture is one where speech is explicit and meanings are taken literally; therefore, the message intended is conveyed primarily by the words spoken alone. The high-context culture is one where meanings are implicit in the words spoken conveyed only a small part of the message (Earley and Ang 2003). The entire meaning of the message therefore needs to be inferred by the listener and is reliant on contextual cues. In individualist cultures, the discourse is direct, whereas the discourse in collectivist cultures is non-textual with emphasis on the use of qualifiers that include statements such as 'may be', 'perhaps', 'probably', and 'slightly'. This notion presents building blocks to investigating the relationship of conflict, ambiguity, and overload to cultural contexts as they apply to error and risk management (RM) highlighting deliberate or purposive behaviours that individuals undertake to detect, avoid, or mitigate error and risk that may be due to underlying assumptions within the organisation, such as beliefs, perceptions, thoughts, and feelings, which ultimately dictate the source of values and actions.

Within the organisational context, Cooke and Rousseau (1988) put forward several cultural styles that form three general types of cultures. The first is the constructive culture, distinguished by encouraging employees to interact with others and approach tasks in a way that will maximise their contentment with the results and include the achievement, self-actualising, humanistic encouraging, and affiliative styles. The second general culture type is the passive/defensive culture, characterised by members interacting in ways that allow them not to be threatened by their environment, trying to avoid confrontation and to establish security and characterised by approval, convention, dependence, and avoidance. The third general culture type is aggressive/defensive culture, where members approach tasks forcefully in order to protect their status and security.

Cross-Cultural Competence: Conflict and Ambiguity

The idea of cross-cultural competence bears relevance in this regard as it is defined as the process by which individuals and systems respond effectively to people of all cultures, languages, classes, races, ethnic backgrounds, religions, and other diversity factors in a way that recognises firms and values the work of individuals and communities to preserve dignity (Earley and Ang 2003). It is therefore viewed as a set of congruent behaviours, attitudes, and policies that mash together to enable the system, agency, of professionals to work effectively in cross-cultural situations. Cross-cultural competence is essentially integration and transformation of knowledge about individuals and groups of people into specific standards, policies, practices, and attitudes used in appropriate cultural settings to ensure high and outcomes. This requires learning new patterns of behaviour and effectively applying them in appropriate settings.

Cultural Intelligence Mega-skills: Conflict, Ambiguity, and Overload

In keeping with this approach, there are mega-skills that have been deemed appropriate components to the concept of cultural intelligence, conflict, and overload (Bucher 2008) The mega-skills put forward by Bucher (2008) suggests understanding self-cultural identity, that is, how individuals think about themselves; checking cultural lenses of recognising the ways in which cultural backgrounds differ on how they influence thinking, behaviour, and assumptions;. Bucher stated that Global consciousness, moving across boundaries and seeing the world from multiple perspectives; shifting perspectives and by an individual putting themselves in the shoes of other cultures Intercultural communication, that is, exchanging ideas and feelings and creating meanings with people from diverse cultural backgrounds; managing cross-cultural conflict, by dealing with conflict among people from differing cultural backgrounds in an effective and constructive manner.

Culture Specificity of Risk and Ambiguity

A culture-specific argument can be used as an explanatory construct that explains variations in performance and perception towards risk due to ambiguity. Risk is about uncertainty and how you manage that uncertainty depends on informed decision-making. Vechhi and Brennan (2009) contend a causal link to differences in priorities, practices, and performance across national cultures when making risk-based decisions. The suggestion here is that differences in priorities and understanding were affected by cultural dimensions (see Fig. 1) such as masculinity and uncertainty avoidance. Leading on from this, individualism and quality practices suggested that individualist cultures displayed a significantly lower level of engagement in quality improvement and control programmes than collectivist countries. The masculinity/femininity dimension also had an effect on quality mechanisms in the level of equity and status between the two. Similarly, uncertainty avoidance had significantly affected quality practices in that high uncertainty avoidance countries tended to rely on resources aimed at quality control. These findings (Vechhi and Brennan 2009) confirmed that quality practices can vary significantly across dimensions of culture due to constructs that include ambiguity.

Socio-technical Considerations to Risk, Conflict, and Ambiguity

Duckers et al. (2009) suggest that the results of these different analysis methods was their reliability and accuracy were limited to the terms of reference in that studies comparing the effectiveness of analysis techniques were not found. With data reporting accepted as a major tool for mitigating risk, risk management may also be influenced by socio-technical considerations that may interfere with the decision-making process caused by ambiguity, conflict, or overload (Malenfant 2009). Here, the belief is that people perceive risks according to their own knowledge, experience, and interests with the aim of making others understand personal perspectives and avoiding conflict.

Hence, an incorporated proposition to consider the dimensions of evaluating a subject at risk is suggested to be contextual with the judgements of the assessor in

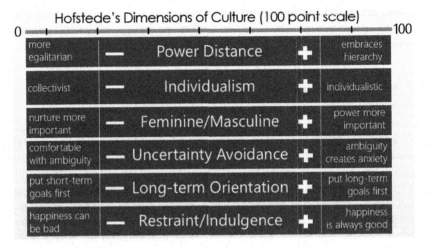

Fig. 1 Hofstede's dimensions of culture

the interventions used. Once again, the idea of assessment and an unambiguous risk approach falls within the realm of a cultural continuum whereby an individual's position could vary over time and contexts (Earle and Cvetkovich 1995). This suggests that multiple cultural narratives of a highly cosmopolitan individual, might easily adjust their risk management judgements and with a clearer approach to risk management tasks, whereby there is an equal expression of concern for localised issues. On the other hand, the pluralistic approach is one that administers concern for the local setting only (Earle and Cvetkovich 1995). This assertion is one that emphasises cognitive representations of an individual in their view of the world, defined as cultural narratives, and is such that a person may have multiplicity of cultural narratives with respect to risk management judgements that avoid the sense of conflict in decision-making. Another construct to this assertion is knowledge, mindfulness, and behavioural ability when combined, interacts effectively across cultures (Ting-Toomey 1999).

The knowledge component to the definition suggests knowledge of processes through which culture influences behaviour. It also identifies knowledge of the processes through which cultural variation affects behaviour, noting that culture influences behaviour through identifiable cognitive and motivational mechanisms. The cognitive frameworks help to organise and process information whereby selective attention to meaning and perceptions is formed (Thomas 2006). The motivational influences are such that individuals seek to ensure that differential motives are lined with their cultural values within the context of their interaction with others who are culturally different (Thomas 2006), minimising the sense of cultural conflict. Mindfulness, on the other hand, is a concept of heightened awareness and enhanced attention to a current experience voiding a sense of ambiguity by adopting a particular approach to cognitive processing by seeking multiple perspectives. Here the belief is that mindfulness is a key link between knowledge and behavioural ability and is key meta-cognitive strategy to understanding self-confident behaviour in the planning and monitoring of performance (Thomas 2006).

Determinants of Risk Taking: Ambiguity and Uncertainty

When examining the determinants of risk taking in an uncertain and ambiguous context, Slattery and Ganster (2002) assert decision-makers who fail to reach their goals often set lower, less risky goals in subsequent decisions. This ambiguity in decision-making was researched in a simulated decision-making environment in which individuals chose more or less risky goals in a complex dynamic task that featured uncertain outcomes yet meaningful consequences. The hypothesis of Slattery and Ganster (2002) utilised several measures of risk propensity designed to assess personal behaviour in hypothetical standardised situations framed as a basic risk paradigm. Measuring a candidate's attitude towards risk included a measure of the subject's self-reported willingness to take risks with the results indicating effective consequences of subsequent choices are influenced by the outcomes experienced in past decisions.

Commensurate to the idea of risk taking and perception in risk-oriented decision-making is the notion of the Fuzzy Trace Theory (FTT) (Reyna 2008). The key concept holds that people rely on the general idea of information (gist) as opposed verbatim details in judgement and decision-making. The notion surmises that precise information about risk may not be effective in encouraging prevention behaviours on the basis that people may perceive certain facts but not derive intended meanings. Based on medical decision-making and health, FTT characterises that human judgement and decision-making is primarily based on imprecise gist that forms the major means by which people indicate and act on their understanding or perception of information.

Formal risk identification (RI), assessment (RA), and management (RM) processes and tools are a useful aid to decision-making in relation to reducing the risk posed by serious offenders. Expectations about risk assessments, decisions, and management must be realistic. No matter how good they appear to be, it is impossible to use the information derived from a formal risk instrument to predict with certainty the behaviour of an individual or the outcome of a particular situation. RI, RA and RM tools should be regarded as an excellent, but limited, means of improving the likelihood of identifying and preventing future offending or victimisation. They can enhance professional judgement but not replace it (see Principle 4 College of Policing Risk).

Indecisiveness and Ambiguity

While the concept of knowledge processing and contextual referencing has often been discussed, Yates, Ji, Oka, Lee, Shinotsuka, and Sieck (1998) offer a perspective to cultural variations in indecisiveness often associated with the construct of ambiguity. The degree of decision-making processes and indecisions by individuals in culturally diverse environments may be paramount to the immediacy of effective risk judgement outcomes. Yates et al. (1998) undertook studies that examined cultural variations linked to indecisiveness among Chinese, Japanese, and Americans. The study obtained through validated self-reporting comprehensively measures indecisiveness and indicated large cultural differences, with Japanese participants exhibiting substantially more indecisiveness than Chinese or Americans. Evidence in the study highlighted cultural variations correspond to variations in people's positive versus negative values for decisive behaviours, suggesting that such values are plausibly an important means for motivating and sustaining cultural differences in indecisiveness. Direct behavioural instances of the differences in indecisiveness are therefore implicated, suggesting that thoroughness might be an important cognitive mechanism, whereby cultural differences in indecision actually occur.

Core to these studies is the proposition that culture is a significant contributor to the indecisiveness; however, as Yates et al. (1998) put forward, the studies indicated differences in Western and Asian culture, where the arguments centred largely on Asian collectivism versus Western individualism with a prediction that indecision would be greater within an Asian culture than in a Western culture. What stands with greatest significance in the study to decision-making are the elements of 'confidence' and 'over-confidence'. In this instance, general knowledge questions were reflected in an individual's probability judgement whereby if an individual is overconfident the bias is greater than zero (bias > 0) and under-confident is indicated where bias is less than zero (bias < 0). As has been indicated, the research methodology highlighted a shortcoming in the thoroughness of participant's reflections.

Yates et al. (1998) suggest that the culture to which people belong can be a powerful predictor of their indecisiveness and that the values of individuals and their cultures can differ considerably in whether and how much they seem to admire or abhor indecisive behaviours, and these values are associated with the incidence of indecisiveness. Similarly, thoroughness may be a plausible mechanism by which indecisiveness may emerge.

Shared Mental Modelling: Task Analysis and Ambiguity

The construct and measurement of shared mental modelling outlines three important characteristics were gauging similarity among team members with respect to their knowledge representations. These characteristics include a method for elicitation, structure representation, and representation of emergence (DeChurch and Mesmer-Magnus 2010). Elicitation may mean the use of ratings and concept maps based on the results of task analysis; however, how the knowledge contained in the model is represented would be based on perception and therefore may be subject to values and beliefs contained in the cultural dimension. This may be similarly in structure representation which captures the degree of association between distinct components of their team or task. Representation of emergence involves how individuals' mental models are collectively considered as constituents of a team mental model in that it is the degree of sharedness in perception and conceptualisation that is of interest (DeChurch and Mesmer-Magnus 2010). The cognitive architecture to shared mental modelling, while improving team and workplace effectiveness, still draws on the relevance of task analysis and individual perceptions.

Summary

This chapter has discussed a number of items that may be considered useful information and providing an understanding to the framework of cultural adaptability and its symbiotic relationship to role stressors in the sphere of law enforcement. Duties that engage multicultural environments and risk-type decision-making require an understanding of being personally resilient to conflict, ambiguity, and overload in roles and tasks. Engaging cultural intelligence in the context of communication, cross-cultural competence, and socio-technical considerations creates the foundations for addressing the determinants of risk and risk taking and the possible stress that can result from a lack of understanding of the environment to the indecisiveness attached to those situations that may have impact on one's emotional and mental state of readiness. Harnessing an understanding of values, perceptions, and belief systems may definitively add to your toolkit of knowledge and the way you apply this knowledge in your everyday policing duties.

Seminar Questions

Why is intercultural communication important in policing?
What are the determinants of risk taking in policing? Why is risk management important?

Exam Questions

What are the socio-technical considerations to risk, conflict, and ambiguity as outlined by the author?

References

Bucher (2008). Building Cultural Intelligence: Nine Megaskills; Pearson.
Cooke, R., & Rousseau, D. (1988). Behavioral Norms and Expectations: A Quantitative Approach to the Assessment of Organizational Culture. Sage Journals.
DeChurch, L. A., & Mesmer-Magnus, J. R. (2010). The cognitive underpinnings of effective teamwork: A meta-analysis. *Journal of Applied Psychology, 95*(1), 32–53.
Duckers, M., Faber, M., Cruijsberg, J., Grol, R., Schoonhoven, L., & Wensing, M. (2009). Safety and risk management interventions in hospitals: A systematic review of the literature. *Medical Care Research and Review, 66*(Suppl. 6), 90S
Earle, T., & Cvetkovich, G. (1995). *Social trust: Toward a cosmopolitan society*. Westport: Praeger.
Earley, P. C., & Ang, S. (2003). *Cultural intelligence: Individual Interactions across cultures*. Stanford: Stanford University.
Hecht, M. L. (1993). A research odyssey: Towards the development of a communication theory of identity. *Communication Monographs, 60*, 76–82.
Hecht, M. L., Collier, M. J., & Ribeau, S. A. (1993). *African American communication: Ethnic identity and cultural interpretation*. Newbury Park: Sage.
Levi, (2000). Stressors at the Workplace Vol 15 Jan March. Hanley & Belfus.

Malenfant, R. (2009). Risk, Control and Gender: Reconciling Production and Reproduction in the Risk Society. Sage.

Neenan, M., & Dryden, W. (2002). *Life coaching: A cognitive behavioural approach.* London: Brunner.

Peterson, M. F., Smith, P. B., Akande, A., Ayestaran, S., et al. (1995). Role conflict, ambiguity, and overload: A 21-nation study. *Academy of Management Journal, 38*, 2; ProQuest.

Reyna, V. (2008, November 19). *A theory of medical decision making and health: Fuzzy trace theory.* Newbury Park: Sage.

Slattery, J. P., & Ganster, D. C. (2002). Determinants of risk taking in a dynamic uncertain context. *Journal of Management, 28*(1), 89–106.

Ting-Toomey, S. (1999, January 22). *Communicating across cultures.* New York: Guilford Press.

Thomas, D. (2006). Domain and Development of Cultural Intelligence: The Importance of Mindfulness. Sage.

Vechhi, A., & Brennan, L. (2009). Quality management: A cross-cultural perspective. *Cross Cultural Management An International Journal, 16*(2), 149–164.

Yates, J. F., Lee, J.-W., Shinotsuka, H., Patalano, A. L., & Sieck, W. R. (1998). Cross-cultural variations in probability judgment accuracy: Beyond general knowledge overconfidence? *Organizational Behavior and Human Decision Processes, 74*, 89–117.

Mental Health Awareness for Police Officers

Mark Roycroft and Lindsey Brine

Law enforcement officers often become involved in stressful situations and these events can impact individuals in different ways. Exposure to traumatic incidents may range from violent domestic disputes or sexual assaults to fatal collisions, homicides, drownings, suicides, terrorist bombings, and natural disasters. All police officers, including specialist officers, may accumulate the effects of this trauma rather quickly or over a lengthy period of time. Identifying stress in colleagues and reducing the impact of police work on individual officers and staff is a key part of modern police management and is a responsibility of all law enforcement officers, regardless of rank. It is incumbent on police officers to identify stress and concerning psychological behavior in their colleagues.

The Metropolitan Police now encourages MIND Blue Light Champions, who are trained to identify stress-related symptoms in colleagues. The vocational aspect of policing means that many officers return to work or keep working after they have experienced a traumatic incident or are suffering from some form of stress. This is often attributed to the police mentality of moving on and getting things done regardless of how tough it is. Significant work to reduce the stigma around mental illness within the police has been done in the UK and in Canada. MIND has published a booklet, 'How to Manage Your Mental Wellbeing', which discusses common stress

M. Roycroft (✉) • L. Brine
Rabdan Academy, Al Bhustan, Abu Dhabi, United Arab Emirates
e-mail: mroycroft@ra.ac.ae

M. Roycroft, L. Brine (eds.), *Modern Police Leadership*,
https://doi.org/10.1007/978-3-030-63930-3_28

factors including repeated exposure to traumatic events, workload pressures, long working hours, lone working, and dealing with physically or verbally abusive people. This is on top of the pressures shown below in an 'ordinary' workplace. Police officers have to be constantly alert and attentive. These demands can lead to a chronic state of hyper-arousal.

> Posttraumatic Stress Disorder (PTSD) is a mental health condition caused by witnessing or experiencing actual or threatened death, serious injury or violence. Being affected by these types of events is normal, however if the thoughts or memories of these events start to seriously affect the life of the person long after the event, that person could be experiencing PTSD. Signs that someone may be experiencing PTSD include nightmares, uncontrollable memories, persistent fear and severe anxiety.
>   It is believed that PTSD is caused by a complex mix of life experiences, including the amount and severity of trauma you have experienced since early childhood; the way your brain regulates the chemicals and hormones your body releases in response to stress; and inherited mental health risks such as an increased risk of anxiety or depression and inherited aspects of your personality or temperament. (https://www.pshsa.ca/resources/ptsd-awareness-for-police-officers)

Often, a chemical or hormonal imbalance caused by the body's response to stress can be effectively treated with medication prescribed by a specialist in PTSD such as psychiatrist or a neurologist. PTSD is a long-standing mental health phenomenon that was originally associated with soldiers in war zones. It has been called many other names such as 'shell-shock', 'combat fatigue', and 'battle fatigue'. Through time and research, it is now understood to impact many different categories of occupations and people including coroners, doctors, firefighters, front-line law enforcement officers, nurses, paramedics, prison guards, and victims and witnesses of violent crime, accidents, and natural or manmade disasters.

People are more at risk for developing PTSD if they

- have a job that increases the likelihood of being exposed to traumatic events
- experience intense or long-lasting trauma
- feel horror, helplessness, or extreme fear
- see people get killed or hurt
- experienced other trauma earlier in life, including childhood abuse or neglect
- have other medical problems such as anxiety or depression
- lack a good support system of family or friends
- deal with extra stress after the event such as loss of a loved one, pain or injury, or loss of job or home
- have biological (blood) relatives with mental health problems including PTSD or depression

Some of the most commons signs and symptoms of PTSD include the following:

- Intrusive memories
- Reliving the event as if it were actually happening
- Nightmares
- Flashbacks
- Physiological symptoms such as increased heart rate and sweating
- Paranoia
- Severe emotional distress
- Hyper-arousal
- Insomnia
- Unexplained feelings of anger or being overwhelmed
- Irritability
- Hypervigilance at all times, often for no reason
- Overwhelming feelings of guilt
- Emotional numbness
- Inability to concentrate
- Self-medicating with alcohol or drugs
- Persistent avoidance
- Trying to avoid thinking about the event
- Avoiding places, objects, activities, or people that remind you of the event
- Losing interest in activities that were enjoyable in the past
- Difficulty maintaining close relationships
- Memory problems including not remembering important aspects of the traumatic event
- Negative cognition and mood
- Distorted sense of blame
- Estrangement from others
- Increased negative feelings about self or others
- Feeling emotionally numb or inability to experience positive or negativeemotions
- Feeling hopeless about the future
- Suicidal thoughts (https://www.pshsa.ca/resources/ptsd-awareness-for-police-officers)

These symptoms may develop rather quickly or over a lengthy period of time. Many front-line police officers who are exposed to trauma on a daily basis become so used to it that they often do not realize they are exhibiting symptoms of

PTSD. The co-author of this chapter, in retrospect, realized that he was exhibiting symptoms of PTSD as early as 2 years into his 29-year career, yet did not seek assistance or treatment until his 27th year in the police. He was diagnosed with severe, chronic, cumulative PTSD as a result of many years of police work. This makes it even more critical for colleagues to care for one another. Possible signs of PTSD in a colleague include the following:

- Trouble remembering or concentrating on tasks
- Difficulty managing time or completing tasks
- Feelings of fear and anxiety about completing usual duties
- Unreasonable reactions to normal situations
- Anger outburst and interpersonal conflict
- Excessive fatigue and abnormal sleep patterns
- Inability to cope with stressful events
- Avoidance of certain job duties that they were comfortable previously performing
- Increased alcohol use after work
- Performance deterioration, lateness, or absenteeism (https://www.pshsa.ca/resources/ptsd-awareness-for-police-officers)

Definitions of Mental Health

The Health and Safety Executive in the UK define 'stress' as 'the adverse reaction a person has to excessive pressure or other types of demand placed upon them'. They give the following reasons for stress:

- The demands of your job
- Your control over your work
- The support you receive from managers and colleagues
- Your relationships at work
- Your role in the organization and how it is managed

The Police Federation (which represents most police officers in the UK) conducted a survey with the assistance of Cambridge University called 'The Job, The Life' of 17,000 police officers, from 47 police forces in the UK. Stress and anxiety was experienced by 79% of officers within the previous 12 months, with 94% of those affected saying the difficulties were caused or made worse by their job. About

44% said they viewed their job as very or extremely stressful—a larger proportion than in the 2016 survey (39%). The main findings were as follows:

- 21% of police officers who responded reported symptoms consistent with PTSD or the more severe complex PTSD (CPTSD);
- 73% of those with PTSD or CPTSD will be unaware that they have it;
- 66% of those reported a psychological or mental health issue which they felt was a direct result of police work;
- 69% of officers feel that trauma is not well managed in their force;
- 93% still go to work even when suffering from a work-related psychological issue.

Police Professional, May 2020, reported on the survey and stated that the Cambridge University survey found that police officers and staff score significantly lower on World Health Organization (WHO) well-being indices than other sectors. The average sickness absence is 20 days over a year, with 'health problems caused or made worse by work' cited as the most frequent reason for calling in sick. 'The Job, The Life' is the first major study to use the WHO-adopted screening questionnaire for complex PTSD. Among the findings, more than half of those surveyed said that they had insufficient time to process incidents before being sent back out on the next call. Stress is not confined to lower ranks, and in 2016, the Police Superintendents Association in the UK carried out a survey of superintendents to try and understand the resilience of members and the realities of day-to-day life as a superintendent.

The figures showed that

- 50% had signs of suffering with anxiety
- 27% experienced symptoms of depression
- 75% were working more than 50 hours per week

The police in Canada face the same mental health challenges the Centre for Addiction and Mental Health (CAMH) found that Canadian police officers are disproportionately affected by mental illness. A substantial number of municipal/provincial police (36.7%) and Royal Canadian Mounted Police (RCMP) (50.2%) report symptoms of mental illness compared to the general population. A study of two urban Canadian police departments found that mental health problems and illnesses were frequently cited by officers:

- 52% reported moderate to severe stress (11% extremely severe);

- 88% reported moderate to severe anxiety (12% extremely severe);
- 87% reported moderate to severe depression (13% extremely severe); and
- 29% were in the clinical diagnostic range for PTSD.

CAMH states that there are a variety of sources of poor mental health in the police. Two of the most widely recognized sources of police stress are operational stress (sometimes referred to as occupational or environmental stress) and organizational stress.

Operational Stress

Operational stress is commonly understood to mean the stress and trauma that police officers encounter in the course of their work. Exposure to traumatic situations such as road traffic collisions, murder scenes, child abuse, sexual assault, and violence can leave officers vulnerable to operational stress injuries. These can produce psychological issues such as anxiety, depression, PTSD, and substance use disorders that directly result from activities performed in the line of duty.

Organizational Stress

Organizational stress is generally recognized as the tension resulting from characteristics of the workplace. Organizational 'stressors' such as ineffective leadership, problematic tenure and promotions processes, understaffing, lack of resources, and organizational culture can cause serious challenges for police officers. In fact, police tend to rank organizational stressors higher than operational stress. Some of the additional stressors faced by Canadian officers in these locations include the following:

- Isolation
- Extreme environmental conditions
- Long distances to travel
- Lack of back-up
- Lack of health and social services
- Communities with high rates of crime and victimization
- Communities with high rates of poverty, mental illness, substance misuse, and family disruption

Coping Mechanisms

According to a US National Institute of Justice report, some other consequences of being a police officer are cynicism and suspiciousness, emotional detachment from aspects of daily life, reduced efficiency, absenteeism and early retirement, excessive aggressiveness, alcoholism and other substance abuse problems, marital or other family problems, post-traumatic stress disorder, and suicide (Dempsy and Forst 2016, p. 174).

In the chapter "Extraterritorial Investigations of Terrorist-Related Kidnappings", Brine discusses the need for regular psychological assessment by trained psychologists in high-risk and high-stress situations. Officers involved in undercover work and other areas of covert operations receive regular psychological assessment. This should also include those conducting duties involving collision reconstruction, homicides, natural disasters, and many others where there is constant exposure to trauma.

It is incumbent on officers and supervisors to recognize officers' behavior, and if there are issues then the advice and support of occupational health or other trained staff should be sought. An increasing part of police managers' work is to monitor the well-being of officers and staff while developing health, safety, and well-being. A leader in a police organization needs to take care of personal qualities and values. Police managers and leaders have a duty to help maintain the well-being and mental health of employees. The police in the UK have launched the national well-being service and this includes support as well as training for forces. It is intended to reduce stigma and improve the knowledge and support available. In chapter "Personal Resilience in High-Risk Domains", the author speaks about 'personal resilience'. Some suggest it is the ability, in the face of difficulty, to retain flexible, cognitive, behavioral, and emotional responses (Neenan and Dryden 2002). Other definitions include the ability to lessen the effects of stress. Chapter "Personal Resilience in High-Risk Domains" talks about role stress and officers may find that during different times in their careers. Certain roles demand more and stress may only manifest itself years later.

Officers have to make critical decisions and this may save lives or cause life to be lost. Recognizing risk and dealing with risk can also have a long-term effect on officers and staff. Officers have to be personally resilient to conflict, ambiguity, and overload in roles. This is not an easy task in the complex world of law enforcement. They are expected to have good cultural intelligence skills and recognize the consequences of their decision making and risk management. Listening to Independent Advisory Groups and minimizing the fallout from critical incidents can help protect officers from further risk from riots and protests. In Appendix 8 the UN principles recommend that 'police supervisors shall ensure that stress counselling is offered to police officers who have been involved in violent situations or who have discharged a firearm'. All policing ranks can suffer stress, and middle managers were seen by the Cranfield School of Management to experience 'feelings of isolation, anxiety, and enormous stress' by acting as a buffer between senior management and the rank and file (Sopow 2019, 'RCMP Leadership in the 21st Century').

Many police organizations have worked to reduce the stigma attributed to mental health. Good practice needs to be emphasized in the training of leaders and encouraging colleagues to be aware of the well-being of their co-workers. Officers should be encouraged to maintain their well-being over a whole career. Cumulative PTSD can build up over years and cause the same symptoms as officers who are coping with one traumatic incident. Appendix 16 illustrates some of the ways that the UK College of Policing suggest that this can be achieved including dietary advice, ensuring adequate breaks during shifts and encouraging individuals to recognize their own limitations in the workplace.

References

Blue Light Wellbeing Framework Organisational Development and International Faculty. (2017, May).

Dempsey, J. S., & Forst, L. S. (2016). An introduction to policing. Cengage Learning. USA.

MIND Blue Light managing well being Police MIND Charity.

Neenan, & Dyrden. (2002). Life Coaching: A Cognitive-Behavioural Approach. Routledge

PTSD Awareness for Police Officers. https://www.pshsa.ca/resources/ptsd-awareness-for-police-officers

Responding to trauma in policing a practical guide. College of Policing.

Sopow, E. (2019). *RCMP leadership in the 21 st century. The need for boundary-spanning leadership*. Canada: University Canada West.

Decision-Making in Law Enforcement

Mark Roycroft

Introduction

Police officers have to face difficult decisions everyday of their working lives, and they learn to prioritise and deal with critical incidents. The police face unique decision-making environments where they encounter rapidly changing conditions. Chaotic and stressful conditions often create difficulties for police officers in prioritising the direction, type, intensity and pace of the actions they will take to effectively control a critical incident or live investigation. This chapter explores how police officers make decisions in a natural environment (naturalistic decision-making) and how they implement those choices. The decision-making can be part of a domestic dispute, firearms incident or a major investigation. The decisions made will influence the outcome of all these incidents, and sometimes, the decisions made at the start of a critical incident influence the progress of that case, either negatively or positively.

Sound decision-thinking practices lead to what must, in turn, be followed by an effective implementation of choices. There is no system of decision-making which guarantees infallibility. Sound decision-making does not ensure success, nor does not allow us to avoid risk, but it can mitigate it. The police decision maker is relied

M. Roycroft (✉)
Rabdan Academy, Al Bhustan, Abu Dhabi, United Arab Emirates
e-mail: mroycroft@ra.ac.ae

M. Roycroft, L. Brine (eds.), *Modern Police Leadership*,
https://doi.org/10.1007/978-3-030-63930-3_29

389

upon to exercise judgement and discretion. For example, simply rounding up the "usual suspects" could exacerbate a local community relationship or minority sensitivities.

Historical Context: Traditional Decision-Making Structures. Case Study Hillsborough Stadium Disaster 1989

Poor decisions can lead to dire consequences. For example, in 1989, fans surging into the Hillsborough football stadium in Sheffield, UK, for a Football Association semi-final match led to people being crushed against retaining fences. This resulted in the deaths of 96 people and injuring of over 700. There were a number of decisions made by the police before and during the match day which impacted upon this incident. These included the decisions made by the police match commander, a chief superintendent, not to delay the kick off and to open an additional entrance, both of which were held to have directly contributed to the subsequent deaths. There followed an apparent cover-up by some police officers which appears contrary to the Code of Ethics (Turner 2016; Scraton 2009). The subsequent Independent Police Complaints Commission (IPCC) report (now Independent Office of Police Conduct (IOPC)) outlined the errors of decision-making on the day of the match on 15 April 1989 and the report was published on 27 June 2017. It is the biggest criminal investigation into alleged police misconduct in England and Wales.

The contemporary police officer has many masters and must comply with legal statute, Human Rights legislation and local policy whilst deciding whether their actions are necessary and proportionate. Irvine and Dunningham (1993) found that the most prevalent error in criminal investigation was the making of decisions.

A former senior UK police officer, Mark (1978), suggested that the police service was the place where problems not wanted by others could be placed; he continued suggesting that a police chief serves five masters, which still persist today:

1. Criminal law
2. Police authorities (now police and crime commissioners)
3. Police (and now also police staff) under their command
4. Public citizens
5. The officer's conscience

Police officers continue to practise a great deal of autonomy in their decision-making based on their professional judgement. The importance of rigorous training, high professional standards and practice does much to assist in such professional decision-making. Their use of naturalistic decision-making sometimes has to rely on "Satisficing"(i.e. doing the best in a limited timeframe).

Naturalistic Decision-Making

Models of naturalistic decision-making place a high premium on situation assessment, prioritisation and strategic action (Klein 1989). This research demonstrates that people solve problems by a selective, heuristic search through large problem spaces and large databases, using means-ends analysis as a principal technique for guiding the search. Proficient decision makers must first try to fill gaps and explain conflict and only then assess the reliability of assumptions. They try to construct complete and coherent situational models. The requirement for police officers to use meta recognition skills to assist with situation assessment is important. Cohen, Freeman and Thompson (1997) state that metacognitive skills are also crucial (p5) in two phases of intuitive decision-making:

- Construction of a situation model or plan when recognition is uncertain
- Verifying the results of recognition

They describe the metacognitive process composed of three stages: the quick test, critiquing and correcting. The quick test is similar to Klein's (1989) idea of "satisfying" (i.e. doing the best in a limited timeframe). National Decision Models (NDMs) assume that the decision situation is usually embedded within a broader environmental and organisational context. Adaptive expertise entails a "deep comprehension of the conceptual structure of the problem domain." Once there appears to be other issues or risks or there are unreliable assumptions, and then the "correcting" stage is entered where more information needs to be collected. This stage requires the collection of additional data to resolve ambiguity. Metacognitive skills are needed in the process of evaluating and assumptions.

A "frame" is a mental construct consisting of elements and the relationship between them. Initial framing may be fairly swift, but when the stakes are high, individuals seldom settle for the first impression. After initial framing, a lot of time is invested in fleshing out and understanding of the situation and making judgements. The decision maker can use a recognition process to deal with previously encountered situations. If the situation is substantially different from previously encountered situations, they set about formulating an action plan that deals with its uniqueness embedding observed events in a context in order to give them meaning is called "framing." Frames are mental structures that guide understanding of a complex reality.

"Satisficing" is another way of reducing the information flow, and it assumes that the decision maker has a minimum set of standards that an option must meet. Simon's vision of bounded rationality has two interlocking components: the limitations of the human mind and the structure of the environments in which the mind operates. Heller (1988:39) states that "the more turbulent the environment the more likely that participative methods of decision-making are used." Heller comments that "the uncertainty created by a turbulent and complex environment leads a manager to conclude that his own knowledge and experience alone are insufficient to make a high quality decision." The research also found that the higher the skills and educational qualifications of managers the greater the degree of participative decision-making. Crego and Harris (2000:261) states that NDM focuses on "experts making decisions in real world environments, these are typically characterised by time pressure, high-risk dynamic problems and inadequate information." He states that Klein's recognition primed decision (RPD) model describes decisions made within high-stakes environment and a short timeframe for action, the retrieval of patterns of typicality within the critical incident that the decision makers recognise from their previous experience. Their selection of a course of action becomes a rapid response.

Principle 5 of the APP on Risk talks of the need for decision-making strategies that can be used in real-life, dynamic, high-stake situations may be significantly different from those that can be applied when the risk can be anticipated and controlled. The police may have to take the least worst option with limited time to gather all the information needed; the law recognises this and cases involving firearms (see McCann case in Firearms Policing chapter "Armed Policing"). This entails making the best decision they can make at the time with limited knowledge and limited intelligence.

Flin and Arbuthnot (2020:278) argue that because of the stakes in critical situations, it is necessary to ensure that decision makers are trained to deal with situations beyond, as well as within, their capabilities. They add that the RPD process is dependent upon valid experience and training. "It is the integrity and underpinning of any system that accepts that commanders must, at times, make rapid intuitive style decisions and that they will be reliable." The Centrex Investigative Doctrine (2005) formulates a model showing the stages of criminal investigations. This starts with the instigation of an enquiry, the initial investigation, the investigative evaluation and progresses to suspect management. This is followed by evidential evaluation, charge, case management and then a court appearance.

Beach (1997) states that an expert can use their experience to "frame situations" rapidly and accurately. Experts recognise meaningful patterns of events and having recognised (framed) them and then use them to perform the tasks that the situation demands. Kind (1987:128), when discussing framing, states that the investigator/ police officer has to draw their boundaries "much tighter to provide a problem which is amenable to investigation knowing." He comments (p132) that the "experienced investigator carries in his mind a frame consisting of two parts, the inner frame and the outer frame. The boundary between the two may be "diffuse" or clear. The idea of frame in Kind's words is "strongly associated with the idea of elimination," that decision makers aim at finding solutions which are "satisfactory rather than optimal." Satisfaction is achieved through simplification, including judicious use of shortcuts or "heuristics." The concept of "bounded rationality" involves decision makers trying to make things easy for themselves by

- reducing problems to manageable proportions,
- concentrating upon only a few options,
- making choice based upon intelligent guesswork, and
- searching for a solution "that will do."

Police investigators and police officers who attend a critical incident have to draw up hypotheses, and the UK College of Policing Core Investigative Doctrine states that hypotheses can assist investigators to progress investigations. Before deciding to use hypotheses, the investigator must consider the following:

- Has all the material been gathered?
- Does the investigator understand all the material?
- Are there any lines of enquiry which have not yet been pursued and which could generate more material?
- What benefit will the use of a hypothesis bring to the investigation?

Risk Management in Law Enforcement

The police need to maintain public safety by competent risk management, which involves identifying, assessing and prioritising risks. The experienced police officer will quickly assess the situation and understand the critical tasks required. Other chapters deal with firearms policing and public order situations, but the management of risk in these situations is usually instant and real. The public entrusts the police to deal with critical incidents and risk professionally.

Some of the components of risk management involve (US COPS) the following:

- Recognition of the critical tasks required
- Prioritisation of tasks required and the decision-making process that goes with that
- Mobilisation is to take action to manage or mitigate the recognised and prioritised risks
- Control, reduce or eliminate identified hazards by effective decision-making (Copple and Copple 2018)

Risk Identification (See Appendix 9)

Principle 1 of the College of Policing app on Risk states that making decisions in an operational context is a form of risk-taking. Viewing decision-making as risk-taking allows the police service to focus on controlling and improving the quality of decision-making. Principle 2 states that the police have a duty to confront risk and to make risk decisions on behalf of the communities they serve. Even though making a decision involves the risk of criticism if harm occurs, this risk to the reputation of a police force or an individual member is secondary to the primary responsibility to protect life. Similarly when a good risk decision produces a poor outcome, this does always mean that the decision was wrong. On occasions the police have to make decisions on flawed intelligence, and they therefore make the best decision they can at that time. The major theme here is the ability to review the decision-making process as per Roycroft's (2019) research into decision-making around murder cases. Good risk management should increase the likelihood of successful decisions but will not, in itself, guarantee that harm will not occur.

Current Professional Practice on Decision-Making

Across England and Wales the main police manuals of guidance for decision-making are authorised professional practice (from an investigative perspective previously known as the Core investigative Doctrine) and the Association of Chief Police Officers (ACPO) (2006) Murder Investigation Manual. These set out advice on dealing with incidents for all ranks regardless of service and all ranks are subject to the Code of Ethics issued by the College of Policing.

Quinton et al. (2000) describe how routinely the decisions taken by police officers on the street when dealing with the public to either enforce or not enforce the law have a great impact on those concerned, but are often invisible to their police supervisors. Smith and Flanagan (2000) defined a number of skill categories essential for police Senior Investigating Officers (SIOs) in order for them to operate effectively, included in which significant importance is placed on effective decision-making. Given this the practice of discretion when making decisions needs better development and support within police practice (Quinton et al. 2000).

Smith and Flanagan (2000) suggest that SIOs should have the ability to think laterally, and they refer to the lack of formal processes by which investigators can learn. The Core Investigative Doctrine states that it provides national guidance on the key principles of criminal investigation along with promoting good practice amongst practitioners. The National Police Chiefs Council (NPCC) Murder Manual (see College of Policing app 2014) breaks the investigative process into five stages as follows:

- Stage 1 Fast-Track Actions
- Stage 2 Theoretical Processes or Investigative Process
- Stage 3 Planned Method of Investigation
- Stage 4 Suspect Enquires
- Stage 5 Disposal

This guidance describes some of the issues that investigators face when making decisions including the need to overcome bias on both an individual level and when verifying information, oversimplifying facts, becoming overwhelmed with information and as a result following non-optimal lines of enquiry. Rossmo (2009) describes how sometimes an individual's simplified methods of quickly processing information can lead to mental errors known as cognitive bias.

Stelfox (2009) explores the range of both reactive and proactive responses to crime investigation, with the latter being particularly appropriate when investigating organised crime. According to the range of guidance available, the "Investigative Mind-set" requires an investigative team to consider a range of approaches when making decisions including a need to understand the source of material, the importance of effective planning and preparation, any examination needs to be thorough, with all actions accurately recorded and collated. It is imperative that subsequent evaluations are effective as this may influence how future decisions are made; additionally, it is fair to suggest that those in the police service are effective at reflecting in action as opposed to that of reflecting on action as outlined by Schon (1983) as this can exacerbate situations.

Across the UK, the police services use the College of Policing (2014) National Decision Model (NDM). There are six key elements with the mnemonic CIAPOAR explaining the key elements of the NDM:

Code of Ethics—Principles and standards of professional behaviour
Information—Gather information and intelligence
Assessment—Assess threat and risk and develop a working strategy
Powers and policy—Consider powers and policy
Options—Identify options and contingencies
Action and review—Take action and review what happened

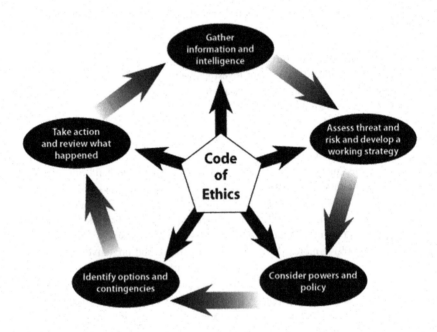

The College of Policing Police Code of Ethics underpins the NDM and sets out the policing principles that members of the police service are expected to uphold and the standards of behaviour they are expected to meet. Many forces have their own values statements, which are complementary to the Code of Ethics.

Throughout any policing decision-making situation, decision makers across all ranks will need to ask themselves a number of questions:

- Are actions consistent with the Code of Ethics?
- What would a victim or community affected expect of me?
- What does the police service expect of me?
- Is this action or decision likely to reflect positively on my professionalism and the wider policing profession?
- Can I explain my action or decision in a public forum?

During the early stages of an incident, the decision maker defines the situation and clarifies matters relating to any initial information and intelligence. They then assess risk and the NDM asks decision makers to consider the following:

- Options that are available
- Immediacy of the threat
- Limitations of the current information
- Time available
- Resources and support available
- Individual's own knowledge, experience and skills
- Impact of an action on the situation and the public
- What action can be taken if things do not happen as anticipated?

The Joint Emergency Services Interoperability Programme (JESIP) has been established to improve the ways in which the three emergency services work together at major and complex incidents (see JESIP app).

When commanders arrive at the scene of a major incident, it is essential that they can quickly establish what is happening around them and jointly agree on a plan of action. The Joint Decision Model (JDM) has been adapted from the NDM to enable this to happen.

The Golden Hour

Experienced investigators often use the term the "Golden Hour" to describe the principle that effective early action should be taken so that significant evidentiary material is identified, secured, by ensuring that it is not lost or destroyed. Where the police are informed of an incident shortly after it has occurred, the offenders may still be in the area. Locating them can provide numerous forensic opportunities that could otherwise be lost. Likewise, the testimony of witnesses can also be obtained while the offence is still fresh in their mind. CCTV images and other data can be collected before it is deleted and action can be taken to secure scenes before they become contaminated. It is important that the decision is taken early to maximise the recovery of evidence. Crego and Harris (2000) describe how the Golden Hour approach ensures that the incident is dealt with decisively.

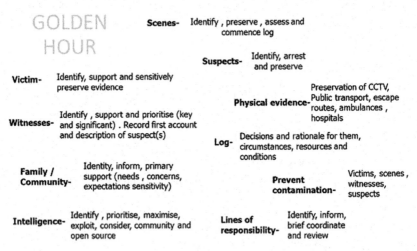

Cook and Tattersall (2016) summarise the doctrine including the importance that nothing should be assumed or believed and that everything should be both challenged and checked, meaning that nothing should be accepted at face value or taken for granted. Investigators must always corroborate, check, constantly review and confirm their findings (ibid.). Rossmo (2009) raises words of caution as to how research has demonstrated how increased information can lead to increased confidence in an individual's analysis of a situation, but not necessarily increased accuracy of the analysis.

Roycroft and Roach (2019) found that experienced senior detectives were concerned with "clearing the ground" beneath their feet once they are engaged in policing an incident, that is, ascertaining all relevant facts before moving on with an investigation. This includes risk assessing the incident. Ansoff (1965) saw strategy as decision-making with imperfect information, and he divided management decision-making into several distinguishable areas, each with requirements to make decisions, these being the need to make strategic decisions, administrative decisions and/or operational decisions.

The modern police decision maker has to take cognisance of all these strategic, administrative and operational issues. Stelfox (2009) discusses the three key decision areas for investigative decision makers to consider: Does the behaviour constitute a criminal offence? Who could be the suspect? What additional information and physical materials should be gathered? In the current environment, a fourth element could also be added, "The political" element or the perception of how that case is being handled is as important as the "mechanical" conduct of the enquiry. The media, the public and local community will (quite rightly) demand updates on all elements of the investigation and all concerns will have to be allayed.

During this stage the decision maker defines the situation (i.e. defines what is happening or has happened) and clarifies matters relating to any initial information and intelligence.

All police decision makers should ask themselves:

* What is happening?
* What do I know so far?
* What do I not know?
* What further information (or intelligence) do I want/need at this moment?
* When did I know?

Recording Decision-Making

All decision makers are accountable for their decisions and must be prepared to provide a rationale for what they did and why. In some circumstances, the need to document decisions is prescribed by statute, required by organisational strategies, policies or local practices, or left to the decision maker's own discretion.

The length and detail of the record should be proportionate to the seriousness of the situation or incident, particularly if this involves a risk of harm to a person.

Conclusion

The range of skills required by police officers and particularly senior detectives involves diagnostic inclination and the ability to build the case with the correct choice of solving factors.

Seminar Questions

1. What are the lessons from the Hillsborough football tragedy in 1989 for police decision-making and leadership?
2. Sir Robert Mark in 1978 described the police as having five masters; how do those five masters apply to the police today?
3. Klein's RPD model talks of "satisficing" decisions; how do police officers use this model to make decisions on a daily basis?
4. Police officers manage risk as part of their daily tasks; what are the components of risk management?

Exam Question

What is naturalistic decision-making and how does it apply to policing both investigations and public order events?

References

ACPO. (2006). *Murder investigation manual.* Wyboston: NPIA.

Ansoff, H. I. (1965). *Corporate strategy.* New York: McGraw Hill.

College of Policing. (2014). *Authorised professional practice: National decision model.* [online]. https://www.app.college.police.uk/app-content/national-decision-model/the-national-decision-model/. Accessed 01 Sep 2018.

Cook, T., & Tattersall, A. (Eds.). (2016). *Blackstone's senior investigating officers handbook* (4th ed.). Oxford: University Press.

Copple, C. K., & Copple, J. E. (2018). *Risk Management in Law Enforcement: Discussions on Identifying and Mitigating Risk for Officers, Departments, and the Public.* Washington, DC: Office of Community Oriented Policing Services.

Crego, J., & Harris, C. (2000). *Do NDM and CDM theories mark the ends of a continuum? Or Does a hybrid approach better describe team-based decision-making problem solving processes with the management of critical incidents?* Draft Paper July 2000. [online]. http://www.calt.demon.co.uk/critical%20incident%20management.htm. Accessed 06 Jan 2019.

Flin, F., & Arbuthnot, K. (2020). Ashgate Incident Command: Tales from the Hot Seat.

Irvine, B., & Dunningham, C. (1993). *Human factors in the quality control of CID investigations research* (Royal Commission on Criminal Justice, Research Study Number 21). London: Home Office

Kind, S. (1987). The Scientific Investigation of Crime John Sherrat and Son Manchester.

Klein, H. J. (1989). An integrated control theory model of work motivation. *The Academy of Management Review, 14*(2), 150–172. https://doi.org/10.2307/258414

Mark, R. (1978). *In the office of constable.* London: Collins.

Quinton, P., Bland, N., & Miller, J. (2000). *Police stops, decision-making and practice* (Police Research Series Paper 130). London: Home Office

Rossmo, D. K. (2009). *Criminal investigative failures.* Boca Raton: CRC Press.

Roycroft, M. (2019). *Decision Making in Police Enquiries and Critical Incidents.* Palgrave Macmillan.

Roycroft, M., & Roach, J. (Eds.). (2019). *Decision making in police enquires and critical incidents: What really works.* London: Palgrave.

Schon, D. (1983). *The reflective practitioner: How professionals think in action.* New York: Basic Books.

Scraton, P. (2009). *Hillsborough – The truth.* Edinburgh: Mainstream Publishing UK.

Smith, N., & Flanagan, C. (2000). *The effective detective: Identifying the skills of an effective SIO.* London: Home Office.

Stelfox, P. (2009). *Criminal investigation: An introduction to principles and practice.* Oxon: Willan.

Turner, R. (2016). *Hillsborough disaster: Five key mistakes.* [online]. https://www.bbc.co.uk/news/uk-england-merseyside-35462767. Accessed 20 Dec 2018.

Part IX

Community Policing

Community Policing

Johannes Oosthuizen

The modern-day concept of community policing has its roots in the concept of re-assurance policing, a notion proposed by the American psychologist Charles Bahn (1974), who sought to define the concept in terms of a subjective feeling of safety, instead of seeking objective measures such as crime statistics or numbers of arrests (Millie 2014, p. 2). Although community policing practices were not widely implemented in the years following Bahn's writings due to the dominance of a performance-based police culture in North America and the UK, things changed in the early 1990s when community-orientated policing started to receive strong federal support in North America (Moraff 2015) and simultaneously found favour with the Home Office in London (Singer 2004).

Whilst there is little evidence to indicate that community policing in North America has gone beyond a pilot or produced a significant shift in the core activities of the police (Zhao et al. 2001), community policing (or neighbourhood policing) in England and Wales ran pilots in 16 wards across 8 forces from October 2003 under the National Reassurance Policing Programme (NRPP), which led to the national launch of the Neighbourhood Policing Programme (NPP) in April 2005 (Quinton and Morris 2008, p. 4). Both the NRPP and the NPP sought to trigger three deliver mechanisms, namely police visibility, community involvement in identifying local priorities and collaborative problem-solving in tackling those

J. Oosthuizen (✉)
Rabdan Academy, Al Bhustan, Abu Dhabi, United Arab Emirates

M. Roycroft, L. Brine (eds.), *Modern Police Leadership*,
https://doi.org/10.1007/978-3-030-63930-3_30

priorities (Quinton and Morris 2008, p. 9), and by 2008, the stage was set with 13,500 dedicated officers operating in 3500 neighbourhood policing teams (NPT) to deliver a 'citizen focus' approach across England and Wales (NPIA 2010, p. 12).

There is a wealth of international evidence that demonstrates how neighbourhood policing reduces crime and improves public confidence in policing, particularly when the public are involved in priority setting and problem-solving (Quinton and Morris 2008, p. 4). An example of this is Dorset Police, who redesigned their neighbourhood policing model in August 2013 under Project Genesis, in order to support their strategic commitment to support neighbourhood policing in urban and rural communities. Their project acknowledged that policing is a dynamic operation that has continued to face a variety of challenges across police forces in England and Wales since its national implementation in 2008, and in order to capture, examine and analyse those aspects at different levels within a single police force, Project Genesis focused on the three main roles within an NPT, namely the sergeant, police constable and Police Community Support Officer (PCSO).

Community Policing in the USA

The modernisation of American police forces is said to have begun during the Reform Era (1930–1970) when police administrators implemented strategies and used technology to increase the distance between their personnel and the citizens they served. During this era, many police departments adopted a hierarchical management style based largely on military models and written policies, and procedures were adopted to define and structure the police role within the community (Fisher-Stewart 2007, p. 3).

The social and political unrest of the Civil Rights movement in the USA characterised their 1960s (NBC News 2008), and the subsequent riots, assassinations, and increased gang violence negatively affected police community relations. The Kerner report (1968) (see chapter "Use of Force and Public Order") on the US riots pointed out that rioting was sparked by a confrontation with a police force seen by the black community as racist, invasive and unconcerned with black citizens. The underlying causes lay in chronic unemployment, unequal health care and education.

Police brutality often led to civil disorder with rising crime rates and the inability of the police to stem the tide. Police administrators realised the need to return to their community roots to improve the pressing issues about crime and disorder. In the 1970s, the community policing era began, and although most law enforcement agencies did not fully embrace the concept until the 1980s (Fisher-Stewart 2007,

p. 3), community-oriented policing in the USA received strong federal support from 1994 when the Department of Justice (DOJ) adopted it as a formal strategy.

The experience of community policing in the USA has been mixed in terms of both implementation and impact as the original emphasis was to improve police community relations but, since the 1990s, has increasingly promoted community-identified priorities and problem-solving (Quinton and Morris 2008, p. 3). According to Skogan and Hartnett (1997a, b, pp. 6–9), community policing in the USA is viewed as a process instead of a product and is organised around four general principles, namely

1. A reliance on organisational decentralisation and a reorientation of local patrol functions to enable more effective communication with that community
2. A commitment to problem-orientated policing (POP)
3. Responsiveness to the local community when setting local priorities and developing tactics to deal with them
4. A commitment to preventing crimes within that community

Challenges of Implementation

Some of the challenges this produces hinge on ensuring that local problem-solving initiatives are effective and the difficulties of implementing this are well documented (Cordner and Bieber 2003). There is also the need to ensure that community engagement is representative of the local communities being policed and that the engagement by the police with those particular communities is able to inform their local policing priorities (Skogan and Steiner 2004).

By 2015, the DOJ's Office of Community-Oriented Policing Services (COPS) had distributed more than $14 billion in grants to thousands of law enforcement agencies to advance a broad range of strategies ostensibly organised around community policing principles, and whilst many of these initiatives have been successful, the programme has not been without challenges (Moraff 2015).

Community Policing in England and Wales

In comparison, the principles of community and neighbourhood policing in England and Wales have a longer history and wider implementation, with significant centralised support from the British government. The UK has a long tradition of consensus policing as encapsulated in the famous principle 'the police are the public and the public are the police' (Longstaff et al. 2015, p. 9). During the second half of the twentieth century, the gap between the police and the communities they served began to widen as car patrols replaced foot patrols and police stations closed or were no longer open 24 hours a day. As a response to this widening gap, community policing began to emerge in a number of forces in the UK, and similar developments were occurring in the 1970s and early 1980s in other countries, especially in the USA and the Netherlands.

According to Wakefield (2006, p. 40), community policing emerged in the UK during the late 1970s as a remedy to the problems associated with the unit-beat strategy (combining the functions of the local foot-patrol officer with that of the mobile 24/7 area car) introduced in the mid-1960s and stressed the importance of improved police-community relations and strengthened police legitimacy (Tilley 2003). John Alderson is often seen as the first senior proponent of community policing in the UK. He was the Chief Constable of Devon and Cornwall, and he produced a 10-point model for his force in 1979. Waddington (1999) describes Alderson's plan as 'a rejection of the technocratic process of professionalisation' of the 1960s and 1970s.

Although traditional foot patrol had come to be regarded as inefficient, it was popular with the public and the changes were misunderstood and resented. In his book *Policing Freedom* he argued,

'The purpose of preventive policing in the broad sense is to find ways of bringing joint resources to bear in times of social change and economic deterioration. Without new ideas and the will to fly in the face of tradition, we may witness a police service beginning to feel unable to cope and having to rely more and more on technologies, "coppery" and response time evaluation for self-esteem. The fusion of social policing and legal policing has a better chance of success than either would enjoy separately. The necessary change must begin in police culture, attitudes and habits and these changes should reflect and be reflected in policies. Police efforts to harness "society against crime" would exhibit care, education, persuasion and ultimately enforcement.'

The lack of community involvement and/or satisfaction was dramatically highlighted in the Scarman report of 1981.

This model of community policing was supported by the Scarman report (1981) on the Brixton riots, which highlighted the police's role in the deterioration of community relations, and in the early version of community policing, crime and disorder reduction was a secondary objective to that of improving community relations with the police (Quinton and Morris 2008, p. 3). It was thought that by increasing police legitimacy, there would be an inevitable reduction in crime, whereas with neighbourhood policing, crime reduction is only considered possible by implementing a process of collaborative problem-solving to deal with locally identified crime and disorder priorities. Community policing also gave more emphasis to community capacity-building as an end in itself, rather than viewing it as a means to support and facilitate the community involvement in problem-solving.

During the mid-1990s, recorded crime levels were falling in England and Wales, reversing a seemingly inexorable pattern of year-on-year rises (HMIC 2001, p. 19), and the British Crime Survey (BCS), now known as the Crime Survey for England and Wales (CSEW), also recorded a significant reduction in the 'worry about crime' by respondents (Allen and Wood 2003) over the same period. However, the Audit Commission (UK Government 2015) argued that recorded crime fell by 14% between 1995 and 1997, but fewer than one person in ten was aware that crime had decreased over this period. This lack of awareness of reducing crime rates, coupled with reduced levels of public confidence in policing reported by Hough (2003, pp. 146–147), became known as the 'reassurance gap' (ACPO 2001) and led to the development of the policy of reassurance policing in early 2000.

An important piece of work responsible for conducting a thematic inspection on enhancing public reassurance by means of a visible and accessible police service was the Her Majestys Inspectorate of Constabulary (HMIC) Report *Open All Hours* led by Sir Keith Povey (HMIC 2001, p. 16). One of the aims of the report was to define the meaning of reassurance within a policing context and did so by saying that this definition extends public reassurance well beyond the remit of policing (HMIC 2001, p. 20).

So, whilst there have been different versions of how reassurance policing can be defined as a concept or how it should be implemented, according to Millie and Herrington (2005, p. 43), there are some common objectives that join them together:

- To reduce the fear of crime
- To increase levels of public confidence in policing
- To support the active citizen approach
- To improve levels of community intelligence
- To reduce anti-social behaviour (ASB)
- To reduce levels of crime

In addition, the *Open All Hours* report (HMIC) also defined reassurance policing as any policing activity that is visible within the community and that specifically requires directed mobile and foot patrols in order to achieve that aim. However, using mobile patrols in order to improve police visibility has its limitations and could be more detrimental than beneficial, even though Bahn (1974) suggested that the sight of a patrol officer could be viewed as a powerful signal for control.

A political imperative was needed to move the concept of reassurance policing into a national model of practice and the imperative that acted as a catalyst for the introduction of neighbourhood policing under the Labour government was the concept of new localism, a notion that aimed to put the community at the heart of political decision making and give communities a say in the provision of local services (Bullock and Leeney 2013, cited in Longstaff et al. 2015).

Neighbourhood policing could therefore be seen as a reinterpretation of an earlier form of community policing, where community involvement is largely about directing the work of local officers towards the crime and disorder problems that cause the most public concern, and which is closely tied to the idea of problem-solving (Quinton and Morris 2008, p. 3).

The Influence of Reassurance Policing

The American psychologist Charles Bahn (1974) sought to define the concept in terms of a subjective feeling of safety, instead of seeking objective measures such as crime statistics or numbers of arrests (Millie 2014, p. 2). Reassurance policing can be described as a broad term used to define any sectoral policing activity that is visible within the community (PA Consulting Group 2001, p. 1), and Bahn (1974, p. 341) defined reassurance as the feelings of safety and security that a citizen experiences when he sees a police officer or a patrol car nearby. Bahn identified accessibility and visibility as key factors for increasing public feelings of safety, and the linked concepts of accessibility, familiarity and visibility were widely cited and used by the Home Office (Robinson 2006, p. 11).

There have been periods leading up to 2008 where very little community or neighbourhood policing was practised which, according to Millie (2014, p. 2), was due to the infusion of a performance-based culture which had enveloped North America and Britain and the subsequent focus on crime control, and prevention (zero-tolerance or intelligence-led policing) was the order of the day. This performance-based culture or practice relied heavily on the police achieving targets of detecting crime and arresting offenders instead of dealing with the causes and influencers of crime and criminals.

What made a performance-based culture even more unsuitable was that crime rates in most Western countries began to fall during the mid-1990s (Millie 2014,

p. 3) (Grove et al. 2012, p. 192) and the expectation that the fear of crime held by citizens did not appear to be happening (Innes 2004).

The Key Elements of Neighbourhood Policing

Neighbourhood policing has been described as being the key building block of effective and legitimate policing (Stevens 2013, p. 3) and provides dedicated police resources to each and every local area, or neighbourhood, in England and Wales. The more popular aspects of local policing, such as visible foot patrols and the presence of familiar police staff, have become more prevalent since the introduction of policing reforms at the turn of the twenty-first century.

According to Quinton and Morris (2008, p. 4), the international evidence base indicates that neighbourhood policing's prospects for success are promising in terms of reducing crime and improving public perceptions, particularly when it involves both the public's participation in priority setting and problem-solving. Both were critical elements for the programme to introduce neighbourhood policing across England and Wales in 2008, as although the BCS at that time indicated that crime had been falling since a historic high in 1995, successive surveys were still showing that public perceptions persisted that crime was rising (Millie and Herrington 2005, p. 41) and that victimisation risks were increasing (Robinson 2006, p. 9). This is what Crawford et al. (2005) referred to as the reassurance paradox, which stubbornly endured despite high police officer numbers and more police staff at the time. Importantly, and as mentioned before, members of the public were becoming concerned about more than just conventional types of crime, and their focus was increasingly turning to the impact and effect of low-level incivilities and anti-social behaviour.

According to the College of Policing (2015a, p. 2), the key elements of neighbourhood policing are public engagement, collaborative problem-solving and targeted foot patrol and evidence from the two studies evaluating the NRPP. These suggested that these three key elements provide a positive impact on public confidence, feelings of safety and crime reduction, going further than the 'woolly' aspirations feared by Millie and Herrington (2005, p. 45)

Public Confidence and Neighbourhood Policing

Within this debate over how to raise levels of public confidence and satisfaction in policing, some caution should be exercised in how achievable much of this may be and this caution is framed in the concept developed by Hunt et al. (2011, p. 13), who stated that public perception is an outcome of policing, not an output. To illustrate the point, they argued that when companies produce goods or services and that service is well communicated and delivered to a customer, the outcome is overall customer satisfaction. However, not all customers will be satisfied and companies have to accept that some customers have preferences that militate against satisfaction with their product, and as a result, it is not beneficial to pursue improvements to products based on customers' dissatisfaction.

According to Sindall and Sturgis (2013, p. 149), the numbers of police officers employed play a significant role in the levels of public confidence in policing, as reported in their study on the comparison between police numbers and police visibility in relation to public confidence in policing, which suggested that any proposed reductions in police officer numbers, regardless of whether they are in frontline or back office roles, would have an adverse effect on the public's confidence in the police. In addition, a 2013 review of neighbourhood policing by the College of Policing (2015a, p. 24) revealed that four police forces were engaged in measuring levels of public confidence and/or satisfaction to assess the performance of their neighbourhood policing teams.

Whether such measures are effective and relevant were questioned previously by the findings of Farrall and Gadd (2004), who suggested that using public confidence as a measure of whether the police are doing a good job is problematic, as policing analysts, if anything, have over-estimated the level of fear of crime held by citizens. Hough (2003) supported these findings by saying that although the public's perceptions of disorder and ASB had increased in the late 1990s before levelling off by 2003, public confidence in policing was declining throughout this period anyway and particularly within a climate of reducing crime rates.

Weatheritt (1983, p. 129) stated that if they (community policing) have any unifying theme, it is that they are all based on the importance of winning and sustaining public confidence in the police as a condition for effective policing. The objective of sustaining and improving public confidence continues to be an important driver of any community policing strategy today, and whilst the BCU evaluation of 2008 stated that foot patrol was important, it was considered insufficient on its own to prompt a large-scale shift in public perceptions, and it was likely that all three delivery mechanisms would need to be delivered in large enough doses across a

BCU, or sufficiently concentrated in local pockets, in order to significantly improve public confidence.

In policing a pandemic, the authors Walton and Falkner (2020) state that maintaining policing presence in neighbourhoods should be a priority and that safer neighbourhood teams (SNTs) routinely engage in local law enforcement, problemsolving and engagement. They often lead multiagency responses at the local level. They provide a reassuring street police presence and routinely address local crime challenges and anti-social behaviour.

Walton and Falkner state that, however, an increase in demand for police emergency response will inevitably result in the stripping back of SNTs by police forces across the country. Neighbourhood officers will be required to backfill emergency response teams and replace other police officers and staff who contract Coronavirus, to assist with crisis management and to fill new roles created as a result of the challenges of the crisis'.

This will leave some communities vulnerable to local disorder and criminal opportunists while reducing the visibility of the police.

Introduction of PCSOs

The HMIC report *Open All Hours* (HMIC 2001) was published in 2001; the White Paper, *Policing a New Century: A Blueprint for Reform* (Home Office 2001a, b), signalled changes in the police service ahead of the Police Reform Act 2002 such as the introduction of the role of PCSO. Although auxiliary patrol officers had been debated as long ago as 1995, proposals for such changes were rejected by ACPO as being unworkable, but by 2001, the climate had changed and the prospect of PCSOs in addition to an increase in the numbers of regular police officers was welcomed at a strategic level (Robinson 2006). The PCSOs played a pivotal role within the strategic plans of the NRPP was launched in 2004 (Home Office 2006, p. 64), which sought very clear outcomes (Tuffin et al. 2006, p. 13) namely

- Reduced anti-social behaviour and improved quality of life;
- Reduced fear of crime and improved sense of safety;
- Increased public satisfaction with, and confidence in, the police; and
- Improved social capacity.

Police Reform Act (PRA) 2002 introduced PCSOs and was an empowering part of a broader police reform agenda arising from not only *Open All Hours*, but also the Policing Bureaucracy Task Force, chaired by Sir David O'Dowd, which reported in 2002 (Home Office 2001a, b).

The first round of government funding was announced for 1206 PCSOs across 27 forces towards the end of 2002, and the first PCSOs came onto the streets in West Yorkshire in March 2003. The numbers rose nationally to 24,000 during the financial year 2007/2008, through the neighbourhood policing fund (NPF). However, due to the impact of public sector austerity, the PCSO workforce began to decrease from 2010 after cuts of 20%. This took the PCSO workforce in England and Wales below the levels of 2008 (Greig-Midlane 2014a, b, p. 14), and the numbers have continued to fall since 2010, to 9547 in 2019, which is a 6%.

For the NRPP, reducing crime and disorder and increasing public reassurance were intrinsically linked and the aim of doing so was to be able to identify the crimes or disorders for an area that act as key signals detrimentally affecting the way the public view the area (Millie and Herrington 2004, p. 4). So, in order to test this hypothesis, the NRPP was initially piloted at a ward level and ran pilots in 16 wards across 8 forces in England under relatively controlled conditions between October 2003 and March 2005 (Quinton and Morris 2008, p. 5). This new concept of neighbourhood policing was considered to be a significant undertaking for the government, police service and their partners, and during the pilot, the Metropolitan Police Service (MPS) produced the Safer Neighbourhoods Programme (2005) which, subsequently evolved into the NPP and contributed towards the introduction of neighbourhood policing in England and Wales in 2008 review of neighbourhood policing by the College of Policing (2015a, p. 25). There were also signs of improved safety, public perceptions of community engagement, police visibility and familiarity with the police (Tuffin et al. 2006, p. 12), and further analysis of the NRPP survey showed that the three key delivery mechanisms were associated with improvements in public confidence, namely

- Targeted foot patrol
- Identifying community priorities for action
- Effective problem-solving

Good neighbourhood policing teams are described by Longstaff et al. (2015, p. 35) as being able to identify suspects, being aware of vulnerable people in their community and relaying community concerns and intelligence to other sections of the force. Research has also identified that the output of policing is one of crime control and prevention, and Diez-Ticio and Mancebon's (2002) review of literature examining police production functions demonstrated that the output of police are public safety and protection of the rights of individuals, with police seeking to maximise this output. Smith et al. (2008, p. 107) argued further by saying that an ideal system of crime control would be one that reduces crime as far as possible, that spreads the benefits of crime reduction as fairly as possible, but, in doing so, preserves the liberties (of movement and of privacy) that society deems to be essential.

Project Genesis: A Study of Neighbourhood Policing in Dorset Police

In 2013, Dorset Police commissioned a review of their neighbourhood policing model, in order to examine the impact of public sector austerity on their neighbourhood policing teams and determine whether critical elements of neighbourhood policing practices such as visible patrols, local problem-solving initiatives and police collaboration with local communities had been negatively affected. The review (Project Genesis) conducted extensive and wide-ranging research.

Project Genesis conducted interviews, surveys and observational studies of their neighbourhood policing teams, and in total, 333 officers participated in the research. One of the outcomes of the observations study (known as the Deep Dive) was that neighbourhood policing officers spent a quarter of their shift time on patrol and attendance at incidents only occupied 15.3% of their time. Post-incident work produced similar figures of 15.2%, with administration taking up 12.1% shift time and briefings and meetings a further 5.9%. However, only 7.7% of the time was recorded as having been spent working with communities with the remaining time spread between meal breaks (4.3%), travelling (2.7%) and a series of other small activities adding up to 11.0%.

Project Genesis also revealed that there were systemic weaknesses in the structure of NPTs across Dorset, ranging from a lack of resources, personnel, support and role-specific training, constant and regular abstractions from duty but particularly in areas of NPTs consulting and engaging the public, as well as attempts to involve the public in problem-solving. With regards to problem-solving within their communities, an element of independence was prevalent across all the ranks. For sergeants, over three quarters of interviewees stated that they were not being required to adhere to any organisational guidelines on how to deal with local issues and were being allowed to develop their own strategies, and for their neighbourhood police officers, of the 94 PCs participating in an e-survey, 80% also said that did not follow any organisational guidelines in this regard.

Finally, the observational exercise revealed that almost 80% of the tasks performed by neighbourhood police officers and PCSOs were self-tasked, with only

5% of their activities being generated by the public and 11% being associated with some form of crime detection or prevention. Whilst the development and utilisation of individual officer discretion is crucial within neighbourhood policing strategies, it is also equally important to ensure that a corporate structure and framework exists within which that discretion may be utilised. This is supported by a 2014 HMIC case study review Dorset Police, which stated that in order to effectively tackle public concerns and improve the quality of life in the neighbourhood, local priorities must feed into force priorities and the Tasking and Coordinating Group (TCG) process and that the force must have systems in place that monitor the effectiveness and impact of this activity.

An absence of defined neighbourhood policing role profiles for sergeants, PCs or PCSOs in Dorset Police was also identified and not only was this raised by officers in their interviews and surveys and viewed as a concern and a contributor for lack of focus, but role profiles for police officers pre-date the NRPP in 2003–2005, and no reason for the absence of profiles could be established. In addition, there was limited induction training being provided for PCSOs and none for sergeants and police officers and no ongoing training for any of the ranks, to refresh their skills or ensure they were being kept updated and abreast of legislative changes or the introduction and application of new laws. There were also no performance frameworks in place to monitor the activities, actions, progress and success of NPTs against force and local priorities, which led to a complete lack of accountability of the NPTs towards their communities, and data suggested that it was also contributing to a lack of focus and accountability for officers and PCSOs. Another concern raised by the findings of this study was the low levels of community engagement and levels of crime-based activities by NPT police officers. This confirmed that NPTs were not being guided by organisational principles or established role profiles but had developed multiple independent methods of dealing with their workloads as they saw fit, and using their warranted powers to deal with local crime was not top of their list. Project Genesis identified a possible risk to Dorset Police that there could be a failure to recognise and support the breadth of expected outputs from NPTs and instead use them to complement those resources already committed to a focus on the investigation of individual crimes. It was also necessary to recognise that neighbourhood policing had become a specialised aspect of local policing that required role-specific skills and training and any comparisons or similarities with community beat policing pre-2006 were no longer valid.

These concerns about the high levels of self-tasking, low levels of community engagement and low levels of crime-based activities suggested that NPTs were acting without organisational guidance and were developing multiple independent methods of dealing with their workloads as they saw fit.

Dorset Police NPT: The Lessons Learnt

Project Genesis produced 44 separate recommendations for a modified neighbourhood policing model in Dorset Police, and the senior management team implemented the changes almost immediately to reverse negative trends and support the local communities throughout Dorset. The new coherent strategic concept of neighbourhood policing was based on the following key issues:

Key Issue 1 There was evidence from the qualitative data to indicate that other police and non-police departments were increasingly using NPTs as the 'final resting place' for some of their work to be done. Examples range from Criminal Investigation department (CID) requests for statements on their behalf, District Councils becoming dependant on the use of PCSOs to cover School Crossing patrols and fill in for council staff on sick leave, requests from Traffic Policing Units (TPU) to use PCSOs on fast-road closures and frontline patrol officers passing the most minor neighbourhood disputes to NPTs even though many can be resolved on first contact by those first responders.

Key Issue 2 (Dorset Police 2013a, b, p. 13) The sustained reduction in the number of incidents attended by patrol officers suggested that patrol officers had the resilience to accommodate some of the work required of NPTs, such as low-level neighbourhood disputes that do not involve repeat medium- and high-risk victims or offenders in that area.

Key Issue 3 The Deep Dive data (observational study) provided good evidence of the diverse level of abstraction and demand on NPTs. Findings determined that the rate of abstracting NPT officers back into frontline duties was unregulated and made it extremely difficult for NPT officers to fulfil their core roles, particularly engaging communities and collaborating with local communities to problem-solve local issues. Interviews revealed that 73% of respondents found the demands being placed on them as being difficult or impossible to manage, which suggested that the declining levels of public satisfaction and confidence Dorset Police were facing at the time were unavoidably linked with the absence of core neighbourhood police activity.

The Threat of Continued Abstractions

The Casey Report (2008, p. 26) highlighted key priorities that the public want from policing, particularly from local policing and the impact that dedicated NPTs provide for communities. It stated that it was essential to have continuity with NPTs in order that the officers and PCSOs get to know their areas and communities well and gain the respect and trust of local communities and thereby ensure that they put the citizen at the centre of what they do (Home Office 2010, p. 13). In addition, there is a weight of evidence to support the continued use of neighbourhood policing and the impact it has had on medium- and long-term crime strategies and ASB, not least of all the findings of the NRPP in 2006. The College of Policing (2014) developed a three-year programme to establish a clear evidence base of 'what works' in the field of local policing, and are also of the opinion that in order to keep the public safe, local policing is vital in ensuring that victims and witnesses of crime have confidence in the service and are satisfied with the handling of their case (College of Policing 2015).

In order to ensure that the success of neighbourhood policing is developed within Dorset, there is a need not only to protect, sustain and embed NPTs within local policing but also to recognise that neighbourhood policing has now become a specialised aspect of local policing that requires role-specific skills and training and can no longer be compared to forms of community beat policing performed 15 years ago. For many 24/7 response officers, neighbourhood policing is still seen as the 'soft side of policing, drinking tea and kicking a football around afield with offenders'. Project Genesis research with sergeants found that 61% (n 11) believed that patrol officers did not have an understanding of what NPTs actually do, and additional e-survey questions to neighbourhood police officers and PCSOs showed similar trends. Many of the core tasks of NPTs revolve around improving public confidence, working in collaboration with local partners to reduce crime and ASB, developing effective strategies to deal with high-risk victims of crime through the Victim First process, ensuring that robust procedures are in place to prevent, detect and reduce crime by the targeted use of NPT constables and the effective engagement of local communities to produce collaborative solutions to local problems. The lack of recognition of neighbourhood policing by the force and fellow officers as a specialist skill, requiring specific skillsets appears to be a contributing factor for the lack of understanding and appreciation of what NPTs do.

Seminar Questions

- What are the key elements of neighbourhood policing?
- What was Operation Genesis in Dorset Police, and how did it improve community policing?
- What were the lessons learnt from the Genesis Project for Dorset Police?
- What were the original aims for introducing police and community support officers in the UK in 2002?

Exam Question

How did the Scarman report of 1982 change community policing in the UK?

References

ACPO. (2001). *Reassurance – Civility first: A proposal for police reform.* London: Association of Chief Police Officers of England, Wales and Northern Ireland.

Allen, J., & Wood, M. (2003). Crime in England & Wales: Quarterly update to June 2003. *Home Office. assets.publishing.service.gov.uk* › uploads › file

Bahn, C. (1974). The reassurance factor in police patrol. *Criminology, 12*(5), 338–345.

Bullock, K., & Leeney, D. (2013). Participation, 'responsivity' and accountability in neighbourhood policing. *Criminology and Criminal Justice, 13*(2), 199–214.

Casey, L. (2008). *Engaging communities in fighting crime.* London: Cabinet Office.

College of Policing. (2015). *College of Policing analysis: Estimating demand on the police service.* London: College of Policing.

College of Policing. (2015a). *Delivering neighbourhood policing – A practice stocktake.* Coventry: College of Policing Limited.

Cordner, G., & Bieber, E. (2003). *Research for practice: Problem-orientated policing in practice.* Washington, DC: National Institute of Justice.

Crawford, A., Lister, S., Blackburn, S., & Burnett, J. (2005). *Plural policing: The mixed economy of visible patrols in England & Wales.* Bristol: Polity Press.

Dorset Police. (2013a, April 6). *Our priorities.* Retrieved July 8, 2014, from Dorset Police: http://www.dorset.police.uk/Default.aspx?page=293

Dorset Police. (2013b). *Declining confidence in Dorset Police? – An emerging issue.* Winfrith: Business Change Department.

Farrall, G., & Gadd, D. (2004). Research note: The frequency of the fear of crime. *British Journal of Criminology, 44*, 127–132.

Fisher-Stewart, G. (2007). *Community policing explained: A guide for local governments.* Washington, DC: US Department of Justice.

Greig-Midlane, J. (2014a). *Changing the beat? The impact of austerity on the neighbour-hood policing workforce.* Cardiff: Cardiff University.

Greig-Midlane, J. (2014b). *Changing the beat? The impact of austerity on the neighbour-hood policing workforce.* Cardiff: USPI.

Grove, L., Tseloni, A., & Tilley, N. (2012). Crime, inequality and change in England and Wales. In J. Van Dijk & A. Tseloni (Eds.), *The international crime drop: New directions in research.* Loughborough: Loughborough University.

HMIC. (2001). *Open all hours: A thematic inspection report on the role of police visibility and accessibility in public reassurance.* London: Home Office.

Home Office. (2001a). *Policing a new century: A blueprint for reform.* London: Home Office.

Home Office. (2001b). *Policing Bureaucracy Taskforce: Change proposals to increase the presence of police in communities.* London: Home Office.

Home Office. (2006). *An evaluation of the impact of the National Reassurance Policing Programme.* London: Home Office.

Hough, M. (2003). Modernisation and public opinion: Some criminal justice paradoxes. *Contemporary Politics, 9*(2), 143–155.

Hunt, P., Irving, B., & Farnia, L. (2011). *Testing the police workforce resilience hypothesis: An application of labour economics to policing management..* Santa

Innes, M. (2004). Reinventing tradition? Reassurance, neighbourhood security and policing. *Criminology & Criminal Justice, 4*(2), 151–171.

Longstaff, A., Willer, J., Chapman, J., Czarnomski, S., & Graham, J. (2015). *Neighbourhood policing: Past, present and future. A review of the literature.* London: The Police Foundation.

Millie, A. (2014). Reassurance policing and signal crimes. In G. Bruinsma & D. Weisburd (Eds.), *Encyclopaedia of criminology and criminal justice* (pp. 4327–4335). New York: Springer.

Millie, A., & Herrington, V. (2004). Reassurance policing: Views from the shop floor. In *British Criminology Conference* (Vol. 7, pp. 1–15). Portsmouth: University of Portsmouth.

Millie, A., & Herrington, V. (2005). Bridging the gap: Understanding reassurance policing. *The Howard Journal, 44*(1), 41–56.

Moraff, C. (2015, June 22). *The US has spent $14B on Community Policing – What have we learned so far?* Yes (Summer 2015).

NBC News. (2008, May 27). *1960–1970s: Civil rights, Vietnam and protest.* Retrieved from NBC News.com: http://www.nbcnews.com/id/24714290/ns/us_newsgut_check/t/s-s-civil-rights-vietnam-protest/#.XiA0c1MzbkI

NPIA. (2010). *Safe and confident neighbourhoods strategy: Next steps in neighbourhood policing.* London: Home Office.

PA Consulting Group. (2001). *Diary of a police officer.* Police research series, paper, pp. 184–196 of 242. Lone-actor terrorism, terrorism and conflict, UK Counter-terrorism, Domestic Security, Terrorism.

Quinton, P., & Morris, J. (2008). *Neighbourhood policing: The impact of piloting and early national implementation.* London: Home Office.

Robinson, A. (2006). *Police community support officers: A literature and policy.* Hallam Centre for Community Justice.

Sindall, K., & Sturgis, P. (2013). Austerity policing: Is visibility more important than absolute numbers in determining public confidence in the police? *European Journal of Criminology, 10*, 2.

Singer, L. (2004). *Reassurance policing: An evaluation of the local management of policing.*

Skogan, W. G., & Hartnett, S. M. (1997a). *Community policing, Chicago Style.* Oxford: Oxford University Press.

Skogan, W., & Hartnett, S. (1997b). *Community policing, Chicago Style.* Oxford: Oxford University Press.

Skogan, W., & Steiner, L. (2004). Community policing in Chicago, Year Ten. In *An evaluation of Chicago's alternative policing strategy.* Chicago: CCPEC.

Smith, S., Le Grand, J., & Propper, C. (2008). *The economics of social problems.* Hampshire: Palgrave Macmillan.

Stevens, J. (2013). *Policing for a better Britain: Report of the Independent Police Commission.* London: Independent Police Commission.

Tilley, N. (2003). Community policing, problem-orientated policing and intelligence-led policing. In T. Newburn (Ed.), *Handbook of policing.* Cullompton: Willan Publishing.

Tuffin, R., Morris, J., & Poole, A. (2006). *An evaluation of the impact of the National Reassurance Policing Programme.* London: Home Office.

UK Government. (2015, March 1). Audit Commission closed in March 2015. Retrieved July 9, 2016, from Gov.uk: https://www.gov.uk/government/organisations/auditcommission

Waddington, P. A. J. (1999). Police (canteen) sub-culture. An appreciation. *The British Journal of Criminology, 39*(2), 287–309. https://doi.org/10.1093/bjc/39.2.287.

Wakefield, A. (2006). *The value of foot patrol: A review of research.* London: The Police Foundation.

Walton, R., & Falkner, S. (2020). *Policing a pandemic.* Policy exchange UK. https://policy-exchange.org.uk › uploads › Policing.

Weatheritt, M. (1983). Community policing: Does it work and how do we know? A review of research. In T. Bennett (Ed.), *The future of policing.* Cambridge: University of Cambridge Institute of Criminology.

Zhao, J., Lovrich, N. P., & Robinson, T. H. (2001). Community policing: Is it changing the basic functions of policing?: Findings from a longitudinal study of 200+ municipal police agencies. *Journal of Criminal Justice, 29*(5), 365–377.

Building Communities from the Inside Out

Nigel Lloyd

> The day after the riots (August 2011) something wonderful began to happen. Quiet, law-abiding citizens everywhere organised themselves through social networking into 'broom armies' and marched as one to reclaim their streets. They cleaned up burnt wrecks, scrubbed away tar in their rubber gloves and shovelled debris into black bags. Many helped weeping shopkeepers clean and restock their shops and donated all manner of items to those who had lost everything. The estimated 13,000 people who caused nearly half a billion pounds of damage to their communities were vastly outnumbered by thousands more who showed the great British backbone I have always said exists out there. And they did it freely and with a collective passion to do what was right, responding instinctively, not because anyone told them to. (Baroness Newlove. 'Building Safe, Active Communities' 2011 (see below))

N. Lloyd (✉)
Rabdan Academy, Al Bhustan, Abu Dhabi, United Arab Emirates
e-mail: mroycroft@ra.ac.ae

© The Author(s), under exclusive license to Springer Nature Switzerland AG 2021

M. Roycroft, L. Brine (eds.), *Modern Police Leadership*,
https://doi.org/10.1007/978-3-030-63930-3_31

Overview of Asset-Based Community Development

Asset-based community development (ABCD) is built upon three decades of community development research by Kretzmann and McKnight (Northwestern University, Chicago, USA) into what actually works in bringing communities together to make a difference to a range of quality of life issues.

It is an approach that sees community members as active agents for change rather than passive beneficiaries of service provision or clients. It uses the skills, passion and commitment of local people to achieve what most benefits their neighbourhood. It asserts that economic, social and safety revitalisation begins with what is already present and available within the neighbourhood and its communities. It supports the national neighbourhood policing model of addressing public priorities and partnership working, and reinforces the strength and traditions of the police service such as Peel's policing principle that the police are the public and the public are the police. Better community engagement will help build trust and confidence and improve the flow and quality of information whether that relates to crime, health or wellbeing. ABCD is a more citizen-focused and community-driven method that enables neighbourhoods to flourish, increasing a sense of belonging and improving community cohesion, social, health and economic potential whilst also increasing safety and reducing harm.

▶ Maidstone's Urban Blue Bus is staffed entirely by volunteers. It saves the NHS ten times its small annual running costs by reducing ambulance calls and A&E admissions. The bus travels around schools and other organisations teaching a range of subjects including alcohol awareness. At weekends, the bus is parked in the town centre helping to reduce pressure on ambulance and A&E services. It has an onboard medical area to treat minor injuries and is a valuable resource for people socialising in the town.

It is an approach that has been successfully employed in some of the most challenging environments in the world, such as Rwanda and Kenya, as well as Sweden, the Netherlands, Canada, Australia and the UK. Their success has reinforced the commitment that the best way to achieve social cohesion is to build more connected communities (Fig. 1).

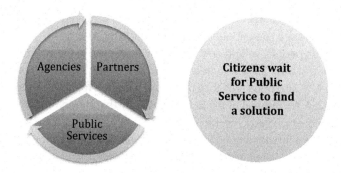

Fig. 1 Traditional services model

Fig. 2 ABCD approach

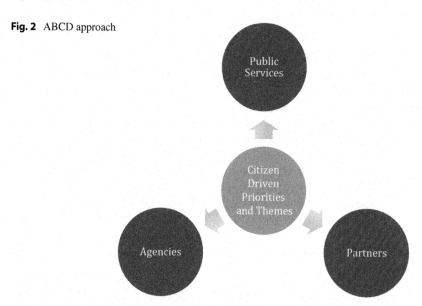

ABCD focuses on what communities can do that is relevant, empowering and cohesive. It is an inclusive community-driven process that engages and shares the local assets, skills, attributes and passions of the people, to achieve the change that makes the greatest impact on their quality of life. The local community is the primary building block for sustainable growth. For public services, it is about listening better to what people and communities think they can do themselves and what they think would be helpful support from the public services (Fig. 2).

▶ Levels of volunteering in the UK are higher compared to many of our European neighbours, **40%** of people living in England (over 17 million people) volunteered formally at least once in the last twelve months with **25%** volunteering formally at least once a month. There is also good evidence that more people would like to get involved. Almost half of the public (**49%**) say that they would like to be more involved in decisions affecting their local area, and another **15%** would, depending on the issue. (*2008/09 Citizenship Survey: Empowered Communities Topic Report*)

Key ABCD Roles

▶ **East Belfast Alternatives** Organisations knew the names of 36 young people allegedly responsible (for anti-social behavior). Tired of punitive action, East Belfast Alternatives (EBA) was asked to help develop a strategic community response instead. EBA, with community groups Walkway Community Centre and Crossroads, invited young people, their parents, local residents, community workers and some statutory agencies to a meeting to decide how to move forward, together. About 70 people came. That night young people committed to hand over weapons, remove graffiti, and stop the anti-social behaviour. Parents promised to keep a closer eye on their children and to be more active and positive in their parenting.

Leadership
The style and type of leadership, group or individual, for example, and how it is formalised is for the community to decide. The challenge is getting the right leadership approach that is inclusive and enabling, rather than becoming a 'gatekeeper' or overly bureaucratic and slowing progression.

Community Builder
A Community Builder is someone who is focused on engaging the skills, knowledge and talents of every community member, as well as the institutional, associational, physical, economic and cultural resources that are part of every community to a greater or lesser extent.

Table 1 Public services model versus ABCD model

Public services model	Community building (asset based) model
Focus on deficiencies	Focus on assets (capacities, skills, relationships and resources)
Problem response	Opportunity identification
Charity orientation	Investment orientation
Grants go to other agencies or are funded to action agency priorities	Match funds, micro-financing, investment for leverage and go-to-action community priorities. 'Sweet equity' seen as a match
More services	More citizen-led action
High emphasis on agencies	Emphasis on associations
Focus on individuals	Focus on communities/neighbourhoods
Focus on maintenance	Focus on development
Sees residents as clients/customers	Sees residents as citizens and co-producers of sustainable hospitable communities
Sees their role as fixing, saving, monitoring and managing people	See their role as coming alongside people to help them develop their potential and connections
Believes programmes are the answer to social and economic challenges	Believes that people are the answer to social and economic challenges and must be supported to identify local response in an inclusive way

Community Connector

Community Connectors are good networkers who are basically people specialists. As the name suggests, they are an essential part of joining and connecting communities, assets and people in general (Table 1).

The primary objective of ABCD is to achieve a stronger, safer and sustainable community-driven approach to addressing those issues that matter most to the local people, supported by public services, and this is achieved through a strategic as well as a local neighbourhood approach.

Baroness Newlove, the Victims' Commissioner for England and Wales, in *Our Vision for Safe and Active Communities* (2011) advocates that communities and individuals should be encouraged and rewarded in playing a more central role in addressing crime and anti-social behaviour. The report argued for change in the public mindset: rather than looking to other authorities to address the local criminal problems, they should do it themselves. This echoes the ABCD police model.

Charlene Ellis, 18, and Letisha Shakespeare, 17, were the innocent victims of a drive-by shooting in Aston, Birmingham, on 2 January 2003. Both were killed. With Charlene's mother, she launched a gun amnesty that produced nearly 44,000 firearms and more than one million rounds of ammunition. She has appeared before a Commons select committee and travelled to New York to discover how the city is tackling gun crime. She felt that the key to solving community problems comes from the community itself. She commented, 'The police can't do their job if they're faced with a brick wall.' The community came together to help stop the gun warfare in Birmingham. The community realised that change had to come from within its own community; therefore, educating the local community and reducing gang violence by mediation were the tools used to disrupt gang activity.

She has been sickened by local fear and apathy, distilled in the commonly expressed view that it is someone else's problem. In Birmingham, she helped to initiate a Safer Lives, Safer Communities campaign, encouraging individuals to challenge criminal behaviour. This has become the Charity Precious Lives concentrating on education in schools.

Strategic Leadership

Leadership, commitment and support are essential to the success of ABCD. There are various ways of doing this, but somebody needs to lead and demonstrate commitment so that the other public services, agencies and volunteer groups see the benefits of participating. Police and Crime Commissioners (PCCs) need to ensure the policing needs of their communities are met as effectively as possible, bringing communities closer to the police and building confidence in the system, while restoring trust is an obvious place to start. This was enhanced under the Police Reform and Social Responsibility Act 2011. PCCs are working with a broad range of organisations and local authorities in building productive partnerships.

Community Safety Partnerships is another key component with their responsibility for taking a strategic approach and their focus on community, increasing safety and reducing harm. The advantages of partnership working are well evidenced with more effective delivery of services whilst also achieving better value for money from existing resources.

The Way Forward

ABCD can be achieved through a range of options including the following:

Strategic Partnership Seminar

- Understand the principles and values of ABCD and the role of partner agencies, public services and volunteer groups.
- Develop a comprehensive strategy to deliver ABCD.
- Develop effective partnership support processes for community-led initiatives and themes.
- Develop effective community engagement strategies to understand public and neighbourhood priorities and maximise support activities.
- Support community led-projects.
- Provide a community of practice forum.

Community Forums

On a geographic basis, deliver training to community leaders, faith groups, key individuals, local practitioners, community networkers and neighbourhood police officers on the principles and values of ABCD including asset mapping, local priorities and themes, community connections and contact management, and collaborative problem solving.

Popular Community Themes that Come Out of the ABCD Process

▶ Participatory Budgeting in High Wycombe   Castlefield & Oakridge in High Wycombe was allocated funding of £55,000 for participatory budgeting. The local Residents Action Group (RAG) came up with a process for allocating money to priorities picked out by the community. The process was supported by the Participatory Budgeting Unit.

Our aims were to use information gathered from local community events to pin down the top issues and needs for the area, and to identify the service providers, groups and agencies who would be willing to undertake projects to meet these community needs. We wanted to allow the community to decide which projects they wanted to see undertaken in their community. And we wanted to help build community spirit – and hopefully encourage the local press to give the community some positive publicity.

1. Health and Wellbeing

Health and wellbeing but also social engagement and networking.

2. Safety and Security

An obvious focus on crime, anti-social behaviour and increasing safety but also understanding the impact of signal crime and control measures.

3. Building Communities

Connecting communities, engagement and contact management, and developing social networks.

4. The Environment

Creating a positive physical environment and increase ways to Reduce, Reuse and Recycle.

5. Nurturing the Local Economy

Encouraging 'Buy Local Produce', reuniting producers with consumers and encouraging small and medium enterprises.

6. Raising Powerfully Connected Children

Supporting development outside professional support, for example, hobbies, sport, education, and so on.

7. Aging Well

Supporting the ageing population and encouraging social engagement and networking.

8. Respond to Natural Disasters

Local knowledge and flexible response to critical situations such as flooding and heavy snow, for example. A business continuity approach to local disasters.

ABCD encourages positive relationships between communities and public services, agencies and volunteer groups; there is a focus on socio-economic wellbeing and community empowerment. It is about connecting communities and developing a sense of commonality around real-life issues supported by more effective and efficient public services.

The principles and values of ABCD support the Police and Crime Commissioner's Police and Crime Plan for West Mercia including the vision:

'A new community spirit with people working together to improve society and prevent crime and disorder in partnership.'

ABCD can enable and support the majority of the strategic aims including the following:

Objective 2: To provide an effective neighbourhood policing model, with a focus on areas of greatest need

Objective 8: To develop a strategy to empower local communities to actively engage in preventing crime and disorder and to provide a strong and powerful voice for the people and victims of crime

Objective 13: To develop and implement a public engagement strategy

ABCD offers that 'new community spirit' and a more inclusive community-focused approach for public sector organisations to engage with the community and support community-led initiatives that make the greatest impact on the quality of people's lives. It is about building stronger and safer communities that make the most effective and efficient use of the public services and leave a lasting legacy for sustainable development.

▶ Top Ten Tips for Community Activists **Think about developing community spirit (not necessarily fighting crime).** Focus on watching out for each other, rather than just watching out for criminals. Research shows that stronger communities where neighbours know and look out for each other have lower levels of crime.

Start with your street and neighbours.

Technology can help. Email, social networking sites, blogs and twitter can all help to create a sense of community and allow you to keep in touch despite your busy lives.

Have a clear purpose.

Try to get everyone involved. The wider the range of people you can get to work together the better.

Don't reinvent the wheel. Look at what local groups already exist and join them. Remember there's strength in numbers. Search for good practice on the internet. Learn from people who are already doing it or have done it and remember to share your successes with others.

Get your Neighbourhood Police and Council working with you. Go out to their meetings, but also get them along to yours, or agree to have joint meetings where everyone is present, including statutory and voluntary sector agencies as well as community representatives. Be clear about the problems in the area and work together on solving them. Hold each other to account if they (or you) fail to deliver. Get the agencies to support activists and to watch out for your safety.

Don't forget about local schools, charities and businesses. They might just be your greatest source of support and resources. Most banks and supermarkets for example will have locally focused volunteering and fundraising. Don't be shy to approach them with your ideas or to ask them for help.

Be imaginative when looking for funding. There is more around than you might imagine, local charities and trusts are a good source. Research online and consider teaming up with another group to apply.

Don't give up!

Changes won't happen overnight, but persevere. Get more and more people involved, including your councillors and your MP. Remember the bigger you are, the louder your voice will be. If no one is listening or helping, go higher and use the local media to highlight your issues.

Our Vision for Safe and Active Communities
Baroness Newlove

Strategic Partnership Seminar

- Understand the principles and values of ABCD and the role of partner agencies, public services and volunteer groups.
- Develop effective partnership support processes for community-led initiatives and themes.
- Develop effective community engagement strategies to understand public and neighbourhood priorities and maximise support activities.
- Support community-led projects.
- Provide a community of practice forum.

Exam Question

- Develop a comprehensive strategy to deliver ABCD.

Part X

Conclusion

Conclusion

Mark Roycroft

This book explores the concept of dispersed or distributed leadership and the operational and strategic policing skills needed for the twenty-first century. How police deal with "new" and "old" demands while engaging with the community and preserving human rights and answering to accountability bodies is a critical question. There is a move to develop the concept of leadership throughout police departments rather than tie it to rank. The need to develop the requisite skills for a particular police discipline cannot be solely dependent on rank; those with the ability and experience are to be encouraged and mentored. As policing becomes more specialized, and more skills and training are required, the days of the "omni-competent" leader are fast disappearing. We now have leaders leading at different levels of the organization. Eli Sopow discusses distributed leadership in his article on boundary shaped police leadership in the twenty-first century (2019).

Recent events, such as Covid-19, Black Lives Matter and the EncroChat crime, highlight the diverse demands on the modern police officer. The skill base and sources needed are far removed from what Sir Robert Peel could have imagined in 1829. Distinct and different policing demands illustrate how police forces must maintain and equip their staff to deal with modern demands. Covid-19 has presented modern policing with one of its more complex challenges since World War

M. Roycroft (✉)
Rabdan Academy, Al Bhustan, Abu Dhabi, United Arab Emirates
e-mail: mroycroft@ra.ac.ae

M. Roycroft, L. Brine (eds.), *Modern Police Leadership*,
https://doi.org/10.1007/978-3-030-63930-3_32

437

2. This has forced the police into maintaining public order, protecting vulnerable people and supporting other emergency services. Covid-19 has seen that the police have faced less acquisitive crime but more domestic violence reports. With more home working, there have been more cyberattacks on less well-protected domestic computers. The police have to adapt and maintain their core functions. The police will have to police in a multipolar world post-Covid-19.

This book clearly illustrates the good practice involved in various police duties including crisis management, public order, and diverse and complex investigations. The "pracademics" who contributed to this book, with their unique blend of operational experience and academic background, demonstrate how police officers need to equip themselves for the new generation of policing. Leadership, intelligence gathering skills and international cooperation are needed on unprecedented scales. There is a set of recurring themes across a panoply of police disciplines. The mere fact that the contributors to this book were able to comment on so many different areas of policing provides a unique insight. While police officers develop through experience and training, their technical skills and knowledge have to be employed in an ethical milieu. The book shows the range of skills and expertise needed for modern policing and how dispersed leadership within an integrated structure is fundamental to coping with this demand. The main themes that have been identified are as follows.

Some of the themes that have emerged (see Table 1) are decision-making skills, intelligence gathering, investigative skills, risk management and cross-cultural skills. Officers also have to have personal resilience, community awareness and technical skills in such areas as counter-terrorism, public order and firearms situations. The pracademics in each chapter looked at the skills needed at and the essential areas of knowledge required at each part of the police structure. This "dispersed" or "distributed" leadership reflects the strength of expertise with modern forces.

Managing Risk

Risk management is a critical component of policing. Table 1 shows the number of chapters where risk management was considered a key part of police officers skills. Chapter "Local Partnerships and International Agencies" on police leadership within high-risk environments shows that there is a requirement for leaders who possess the required tactical and technical knowledge, who have high standards, who can think outside the box and who have the ability to motivate and inspire others to achieve results. Managing risk is critical in many areas of policing, from

Table 1 Skills described in the chapters

Relevant skills	Relevant chapter
Risk management	"Use of Force/Public Order"Chapter 5 , "Armed Policing Chapter 6 ", "Management of Deadly Force Chapter 7", "The Grainger Firearms Case Study Chapter 8", "Investigation Chapter 12 ", "Cybercrime Chapter 11", "Sexual Assault in the UK and Canada Chapetr 15 ", "Investigative Interviewing Chapter 16 ", "Forensics the Golden Hour Chapter 18 (Rose)", "The Crime Scene Expert Chapter 19 " and "Forensic Intelligence Chapter 20 "
Personal resilience	"Personal Resilience in High-Risk Domains Chapter 27 " and "Mental Health Awareness for Police Officers Chapter 28 "
Decision-making	"Local Partnerships and International Agencies"Chapter 4 , "Use of Force/Public Order"Chapter 5 , "Armed Policing Chapter 6", "Management of Deadly Force Chapter 7 ", "Cybercrime Chapter 13 ", "Investigative Interviewing Chapter 16", "Police Practice in Dealing with Severe Addictions and/or Mental Illness: Treatment or Arrest?", "The Crime Scene Expert Chapter 19" and "Decision-Making Chapter 29 "
Cultural awareness/ community policing	"Community Policing Chapter 31 " and "Building Communities from the Inside Out"Neighbourhood Policing Chapter 30
Technical skills	"Local Partnerships and International Agencies Chapter 4 ", "Use of Force/Public Order", "Armed Policing", "Management of Deadly Force", "The Grainger Firearms Case Study", "Crisis and Disaster Management and Disaster Victim Identification (DVI) Chapter 10" and "Cybercrime Chapter 13(delete rest of title) in the Age of Digital Transformation, Rising Nationalism and the Demise of Global Governance"
Leadership skills	"Use of Force/Public Order", "Armed Policing Chapter 6", "Management of Deadly Force", "The Grainger Firearms Case Study", "UN Peacekeeping Operations Chapter 9", "Crisis and Disaster Management and Disaster Victim Identification (DVI) Chapter 10", "Investigation Chapter 12", "Child Protection Chapter 14", "The Crime Scene Expert"Chapter 19, "Counter-Terrorism Chapter 21", "Extraterritorial Investigations of Terrorist-Related Kidnappings"Chapter 24, and "Global Policing Leadership and Security Sector Reform Chapter 26 "
Investigative skills	"Investigation Chapter 12 ", "Cybercrime", "Child Protection", "Sexual Assault in the UK and Canada Chapter 15", "Investigative Interviewing", "Forensics the Golden Hour (Rose)", "The Crime Scene Expert Chapter 19 ", and "Forensic Intelligence Chapter 20"
Knowledge of subject matter	All chapters
Firearms command skills	"Management of Deadly Force Chapter 7 " and "The Grainger Firearms Case Study Chapter 8"
Public order management skills	"Use of Force/Public Order Chapter 5"

(continued)

Table 1 (continued)

Relevant skills	Relevant chapter
Knowledge of legal powers	All chapters
Intelligence gathering	"Homegrown and Lone-Actor Terrorism Chapter 22" and "The Nexus Between Terrorist Organizations and Organized Crime"Chapter 23
Cyber skills	"Cybercrime Chapter 13", "Child Protection Chapter 14 " and "Sexual Assault in the UK and Canada Chapter 15"
Partnership development	"Introduction" and "Accountability and Governance Chapter 3"

child protection to counter-terrorism and everything in between. The crisis management chapter states that "risk management is a process that assists with the identification and management of potential risks and liability that an organization may encounter. Risk identification and management are an essential part of dealing with crises and disasters." The case study on the police response to Hurricane Katrina in New Orleans illustrates this.

Globalization

- Impact of networks of information and communication has changed the environment of policing.
- The disorder impacts on a global stage instability.

Globalization has a continuing and significant influence on organized crime, primarily through the integration of markets. The police will have to police in a multipolar world post-Covid-19.

Developing the Policing Model

In the chapter on UN peacekeeping (Chapter 9), or in some cases peacemaking, Brine demonstrates that the UN mission in Haiti was partly there to assist the Haitian authorities in developing a "sustainable police service based on democratic norms, and sound principles of governance and the rule of law" and to provide the Haitian force with a more dynamic approach to operational support and mentoring. As an increasingly globalized world, nations with successful economies and sustainable democracy have an obligation to help and mentor fledging nations.

One of the main themes considered in the book was the management of risk in the police service. Table 1 shows the number of chapters where risk management was considered a key part of police officers skills. In Chapter 10"Crisis and Disaster Management and Disaster Victim Identification (DVI)" police leadership within high-risk environments requires leaders who possess the required tactical and technical knowledge. The introduction mentioned Principle 3 of the management of Risk from the UK College of Policing. Managing risk is an important issue in child protection issues, and these points are mentioned in Chapter "Child Protection".

The crisis management chapter (Chapter 10 "Crisis and Disaster Management and Disaster Victim Identification (DVI)") states that "risk management is a process that assists with the identification and management of potential risks and liability that an organization may encounter. Risk identification and management are highlighted, and a case study of Hurricane Katrina in New Orleans in 2005 illustrates the need for good communications and risk management.

Officers have to contend with globalization, and the impact of networks of information and communication has changed the environment of policing particularly on investigations. Similarly, social media has allowed disorder to impact on a global stage. Globalization will also have a significant influence on organized crime, primarily through the integration of markets.

Developing the Policing Model

The policing model used in Haiti by the UN (see Chapter "UN Peacekeeping Operations") stated that the UN mission was partly there to assist the Haitian authorities in developing a "sustainable police service based on democratic norms, and sound principles of governance and the rule of law" and to provide the Haitian force with a more dynamic approach to operational support and mentoring. The book has shown that modern policing encapsulates policing by consent models, crime control models and community-based models. These are not mutually exclusive but form part of the modern approach to policing. The UN mission described the wish of developing nations to harness these models to augment their institutions.

Investigative Skills

The skills required by all police officers in the twenty-first century are far removed from Peel's early "Bobbies" in 1829. The plethora of crimes and the means by which they are undertaken presents the modern officer with huge challenges.

Officers need to collect intelligence, interview and arrest and then prepare case files for the prosecuting agencies. Modern investigators face new demands and the check and balances in the modern era, that is, disclosure of evidence to the defence and tests of evidence (see Chapter "Investigation") are appropriate for a democratic society. So the traditional evidence-gathering process remains the same, but the police are faced with new crimes such as child sexual exploitation (CSE), human trafficking and cybercrime. These require new skills. The cybercrime chapter (Chapter "Cybercrime") looked at two types of cybercrime: cyber-dependant and cyber-enabled crime. While these are new crimes, the traditional investigative process still applies with officers collecting intelligence and evidence on the suspects albeit on a transnational scale. Chapter "Investigation" mentioned the seven major themes from 40 years of public inquires and reviews in the UK: these are as follows:

- The clarity and leadership needed among senior officers
- The skills of senior investigating officers required
- Systematic failures
- The phasing of enquires required
- The role of the major incident room(MIR)
- Information management
- Individual investigative strategy failures

These seven are often repeated in modern investigations, and Chapter "Child Protection" described the Poppi Worthington case in Cumbria and how it repeated earlier mistakes from the Victoria Climbie case and Baby P case. Child protection policies (Chapter "Child Protection") need cooperation between other agencies such as medical, teaching or residential care staff in terms of reporting suspicions or protecting children. Policy formulation in this area of police work is driven by (inter-alia) new legislation and research.

Cybercrime

Protrka (Chapter 13 "Cybercrime") discusses cyber-dependant crime and cyber-enabled crime. Cybercrime has now become the volume reported crime and means that a victim can be in one country and the suspect in another. The police need new skills to deal with this type of crime. Cyber criminals (NCSC 2017) may directly steal money or monetize their capabilities indirectly through intellectual property theft, through extortion (issuing ransom demands following denial of service or data theft) or through malware. As technologies advance, there are clearly new opportunities to be had via routes such as the Internet of Things (IoT), smart homes and autonomous vehicles. The police will have to keep abreast of these developments and work with private companies to ensure the safety and privacy of the general public. The investigation of cybercrime by nominated detectives will be vital in all future enquires. Data collection and data evidence are the most sensitive steps of computer forensic analysis (CFA). Poe, in Chapter "Cybercrime in the Age of Digital Transformation, Rising Nationalism and the Demise of Global Governance", states that the duality of benefit and "peril" of the digital transformation of society is best exemplified by the under-regulated rise of social media and the role it has played in spectacular crimes, most notably mass shootings in the USA (Charleston, El Paso and Pittsburgh) and New Zealand (Christchurch). Poe's chapter talks of the threat from state-sponsored cybercrime and the need for international cooperation that builds on Roycroft's chapter (Chapter "Local Partnerships and International Agencies") on partnership. Problems like cybercrime and terrorism cannot be solved by the police themselves and require remedies from both the private and public sectors. Bowling and Sheptycki (2012) talk of "glocal" policing where the local and global policing worlds converge.

Cultural Awareness

Child protection, counter-terrorism, peacekeeping, community policing, all require a heightened degree of cultural awareness. The societies we police comprised diverse religious, ethnic, economic and social stakeholders. The police must learn to identify with these different groups to understand their needs.

Intelligence Gathering

This book speaks of how the police gather intelligence and collect evidence. Increasingly, the modern officer must know how to gather intelligence, collect evidence, analyse evidence and then arrest or disrupt criminal activity. All this must be done with human rights at the forefront of the thought process. And, the police must be held accountable for their actions and decisions while ensuring that they are proportionate, necessary and ethical.

An increased use of technology, such as body-worn cameras, CCTV and drones, allows the police to gather information and turns it into actionable intelligence and evidence. Facial recognition technology can pick suspects out in a crowd and contributes to public safety. All of these new technologies come with privacy concerns, and the officer has to contend with preserving those rights and dealing with suspects and witnesses judiciously. The officer becomes an arbiter of how these seemingly conflicting themes can be reconciled.

Intelligence gathering has led to the clear conclusion that there is a nexus between organized crime and terrorist groups. This stretches police resources to the limit and requires a coordinated international and partnering response. There are many international and regional policing agencies that assist in this effort.

Chapter "Knowledge Management (KM Chapter 25) and Intelligence-Led Policing (ILP)" looked at the issue of intelligence gathering, and various chapters illustrated the need for intelligence collection and analysis. The five regimes of intelligence (Delpeuch, T & Ross J.E 2016) includes public order intelligence, criminal intelligence, public tranquillity, partnership intelligence and strategic intelligence.

There is a critical need for up to date and real time intelligence in virtually every area of policing. This enables the development of specific responses to individual problems" (2020 Pepper). Intelligence-driven crime reduction is a three-stage process, requiring that law enforcement:

1. interpret the criminal environment
2. influence decision-makers
3. decision-makers impact the criminal environment

We have looked on how the police gather intelligence and collect evidence. Increasingly, therefore, the modern officer requires the skill to analyse and filter the intelligence gathered and then arrest or disrupt activity (see Chapter "Knowledge Management (KM) and Intelligence-Led Policing (ILP)"). The goal is to protect the public from dangerous people. The police must do this while balancing human rights (as seen in Chapter "Human Rights"). It is only right that the police are held accountable for their actions. The concepts of proportionality and necessity are essential for ethical decision-making.

Intelligence gathering has led to the clear conclusion that there is a nexus between organized crime and terrorist groups. This stretches police resources to the limit and requires a coordinated international and partnering response. There are many international and regional policing agencies that assist in this effort.

Chapter "The Nexus Between Terrorist Organizations and Organized Crime" brought home the nexus between organized crime group (OCGs) and terrorist groups. These "poly crime" groups (Europol) stretch police resources across the globe and mean that partnership working is just not carried out at a local level but on an international basis. Poe and Roycroft (Chapters "Cybercrime in the Age of Digital Transformation, Rising Nationalism and the Demise of Global Governance" and "Local Partnerships and International Agencies") describe some of the international agencies and bodies involved. The modern officer therefore needs a combination of good decision-making qualities, intelligence gathering and leadership sometimes on a transnational basis to advance the international response to crimes such as human trafficking and the exploitation of vulnerable people whether through sexual abuse or the trafficking of human beings.

Public Order

Officers still face public protest albeit it is harder to predict due to social media and the mobility it gives protestors. "Sousveillance" means that the police are under constant scrutiny, and their own body-worn cameras provide not only a check of their work but also fresh evidence-gathering opportunities. Public protest is still prevalent, albeit much harder to predict and control. Social media and increased mobility make it difficult for the police to keep ahead of revolving or rotating protestors. In addition, the police are under increased scrutiny by virtue of their own body-worn cameras.

Personal decision-making mentioned in Chapter 29 discusses "Decision--Making in Law Enforcement" The "Yellow Vest" protests began in France in December 2018. The unrest began in response to rising gas taxes, but with little organization and relying mostly on social media, the protests moved spontaneously from France's rural regions to Paris. This emphasizes the globalization of policing disorder. The impact of networks of information and communication has changed the environment of policing, the disorder impacts on a global stage.

The reasons for the Summer Riots in the UK in Summer of 2011 were researched by the Rowntree Foundation and the *Guardian* newspaper (2012). The riots were a watershed in the way police in the UK responded to mass evidence gathering via smartphone cameras and how they coordinated their response to people using social media to organize and carry out the riot.

Firearms Policing

Firearms, regardless of whether the police officer is armed and on the front line (e.g. Australia, Canada, Northern Ireland, USA, etc.) or from a specialist firearms unit (e.g. England, New Zealand, Scotland, Wales, etc.), involves a thorough risk assessment coupled with a good communication strategy. Judgement decisions are made on an "awareness" of a situation, and awareness is a combination of "prior knowledge" and a "perception of the reality." Prior knowledge is to do with training and experience, and perceptions of reality are firmly grounded in the information you know about a particular event. It may take a long time to assemble all the information one needs to make an informed decision. This often means that decisions are either (a) taken too early or (b) too late, which means one runs the risk of making the decision too late (Bell RUSI 2007). Police officers in countries where all police are armed are generally quite adept at determining when lethal force can be justified.

Protecting the Vulnerable

The police role is about protecting the vulnerable including children and the disadvantaged. Modern crimes include the trafficking of children and young women while child protection was dealt with in Chapter "Child Protection" and the expertise and skills needed were discussed. Similarly, mental health was raised in chapter. The interviewees in "Police Chiefs in the UK" (2016) advocated that there was a greater need for integration and cross-agency working to protect the vulnerable in society. One example is the Cardiff Model (www.cdc.gov), which allows for deeper integration with children's services, mental health professionals and the National Health Service (NHS). Dr Shephard who formed the unit in 1997 felt that this was essential to deal with the threat, harm and risk.

Chapter "Sexual Assault in the UK and Canada" looked at the development of policies on rape and sexual assault. In the UK, the police have come a long way from the Roger Graef documentary of 1982 that led to changes in sexual assault investigation. However, the "attrition" rate of cases that proceed to court remains high. The law has changed both in Canada and in the UK, but many court trials hinge on "consent" between the parties. Social changes and the rise of technology have seen a "tsunami" of social media messages in such cases. The diversity of investigations and the skills required both technically and emotionally are shown in this chapter about sexual assault cases.

Detectives and police officers regularly interview suspects and witnesses of crimes. This is another "skill" with officers trained and developed by the police force. Bailey here talks of the PEACE model and ABE or achieving best evidence interview. A confession or first-hand account of an incident is still crucial to an investigation and can corroborate or disprove the version given by the suspect. The management of witnesses was one of the key solving factors in Roycroft's research (2019) of murder cases in London. The interviewing and management of witnesses is crucial to the successful conclusion of cases, and the interviews can provide crucial evidence to the Major Incident Room.

Forensic

The chapters by Fairgreave, Williamson and Rose highlight the importance of forensic investigation and expertise in all levels of police investigations. Roycroft in his research on 166 murder cases (2019) found that forensic material was still the highest solving factor in murder cases. Digital investigations involving smartphones and computers have made this even more critical for the modern police officer. Many forces struggle to cope with the level of material to be examined, and in the UK, disclosure of that material to the defence has exacerbated the issue. The rape trail of Liam Allen in 2018 in the UK revealed that over 50,000 social media messages had not been fully investigated by the police. The modern police officer has to oversee and deal with all these issues. The importance of forensic investigation and expertise cannot be understated. Accountability, the needs of the victim and the behaviour of the suspect can make this even more difficult. Trace evidence at a crime scene remains a significant part of any investigation and the "Golden Hour" must be considered in every investigation. Equally important is the role of non-police forensic experts such as anthropologists who discover, document, recover and analyse human remains that have undergone significant decomposition. He further describes how the police use "experts" or expert witnesses to assist an investigation. The victim's needs, accountability and the suspect's behaviour in such cases can make these complex cases even more difficult. Chapter "The Crime Scene Expert" describes how the police use "experts" or expert witnesses to assist an investigation. Kind (1987) described the role of expert witnesses and that the senior investigating officer (SIO) must keep in mind the "conditions which are associated with his use of specialists; these include the following:

- formulating the problem as clearly as possible
- listening attentively and patiently to any reply
- accepting that the answer may not be the one the SIO wants or expects

Professor Fairgreave describes the established process for having a non-police expert in a particular area of forensic science. The key aspect of this process is to have a system in place to evaluate the credentials of forensic experts prior needing them to respond to an incident.

One of the central themes of the book is the growth of technology, and this applies to trace evidence at crime scenes. As DNA advances, it is more important that all initial evidence is gathered in the Golden Hour period. Williamson's chapter dealt with two main themes of the book: forensics and intelligence gathering under the guise of forensic intelligence or FORINT. He states that "FORINT has been used with some success in both a national and international context to supplement criminal intelligence, though it has still to be valued and absorbed entirely into ILP as a proactive product in the UK."

Requirements for Different Types of Leadership at Different Levels

To help develop a new type of resilient and adaptable global policing leader, it is necessary to better understand the traits expected of such a person today: someone driven by the core values of engagement, open to challenge, flexible, emotionally intelligent and with the ability to understand and exploit the benefits of partnership, technology and good business practices. This leader must be open to a "whole of government approach" and local, regional and international partnerships. This is especially important in a globalized world with threats such as terrorism—regardless of what the motivator of terrorism is. This can include lone-actor (wolf) terrorism which is difficult to detect. Deradicalization is key to this challenge.

Policing and Leadership Skills Required for the Twenty-First Century

Leadership skills needed to perform modern policing duties include four pillars of capability: professional development, support, partnership development and e-learning. This assists capacity building and tackling issues such as public order, terrorism investigation, intelligence and transnational threats. Crisis management also requires the basic values of honesty, integrity, professionalism, compassion, accountability and respect. In addition, the competencies of thinking skills and people skills are critical. Thinking skills incorporate planning and organizing, problem solving, strategic thinking and decisiveness. Eyre and Kubicek gave details of the skills needed to perform modern policing duties. To help develop a new type of resilient and adaptable global policing, certain traits are expected of such a person today: someone driven by the core values of international engagement, open to challenge, flexible, emotionally intelligent and with the ability to understand and exploit the benefits of partnership, technology and good business practices

Brine talks of the Canadian "whole of government approach" to combating terrorism, while Poe mentions the usefulness of international cooperation from treaties such as the Five Eyes intelligence sharing community and international bodies such as the UN. Poe talks of regional responses in law enforcements such as Europol, ASEAN and Gulf Cooperation Council (GCC). These bodies all perform specific functions in certain geographical areas with "reach" into other parts of the globe. As Bowling et al. state, a global police force is a chimera, but global policing is a reality; they further talk of "Glocal" policing and the global policing architecture.

Naturalistic decision-making and how police officers make decisions in real-life situations are part of Chapter "Decision-Making in Law Enforcement". Sound decision-thinking practices lead to what must, in turn, be followed by an effective implementation of choices. The 166 murder cases looked at in this research showed that there were potentially 41 individual solving factors and the senior detective has to prioritize these factors.

Resilience and Operational Stress Injuries

While the narrative of resilience may be simplified, confusion may rest with an outward persona of having everything under control; however, the inner self is in total chaos. This may be exemplified by poor decision-making, non-filtering of conflicting tasks, ambiguity of the tasks and being overloaded by tasks to the point of despondency. Such experiences may be felt on the first day of candidacy at the police academy or at executive decision-making level within the police organization. Police officers are exposed to a significant amount of trauma and death. Regardless of the experience, ensuring a conscious effort to effectively manage those role stressors and harness an inner strength in a cross-cultural environment will help you rebound and reset your mental state. It is critical that police, at all levels, recognize that this is a legitimate hazard of the job and offer assistance to those who may be impacted by it.

The main skills described in relation to police chiefs (Roycroft, 2019) are the following:

- Intelligence, intellectual agility and intellectual firepower (95%)
- Resilience (95%)
- Having a sense of humour (94%)
- Political acumen (90%)

- Financial skills (87.5%)
- Humility (67.5%)
- Values and integrity (92.5%)
- Sharing Glory with the team (65%)
- Dealing with the expectations of your staff (70%)
- Intelligence/intellectual horsepower (85%)

Sergeants

The first-line supervisor leadership role is critical for the stability and future of any police service. It is crucial that sergeants realize that they are a critical part of the management team and, as such, are responsible for maintaining policy and procedure compliance, instilling core values and "selling" middle and upper management operational and strategic goals and objectives (Waters, 2004). Sergeants must also realize that their direct contact with police officers transcends into a great amount of influence, and according to Tully (1998), every comment, gesture or non-verbal communication is interpreted by their subordinates as either support for or rejection of a management position.

Part of the role of a first-line supervisor is to be fair and impartial in handling all issues related to job performance of their subordinates. They must treat each incident and proposed resolution without bias or preference and concentrate strictly on the circumstances of the issue. First-line supervisors who take a fair and impartial stance with their subordinates will inevitably encounter fewer issues and be able to promote a sense of equality among their subordinates. However, sergeants who fail to abide by fair and impartial standards could be seen as promoting the negative aspects of police culture or the "old boys club," which tends to devalue the professionalism of an organization (Waters, 2004).

The Future

Policing in the future must bridge the gap between domestic policing and international policing. We must learn from each other about how to use most advanced equipment and training and legal standards to fight all forms of international crime and corruption. Policing Scotland 2026 predicts that in 2026 in the UK, living alone will be more common, and the transport sector will become semi-autonomous, 140 plus languages will be spoken in homes, and there will be 30% more people over 75%. These will consume more police resources.

The dynamics of policing do not change, but it is set against increasing demand for policing services. We must develop a global consensus to deal with global crime: 80% of IT is in private hands. Globally, we need to look at all aspects of international law and allow for seizure of criminal assets to disrupt and deter criminals. Modern policing includes mentoring and fostering other nations in capacity development.

Community policing or neighbourhood policing teams are discussed in Chapter "Community Policing", and the author Oosthuizen talks of the fusion of social policing and legal policing; the combined model has a better chance of success than either would enjoy separately. The key elements of successful community policing are illustrated, and these align with the intelligence gathering needed.

The United Nations conducts targeted firearms trafficking hotspots and have unravelled the link between organized crime and terrorism. There have been numerous versions of Operation Trigger, and Trigger V (September 2019) took place across eight countries in Latin America—Belize, Colombia, Costa Rica, El Salvador, Guatemala, Honduras, Mexico and Panama. About 42,000 checks were carried out at known trafficking hotspots including land, air and sea border points. Some 850 firearms were recovered and 560 individuals were arrested.

Case Study Operation Trigger IV—MENA

18–26 September 2018

This took place across four countries in the Middle East and North African region—Iraq, Jordan, Lebanon and Morocco. Checks were carried out at known trafficking hotspots including land, air and sea border points. Some 57 firearms were recovered and 17 individuals arrested for firearms offences. Operation Trigger IV took place across Iraq, Jordan, Lebanon and Morocco.

Summary

Policing in the future must bridge the gap between domestic policing and international policing. The police need new skills for the twenty-first century, including cyber detectives. Some argue that we need fourth-generation undercover officers online to cope with CSE, fraud online and identity theft. Future police officers must display personal resilience and cultural awareness; the panoply of skills needed by individual police officers to police the twenty-first century has been well highlighted here. Summary of this book, written by "pracademics," demonstrates the operational and strategic complexity of policing in the twenty-first century.

Seminar Questions

- What skills are needed for policing in the twenty-first century? Why police leadership is so important?
- What is good police leadership?
- Which are the most important competencies of police leader?
- Why police leader's personal well-being is so important?
- What do we mean by dispersed or distributed leadership within the police force?

Exam Question

- Definition of police leadership

References

Bowling, B., & Sheptycki, J. (2012). *Global policing*. SAGE Publications Ltd, https://doi.org/10.4135/9781446251775

Bratton, J., & Gold, J. (2017). *Human resource management. Theory and practice*. Palgrave.

Centres: Leading for Those We Serve. The police leadership qualities framework.

Kind, S., (1987). The Scientific Investigation of Crime John Sherrat and Son Manchester

Koivuniemi, T. (2018). Management and leadership training in police organization: The EMBA in policing

Melo, R. C., Silva, M. J., & Parreira, P. (2014). Effective leadership: Competing values framework. *Procedia Technology, 16*, 921–928.

Morais, L. F., & Graça, L. M. (2013). A glance at the competing values framework of Quinn and the Miles & Snow strategic models: Case studies in health organizations. *Revista Portuguesa de Saúde Pública, 31*(2), 129–144.

Quinn, R. E., Faerman, S. R., Thompson, M. P., & McGrath, M. R. (2003). *Becoming a master manager: A competency approach* (3rd ed.). Hoboken: Wiley.

Quinn, R. E., Faerman, S. R., Thompson, M. P., McGrath, M. R., & Clair, L. S. (2011). *Becoming a master manager: A competing values approach*. Hoboken: Wiley.

Roberts, K., Herrington, V., Jones, W., White, J., & Day, D. (2016). Police leadership in 2045: The value of education in developing leadership. *Policing: A Journal of Policy and Practice, 10*(1), 26–33.

Roycroft, M., & Roach, J. Ed. (2019). Decision making in Police Enquires and Critical Incidents: What really works. London: Palgrave

Tully B. Applied and Forensic Psychological Contributions to Policing and Expert Witness Work 1998: Collaboration and Conflict. *International Journal of Police Science & Management, 1*(2):192–200. https://doi.org/10.1177/146135579900100208

Glossary

ACC	Assistant Chief Constable
	Glossary Chapter 13 Cyber Crime
ACPO	Association of Chief Police Officers
ANPR	Automatic Number Plate recognition
ANACAPA	(intelligence principles and analytical techniques to enable critical thinking skills)
APCC	Association of Police and Crime Commissioners
ARV	Armed response vehicle
ASBO	Anti Social Behaviour Orders
AQ	Al Qaeda
AQIM	Al Qaeda in the Islamic Maghreb (Northwest Africa)
BAME	Black and Ethnic Minorities
BCU	Borough Command
BWC	Body Worn Cameras
CC	Chief Constable
CEOP	Child Exploitation and Online Protection agency
CEW	conducted energy weapon (also known as a TASER)
CHIS's	Covert Human Intelligence Sources
CIA	Central Intelligence Agency (USA)
CID	Criminal Investigation Department
CJ system	Criminal Justice system
CoPaCC	Comparing the office of Police and Crime Commissioners

M. Roycroft, L. Brine (eds.), *Modern Police Leadership*,
https://doi.org/10.1007/978-3-030-63930-3

CSE	Child Sexual Exploitation
CSP	Community Safety Partnership
CSR	Comprehensive Spending Review (CSR)
CVE	Countering Violent extremism
	Darknet Criminal web
DCC	Deputy Chief Constable
DEA	Drug Enforcement Agency
ECHR	European Charter of Human Rights
EBP	Evidence Based Policing
EOKA	Ethnikí Orgánosis Kipriakoú Agónos (Greek: National Organization of Cypriot Struggle
Europol	European Union's law enforcement agency. Headquartered in The Hague
FA	Forensic Anthropologist
FBI	Federal Bureau of Investigation
FEMA	Federal Emergency Management Agency USA
FININT	Financial Intelligence
FOI	Freedom of Information
FORINT	Forensic Intelligence
Four IR (4IR)	Fourt Industrial revolution
	Frontex European border and Coast Guard Agency
FLQ	The Front de la Liberation du Quebec (FLQ), or the Front for the Liberation of Quebec,
FVEY	Five Eyes Intelligence Community
GCC POL	Gulf Cooperation Council
	Golden Hour: Preserving the Crime Scene early in the investigation.
HASC	Home Affairs Select Committee
HMIC	Her Majesty's Inspectorate of Constabulary
HMICFRS	Her Majesty's Inspectorate of Constabulary and Fire and Rescue
HMICFRS	Post Her Majesty's Inspectorate of Constabulary and Fire Service
HUMINT	Human intelligence
IAG	Independent Advisory Group Interpol
ICAP	International Association of Chiefs of Police
IDVA	Independent Domestic Violence Advisor
IPCC	Independent Police Complaints Commission
IOPC	Independent Office of Police Conduct
ILP	Intelligence Led Policing
IRA	Irish Republican Party

IRTL	Independent Reviewer of Terrorist Legislation
ISIL	Islamic State of Iraq and the Levant
IPOC	Independent Office of Police Conduct
JSP	Joint Services Specialist Firearms Commander Programme (JSP) (JSSFCDP)
JTAC	Joint Terrorist Analysis Centre
MAPPA	Multi Agency Protection Panels
MARAC	Multi Agency Risk Assessment Conference
MASH	Multi Agency Safeguarding Hub
MASINT	Measures and signals intelligence
MASTS	Mobile Armed Surveillance Team
MIR	Major Incident Room
MIT	Major Incident Team
MINUSTAH	United Nations Stabilization Mission in Haiti
MOPAC	Mayors Office for Policing and Crime
NABIS	National Ballistics Intelligence Service
NCA	National Crime Agency
NIM	National Intelligence Model
NPCC	National Police Chiefs Council
NPoCC	National Police Coordination Centre
OCG	Organised Crime Group
OFC	Operational Firearms Commander
OSINT	Open source intelligence
OPC	Office of Professional Conduct
PACE	Police and Criminal Evidence Act
PCC	Police and Crime Commissioner
PCSO	Police Community Support Officer
PEEL	Police Effectiveness, Efficiency and Legitimacy HMIC programme
PTSD	Post Traumatic Stress Disorder
PCSO	Police Community Support Officer
PIRC	Police Investigations and Review Commissioner
PNAC	Police National Assessment Centre
PONI	The Policing Ombudsman Office of Northern Ireland
PSD	Professional Standards Department
PSU	Police Support Units
PSNI	Police Service of Northern Ireland

Ransomware	Ransomware is a type of malicious software (malware) designed to deny access to a computer
RCMP	Royal Canadian Mounted Police
RIPA	Regulation of Investigatory Powers Act
ROCU	Regional Organised Crime Units
SIGINT	Signals intelligence
SSR	Security Sector Reform
(SFO)	Specialist Firearms Operations
SIO	Senior Investigating Officer
SOCA	Serious and Organised Crime Unit
SOCTA	Serious and Organized Crime Threat Assessment report
SPR	Strategic Police Requirement (see Appendix 6)
TASER	Thomas Swift Electric Rifle (also known as a CEW)
TFC	Tactical Firearms Commander
TOC	Transnational organized Crime
TO	Terrorist Organisation
UNPOL	United Nations Police
WEF	World Economic Forum
WISCI	Witness interview strategies for critical incidents

Appendices

Appendix 1: Peelian Principles from Introduction Chapter

Policing by Consent: Home Office

These nine principles describe the 'policing by consent'; the Home Secretary was referring to a long standing philosophy of British policing, known as the Robert Peel's 9 Principles of Policing. However, there is no evidence of any link to Robert Peel and it was likely devised by the first Commissioners of Police of the Metropolis (Charles Rowan and Richard Mayne). The principles were set out in the 'General Instructions' that were issued to every new police officer from 1829 were: see Introduction and Appendix

1. To prevent crime and disorder, as an alternative to their repression by military force and severity of legal punishment.
2. To recognise always that the power of the police to fulfil their functions and duties is dependent on public approval of their existence, actions and behaviour and on their ability to secure and maintain public respect.
3. To recognise always that to secure and maintain the respect and approval of the public means also the securing of the willing co-operation of the public in the task of securing observance of laws.
4. To recognise always that the extent to which the co-operation of the public can be secured diminishes proportionately the necessity of the use of physical force and compulsion for achieving police objectives.

M. Roycroft, L. Brine (eds.), *Modern Police Leadership*,
https://doi.org/10.1007/978-3-030-63930-3

5. To seek and preserve public favour, not by pandering to public opinion; but by constantly demonstrating absolutely impartial service to law, in complete independence of policy, and without regard to the justice or injustice of the substance of individual laws, by ready offering of individual service and friendship to all members of the public without regard to their wealth or social standing, by ready exercise of courtesy and friendly good humour; and by ready offering of individual sacrifice in protecting and preserving life.

6. To use physical force only when the exercise of persuasion, advice and warning is found to be insufficient to obtain public co-operation to an extent necessary to secure observance of law or to restore order, and to use only the minimum degree of physical force which is necessary on any particular occasion for achieving a police objective.

7. To maintain at all times a relationship with the public that gives reality to the historic tradition that the police are the public and that the public are the police, the police being only members of the public who are paid to give full time attention to duties which are incumbent on every citizen in the interests of community welfare and existence.

8. To recognise always the need for strict adherence to police-executive functions, and to refrain from even seeming to usurp the powers of the judiciary of avenging individuals or the State, and of authoritatively judging guilt and punishing the guilty.

9. To recognise always that the test of police efficiency is the absence of crime and disorder, and not the visible evidence of police action in dealing with them.

(https://www.gov.uk/government/publications/policing-by-consent/definition-of-policing-by-consent)

Appendix 2: Code of Police Ethics UK

The UK police have a Code of Ethics based on the following policing principles (See Code of Ethics College of Policing app www.college.police.uk).
Accountability: You are answerable for your decisions, actions and omissions.
Fairness: You treat people fairly.
Honesty: You are truthful and trustworthy.
Integrity: You always do the right thing.
Leadership: You lead by good example.
Objectivity: You make choices on evidence and your best professional judgement.
Openness: You are open and transparent in your actions and decisions.
Respect: You treat everyone with respect.
Selflessness: You act in the public interest.

Appendix 3: The Royal Canadian Mounted Police Code of Conduct (See www.rcmp-grc.gc.ca)

The guiding principles of the RCMP are its core values: Honesty, Integrity, Professionalism, Compassion, Accountability and Respect (HIPCAR)

Honesty

Being truthful in character and behaviour.

Integrity

Acting consistently with our other core values upholding the ethical and social norms of the RCMP.

Professionalism

Having a conscientious awareness of our role, image, skills and knowledge in our commitment to quality client oriented service.

Compassion

Demonstrating care and sensitivity in word and action.

Accountability

There are two components of accountability. The first is the process of rendering an account to those from whom we derive our authority of what we did, why we did it, how we did it and what we are doing to improve performance or results. The second component is "answerability"—the obligation to provide information to others in our communities of interest with respect to our decisions, actions and results in light of clear, previously agreed upon understandings and expectations.

Respect

The objective, unbiased consideration and regard for the rights, values, beliefs and property of all people.

Within the Royal Canadian Mounted Police Act, police officers also have the following:

Responsibilities

It is the responsibility of every member

(a) to respect the rights of all persons;

(b) to maintain the integrity of the law, law enforcement and the administration of justice;

(c) to perform the member's duties promptly, impartially and diligently, in accordance with the law and without abusing the member's authority;

(d) to avoid any actual, apparent or potential conflict of interests;

(e) to ensure that any improper or unlawful conduct of any member is not concealed or permitted to continue;

(f) to be incorruptible, never accepting or seeking special privilege in the performance of the member's duties or otherwise placing the member under any
obligation that may prejudice the proper performance of the member's duties;

(g) to act at all times in a courteous, respectful and honourable manner; and

(h) to maintain the honour of the Force and its principles and purposes.

(https://laws-lois.justice.gc.ca/eng/acts/R-10/page-7.html#h-421417)
This is aimed as a guide to assist the ethical decision making of members.

Appendix 4: Legal Rights Embedded in the Canadian Charter of Rights and Freedoms (https://www.justice.gc.ca/eng/csj-sjc/rfc-dlc/ccrf-ccdl/rfcp-cdlp.html#s4)

Life, liberty and security of person

7. Everyone has the right to life, liberty and security of the person and the right not
to be deprived thereof except in accordance with the principles of fundamental
justice.

Marginal note: Search or seizure

8. Everyone has the right to be secure against unreasonable search or seizure.

Marginal note: Detention or imprisonment

9. Everyone has the right not to be arbitrarily detained or imprisoned.

Marginal note: Arrest or detention

10. Everyone has the right on arrest or detention

(a) to be informed promptly of the reasons therefor;

(b) to retain and instruct counsel without delay and to be informed of that
right; and

(c) to have the validity of the detention determined by way of habeas corpus
and to be released if the detention is not lawful.

Marginal note: Proceedings in criminal and penal matters

11. Any person charged with an offence has the right

(a) to be informed without unreasonable delay of the specific offence;

(b) to be tried within a reasonable time;

(c) not to be compelled to be a witness in proceedings against that person in respect of the offence;

(d) to be presumed innocent until proven guilty according to law in a fair and public hearing by an independent and impartial tribunal;

(e) not to be denied reasonable bail without just cause;

(f) except in the case of an offence under military law tried before a military tribunal, to the benefit of trial by jury where the maximum punishment for the offence is imprisonment for five years or a more severe punishment;

(g) not to be found guilty on account of any act or omission unless, at the time of the act or omission, it constituted an offence under Canadian or international law or was criminal according to the general principles of law recognized by the community of nations;

(h) if finally acquitted of the offence, not to be tried for it again and, if finally found guilty and punished for the offence, not to be tried or punished for it again; and

(i) if found guilty of the offence and if the punishment for the offence has been varied between the time of commission and the time of sentencing, to the benefit of the lesser punishment.

Marginal note: Treatment or punishment

12. Everyone has the right not to be subjected to any cruel and unusual treatment or punishment.

Marginal note: Self-crimination

13. A witness who testifies in any proceedings has the right not to have any incriminating evidence so given used to incriminate that witness in any other proceedings, except in a prosecution for perjury or for the giving of contradictory evidence.

Marginal note: Interpreter

14. A party or witness in any proceedings who does not understand or speak the language in which the proceedings are conducted or who is deaf has the right to the assistance of an interpreter.

(https://laws.justice.gc.ca/eng/regulations/SOR-2014-281/page-6.html)

Appendix 5: Royal Canadian Mounted Police Regulations, 2014

Schedule (Section 18 and Subsection 23(1)) Code of Conduct of the Royal Canadian Mounted Police

Statement of Objectives

Maintaining the confidence of Canadians in the Royal Canadian Mounted Police is essential.

Members of the Royal Canadian Mounted Police are responsible for the promotion and maintenance of good conduct in the Force.

This Code of Conduct sets out responsibilities, consistent with section 37 of the *Royal Canadian Mounted Police Act*, that reinforce the high standard of conduct expected of members of the Force.

1. APPLICATION This Code applies to every member of the Force and establishes responsibilities and the standard of conduct for members, on and off duty, in and outside Canada.
2. RESPECT AND COURTESY Members treat every person with respect and courtesy and do not engage in discrimination or harassment.
3. RESPECT FOR THE LAW AND THE ADMINISTRATION OF JUSTICE Members respect the law and the rights of all individuals. Members act with integrity, fairness and impartiality, and do not compromise or abuse their authority, power or position.
4. DUTIES AND RESPONSIBILITIES Members are diligent in the performance of their duties and the carrying out of their responsibilities, including taking appropriate action to aid any person who is exposed to potential, imminent or actual danger.
5. USE OF FORCE Members use only as much force as is reasonably necessary in the circumstances.
6. CONFLICT OF INTEREST Members avoid actual, apparent or potential conflicts between their professional responsibilities and private interests.
7. DISCREDITABLE CONDUCT Members behave in a manner that is not likely to discredit the Force.

Appendix 6: The UK Strategic Police Requirements

The 5 Cs Capacity and contribution, Capability, Consistency, Connectivity.

The particular threats specified in Part A of the SPR, and referred to as the national threats in this report, are: • terrorism; • civil emergencies; • organised crime; • public order threats; and • large-scale cyber incidents. Part B specifies the policing response that is required nationally, in conjunction with other national agencies, to counter these threats.

Appendix 7: ECHR Articles 1–11 www.echr.coe.int

Article 2 | Right to life Article 2(1) European Convention of Human Rights states:

> *Everyone's right to life shall be protected by law. No one shall be deprived of his life intentionally save in the execution of a sentence of a court following his conviction of a crime for which this penalty is provided by law.*

Article 3 | Anti-torture and inhumane treatment: No one shall be subjected to torture or to inhuman or degrading treatment or punishment

Article 4 | Anti-slavery

Article 5 | Right to liberty and security of the person Everyone has the right to liberty and security of person. No one shall be deprived of his liberty save in the following cases and in accordance with a procedure prescribed by law:

Article 6 | Right to a fair trial Everyone charged with a criminal offence shall be presumed innocent until proven guilty according to law.

Article 7 | Anti-retrospective conviction

Article 8 | Right to private and family life i.e. "everyone has the right to respect for his private and family life, his home and his correspondence

Article 9 | Right to freedom of thought, conscience and religion

Article 10 | Right to freedom of expression

Article 11 | Right to freedom of assembly and association

Appendix 8: United Nations Basic Principles on the Use of Force and Firearms by Law Enforcement Officials

4.1 **Police officers, in carrying out their duties, shall as far as possible apply non-violent methods before resorting to any use of force. Any use of force shall be the minimum appropriate in the circumstances and shall reflect a graduated and flexible response to the threat. Police officers may use force only if other means remain ineffective or have no realistic chance of achieving the intended result.** *(Sourced from: Article 4 United Nations Basic Principles on the Use of Force and Firearms by Law Enforcement Officials.)*

4.2 Police officers responsible for the planning and control of operations where the use of force is a possibility shall so far as possible plan and control them to minimise recourse to the use of force, in particular, potentially lethal force. Consideration shall be given during the planning of an operation to the need for medical assistance to be available.

(Sourced from: European Court of Human Rights: McCann-v-UK (1995) 21 EHRR paragraph 194.)

4.3 Wherever it is necessary for police officers to resort to the lawful use of force or firearms, they shall:
   (a) exercise restraint in such use and act in proportion to the seriousness of the offence and the legitimate object to be achieved;
   (b) minimise damage and injury, and respect and preserve human life;
   (c) ensure that assistance and medical aid are secured to any injured person at the earliest possible opportunity;
   (d) ensure that relatives or close friends of the injured or affected person are notified at the earliest possible opportunity;
   (e) report the incident promptly to their supervisors;
   (f) comply with Police Service policy, procedure and guidance.

(Sourced from: Article 5(A)-(C), Article 6 United Nations Basic Principles on the Use of Force and Firearms by Law Enforcement Officials.)

4.4 A police officer shall discharge a firearm only where the officer honestly believes it is absolutely necessary to do so in order to save life or prevent serious injury, unless the discharge is for training purposes or the destruction of animals

(Sourced from: European Court of Human Rights: Andronicou and Constantinou –v- Cyprus (1997) 25 EHRR; Article 9 United Nations Basic Principles on the Use of Force and Firearms by Law Enforcement Officials.)

4.5 Before police officers resort to the use of firearms, they shall identify themselves and give a clear warning of their intent to us firearms, with sufficient time for the warnings to be observed, unless to do so:

(a) would unduly place any person at a risk of death or serious injury; or
(b) would be clearly inappropriate or pointless in the circumstances of the incident.

(Sourced from: Article 10 United Nations Basic Principles on the Use of Force and Firearms by Law Enforcement Officials.)

4.6 Police supervisors shall ensure that stress counselling is offered to police officers who have been involved in violent situations or who have discharged a firearm.

(Sourced from: Article 21 United Nations Basic Principles on the Use of Force and Firearms by Law Enforcement Officials.)

Appendix 9: Ten Principles of Risk Management (College of Policing)

Principle 1
1. Uncertainty is an inherent feature of operational decision making
Operational incidents are by their nature dynamic. Making decisions in an operational context is a form of risk taking. Risk taking offers the possibility of harm but also the chance of success. As professional risk takers, members of the police service must be willing to take risks rather than avoid them.

Principle 2
Maintaining or achieving the safety, security and wellbeing of individuals and communities is a primary consideration in risk decision making. The police have a duty to confront risks and to make risk decisions on behalf of the communities they serve. The standard is based on reasonableness, which brings in consideration of the circumstances of the case, the ease or difficulty of taking precautions and the resources available.

Principle 3

Risk taking involves judgement and balance. Decision makers are required to consider the value and likelihood of the possible benefits of a particular decision against the seriousness and likelihood of the possible harms. Risk takers should consider and compare the value of the likely benefits and the possible harms of their proposed decision. Decision makers must be able to exercise sound judgement in coming to an appropriate decision. The rigour of operational decision making must be **proportionate** to the seriousness of the risks involved and be supported by appropriate, considered and robust systems.

Forces are responsible for ensuring officers and staff are able to apply a range of risk-related knowledge, skills and techniques when dealing with operational incidents. This includes:

- establishing partnerships between the police and others, e.g., multi-agency public protection arrangements (MAPPA) and multi-agency risk assessment conferences (MARAC)
- enabling senior officers—through training, assessment and monitoring—to provide effective leadership when commanding operational situations.

Principle 4

Harm can never be totally prevented. Risk decisions should, therefore, be judged by the quality of the decision making, not by the outcome. The fact that a good risk decision sometimes has a poor outcome does not mean the decision was wrong. Even when all the right and appropriate precautions have been taken, injuries and deaths may still occur. Good risk management should increase the likelihood of successful decisions but will not, in itself, guarantee that harm will not occur.

Good risk-making tools can help to ensure quality decision making

- Formal risk identification (RI), assessment (RA) and management (RM) processes and tools are a useful aid to decision making in relation to:
  - reducing the risk posed by serious offenders
  - increasing the protection available to vulnerable people
  - improving the identification and management of 'risky' locations.

Principle 5

Making risk decisions, and reviewing others' risk decision making, is difficult. This needs to take into account whether they involved dilemmas or emergencies, were part of a sequence of decisions or might appropriately be taken by other agencies. When a risk decision is being reviewed, the full conditions and influences existing at the time should be identified and examined to determine whether the action taken was reasonable in those circumstances.

Principle 6
The standard expected and required of members of the police service is that their risk decisions should be consistent with those a body of officers of similar rank, specialism or experience would have taken in the same circumstances. Total agreement between all members of the police service on the most appropriate solution in a risk situation is neither possible nor required. The standard of care is that which a **reasonable** police officer would take in the particular circumstances. Police officers and staff must make reasonable risk decisions.

Principle 7
Whether to record a decision is a risk decision in itself which should be left to professional judgement. The decision whether or not to make a record, and the extent of that record, should be made after considering the likelihood of harm occurring and its seriousness. **It is impossible to record all decisions.**

Principle 8
To reduce risk aversion and improve decision making, policing needs a culture that learns from successes as well as failures. Good risk taking should be identified, recognised and shared. More valuable lessons can be learned from examples of successful decisions rather than from the much rarer ones that lead to loss or harm.

- Most risk decisions have successful outcomes, and experience shows that people learn more useful lessons from what works than from what does not work.
- Rather than focus on poor decisions, therefore, (especially where harm has occurred) a risk management approach needs decision makers to have access to lessons learned and good practice.

Principle 9
Sharing information about individuals between public authorities is essential to keeping people safe. Good quality information exchange and shared risk assessment and risk management planning between government agencies, non-government organisations, community groups and service providers is essential to managing risk effectively. This requires relevant agencies to work collaboratively in relation to people who pose a risk of harm to others, or are deemed to be at risk of harm.

Principle 10
Members of the police service who make decisions consistent with these principles
should receive the encouragement, approval and support of their organisation.

Appendix 10

Ten Key Principles Governing the Use of Force by the Police Service

1. Police officers owe a general duty to protect persons and property, to preserve
   order, to prevent the commission of offences and, where an offence has been
   committed, to take measures to bring the offender to justice;
2. Police officers may, consistent with this duty, use force in the exercise of particular statutory powers, for the prevention of crime or in effecting a lawful
   arrest. They may also do so in self defence or the defence of others;
3. Police officers shall, as far as possible, apply non-violent methods before resorting to any use of force. They should use force only when other methods
   have proved ineffective;
4. When force is used it shall be exercised with restraint. It shall be the minimum
   honestly and reasonably judged to be necessary to attain the lawful objective;
5. Lethal or potentially lethal force should only be used when absolutely necessary in self- defence, or in the defence of others against the threat of death or
   serious injury;
6. Any decision relating to the use of force which may affect children, or other
   vulnerable persons, must take into account the implications of such status including, in particular, the potentially greater impact of force on them;
7. Police officers should plan and control operations to minimise, to the greatest
   extent possible, recourse to lethal force, and to provide for the adoption of a
   consistent approach to the use of force by all officers. Such planning and control will include the provision to officers of a sufficient range of non-lethal
   equipment and the availability of adequate medical expertise to respond to
   harm caused by the use of force;
8. Individual officers are accountable and responsible for any use of force, and
   must be able to justify their actions in law;
9. In order to promote accountability and best practice all decisions relating to
   the use of force, and all instances of the use of force, should be reported and
   recorded either contemporaneously, or as soon as reasonably practicable;
10. Any decision relating to the use of force by police officers must have regard to
    the duty of care owed by the relevant police service to each individual police

officer in the discharge of his duties. Deployment of police officers in a public order context where force may be used can carry grave risks to their own safety, and so must be the subject of rigorous control for that reason also.

(Source: HMIC (2011) The rules of engagement: A review of the August 2011 disorders, © Crown copyright.)

Appendix 11: Timeline of Significant Modern Terrorism Events Throughout the World

- 1858 First Fenian terrorist attack in London
- 7 April 1868—Thomas D'Arcy McGee is assassinated in Ottawa by an alleged Irish nationalist or Fenian rebel sympathizer named Patrick J. Whelan
- 1963–1970 FLQ Crisis—Canada. Separatists detonated over 900 bombs and committed two high profile kidnappings of 2 government members, one of whom was killed.
- 31 October 1971 Bomb explodes Post Office Tower, bomb left by IRA
- 19 September 1972: Black September post a bomb to the Israeli embassy in London
- 5 October 1974:Guildford Pub bombings by the IRA
- 21 November 1974: Birmingham Pub Bombings UK
- Introduction of the Prevention of Terrorism Act
- 30 March 1979 NI Secretary Airey Neave killed by bomb under his car in the House of Commons
- 27 August 1979 Warrenpoint massacre and Lord Mountbatten killed, 18 soldiers killed.
- June 1982 Abu Nidal kills the Israeli ambassador in London
- 23 August 23-Turkish military attaché to Canada assassinated by Armenian militants in Ottawa while sitting in his vehicle at a traffic light.
- 14 October 1982—The anarchist group Squamish Five bombs a factory in Toronto, Canada that is manufactures components of American cruise missiles.
- 30 November 1982 Animal Rights militia send a letter bomb to PM Margaret Thatcher
- 17 December 1983 Harrods bomb
- 12 October 1984 Brighton bomb at Tory Party conference
- 23 June 1985 Simultaneous bombing of two Air India flights originating in Canada.

- 21 December 1988 Lockerbie bomb in Pan Am flight 103 in London to the US from London
- 20 July 1990 Stock exchange bombed by IRA
- 7 February 1991 IRA mortar 10 Downing Street
- 10 April 1992 Baltic Exchange Bombing
- 3/12/92 IRA detonate bomb in Manchester
- 20 March 1995 Attack on **Tokyo** subway Terrorist group Aum Shinrikyo (Religion of Truth) released by Sarin gas on five trains on the Tokyo subway, attack focused on trains between Kasumigaseki and Ngatacho stations, home to the Japanese government
- 9 February 1996 Docklands bombings in London
- 11 September 2001 World Trade centre bombings New York, Pentagon Washington DC
- 29 March 2004 the arrest of the Digi bomber, Momin Khawaja in 2004 as a result of Operation Awaken
- 11 March 2004 Madrid Railway bombings in Spain
- 7 July 2005 London Bombings 7 July 2005: 7 July bombings: A series of four coordinated suicide attacks in central London in which three bombs exploded on Underground trains A double-decker bus at Tavistock Square was also destroyed. The bombs were detonated by four British Islamist suicide bombers. The explosions killed 52 people and resulted in over 700 injuries (see 2014 Stainforth p76 for full description of 7/7 bombings).
- 30 June 2007 Glasgow Airport attack carried out by Islamic extremist
- 22 May 2008 Exeter bombings by Islamist extremists
- 26 November 2008 to 29/11/08 **Mumbai** attacks India, Killed 175 people case Study Preventing Terrorism and Violent Extremism A Stainforth 2014
- 22 May 2013 Killing of Soldier Lee Rigby by Islamic extremists
- 13 November 2015 Paris attacks: A series of co-ordinated attacks began over about 35 minutes at six locations in central Paris. The first shooting attack occurred in a restaurant and a bar in the 10th arrondissement of Paris. There was shooting and a bomb detonated at Bataclan theatre in the 11th arrondissement during a rock concert. Approximately 100 hostages were then taken and overall 90 were killed there. Other bombings took place outside the Stade de France stadium in the suburb of Saint-Denis during a football match between France and Germany.
- 21 July 2005: 21 July attempted bombings: Four more bombings, unconnected with those on 7 July, were attempted on 21 July 2005 at Shepherd's Bush, Warren Street and Oval stations, as well as on a bus in Shoreditch. In these incidents, each bomb detonator fired, but did not ignite the main explosive charge.

- 2 June 2006 Attacks against targets in S Ontario, Canada led to the arrest of 18 people see *Domestic Extremism and the Case of the Toronto 18.*, Kowalski., Palgrave Macmillan 2016
- 20 October 2014, two Canadian Forces members killed in a ramming attack by a recent radicalized Muslim convert
- 22 March 2016, three coordinated suicide bombings occurred in Belgium: two at Brussels Airport in Zaventem, and one at Maalbeek metro in central Brussels. 32 civilians and 3 suspects killed, and more than 300 people were injured.
- 22 March 2017: Khalid Masood, drove a car into pedestrians on Westminster Bridge before crashing the car into the perimeter fence of the British Parliament in Westminster London. Masood then exited the vehicle and stabbed a police officer before being shot dead by police. About 40 people were injured and there were 6 deaths.
- 3 June 2017: a van with three attackers inside was driven into pedestrians on London Bridge After exiting the vehicle, the attackers stabbed people in pubs and restaurants in nearby Borough Market before being shot dead by police. Eleven people, including the three attackers, were killed and 48 people were injured.
- 19 June 2017: a van driven by Darren Osborne drove into people walking near Finsbury Park Mosque in London. There were eleven injuries and one person died.
- 14 August 2018, 2018 Westminster car attack: A Ford Fiesta swerved into pedestrians outside the palace of Westminster. The car then crossed over a traffic island before crashing into a security barrier.
- March 2019 Shooting by Brenton Tarrant in a mosques in Christchurch, New Zealand. 51 People killed.
- 2 February 2020, Streatham stabbing: Three people were stabbed before Police shot the suspect, Sudesh Amman.

Appendix 12: Counter Terrorism Organisations

The UK
SO15 (Specialist Operations 15) Counter-Terrorism Branch.

The Metropolitan Police combined a number of terrorist related functions after the 7 July 2005 terrorist suicide attack in London, England. This unit has a nationwide responsibility and primacy in respect of counter terrorism work and is headed by an Assistant Commissioner (the equivalent of a Chief Constable). There are eleven regional Counter Terrorism Units (CTUs) and Intelligence Units (CTIUs). These units mirror the regional structure of Internal Intelligence Service MI5.

Canada

The National Security Criminal Investigations program of the Royal Canadian Mounted Police is founded on its capacity and capability (see Kurt Chapter) to conduct criminal investigations into national security-related terrorist and criminal activity. (Why)The Royal Canadian Mounted Police and the Metropolitan police in the UK have become leaders in proactive disruption, international training, and complex investigations. The RCMP is involved in many that are extra-territorial. It is uniquely Canadian that the word 'terrorism' is not found in the title. This is a strategic approach that allows Canada to not raise alarms with the general public that there is a clear and present terrorist threat in Canada. National Security Criminal Investigations governs all terrorist related criminal investigations in Canada and abroad by providing oversight, guidance, and direction by utilizing a centralized control structure. Overall, the intent of the National Security policing program is "to reduce the threat of terrorist criminal activity in Canada and abroad by preventing, detecting, investigating, and gathering evidence to support the prosecution of those involved in national security-related criminal acts" (Royal Canadian Mounted Police, 2019). Like the United Kingdom model (Innes and Thiel, 2012), in the event of any terrorist investigation or attack, the Royal Canadian Mounted Police is legislated to take the primary criminal investigative lead both domestically and overseas. This often is demoralizing to the local police agency where the event is occurring

5 Eyes Intelligence Community

Australia, Canada, New Zealand, United Kingdom and the USA form the 5 Eyes Intelligence community. This arrangement facilitates information and intelligence sharing and collaboration between the five countries. This requires a response and input from local, national and regional levels, including both police organisations and intelligence services. The 5 Eyes is overseen by an Intelligence and Oversight Review Council. The 5 Eyes partnership exchanges views on subjects of mutual interest and concern and compares best practices in review and oversight methodology

France

There are two national police forces in France: the Gendarmerie Nationale (which is a branch of the French armed forces, and the Police Nationale (which is a civilian police force). There are two main units that deal with counter terrorism: GIGN (Groupe d'intervention de la Gendarmerie nationale) and RAID (National Police—Recherche, Assistance, Intervention, Dissuasion). The GIGN was formed in 1974 following the Palestinian militants' deadly attack against Israeli athletes at the 1972 Munich Olympics. It has been deployed abroad. RAID is an elite tactical unit and is limited to domestic crises.

Intelligence gathering for counterterrorism is the responsibility of the Central Directorate of Interior Intelligence (DCRI).

Germany

The Bundeskriminalamt (BKA—Federal Criminal Police Office) is mandated with counter-terrorism, international drug trafficking, combating organized crime and many other crimes. It also acts as the communications, information, and criminal intelligence service for the country. It provides support to police forces in Germany and, at times, will take over responsibility for major investigations. The BKA forms part of the "Joint Counter-Terrorism Centre" (GTAZ) in cooperation with other agencies.

Europol

In 2018, all thirteen fatalities from terrorism were the result of jihadist attacks. In addition, 46 people were injured. Europol's counter-terrorism efforts are coordinated by the European Counter Terrorism Centre (ECTC) which seeks to enhanced cross-border cooperation between relevant counter-terrorist authorities.

Interpol

INTERPOL's agreement with the United Nations' Counter-Terrorism Committee Executive Directorate (CTED) means the two bodies we can work closely together https://www.interpol.int/en/Crimes/Terrorism/Partnerships-against-terrorism

UN Office of Counter terrorism; www.un.org › counterterrorism.

Appendix 13: American Definition of Child Abuse

Federal legislation provides guidance to States by identifying a minimum set of acts or behaviors that define child abuse and neglect. The Federal Child Abuse Prevention and Treatment Act (CAPTA) (42 U.S.C.A. § 5106 g), as amended by the CAPTA Reauthorization Act of 2010, defines child abuse and neglect as, at minimum:

- "Any recent act or failure to act on the part of a parent or caretaker which results in death, serious physical or emotional harm, sexual abuse or exploitation"; or
- "An act or failure to act which presents an imminent risk of serious harm."

This definition of child abuse and neglect refers specifically to parents and other caregivers. A "child" under this definition generally means a person who is younger than age 18 or who is not an emancipated minor.

Appendix 14: A List of Child Abuse Enquires and the Relevant Websites

Cleveland Inquiry. https://www.ncbi.nlm.nih.gov/pmc/articles/PMC1834212/pdf/bmj00295-0046.pdf

Orkney. https://assets.publishing.service.gov.uk/government/uploads/system/uploads/attachment_data/file/235702/0195.pdf

North Wales. https://www.theguardian.com/society/2012/nov/06/wales-child-abuse-scandal-questions

Victoria Climbie—(Laming Report). Laming, W. H. (2003). *The Victoria Climbie inquiry: Report of an inquiry by Lord Laming* (Cm. 5730). London: The Stationery Office.

Bichard Inquiry/Soham Murders (2003), https://dera.ioe.ac.uk/6394/1/report.pdf

Historical Institutional Abuse Inquiry (2012) https://www.hiainquiry.org/background-legislation-protocols-procedures-and-rulings

Poppiy Worthington (2012)—Independent Police Complaints Commission Report into the case (2017) https://www.independent.co.uk/news/uk/crime/poppi-worthington-toddler-death-sex-abuse-allegations-ipcc-report-bungled-police-investigation-not-a7608486.html

Giving Victims a Voice NSPCC/MPS

HMIC's review into allegations and intelligence re J Saville 1964 to 2012 March 2013 www.hmic.gov.uk

Appendix 15: 7 Principles of Investigative Interviewing

Principle 1

The aim of investigative interviewing is to obtain accurate and reliable accounts from victims, witnesses or suspects about matters under police investigation. To be accurate, information should be as complete as possible without any omissions or distortion. To be reliable, the information must have been given truthfully and be able to withstand further scrutiny, e.g., in court.

Principle 2

Working with victims and witnesses

Investigators must act fairly when questioning victims, witnesses or suspects. They must ensure that they comply with all the provisions and duties under the Equality Act 2010 and the Human Rights Act 1998.

Principle 3

Investigative interviewing should be approached with an investigative mindset. Accounts obtained from the person who is being interviewed should always be tested against what the interviewer already knows or what can be reasonably established.

Principle 4

Investigators are free to ask a wide range of questions in an interview in order to obtain material which may assist an investigation and provide sufficient evidence or information.

In R v Fulling [1987] 2 ALLER 65, Lord Chief Justice Taylor stated that oppression is defined as: the exercise of authority or power in a burdensome, harsh, or wrongful manner, or unjust or cruel treatment of subjects or inferiors, or the imposition of unreasonable or unjust burdens in circumstances which would almost always entail some impropriety on the part of the [interviewer].

Principle 5

Investigators should recognise the positive impact of an early admission in the context of the criminal justice system.

Principle 6

Investigators are not bound to accept the first answer given. Questioning is not unfair merely because it is persistent. An investigating officer has the duty to obtain accurate and reliable information. A complete and reliable account from witnesses, victims and suspects may not always be easy to obtain. See PACE Code C paragraph 10.9 and paragraph 11.5 for clarification.

Principle 7

Even when a suspect exercises the right to silence, investigators have a responsibility to put questions to them. This principle extends the right of an investigator to put questions to those they believe can help them to establish the truth of a matter under investigation.

Appendix 16: Resilience from the Well Being Framework 2017

Resilience training is available to help all employees identify potential issues

1. The organisation actively promotes improving personal resilience and openly commits to workplace wellbeing programmes
2. The organisation actively seeks ways to reduce sleep deprivation, for example, overtime policies, turnaround times and working day limits
3. Any on-site catering facilities provide healthier options that are actively promoted
4. Rolling schedule of planned events to promote importance of healthy eating is in place
5. Internal or external support is on offer for those who wish to lose weight and commit to a healthier lifestyle
6. Information is made available on the benefits of physical activity and the organisation actively promotes physical activity
7. The importance of minimum legally required breaks taken by all staff is communicated at all levels and employees are encouraged to undertake physical activity if they are engaged in sedentary roles, for example, office-based
8. Staff are encouraged to take part in regular physical activity and opportunities to do so are actively promoted, for example, social, sports, leisure facilities
9. Physical activity in the workplace and in the local area is actively encouraged and supported by the physical environment
10. The organisation provides appropriate, acceptable and accessible information on healthy eating
11. The organisation offers tailored programmes to improve understanding and take-up of physical activity
12. The organisation promotes self-efficacy and encourages individuals to recognise their own limitations in the workplace
13. The organisation promotes alternative methods of travel

Glossary Chapter 13 Cyber Crime

API Application programming interface, a set of functions and procedures allowing the creation of applications that access the features or data of an operating system, application, or other service.—Automated Teller Machines.

Blockchain A system in which a record of transactions made in Bitcoin or another cryptocurrency are maintained across several computers that are linked in a peer-to-peer network. Essentially a distributed database. Information within a blockchain is publicly shared across all participating users or machines. The bitcoin blockchain is a public record of all bitcoin transactions, which helps to verify transactions and prevent double spending.

Cryptocurrencies A digital currency in which encryption techniques are used to regulate the generation of units of currency and verify the transfer of funds, operating independently of a central bank.

Darknet A computer network with restricted access that is used chiefly for illegal peer-to-peer file sharing.

DDoS Distributed Denial of Service, the intentional paralysing of a computer network by flooding it with data sent simultaneously from many individual computers.

Deep Web A part of the internet not accessible to conventional search engines; the only way to access the deep web is by conducting a search within a particular website. For example, government databases and libraries contain huge amounts of deep-web data.

DoS Denial of Service, an interruption in an authorized user's access to a computer network, typically one caused with malicious intent.

© The Author(s), under exclusive license to Springer Nature Switzerland AG 2021
M. Roycroft, L. Brine (eds.), *Modern Police Leadership*,
https://doi.org/10.1007/978-3-030-63930-3

GDPR   The General Data Protection Regulation 2016/679 is a regulation in EU law on data protection and privacy for all individual citizens of the European Union and the European Economic Area. It also addresses the transfer of personal data outside the EU and EEA areas.

Hacking   The gaining of unauthorized access to data in a system or computer.

HIPAA   Health Insurance Portability and Accountability Act of 1996 is United States legislation that provides data privacy and security provisions for safeguarding medical information.

ICT   Information and Communication Technology.

IoT   Internet of things.

IP   Internet Protocol. A digital media transport system that runs over standard IP networks.

ITAC   Canadain Integra\ted Assessment centre.

Malware   Malicious Software or software that is specifically designed to disrupt, damage, or gain unauthorized access to a computer system.

MD5   The MD5 hashing algorithm is a one-way cryptographic function that accepts a message of any length as input and returns as output a fixed-length digest value to be used for authenticating the original message.

Phishing   The fraudulent practice of sending emails purporting to be from reputable companies in order to induce individuals to reveal personal information, such as passwords and credit card numbers.

Ransomware   Type of malicious software designed to block access to a computer system until a sum of money is paid.

SHA1   Secure Hash Algorithm 1 is a cryptographic hash function which takes an input and produces a 160-bit (20-byte) hash value known as a message digest—typically rendered as a hexadecimal number, 40 digits long.

Spam   Irrelevant or unsolicited messages sent over the Internet, typically to a large number of users, for the purposes of advertising, phishing, spreading malware, etc.

Spyware   Software that enables a user to obtain covert information about another's computer activities by transmitting data covertly from their system.

TOR   The Onion Router (Tor) is an open-source software program that allows users to protect their privacy and security against a common form of Internet surveillance known as traffic analysis. Tor was originally developed for the U.S. Navy in an effort to protect government communications. The name of the software originated as an acronym for the The Onion Router, but Tor is now the official name of the program.

Trojan A type of malicious code or software that looks legitimate but can take control of your computer. A Trojan is designed to damage, disrupt, steal, or in general inflict some other harmful action on your data or network.

UID A unique identifier (UID) is a numeric or alphanumeric string that is associated with a single entity within a given system. UIDs make it possible to address that entity, so that it can be accessed and interacted with.

Virus Small software program that can spread from one computer system to another and cause interferences with computer operations.

Worms A computer worm is a type of malware that spreads copies of itself from computer to computer. A worm can replicate itself without any human interaction.

References

Adams, A., Thorp, G., & Heavens, S. (2014). *Rural 3 squad training days*. Winfrith.

Alba, Davey, et al. (2020 May 29). Twitter adds warnings to Trump and White House tweets, fueling tensions. *The New York Times*, www.nytimes.com/2020/05/29/technology/trump-twitter-minneapolis-george-floyd.html

Alhomoud, A., Awan, I., Disso, J. P., & Younas, M. (2013). Cyber security next generation toolkit against botnets. *Computer, 46*(4), 62–66. Available at: https://www.researchgate.net/publication/260584111_A_Next-Generation_Approach_t o_Combating_Botnets.

Al-Khafaji, K., Loy, J., & Kelly, A. M. (2014). Characteristics and outcome of patients brought to an emergency department by police under the provisions (section 10) of the mental health act in Victoria, Australia. *International Journal of Law and Psychiatry, 37*(4), 415–419.

Allen, J., & Wood, M. (2003). Crime in England & Wales: Quarterly update to June 2003. *Home Office. assets.publishing.service.gov.uk* › uploads › file

Almog, J. (2014). Forensics as a proactive science. *Science and Justice*, 325–326. Retrieved from https://doi.org/10.1016/j.scijus.2014.05.008

Almog, J., & Levinson, J. (2008). Forensic science and terrorism. *Journal of Applied Security Research, 3*, 25–35.

Alpert, G., et al. (1994). How reasonable is the reasonable man?: Police and excessive force. *The Journal of Criminal Law and Criminology*, 481–501.

Alpert, G., et al. (2004). *Understanding police use of force: Officers, suspects and reciprocity*. Cambridge: Cambridge University Press.

Aly, A., Macdonald, S., Lee, J., & Chen, T. M. (2017). Introduction to the special issue: Terrorist online propaganda and radicalization. *Studies in Conflict & Terrorism, 40*, 1–9.

Amankwaa, A. O., & McCartney, C. (2018, January). The UK national DNA database: Implementation of the protection of freedoms act 2012. *Forensic Science International, 284*, 117–128.

Anderson, G. (1996). *Fundamentals of educational research*. London: Falmer.

M. Roycroft, L. Brine (eds.), *Modern Police Leadership*,
https://doi.org/10.1007/978-3-030-63930-3

Ansoff, H. I. (1965). *Corporate strategy*. New York: McGraw Hill.

Application of the Multiactivity Model. *Applied Economics*, 351–362. Routledge.

Arnold, S., Clark, P., & Cooley, D. (2010). *Sharing common ground: Review of Yukon's police force: Executive summary*. Retrieved from the Yukon Government website: http://www.policereview2010.gov.yk.ca/

Asselin, M. E. (2003). *Insider research: Issues to consider when doing qualitative association of chief police officers of England, Wales and Northern Ireland*. National Library Medicine.

Aven, T. (2015). Implications of black swans to the foundations and practice of risk assessment and management. *Reliability Engineering and System Safety, 134*, 83–91.

Bahn, C. (1974). The reassurance factor in police patrol. *Criminology, 12*(5), 338–345.

Bailey, A. (2001). *Factors influencing police investigation of sexual crimes committed against people who have a learning disability and implications for public policy*. Ph.D. Thesis. Unpublished.

Bailey PhD ref Protocol on the Procedure in case of Abuse and Neglect of Children (Croatia). https://www.mup.hr/UserDocsImages/Savjeti/2015/PROTOCOL%20ON%20THE%20PROCEDURE%20IN%20CASE%20OF%20ABUSE%20AND%20NEGLECT%20OF%20CHILDREN%20(2).puff. Accessed Sept 2019.

Bailey, A., Barr, O., & Bunting, B. (2001). Police attitudes toward people who have intellectual disabilities an evaluation of awareness training – Intellectual disability. *Research, 45*, 1–7.

Ball, D. J., & Watt, J. (2013). Further thoughts on the utility of risk matrices. *Risk Analysis, 33*(11), 2068–2078.

Bao, C., et al. (2017). Comparison of different methods to design risk matrices from the perspective of applicability. *Information Technology and Quantitative Management (ITQM 2017), 122*, 455–462.

Baron, J. (2008). *Thinking and deciding* (4th ed.). New York: Cambridge University Press.

Barrett, D., Lines, R., Schleifer, R., Elliott, R., & Bewley-Taylor, D. (2008). *Recalibrating the regime: The need for a human rights-based approach to drug policy*. London: Beckley Foundation and International Harm Reduction Association.

Bates, R. A. (2012). Dancing with wolves: Today's lone wolf terrorists. *The Journal of Public and Professional Sociology, 4*(1), 1–15.

Bayley, D. (2006). *Changing of the guard: Developing democratic police abroad*. New York: Oxford University Press UK.

Bilton, M. (2003). *Wicked beyond belief: The hunt for the Yorkshire Ripper*. London: Harper Collins UK.

Bland, N. (1997). *Measuring public expectations of policing: An evaluation of gap*. National Library Medicine.

Blazevska Andonovska, V., & Glavinov, A. (2016). Connection between organized crime and terrorism as a new security threat. *Contemporary Macedonian Defence, 16*(30), 97–110.

Blunkett, D. (2001, September 11). *A speech by the home secretary to the police federation, policing for the 21st Century – UKPOL.CO.UK*. Home secretary: Speech to police superintendents' conference.

Bolan, K. (2017). Air India Flight 182 bombing. *Air India Flight 182 Bombing | The Canadian Encyclopedia*. Available at: https://thecanadianencyclopedia.ca/en/article/air-india-flight-182-bombing. Accessed 15 Sept 2019.

Borum, R. (2011). Radicalization into violent extremism: A review of social science theories. *Journal of Strategic Security, 4*(4), 7–36. http://scholarcommons.usf.edu/cgi/viewcontent.cgi?article.

Bradford, B. (2014). *Mounted police units in neighbourhoods 'boost public trust'*. University Oxford Press.

Bradley, K. (2009). *The Bradley report: Lord Bradley's review of people with mental health problems or learning disabilities in the criminal justice system.* Retrieved from https://webarchive.nationalarchives.gov.uk/20130105193845/http://www.dh.gov.uk/prod_consum_dh/groups/dh_digitalassets/documents/digitalasset/

Brink, J., Livingston, J., Desmarais, S., Greaves, C., Maxwell, V., Michalak, E., Parent, R., Verdun-Jones, S., & Weaver, C. (2011). *A study of how people with mental illness perceive and interact with the police.* Calgary: Mental Health Commission of Canada.

Brogden, M., & Nijhar, P. (2013). *Community policing: National and international models.* Routledge.

Brown, J. (Ed.). (2013). *The future of policing.* London: Routledge.

Bryant, R., Bryant, S., Graça, S., Lawton-Barrett, K., Gilbert, P., Hooper, G., Jones, N., Blackburn, B., McCormack, T., & Mitchell, S. (2017). Blackstone's Handbook for Policing Students 2018.

Bucke, T (2008: 142). *Dictionary of policing.* Willan Publishing: Cullompton

Buckley (2014). *Managing intelligence. A guide for law enforcement professionals.* CRC Press.

Bullock, K., & Leeney, D. Participation, 'responsivity' and accountability in neighbourhood policing. *Criminology and Criminal Justice, 13*(2), 199–214.

Burton, N. (2012, May 23). Our hierarchy of needs. *Psychology Today.* https://www.psychologytoday.com/us/blog/hide-and-seek/201205/our-hierarchy-needs. Accessed 2 June 2018.

Button, M. (2019). *Private policing* (2nd ed.). Oxford: Routledge.

Byard, Roger W., James, H., Berketa, J., & Heath, K. (2016, March). Locard's principle of exchange, dental examination and fragments of skin. *Journal of Forensic Sciences, 61* (2), 545–547.

Caless, B. (2015). *Leading policing in Europe an empirical study of strategic police management.* Policy Press.

Callimachi, R. (2014). Paying ransoms, Europe bankrolls Qaeda terror. *The New York Times.* Available at: https://www.nytimes.com/2014/07/30/world/africa/ransoming-citizens-europe-becomes-al-qaedas-patron.html. Accessed 16 Sept 2019.

Campbell, I., & Kodz, J. (2011). *What makes great police leadership? What research can tell us about the effectiveness of different leadership styles, competencies and behaviours: A rapid evidence review.* London: National Police Improvement Agency.

Carrabine, Cox et al. (2014: 208). *Criminology a sociological introduction.* London: Routledge.

Casey, L. (2008). *Engaging communities in fighting crime.* London: Cabinet Office.

Casey, L. (2016). Review into opportunity and integration, department for communities and local government, London. https://www.gov.uk/government/publications/the-casey-review-a

Charles, J. (2013a, October 15). *Armed bandits testing Haiti's understaffed police forces. Miami herald.* Retrieved from http://www.miamiherald.com/2013/10/15/3691691/armed-bandits-testing-haitis.html

Chernenko, Elena. *Increasing international cooperation in cybersecurity and adapting cyber norms 2018 CFR*. https://www.cfr.org/report/increasing-international-cooperation-cyber

Chikhi, L. (2010, February 22). Algeria says al Qaeda guards Sahara drug smugglers *Reuters*. Available at: https://www.reuters.com/article/us-security-qaeda-algeria/algeria-says-al-qaeda-guards-sahara-drug-smugglers-. Accessed 15 Nov 2019.

Chu, B. (2018, October 3). *Can Theresa May legitimately say that 'austerity' is over?* Citizenship and immigration Canada (2014), Canada's history. Retrieved from http://www.cic.gc.ca/english/resources/publications/discover/section-06.asp

Clapper, J. R. Senate Select Committee on Intelligence, Director of National Intelligence. (2013). *Worldwide threat assessment of the US intelligence community*. Retrieved from website: http://www.intelligence.senate.gov/130312/clapper.pdf

Clarke, C. P. (2018, July). *Investigating and prosecuting cases of the Nexus between organized crime and terrorism: Best practices and lessons learned for practitioners*. International Center for Counter-Terrorism – The Hague report. Available at: https://icct.nl/publication/investigating-and-prosecuting-cases-of-the-nexus-between-organised-crime-and-terrorism-best-practices-and-lessons-learned-for-practitioners/. Accessed 12 Dec 2019.

Coleman, T., & Cotton, D. (2014). TEMPO: A contemporary model for police education and training about mental illness. *International Journal of Law and Psychiatry, 37*(4), 325–333.

Cook, T., & Tattersall, A. (Eds.). (2016). *Blackstone's senior investigating officers' handbook* (4th ed.). Oxford: Oxford University Press.

Cooke R. A., & Rousseau, D. M. (1988). Behavioral norms and expectations: A quantitative approach to the assessment of organizational culture. *Group & Organization Studies, 13*(3), 245–273. https://doi.org/10.1177/105960118801300302.

Cope, N. (2004, March). 'Intelligence Led Policing or Policing Led Intelligence?': Integrating volume crime analysis into policing. *The British Journal of Criminology, 44*(2), 188–203. Available at SSRN: https://ssrn.com/abstract=1160516

Cordner, G., & Bieber, E. (2003). *Research for practice: Problem-orientated policing in practice*. See www.ncjrs.org

Cotton, D., & Coleman, T. G. (2010). Canadian police agencies and their interactions with persons with a mental illness: A systems approach. *Police Practice and Research, 11*(4), 301–314.

Council of Europe Recommendation (2001/11). Concerning guiding principles on the fight against organized crime [GPFOC], 19 September 2001. Available at: https://rm.coe.int/1680092b86. Accessed 4 Jan 2020.

Cox, L. A. (2008). What's wrong with risk matrices? *Risk Analysis, 28*(2), 497–512. https://doi.org/10.1111/j.1539-6924.2008.01030.x.

Cox, M., Malcolm, M., & Fairgrieve, S. (2009). A new digital method for the objective comparison of frontal sinuses for identification. *Journal of Forensic Sciences, 54*(4), 761–772. https://doi.org/10.1111/j.1556-4029.2009.01075.x.

Crawford, A., & Cunningham, M. (2015). 'Working in Partnership: The challenges of working across organisational boundaries, cultures and practices', in J. Fleming (ed.) Police Leadership - Rising to the Top, Oxford: Oxford University Press, pp. 71–94.

Crawford, A., Lister, S., Blackburn, S., & Burnett, J. (2005). *Plural policing: The mixed economy of visible patrols in England and Wales*. Bristol: Policy Press.

Crawshaw, R. (1999). International standards on the right to life and the use of force by police. *The International Journal of Human Rights, 3*: 4. Routledge, London. p. 67.

Crawshaw, R. (2009). *Police and human rights a manual for teachers, resource persons and participants in human rights programmes* (2nd ed., p. 76). Lisbon: Martinus Nijhoff Publishers.

Crawshaw et al. (1998). *Human rights and policing. Standards for good behaviour and a strategy for change.* London: Kluwer Law International.

Crego, J. & Harris, C. (2000, July). *Do NDM and CDM theories mark the ends of a continuum? Or does a hybrid approach better describe team-based decision-making problem solving processes with the management of critical incidents?* Draft paper 2000. [Online] http://www.calt.demon.co.uk/critical%20incident%20management.htm. 06 Jan 2019.

Crocker, A. G., Hartford, K., & Heslop, L. (2009). Gender differences in police encounters among persons with and without serious mental illness. *Psychiatric Services* (Washington, DC), *60*(1), 86–93.

Cross, T. P., Finkelhor, D., & Ormrod, R. (2005a). Police involvement in child protective services investigations: Literature review and secondary data analysis. *Child Maltreatment, 10*(3), 1–21. Retrieved from http://www.unh.edu/ccrc/pdf/CV83.pdf.

Crowley, M. (2011). *Lead from the Heart.* Bloomington: Balboa Press.

Cusson, M. (2018a). A method that combines criminology and forensic science. Considering the case of antiterrorism. In Q. Rossy (Ed.), The Routledge international handbook of forensic intelligence and criminology (Routledge international handbooks) (pp. 39–46). London/New York: Taylor & Francis. Kindle Edition.

Cusson, M. (2018b). The Routledge international handbook of forensic intelligence and criminology. (Q. Rossy, D. Decary-Hetu, O. Delemont, & M. Mulone, Eds.). New York: Routledge.

Daragahi, B. (2019, January 27). Colombia of Europe: How tiny Albania became the continent's drug trafficking headquarters. *Independent.* Available at: https://www.independent.co.uk/news/world/europe/albania-drug-cannabis-trafficking-hu b-europe-adriatic-sea-a8747036.html. Accessed 5 Jan 2020.

Davies, M., & Johnson, J (2015). Navigating the one-on-one model of accountability: Lessons for police and crime commissioners and chief constables through the lens of principal–agent theory. *Policing: A Journal of Policy and Practice.* 2016 – academic.oup.com

Dawes, M. (2006). *Understanding reasonable force.* Derbyshire: The Derwent Press.

De Church, L., & Mesmer-Magnus, J. (2010, January). The cognitive underpinnings of effective teamwork: A meta-analysis Pub Med.gov. *The Journal of Applied Psychology, 95*(1), 32–53.

Deadman, D., & MacDonald, Z. (2004). *Offenders as victims of crime?: An investigation death investigations in Ontario.* https://www.mcscs.jus.gov.on.ca/english/DeathInvestigations/Pathology/pathology_main.html. Accessed 23 Sept 2019.

Fahsing, I. (2013, June). Decision making and decisional tipping points in homicide investigations: An interview study of British and Norwegian detectives. *Journal of Investigative Psychology and Offender Profiling, 10*(2):155–165.

Deloitte Policing 4.0. *Deciding the future of policing in the UK.* www2.deloitte.com › pages › articles ›project-policing

Delpeuch, T., & Ross, J. E. (2016). *Comparing the democratic governance of police intelligence.* Elgar Publishing.

Dempsey, J. (2019). *Stress in the police force: Causes and effects: Criminology.* National Library Medicine.

Denscombe, M. (2007). *The good research guide for small-scale social research.* National Library Medicine.

Dhani, A., & Kaiza, P. (2011, March 31). *Police service strength: England and Wales.* National Library Medicine.

Diallo, T. (2014). *French air strikes kill wanted Islamist militant 'Red Beard' in Mali.* [Online] U.S. Available at: https://www.reuters.com/article/us-mali-islamists/french-air-strikes-kill-wanted-islamist-militant-red-beard-in-mali-idUSBREA2D13Z20140314. Accessed 16 Sep 2019.

Digest of Terrorist Cases [UNODC Digest of Terrorist Cases]. (2010). *United Nations Office on Drugs and Crime.* Available at: https://www.unodc.org/documents/terrorism/Publications/Digest_of_Terrorist_Cases/English.pdf. Accessed 10 Dec 2019.

Donati, J., & Harooni, M. (2014, January 17). Up to 15, mostly foreigners, killed in Kabul suicide attack. *Reuters.* Retrieved from (2009) http://www.reuters.com/article/2014/01/17/us-

Downing, P. (2009a, February). *Methods: Information, systems and contexts.* Oxford: Chandos Publishing.

Downing, P. (2009b, February). Policing terrorism in the United States: The Los Angeles police department's convergence strategy. *Police Chief, 76*(2) 28,30–36,39,40,43.

Drye. (2005). *Hurricane Katrina the essential timeline.* National Geographic

Duckers, M., Faber, M., Cruijsberg, J., Grol, R., Schoonhoven, L., & Wensing, M. (2009). Safety and risk management interventions in hospitals: A systematic review of the literature. *Medical Care Research and Review, 66*(Suppl. 6), 90S.

Durbin, J., Lin, E., & Zaslavaska, N. (2010). Police-citizen encounters that involve mental health concerns: Results of an Ontario police services survey. *Canadian Journal of Community Mental Health, 29,* 53–72.

Dwyer, S., & Buckle, J. (2009). The space between: On being an insider-outsider in qualitative research. *International Journal of Qualitative Methods, 8,* 54–63.

Earle, T., & Cvetkovich, C. (1997). Culture, cosmopolitanism and risk management. *Risk Analysis, 17*(1), 55–65. APA PsycNet.

Earley, P., & Ang, S. (2003). *Cultural intelligence: Individual interactions across cultures.* Stanford: Stanford Business Books.

Edirisingha, P. (2019, July 18). *Interpretivism and positivism (ontological and edition).* London: Home Office.

Ellis, Clare, Raffaello Pantucci, van Zuijdewijn J. de Roy, Edwin Bakker, Benoît Gomis, Simon Palombi, & Melanie Smith. (2016). *Lone-actor terrorism: Analysis paper. Countering lone-actor terrorism series* (2016): 24.

Elmsley, C. (2003). The birth and development of the police. In T. Newburn (Ed.), *A handbook of policing.* Uffculme: Willan Publishing.

Erikson, F. (1986). *Europe's crime-terror Nexus: Links between terrorist and organized crime groups in the European Union* [Europe's crime-terror nexus]. 2012. Available at: https://www.europarl.europa.eu/RegData/etudes/etudes/join/2012/462503/IPOL-LIBE_ET (2012)462503_EN.pdf. Accessed 10 Dec 2019.

European Union Council *Framework Decision 2002/475/JHA, on combating terrorism* [EU CFDCT]. (2002, June 13). Available at: https://eur-lex.europa.eu/legal-content/EN/TXT/?uri=CELEX:02002F0475-20081209. Accessed 10 Nov 2019.

Eva, B., Sameer, P., Alastair, R., Marie, M., O'Malley Troy, Anthony, R. M., Olivier, R., Patrick, R. C., & Simon, W. (2016). The intelligent use of forensic data: An introduction to the principles. *Forensic Science Policy & Management: An International Journal, 7*(1–2), 21–29. https://doi.org/10.1080/19409044.2015.1084405.

Eyre, K (2017). *SSR-PSO PKTC draft Concept Paper – Global SSR policies, interoperability, PSO organisational and operational practice development.*

Fahsing, I., & Ask, K. (2016). The making of an expert detective: The role of experience in English and Norwegian police officers' investigative decision-making. *Psychology, Crime & Law, 22*(3), 203–223.

Fairgrieve, S. (2008). *Forensic cremation analysis and interpretation.* Boca Raton: CRC Press Inc..

Faller, K. C. (2015). Forty years of forensic interviewing of children suspected of sexual abuse. *Social Science, 4,* 34–65.

Fanusie, Y., & Entz, A., 2017. Al-Qaeda in the Islamic Maghreb – s3.us-east-2.amazonaws.com. Available at: https://s3.us-east-2.amazonaws.com/defenddemocracy/uploads/documents/CSIFTFBB_AQIM.pdf. Accessed 16 Sept 2019.

Farrall, G., & Gadd, D. (2004). 'Research note: The frequency of the fear of crime. *British Journal of Criminology, 44,* 127–132.

Ferry, L., & Eckersley, P. (2011). Budgeting and governing for deficit reduction in the *finance and management. Public Services, 10*(1), 14–23.

Finklehor, D. (1986). *A sourcebook on child sexual abuse.* London: Sage.

Fisher, R. P., Geiselman, R. E., & Amador, M. (1989). Field test of the cognitive interview: Enhancing the recollection of actual victims and witnesses of crime. *Journal of Applied Psychology, 74*(5), 722–727.

Fisher-Stewart, G. (2007). *Community policing explained: A guide for local governments,* COPS. Washington, DC: US Department of Justice

FitzGerald, M., Hough, M., Joseph, I., & Qureshi, T. (2002). *Policing for London.* London: Taylor and Francis.

Fleetwood, J., & Lea, J. *De-funding the police in the UK Goldsmiths.* University of *www.britsoccrim.org*

Fleming, J. (2015). *Police leadership, rising to the top.* London: Oxford University Press.

Fletcher, J. K. (2007). Leadership, power, and positive relationships. In J. E. Dutton & B. R. Ragins (Eds.), *LEA's organization and management series. Exploring positive relationships at work: Building a theoretical and research foundation* (pp. 347–371). Lawrence Erlbaum Associates Publishers.

Ford, J. D. (1999). Organizational change as shifting conversations. *Journal of Organizational Change Management, 12,* 480–500.

Foschini, G., & Tonacci, F. (2017, July 31). 'Il petrolio dell'Isis finisce in Italia: la Guardia di Finanza indaga sulle 'navi fantasma.' *la Repubblica.* Available at: https://www.repubblica.it/cronaca/2017/07/31/news/il_petrolio_dell_isis_finisce_in_italia. Accessed 15 Nov 2019.

Fowler, R. (2012). *A season in Hell* [Kindle]. Toronto: Harper Perennials.

Freeze, C., & Perreaux, L. (2013). *Bandit with ties to al-Qaeda charged by RCMP for abducting diplomats.* [Online] The Globe and Mail. Available at: https://www.theglobeandmail.com/news/national/bandit-with-ties-to-al-qaeda-charged-by-rcmp-for-abducting-diplomats/article12820184/. Accessed 16 Sep 2019.

Friedman, L. (2015). *Strategy, a history*. Oxford University Press.

Furnel, S.M. (2019). Cyber crime: A portrait of the landscape. *Journal of Criminological Research, Policy and Practice, 5*, 13–26. University of Plymouth

Garrod, S. (2017, November 8). *Force replaces neighbourhood policing teams*. Police Oracle

Gash, T. (2008). *The new bill: Modernising the police force*. London: IPPR Institute for Public research. www.ippr.org.

Gerspacher, N., et al. (2017, January). *Sustainable capacity building: Guidelines for planning and project design communities*. US Institute of Peace manuscript.

Gill, P., Horgan, J., & Deckert, P. (2014). Bombing alone: Tracing the motivations and antecedent behaviors of lone-actor terrorists. *Journal of Forensic Sciences, 59*(2), 425–435.

Gold, Josh. (2020). Amid COVID-related cyber threats, the Netherlands leads UN efforts. https://www.cfr.org/blog/amid-covid-related-cyber-threats-netherlands.

Goldstein, H. (1990). *Problem orientated policing*. New York: McGraw Hill.

Goldstein, H. (1997). *Policing a Free Society*. Ballinger Press.

Goodchild, M. (2013, December 5). *Future of Gillingham police desk 'hanging in the balance'*. Retrieved July 8, 2014, from Western Gazette: http://www.westerngazette.co.uk/Future-Gillingham-police-desk-8216hanging/ story-20266479-detail/story.html

Goodley, D., Lawthorn, R., Clough, P., & Moore, M. (2004). *Researching life stories*. Routledge.

Goudge, Stephen T. (2008). *The inquiry into pediatric forensic pathology in Ontario*. http://www.attorneygeneral.jus.gov.on.ca/inquiries/goudge/index.html. Accessed 11 Mar 2020.

Graca, S., Bryant, R., Lawton-Barrett, K., Gilbert, P., Hooper, G., Jones, N., Blackburn, B., McCormack, T., Mitchell, S., Nunn, J., O'Neill, M., Owens, J., Bryant, S., & Bryant, R. (Eds.). (2017). *Blackstone's handbook for policing students 2018*. Oxford: Oxford University Press.

Greig-Midlane, Jack 2014. *Changing the beat? The impact of austerity on the neighbourhood policing workforce*. [Project Report]. Cardiff: Universities' Police Science Institute.

Gros, J. (2003). Trouble in paradise: Crime and collapsed states in the age of globalization. *British Journal of Criminology, 43*, 63–80. Retrieved from http://bjc.oxford journal.

Grossman, D., et al. (1999). *Behavioral psychology. Encyclopaedia of violence, peace and conflict*. L.R. Kurtz Academic Press California.

Grossman, D., et al. (2007). *On combat: The psychology and physiology of deadly conflict in war and in peace*. Belleville: PPCT Research Publications.

Guidère, M. (2014). The Timbuktu letters: New insights about AQIM. *Res Militaris*. Available at: https://hal.archives-ouvertes.fr/hal-01081769/document. Accessed 16 Sept 2019.

Gur, O. M. (2010). Persons with mental illness in the criminal justice system: Police interventions to prevent violence and criminalization. *Journal of Police Crisis Negotiations, 10*(1–2), 220–240.

Ha, T. T., Freeze, C., & Leblanc, D. (2013, April 22). Rcmp arrest two for 'al-Qaeda-supported' plot to bomb via train. *The Globe and Mail*. Retrieved from http://www.theglobeandmail.com/news/national/rcmp-arrest-two-for-al-qaeda-supported-plot- to-bomb-via-train/article11465138/

Habermas, J. (1972). *Knowledge and human interests*. London: Heinemann.

Hagan, J. (1993). *The social embeddedness of crime and unemployment. Criminology*. UK: Wiley.

Hamer, D. (2007, March). The Presumption of innocence and reverse burdens: A balancing Act. *The Cambridge Law Journal, 66*(1). Hampshire: Palgrave Macmillan

Hecht, L. M. (2001). Role conflict and role overload: Different concepts, different consequences. *Sociological Inquiry, 71*, 111–121. https://doi.org/10.1111/soin.2001.71.issue-1.

Herrington, V. (2012). Inter-agency cooperation and joined-up working in police responses to persons with a mental illness: Lessons from new South Wales. *Policing, 6*(4), 388–397.

Herschinger, E. (2003). A battlefield of meanings: The struggle for identity in the UN debates on a definition of international terrorism. *Terrorism and Political Violence, 25*(2), 183–201.

Higgins, G. (2009). Quantitative versus Qualitative Methods: Understanding why Quantitative Methods are Predominant in Criminology and Criminal Justice. *Journal of Theoretical and Philosophical Criminology, 1*, 23–27.

Hodgson, P. (1987). *A practical guide to successful interviewing.* Maidenhead: McGraw Hill.

Holden, M., & Lynch, P. (2004). *Choosing the appropriate methodology: Understanding research philosophy.* Ireland: Waterford Institute of Technology.

Horkheimer, M. (1972). *Critical theory: Selected essays.* New York: Herder & Herder.

Hough, M. (2003). Modernisation and public opinion: Some criminal justice paradoxes. *Contemporary Politics, 9*(2), 143–155.

Hough, M., Jackson, J., Bradford, B., Myhill, A., & Quinton, P. (2010). *Procedural justice.* Routledge.

Howden, D. (2011). British holidaymaker is 'beheaded by al-Qa'ida'. *The Independent.* Available at: https://www.independent.co.uk/news/world/africa/british-holidaymaker-is-beheaded-by-al-qaida-1696414.html. Accessed 16 Sept 2019.

Hunt, P., Irving, B., & Farnia, L. (2011). *Testing the police workforce resilience hypothesis: An application of labour economics to policing management.* Santa. Routledge.

Iacobucci, F. (2014). *Police encounters with people in crisis: An independent review of the use of lethal force by the Toronto police service.* Retrieved from http://www.tpsreview.ca/docs/Police-Encounters-With-People-In-Crisis.pdf

Identifying lessons in United Nations international policing missions (Policy Paper No. 9). Retrieved from website: http://www.dcaf.ch/Publications/Identifying-Lessons-in-United-Nations-International-Policing-Missions

Independent Police Commission. (2013). *Policing for a better Britain.* Essex: Anton. See www.statewatch.org › uk-police-commission-report

Innes, M. (2003). *Investigating murder: Detective work and the police response to criminal homicide. Clarendon studies in criminology.* Oxford: OUP.

Innes, M. (2004). Reinventing tradition?: Reassurance, neighbourhood security and policing. *Criminology and Criminal Justice, 4*, 151–171.

Innes, M., & Thiel, D. (2012). Policing terror. In T. Newburn (Ed.), *Handbook of policing* (pp. 553–579). Hoboken: Taylor and Francis.

Institute for Government. (2018). *Performance tracker 2018: Police.* Retrieved from Institute for Government: https://www.instituteforgovernment.org.uk/.../performance-tracker-2018

Irving, B., & Dunningham, C. (1993). Human factors in the quality control of CID investigations research. In *Royal commission on criminal justice, research study number 21.* London: Home Office.

James, A., Phythian, M., Wadie, F., & Richards, J. (2017). The road not taken: Understanding barriers to the development of police intelligence practice. *The International Journal of Intelligence, Security, and Public Affairs, 19*(2), 77–91.

Jay. (2014). *Independent inquiry into child sexual exploitation in Rotherham (England) 1997–2013*. Rotherham: Rotherham Metropolitan Borough Council.

Johnson, P. L. (2019). The crime and state terrorism Nexus: How organized crime appropriates counterinsurgency violence. *Perspectives on Terrorism, XIII*(6), 16–26.

Johnson, N., & Politowski, B. (2016). *Police funding*. London: House of Commons.

Jones, T., & Newburn, T. (2002). The transformation of policing? Understanding current trends in policing systems. *The British Journal of Criminology, 42*, 129–146.

Jones, D., Grieve, J., & Milne, B. (2008). The case to review murder investigations. *Policing, 2*(4), 470–480.

Kadono, N. (1999). How can we fight 21st century crime? International cooperation against transnational organized crime. In CSCAP/ISDS (Eds.), *Transnational crime and regional security in the Asia Pacific* (pp. 119–125). Manila.

Katulić, T., & Protrka, N. (2019).*Information security in principles and provisions of the EU data protection law*. 42nd international convention on information and communication technology, electronics and microelectronics (MIPRO), Opatija, Croatia, pp. 1420–1426. Available at: https://ieeexplore.ieee.org/document/8757153

Kelling, G., Pate, T., Dieckman, D., & Brown, C. (1974). *The Kansas city preventative model www.ncjrs.gov*

Kelling, G., Pate, A., Ferrara, A., Utne, M., & Brown, C. (1981). *Newark foot patrol www. ncjrs.gov*

Kerstetter, K. (2012). Insider, outsider, or somewhere between: The impact of researchers' identities on the community-based research process. *Journal of Rural Social Sciences, 27*(2), Article 7. Available at: https://egrove.olemiss.edu/jrss/vol27/iss2/7.

Khan, J. (2013). *Policing and crime reduction: The evidence and its implications for practice: The police foundation*. National Library Medicine.

Kind, S. (1987). In J. Sherrat & S. Manchester (Eds.), *The scientific investigation of crime*. National Library Medicine.

Kirby, S. (2013). *Effective policing. Implementation in theory and practice*. Palgrave.

Kirby, M. J., & Keon, W. J. (2006). *Out of the shadows at last: Transforming mental health, mental illness and addiction services in Canada*. Retrieved from http://www.mentalhealthcommission.ca/English/system/files/private/t/out_of_the_shadows_at_last_-_full_0.pdf

Knake, Robert K. (2020, May 29). *Banning covert foreign election interference*. Council on foreign relations. www.cfr.org/report/banning-covert-foreign-election-interference

Knake, Robert K. *Banning covert foreign election interference*. Council on Foreign Affairs. https://www.cfr.org/blog/new-cyber-brief-banning-covert-foreign...

Kolditz. (2007). *In extremis leadership: Leading as if your life depended on it*. HB Printing.

Kolditz, T., Karrasch, A., Levine, A., & Kolditz, T. A. (2011). Leadership when it matters most: Lessons on influence from in extremis contexts. In P. Sweeney, M. Matthews, & P. Lester (Eds.), *Leading in dangerous contexts* (pp. 218–229). Annapolis: Naval Institute Press.

Lampe, K. (2001). Not a process of enlightenment: The conceptual history of organized crime in Germany and the United States of America. *Forum on Crime and Society, 1*, 99–116.

Landau, T. (1996). Policing and security in four remote aboriginal communities: A challenge to coercive models of police work. *Canadian Journal of Criminology, 38*(1), 1–32.

Laremont, R. (2011). Al Qaeda in the Islamic Maghreb: Terrorism and counterterrorism in the Sahel. *Taylor & Francis.* Available at: https://www.tandfonline.com/doi/full/10.1080 /19392206.2011.628630. Accessed 16 Sept 2019.

Laub, Zachary. (2019). *Hate speech on social media: Global comparisons.* Council on Foreign Relations. www.cfr.org/backgrounder/hate-speech-social-media-global-comparisons

Lee, S., Brunero, S., Fairbrother, G., & Cowan, D. (2008). Profiling police presentations of mental health consumers to an emergency department. *International Journal of Mental Health Nursing, 17,* 311–316.

Legrand, T., & Vogel, L. (2014a, December). Forensic intelligence. Retrieved from ResearchGate. https://www.researchgate.net/publication/271820268

Legrand, T., & Vogel, L. (2014b, June 23). The landscape of forensic intelligence research. Retrieved from Taylor & Francis Online: https://doi.org/10.1080/00450618.2014.928830

Lehto, M. R., & Nah, F. (2006). *Decision-making models and decision support.* In G. Salvendy (Ed.), *Handbook of human factors and ergonomics* (pp. 191–242). John Wiley & Sons, Inc.. https://doi.org/10.1002/0470048204.ch8.

Leveson. (2015). *Lord justice review of efficiency in criminal proceedings www.gov.uk*

Levi. (2000, January–March 16). *Stressors at the workplace.* Hanley & Belfus.

Levy, I., & Robinson, C. (2019, October 31). *Principles for a more informed exceptional access debate: Lawfare Lawfare.* www.lawfareblog.com/principles-more-informed-exceptional

Ligeti, K., & Lassalle, M. (2018). The organised crime-terror nexus: How to address the issue of ISIS benefitting from lucrative criminal activities? *Law Working Paper Series, 009,* 2–26.

Lomardo, R., & Donner, M. (2018). Can community policing increase residents' informal social control? Testing the impact of the Chicago alternative policing strategy. *Police Practice and Research: An International Journal, 19*(5), 427–442.

Longstaff, A., Willer, J., Chapman, J., Czarnomski, S., & Graham, J. (2015, May). *The police foundation.*

Lord Laming Report. (2003). The Victoria Climbie inquiry: Report of an inquiry by Lord Laming. https://www.gov.uk/government/publications/the-victoria-climbie-inquiry-report-of-an-inquiry-by-lord-laming

Loveday, B. (2006). *Workforce modernisation: Implications for the police service.* Macmillan Press.

Lowe, T., & Innes, M. (2012). Can we speak in confidence? Community intelligence and neighbourhood policing v2.0. *Policing and Society, 22*(3), 295–316.

Lurigio, A. J., Smith, A., & Harris, A. (2008). The challenge of responding to people with mental illness: Police officer training and special programmes. *The Police Journal, 81,* 295–323. https://doi.org/10.1358/pojo.2008.81.4.431.

MacPherson, W. (1999). *The Stephen Lawrence inquiry. Cm 4262-I.* London: Home Office.

Makarenko, T. (2004). The crime-terror continuum: Tracing the interplay between transnational organized crime and terrorism. *Global Crime, 6*(1), 129–145.

Malenfant, R. (2009). *Risk, control and gender: Reconciling production and reproduction in the risk society.* Newbury Park: Sage.

Manjoo, F., Rockwell, P. & Kinney, A. (2005, September 15). Timeline to disaster. *Salon*. Retrieved from http://www.salon.com/2005/09/15/katrina_timeline/

Manning. (2008). *The technology of policing*. London: Policing Journal.

Margolin, J. (1977). Psychological perspectives in terrorism. In Y. Alexander & S. M. Finger (Eds.), *Terrorism: Interdisciplinary perspectives* (pp. 273–274). New York: John Jay.

Mark, R. (1978). *In the office of constable*. London: Collins.

Marshall, C., & Rossman, G. (2006). *Designing qualitative research* (4th ed.). London.

McAllister, A., Bailey, A., & Barr, O. (2002). Training in joint investigation of alleged crimes against people with learning disabilities in Northern Ireland. *Journal of Adult Protection, 4*(2). Pre-Crime and Counter-Terrorism: Imagining Future Crime in the 'War on Terror'.

McCauley, C., Moskalenko, S., & Van Son, B. (2013). Characteristics of lone-wolf violent offenders: A comparison of assassins and school attackers. *Perspectives on Terrorism, 7*(1), 4–24.

McGarrell, E., Freilich, J., & Chermak, S. (2007). Intelligence-led policing as a framework for responding to terrorism. *Journal of Contemporary Criminal Justice, 23*(2), 142–158.

McGuire, M., & Dowling, S. (2013). *Home office UK. "Cyber crime: A review of the evidence"*. Research report 75, Chapter 1: Cyber-dependent crimes, Home Office, London. Available at: https://www.gov.uk/government/publications/cyber-crime-a-review-of-the-evidence

Mcknight, D., & Chervany, N. (1996). *The meanings of trust* (University of Minnesota MIS Research Center Working Paper series, WP 96-04).

McLennan, W. (2018, April 13). *Police numbers: How cuts have made officers less*. Routledge.

McNulty, E. (2014, August 11). The importance of putting people first. Strategy + Business. https://www.strategy-business.com/blog/The-Importance-of-Putting-People-First?gko=3d0b5. Accessed 3 June 2018.

Meleagrou-Hitchens, A., & Kaderbhai, N. (2017). *Research perspectives on online radicalistaion: A literature review, 2006–2016*. London: Vox Pol International Centre for the Study of Radicalisation (ICSR), King's College.

Melo, R. C., Silva, M. J., & Parreira, P. (2014). Effective leadership: Competing values framework. *Procedia Technology, 16*, 921–928.

Meloy, J. R., & Gill, P. (2016). The lone-actor terrorist and the TRAP-18. *Journal of Threat Assessment and Management, 3*(1), 37.

Memon, A., & Higham, P. A. (1999). A review of the cognitive interview. *Psychology, Crime and Law, 5*(1–2), 177–196.

Mercer Kollar, L. M., Jacoby, S. F., Ridgeway, G., & Sumner, S. A. (2017). *Cardiff model toolkit: Community guidance for violence prevention*. Atlanta: Division of Violence Prevention, National Center for Injury Prevention and Control, Centers for Disease Control and Prevention.

Millie, A. (2018). *Reassurance policing and signal crimes*. London: Springer.

Millie, A., & Herrington, V. (2005). *Bridging the gap: Understanding reassurance policing*. Wiley.

Milne, B., & Bull, R. (2006). Interviewing victims, including children and people with intellectual disabilities. In G. Davies & M. Kebbell (Eds.), *Practical psychology for forensic investigations* (pp. 8–23). Chichester: Wiley.

Ministerie van Algemene Zaken. (2018, October 4). *MH17 Incident*. Government.nl, Ministerie Van Algemene. www.government.nl/latest/news/2018/10/04/netherlands-defence-

MINUSTAH (Mission des Nations Unies pour la stabilisation en Haiti). (2013). Developpement de la police nationale d'haiti: cap sur 2016. Retrieved from website: http://www. minustah.org/developpement-de-la-police-nationale-dhaiti-cap-sur-2016/

Mind. (2013a). *At risk, yet dismissed: The criminal victimisation of people with mental health problems*. Retrieved from https://www.mind.org.uk/media-a/4121/at-risk-yet-dismissed-report.pdf

Mind. (2013b). *Police and mental health: How to get it right locally*. Retrieved from http:// forwardforlife.org/wp-content/uploads/2014/03/2013-12-03-Mind_police_final_web. pdf

Mobekk, E. Geneva Centre for the Democratic Control of Armed Forces (DCAF). (2005). Identifying lessons in United Nations international policing missions (Policy paper no. 9). Retrieved from website: http://www.dcaf.ch/Publications/Identifying-Lessons-in-United-Nations-International-Policing-Missions

Moore, M. L., Clough, R., & Goodley, P. (2004). *Researching life storiesmethod, theory and analyses in a biographical age*. Routledge.

Moraff, C. (2015, June 22). *The US has spent $14B on Community Policing – What have we learned so far?* Yes (Summer 2015).

Morais, L. F., & Graça, L. M. (2013). A glance at the competing values framework of Quinn and the Miles & Snow strategic models: Case studies in health organizations. *Revista Portuguesa de SaúdePública, 31*(2), 129–144.

Morin, R., Parker, K., Stepler, R., & Mercer, A. (2017, January 11). *Behind the badge*. Pew Research Center. http://www.pewsocialtrends.org/2017/01/11/behind-the-badge/. Accessed 29 May 2018.

Motson et al. (1992 published 1993). The effects of case characteristics on suspect behaviour during police questioning. *British Journal of Criminology, 32*(1), 23–40 https://doi. org/10.1093/oxfordjournals.bjc.a048178

Muggah, Robert. (2019). Our cities are under cyberattack. Here's why – And what they should do world economic forum. https://www.weforum.org › agenda › 2019/09

Mullins, S., Wither, J. K., & Monaco, S. R. (2016). Terrorism and crime. In J. K. Wither & S. Mullins (Eds.), *Combating transnational terrorism* (pp. 67–84). Sofia: Procon Ltd.

Murray, K. (2004). *Training at the speed of life volume one*. Florida: Armiger Publications, Inc.

Murray, K. R. (2006). *Training at the speed of life. The definitive textbook for military and law enforcement reality based training*. Gotha: Florida Armiger Publications.

Nacos, B. L. (2019). *Terrorism and counterterrorism* (5th ed.). Routledge.

Nakamoto, S. 2009. *Bitcoin: A peer-to-peer electronic cash system*. Bitcoin. Available at: https://bitcoin.org/bitcoin.pdf

Neenan and Dyrden. (2002). *Life coaching: A cognitive-behavioural approach*. Routledge.

Nesbitt, M. (2019). *An empirical study of terrorism charges and terrorism trials in Canada between September 2001 and September 2018*. [Online] Papers.ssrn.com. Available at: https://papers.ssrn.com/sol3/papers.cfm?abstract_id=3325956. Accessed 16 Sep 2019. New York: Springer.

Newburn, T., & Peter, N. (2008). *Dictionary of policing*. Abington: Routledge.

News, BBC. (2020, June 3). www.bbc.com/news/technology-52912881

Neyroud, P., et al. (2001). *Policing, ethics and human rights* (p. 137). Willan Publishing.

Nicholas, S., & Walker, A. (2004). *Crime in England and Wales 2002/2003*. Routledge.

Noor, K. (2008). Case study: A strategic research methodology. *American Journal of Applied Sciences, 5*(11), 1602–1604.

Norms. (2018, February). Council on foreign relations, council on foreign relations.

Norris, E., & Shepheard, M. (2017). *How public inquiries lead to change*. London: Institute for Government.

North Atlantic Military Committee Final Decision 0472/1, Concept for Counter-Terrorism [NATO MCD]. (2016). Available at: https://www.nato.int/cps/en/natohq/topics_69482. htm. Accessed 12 Jan 2020.

O'Rawe et al. (2007, October). *Human rights and policing, a guide for police trainers*. Transitional Justice Institute, UUJ.

Odeljan, R., Butorac, K., & Bailey, A. (2015). Investigative interviews with children. *European Law Enforcement Research Bulletin, 12*, 18–24.

O'Neill, M. (2013, March 1). *PCSO's as the paraprofessionals of policing*. Scottish Institute for Policing Research (SIPR).

Oosthuizen, J., Lewis, C., Kapend, R., & Ellis-Nee, C. (2015). *Analysis of data collected. Organizational Change Management, 12*(6), 61–62.

Overton, I. (2019). *The price of paradise*. Oxford University Press.

PA Consulting Group. (2001). *Diary of a police officer.* Police research series, paper, pp. 184–196 of 242. Lone-actor terrorism, terrorism and conflict, UK Counter-terrorism, Domestic Security, Terrorism.

Pantucci, R., Ellis, C., et al. (2016). *Lone-actor terrorism* (Countering Lone-Actor Terrorism Series No. 11). RUSI.

Patrol Experiment: A Summary Report. Washington, DC: Police Foundation. https://www. policefoundation.org/wp-content/uploads/2015/07/Kellin…

Peace Palace Library. (2013). *Transnational crime*. Retrieved from website: http://www. peacepalacelibrary.nl/research-guides/international-criminal-law/ transnational-crime/

Pepper, I., & McGrath, R. *Introduction to professional policing examining the evidence base*. Routledge.

Peterson, M. F., Smith, P. B., Akande, A., Ayestaran, S., Bochner, S., Callan, V., … Setiadi, B. (1995). Role conflict, ambiguity, and overload: A 21 nation study. *Academy of Management Journal, 38*, 429–452.

Pettitt, B., Greenhead, S., Khalifeh, H., Drennan, V., Hart, T., Hogg, J., Borschmann, R., Mamo, E., & Moran, P. (2013). At risk, yet dismissed: The criminal victimisation of people with mental health problems (Project Report). London: Victim Support, Mind.

Policing Newburn, T. (Ed.). *Handbook of Policing*. Cullompton: Willan Publishing. Policing. *The Howard Journal, 44*(1), 41–56.

*Policing?*Rosenbaum, D. (Ed.). *The challenges of community policing: Testing the policy forum* (pp. 1–21). Oxford: College of Policing.

Policy Toolkit on the Hague Good Practices on the Nexus between Transnational Organized Crime and Terrorism [UNICRI]. (2019). United Nations Interregional Crime and Justice Research Institute. Available at: http://www.unicri.it/news/article/Toolkit_nexus_crime_ terrorism. Accessed 2 Feb 2020. *Political and Social Science, 593*, 84–99.

Povey *Open all Hours* Home Office HMIC report. (2001).

Precey, R., Jackson C., Vincent G., & Harpy G. (2012). *Harnessing the power of diversity and complexity to build effective leadership capacity: Learning across cultural and professional divides.* European Studies in Education Management Vol. 1

Price Waterhouse (PWC). 2018. *Policing in a connected world.* https://www.pwc.com › gx › en › industries › government-public-services › public

Protocol for joint investigation by social workers and police officers of alleged or suspected cases of child abuse – Northern Ireland, PSNI/HSC.

Protrka, N. (2018). *International cooperation and security in combating crime in cyberspace.* Available at: https://urn.nsk.hr/urn:nbn:hr:162:834428

Psychology Today. (2018). *Emotional intelligence.* https://www.psychologytoday.com/us/basics/emotional-intelligence. Accessed 25 June 2018.

Public Safety Canada. (2018). 2018 public report on the terrorism threat to Canada. *Public Safety Canada/Sécurité publique Canada.* Available at: https://www.publicsafety.gc.ca/cnt/rsrcs/pblctns/pblc-rprt-trrrsm-thrt-cnd-2018/index-en.aspx. Accessed 15 Sept 2019.

Puttonen, R. & Romiti F. 2020. *The Linkages between organized crime and terrorism.* Studies in conflict & terrorism. Available at: https://doi.org/10.1080/1057610X.2019.1678871. Accessed 20 Feb 2020.

Quinton, P. (2014). *Does neighbourhood policing have a future? 16th Oxford Policing.* Routledge.

Quinton, P., & Morris, J. (2008). Neighbourhood policing: The impact of piloting and early national implementation. London: Home Office.

Quinton, P., Bland, N., & Miller, J. (2000). *Police stops, decision-making and practice* (Police research series paper 130). London: Home Office.

Raddon, A. (2010, February). *Early stage research training: Epistemology & ontology.* Routledge.

Raffaello, P., Ellis, C., & Chaplais, C. (2016). *Lone-actor terrorism.* RUSI. *What have we learned about lone wolves from Anders Behring Breivik?. Perspectives on Terrorism,* 5(5–6). (2011).

Rajasegaran, J. and others. (2019). *A multi-modal neural embeddings approach for detecting mobile counterfeit apps* (pp. 3165–3171). WWW '19 the world wide web conference, San Francisco. Available at: https://dl.acm.org/citation.cfm?id=3313427

Rand Corporation. (2015, March 9). *Assessing the value of mounted police units.* Routledge.

Rapoport, D. C. (2002). The four waves of rebel terror and September 11. *Journal of Generative Anthropology,* (Spring/summer).

Rawlings, P. (2002). *Policing a Short History.* Cullompton: Willan.

RCMP continuum of force The RCMP Incident Management Intervention Model' (IMIM) model o https://www.rcmp-grc.gc.ca › en › use-force Force

Reaves, B. (2011). *Census of state and local law enforcement agencies, 2008.* National Library Medicine.

Recantation and False Allegations of Child Abuse. (2011). The national children's advocacy center US. https://www.icmec.org/wp-content/uploads/2015/10/Recantations-and-False-Allegations-Bibliography.pdf. Accessed August 2019.

Reiner, R. (2000). *The politics of the police* (3rd ed.). Oxford: Oxford University.

Reines, J. (2018, October 3). *Police force merger would increase your taxes and you may get no extra officers.* Retrieved from Cornwall Live. Routledge.

research. In T. Bennett, *The future of policing.* University of Cambridge.

Research perspectives on online radicalisation: A literature review 2006–2016 (2017) IC

Ribaux, O. (2010). Intelligence-led crime scene processing. Part I: Forensic intelligence. *Forensic Science International*, 10–16.

Reuland, M. M., Schwarzfeld, M., & Draper, L. (2009). *Law enforcement responses to people with mental illnesses: A guide to research-informed policy and practice.* Retrieved from https://www.bja.gov/Publications/CSG_le-research.pdf

Ribaux, O. (2010). Intelligence-led crime scene processing. Part II: Intelligence and crime scene examination. *Forensic Science International*, 63–71.

Ribaux, O., & Benjamin, T. (2014, December). Expanding forensic science through forensic intelligence. *Science & Justice, 54*(6), 494–501.

Ribaux, O., & Caneppele, S. (2018). In Q. Rossy, D. Decary-Hetu, O. Delemont, & M. Mulone (Eds.), *The Routledge international handbook of forensic intelligence and criminology.* New York: Routledge.

Ribaux, O., Walsh, S., & Margot, P. (2004). The contribution of forensic science to crime analysis and investigation: Forensic intelligence. *Forensic Science International, 156,* 171–181.

Ribaux, O., Crispino, F., & Roux, C. (2014). Forensic intelligence: Deregulation or return to the roots of forensic science? *Australian Journal of Forensic Sciences*, 1–15. https://www.tandfonline.com/doi/full/10.1080/00450618.2014.906656

Rice, X., 2009. Briton among four tourists seized by rebels after festival in Mali. *The Guardian.* Available at: https://www.theguardian.com/world/2009/jan/24/mali-niger-hostages. Accessed 15 Sept 2019.

Ritter, C., Teller, J. L. S., Marcussen, K., Munetz, M. R., & Teasdale, B. (2011). Crisis intervention team officer dispatch, assessment, and disposition: Interactions with individuals with severe mental illness. *International Journal of Law and Psychiatry, 34*(1), 30–38. https://doi.org/10.1016/j.ijlp.2010.11.005.

Rix, A., Faye, J., Maguire, M., & Morton, S. (2009). *Improving public confidence in the police: A review of the evidence.* https://assets.publishing.service.gov.uk/government/uploads/system

Robaton, A. (2017, March 31). Why so many Americans hate their jobs. *Moneywatch.* https://www.cbsnews.com/news/why-so-many-americans-hate-their-jobs/. Accessed 28 May 2018.

Robbers, Monica L. P. *Blinded by science: The social construction of reality in forensic television shows and its effect on criminal jury trials.* https://doi.org/10.1177/0887403407305982.

Robert, R. (1994). Police & society. USA: Wadsworth Publishing Company.

Robinson, A. (2006). *Police community support officers: A literature and policy.* Hallam Centre for Community Justice.

Robson, C. (2002). *Real world research: A resource for social scientists and* role of educators. *South African Journal of Education, 28,* 321–333.

Rosenbaum, D. (1994). *The challenge of community policing: Testing the promises.* Sage.

Rosenbaum, D., & Lurigio, A. (2000). An inside look at community policing reform – Definitions, organisational changes, and evaluation findings. In G. Alpert & A. Piquero (Eds.), *Community policing – Contemporary readings.* Prospect Heights: Waveland Press.

Ross, A. (2015, July 18). Elements of a forensic intelligence model. *Australian Journal of Forensic Sciences, 47*(1), 8–15.

Rossmo, D. K. (2009). *Criminal investigative failures.* Boca Raton: CRC Press.

Roulston, K. (2010). *Reflective interviewing.* London: Sage.

Royal Canadian Mounted Police. (2013). *International peace operations branch – Current operations.* Retrieved from http://www.rcmp-grc.gc.ca/po-mp/missions-curr-cour-eng.htm#n4

Roycroft, M. (2016). *Police chiefs in the UK (2016) Bureaucrats, HR managers or Cops?* London: Palgrave.

Roycroft, M., & Roach, J. (Eds.). (2019). *Decision making in police enquires and critical incidents: What really works.* London: Palgrave.

RSA. (2018). White paper 2018. *Current state of cybercrime.* Available at: https://www.rsa.com/content/dam/premium/en/white-paper/2018-current-state-of-cybercrime.pdf

Sallot, J. (2006). Canadian security intelligence service. *Canadian security intelligence service the Canadian encyclopedia.* Available at: https://www.thecanadianencyclopedia.ca/en/article/canadian-security-intelligence-service. Accessed 15 Sept 2019.

Sandberg, S. (2013). Are self-narratives strategic or determined, unified or fragmented? Reading Breivik's Manifesto in light of narrative criminology. *Sage Acta Sociologica, 56*(1), 69–83.

Savage, S., & Milne, R. (2007). Miscarriages of justice: The role of the investigative process. In T. Newburn, T. Williamson, & A. Wright (Eds.), *Handbook of criminal investigation* (pp. 610–627). Cullompton: Willan.

Schmall, E. (2010, November 28). Allegations of fraud and corruption mar Haiti elections. *The Huffington Post.* Retrieved from http://www.huffingtonpost.com/emily-schmall/allegations-of-fraud-corr_. www.dhs.gov

Schmid, A. P. (2016). Defining terrorism. In J. K. Wither & S. Mullins (Eds.), *Combating transnational terrorism* (pp. 1–16). Sofia: Procon Ltd.

Schmid, A. P. (2018). *Revisiting the relationship between international terrorism and transnational organized crime 22 years later [ICCT].* International Centre for Counter-Terrorism – The Hague research paper. Available at: https://icct.nl/publication/revisiting-the-relationship-between-international-terrorism-and-transnational-organised-crime-22-years-later/. Accessed 10 Jan 2020.

Schon, D. (1983). *The reflective practitioner: How professionals think in action.* Michigan: Basic Books.

Schwab, Klaus. The fourth industrial revolution: What it means and how to respond. World Economic Forum www.weforum.org › agenda › 2016/01 › the-fourth-industrial-revolution

Scraton, P. (2009). *Hillsborough – The truth.* London: Mainstream Publishing.

Segal, A., & Pitts, H. (2018). *Cyber conflict after Stuxnet: Essays from the other bank of the Rubicon CCSA*

Serfaty, D., MacMillan, J., Entin, E. E., & Entin, E. B. (1997). *The decision-making expertise of battle commanders.* In C. E. Zsambok & G. Klein (Eds.), *Expertise: Research and applications. Naturalistic decision making* (pp. 233–246). Lawrence Erlbaum Associates, Inc..

Shaw, E. D. (1986). Political terrorists: Dangers of diagnosis and an alternative to the psychopathology model. *International Journal of Law and Psychiatry, 8,* 359–368.

Sherman, L. W. (1998). *Evidence based policing.* Washington, DC: Police Foundation.

Shropshire Star. (2018, October 10). *Policing has reached its tipping point, chief.*

Shull, Aaron. (2019, August 11). *Governing cyberspace during a crisis in trust.* www.cigionline.org/articles/governing-cyberspace-during-crisis-trust

Siddle, B. (1995). *Sharpening the warriors edge: The psychology and science of training*. Belleville: PPCT Research Publications.

Siebel, Thomas M. (2018). *Digital transformation: Survive and thrive in an era of mass extinction*.

Silke, A. (2014). *Terrorism all that matters*. London: Hodder and Stoughton.

Sills, G. L., Vroman, N. D., Wahl, P. E., & Schwanz, P. E. (2008). Overview of New Orleans levee failures: Lessons learned and their impact on national levee design and assessment. *Journal of Geotechnical and Geoenvironmental Engineering, 134*(5), 556–565. Retrieved from http://champs.cecs.ucf.edu/Library/Journal_Articles/pdfs/Sills_Overview_of_New_Orleans.pdf.

Sindall, K., & Sturgis, P. (2013). Austerity policing: Is visibility more important than absolute numbers in determining public confidence in the police? *European Journal of Criminology, 10*, 2.

Singer, L. (2004). *Reassurance policing: An evaluation of the local management of policing*. Routledge.

Skogan, W., & Hartnett, S. (1997). *Community policing, Chicago style*. Oxford University Press: Oxford.

Smith, J. (2003). *The shipman inquiry 2nd report: The police investigation of March 1998, CM 5853*. London: HMSO.

Smith & Milne. (2018). Witness interview strategy for critical incidents (WISCI). *Journal of Forensic Practice, 20*(2) https://www.researchgate.net/deref/https%3A%2F%2Fdoi.org%2F10.1108%2FJFP-03-2018-0007.

Smith, N., & Flanagan, C. (2000). *The effective detective: Identifying the skills of an effective SIO*. London: Home Office.

Smith, K., & Milne, B. *The Journal of Forensic Practice 2018 Witness Interview Strategy*. Routledge.

Smith, M. J., & Tilley, N. (Eds.). (2002). *Crime science: New approaches to preventing and detecting crime* (pp. 191–207). Cullompton, Devon: Willan Stevens, J.

Smith, S., Le Grand, J., & Propper, C. (2008). *The economics of social problems*. Hampshire: Palgrave Macmillan.

Spaaij, R. (2012). *Understanding lone wolf terrorism: Global patterns, motivations and prevention*. Springer.

Starmer, K. (1999). *European human rights law. The human rights act 1998 and the European convention on human rights*. London: Legal Action Group.

Statistics Canada. (2007). *The Haitian community in Canada*. Retrieved from: http://www.statcan.gc.ca/pub/89-621-x/89-621-x2007011-eng.htm

Statistics Canada. (2014). *Religion*. Retrieved from: http://www.statcan.gc.ca/search-recherche/bb/info/3000017-eng.htm

Stelfox, P., & Pease, K. (2005). Cognition and detection: Reluctant bedfellows? In M. Smith & N. Tilley (Eds.), *Crime science: New approaches to preventing and detecting crime* (pp. 194–210). Cullompton: Willan Publishing.

Stelfox, P., & Pease, K. (2005). Cognition and detection: Reluctant bedfellows? In.

Stenning, P. (1996). *Police governance in first nations in Ontario*. Toronto: Centre of Criminology, University of Toronto.

Stenning, P. (2016). The idea of the political 'independence' of the police: International interpretations and experiences. In M. E. Beare & T. Murray (Eds.), Police and government relations (pp. 183–256). Toronto: University of Toronto Press. https://doi. org/10.3138/9781442684690-008.

Stevens, J. (2002). Damilola Taylor: The review of the investigation and prosecution arising from the murder of Damilola Taylor. London: New Scotland Yard. http://image.guardian. co.uk/sys-files/Guardian/documents/2002/12/09/damilola.pdf

Stevens, J. (2013). *Policing for a better Britain: Report of the independent police.*

Stewart, E. (2015, June 8). Morale and organizational stress. *LinkedIn.* https://www.linkedin.com/pulse/traditional-law-enforcement-management-root-cause-low-eric-stewart/. Accessed 29 May 2018.

Stibli, F. (2010). Terrorism in the context of globalization. *Academic and Applied Research in Military Science, 9*(1), 1–7. Retrieved from http://www.zmne.hu/aarms/docs/Volume9/Issue1/pdf/01.pdf.

Stone, Christopher., & Travis, Jeremy. (2011, March). *Toward a new professionalism in policing. New Perspectives in Policing.* Executive session on policing and public safety.

Suboch, G. (2016). *Real-world crime scene investigation: A step-by-step procedure manual.* CRC Press.

Sullivan, G., & Spritzer, K. (1997). The criminalization of persons with serious mental illness living in rural areas. *The Journal of Rural Health: Official Journal of the American Rural Health Association and the National Rural Health Care Association, 13*(1), 6–13.

Sutton, R., Trueman, K., & Moran, C. (2017). *Crime scene management: Scene specific methods.* London: Wiley.

Symantec. (2018). *FASTCash: How the Lazarus Group is emptying millions from ATMs.* Available at: https://www.symantec.com/blogs/threat-intelligence/fastcash-lazarus-atm-malware

Teijlingen, E., & Hundley, V. (2001). *The importance of pilot studies.* University of.

Temkin and Krahe. (2008: 32) Elisabeth McDonald, Temkin & Krahe. Sexual assault and the justice gap: A question of attitude, 29 Pace L. Rev. 349 (2009) Tensions. *The New York Times*, The New York Times, 29 May 2020.

Theil, D. (2016). *Policing terrorism a review of the evidence Darren police foundation.* London.

Thomas, D. (2006). *Domain and development of cultural intelligence: The importance of mindfulness.* Sage.

Ticio-Diez, A., & Mancebon, M. J. (2010). *The efficiency of the Spanish police service: An application of the multiactivity DEA model* (pp. 351–362) Published online: 04 Oct 2010 Applied Economics Volume 34, 2002 – Issue 3.

Tilley, N. (2002). Uses and abuses of evidence in crime prevention. *Community Safety Journal, 1*(1), 13–21.

Tilley, N. (2003). Community policing, problem-orientated policing and intelligence-led transnational organized crime. *Director of National Intelligence.* Available at: https://www.dni.gov/. Accessed 15 Sept 2019.

Tilley, N. (2008). Modern approaches to policing: Community, problem-oriented and intelligence-led. In T. Newburn (Ed.), *Handbook of Policing.* Willan.

Ting-Toomey, S. (1999). *Communicating across cultures* (p. 261). New York: The Guilford Press.

Transparency International. (2013). *Corruption perceptions index 2013.* Retrieved from http://www.transparency.org/cpi2013/results

Transparency International. (2019). *Corruption perceptions index 2018.* Retrieved from http://www.transparency.org/cpi2018/results

Trayner, K., et al. (2020). High willingness to use drug consumption rooms among people who inject drugs in Scotland: Findings from a national bio-behavioural survey among people who inject drugs. *International Journal of Drug Policy.* https://doi.org/10.1016/j. drugpo.2020.102731.

Treverton, G. F., Wollman, M., Wilke, E., & Lai, D. (2011). *Moving toward the future of Policing.* Rand.

Tuffin, R., Morris, J., & Poole, A. (2006). *An evaluation of the impact of the National.*

Turner, R. (2016). *Hillsborough disaster: Five key mistakes.* [Online] https://www.bbc. co.uk/news/uk-england-merseyside-35462767. 20 Dec 2018.

Tyler, T. (2004). Enhancing police legitimacy. *Annals of the American Academy of Political and Social science, AAPSS.*

UK Public Sector: Act One 'The Comprehensive Spending Review'. *Journal of UK.* Retrieved October 17, 2016, from Rand Corporation:

Ulrich, D. (2018). *Creating business value through learning innovations in a disruptive workplace.* HRD Connect USA

University of Oxford. (2014, November 17). *Mounted police units in neighbourhoods.* University Press.

US Department of Homeland Security and UK National Cyber Security Center. (2020). Alert (AA20-). Cybersecurity and Infrastructure Security Agency CISA. www.dhs.gov

US Department of Homeland Security and UK National Cyber Security Center. Alert (AA20-.

Using Technology Global Internet Forum to Counter Terrorism (GIFCT),

Van Dijk., & Tseloni, A. (2018). *The international crime drop: New directions in research.* London: P Waters

Vance, Cyrus. (2019, December 10). *Written testimony for the United States senate committee on the judiciary on smartphone encryption and public safety.* Manhattan District Attorney's Office. www.manhattanda.org/written-testimony-for-the-united-states-senate-committee-on-the-judiciary-on-smartphone-encryption-and-public-safety/

Vechhi, A., & Brennan. (2009). Quality management: A cross-cultural perspective. *Cross Cultural Management An International Journal, 16*(2), 149–164.

Veldhuis, T., & Staun, J. (2009). *Islamist radicalisation: A root cause model.* The Hague: Netherlands Institute of International Relations Clingendael.

Vidino, L., & Brandon, J. (2012). *Countering radicalization in Europe* (Vol. 9). London: The International Centre for the Study of Radicalisation and Political Violence.

Vogel, L., & Legrand, T. (2014). The landscape of forensic intelligence research. *Australian Journal of Forensic Sciences, 47*(1), 16–26. https://doi.org/10.1080/00450618.2014.92 8830.

WADA Confirms Attack by Russian Cyber Espionage Group | World. Retrieved July 5, 2020.

Waddington, P. A. J. (1999). *Policing citizens.* London: UCL Press.

Wakefield, A. (2006). *The value of foot patrol: A review of research.* London: The Police Foundation.

Wakefield, A., & Fleming, J. (2009). *The Sage dictionary of policing.* London: Sage.

Walker, P., & English, C. (2015). Mali attack: More than 20 dead after terrorist raid on Bamako hotel. *The Guardian.*

Walklate. (2004). *Gender, crime, and criminal justice.* Willan.

Wallenfeldt, J. The Troubles. *Encyclopædia Britannica.* Available at: https://www.britannica.com/event/The-Troubles-Northern-Ireland-history. Accessed 15 Sept 2019.

Walton, R., & Falkner, S. (2020). *Policing a pandemic.* Policy exchange UK.

Wardlaw, G. (1989). *Political terrorism: Theory, tactics and counter-measures*. Cambridge: Cambridge University Press.

Weatheritt, M. (1983a). Community policing: Does it work and how do we know? In T. H. Bennett (Ed.), *The future of policing* (Cropwood conference series no.15) (pp. 127–142). Cambridge: Institute of Criminology. Palgrave Macmillan, 14 Nov 2012 – Political Science.

Weatheritt, M. (1983b). *Community policing: Does it work and how do we know? A review*

Weatheritt, M. (1988). Community policing: Rhetoric of reality? In J. Greene & S. Mastofski (Eds.), *Community policing: Reality of rhetoric?* New York: Praeger.

Weisburd, D., & Eck, J. (2004). What can police do to reduce crime, disorder & fear. *Encyclopaedia of Criminology and Criminal Justice*, 4327–4335.

Wellington, J. (2000). *Educational research: Contemporary issues and practical approaches*. London: Continuum.

Wells, W., & Schafer, J. A. (2006). Officer perceptions of police responses to persons with a mental illness. *Policing: An International Journal of Police Strategies & Management, 29*(4), 578–601. https://www.theguardian.com/world/2015/nov/20/mali-attack-highlights-global-spread-extremist-violence.

Wherry, A. (2009). *A negotiated release of the hostages was preferable to just about every other conceivable option. Macleans.ca*. Available at: https://www.macleans.ca/uncategorized/a-negotiated-release-of-the-hostages-was-preferable-to-just-about-every-other-conceivable-option/. Accessed 16 Sept 2019.

White, K. (2007). The Canadian contribution to United Nations peacekeeping. Retrieved from United Nations Association in Canada website: http://peacekeeping.unac.org:8080/en/pdf/CdnUNPkpgBooklet_e.pdf

Wilkinson, D., & Birmingham, P. (2003). *Using research instruments: A guide for.*

Williams, E., Norman, J., & Nixon, K. (2018). Violence against women: Public health or law enforcement problem or both? *International Journal of Police Science & Management, 20*(3), 196–206.

Williamson, T. (1993). *From interrogation to investigative interviewing; strategic trends in police questioning. Journal of Community and Applied Social Psychology, 3*, 89–99.

Williamson, K. (2018). Research concepts. In K. Williamson & G. Johanson (Eds.).

Wilson-Bates, F. (2008). *Lost in transition: How a lack of capacity in the mental health system is failing Vancouver's mentally ill and draining police resources*. Retrieved from http://vancouver.ca/police/assets/pdf/reports-policies/vpd-lost-in-transition.pdf

Wojtanik, A., (2015). *Mokhtar Belmokhtar: One-eyed firebrand of North Africa and the Sahel*. [Online] Ctc.usma.edu. Available at: https://ctc.usma.edu/app/uploads/2018/01/CTC_Mokhtar-Belmokhtar-Jihadi-Bio-February2015-2.pdf. Accessed 15 Sep 2019.

Wood, D. S., & Trostle, L. C. (1997). The nonenforcement role of police in western Alaska and the eastern Canadian arctic: An analysis of police tasks in remote arctic communities. *Journal of Criminal Justice, 25*(5), 367–379.

Yates, J. F., Ji. L.-J., Oka, T., Lee, J.-W., Shinotsuka, H., & Sieck, W. R. (2010). Indecisiveness and culture: Incidence, values, and thoroughness. *Journal of Cross-Cultural Psychology, 41*(3), 428–444. https://doi.org/10.1177/0022022109359692.

Yigit, M. F., & Tarman, B. (2013a). The impact of social media on globalization, democratisation, and participative leadership. *Journal of Social Science Education, 12*(1), 75–80. Retrieved from http://www.jsse.org/index.php/jsse/article/view/84/1169.

York, G. (2009). The secret Mali deal to release two Canadians. *The Globe and Mail*. Available at: https://beta.theglobeandmail.com/news/politics/the-secret-mali-deal-to-release-two-canadians/article4248750/?ref=http://www.theglobeandmail.com&. Accessed 16 Sept 2019.

Zhao, J., Lovrich, N. P., & Robinson, T. H. (2001). Community policing: Is it changing the basic functions of policing?: Findings from a longitudinal study of 200+ municipal police agencies. *Journal of Criminal Justice, 29*(5), 365–377.

Reports

Achieving Best Evidence in Criminal Proceedings. (2011). Guidance on interviewing victims and witnesses, and guidance on using special measures. Ministry of Justice. https://www.cps.gov.uk/sites/default/files/documents/legal_guidance/best_evidence_in_criminal_proceedings.pdf. Accessed Aug 2019.

Allen, G., & Dempsey, N. (2016). *Police service strength*. London: House of Commons. See *commonslibrary.parliament.uk* ›... › Research Briefing

Allen, G., & Zayed, Y. (2019). *Police service strength*. London: House of Commons. See *commonslibrary.parliament.uk* ›... › Research Briefing

Basic Principles on the Use of Force and Firearms by Law Enforcement Officials, adopted by the eighth United Nations congress on the prevention of crime and the treatment of offenders, Havana, Cuba, 27 August to 7 September 1990.

Canadian Broadcasting Corporation CBC. (2019). *The October crisis*. Canadian Broadcasting Corporation. Available at: https://www.cbc.ca/history/EPISCONTENTSE1EP16CH-1PA4LE.html. Accessed 11 Sept 2019.

CBC News. (2009a). Transcript 1: Robert Fowler interview Sept. 8, 2009 | CBC News. *CBCnews*. Available at: https://www.cbc.ca/news/canada/transcript-1-robert-fowler-interview-sept-8-2009-1.8 64625. Accessed 16 Sept 2019.

CBC News. (2009b). Transcript 2: Robert Fowler interview Sept. 9, 2009 | CBC News. *CBCnews*. Available at: https://www.cbc.ca/news/canada/transcript-2-robert-fowler-interview-sept-9-2009-1.8 63593. Accessed 16 Sept 2019.

Cleveland Inquiry. See https://www.thetcj.org/child-care-history-policy/the-cleveland-reportby-judge-elizabeth-butler-sloss. Accessed Aug 2019.

Commission of Inquiry into the Investigation into the Bombing of Air India Flight 182 the. (2015, December 8). www.publicsafety.gc.ca › cnt › rspns-cmmssn › index-en

Convention against Transnational Organized Crime [UNTOC]. (2000, November 15). United Nations, Palermo. Available at: https://www.unodc.org/unodc/en/organized-crime/intro/UNTOC.html#Fulltext. Accessed 5 Dec 2019.

Convention for the Prevention and Punishment of Terrorism [CPPT]. (1937, November 16). *The league of nations*, Geneva. Available at: https://www.wdl.org/en/item/11579/. Accessed 10 Dec 2019.

Countering Terrorism, Protecting Human Rights. A manual [OSCE CTPHR]. (2007). Available at: https://www.osce.org/odihr/countering-terrorism. Accessed 10 Jan 2020.

Cross, T. P., Finkelhor, D., & Ormrod, R. (2005b). *Child maltreatment, police involvement in child protective services investigations*. journals.sagepub.com

Crown Prosecution Service CPS. *The CPS (ABE in Criminal Proceedings) Joint Inspection 2004* HMIC/HMCP www.justiceinspectorates.gov.uk › CJJI_ABE_Dec14_rpt

Dorset Police. (2013, April 6). *Our priorities*. Retrieved July 8, 2014, from Dorset Police:

Dorset Police. (2014). *Total resource management review*. Winfrith: Dorset Police.

Dorset Police. (2019, December 26). *Minimum standards*.

Evaluation of Chicago's alternative policing strategy experiment. Washington, DC: The Police Foundation. (2000)

Flanagan, R. (2004). *A report on the investigation by Cambridgeshire constabulary into the murders of Jessica Chapman and Holly Wells at Soham on 4 August 2002*. London: HMIC

Foreign Affairs Canada, Trade and Development Canada. (2013a). *Aid effectiveness agenda*. Retrieved from http://www.acdi-cida.gc.ca/acdi-cida/ACDI-CIDA.nsf/eng/

Foreign Affairs Canada, Trade and Development Canada. (2013b). *Haiti – Facts at a glance*. Retrieved from www.international.gc.ca › dev-eval-canada-haiti01

Government of Canada Treasury Board Secretariat. (2019). *Standard on security screening*. [Online] Available at: https://www.tbs-sct.gc.ca/pol/doc-eng.aspx?id=28115§ion=glossary. Accessed 11 Sept 2019.

Guidance on Interviewing Suspects (the P.E.A.C.E. Model). https://assets.publishing.service.gov.uk/government/uploads/system/uploads/attachme nt_data/file/757585/BAGT-Interviewing-suspects-v4.0ext_archive.pdf. Accessed Aug 2019.

Guidance on the UN Convention on the Rights of the Child. https://www.ohchr.org/en/professionalinterest/pages/crc.aspx. Accessed Aug 2019.

HM Treasury. (2007). *2007 Pre-budget report and comprehensive spending review*. www.gov.uk

HMIC. (2001). *A thematic inspection report on the role of police visibility and accessibility in public reassurance*

HMIC. (2004). *Modernising the police service: A thematic inspection of workforce* HMIC. (2008, September 1). *Her majesty's inspectorate of constabulary*. Retrieved HMIC. (2011). *Policing in Austerity: One year on*. London: HMIC.

HMIC. (2011a). *Use of force the rules of engagement: A review of the August 2011 disorders*. © Crown copyright.

HMIC. (2011b). *Adapting to austerity*. London: HMIC.

HMIC. (2012). *Increasing efficiency in the police service*. London: HMIC.

HMIC. (2013a). *Dorset Police's response to the funding challenge*. London: HMIC.

HMIC. (2013b). *Policing in austerity: Rising to the challenge*. London: HMIC.

HMIC. (2014a). *Core business: An inspection into crime prevention, police attendance*

HMIC. (2014b). *The strategic policing requirement: An inspection of how police forces in England and Wales deal with threats of a large-scale cyber incident (including criminal attack)*. London: Her Majesty's Inspectorate of Constabulary.

HMIC. (2016). *PEEL: Police effectiveness 2015: An inspection of Dorset Police*. London: Home Office publications.parliament.uk.

HMIC Her Majesty's Inspectorate of Constabulary. (2008, September 1). *HMIC inspection of forces for neighbourhood policing*.

HMIC report. (2001). *Open all hours*. HMIC.

HMIC.reports. See www.justiceinspectorates.gov.uk › hmicfrs

Home Office. (2001). *Policing a new century: A blueprint for Reform*. London: Home Office

Home Office. (2004). *Building communities, beating crime: A better police service for the 21st century*

Home Office. (2006a). An evaluation of the impact of the national reassurance policing programme

Home Office. (2006b). *An evaluation of the impact of the National Reassurance Policing*

Home Office. (2006c). FOI: 1941. *Sir Lawrence Byford report into the police handling of the Yorkshire Ripper case*. [Online] https://www.gov.uk/government/publications/sir-lawrence-byford-report-into-the-police-handling-of-the-yorkshire-ripper-case (03 Feb 2019)

Home Office. (2019a). *Home office evidence to the police remuneration review body:*

Home Office. (2019b). *Police workforce, England and Wales, 31 March 2019:*

Home Office circular 114/83. https://discovery.nationalarchives.gov.uk

Home Office Research Study. (2005) *Home office research study 293 a gap or a chasm? Attrition in reported rape cases*

Home Office Statistical Bulletin 13/03. London: Homicides, Firearm Offences and Intimate Violence 2010/11: Home Office.

IPCC Worboys Rapist report. http://www.ipcc.gov.uk/news/pr200110_worboys-2.htm

Kerslake enquiry. (2019). *Kerslake arena attack review*. www.kerslakearenareview.co.uk

Lord Laming report. *The Victoria Climbie inquiry: Report of an inquiry by Lord Laming...* www.dhs.gov

MH17 Incident I Government.nl www.government.nl › Topics › mh17-incident

Morgan, J. (1991). *'Morgan Report' – Safer communities: The local delivery of crime prevention through the partnership approach*. London: Home Office.

National Crime Agency. NCA and police smash thousands of criminal conspiracies after nationalcrimeagency.gov.uk

National Police Chiefs' Council. (2016, July 1). *About the NPCC*. Retrieved July 9, 2016, www.npcc.police.uk

NBC News. (2008, May 27). *1960–1970s: Civil rights, Vietnam and protest*. Retrieved NBC News.com: http://www.nbcnews.com/id/24714290/ns/us_newsgut_Neighbourhood Engagement Contracts:

Orkney Inquiry. https://www.gov.uk/government/publications/inquiry-into-the-removal-of-children-fro m-orkney-in-february-1991. Accessed Aug 2019.

RCMP. (2014a). *2011–2012 departmental performance report*. Retrieved from http://www.rcmp-grc.gc.ca/dpr-rmr/2011-2012/2012-eng.pdf

RCMP. (2014b). *National security criminal investigations program*. Retrieved from website http://www.rcmp-grc.gc.ca/nsci-ecsn/index-eng.htm

SOCTA serious and organised crime threat assessment report 2019. www.europol.europa.eu

Taylor, D. *The review of the investigation and prosecution arising from the murder of Damilola Taylor*. London: New Scotland Yard. See image.guardian.co.uk › documents › 2002/12/09 › damiolataylor.

The Shipman Inquiry 2nd Report: The Police Investigation of March 1998, CM 5853. London: HMSO.

Websites

BBC. (2013). Profile: Al-Qaeda in North Africa. *BBC News*. Available at: https://www.bbc.com/news/world-africa-17308138. Accessed 15 Sept 2019.

BBC. (2014, December 17). *Police in England and Wales to get 5% funding cut.*

BBC. (2015). Mali bar attack kills five in Bamako. *BBC News*. Available at: https://www.bbc.com/news/world-africa-31775679. Accessed 15 Sept 2019.

BBC. (2019, July 26). *Recruitment of 20,000 new police officers to begin 'within weeks'.* Berkshire: Open University Press.

BBC News. (2016, July 18). *US police shootings: How many die each year?*.

BBC News. (2020, June 3). George Floyd death: Anti-racism sites hit by wave of cyber-attacks. *BBC News*, BBC. www.bbc.com/news/technology-52912881.

BBC News – Ian Tomlinson unlawfully killed by Pc at G20 protests. http://www.bbc.co.uk/news/uk-13268633

CBC. (2019). *The October crisis. Canadian broadcasting corporation.* Available at: https://www.cbc.ca/history/EPISCONTENTSE1EP16CH1PA4LE.html. Accessed 11 Sept 2019.

Charles, J. (2013b, October 15). Armed bandits testing Haiti understaffed police forces. *Miami Herald*. Retrieved from http://www.miamiherald.com/2013/10/15/3691691/

Child Welfare Information Gateway see (2016) Merseyside crime prevention fund. https://www.merseysidepcc.info/CrimePreventionFund.aspx

College of Policing

ACPO. *Murder investigation manual.* www.app.college.police.uk › app-content › homicide

Association of Chief Police Officers (ACPO). (2009). *Guidance on command and control* (p. 11). London: ACPO College of Policing app website. www.app.college.police.ac.uk; www.app.college.police.uk.

Association of Chief Police Officers (ACPO). *Manual of guidance on police use of firearms,* (ACPO) *firearms.* www.app.college.police.uk/app-content/armed-policing/

Commission of Inquiry into the Investigation into the Bombing of Air India Flight 182 https://www.google.co.uk/url?sa=t&rct=j&q=&esrc=s&source=web&cd=&cad=rja&uact=8&ved=2ahUKEwju5eHo8_vxAhVRTcAKHZH2DrsQFjAAegQIBhAD&url=https%3A%2F%2F. www.ontario.ca%2Flaws%2Fstatute%2F90c37&usg=AOvVaw3GZqt74hgLLj_A7NTpset Coroner's Act of Ontario R.S.O. 1990, C. C.37, s. 31(1).

Conventions on Cyber Crime. www.coe.int/en/web/conventions/full-list/-/conventions/treaty/185/signatures

Criminal Code of Canada Legislative Services Branch. 2019. *Criminal code.* Available at: https://laws-lois.justice.gc.ca/eng/acts/C-46/. Accessed 15 Sept 2019.

DDI Global Leadership Forecast 2014|2015. https www.ddiworld.com/glf2014

Europol. 2017. *Drugs and the darknet, perspectives for enforcement, research and policy.* Available at: https://www.europol.europa.eu/sites/default/files/documents/drugs_and_the_darknet_-_td0417834enn.pdf

Flanagan, R. (2007). *The review of policing.* Home Office: London. www.justiceinspectorates.gov.uk › hmicfrs › media.

Foreign Affairs, Trade and Development Canada. (2013a). *Aid effectiveness agenda.* Retrieved from http://www.acdi-cida.gc.ca/acdi-cida/ACDI-CIDA.nsf/eng/

Foreign Affairs, Trade and Development Canada. (2013b). *Haiti – Facts at a glance.* Retrieved from http://www.acdi-cida.gc.ca/acdi-cida/acdi-cida.nsf/En/ NIC-223124146-NRN

Frozen watchfulness. http://www.body-languages.net/2014/02/frozen-watchfulness/.

Globe and Mail (3/2/17) newspaper Canada. Sexual assault.

Guardian.Bindell (28.2.14) Rape Cases.

Handbook on Research on Teaching. (3 ed., pp. 119–161). New York, NY. hanging/story-20266479-detail/story.html

Internet Organised Crime threat report (IOCTA) published by EC3 www.europol.europa.eu › iocta-report

Interpol Investigative support for Cybercrime. https://www.interpol.int/en/Crimes/Cybercrime/Investigative-support-for-cybercrime

Investigative interviewing – College of Policing APP. www.app.college.police.uk › app-content › investigations. www.dhs.gov

Labour Party. (2005). *Britain, forward not back: The Labour Party manifesto 2005.*

Laming, L. (2003). *The Victoria Climbie inquiry.* Norwich: TSO.

Leveson, B Lord Justice. (2015). *Review of efficiency in criminal proceedings.* www.judiciary.uk › publications › review-of-efficiency...

Major Incidents.https://www.app.college.police.uk/app-content/civil-emergencies/DVIpolicy

Merseyside Crime Prevention Fund (PCC) from the city of Liverpool in the UK. See https://www.merseysidepcc.info/CrimePreventionFund.aspx

Ministerie van Algemene Zaken. (2018a, May 25). MH17 incident. *Government.nl,* Ministerie Van Algemene Zaken. www.government.nl/topics/mh17-incident

Ministerie van Algemene Zaken. (2018b, October 4). Netherlands defence intelligence and security service disrupts Russian cyber operation targeting OPCW. *News Item | Government.nl,* Ministerie. www.government.nl/latest/news/2018/10/04/netherlands-defence-intelligence-and-security-service-disrupts-russian-cyber-operation-targeting-opcw

MINUSTAH (Mission des Nations Unies pour la stabilisation en Haiti). (2013). Developpement de la police nationale di'Haiti: cap sur 2016. Retrieved from website: http://www.minustah.org/developpement-de-la-police-nationale-dhaiti-cap-.

Mobekk, E. Geneva Centre for the Democratic Control of Armed Forces (DCAF). (2005). *Identifying lessons in United Nations international policing missions* (Policy paper no. 9). Retrieved from website: http://www.dcaf.ch/Publications/Identifying-Lessons-in-United-Nations-International-Policing-Missions

National Crime Agency. (2020, July 2). NCA and police smash thousands of criminal conspiracies after infiltration of encrypted communication platform in UK's biggest ever law enforcement operation. *National Crime Agency.* www.nationalcrimeagency.gov.uk/news/operation-venetic.

National decision making model. See College of Policing App www.app.college.police.uk › app-content › national-decision-making – Model national implementation. London: Home Office.

PBS. (2010). *Hurricane Katrina crime and disorder and the storm.* www.pbs.org, USA.

Police Encounters with People in Crisis – Toronto Police Service. https://www.torontopolice.on.ca/publications/files/reports/police_encounters_with_people_in_crisis_2014.pdf

Ransomware Europe's Largest Private Hospital Operator Fresenius Hit by Ransomware. *krebsonsecurity.com* › 2020/05 › europes-largest-private

Serious and Organized Crime Threat Assessment [SOCTA]. (2017). Available at: https://www.europol.europa.eu/socta-report. Accessed 5 Feb 2020.

Smartphone Encryption and Public Safety. Manhattan District Attorney's Office, 10 Dec.

Terrorism the Canadian Encyclopedia. (2014). *Terrorism.* Retrieved from http://thecanadianencyclopedia.com/en/article/terrorism/

The Reference Dictionary. (2013). *Definition of 'failed state'.* Retrieved from http://dictionary.reference.com/browse/failedstate

Tulloch, Michael H. 2017 Report of the independent police oversight review. Queen's Printer for Ontario. https://www.attorneygeneral.jus.gov.on.ca/english/about/pubs/police_oversight_review/

United Nations

UN Basic principles on the use of Force and firearms by Law enforcement Officers (1990).

UN Convention of the Rights of the Child. https://www.ohchr.org/en/professionalinterest/pages/crc.aspx. Accessed Aug 2019.

UN Human Rights. https://www.un.org/en/sections/issues-depth/human-rights/

UN Police Dept. – Police Monitoring, Mentoring and Advising in Peace (Manual) 2017 Operations.

United Nations. (2013). MINUSTAH – Facts and figures. Retrieved from http://www.un.org/en/peacekeeping/missions/minustah/facts.shtml

United Nations. (2016). *Secretary-general's high-level panel on digital cooperation.* United Nations.

United Nations. (2019a). Secretary-general's high-level panel on digital cooperation. *United Nations.* www.un.org/en/digital-cooperation-panel/

United Nations. (2019b). www.un.org/en/digital-cooperation-panel/

United Nations Department of Peacekeeping Operations (2010). *Concept of operations.*

United Nations General Assembly resolution A/59/894, Measures to eliminate international terrorism – Appendix II – Draft Comprehensive Convention against International Terrorism [CCIT]. (2005, August 12). Available at: https://undocs.org/pdf?symbol=en/A/59/894. Accessed 2 Dec 2019.

United Nations Office on Drugs and Crime. (2015). *Total police personnel at the national.*

United Nations Secretariat. (1995a, April). *Action against national and transnational economic and organized crime. Ninth UN congress on the prevention of crime and the treatment of offenders.* Egypt: Cairo. Retrieved from http://www.asc41.com/UN_congress/9th

United Nations Secretariat. (1995b, April). *Action against national and transnational economic and organized crime. Ninth United Nations congress on the prevention of crime and the treatment of offenders,* Cairo, Egypt. Retrieved from http://www.asc41.com/UN_congress/9th UN congress on the prevention of crime/018 ACONF.169.15.ADD.1 Strengthening the Rule of Law.pdf.

United Nations Secretariat. (1995c, April). *Action against national and transnational economic and organized crime. Ninth United Nations congress on the prevention of crime and the treatment of offenders*, Cairo, Egypt. Retrieved from http://www.asc41.com/UN_congress/9th UN congress on the prevention of crime/018 ACONF.169.15.ADD.1 Strengthening the Rule of Law.pdf.

United Nations Security Council resolution [S/RES/2195].(2014, December 19). *Threats to international peace and security*. Available at: http://unscr.com/en/resolutions/2195. Accessed 5 Dec 2019.

United Nations Security Council resolution [S/RES/2482]. (2019, July 19). *Threats to international peace and security*. Available at: http://unscr.com/en/resolutions/2482. Accessed 5 Jan 2020.

United States Department of State. (2014). Country reports on terrorism, western hemisphere, Canada. Retrieved from http://www.state.gov/j/ct/rls/crt/2012/209984.htm

United States Department of State, Bureau of Diplomatic Security. (2013). *Haiti 2013 crime and safety report*. Retrieved from https://www.osac.gov/pages/ContentRe portDetails.aspx?cid=14000

UNODC Global Report on Crime & Justice 1999. www.dhs.gov

UNODC. Adversarial versus inquisitorial legal systems. https://www.unodc.org/e4j/en/organized-crime/module-9/key-issues/adversarial-vs-inquisitorial-legal-systems.html

UNODC Transnational Organised Crime. www.unodc.org › 2019 › SEA_TOCTA_2019

Wademas Law Children's safety – The Official Portal of the UAE Government *u.ae* › justice-safety-and-the-law › children-safety. www.dhs.gov

Yigit, M. F., & Tarman, B. (2013b). The impact of social media on globalization, democratization, and participative leadership. *Journal of Social Science Education, 12*(1), 75–80. Retrieved from http://www.jsse.org/index.php/jsse/article/view/84/1169.

Index

A

Alderson, J. (Devon and Cornwall), 408
Al Qaeda in the Islamic Maghreb (AQIM)
    (Northwest Africa), 298, 305,
    306, 308, 310–314, 317
Amanda, 316
Analysis, 39, 40, 98, 114, 116, 133, 139,
    152, 160, 179, 206, 237,
    239–241, 247, 248, 250,
    255–257, 282, 284, 287, 290,
    291, 299, 329, 330, 334,
    336–338, 340, 341, 354, 361,
    373, 377, 391, 398, 414, 444
Anderson, D. QC (The Terrorism
    Regulator), 6, 250, 272
Anthropology, 237, 241
Armed response vehicles (ARVs), 68–70
Association of Chief Police Officers
    (ACPO), 56, 67, 77, 153, 189,
    394, 409, 413

B

Bird, Derrick (shootings Cumbria, Blair, I.),
    59, 67
Breivik, A. (Norway), 289
Brennan, Nigel, 316–318, 373

C

Canadian Security Intelligence Services
    (CSIS), 305, 307
Code, 116, 172, 188, 264, 304,
    313–315, 390,
    396, 397
College of Policing APPs, 55,
    62, 76, 106, 185,
    394, 395
    firearms, 62
The College of Policing Code of Ethics,
    394, 396
Community policing, 6, 9, 102,
    252, 271, 272, 405–419,
    443, 451
    intelligence, 451
Community Safety Partnerships (CSPs), 32,
    36, 428
Continum Force Model, 63
Counter Terrorism Internet Referral Unit
    (CTIRU), 274
County Lines drug trade, 139
Covert Human Intelligence Sources
    (CHIS), 337
Crime Survey of England and Wales
    (CSEW), 409
Cyber Crime, 145, 442–443

D
Deployment of Armed Officers, 276
Deputy Mayors Office for London, 22, 33
Digibomber, 305
Dunblane, 67, 69

E
ECHR, 16, 35, 62
8Chan website, 283
El Paso Shooting, Patrick Crusis, 117, 122,
        443
Encrochat, 41–42, 437
Europol, 9, 40, 139, 140, 145, 146, 293,
        444, 449
Evidence based Policing (EBP), 136, 200,
        201, 336–339

F
Financial Action Task Force (FATF), 41, 273
Firearms Policing, 62, 392, 393, 445–446
5 Eyes (FVEY), 40, 110, 117–123, 310,
        318, 449
Five Eyes Intelligence sharing Treaty, 110
Floyd, George Public Order Chapter and
        LL Poe, 3, 48, 51, 115, 121, 406
Fowler, Robert (Canadain kidnap victim),
        306, 307, 310, 312–318
Frontex, 41, 139

G
G8, 93, 319
G20, 48
Gibraltar 3, 1988. The IRA, *see* McGann
        acse members; Mairead Farrell

H
Her Majesties Inspectorate of
        Constabularies (HMIC), 175,
        333, 409, 413, 416
Home Affairs Select Committee, 33
Human Trafficking, 9, 15, 41, 264, 272,
        303, 308, 442, 445
Hungerford shooting, 67, 69

I
Independent advisory Groups (IAG), 35,
        387
Independent office for Police Conduct
        (IOPC), 20–21, 390
Intelligence Led Policing (ILP), 245,
        247–248, 252, 253,
        255, 273–274, 327–343,
        410, 448
Interpol, 40, 41, 105, 106, 140, 146

L
Leadership, Advisory and Professional
        Development (LAPD), 360–364
Lindhout, Amanda, 316–318
Louis, Guay (Canadain kidnap victim), 306

M
Mairead Farrell, 63
Mark, Sir Robert, 390
McGann acse members, 63
Mental health police, 204
Michael Alun PCC South Wales, 29
Millennium Bomber, 304
        Ressam, Ahmed, 304
Morgan Report, 33
Multi-agency risk assessment, 30
Multi-agency risk assessment conferences
        (MARAC), 31, 32
Multi Agency Safeguarding Hubs (MASH),
        31

N
The National Crime Agency (NCA), 41,
        145, 179, 188
National Intelligence Model (NIM), 337
National Police Chiefs Council (NPCC),
        27, 67, 106, 395
National Police Coordination Centre
        (NPoCC), 106
Neighbourhood policing teams (NPT), 30,
        33, 275, 406, 412,
        414–418, 451
Neyroud, P., 48, 52

O
Office for National Statistics (ONS), 173
On armed policing, 62
Operation Kratos, 66
Orde, Hugh, 67
Organised crime groups (OCGS), 67, 141,
    164, 336

P
Peelian Principles, 4, 9
Poe, LL, 443, 444, 449
Police and Community Support Officers
    (PCSOs), 25, 271, 274, 275, 337,
    406, 413–418
Police and Crime Commissioners (PCCs),
    19, 20, 22–23, 27, 29, 32,
    33, 59, 69, 70, 179, 201,
    202, 204, 215, 271,
    272, 390, 428
Police and Criminal Evidence Act of 1984
    (PACE), 184, 188, 197
Police Effectiveness, Efficiency and
    Legitimacy (PEEL), 22
Police Investigations & Review
    Commissioner (PIRC) Scotland,
    21–22
Police Ombudsman Office for Northern
    Ireland (PONI), 21
Police Reform and Social Responsibility
    Act 2011, 22, 32, 428
Police Service of Northern Ireland (PSNI),
    Crime Operations PSNI, 51, 55,
    59, 80
Prevent, the 4Ps counter terrorism strategy
    Organized Crime Strategy, 277
Problem orientated Policing Model (POP),
    31, 252, 338, 339, 407

R
Reiner, Robert, 20
Roads Policing, 27, 63, 87, 89, 90,
    105–107, 175, 206, 267–269,
    304

Royal Canadian Mounted Police (RCMP),
    4, 20, 23, 24, 63, 65, 67,
    104–107, 175, 206, 304–310,
    312–314, 316–318, 385, 388
Royal Ulster Constabulary (RUC), 270

S
SARA model, 338
Scene of Crime Officer (SOCO), 226, 253
The Scottish Police Authority (SPA), 21
Section 38 Powers, 20
Sexual assault Investigations, 171–182,
    194, 446
SSR Strategic, 354
Strategic policing requirement, 23, 202
Summer Riots London 2011, 445

T
Tasers, 69, 70
Trap 18 terrorist analysis, 286, 287, 289,
    291

U
UN Convention against Transnational
    Organized Crime (UNTOC), 295
United Nations (UN), 13, 14, 40, 50, 51,
    62, 63, 66, 86–94, 110, 115, 116,
    139, 140, 172, 212, 277,
    293–298, 303, 306, 307, 309,
    317, 319, 357, 387, 440, 441,
    449, 451
United Nations Office of Drugs and Crime
    (UNODC), 40, 212, 341
United States (US), 110
UN Security Resolution, 88, 94, 140, 295,
    296, 298

W
Waldorf, Stephen (shooting of film editor),
    62, 63
Winsor, Sir Tom (HMIC), 22

Printed by Printforce, United Kingdom